Advanced Race Guide

CREDITS

Lead Designer: Jason Bulmahn
Designers: Dennis Baker, Jesse Benner, Benjamin Bruck, Adam Daigle, Jim Groves, Tim Hitchcock, Hal MacLean, Jason Nelson, Stephen Radney-MacFarland, Owen K.C. Stephens, Todd Stewart, and Russ Taylor

Cover Artist: Wayne Reynolds
Interior Artists: Dave Allsop, Alex Aparin, Yngvar Asplund, Rayph Beisner, Eric Belisle, Eric Braddock, Christopher Burdett, Anna Christenson, Jorge Fares, Sara Forlenza, Grafit, Paul Guzenko, Andrew Hou, Mathias Kollros, Emiliano Petrozzi, Steve Prescott, Dmitry Prosvirnin, Klaus Sherwinski and Luisa Preissler, Marc Simonetti, J. P. Targete, Ben Wootten, Kieran Yanner, and Ilker Serdar Yildiz

Creative Director: James Jacobs
Managing Editor: F. Wesley Schneider
Development: Jason Bulmahn, Patrick Renie, Stephen Radney-MacFarland, and Sean K Reynolds
Editing: Judy Bauer, Christopher Carey, Erik Mona, and James L. Sutter
Editorial Assistance: Rob McCreary and Mark Moreland
Editorial Interns: Meredith Kniest, Alexandra Schecterson, and Jerome Virnich

Senior Art Director: Sarah E. Robinson
Graphic Designer: Andrew Vallas
Production Specialist: Crystal Frasier

Publisher: Erik Mona
Paizo CEO: Lisa Stevens
Vice President of Operations: Jeffrey Alvarez
Director of Sales: Pierce Watters
Finance Manager: Christopher Self
Staff Accountant: Kunji Sedo
Technical Director: Vic Wertz
Senior Software Developer: Gary Teter
Campaign Coordinator: Mike Brock

Website Team: Ross Byers, Liz Courts, Lissa Guillet, and Chris Lambertz
Warehouse Team: Will Chase, Michael Kenway, Jeff Strand, and Kevin Underwood
Customer Service Team: Cosmo Eisele, Erik Keith, and Sara Marie Teter

Special Thanks: Ryan Dancey; Clark Peterson; the KublaCon Development Workshop—Dawn R. Fischer, Richard Flynn, Gabriel S. García, Bruce Higa, Jennifer Krull, Daniel Langton, Nicholas Lundback, Sarah Lundback, Ian McNear, Jason Nelson-Wolfe, Anthony Perinoni, Richard Pratt, Ryan Rivers, Richard Tishler, and Michael Weller—and the proud participants of the open gaming movement.

This game is dedicated to Gary Gygax and Dave Arneson.

Based on the original roleplaying game rules designed by Gary Gygax and Dave Arneson and inspired by the third edition of the game designed by Monte Cook, Jonathan Tweet, Skip Williams, Richard Baker, and Peter Adkison.

This game would not be possible without the passion and dedication of the thousands of gamers who helped playtest and develop it. Thank you for all of your time and effort.

Paizo Publishing, LLC
7120 185th Ave NE, Ste 120
Redmond, WA 98052-0577
paizo.com

TABLE OF CONTENTS

INTRODUCTION

In fantasy roleplaying games, race is fundamental. It both provides a starting point for character creation and sets the tone for a character as it progresses.

Race in the Pathfinder Roleplaying Game mixes biology and culture, then translates those concepts into racial traits. Yet since both biology and culture are mutable—especially when one considers the powerful forces of magic—racial traits can be so diverse that two elves can be extremely different while still manifesting aspects of their shared heritage and culture. A race's traits, its history, its relations with other races, and the culture that all of these things imply—all of these frame your character.

This is true whether you play to or against the stereotypes. A savage and bloodthirsty half-orc who lives only for battle is fun to play, but so is a stern and conflicted half-orc paladin constantly struggling to keep her bloodlust in check. Both fit comfortably within the theme of half-orc, but come off as very different characters around the game table. The *Advanced Race*

Guide allows for both typical members of a race and the interesting outliers that many players love to portray. In purely mechanical terms, it provides a wealth of new game material for the Pathfinder RPG's playable races, many available only to specific races in order to showcase those aspects that make the races unique.

But the *Advanced Race Guide* is more than that. While the Pathfinder RPG has always featured a variety of races for players to roleplay, this book alone offers 36 different playable races, not counting subraces, and this is merely a starting point. Virtually all worlds and campaign settings include open environmental and cultural niches that could be filled by new races and cultures uniquely tailored to them. Thus, this book also presents the race builder—a system that enables you to create brand-new races for your campaign worlds. These new rules allow you to make an unlimited number of new races, both equivalent in power to the races already in the game or more powerful if you want to experiment with dangerously exotic new characters.

You hold in your hands a toolbox—a lexicon of the various cultures and people who become heroes in the world of Pathfinder, as well as everything you need to create your own. Take your game someplace new, or return to the old classics and see them as you've never seen them before.

NAVIGATING THIS BOOK

This book is organized a little differently than other Pathfinder RPG supplements. Typically, a book like this is divided into separate chapters on classes, feats, equipment, spells, and magic items. But since the main theme of this book is race, most chapters instead present a number of races, with each race's entry containing new alternate racial traits, favored class rewards, archetypes, feats, equipment, magic items, spells, and more. Chapter 4 presents the exciting new race builder rules, and at the end of the book you'll find a table to aid you in quickly locating the various spells presented in this book, along with a standard index that includes feats and magic items.

Chapter 1—Core Races: This chapter reintroduces the core races of the Pathfinder RPG. Each section of this chapter presents one of the seven core races—dwarves, elves, gnomes, half-elves, half-orcs, halflings, and humans—reprinting and expanding upon the information about those races found in the *Pathfinder RPG Core Rulebook* and the *Pathfinder RPG Advanced Player's Guide*. Here you'll find all the background material for each of these races and the standard racial traits, as well as a number of alternative racial traits and favored class rewards.

Furthermore, each of the core races takes the idea of alternate racial traits a step further by presenting a number of subraces for those races. These subraces bundle a group of alternate class features together into thematic categories that provide new takes on the existing core races. From imperious humans to arctic elves to gear gnomes, each subrace gives players a chance to play a core race in a way that's completely out of the ordinary.

But races are not all about racial traits and favored class rewards. Each of the core races comes from a vibrant culture with its own history, norms, and adventuring outlooks. To represent this, each race's entry presents a number of new character options, such as race-specific archetypes, adventuring equipment, feats, magic items, and spells.

Chapter 2—Featured Races: Following the detailed information on the core races, Chapter 2 provides a selection of 15 featured races. From the celestial aasimar to the fiendish tiefling, and from the feathery and mischievous tengu to the shadowy and spiteful drow, featured races are those peoples just beyond the core races in their exoticism, who despite their relative rarity are still likely familiar faces for adventuring groups. As in Chapter 1, each of these entries presents information on the race's culture, society, interactions with other races, and how the race fits into Pathfinder's cosmology. Each section details a number of alternate racial traits, favored class rewards, archetypes, feats, equipment, magic items, and spells designed specifically for those players interested in creating such characters.

Chapter 3—Uncommon Races: Some races are so rare as to seem strange and monstrous to many of the core races, yet that doesn't mean they can't make for fun and exciting characters. Many of them, like the gripplis, rarely leave their isolated homes, while others, like the kitsune, nagaji, and samsarans, may be more common in far-off lands, but are rare and wondrous in a baseline campaign. While the entries for the uncommon races are shorter than those of either the core or featured races, they provide a number of new options for those who want to play a truly exotic race. Each of the 14 uncommon race entries presented here feature a handful of alternate racial traits and favored class rewards; a single archetype; and a mix of feats, equipment, magic items, and spells.

Chapter 4—Race Builder: The last chapter of this book introduces a new race-creation system that was extensively playtested by the gaming community at **paizo.com**. This race builder allows you to mix and match new and existing racial traits using a Race Point system to create new playable races for your campaign. This system is not merely a matrix of costs and values, but also an essential tool for crafting your race's story and finding its niche within your game world. In this chapter you'll find the point costs for the racial abilities and traits of the races described in the other chapters of the *Advanced Race Guide*—these examples are there to provide you with benchmarks for your own race creation. Use them to make sure your new races are balanced, or treat them as a foundation from which you can build more powerful versions of existing races by increasing the Race Point value and adding new and appropriately themed racial traits. This is especially useful if you want to create the possibility of more monstrous races coexisting with standard races—you can create supercharged versions of dwarves, elves, halflings, and other core races, with each variant roughly balanced against the others, thus providing a high-powered but roughly even playing field.

Lastly, a few examples of new and monstrous races are presented throughout the chapter, allowing you to insert even more racial diversity into your Pathfinder game without having to build a new race from whole cloth. Incorporate them as presented, or pick them apart and rebuild them yourself. You have the tools now—the possibilities are endless.

1 CORE RACES

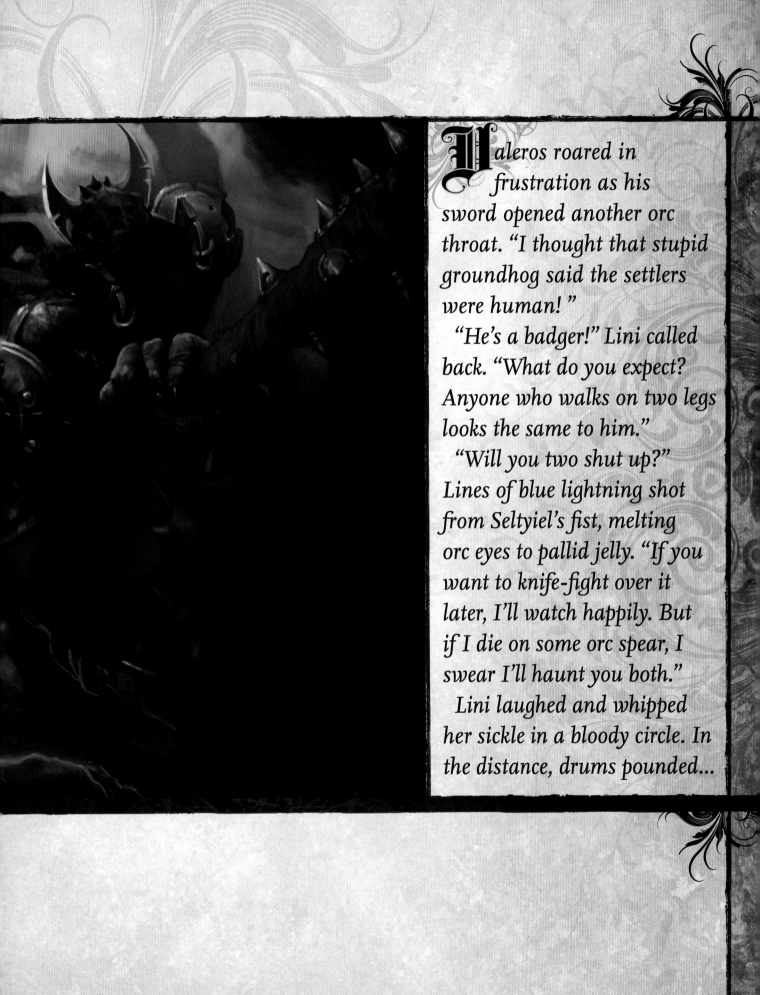

aleros roared in frustration as his sword opened another orc throat. "I thought that stupid groundhog said the settlers were human!"

"He's a badger!" Lini called back. "What do you expect? Anyone who walks on two legs looks the same to him."

"Will you two shut up?" Lines of blue lightning shot from Seltyiel's fist, melting orc eyes to pallid jelly. "If you want to knife-fight over it later, I'll watch happily. But if I die on some orc spear, I swear I'll haunt you both."

Lini laughed and whipped her sickle in a bloody circle. In the distance, drums pounded...

Core Races

Race is an important part of what makes characters who they are, yet it's often all too easy to gloss over the details. After all, most people know the basics: dwarves are short, elves live a long time, and gnomes are dangerously curious. Half-orcs are ugly. Humans are—well, human. To some players, choosing a race is simply a matter of finding which racial modifiers best fit a character's class.

Yet there's so much more to race than that. From their deep halls beneath craggy mountains, dwarves sing mournful ballads that teach children of the heroes of old, helping them dream of the day when they might give their own lives in the stronghold's defense. In the spires of their forest cities, elves find a kinship with nature, as the great trees are some of the few non-elven friends who won't grow old and wither before their eyes. By exploring the cultures and traditions of a character's race, we can better understand where she comes from and what makes her tick, thus immersing ourselves that much deeper in the campaign world.

This chapter is designed to help you get the most out of the seven core races presented in the *Pathfinder RPG Core Rulebook*, in terms of both mechanics and flavor. Herein you will find all the racial information presented in that book and the *Advanced Player's Guide*, along with a number of new rules options such as new alternate racial traits and favored class rewards, explorations of racial subtypes, new racial archetypes, and more. The races covered in this chapter include the following.

Dwarves: These short and stocky defenders of mountain fortresses are often seen as stern and humorless. Known for mining the earth's treasures and crafting magnificent items from ore and gemstones, they have an unrivaled affinity for the bounties of the deep earth. Dwarves also have a tendency toward traditionalism and isolation that sometimes manifests as xenophobia.

Elves: Tall, noble, and often haughty, elves are long-lived and subtle masters of the wilderness. Elves excel in the arcane arts. Often they use their intrinsic link to nature to forge new spells and create wondrous items that, like their creators, seem nearly impervious to the ravages of time. A private and often introverted race, elves can give the impression they are indifferent to the plights of others.

Gnomes: Expatriates of the strange land of fey, these small folk have a reputation for flighty and eccentric behavior. Many gnomes are whimsical artisans and tinkers, creating strange devices powered by magic, alchemy, and their quirky imagination. Gnomes have an insatiable need for new experiences that often gets them in trouble.

Half-Elves: Often caught between the worlds of their progenitor races, half-elves are a race of both grace and contradiction. Their dual heritage and natural gifts often create brilliant diplomats and peacemakers, but half-elves are often susceptible to an intense and even melancholic isolation, realizing that they are never truly part of elven or human society.

Half-Orcs: Often fierce and savage, sometimes noble and resolute, half-orcs can manifest the best and worst qualities of their parent races. Many half-orcs struggle to keep their more bestial natures in check in order to epitomize the most heroic values of humanity. Unfortunately, many outsiders see half-orcs as hopeless abominations devoid of civility, if not monsters unworthy of pity or parley.

Halflings: Members of this diminutive race find strength in family, community, and their own innate and seemingly inexhaustible luck. While their fierce curiosity is sometimes at odds with their intrinsic common sense, halflings are eternal optimists and cunning opportunists with an incredible knack for getting out the worst situations.

Humans: Ambitious, sometimes heroic, and always confident, humans have an ability to work together toward common goals that makes them a force to be reckoned with. Though short-lived compared to other races, their boundless energy and drive allow them to accomplish much in their brief lifetimes.

GENERAL DESCRIPTION

Each race's entry begins with a general description of the race, followed by specific entries for the race's physical description, society, relations with other races, alignment and religion, and members' common motivation for adventuring.

RACIAL TRAITS

Each race's entry features a sidebar listing the race's standard racial traits. This information includes the race's type, size, vision, and base speed, as well as a number of other traits common to most members of the race. With your GM's permission, you will also have the option to exchange these standard racial traits for a number of alternate racial traits, the rules for which are provided in the section below.

ALTERNATE RACIAL RULES

Alternate racial rules allow you to exchange existing racial traits for new ones or gain new favored class rewards based on your character's race. The general rules for alternate racial traits and alternate favored class options are summarized below.

Alternate Racial Traits: This section lists alternate racial traits for each of the seven core races. Many of them play on racial themes not reflected in the standard racial traits, like the elven alternate racial trait fleet-footed, which grants the Run feat and a bonus on initiative checks instead of the normal keen senses and weapon familiarity traits, reflecting the grace and uncanny reflexes of that race. To take one of these alternate racial traits, you must exchange one or more of the existing standard racial traits available to the race. You can exchange one or several of the standard racial traits, but you cannot exchange the same racial trait more than once. For example, an elf who takes the fleet-footed racial trait cannot take the urbanite racial trait, because the latter trait also replaces keen senses.

Racial Subtypes: This section presents a number of select racial subtypes for each of the core races. Racial subtypes give a brief description of what makes the subrace different and presents a suite of alternate racial traits that subrace gains instead of the race's standard racial traits.

Favored Class Options: These rules allow each race to take alternate rewards when a member of that race gains a level in her favored class. Each of these replaces the normal reward for having a level in a favored class—either gaining 1 extra hit point or 1 extra skill rank each time a member of the race takes a level in that class. Unlike those general rewards, the alternate favored class options usually speak directly to the features and options of the class in question. Most of them are plays on the flavor of the race, such as a gnome's curiosity about alchemical devices or a halfling's innate luck.

When choosing one of these favored class options, the reward is gained on a level-by-level basis. Unless otherwise noted, these benefits always stack with themselves. For example, a halfling fighter adds +1 to his CMD when resisting a trip or a grapple each time he gains a level; choosing this benefit twice increases the bonus to a total of +2, choosing it 10 times increases the bonus to a total of +10, and so on.

In other cases, these rewards may have a fixed numerical limit, after which selecting such a favored class reward again has no effect. In these cases you can always select the standard reward for taking a level in a favored class.

Some of these alternate class rewards only add +1/2, +1/3, +1/4, or +1/6 on a roll (rather than +1) each time the reward is selected. When applying this type of result to a die roll, always round down (minimum 0). For example, a half-orc with gunslinger as her favored class adds a +1/4 bonus on attack rolls and a +1/2 bonus on damage rolls when using the pistol whip deed each time she selects that favored class bonus, though this means the net effect is +0 on each after selecting it once (because both +1/4 and +1/2 rounds down to 0). After 20 levels, this benefit gives the half-orc a +5 bonus on attack rolls and a +10 bonus on damage rolls when using the pistol whip deed (in addition to the base value from being a 20th-level gunslinger).

RACIAL ARCHETYPES

This section presents two archetypes for each of the expanded races. Sometimes, an entry in this section presents a new cavalier order or sorcerer bloodline instead

of an archetype. Typically, only members of the section's race can take the listed archetype, bloodline, or order, though such options rarely interact with the racial traits or alternate racial traits of that race. An archetype usually features a thematic link to the race, granting it class features that complement the abilities and the background of the race. Because adventurers are often societal outliers, sometimes these archetypes feature a theme that is the exception to the norm for racial tendencies. The following is a list of all the archetypes featured in this chapter, listed by race. The class for each archetype is listed in parentheses. If the option is a sorcerer bloodline instead of an archetype, this is also called out in parentheses.

Dwarves: Exarch (inquisitor), forgemaster (cleric), stonelord (paladin).

Elves: Ancient lorekeeper (oracle), spell dancer (magus), spellbinder (wizard), treesinger (druid).

Gnomes: Experimental gunsmith (gunslinger), prankster (bard), saboteur (alchemist).

Half-Elves: Bramble brewer (alchemist), bonded witch (witch), wild caller (summoner), wild shadow (ranger).

Half-Orcs: Blood god disciple (summoner), hateful rager (barbarian), redeemer (paladin), skulking slayer (rogue).

Halflings: Community guardian (oracle), filcher (rogue), order of the paw (cavalier), underfoot adept (monk).

Humans: Buccaneer (gunslinger), feral child (druid), imperious bloodline (sorcerer), wanderer (monk).

NEW RACIAL RULES

The final section of each race entry provides new rules options for the race other than archetypes. The new racial rules are split up into four sections, each described below.

Equipment: The equipment section for each race provides new rules for standard and alchemical equipment available to the race. Often such equipment is available on the open market and members of other races can purchase it, but many times, especially in the case of alchemical equipment, it has no effect, lesser effects, or even detrimental effects on members of other races.

Feats: This section provides new racial feats for members of this race. These feats often play off a particular theme of the race and in many cases expand or empower racial traits of that race. All of these feats have the race in their prerequisites, so members of other races cannot take them.

Magic Items: Magic items provided in this section are often created and used exclusively by members of the race. Some have effects that interact with racial traits, but others have broader uses, and can be used by members of other races.

Spells: The spells in this section are common to spellcasting members of the race. Sometimes they only target members of the race, but often they are just the race's well guarded secrets; members of other races can learn to cast them with GM permission.

DWARVES

Dwarves are a stoic but stern race, ensconced in cities carved from the hearts of mountains and fiercely determined to repel the depredations of savage races like orcs and goblins. More than any other race, dwarves have acquired a reputation as dour and humorless artisans of the earth. It could be said that their history shapes the dark disposition of many dwarves, for they reside in high mountains and dangerous realms below the earth, constantly at war with giants, goblins, and other such horrors.

Dwarves are lovers of history and tradition, and their long lifespan leads to far less in the way of generational shifts in attitudes, styles, fashions, and trends than shorter-lived races exhibit. If a thing is not broken, they do not fix it or change it; and if it is broken, they fix it rather than replace it. Thrifty as a rule, dwarves are loath to discard anything unless it is truly ruined and unable to be fixed. At the same time, dwarves' meticulous, near-obsessive attention to detail and durability in their craftsmanship makes that a rare occurrence, as the things they make are built to last. As a result, buildings, artwork, tools, housewares, garments, weapons, and virtually everything else made by dwarves still sees regular use at an age when such items would be relegated to museum pieces, dusty antique shelves, or junkyard fodder by other races. Taken together, these traits create the impression that dwarves are a race frozen in time.

Nothing could be further from the truth, however, as dwarves are both thoughtful and imaginative, willing to experiment, if always keen to refine and perfect a new technique or product before moving on to the next one. Dwarves have achieved feats of metallurgy, stonework, and engineering that have consistently outpaced the technological advances of other races, though some non-dwarven races have used magic to supplement and perfect their own creations to achieve the same ends through

DWARF RACIAL TRAITS

+2 Constitution, +2 Wisdom, –2 Charisma: Dwarves are both tough and wise, but also a bit gruff.

Medium: Dwarves are Medium creatures and receive no bonuses or penalties due to their size.

Slow and Steady: Dwarves have a base speed of 20 feet, but their speed is never modified by armor or encumbrance.

Darkvision: Dwarves can see in the dark up to 60 feet.

Defensive Training: Dwarves gain a +4 dodge bonus to AC against monsters of the giant subtype.

Greed: Dwarves gain a +2 racial bonus on Appraise checks made to determine the price of nonmagical goods that contain precious metals or gemstones.

Hatred: Dwarves gain a +1 racial bonus on attack rolls against humanoid creatures of the orc and goblinoid subtypes because of their special training against these hated foes.

Hardy: Dwarves gain a +2 racial bonus on saving throws against poison, spells, and spell-like abilities.

Stability: Dwarves gain a +4 racial bonus to their Combat Maneuver Defense when resisting a bull rush or trip attempt while standing on the ground.

Stonecunning: Dwarves gain a +2 bonus on Perception checks to notice unusual stonework, such as traps and hidden doors located in stone walls or floors. They receive a check to notice such features whenever they pass within 10 feet of them, whether or not they are actively looking.

Weapon Familiarity: Dwarves are proficient with battleaxes, heavy picks, and warhammers, and treat any weapon with the word "dwarven" in its name as a martial weapon.

Languages: Dwarves begin play speaking Common and Dwarven. Dwarves with high Intelligence scores can choose from the following: Giant, Gnome, Goblin, Orc, Terran, and Undercommon.

mystical rather than mundane means. They are also a race typified by stubborn courage and dedication to seeing tasks through to completion, whatever the risks. These traits have led dwarves to explore and settle in extreme environments that would cause other races to quail and retreat. From the darkest depths of the underworld to the highest mountain peaks, from rusting iron citadels along desolate rocky coasts to squat jungle ziggurats, dwarves have established their enclaves and redoubts, holding them against all comers or perishing to the last and leaving only their enduring monuments to stand as their legacy.

While it is said that dwarves are not venturesome or inventive, it would be more accurate to say that they maintain a focus on and dedication to each task they undertake and every change they adopt, vetting such changes thoroughly before adopting them wholeheartedly. When faced with new circumstances and new needs, they react by applying tried and true tools and techniques systematically, using existing methods whenever possible rather than trying to invent novel solutions for every situation. If necessity requires, however, they throw themselves with equal vigor into developing the next perfect procedure for demolishing the obstacles that get in their way. Once their desired goal is obtained, they focus on consolidating each new piece of territory or conceptual advance. Dwarves thus rarely overextend themselves, but they also may miss opportunities to seize the initiative and maximize the advantages they create.

Physical Description: Dwarves are a short and stocky race, and stand about a foot shorter than most humans, with wide, compact bodies that account for their burly appearance. Male and female dwarves pride themselves on the long length of their hair, and men often decorate their beards with a variety of clasps and intricate braids. Clean-shavenness on a male dwarf is a sure sign of madness, or worse—no one familiar with their race trusts a beardless dwarven man.

Society: The great distances between dwarves' mountain citadels account for many of the cultural differences that exist within their society. Despite these schisms, dwarves throughout the world are characterized by their love of stonework, their passion for stone- and metal-based craftsmanship and architecture, and their fierce hatred of giants, orcs, and goblinoids. In some remote enclaves, such as those areas where these races are uncommon or unheard of, dwarves' fixation on security and safety combined with their rather pugnacious nature leads them to find enemies or at least rivals wherever they settle. While they are not precisely militaristic, they learned long ago that those without axes can be hewn apart by them, and thus dwarves everywhere are schooled to be ready to enforce their rights and claims by force of arms. When their patience with diplomacy is exhausted,

dwarves do not hesitate to adopt what they call "aggressive negotiations."

Relations: Dwarves and orcs have long dwelt in proximity to one another, and share a history of violence as old as both races. Dwarves generally distrust and shun half-orcs. They find elves, gnomes, and halflings to be too frail, flighty, or "pretty" to be worthy of proper respect. It is with humans that dwarves share the strongest link, for humans' industrious nature and hearty appetites come closest to matching those of the dwarven ideal.

Alignment and Religion: Dwarves are driven by honor and tradition. While they are often stereotyped as standoffish, they have a strong sense of friendship and justice, and those who win their trust understand that while they work hard, they play even harder—especially when good ale is involved. Most dwarves are lawful good.

Adventurers: Although dwarven adventurers are rare compared to humans, they can be found in most regions of the world. Dwarves often leave the confines of their redoubts to seek glory for their clans, to find wealth with which to enrich the fortress-homes of their birth, or to reclaim fallen dwarven citadels from racial enemies. Dwarven warfare is often characterized by tunnel fighting and melee combat, and as such most dwarves tend toward classes such as fighters and barbarians.

Male Names: Dolgrin, Grunyar, Harsk, Kazmuk, Morgrym, Rogar.

Female Names: Agna, Bodill, Ingra, Kotri, Rusilka, Yangrit.

ALTERNATE RACIAL RULES
While most think of dwarves as a relatively homogenous race, many clans have adapted over the years to better survive in harsh and varied environments. The following options represent some of that customization, and can be taken by any dwarf character.

Alternate Racial Traits
The following racial traits may be selected instead of the standard dwarf racial traits. Consult your GM before selecting any of these new options.

Ancient Enmity: Dwarves have long been in conflict with elves, especially the hated drow. Dwarves with this racial trait receive a +1 racial bonus on attack rolls against humanoid creatures of the elf subtype. This racial trait replaces hatred.

Craftsman: Dwarves are known for their superior craftsmanship when it comes to metallurgy and stonework. Dwarves with this racial trait receive a +2 racial bonus on all Craft or Profession checks related to metal or stone. This racial trait replaces greed.

Deep Warrior: Dwarves with this racial trait grew up facing the abominations that live deep beneath the surface. They receive a +2 dodge bonus to AC against monsters of the

aberration type and a +2 racial bonus on combat maneuver checks made to grapple such creatures (or to continue a grapple). This racial trait replaces defensive training.

Giant Hunter: Dwarves with this racial trait gain a +1 bonus on attack rolls against humanoids with the giant subtype. Furthermore, they gain a +2 bonus on Survival checks to find and follow tracks made by humanoids with the giant subtype. This racial trait replaces the hatred racial trait.

Lorekeeper: Dwarves keep extensive records about their history and the world around them. Dwarves with this racial trait receive a +2 racial bonus on Knowledge (history) checks that pertain to dwarves or their enemies. They can make such skill checks untrained. This racial trait replaces greed.

Magic Resistant: Some of the older dwarven clans are particularly resistant to magic. Dwarves with this racial trait gain spell resistance equal to 5 + their character level. This resistance can be lowered for 1 round as a standard action. Dwarves with this racial trait take a –2 penalty on all concentration checks made in relation to arcane spells. This racial trait replaces hardy.

Minesight: Dwarves with this racial trait increase the range of their darkvision to 90 feet; however, they are automatically dazzled in bright light and take a –2 penalty on saving throws against effects with the light descriptor. This racial trait replaces darkvision.

Mountaineer: Mountain dwarves are skilled at climbing and navigating narrow ledges. Dwarves with this racial trait are immune to altitude sickness and do not lose their Dexterity bonus to AC when making Climb or Acrobatics checks to cross narrow or slippery surfaces. This racial trait replaces stability.

Relentless: Dwarves are skilled at pushing their way through a battlefield, tossing aside lesser foes with ease. Dwarves with this racial trait receive a +2 bonus on combat maneuver checks made to bull rush or overrun an opponent. This bonus only applies while both the dwarf and his opponent are standing on the ground. This racial trait replaces stability.

Rock Stepper: Dwarves with this racial trait can skillfully negotiate rocky terrain. They can ignore difficult terrain created by rubble, broken ground, or steep stairs when they take a 5-foot step. This racial trait replaces stonecunning.

Saltbeard: Dwarves occasionally found iron cities along rugged seacoasts, and natives of such cities gain a +2 bonus on Profession (sailor) and Survival checks while at sea. They gain a +1 racial bonus on attack rolls and a +2 dodge bonus to AC against creatures with the aquatic or water subtype. Their greed racial trait applies only to treasure found in or under the water, but applies to all such treasure regardless of whether or not it contains metal or gemstones. This racial trait replaces defensive training, hatred, and stonecunning.

Sky Sentinel: As creatures with a deep affinity for the ground, dwarves are wary of attacks from above. Enemies on higher ground gain no attack roll bonus against dwarves with this racial trait, and they gain a +1 racial bonus on attack rolls, a +2 dodge bonus to AC, and a +2 bonus on Perception checks against flying creatures. This racial trait replaces defensive training, hatred, and stonecunning.

Stonesinger: Some dwarves' affinity for the earth grants them greater powers. Dwarves with this racial trait are treated as one level higher when casting spells with the earth descriptor or using granted powers of the Earth domain, the bloodline powers of the earth elemental bloodline, and revelations of the oracle's stone mystery. This ability does not give them early access to level-based powers; it only affects the powers they could use without this ability. This racial trait replaces stonecunning.

Stubborn: Dwarves are renowned for their stubbornness. Dwarves with this racial trait receive a +2 racial bonus on Will saves to resist spells and spell-like abilities of the enchantment (charm) and enchantment (compulsion) schools. In addition, if they fail such a save, they receive another save 1 round later to prematurely end the effect (assuming it has a duration greater than 1 round). This second save is made at the same DC as the first. If the dwarf has a similar ability from another source (such as a rogue's slippery mind), he can only use one of these abilities per round, but he can try the other on the second round if the first reroll ability fails. This racial trait replaces hardy.

Surface Survivalist: Some dwarves have dwelt so long aboveground they have lost their ability to see at night. However, their adaptation to extreme environments allows them to treat wind conditions (when determining whether or not they are checked or blown away) and either hot or cold climates (choose one) as one step less severe. This racial trait replaces darkvision.

Xenophobic: Isolationist dwarves despise non-dwarven humanoids. They speak only Dwarven and do not gain any bonus languages from possessing a high Intelligence score. In addition, they learn only one language per 2 ranks of Linguistics they possess. However, their untrusting nature gives them a +1 bonus against mind-affecting effects, except for fear affects. This racial trait replaces a dwarf's normal languages.

Wyrmscourged: Dwarves with this racial trait gain a +1 bonus on attack rolls and a +2 dodge bonus to AC and on saving throws against the exceptional, supernatural, and spell-like abilities of dragons. They also gain a +2 racial bonus on Knowledge (arcana) checks to identify dragons and can make such checks untrained. This racial trait replaces defensive training, hatred, and stonecunning.

Racial Subtypes

You can combine various alternate racial traits to create dwarven subraces or variant races, such as the following.

Deep Delver: Dwarves living far below the earth have the minesight and deep warrior racial traits. Deep delver spellcasters may exchange stonecunning for the stonesinger trait.

Elder Dwarf: Traditionalist dwarves of ancient lineage have the ancient enmity, lorekeeper, and either the magic resistant or stubborn racial traits.

Exiled Dwarf: Dwarves who have lost their homelands usually have the relentless and stubborn racial traits, and often have wyrmscourged as well.

Mountain Dwarf: Dwarves living atop high peaks have the mountaineer racial trait and often surface survivalist as well. Mountain dwarves are also trained to defend their homes, and may take the sky sentinel and xenophobic traits instead.

Favored Class Options

Instead of receiving an additional skill rank or hit point whenever they gain a level in a favored class, dwarves have the option of choosing from a number of other bonuses, depending upon the character's favored class. The following options are available to all dwarves who have the listed favored class, and unless otherwise stated, the bonus applies each time you select the listed favored class reward.

Alchemist: Add +1/4 to the alchemist's natural armor bonus when using his mutagen.

Barbarian: Add +1 to the barbarian's total number of rage rounds per day.

Bard: Reduce arcane spell failure chance for casting bard spells when wearing medium armor by +1%. Once the total reaches 10%, the bard also receives Medium Armor Proficiency, if he does not already possess it.

Cavalier: Add +1/2 to the cavalier's bonus to damage against targets of his challenge.

Cleric: Select one domain power granted at 1st level that is normally usable a number of times per day equal to 3 + the cleric's Wisdom modifier. The cleric adds +1/2 to the number of uses per day of that domain power.

Druid: Select one domain power granted at 1st level that is normally usable a number of times per day equal to 3 + the druid's Wisdom modifier. The druid adds +1/2 to the number of uses per day of that domain power.

Fighter: Add +1 to the fighter's CMD when resisting a bull rush or trip.

Gunslinger: Reduce the misfire chance for one type of firearm by 1/4. You cannot reduce the misfire chance of a firearm below 1.

Inquisitor: Add +1/2 to the inquisitor's level for the purpose of determining the effects of one type of judgment.

Magus: Select one known magus arcana usable only once per day. The magus adds +1/6 to the number of times it can be used per day. Once that magus arcana is usable twice per day, the magus must select a different magus arcana.

Monk: Reduce the Hardness of any object made of clay, stone, or metal by 1 whenever the object is struck by the monk's unarmed strike (minimum of 0).

Oracle: Reduce the penalty for not being proficient with one weapon by 1. When the nonproficiency penalty for a weapon becomes 0 because of this ability, the oracle is treated as having the appropriate Martial or Exotic Weapon Proficiency feat with that weapon.

Paladin: Add a +1 bonus on concentration checks when casting paladin spells.

Ranger: Add a +1/2 bonus on wild empathy checks to influence animals and magical beasts that live underground.

Rogue: Add a +1/2 bonus on Disable Device checks regarding stone traps and a +1/2 bonus to trap sense regarding stone traps.

Sorcerer: Add +1/2 to acid and earth spell or spell-like ability damage.

Summoner: Add a +1/4 natural armor bonus to the AC of the summoner's eidolon.

Witch: Add +1/4 natural armor bonus to the AC of the witch's familiar.

Wizard: Select one item creation feat known by the wizard. Whenever he crafts an item using that feat, the amount of progress he makes in an 8-hour period increases by 200 gp (50 gp if crafting while adventuring). This does not reduce the cost of the item; it just increases the rate at which the item is crafted.

RACIAL ARCHETYPES

The following racial archetypes are available to dwarves.

Exarch (Inquisitor)

The gruff traditionalism of most dwarves finds its apex in those who adhere to a strict orthodoxy rooted in ancient principles and practices and who are not amenable whatsoever to change or innovation.

Spells: Exarchs cannot cast spells with the chaotic descriptor.

Inflexible Will (Ex): At 1st level, an exarch gains a +2 bonus on saving throws against *confusion* and *insanity* effects and effects with the chaotic descriptor. This ability replaces monster lore.

Detect Chaos (Sp): At will, an exarch can use *detect chaos*. This ability replaces detect alignment.

Fearsome Jurist (Su): At 5th level, an exarch can imbue one of her weapons with the *jurist* or *menacing* weapon special ability as a swift action, and may switch between these properties as a swift action. When using either special ability, her weapon's critical threat range doubles

against chaotic creatures. This does not stack with *keen edge*, Improved Critical, or similar effects. This ability otherwise functions as and replaces bane.

Aura of Repetition (Su): At 8th level, once per day while using her judgment, an exarch can project an aura of repetition, as the Toil subdomain power (*Advanced Player's Guide* 97). If the exarch takes Artifice (Toil) as her domain, the save DC of her aura increases by 2 but its duration does not increase. This ability replaces her second judgment.

Double Jeopardy (Su): At 12th level, whenever an exarch uses her fearsome jurist ability, she may choose to affect two weapons, with one gaining the *jurist* weapon special ability and the other the *menacing* special ability as above. Both special abilities may be combined in a single weapon, whose critical threat range doubles. This does not stack with *keen edge*, Improved Critical, or similar effects. This ability replaces greater bane.

Aura of Reversion (Su): At 16th level, while using her judgment, an exarch can project a 30-foot-radius emanation for a number of rounds per day equal to her inquisitor level. Any creature other than the exarch that is using a transmutation effect within this aura at the beginning of its turn becomes sickened, or sickened and nauseated if using a polymorph effect, including the change shape ability (Fortitude negates; DC 10 + 1/2 the exarch's level + her Wisdom modifier). Continuous effects from permanent magical items do not cause this effect. Within the aura, dispel checks against transmutation effects gain a +4 bonus. This ability cannot be used simultaneously with aura of repetition. This ability replaces her third judgment.

Foehammer (Fighter)

While the axe is the most famous dwarven weapon, the hammer is at the heart of dwarves' heritage as forgemasters and warriors alike.

Sledgehammer (Ex): At 3rd level, a foehammer wielding a hammer gains a +2 circumstance bonus on combat maneuver checks made to bull rush, overrun, sunder, or trip. This ability replaces armor training 1.

Weapon Training (Ex): At 5th level, a foehammer must select hammers and does not gain weapon training with other groups, though his weapon training bonus improves by +1 every four levels after 5th.

Hammer to the Ground (Ex): At 7th level, when a foehammer succeeds at a bull rush combat maneuver, he can make a trip combat maneuver at the end of the bull rush. If he does not move with the target, the force of his blow may still trip his foe, but he takes a −5 penalty on the combat maneuver check to trip.

At 15th level, any creature a foehammer successfully bull rushes is automatically knocked prone at the end of the bull rush. This ability replaces armor training 2 and 4.

Rhythmic Blows (Ex): At 9th level, each time that a foehammer hits a target, he gains a +1 bonus on attack rolls against that target. This bonus stacks with each hit against that target, but lasts only until the end of the foehammer's turn. This ability replaces weapon training 2.

Piledriver (Ex): At 11th level, as a standard action, a foehammer may make a single melee attack with a weapon from the hammer weapon training group. If the attack hits, he may make a bull rush or trip combat maneuver against the target of his attack as a free action that does not provoke an attack of opportunity. This ability replaces armor training 3.

Ground Breaker (Ex): At 13th level, as a full-round action, a foehammer may strike the ground with his hammer. If the attack deals more damage than the floor's hardness, the space he occupies and all adjacent squares become difficult terrain. Creatures in those squares, except for the foehammer, are knocked prone (DC 15 Reflex negates). This ability replaces weapon training 3.

Hammer Master (Ex): At 17th level, any combat feats a foehammer has learned with any weapon from the hammer weapon training group (e.g., Improved Critical, Weapon Focus) apply to all weapons from that group. This ability replaces weapon training 4.

Devastating Blow (Ex): At 19th level, as a standard action, a foehammer may make a single melee attack with a weapon from the hammer weapon training group at a –5 penalty. If the attack hits, it is treated as a critical threat. Weapon special abilities that only activate on a critical hit do not activate if this critical hit is confirmed. This ability replaces armor mastery.

Weapon Mastery (Ex): A foehammer must choose a weapon from the hammer group.

Forgemaster (Cleric)

Forgemasters are priestly dwarves who are ritual casters and expert enchanters, able to produce their rune-graven armaments with astonishing speed.

Artificer: A forgemaster gains only one domain, which must be the Artifice domain (not including subdomains). If she worships a deity, it must grant the Artifice domain.

Steel Spells: A forgemaster adds the following spells to her spell list (spells marked with an asterisk [*] are found in the *Advanced Player's Guide*): 1st—*crafter's curse*, *crafter's fortune*, *lead blades*; 2nd—*chill metal*, *heat metal*, *shatter*; 3rd—*keen edge*, *versatile weapon*; 8th—*iron body*, *repel metal or stone*.

Divine Smith (Su): Whenever a forgemaster casts a spell that targets a weapon, shield, or armor, the spell takes effect at +1 caster level. If the spell has one or more metamagic feats applied, she reduces the total level adjustment to the spell by 1 (minimum 0).

Runeforger (Su): A forgemaster may inscribe mystical runes upon a suit of armor, shield, or weapon as full-round action, using this ability a number of times per day equal to 3 + her Intelligence modifier. These runes last 1 round per cleric level, but inscribing the same rune twice on an item increases this duration to 1 minute per level, three times to 10 minutes per level, and four times to 1 hour per level. *Erase* affects runes as magical writing. A forgemaster learns forgemaster's blessing at 1st level and may learn one additional rune at 2nd level and every 2 levels thereafter. Only one type of rune marked with an asterisk (*) may be placed on an item at any given time. This ability replaces channel energy.

Ancient Splendor: The inscribed weapon, armor, or shield grants a +2 circumstance bonus on Diplomacy and Intimidate checks (+4 when interacting with dwarves).

Bloodthirst*: The inscribed piercing or slashing weapon functions as if it had the *wounding* special ability, even if nonmagical. The forgemaster must be at least 4th level before learning this rune.

Deathstrike: The inscribed weapon stores a *death knell* spell that triggers immediately if a blow from the weapon reduces a target to negative hit points. This expends all deathstrike runes on the weapon. The forgemaster must be at least 4th level before learning this rune.

Durability: The inscribed item's hardness increases by an amount equal to the forgemaster's Wisdom modifier, and its hit points increase by an amount equal to twice her level.

Featherlight: The inscribed item's weight is halved; a metal item's weight is reduced to 1/4 normal. If inscribed on a suit of armor, its armor check penalty for Acrobatics, Climb, and Jump checks is halved.

Forgemaster's Blessing: The inscribed nonmagical item functions as a masterwork item.

Ghostglyph*: The inscribed weapon, shield, or armor gains the *ghost touch* special ability. The forgemaster must be at least 4th level before learning this rune.

Glowglyph: The inscribed item sheds light as a torch. As a standard action, the bearer can command the rune to erupt in a burst of light as a shield with the *blinding* special ability with a burst radius of 5 feet per glowglyph rune inscribed on the item. This expends all glowglyph runes on the item.

Invulnerability*: The inscribed armor grants its wearer DR/magic equal to 1/2 her cleric level. The forgemaster must be at least 8th level before learning this rune.

Powerstrike*: The inscribed weapon's critical threat range doubles. This does not stack with *keen edge*, Improved Critical, or similar effects. The forgemaster must be at least 6th level before learning this rune.

Return*: The inscribed weapon gains the *returning* weapon special ability. The forgemaster must be at least 4th level before learning this rune.

Spellguard: The inscribed item gains spell resistance equal to 11 + her cleric level. This applies only to effects targeting the item itself.

Spellglyph*: The inscribed weapon gains the *spell storing* special ability. The forgemaster must be at least 4th level before learning this rune.

Thief-Curse: The forgemaster designates one creature as the rightful owner of an item. Any other creature that intentionally grasps the item is cursed (as *bestow curse*) for the duration of the rune. The forgemaster must be at least 6th level before learning this rune.

Tracer: For as long as the rune lasts, the cleric may sense its location at will as a standard action, as if using *locate object*.

Craft Magic Arms and Armor: The forgemaster gains this as a bonus feat at 3rd level.

Master Smith (Ex): At 5th level, a forgemaster can craft mundane metal items quickly, using half their gp value to determine progress, and can craft magical metal items in half the normal amount of time.

Stonelord (Paladin)

A stonelord is a devoted sentinel of dwarven enclaves, drawing the power of the earth and ancient stone to protect her people.

Stonestrike (Su): Once per day per paladin level, a stonelord can draw upon the power of the living rock. As a swift action, she treats her melee attacks until the beginning of her next turn (whether armed or unarmed) as magical and adamantine, including ignoring hardness up to twice her paladin level, with a +1 bonus on attack and damage rolls, as well as on combat maneuver checks. This bonus also applies to her CMD if she or her target is touching the ground or a stone structure. This bonus increases by +1 at 5th level and every 5 levels thereafter. This ability replaces smite evil.

Heartstone (Ex): At 2nd level, a stonelord's flesh becomes progressively rockier. She gains a +1 natural armor bonus to AC and DR/adamantine equal to 1/2 her paladin level. The natural armor bonus increases by +1 at 6th level, and every four levels thereafter, to a maximum of +5 at 18th level. These benefits are halved when not touching the ground or a stone structure. This ability replaces divine grace.

Stoneblood (Ex): At 3rd level, a stonelord's vitals begin to calcify and her blood transforms into liquid stone. She adds her paladin level on checks to stabilize at negative hit points and gains a 25% chance to ignore a critical hit or precision damage. This does not stack with *fortification* armor or similar effects. At 9th level, this chance increases to 50% and she becomes immune to petrification. At 15th level, this chance increases to 75% and she becomes immune to bleed and blood drain effects. This ability replaces divine health and her mercies gained at 3rd, 9th, and 15th level.

Defensive Stance (Ex): At 4th level, a stonelord gains the defensive stance ability, as a stalwart defender (*Advanced Player's Guide* 277), and may select one defensive power at 8th level and every four levels thereafter. Levels of stalwart defender stack with her paladin levels when determining the total number of rounds that she can maintain her defensive stance per day. A stonelord does not gain any spells or spellcasting abilities, does not have a caster level, and cannot use spell trigger or spell completion magic items.

Earth Channel (Su): At 4th level, a stonelord gains Elemental Channel (earth) as a bonus feat, which she may activate by spending two uses of her lay on hands ability, using her paladin level as her effective cleric level. This ability replaces channel positive energy.

TABLE 1-1: DWARVEN WEAPONS

Exotic Weapons	Cost	Dmg (S)	Dmg (M)	Critical	Range	Weight	Type	Special
Light Melee Weapons								
Helmet, dwarven boulder	20 gp	1d3	1d4	×2	—	10 lbs.	B	see text
One-Handed Melee Weapons								
Waraxe, dwarven double	60 gp	1d8	1d10	×3	—	12 lbs.	S	see text
Two-Handed Melee Weapons								
Longaxe, dwarven	50 gp	1d10	1d12	×3	—	14 lbs.	S	reach
Longhammer, dwarven	70 gp	1d10	2d6	×3	—	20 lbs.	B	reach

Stone Servant (Su): At 5th level, a stonelord may call a Small earth elemental to her side, as a paladin calls her mount. This earth elemental is Lawful Good in alignment and possesses the celestial template, and it increases in size as the stonelord gains levels, becoming Medium at 8th level, Large at 11th level, Huge at 14th level, Greater at 17th level, and Elder at 20th level. This ability replaces divine bond.

Stonebane (Su): At 11th level, when using stonestrike, a stonelord's attack gains the *bane* weapon special ability against creatures with the earth subtype and constructs or objects made of earth or stone. This ability replaces aura of justice.

Phase Strike (Su): At 12th level, a stonelord's stonestrike may pass through stone and metal as if they weren't there. By spending 2 uses of her stonestrike ability, she may ignore any cover less than total cover provided by stone or metal, and she ignores any AC bonus from stone or metal armor or shields as if wielding a *brilliant energy* weapon. A phase strike cannot damage constructs, objects, or creatures with the earth subtype, but unlike a *brilliant energy* weapon, it can harm undead. This ability replaces her 12th-level mercy.

Mobile Defense (Ex): At 18th level, a stonelord can make one 5-foot step per round while maintaining her defensive stance. This ability replaces her 18th-level mercy.

Stone Body (Ex): At 20th level, a stonelord's body transforms into living stone. She no longer needs to eat, drink, breathe, or sleep, and she becomes immune to paralysis, poison, and stunning. She is also no longer subject to critical hits or precision-based damage. This ability replaces holy champion.

NEW RACIAL RULES

The following options are available to dwarves. At the GM's discretion, other appropriate races may also make use of some of these.

Dwarven Equipment

Dwarves have access to the following equipment.

Helmet, Dwarven Boulder: This heavy, reinforced helmet can be used to make melee attacks. The wearer may also use the helmet when attempting bull rush maneuvers, granting a +2 circumstance bonus on the check, but after completing the maneuver (whether successful or not), the wearer is staggered until the end of his next turn. In addition, the helmet grants a +2 circumstance bonus to the wearer's AC against critical hit confirmation rolls. A dwarven boulder helmet adds 20% to the wearer's arcane spell failure chance. It occupies the head slot and is made of metal, not stone, meaning that it can be crafted from unusual materials as a metal weapon. A dwarven boulder helmet can be enchanted as a weapon (not as armor, despite providing some protection).

Longaxe, Dwarven: These ornate and heavy blades are mounted atop a long, steel-shod haft for greater reach. They are rare among cave-dwelling dwarves but common in mountain dwarf clans that commonly feud with giants.

Longhammer, Dwarven: These heavy-headed bludgeons are often carved or cast with monstrous faces or drilled with tiny holes to create a menacing whistling as they are swung through the air.

Waraxe, Dwarven Double: This hefty waraxe is similar to the common dwarven waraxe, but its recurved blade spans forward and back from its head like a deadly butterfly. A dwarven double waraxe grants a +1 bonus on all attack rolls after the first when using Cleave or Great Cleave.

Dwarven Feats

Over their long history, dwarves have faced many enemies from both above and below. As a result, they have developed a number of tricks and abilities to help them survive in the face of such threats.

Brewmaster

You can concoct potent brews.

Prerequisites: Craft (alchemy) 1 rank, Profession (brewer) 1 rank, dwarf.

Benefit: You gain a +2 bonus on Craft (alchemy) and Profession (brewer) checks, and you add +1 to the DC of any ingested poison you create.

Cleave Through (Combat)
You are ferocious at hewing smaller opponents.

Prerequisites: Str 13, Cleave, Power Attack, base attack bonus +11, dwarf.

Benefit: When using Cleave or Great Cleave, if your initial attack hits, you may take a single 5-foot step as a free action before making your additional attacks. If doing so places a creature within your threatened area, that creature becomes a legal target for your additional Cleave attack(s) as long as it meets all the other prerequisites.

Normal: You may only make additional attacks with Cleave against creatures you threaten when you make your initial attack.

Cloven Helm (Combat)
Your helm turns aside lethal blows.

Prerequisites: Dented Helm, Hard-Headed, base attack bonus +11, dwarf.

Benefit: When wearing a helmet, you add +1 to your AC against critical hit confirmation rolls; this benefit stacks with Dented Helm. When you use Dented Helm to deflect a critical hit, you may apply all damage from the critical hit to your helmet before applying any damage to yourself. If you take no damage, any additional effects, such as critical feats or poison, are negated.

Dented Helm (Combat)
Your helm protects you from hard hits.

Prerequisites: Hard-Headed, base attack bonus +6, dwarf.

Benefit: When wearing a helmet, you add +1 to your AC against critical hit confirmation rolls. When a critical hit is confirmed against you, as an immediate action, you can apply half of the damage from the attack to your helmet rather than yourself, applying hardness as normal. If the damage destroys your helmet, any leftover damage is applied to you. After using this feat, you are staggered until the end of your next turn. You may not use this feat if your helmet has the broken condition or the attack ignores armor bonuses to AC.

Giant Killer (Combat)
Your cleaving strokes menace giants and larger foes.

Prerequisites: Str 13, Cleave, Goblin Cleaver, Orc Hewer, Power Attack, Strike Back, base attack bonus +11, dwarf.

Benefit: This functions as Goblin Cleaver, but your additional attacks can be made against creatures one size category larger than you or smaller. In addition, any such attacks made against humanoids (giant) gain a +2 circumstance bonus on attack rolls.

Goblin Cleaver (Combat)
You are ferocious at hewing smaller opponents.

Prerequisites: Str 13, Cleave, Power Attack, dwarf.

Benefit: When using Cleave or Great Cleave, if your initial attack hits, you may take your additional attacks against any creature smaller than you that you threaten; your targets need not be adjacent to one another. Additional attacks you make against humanoids (goblinoid) gain a +2 circumstance bonus on attack rolls.

Hard-Headed (Combat)
Your thick skull is almost a weapon unto itself.

Prerequisites: Base attack bonus +1, dwarf.

Benefit: You gain a +1 bonus on attack rolls and combat maneuver checks made using a helmet. You receive a +2 bonus on saves against spells and special abilities that cause you to become staggered or stunned.

Ledge Walker
You negotiate tiny ledges like a mountain goat.

Prerequisites: Dex 13, dwarf, mountaineer or stability racial trait.

Benefit: You can move at full speed while using Acrobatics to balance on narrow surfaces, and you gain a +4 bonus on Climb checks to catch yourself or another creature while falling. You also gain a +4 bonus on saving throws against effects that would cause you to fall prone (such as earthquakes). This bonus does not apply to your CMD against bull rush or trip attacks.

Orc Hewer (Combat)
You are ferocious at hewing your enemies, especially orcs.

Prerequisites: Str 13, Cleave, Goblin Cleaver, Power Attack, dwarf.

Benefit: This feat functions as Goblin Cleaver, but your additional attacks can be made against creatures your size or smaller. In addition, any such attacks that you make against humanoids (orc) gain a +2 circumstance bonus on attack rolls.

Shatterspell (Combat)
Your mighty blows shatter your enemy's magic.

Prerequisites: Disruptive, Spellbreaker, dwarf, 10th-level fighter.

Benefit: As a standard action, you can attempt to sunder an ongoing spell effect as if you had the spell sunder rage power (*Ultimate Combat* 28). You may use this feat once per day, plus one additional time per day for every 5 points by which your base attack bonus exceeds +10.

Toxic Recovery
Your system recuperates from the effects of poisons with astonishing speed.

Prerequisites: Dwarf, hardy racial trait.

Benefit: Whenever you succeed at a saving throw against poison, you heal 1 point of ability damage of the type dealt by the poison. Whenever you heal ability damage naturally or magically, you heal 1 additional point of ability damage. This feat has no effect on penalties to ability scores or ability drain.

Dwarven Magic Items

Dwarven magic often involves earth and stone, and is tailored to overcome the challenges they face in everyday life. It should therefore come as no surprise that dwarves' magic items often deal with these as well. The following magic items were invented by dwarven crafters, and are rare outside their communities.

ELIXIR OF DARKSIGHT

Aura moderate transmutation; **CL** 6th

Slot none; **Price** 1,200 gp; **Weight** —

DESCRIPTION

This dark, syrupy draught doubles the range of the drinker's darkvision and also enables her to see through *deeper darkness* when using darkvision. The effects last for 1 hour.

CONSTRUCTION

Requirements Craft Wondrous Item, *darkvision, deeper darkness*; **Cost** 600 gp

ROD OF DWARVEN MIGHT

Aura strong transmutation; **CL** 19th

Slot none; **Price** 80,000 gp; **Weight** 10 lbs.

DESCRIPTION

This dwarven version of the more famous *rod of lordly might* has no spell-like powers; however, when wielded by a dwarf, it increases all AC, attack roll, CMD, CMB, and saving throw bonuses from a dwarf's racial traits by +1. The rod shares the mundane powers of a *rod of lordly might*, but its magical weapon forms are tailored to dwarven preferences.

- In its normal form, the rod can be used as a +1 *returning light hammer*.
- When button 1 is pushed, the rod becomes a +3 *dwarven longhammer*.
- When button 2 is pushed, the rod becomes a +4 *dwarven waraxe*.
- When button 3 is pushed, the rod becomes a +2 *light crossbow* or +2 *heavy crossbow*.

CONSTRUCTION

Requirements Craft Magic Arms and Armor, Craft Rod, *bull's strength, telekinesis*, creator must be a dwarf; **Cost** 40,000 gp

Dwarven Spells

Dwarven spellcasters are renowned for shaping the ground beneath them, molding metal, and using magic to aid their craft. These spells are just a sample of such magics.

GROUNDSWELL

School transmutation [earth]; **Level** cleric 2, druid 2, magus 2, ranger 2

Casting Time 1 standard action

Components V, S

Range touch

Target creature touched

Duration 1 minute/level

Save Fortitude negates (harmless); **Spell Resistance** yes (harmless)

This spell allows the target to cause the ground to rise up beneath him. As a swift action, the target can cause the ground to rise 5 feet, while all adjacent squares are treated as steep slopes (*Core Rulebook* 428). The *groundswell* precludes flanking from creatures standing at lower elevations than the target. If the target moves after creating a *groundswell*, the ground returns to its normal elevation at the end of his turn; otherwise, it remains in place until the target moves or uses a swift action to return the ground to normal. A *groundswell* cannot increase elevation of the ground beyond 5 feet.

IRONBEARD

School transmutation; **Level** antipaladin 1, cleric 1, magus 1, paladin 1, ranger 1

Casting Time 1 standard action

Components V, S

Range touch

Target creature touched

Duration 1 minute/level

Save Fortitude negates (harmless); **Spell Resistance** yes (harmless)

This spell causes a brushy beard of stiff iron to erupt from the face of a willing target. The *ironbeard* grants a +1 armor bonus to AC, and this bonus stacks with any armor worn by the creature. The *ironbeard* may also be used as a weapon equivalent to cold iron armor spikes. The *ironbeard* makes it difficult to speak, so any spellcasting with a verbal component has a 20% spell failure chance.

TOILSOME CHANT

School enchantment (compulsion)[mind-affecting]; **Level** bard 1

Casting Time see text

Components V, S

Range close (25 ft. + 5 ft./2 levels)

Target one living creature

Duration see text

Saving Throw Will negates (harmless); **Spell Resistance** yes (harmless)

You can cast this spell as part of the action to begin an inspire competence bardic performance. The benefit of inspire competence persists for as long as is necessary to complete the target's next skill check using the chosen skill (up to a maximum of 1 hour per caster level), even if you cease your bardic performance.

Elves

The long-lived elves are children of the natural world, similar in many superficial ways to fey creatures, though with key differences. While fey are truly linked to the flora and fauna of their homes, existing as the nearly immortal voices and guardians of the wilderness, elves are instead mortals who are in tune with the natural world around them. Elves seek to live in balance with the wild and understand it better than most other mortals. Some of this understanding is mystical, but an equal part comes from the elves' long lifespans, which in turn gives them long-ranging outlooks. Elves can expect to remain active in the same locale for centuries. By necessity, they must learn to maintain sustainable lifestyles, and this is most easily done when they work with nature, rather than attempting to bend it to their will.

However, their links to nature are not entirely driven by pragmatism. Elves' bodies slowly change over time, taking on a physical representation of their mental and spiritual states, and those who dwell in a region for a long period of time find themselves physically adapting to match their surroundings, most noticeably taking on coloration that reflects the local environment.

Elves value their privacy and traditions, and while they are often slow to make friends at both the personal and national levels, once an outsider is accepted as a comrade, the resulting alliances can last for generations. Elves take great joy in forging alliances with races that share or exceed their long lifetimes, and often work to befriend dragons, outsiders, and fey. Those elves who spend their lives among the short-lived races, on the other hand, often develop a skewed perception of mortality and become morose, the result of watching wave after wave of companions age and die before their eyes.

Physical Description: Generally taller than humans, elves possess a graceful, slender physique that is accentuated by their long, pointed ears. It is a mistake, however, to consider them weak or feeble, as the thin limbs of an elf can contain surprising power. Their eyes are wide and almond-shaped, and filled with large, vibrantly colored pupils. The coloration of elves as a whole varies wildly, and is much more diverse than that of human populations. However, as their coloration often matches their surroundings, the elves

Elf Racial Traits

+2 Dexterity, +2 Intelligence, –2 Constitution: Elves are nimble, both in body and mind, but their form is frail.

Medium: Elves are Medium creatures and receive no bonuses or penalties due to their size.

Normal Speed: Elves have a base speed of 30 feet.

Low-Light Vision: Elves can see twice as far as humans in conditions of dim light.

Elven Immunities: Elves are immune to magic sleep effects and gain a +2 racial saving throw bonus against enchantment spells and effects.

Elven Magic: Elves receive a +2 racial bonus on caster level checks made to overcome spell resistance. In addition, elves receive a +2 racial bonus on Spellcraft skill checks made to identify the properties of magic items.

Keen Senses: Elves receive a +2 racial bonus on Perception checks.

Weapon Familiarity: Elves are proficient with longbows (including composite longbows), longswords, rapiers, and shortbows (including composite shortbows), and treat any weapon with the word "elven" in its name as a martial weapon.

Languages: Elves begin play speaking Common and Elven. Elves with high Intelligence scores can choose from the following: Celestial, Draconic, Gnoll, Gnome, Goblin, Orc, and Sylvan.

of a single community may appear quite similar. Forest-dwelling elves often have variations of green, brown, and tan in their hair, eye, and even skin tones.

While elven clothing often plays off the beauty of the natural world, those elves who live in cities tend to bedeck themselves in the latest fashions. Where city-dwelling elves encounter other urbanites, the elves are often fashion trendsetters.

Society: Many elves feel a bond with nature and strive to live in harmony with the natural world. Although, like most, elves prefer bountiful lands where resources are plentiful, when driven to live in harsher climates, they work hard to protect and shepherd the region's bounty, and learn how to maximize the benefit they receive from what little can be harvested. When they can carve out a sustainable, reliable life in deserts and wastelands, they take pride as a society in the accomplishment. While this can make them excellent guides to outsiders they befriend who must travel through such lands, their disdain of those who have not learned to live off the scant land as they have makes such friends rare.

Elves have an innate gift for craftsmanship and artistry, especially when working in wood, bone, ivory, or leather. Most, however, find manipulating earth and stone to be distasteful, and prefer to avoid forging, stonework, and pottery. When such work must be done within a community, a few elves may find themselves drawn to it, but regardless of their craftsmanship, such "dirt-wrights" are generally seen by other elves as being a bit off. In the most insular of elven societies, they may even be treated as lower class.

Elves also have an appreciation for the written word, magic, and painstaking research. Their naturally keen minds and senses, combined with their inborn patience, make them particularly suited to wizardry. Arcane research and accomplishment are seen as both practical goals, in line with being a soldier or architect, and artistic endeavors as great as poetry or sculpture. Within elven society, wizards are held in extremely high regard as masters of an art both powerful and aesthetically valued. Other spellcasters are not disdained, but do not gain the praise lavished upon elven wizards.

Relations: Elves are prone to dismissing other races, writing them off as rash and impulsive, yet on an individual level, they are excellent judges of character. In many cases an elf will come to value a specific member of another race, seeing that individual as deserving and respectable, while still dismissing the race as a whole. If called on this behavior, the elf often doesn't understand why his "special friend" is upset the elf has noticed the friend is "so much better than the rest of his kind." Even elves who see such prejudice for what it is must constantly watch themselves to prevent such views from coloring their thinking.

Elves are not foolish enough, however, to dismiss all aspects of other races and cultures. An elf might not want a dwarf neighbor, but would be the first to acknowledge dwarves' skill at smithing and their tenacity in facing orc threats. Elves regard gnomes as strange (and sometimes dangerous) curiosities, but regard their magical talent as being worthy of praise and respect. Halflings are often viewed with a measure of pity, for these small folk seem to the elves to be adrift, without a traditional home. Elves are fascinated with humans, who seem to live in a few short years as full a life as an elf manages in centuries. In fact, many elves become infatuated with humans, as evidenced by the number of half-elves in the world. Elves have difficulty accepting crossbreeds of any sort, however, and usually disown such offspring. They similarly regard half-orcs with distrust and suspicion, assuming they possess the worst aspects of orc and human personalities.

Alignment and Religion: Elves are emotional and capricious, yet value kindness and beauty. Most elves are chaotic good, wishing all creatures to be safe and happy, but unwilling to sacrifice personal freedom or choice to accomplish such goals. They prefer deities who share their love of the mystic qualities of the world—Desna and Nethys are particular favorites, the former for her wonder and love of the wild places, and the latter for his mastery of magic. Calistria is perhaps the most notorious of elven deities, for she represents elven ideals taken to an extreme. Elves accept in Calistria (and her priests) behavior they would denounce in others, because Calistria is clearly (to elves' perceptions) serving as an example of personal artistry and freedom of expressions, rather than seeking some base physical gratification.

Adventurers: Many elves embark on adventures out of a desire to explore the world, leaving their secluded realms to reclaim forgotten elven magic or search out lost kingdoms established millennia ago by their ancestors. This need to see a wider world is accepted by their societies as a natural part of becoming mature and experienced individuals. Such elves are expected to return in some few decades and take up lives in their homelands once more, enriched both in treasure and in worldview. For those elves raised among humans, however, life within their homes—watching friends and family swiftly age and die—is often stifling, and the ephemeral and unfettered life of an adventurer holds a natural appeal.

Elves generally eschew melee because of their relative frailty, preferring instead to engage enemies at range. Most see combat as unpleasant even when needful, and prefer it be done as quickly as possible, preferably without getting close enough to smell their foes. This preference for making war at a distance, coupled with their natural accuracy and grasp of the arcane, encourages elves to pursue classes such as wizards and rangers.

Male Names: Caladrel, Heldalel, Lanliss, Meirdrarel, Seldlon, Talathel, Variel, Zordlon.

Female Names: Amrunelara, Dardlara, Faunra, Jathal, Merisiel, Oparal, Soumral, Tessara, Yalandlara.

ALTERNATE RACIAL RULES

Elves, by their very nature, are a race with a wide variety of traits and features, many of which are drawn from the environment in which they live. The following rules represent some of those varied aspects, and while many are themed to one environment or another, they can be taken by any elf character.

Alternate Racial Traits

The following racial traits may be selected instead of the standard elf racial traits. Consult your GM before selecting any of these new options.

Arcane Focus: Some elven families have such long traditions of producing wizards (and other arcane spellcasters) that they raise their children with the assumption each is destined to be a powerful magic-user, with little need for mundane concerns such as skill with weapons. Elves with this racial trait gain a +2 racial bonus on concentration checks made to cast arcane spells defensively. This racial trait replaces weapon familiarity.

Darkvision: Though uncommon, some groups of elves are born with darkvision, rather than low-light vision. In many cases this is taken as a sign of a drow in the elf's ancestry, and can lead to persecution within the elf's home community. Elves with this racial trait gain darkvision with a range of 60 feet, but also gain sensitivity to light and are dazzled in areas of bright light or within the radius of a *daylight* spell. This racial trait replaces low-light vision.

Desert Runner: Some elves thrive in the deepest deserts, forever roaming across burned and parched lands. Elves with this racial trait receive a +4 racial bonus on Constitution checks and Fortitude saves to avoid fatigue, exhaustion, or ill effects from running, forced marches, starvation, thirst, or hot or cold environments. This racial trait replaces elven magic.

Dreamspeaker: A few elves have the ability to tap into the power of sleep, dreams, and prescient reverie. Elves with this racial trait add +1 to the saving throw DCs of spells of the divination school and sleep effects they cast. In addition, elves with Charisma scores of 15 or higher may use *dream* once per day as a spell-like ability (caster level is equal to the elf's character level). This racial trait replaces elven immunities.

Elemental Resistance: Elves who dwell in the most extreme environments, from arctic wastelands to volcanic plains, develop natural resistance to the dangers of their homelands over the course of a few generations. Elves with this racial trait gain elemental resistance 5 to acid, cold, electricity, or fire. This choice is made at character creation, and once made it cannot be changed. This racial trait replaces elven immunities.

Envoy: Elves often have trouble relating to neighbors of other races, especially those with much shorter lifespans. As a result, some are trained in minor magics that are particularly useful when dealing with non-elves. Elves with this racial trait and an Intelligence score of 11 or higher gain the following spell-like abilities once per day: *comprehend languages*, *detect magic*, *detect poison*, and *read magic*. The caster level for these effects is equal to the elf's level. This racial trait replaces elven magic.

Eternal Grudge: Some elves grow up in secluded, isolationist communities where generations-old slights and quarrels linger as eternal blood feuds. Elves with this racial trait receive a +1 bonus on attack rolls against humanoids of the dwarf and orc subtypes because of special training against these hated foes. This racial trait replaces elven magic.

Fleet-Footed: While all elves are naturally lithe and agile, some also are naturally speedy and have a strong desire to rush into situations rather than worrying about looking ahead. Elves with this racial trait receive Run as a bonus feat and a +2 racial bonus on initiative checks. This racial trait replaces keen senses and weapon familiarity.

Lightbringer: Many elves revere the sun, moon, and stars, but some are literally infused with the radiant power of the heavens. Elves with this racial trait are immune to light-based blindness and dazzle effects, and are treated as one level higher when determining the effects of any light-based spell or effect they cast (including spell-like and supernatural abilities). Elves with Intelligence scores of 10 or higher may use *light* at will as a spell-like ability. This racial trait replaces the elven immunities and elven magic racial traits.

Silent Hunter: Elves are renowned for their subtlety and skill. Elves with this racial trait reduce the penalty for using Stealth while moving by 5 and can make Stealth checks while running at a −20 penalty (this number includes the penalty reduction from this racial trait). This racial trait replaces elven magic.

Spirit of the Waters: Some elves have adapted to life in tune with the sea or along the reedy depths of wild rivers and lakes. They gain a +4 racial bonus on Swim checks, can always take 10 while swimming, and may choose Aquan as a bonus language. They are proficient with longspear, trident, and net. This racial trait replaces elven magic and weapon familiarity.

Urbanite: Elves who live in cities for more than a century can grow to know the ebb and flow of social situations just as their forest-dwelling cousins know the rules of the wild. Elves with this racial trait gain a +2 racial bonus on Diplomacy checks made to gather information and

Sense Motive checks made to get a hunch about a social situation. This racial trait replaces keen senses.

Woodcraft: Elves know the deep secrets of the wild like no others, especially secrets of the forests. Elves with this racial trait gain a +1 racial bonus on Knowledge (nature) and Survival checks. In forest terrain, these bonuses improve to +2. This racial trait replaces elven magic.

Racial Subtypes

You can combine various alternate racial traits to create elven subraces or variant races, such as the following.

Arctic Elf: These elves were born and raised in the frozen lands of the far north or south, and have dealt with freezing deserts, nights that last for weeks, and the horrors that roam the cold terrain. These elves have the darkvision, desert runner, and elemental resistance alternate racial traits.

Dusk Elf: Rather than being tied to the terrain around them, some elves are linked to the night itself. Though not tied to demon worship and evil as drow are, these elves are similarly attuned to the magical concepts of darkness and shadow. These elves have the arcane focus, darkvision, dreamspeaker, and silent hunter alternate racial traits.

Savage Elf: In lands where every day is a constant struggle to survive and the niceties of civilization are rare, elves adapt to depend on swift strikes and lifelong vigilance to keep their families alive. These elves have the eternal grudge and fleet-footed alternate racial traits.

Tower Elf: Some elven institutions of magical learning date back centuries, and entire clans of elves have lived for generations as caretakers, students, and instructors of these self-sufficient schools of wizardry. These elves have the arcane focus and urbanite alternate racial traits.

Favored Class Options

The following options are available to all elves who have the listed favored class, and unless otherwise stated, the bonus applies each time you select the class reward.

Alchemist: Add one extract formula from the alchemist's list to his formula book. This formula must be at least one level lower than the highest-level formula the alchemist can create.

Barbarian: Add +1 to the barbarian's base speed. In combat this option has no effect unless the barbarian has selected it five times (or another increment of five). This bonus stacks with the barbarian's fast movement feature and applies under the same conditions as that feature.

Bard: Add +1 to the bard's CMD when resisting a disarm or sunder attempt.

Cavalier: Add +1 hit point to the cavalier's mount. If the cavalier ever replaces his mount, the new mount gains these bonus hit points.

Cleric: Select one domain power granted at 1st level that is normally usable a number of times per day equal to 3 + the cleric's Wisdom modifier. The cleric adds +1/2 to the number of uses per day of that domain power.

Druid: Add +1/3 to the druid's natural armor bonus when using wild shape.

Fighter: Add +1 to the fighter's CMD when resisting a disarm or sunder attempt.

Gunslinger: Add +1/3 on critical hit confirmation rolls made with firearms (maximum bonus of +5). This bonus does not stack with Critical Focus.

Inquisitor: Add one spell known from the inquisitor's spell list. This spell must be at least one level below the highest-level spell the inquisitor can cast.

Magus: The magus gains 1/6 of a new magus arcana.

Monk: Add +1 to the monk's base speed. In combat this option has no effect unless the monk has selected it five times (or another increment of five). This bonus stacks with the monk's fast movement class feature and applies under the same conditions as that feature.

Oracle: Add +1/2 to the oracle's level for the purpose of determining the effects of one revelation.

Paladin: Add +1/2 hit point to the paladin's lay on hands ability (whether using it to heal or harm).

Ranger: Choose a weapon from the following list: longbow, longsword, rapier, shortbow, short sword, or any weapon with "elven" in its name. Add +1/2 on critical hit confirmation rolls made while using that weapon (maximum bonus of +4). This bonus does not stack with Critical Focus.

Rogue: Add +1 to the number of times per day the rogue can cast a cantrip or 1st-level spell gained from the minor magic or major magic talent. The number of times this bonus is selected for the major magic talent cannot exceed the number of times it is selected for the minor magic talent. The rogue must possess the associated rogue talent to select these options.

Sorcerer: Select one bloodline power at 1st level that is normally usable a number of times per day equal to 3 + the sorcerer's Charisma modifier. The sorcerer adds +1/2 to the number of uses per day of that bloodline power.

Summoner: The amount of time the summoner must spend to summon his eidolon is reduced by 1 round, to a minimum of 1 round.

Witch: Add one spell from the witch spell list to the witch's familiar. This spell must be at least one level lower than the highest-level spell she can cast. If the witch ever replaces her familiar, the new familiar knows these bonus spells.

Wizard: Select one arcane school power at 1st level that is normally usable a number of times per day equal to 3 + the wizard's Intelligence modifier. The wizard adds +1/2 to the number of uses per day of that arcane school power.

RACIAL ARCHETYPES

The following racial archetypes are available to elves.

Ancient Lorekeeper (Oracle)

The ancient lorekeeper is a repository for all the beliefs and vast knowledge of an elven people. She shows a strong interest in and understanding of histories and creation legends at a young age, and as she matures her calling to serve as the memory of her long-lived people becomes clear to all who know her. An ancient lorekeeper has the following class features.

Class Skills: An ancient lorekeeper adds Knowledge (arcane) and Knowledge (local) to her list of class skills. Whenever she makes a Knowledge check of any kind about a question regarding elves (creatures of the elf subtype), the ancient lorekeeper adds half her class level on her check. This replaces the bonus skills the ancient lorekeeper gains from her mystery.

Elven Arcana (Ex): At 2nd level, an ancient lorekeeper's mastery of elven legends and philosophy has allowed her to master one spell used by elven wizards. She selects one spell from the sorcerer/wizard spell list that is at least one level lower than the highest-level oracle spell she can cast. The ancient lorekeeper gains this as a bonus spell known. The spell is treated as one level higher than its true level for all purposes. The ancient lorekeeper may choose an additional spell at 4th, 6th, 8th, 10th, 12th, 14th, 16th, and 18th levels. This ability replaces the bonus spells she would normally gain at these levels from her chosen mystery.

Mysteries: The following oracle mysteries complement the ancient lorekeeper archetype: Lore, Nature, Waves, Wind (*Advanced Player's Guide*); Ancestor, Time, Wood (*Ultimate Magic*).

Spell Dancer (Magus)

The strong emphasis on wizards within elven culture influences how even non-wizard elves see themselves. Many elven magi do not consider themselves masters of a blend of martial and magical talents, but rather a sub-category of wizards who study the effect of physical movement and techniques upon spellcasting ability. They believe their ability to cast spells while fighting is an outgrowth of the concept of the "spell dance," which itself is just another kind of wizardry. A spell dancer has the following class features.

Class Skills: A spell dancer adds Acrobatics and Perform (dance) to his list of class skills and removes Intimidate and Ride from his list of class skills.

Spell Dance (Su): At 1st level, a spell dancer gains the ability to expend 1 point from his arcane pool as a swift action to gain a +10 enhancement bonus to his movement rate and a +2 dodge bonus to Armor Class against attacks of opportunity provoked by moving through threatened spaces for 1 minute. For every four levels beyond 1st, the spell dancer gains another +10 enhancement bonus to movement and +2 to AC against attacks of opportunity provoked from movement.

At 5th level, once per spell dance as a swift action, the spell dancer may use one of the following on himself as a swift action: *blur*, *fly*, or *haste*. These abilities last for 1 round. At 9th level, the spell dancer may instead take a swift action to use *dimension door* as a spell-like ability once during a spelldance. At 13th level, the spell dancer may instead choose to take a swift action to gain *freedom of movement* for 1d4 rounds.

This ability replaces the magus's ability to expend points from his arcane pool as a swift action to grant any weapon he is holding magic bonuses for 1 minute.

Arcane Movement (Su): At 5th level, whenever a spell dancer casts a magus spell, he gains a competence bonus on

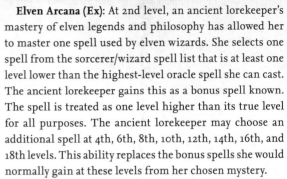

Acrobatics, Climb, Escape Artist, and Stealth checks equal to the spell's level until the beginning of his next turn. This ability replaces the bonus feat a magus receives at 5th level.

Dance of Avoidance (Su): At 7th level, while wearing light armor or no armor, a spell dancer gains a +2 insight bonus to Armor Class. This ability replaces the medium armor class feature.

Greater Dance of Avoidance (Su): At 13th level, while wearing light armor or no armor, a spell dancer's insight bonus to Armor Class increases to +4. This ability replaces the heavy armor class feature.

Magus Arcana: The following magus arcana complement the spell dancer archetype: arcane cloak, prescient defense (*Ultimate Combat*); close range, concentrate, hasted assault, spell shield (*Ultimate Magic*).

Spellbinder (Wizard)

A spellbinder is an elven wizard who forges an arcane bond between himself and one or more wizard spells. These spells become so well understood by the spellbinder that he can prepare them in spell slots that already have other spells prepared in them.

Spell Bond (Su): At 1st level, a spellbinder selects any one spell that he knows as a bonded spell. As a full-round action, the spellbinder may replace a spell of the same or higher level as his bonded spell with his bonded spell. For example, a spellbinder who selects *magic missile* as his bonded spell could spend a full-round action to exchange any 1st-level or higher spell that he has prepared with *magic missile*. At 3rd level, and every two levels thereafter, a spellbinder may select another spell he knows and add it to his list of bonded spells, to a maximum of nine bonded spells at 17th level.

Upon reaching 4th level, and every two levels thereafter, a spellbinder can choose to select a new spell as a bonded spell in place of one with which he is already bonded. In effect, the spellbinder loses the bond with the old spell (though it is still one of his spells known) in exchange for forging a spell bond with a new spell. The new spell's level must be the same as that of the spell being exchanged. A spellbinder may swap only one spell bond at any given level, and must choose whether or not to swap the spell bond at the same time that he gains two new spells known for the level.

This ability replaces arcane bond.

Discoveries: The following discoveries complement the spellbinder archetype: Fast Study, Split Slot (*Ultimate Magic*).

Treesinger (Druid)

Elves live far longer than other common races, and a single elf may see whole empires rise and fall. Given the impermanence of the cultures around them, it's small wonder that some elves turn to the timeless growth of nature for solace, finding allies among the great trees themselves, and even leading the forest's plants into combat. A treesinger has the following class features.

Plant Bond (Ex): At 1st level, a treesinger forms a mystic bond with plant life. This bond can take one of two forms. The first grants the treesinger one of the following domains: Plant (*Core Rulebook*); Growth (*Advanced Player's Guide*); Jungle, Swamp (*Ultimate Magic*). When determining the powers and bonus spells granted by this domain, the treesinger's effective cleric level is equal to her druid level. A treesinger who selects this option also receives additional domain spell slots, just like a cleric. She must prepare the spell from her domain in this slot, and this spell cannot be used to cast a spell spontaneously.

The second option is to form a close bond with a plant companion. A treesinger may begin play with any of the plants listed in Plant Companions (see page 26). This plant is a loyal companion that accompanies the treesinger on her adventures. Except for the companion being a creature of the plant type, drawn from the list of plant companions, this ability otherwise works like the standard druid's animal companion ability.

Plant bond replaces the druid's nature bond ability.

Green Empathy (Ex): At 1st level, a treesinger can improve the attitude of a plant creature. This ability functions just like a Diplomacy check made to improve the attitude of a person. The treesinger rolls 1d20 and adds her druid level and her Charisma modifier to determine the wild empathy check result. The typical wild plant creature has a starting attitude of indifferent.

To use green empathy, the treesinger and the plant creature must be within 30 feet of one another under normal conditions. Generally, influencing a plant creature in this way takes 1 minute but, as with influencing people, it might take more or less time.

A treesinger can also use this ability to influence an animal, but she takes a –4 penalty on the check. This ability replaces the wild empathy class feature.

Wild Shape (Su): At 4th level, a treesinger gains the ability to wild shape. This ability functions at her actual druid level. A treesinger cannot use wild shape to adopt an animal or elemental form. Instead, when she gains this ability at 4th level, she can assume the form of a Small or Medium plant. This functions as *plant shape I*, except the treesinger does not yet gain access to the constrict or poison abilities of the plant form assumed. At 8th level, the treesinger's wild shape gains the full range of abilities available from *plant shape I*. At 10th level, a treesinger can assume the form of a Large or Tiny plant. Her wild shape ability now functions like *plant shape II*. At 12th level, a treesinger can assume the form of a Huge plant. Her wild shape ability now functions like *plant shape III*. This ability replaces, and otherwise functions like, the normal druid wild shape ability.

Plant Companions

Each plant companion has different starting sizes, speed, attacks, ability scores, and special qualities. All plant attacks are made using the creature's full base attack bonus unless otherwise noted. Plant attacks add the plant's Strength modifier on the damage roll, unless it has only one attack, in which case it adds 1-1/2 times its Strength modifier. Some plant companions have special abilities, such as scent. Plant companions cannot gain armor or weapon proficiency feats, even as they advance in hit dice, and cannot use manufactured weapons at all unless their description says otherwise.

As you gain levels, your plant companion grows in power as well. It gains the same bonuses that are gained by animal

companions, noted on Table 3–8: Animal Companion Base Statistics on page 52 of the *Core Rulebook*. Each plant companion gains an additional bonus, usually at 4th or 7th level, as listed with each plant choice. Instead of taking the listed benefit at 4th level, you can instead choose to increase the companion's Strength and Constitution by 2.

Carnivorous Flower

Starting Statistics: Size Small; **Speed** 30 ft., climb 10 ft.; **AC** +2 natural armor; **Attack** bite (1d6); **Ability Scores** Str 10, Dex 17, Con 15, Int 2, Wis 12, Cha 10; **Special Qualities** low-light vision, scent.

4th-Level Advancement: Size Medium; **Attack** bite (2d6); **Ability Scores** Str +4, Dex –2, Con +2; **Special Attacks** rage (1/day, as the barbarian class feature for 6 rounds).

Crawling Vine

Starting Statistics: Size Medium; **Speed** 20 ft., climb 20 ft.; **AC** +2 natural armor; **Attack** slam (1d4); **Ability Scores** Str 13, Dex 17, Con 13, Int 1, Wis 12, Cha 2; **Special Attacks** grab; **Special Qualities** low-light vision, scent.

4th-Level Advancement: Size Large; **AC** +1 natural armor; **Attack** slam (1d6); **Ability Scores** Str +8, Dex –2, Con +4; **Special Attacks** constrict 1d6.

Puffball (Floating Fungus)

Starting Statistics: Size Small; **Speed** 20 ft., fly 60 ft. (average); **AC** +1 natural armor; **Attack** thorn (1d4 plus poison); **Ability Scores** Str 10, Dex 15, Con 12, Int 2, Wis 14, Cha 6; **Special Attacks** poison (*Frequency* 1 round [6], *Effect* 1 Con damage, *Cure* 1 save, Con-based DC); **Special Qualities** low-light vision.

4th-Level Advancement: Ability Scores Str +2, Con +2.

Sapling Treant

Starting Statistics: Size Medium; **Speed** 30 ft., climb 30 ft.; **AC** +1 natural armor; **Attack** 2 slams (1d6); **Ability Scores** Str 15, Dex 10, Con 12, Int 2, Wis 12, Cha 7; **Special Qualities** double damage against objects, low-light vision.

4th-Level Advancement: Size Large; **AC** +2 natural armor; **Attack** 2 slams (1d8); **Ability Scores** Str +8, Dex –2, Con +4.

NEW RACIAL RULES

The following options are available to elves. At the GM's discretion, other appropriate races may also make use of some of these.

Elven Equipment

Elves have access to the following equipment.

Arcane Family Workbook: The elven predilection for becoming wizards and the social benefits that elven wizards enjoy often encourages families to dedicate themselves to wizardly studies for multiple generations. Older elven wizards take note of their own insights into the secrets of arcane magic and compile these thoughts with the ideas of earlier generations to form family workbooks. When used as a reference (an action that typically takes 1d4 full rounds of searching the text), an arcane family workbook grants a +2 circumstance bonus on a Spellcraft checks. This bonus increases to +4 if 1d4 hours are spent referencing the book.

Artificer's Lab, Portable: The portable artificer's lab contains everything needed to create magic items, though many of the tools and implements are of only the most basic type. This lab allows the artificer to spend 4 hours crafting each night while out adventuring, and net 3 hours' worth of work (instead of 2). However, because the tools are all designed to fulfill multiple functions and the portable lab lacks the space and quiet that provide ideal circumstances for creating magic items, the skill check to complete a magic item that had any of its work done using a portable lab takes a −5 penalty.

Bag, Bear: These sacks each include a 20-foot-long rope, from which they may be easily suspended from a tree limb or similar anchor point. Placing foodstuffs or fragile materials in hanging sacks is often considered a basic precaution when camping in the wild, to prevent bears and other predators from rooting through the sack's contents.

Spellbook, Compact: The need to be able to record and travel with dozens or even hundreds of spells often forces elven wizards to seek lighter spellbooks. Compact spellbooks hold only 70 pages of spells, but they weigh significantly less than an ordinary spellbook.

Tent, Hanging: A hanging tent is a small tent (able to comfortably house a single Medium creature) with a teardrop shape, which hangs from a sturdy anchor rope. The rope can be tied to a tree limb, grappling hook, or even a piton hammered into a cliff side. Hanging tents are used primarily in mountainous terrain (where no flat surface may be available for camping) and swamps (where no dry ground may be available). Climbing in or out of a hanging tent is a full-round action that requires a DC 10 Climb check. Failure indicates another attempt must be made, while failure by 5 or more indicates the camper has fallen from the tent.

Elven Equipment

Item	Cost	Weight
Arcane family workbook	300 gp	3 lbs.
Artificer's lab, portable	300 gp	40 lbs.
Bag, bear	2 gp	3 lbs.*
Spellbook, compact (blank)	50 gp	1 lb.
Tent, hanging	20 gp	15 lbs.*

* These items weigh 1/4 this amount when made for Small characters. Containers for Small characters also carry 1/4 the normal amount.

Elven Special Materials

Given their strong ties to nature and inclination for arcane arts, it's not surprising that elves have developed a few special materials well suited to their needs and homelands.

Darkleaf Cloth: Darkleaf cloth is a special form of flexible material made by weaving together leaves and thin strips of bark from darkwood trees, then treating the resulting fabric with special alchemical processes. The resulting material is tough as cured hide but much lighter, making it an excellent material from which to create armor. Spell failure chances for armors made from darkleaf cloth decrease by 10% (to a minimum of 5%), maximum Dexterity bonuses increase by 2, and armor check penalties decrease by 3 (to a minimum of 0).

An item made from darkleaf cloth weighs half as much as the same item made from normal cured leather, furs, or hides. Items not primarily constructed of leather, fur, or hide are not meaningfully affected by being partially made of darkleaf cloth. As such padded, leather, studded leather, and hide armor can be made out of darkleaf cloth (although other types of armor made of leather or hide might be possible). Because darkleaf cloth remains flexible, it cannot be used to construct rigid items such as shields or metal armors. Armors fashioned from darkleaf cloth are always masterwork items as well; the masterwork cost is included in the prices given below.

Darkleaf cloth has 20 hit points per inch of thickness and hardness 10.

Wyroot: The root of the wyrwood tree has a peculiar quality. When a weapon constructed of wyroot confirms a critical hit, it absorbs some of the life force of the creature hit. The creature hit is unharmed and the wyroot weapon gains 1 life point. As a swift action, a wielder with a *ki* pool or an arcane pool can absorb 1 life point from the wyrwood weapon and convert it into either 1 *ki* point or 1 arcane pool point. Most wyroot weapons can only hold 1 life point at a time, but higher-quality wyroot does exist. The most powerful wyroot weapons can hold up to 3 life points at a time. Any unspent life points dissipate at dusk.

Wyroot can be used to construct any melee weapon made entirely of wood or a melee weapon with a wooden haft. Constructing a wyroot weapon that can hold 1 life point increases the weapon's cost by 1,000 gp, constructing one that can hold up to 2 life points increases the weapon's cost by 2,000 gp, and constructing one that can hold up to 3 life points increases the weapon's cost by 4,000 gp.

Type of Darkleaf Cloth Item	Cost Modifier
Clothing	+500 gp
Light armor	+750 gp
Medium armor	+1,500 gp
Other items	+375 gp/lb.

Elven Feats

Elves have access to the following feats.

Attuned to the Wild

You share a strong mystic connection with one type of wilderness terrain.

Prerequisite: Elf.

Benefit: Select one type of terrain from the ranger class's favored terrain class feature (except urban). While you are in your selected terrain type, your natural healing rate (the amount of hit points and ability damage you heal from a full night's rest) doubles.

Special: You can take this feat multiple times. Its effects do not stack. Each time you take it, it applies to a different terrain type.

Elven Battle Training (Combat)

You have been specially trained to wield a variety of traditional elven weapons.

Prerequisites: Base attack bonus +1, elf.

Benefit: You have received special training with traditional elven weapons (longbows, composite longbows, longswords, rapiers, shortbows, composite shortbows, and any weapon with the word "elven" in its name). You receive a +2 bonus to your CMD against disarm and sunder maneuvers directed at one of these weapons you are wielding. In addition, if you are wielding one of these melee weapons, you may make an additional attack of opportunity each round (this bonus stacks with Combat Reflexes).

Guardian of the Wild

Your mystic connection with the wilderness enhances your ability to react to threats.

Prerequisites: Attuned to the Wild, elf.

Benefit: When you are in a terrain type you have selected the Attuned to the Wild feat for, you gain a +2 dodge bonus to Armor Class. If you are in an area that qualifies as more than one kind of terrain, these bonuses do not stack; you receive the bonus for only one of the terrain types.

Mage of the Wild

Your mystic connection with the wilderness enhances your spellcasting.

Prerequisites: Attuned to the Wild, elf.

Benefit: When you are in a terrain type you have selected the Attuned to the Wild feat for, you gain a +2 bonus on caster level checks, concentration checks, and, Knowledge (arcana) and Spellcraft checks. If you are in an area that qualifies as more than one kind of terrain, these bonuses do not stack; you receive the bonus for only one of the terrain types.

Spirit of the Wild

Your mystic connection with one type of wilderness has grown even stronger.

Prerequisites: Attuned to the Wild, Guardian of the Wild, elf.

Benefit: When you are in a terrain type you have selected the Attuned to the Wild feat for, you gain a +4 bonus on Perception checks made to act in the surprise round of combat. If you act in the surprise round, you gain blindsense out to a range of 30 feet during the surprise round. If you are in an area that qualifies as more than one kind of terrain, these bonuses do not stack; you receive the bonus for only one terrain type.

Elven Magic Items

Elves are renowned for their skill at crafting beautiful and deadly magic items. The following examples are made by many elven crafters.

BRACERS OF SWORN VENGEANCE

Aura strong evocation; **CL** 15th

Slot wrists; **Price** 25,000 gp; **Weight** 1 lb.

DESCRIPTION

These white leather bracers have delicate elven runes etched upon them, one reading "swift defeat" and the other "vengeance." Once per day, as an immediate action when the wearer takes hit point damage from a target, she may cry out, "Death to those who wrong me!", swearing vengeance against the attacker. The wearer gains a +1 competence bonus on weapon attack rolls made against the target of his sworn vengeance, and deals an additional 2d6 points of damage on successful weapon attack rolls.

For the duration of the effect, the wearer takes a –2 penalty on attack rolls against any target other than his sworn enemy. These bonuses and penalties last for 24 hours or until the sworn enemy is slain or destroyed by the wearer of the bracers, whichever comes first. If the wearer fails to slay the target of his oath, these bracers cannot be used again until 7 days have passed.

CONSTRUCTION

Requirements Craft Wondrous Item, *shout*, creator must be an elf; **Cost** 12,500 gp

GAUNTLETS OF SKILL AT ARMS

Aura moderate transmutation; **CL** 8th

Slot wrists; **Price** 30,000 gp; **Weight** 1 lb.

DESCRIPTION

These finely crafted leather gauntlets have plates of silvered steel covering the back, and silver buckles at the wrist and forearm. The gloves enable the wearer to use any traditional elven weapon (longbows, composite longbows, longswords, rapiers, shortbows, composite shortbows, and any weapon with the word "elven" in its name) as if he were proficient in its use. If he uses such a weapon and is already proficient with it, he gains a +1 competence bonus on attack and damage rolls. Both gloves must be worn for the magic to be effective.

CONSTRUCTION

Requirements Craft Wondrous Item, Craft Magic Arms and Armor, creator must be an elf; **Cost** 15,000 gp

GLOVES OF ELVENKIND

Aura moderate transmutation; **CL** 8th
Slot hands; **Price** 7,500 gp; **Weight** —

DESCRIPTION

These plain gray leather gloves grant a +5 competence bonus on Spellcraft checks and concentration checks made to cast a spell defensively. Both gloves must be worn for the magic to be effective.

CONSTRUCTION

Requirements Combat Casting, Craft Wondrous Item, creator must be an elf; **Cost** 3,500 gp

Elven Spells

Most know of elven magic for its power, but those who delve deeper discover its elegance and ties to the natural world. The following spells are just a few that the elves are known for.

BLEND

School illusion (glamer); **Level** alchemist 1, druid 1, magus 1, ranger 1, sorcerer/wizard 1, witch 1
Casting Time 1 standard action
Components S
Range personal
Target you
Duration 10 minutes/level
You draw upon your elven link to the wilderness to change the coloration of yourself and your equipment to match that of your surroundings. This grants you a +4 circumstance bonus on Stealth checks and allows you to make Stealth checks without cover or concealment, but only while you move no more than half your base speed or less. If you move more than half your base speed on your turn, you gain no benefit from this spell until the start of your next turn. If you make an attack, this spell ends (as *invisibility*).

WARD OF THE SEASON

School abjuration; **Level** cleric 4, druid 3, ranger 3, witch 3
Casting Time 1 standard action
Components V, S
Range touch
Target one creature
Duration 1 hour/level
Saving Throw Will negates (harmless); **Spell Resistance** no
This spell harnesses the power of the seasons to protect the target and grant a number of bonuses. This spell has one of

four different effects. The caster of the spell can select any one of the following four effects, but can change the effect as a standard action that reduces the total remaining duration by 1 hour.

Spring: The target is wrapped in light vines, culminating in a crown of bright, beautiful flowers. While the spell remains in effect, the target is immune to bleed effects and regains 1 hit point per round whenever below 0 hit points, as long as the target is still alive. This stabilizes the target. For each hit point restored in this way, the spell's total remaining duration is reduced by 1 hour.

Summer: The target is surrounded by tiny motes of light. While the spell remains in effect, the target's base speed increases 10 feet. The target may instead increase its base speed by 30 feet for 1 round by reducing the spell's total remaining duration by 1 hour.

Fall: A cloak of autumn leaves appears on the target. While the spell remains in effect, the target gains a +2 morale bonus on Fortitude saves. The target can decide to roll twice on any saving throw against disease or poison and take the higher result by reducing the spell's total remaining duration by 1 hour.

Winter: A flutter of snow and crisp air surrounds the target. While this spell remains in effect, the target automatically succeeds at Acrobatics skill checks made to avoid falling while moving across slick or narrow surfaces. The target can move freely through difficult terrain for 1 round by reducing the spell's remaining duration by 1 hour. Difficult terrain created by magic affects the target normally.

WHISPERING LORE

School divination; **Level** cleric 2, druid 1, ranger 1, witch 1
Casting Time 1 full-round action
Components V, S, M/DF (an owl's beak)
Range personal
Target you
Duration 10 minutes/level (D)
Upon casting this spell, you are able to gain knowledge from the land itself. As you walk through the terrain, it whisper information in a language you understand, though the whispering is so rambling it is hard to distinguish useful information. This whispering grants you a +4 insight bonus on a single Knowledge skill type appropriate to the type of terrain you are in. If you are within a cold, desert, forest, jungle, mountain, plains, swamp, or water environment, you gain the bonus on Knowledge (nature) checks. If you are within an underground environment, you gain the bonus on Knowledge (dungeoneering) checks. If you are within an urban environment, you gain the bonus on Knowledge (local) checks. If you are on a plane other than the Material Plane, you gain the bonus on Knowledge (planes) checks. If you enter a new terrain, you lose the previous terrain's skill bonus and gain the new bonus.

GNOMES

Gnomes are distant relatives of the fey, and their history tells of a time when they lived in the fey's mysterious realm, a place where colors are brighter, the wildlands wilder, and emotions more primal. Unknown forces drove the ancient gnomes from that realm long ago, forcing them to seek refuge in this world; despite this, the gnomes have never completely abandoned their fey roots or adapted to mortal culture. Though gnomes are no longer truly fey, their fey heritage can be seen in their innate magic powers, their oft-capricious natures, and their outlooks on life and the world.

Gnomes can have the same concerns and motivations as members of other races, but just as often they are driven by passions and desires that non-gnomes see as eccentric at best, and nonsensical at worst. A gnome may risk his life to taste the food at a giant's table, to reach the bottom of a pit just because it would be the lowest place he's ever been, or to tell jokes to a dragon—and to the gnome those goals are as worthy as researching a new spell, gaining vast wealth, or putting down a powerful evil force. While such apparently fickle and impulsive acts are not universal among gnomes, they are common enough for the race as a whole to have earned a reputation for being impetuous and at least a little mad.

Combined with their diminutive sizes, vibrant coloration, and lack of concern for the opinions of others, these attitudes have caused gnomes to be widely regarded by the other races as alien and strange. Gnomes, in turn, are often amazed how alike other common, civilized races are. It seems stranger to a gnome that humans and elves share so many similarities than that the gnomes do not. Indeed, gnomes often confound their allies by treating

GNOME RACIAL TRAITS

+2 Constitution, +2 Charisma, –2 Strength: Gnomes are physically weak but surprisingly hardy, and their attitude makes them naturally agreeable.

Small: Gnomes are Small creatures and gain a +1 size bonus to their AC, a +1 size bonus on attack rolls, a –1 penalty to their Combat Maneuver Bonus and Combat Maneuver Defense, and a +4 size bonus on Stealth checks.

Slow Speed: Gnomes have a base speed of 20 feet.

Low-Light Vision: Gnomes can see twice as far as humans in conditions of dim light.

Defensive Training: Gnomes gain a +4 dodge bonus to AC against monsters of the giant subtype.

Gnome Magic: Gnomes add +1 to the DC of any saving throws against illusion spells that they cast. Gnomes with Charisma scores of 11 or higher also gain the following spell-like abilities: 1/day—*dancing lights, ghost sound, prestidigitation,* and *speak with animals.* The caster level for these effects is equal to the gnome's level. The DC for these spells is equal to 10 + the spell's level + the gnome's Charisma modifier.

Hatred: Gnomes receive a +1 bonus on attack rolls against humanoid creatures of the reptilian and goblinoid subtypes because of their special training against these hated foes.

Illusion Resistance: Gnomes gain a +2 racial saving throw bonus against illusion spells and effects.

Keen Senses: Gnomes receive a +2 racial bonus on Perception checks.

Obsessive: Gnomes receive a +2 racial bonus on a Craft or Profession skill of their choice.

Weapon Familiarity: Gnomes treat any weapon with the word "gnome" in its name as a martial weapon.

Languages: Gnomes begin play speaking Common, Gnome, and Sylvan. Gnomes with high Intelligence scores can choose from the following: Draconic, Dwarven, Elven, Giant, Goblin, and Orc.

everyone who is not a gnome as part of a single, vast non-gnome collective race.

Physical Description: Gnomes are one of the smallest of the common races, generally standing just over 3 feet in height. Despite their small frames, however, gnomes are extremely resilient, and not as weak as many of their foes assume. Though their diminutive stature reduces their ability to move quickly, gnomes often train to take advantage of their size, especially when fighting foes much larger than themselves.

The coloration of gnomes varies so wildly that many outsiders assume gnomes commonly use dyes and illusions to change their skin and hair tones. While gnomes are certainly not above cosmetic enhancement (and may wish to change their appearance just to see how outlandish they can look), their natural hues truly range over a rainbow of coloration. Their hair tends toward vibrant colors such as the fiery orange of autumn leaves, the verdant green of forests at springtime, or the deep reds and purples of wildflowers in bloom. Similarly, their flesh tones range from earthy browns to floral pinks, and gnomes with black, pastel blue, or even green skin are not unknown. Gnomes' coloration has little regard for heredity, with the color of a gnome's parents and other kin having no apparent bearing on the gnome's appearance.

Gnomes possess highly mutable facial characteristics, and their proportions often don't match the norm of other humanoid races. Many have overly large mouths and eyes, an effect which can be both disturbing and stunning, depending on the individual. Others may have extremely small features spread over an otherwise blank expanse of face, or may mix shockingly large eyes with a tiny, pursed mouth and a pert button of a nose. Gnomes rarely take pride in or show embarrassment about their features, but members of other races often fixate on a gnome's most prominent feature and attempt to use it as the focus of insults or endearments.

Society: Unlike most races, gnomes do not generally organize themselves within classic societal structures. Gnome cities are unusual and gnome kingdoms almost unknown. Further, gnomes have no particular tendency to gather in specific neighborhoods even when a large number of them live among other races. While specific laws meant to contain the potential impact of gnomes on a society may require a "gnome quarter," and societal pressure sometimes causes all non-gnomes to move away from areas with high gnome populations, left to their own devices, gnomes tend to spread evenly throughout communities that allow them.

However, even when gnomes are common within a community as a group, individual gnomes tend to be always on the move. Whimsical creatures at heart, they typically travel alone or with temporary companions, ever seeking new and more exciting experiences. They rarely form enduring relationships among themselves or with members of other races, instead pursuing crafts, professions, or collections with a passion that borders on zealotry. If a gnome does settle in an area or stay with a group for a longer period, it is almost always the result of some benefit that area gives to a vocation or obsession to which the gnome had dedicated himself.

Despite their extremely varied backgrounds and lack of a unifying homeland, gnomes do possess some common cultural traits. Male gnomes have a strange fondness for unusual hats and headgear, often wearing the most expensive and ostentatious head-covering they can afford (and that their chosen careers will allow them to wear without causing problems). Females rarely cover their heads, but proudly wear elaborate and eccentric hairstyles that often include intricate jeweled combs and headpieces.

Relations: Gnomes have difficulty interacting with the other races, on both emotional and physical levels. In many ways the very fact other races see gnomes as odd is itself the thing gnomes find most odd about other races, and this leads to a strong lack of common ground upon which understanding and relationships can be built. When two gnomes encounter one another, they generally assume some mutually beneficial arrangement can be reached, no matter how different their beliefs and traditions may be. Even if this turns out not to be the case, the gnomes continue to look for commonalities in their dealings with each other. The inability or unwillingness of members of other races to make the same effort when dealing with gnomes is both frustrating and confusing to most gnomes.

In many ways, it is gnomes' strong connection to a wide range of apparently unconnected ideas that makes it difficult for other races to build relationships with them. Gnome humor, for example, is often focused on physical pranks, nonsensical rhyming nicknames, and efforts to convince others of outrageous lies that strain all credibility. Gnomes find such efforts hysterically funny, but their pranks often come across as malicious or senseless to other races, while gnomes in turn tend to think of the taller races as dull and lumbering giants.

Gnomes get along reasonably well with halflings and humans, who at least have some traditions of bizarre, gnomelike humor. Gnomes generally feel dwarves and half-orcs need to lighten up, and attempt to bring levity into their lives with tricks, jokes, and outrageous tales the more dour races simply cannot see the sense of. Gnomes respect elves, but often grow frustrated with the slow pace at which members of the long-lived race make decisions. To gnomes, action is always better than inaction, and many gnomes carry several highly involved projects with them at all times to keep themselves entertained during rest periods.

Alignment and Religion: Although gnomes are impulsive tricksters, with sometimes inscrutable motives and equally confusing methods, their hearts are generally

in the right place. What may seem a malicious act to a non-gnome is more likely an effort to introduce new acquaintances to new experiences, however unpleasant the experiences may be. Gnomes are prone to powerful fits of emotion, and find themselves most at peace within the natural world. They are usually neutral good, and prefer to worship deities who value individuality and nature, such as Cayden Cailean, Desna, Gozreh, and Shelyn.

Adventurers: Gnomes' propensity for wanderlust, deep curiosity, and desire to master odd or esoteric skills and languages make them natural adventurers. They often become wanderers to experience new aspects of life, for nothing is as novel as the uncounted dangers facing adventurers. Many gnomes see adventuring as the only worthwhile purpose in life, and seek out adventures for no other motive than to experience them. Other gnomes desire to find some lost lore or material that has ties to their chosen vocation and believe only dragon hoards and ancient ruins can contain the lore they need, which can result in gnomes who think of themselves as bakers or weavers being just as accomplished adventurers as those who declare themselves to be mages or scouts.

Gnomes are physically weak compared to many races, and see this as a simple fact of life to be planned for accordingly. Most adventuring gnomes make up for their weakness with a proclivity for sorcery or bardic music, while others turn to alchemy or exotic weapons to grant them an edge in conflicts.

Male Names: Abroshtor, Bastargre, Halungalom, Krolmnite, Poshment, Zarzuket, Zatqualmie.

Female Names: Besh, Fijit, Lini, Majet, Neji, Pai, Queck, Trig.

ALTERNATE RACIAL RULES

Gnomes are a wildly varied and independent race. As a result, there are many variations in their abilities, outlooks, and styles. The following rules are just some of the different traits that manifest in gnomes, frequently without regard for heritage or training.

Alternate Racial Traits

The following racial traits may be selected instead of standard gnome racial traits. Consult your GM before selecting any of these new options.

Academician: Some gnomes are more academically inclined than their kin. Gnomes with this racial trait gain a +2 bonus on any single Knowledge skill. This racial trait replaces the obsessive racial trait.

Bond to the Land: Some gnomes have strong ties to specific kinds of terrain, as a holdover from their fey origins. These gnomes gain a +2 dodge bonus to AC when in a specific terrain type selected from the ranger list of favored terrains. This choice is made at character creation,

and cannot be changed. This racial trait replaces defensive training and hatred.

Darkvision: Some gnome strains have lived in the underground depths for so long they have given up on light entirely and gained darkvision with a range of 60 feet. This racial trait replaces low-light vision and keen senses.

Eternal Hope: Gnomes rarely lose hope and are always confident that even hopeless situations will work out. Gnomes with this racial trait receive a +2 racial bonus on saving throws against fear and despair effects. Once per day, after rolling a 1 on a d20, the gnome may reroll and use the second result. This racial trait replaces defensive training and hatred.

Explorer: Many gnomes are obsessed with seeing as much of the world as possible, rather than perfecting some specific talent or vocation. These gnomes gain a +2 racial bonus on Climb checks and checks for one Knowledge skill of their choice. This racial trait replaces hatred and obsessive.

Fell Magic: Gnomes add +1 to the DC of any saving throws against necromancy spells that they cast. Gnomes with Wisdom scores of 11 or higher also gain the following spell-like abilities: 1/day—*bleed, chill touch, detect poison,* and *touch of fatigue.* The caster level for these effects is equal to the gnome's level. The DC for these spells is equal to 10 + the spell's level + the gnome's Wisdom modifier. This racial trait replaces gnome magic.

Gift of Tongues: Gnomes love languages and learning about those they meet. Gnomes with this racial trait gain a +1 bonus on Bluff and Diplomacy checks, and they learn one additional language every time they put a rank in the Linguistics skill. This racial trait replaces defensive training and hatred.

Knack with Poison: Some gnomes have an instinctive understanding of poisons and their uses. Gnomes gain a +2 racial bonus on Fortitude saves against poison and a +2 bonus on Craft (alchemy) checks to make poison. The bonus on Fortitude saving throws against poisons increases to +4 if the gnome accidentally poisons himself when applying or readying the substance. This racial trait replaces illusion resistance and obsessive.

Magical Linguist: Gnomes study languages in both their mundane and supernatural manifestations. Gnomes with this racial trait add +1 to the DC of spells they cast with the language-dependent descriptor or those that create glyphs, symbols, or other magical writings. They gain a +2 racial bonus on saving throws against such spells. Gnomes with Charisma scores of 11 or higher also gain the following spell-like abilities: 1/day—*arcane mark, comprehend languages, message, read magic.* The caster level for these effects is equal to the gnome's level. This racial trait replaces gnome magic and illusion resistance.

Master Tinker: Gnomes experiment with all manner of mechanical devices. Gnomes with this racial trait gain a

+1 bonus on Disable Device and Knowledge (engineering) checks. They are treated as proficient with any weapon they have personally crafted. This racial trait replaces defensive training and hatred.

Pyromaniac: Gnomes with this racial trait are treated as one level higher when casting spells with the fire descriptor, using granted powers of the Fire domain, using the bloodline powers of the fire elemental bloodline or the revelations of the oracle's flame mystery, and determining the damage of alchemist bombs that deal fire damage (this ability does not give gnomes early access to level-based powers; it only affects the powers they could use without this ability). Gnomes with Charisma scores of 11 or higher also gain the following spell-like abilities: 1/day—*dancing lights, flare, prestidigitation, produce flame.* The caster level for these effects is equal to the gnome's level; the DCs are Charisma-based. This racial trait replaces gnome magic and illusion resistance.

Warden of Nature: Gnomes must often protect their homes against unnatural or pestilential infestations. Gnomes with this racial trait gain a +2 dodge bonus to AC against aberrations, oozes, and vermin, and a +1 bonus on attack rolls against them because of their special training. This racial trait replaces defensive training and hatred.

Racial Subtypes

You can combine various alternate racial traits to create gnome subraces or variant races, such as the following.

Dread Gnomes: Moodier, less forgiving, and often crueler than other gnomes, dread gnomes trace their heritage to the darker, more bloodthirsty lines of fey. Though not all dread gnomes are evil, they all find humor in watching others suffer, and have little use for the bright colors and joyful pursuits of their more cheerful cousins. Dread gnomes have the fell magic and knack for poison alternate racial traits.

Gear Gnomes: Sometimes rather than a single gnome becoming obsessed with a project, whole families of gnomes undertake a project so massive it requires generations of artisans to complete. Such projects often involve complex clockwork devices (or entire clockwork buildings), and those born into families dedicated to lifetimes of work on them are known as gear gnomes. Gear gnomes have the academician and master tinker alternate racial traits.

Lava Gnomes: Fascinated by the power of magma and living in vast caverns beneath active volcanoes, lava gnomes are considered hot-tempered and dangerously unstable even by other gnomes. Lava gnomes have the darkvision and pyromaniac alternate racial traits.

Traveler Gnomes: These gnomes were born on the move, their families living on a ship or in a caravan wagon. These gnomes have the magical linguist and either the explorer or the gift of tongues alternate racial traits.

Favored Class Options

The following options are available to all gnomes who have the listed favored class, and unless otherwise stated, the bonus applies each time you select the class reward.

Alchemist: Add +1/2 to the number of bombs per day the alchemist can create.

Barbarian: Add a +1/2 bonus to the barbarian's trap sense.

Bard: Add +1 to the bard's total number of bardic performance rounds per day.

Cavalier: Add +1 to the cavalier's mounted base speed. In combat this has no effect unless the cavalier has selected this reward five times (or another increment of five). If the cavalier ever replaces his mount, the new mount gains this bonus to its speed.

Cleric: Add +1/2 to the cleric's channeled energy total when healing creatures of the animal, fey, and plant types.

Druid: The druid gains energy resistance 1 against acid, cold, electricity, or fire. Each time the druid selects this reward, increase her resistance to one of these energy types by +1 (maximum 10 for any one type).

Fighter: Add +1 to the fighter's CMD when resisting a dirty trick or steal attempt.

Gunslinger: The gunslinger reduces the amount of time needed to restore a broken firearm using the Gunsmithing feat by 5 minutes (maximum reduction of 50 minutes).

Inquisitor: Add a +1 bonus on concentration checks when casting inquisitor spells.

Magus: Add one of the following weapon special abilities to the list of weapon special abilities the magus may add to his weapon using his arcane pool: *defending, ghost touch, merciful, mighty cleaving, vicious* (*Core Rulebook*); *allying, conductive, corrosive, corrosive burst, menacing* (*Advanced Player's Guide*). Once an ability has been selected with this reward, it cannot be changed.

Monk: Add +1 to the monk's Acrobatics check bonus gained by spending a point from his *ki* pool. A monk must be at least 5th level to select this benefit.

Oracle: Add +1/2 to the oracle's level for the purpose of determining the effects of the oracle's curse ability.

Paladin: Add +1/2 hit point to the paladin's lay on hands ability (whether using it to heal or harm).

Ranger: Add DR 1/magic to the ranger's animal companion. Each additional time the ranger selects this benefit, the DR/magic increases by +1/2 (maximum DR 10/magic). If the ranger ever replaces his animal companion, the new companion gains this DR.

Rogue: The rogue gains a +1/2 bonus on Disable Device and Use Magic Device checks related to glyphs, symbols, scrolls, and other magical writings.

Sorcerer: Select one bloodline power at 1st level that is normally usable a number of times per day equal to 3 + the sorcerer's Charisma modifier. The sorcerer adds +1/2 to the number of uses per day of that bloodline power.

Summoner: Add +1 hit point to the summoner's eidolon.

Witch: The witch gains 1/6 of a new witch hex.

Wizard: Select one arcane school power at 1st level that is normally usable a number of times per day equal to 3 + the wizard's Intelligence modifier. The wizard adds +1/2 to the number of uses per day of that arcane school power.

RACIAL ARCHETYPES

The following racial archetypes are available to gnomes.

Experimental Gunsmith (Gunslinger)

The experimental gunsmith is obsessed with creating the ultimate firearm, and is willing to take risks to work the kinks out of her design. An experimental gunsmith has the following class features.

Experimental Firearm (Ex): At 1st level, an experimental gunsmith begins play with an experimental firearm. This acts as the gunslinger's gunsmith ability, but the firearm the experimental gunsmith begins with has one innovation (see below). Further, the experimental gunsmith is treated as having the Gunsmithing feat, but only in regard to his beginning firearm (or the construction of a replacement firearm of the same design, if the original is lost). This ability otherwise works like the standard gunslinger's gunsmith and Gunsmithing abilities and replaces those abilities.

Innovations (Ex): An experimental gunsmith starts play with one innovation she can make to her experimental firearms, selected from the list below. This innovation is a radical change to the typical design of a firearm, and comes with both additional benefits and noteworthy drawbacks. The experimental gunsmith can maintain only one experimental firearm modified with one or more innovations, as it requires constant adjustments and much of her time is spent maintaining the weapon. If the experimental gunsmith takes the Gunsmithing feat, she can create other firearms using a single innovation she knows (or add one innovation to an existing firearm), though such weapons become unreliable over time. The misfire value of such weapons increases by 1 for each week after its creation, although the experimental gunsmith can return the misfire rate to normal by spending 1 day maintaining the weapon and spending 50 gp in raw materials. For the purposes of crafting such firearms, each innovation is treated as the masterwork weapon quality (with a value of 300 gp).

At 5th level, and every four levels after that (9th, 13th, and 17th level), the experimental gunsmith learns one additional innovation from the list below. These represent constant and increasingly skilled tinkering with a single firearm in her possession, and when the experimental gunsmith gains an innovation, she may immediately apply it to her experimental firearm. Once an innovation has been selected, it cannot be changed. This ability replaces gun training.

Expanded Capacity: The experimental gunsmith increases her firearm's capacity by one (generally by adding another barrel, depending on the weapon's design). She also increases its weight by 50%. Because of the complexity of increasing its capacity, her weapon is more prone to misfire, and its misfire value increases by 1 (this is in addition to any misfire increase if the weapon is made with the Gunsmithing feat).

Expanded Chamber: The experimental gunsmith's firearm has a much larger than normal chamber for black powder, allowing her to use 2 doses of powder with each shot. The weapon grants a +1 circumstance bonus on damage rolls. However, when the weapon misfires, it causes a flashburn. This is the same as the weapon exploding (dealing damage from a corner of the experimental gunsmith's square), except the weapon is not automatically destroyed. If a broken weapon misfires, it is destroyed as normal.

Grapple Launcher: The experimental gunsmith's firearm includes a special set of rails that allows her to slide a grappling hook over the barrel and fire it as a full-round action. The grappling hook anchors into anything she successfully hits with an attack roll, and the DC of the Strength check required to pull the grappling hook loose is equal to her attack roll to lodge it in place. A Disable Device check can remove it with a +5 bonus on the check, and a creature struck by the hook can escape it with a combat maneuver check or Escape Artist check with a +5 bonus on the check. The firearm is powerful enough to fire a hook trailing up to 100 feet of rope, but throws off the balance of the experimental gunsmith's firearm, reducing its range increment by 50%.

Recoilless: The experimental gunsmith's firearm includes a series of gears, springs, and pistons designed to reduce its recoil and thus improve accuracy. The range increment of the weapon increases by 10 feet. However, the system is fragile, and easily damaged. Anytime the weapon misfires, this system becomes broken and does not function until the experimental gunsmith spends 1 hour repairing it.

Vial Launcher: The experimental gunsmith adds a special tube onto her firearm that can hold 1 vial of alchemical material, such as alchemist's fire, a tanglefoot bag, or a thunderstone. A special trigger allows her to channel the force of black powder into this tube to launch the vial as a ranged attack with half the range increment of her firearm. The experimental gunsmith can take this action in place of any single ranged attack, and may use the same attack bonus that she can apply to the firearm. If the alchemical substance has a save DC, it becomes 10 + 1/2 her experimental gunsmith level + her Wisdom modifier when she launches the vial from her firearm. This increase only applies to the initial saving throw. If additional saving throws are called for, they are resolved as normal. Reloading the tube is a time-consuming process and requires two full-round actions. If the weapon misfires while loaded with an alchemical substance, it detonates with the experimental gunsmith (and the firearm) as the target.

Prankster (Bard)

The prankster sees humor as the highest form or art, and pranks as the highest form of humor. In addition to setting friends up for light-hearted pranks, the prankster can use his quick wit and cruel sense of humor to enrage foes before incapacitating them with a clever turn of phrase.

Bardic Performance: A prankster's bardic performance functions like a bard's, but some of its performances are exchanged for those listed below.

Mock (Su): At 1st level, the prankster can use his performance to cause one or more creatures to become furious with him. Each creature to be mocked must be within 90 feet, able to see, hear, and understand the prankster, and capable of paying attention to him. The prankster must also be able to see the creatures affected. For every three levels the prankster has attained beyond 1st, he can target one additional creature with this ability.

Each creature within range receives a Will save (DC 10 + 1/2 the prankster's level + the prankster's Charisma modifier) to negate the effect. If a creature's saving throw succeeds, the prankster cannot successfully mock that creature for 24 hours. If its saving throw fails, the creature is angered by the performance and seeks to harm the prankster. While the prankster maintains the mocking, the target takes a –2 penalty on all attack rolls and skill checks until it has successfully attacked the prankster with a melee or ranged attack, or has harmed the creature with a spell that deals damage.

Mock is an enchantment (compulsion) mind-affecting ability. Mock relies on audible and visual components in order to function. This ability replaces fascinate.

Punchline (Sp): At 6th level, the prankster can use his performance to tell a punchline to amuse a creature he has already mocked (see above), goading it into *hideous laughter* (as the spell). Using this ability does not disrupt the mock effect, but it does require a standard action to activate (in addition to the free action to continue the mock effect). A prankster can use this ability more than once against an individual creature during an individual performance.

Telling a punchline does not count against a prankster's daily use of bardic performance. A Will saving throw (DC 10 + 1/2 the bard's level + the bard's Charisma modifier) negates the effect. This ability affects only a single creature. Punchline is an enchantment (compulsion), mind affecting, language-dependent ability and relies on audible components. This ability replaces the suggestion ability.

Mass Punchline (Sp): This ability functions just like punchline, but allows a prankster of 18th level or higher to use *hideous laughter* simultaneously against any number of creatures that he has mocked. This ability replaces the mass suggestion ability.

Swap (Ex): A prankster can steal an object from a creature and replace it with another object of the same size or smaller that the prankster has in his hand. This functions as the steal combat maneuver (*Advanced Player's Guide* 322), but the prankster does not provoke an attack of opportunity, and may use his Sleight of Hand check

in place of his combat maneuver check. If the prankster's check exceeds the target's CMD by 10 or more, the target is unaware the swap has been made until it tries to use the swapped object or the end of its next turn (whichever happens first). This ability replaces lore master.

Saboteur (Alchemist)

The saboteur is an alchemist who specializes in destroying the plans, materials, and allies of his enemies. A saboteur has focused his alchemical research toward new ways to conceal his presence, sow confusion, and blow up large structures.

Class Skills: A saboteur adds Knowledge (engineering) to his list of class skills and removes Knowledge (nature) from his list of class skills.

Chameleon Mutagen (Su): At 1st level, a saboteur discovers how to create a special elixir that he can imbibe in order to heighten his ability to move undetected and his mobility at the cost of his physical might. When consumed, the elixir causes the saboteur's skin to change color to match the background and causes his hands and feet to secrete a sticky residue. This grants him a circumstance bonus on Stealth checks equal to half his alchemist level (minimum +1), as well as granting him a climb speed equal to half his base speed, for 10 minutes per saboteur level. In addition, while the chameleon extract is in effect, the saboteur takes a –2 penalty to his Strength.

This ability replaces mutagen. A saboteur who drinks an alchemist's mutagen is treated as a non-alchemist. All limitations to mutagens apply to chameleon mutagen as if it were the same ability. The infuse mutagen discovery and persistent mutagen class ability apply to the chameleon mutagen.

Saboteur Discoveries: The following new options may be taken as discoveries by a saboteur.

Bore Bomb*: When the saboteur creates a bomb, he may choose to make it a bore bomb. If a bore bomb strikes a wall, gate, siege engine, or similar large, solid, inanimate structure, it ignores half the target's hardness and deals 1 point of damage per saboteur level. If a bore bomb reduces an inanimate target to half its hit points or fewer, it blows a hole 5 feet wide and 5 feet deep in the target.

Complex Bomb: When the saboteur creates a bomb, he can choose to have it modified by two different discoveries that modify a bomb's damage (those discoveries marked with an asterisk). Each discovery modifies half the bomb's damage dice, rounding down. For example, a concussive/frost bomb from a 9th-level saboteur deals 2d4 points of sonic damage + 2d6 points of frost damage. Creating a complex bomb counts as 2 daily uses of the bomb ability.

Grand Chameleon Mutagen: The saboteur's chameleon mutagen now grants him a circumstance bonus on Stealth checks equal to his alchemist level, as well as granting him a climb speed equal to his normal movement speed. The saboteur must possess the greater chameleon mutagen discovery and be at least 16th level to select this discovery.

Greater Chameleon Mutagen: The saboteur's chameleon mutagen now also grants the saboteur the hide in plain sight ability, as the ranger ability of the same name, but it functions in any terrain. The saboteur must be at least 12th level to select this discovery.

Grand Discoveries: A saboteur may select the following grand discovery.

True Chameleon Mutagen: The saboteur's chameleon mutagen now acts as if he was under the effects of the *improved invisibility* and *spider climb* spells, using his alchemist level as the caster level, for the duration of the mutagen. The saboteur must possess the grand chameleon mutagen discovery to select this grand discovery.

Discoveries: The following discoveries complement the saboteur archetype: acid bomb, concussive bomb, delayed bomb, explosive bomb, fast bombs, inferno bomb, madness bomb, precise bombs, smoke bomb, stink bomb (*Advanced Player's Guide*); explosive missile, immolation bomb, siege bomb (*Ultimate Combat*); blinding bomb, cognatogen, confusion bomb, tanglefoot bomb (*Ultimate Magic*).

NEW RACIAL RULES

The following options are available to gnomes. At the GM's discretion, other appropriate races may also make use of some of these.

Gnome Equipment

Gnomes have access tot he following equipment.

Dilettante's Outfit: These clothes are favored by gnome inventors and wanderers, and consist of sturdy boots, a pair of stout linen pants or skirt, a cloth shirt, leather gloves, a hat and cloak, and numerous belts, straps, and accessories (such as scarves, a vest, bits of rope or twine, and bandoleers). These items are generally mismatched, each having been selected as "superior" from some other set of clothing, and are rife with pockets and small hidey-holes. It the wearer a +2 circumstance bonus on Sleight of Hand checks made to conceal a small object on her body.

Hound's Blood: If you apply the thick, red paste known as hound's blood to your nostrils or upper lip, it greatly enhances your sense of smell. For most creatures, this grants a +2 circumstance bonus on Perception checks for 1 hour. For gnomes, it briefly grants a super-heightened sense of smell, granting the

36

scent ability for 5 minutes, before the potency is reduced to a +2 circumstance bonus on Perception checks for an additional 1 hour.

Moonrod: This 1-foot-long, silver-tipped tin rod glows dimly when struck as a standard action. It sheds dim light in a 30-foot radius. However, the light given off by a moonrod is particularly easily to perceive for creatures with low-light vision. For such creatures, a moonrod increases the light level by one step (to a maximum of normal) for a 60-foot radius. It glows for 6 hours, after which the silver tip is burned out and worthless.

Obsession Log: Gnomes use these small books to record information about their obsessions. When a gnome consults her obsession log (taking 1 minute), she gains a +2 circumstance bonus on the next Craft or Profession check she makes, as long as that skill was the one chosen for her obsessive racial trait.

Scentbane Incense: Scentbane incense is a form of smokestick that also blocks most scents. As long as the smoke lasts, creatures with the scent special ability must make Perception checks, opposed by the Stealth checks of any creatures within the smoke, to use scent to locate creatures within the smoke. If a creature remains in scentbane incense for 5 rounds or more, the smoke clings to it for 1 round after it leaves, making it similarly difficult to find by scent during that time.

Sheriff's Whistle: Used most often by gnome sheriffs and rangers, a sheriff's whistle gives off a piercing shriek that can easily be heard up to 1,000 feet away under ordinary circumstances. However, the frequency of the shriek is such that it can only be heard by badgers, dogs, and gnomes.

Gnome Equipment

Item	Cost	Weight	Craft DC
Dilettante's outfit	20 gp	8 lbs.*	—
Hound's blood (vial)	110 gp	—	20
Moonrod	10 gp	1 lb.	25
Obsession log	25 gp	1 lb.	—
Scentbane incense	80 gp	—	20
Sheriff's whistle	1 gp	—	—

* This items weighs 1/4 of this amount when made for Small characters.

Gnome Feats

Gnomes have access to the following feats.

Casual Illusionist

You can use your innate magic to create minor illusions that augment your efforts at trickery and deceit.

Prerequisites: Gnome, gnome magic racial trait.

Benefit: As long as you have at least one spell-like ability unused from your gnome magic racial trait, you gain a +2 racial bonus on all Bluff, Disguise, and Sleight of Hand checks you make. At 10th level, these bonuses increase to +4.

Special: This feat counts as the Deceitful feat for the purposes of all prerequisites.

Expanded Resistance

You have expanded your natural resistance to magic to encompass different kinds of magic.

Prerequisites: Gnome, illusion resistance racial trait.

Benefit: Select one school of magic other than illusion. You gain a +2 racial bonus on saving throws against spells or effects from the selected school.

Special: You may select this feat more than once. Its effects do not stack. Each time you select it, it applies to a different school of magic.

Gnome Weapon Focus (Combat)

Your extensive training with traditional gnome weapons gives you an advantage.

Prerequisites: Base attack bonus +1, gnome, proficient with all martial weapons.

Benefit: You gain a +1 bonus on attack rolls with gnome weapons (weapons with "gnome" in the title).

Great Hatred (Combat)

Your rage burns with vast intensity.

Prerequisites: Gnome, hatred racial trait.

Benefit: You gain an additional +1 bonus on melee and thrown weapon attacks against targets of your hatred racial trait.

Vast Hatred (Combat)

Your rage stretches beyond normal bounds.

Prerequisites: Gnome, hatred racial trait.

Benefit: Select two creature types (and subtypes where appropriate) from the list of potential favored enemies from the ranger class ability. Your +1 attack bonus from the hatred racial trait applies to creatures of the selected types (and subtypes).

Special: You may take this feat more than once. Its benefits do not stack. Each time you select this feat, you select two additional creature types to which your hatred racial trait applies.

Gnome Magic Items

Magic items crafted by gnomes are often useful tools to assist them in their labors or items that take advantage of their innate magical abilities.

AMAZING TOOLS OF MANUFACTURE

Aura faint transmutation; **CL** 3rd
Slot none; **Price** 12,000 gp; **Weight** 1 lb.

DESCRIPTION

Tools of this type always appear to be of the highest quality and wrought of the finest materials, most often mithral, darkwood, and adamantine. In the hands of a casual wielder, these items simply appear to be magically enhanced masterwork tools for a specific Craft skill (determined randomly), granting a +4 circumstance bonus on such skill checks.

However, in the hands of a craftsman with 6 or more ranks in the selected Craft skill, the greater power of the *amazing tools of manufacture* becomes apparent. The wielder may use the tools to create items using the Craft skill much more surely and quickly. The wielder may take raw materials with a value equal to half the price of an object to be crafted, and produce a finished object in as little as 1 hour for an item with a final cost of 2,000 gp or less. For objects with a final cost of more

than 2,000 gp, the wielder can perform 2,000 gp worth of work in a single hour, but only once each day. Only a single skill check is required to successfully complete the item, made on the last day of crafting and gaining the +4 circumstance bonus granted by the tools.

CONSTRUCTION

Requirements Craft Wondrous Item, Master Craftsman; **Cost** 6,000 gp

BOOTS OF ESCAPE

Aura faint conjuration; **CL** 5th
Slot feet; **Price** 8,000 gp; **Weight** 1 lb.

DESCRIPTION

These sturdy, leather-soled cloth boots have straps at the ankles and calves to ensure a snug fit. Once per day, when the wearer of the boots is grappled, pinned, or entangled, he may transfer himself to any spot within 30 feet. This acts as if the wearer had used a *dimension door* spell. A gnome wearing these boots may instead transfer himself up to 400 feet.

CONSTRUCTION

Requirements Craft Wondrous Item, creator must be a gnome or a wizard specialized in the school of conjuration; **Cost** 4,000 gp

PHANTASMAL GEM

Aura faint illusion; **CL** 3rd
Slot none; **Price** 4,000 gp; **Weight** 1 lb.

DESCRIPTION

This small cut crystal appears to be filled with hazy, indistinct images that constantly shift and vary. If a spellcaster holding the *phantasmal gem* casts an illusion spell with a duration of concentration (or concentration + a number of rounds), the illusion lasts up to an additional 10 rounds after the spellcaster ceases concentrating on it. The spellcaster may end the illusion early as a swift action. The *phantasmal gem* can be used multiple times in a day, but cannot grant more than a total of 10 additional rounds of illusion spells per day. A gnome using a *phantasmal gem* can recharge it by expending uses of spell-like abilities gained through the gnome magic racial trait. Each spell-like ability expended as a standard action recharges 1 round of duration to the *phantasmal gem* (up to a maximum of 10 rounds).

CONSTRUCTION

Requirements Craft Wondrous Item, creator must be a gnome or a wizard specialized in the school of illusion; **Cost** 2,000 gp

RING OF CRAFT MAGIC

Aura faint transmutation; **CL** 3rd
Slot ring; **Price** 12,000 gp; **Weight** 1 lb.

DESCRIPTION

A ring of craft magic always bears some sort of tool-like design in its craftsmanship. The wearer of the ring sees spells as similar to crafts, and vice versa. The wearer of this ring may make a Craft check in place of a Spellcraft check to identify an item that could be created with the Craft skill. The wearer may also expend a spell slot or prepared spell to gain an enhancement bonus equal to the level of the expended spell on a single Craft or Profession check (regardless of the amount of time needed to make the check).

CONSTRUCTION

Requirements Forge Ring, creator must have the obsession racial trait; **Cost** 6,000 gp

Gnome Spells

Gnomes have access to the following spells.

DEATH FROM BELOW

School abjuration; **Level** bard 3, sorcerer/wizard 2
Casting Time 1 standard action
Components V, S
Range touch
Target creature touched
Duration 1 round/level
Save Fortitude negates (harmless); **Spell Resistance** yes (harmless)

You grant the target a dodge bonus to its Armor Class against attacks from larger creatures. The bonus is equal to +1 for every size category the attacker is larger than the target of the spell, to a maximum of +1 per 3 caster levels. If the spell's target is a gnome, the maximum bonus is equal to +1 per 2 caster levels.

JITTERBUGS

School illusion (figment) [mind-affecting]; **Level** bard 1, sorcerer/wizard 2
Casting Time 1 standard action
Components V, S
Range short (25 ft. +5 ft. 2/levels)
Target one creature
Duration 1 round/level
Save Will negates **Spell Resistance** yes

You cause the target to perceive itself as being covered in creeping, crawling, stinging bugs. This causes the target to become jittery and unable to stay still, forcing it to constantly move and twitch. The target takes a −4 penalty on all Dexterity checks and Dexterity-based skill checks, and cannot take the delay, ready, or total defense actions.

MAJOR PHANTOM OBJECT

School illusion (figment) [mind-affecting]; **Level** sorcerer/wizard 5
Casting Time 10 minutes
Range close (25 ft. + 5 ft./2 levels)
Effect phantasmal, unattended, nonmagical object, up to 1 cu. ft./level

Duration 10 minutes/level (D)
Save Will negates; **Spell Resistance** yes

This spell functions as the *major creation spell*, except as noted above and the object created is a semi-real phantasm. Any creature that interacts with the object may make a Will save, with success causing the object to cease to exist. A gnome casting this spell may make a Spellcraft check in place of any Craft check required to make a complex item.

MINOR DREAM

School illusion (figment) [mind-affecting]; **Level** alchemist 2, bard 3, sorcerer/wizard 3, witch 2
Casting Time 1 minute
Components V, S
Range unlimited
Target you or one gnome touched
Duration see text
Save none; **Spell Resistance** yes

This spell functions as the *dream spell*, except as follows. The messenger must be yourself or a gnome touched. The message can be no longer than 20 words. If the recipient of the message is not asleep when the spell is cast, the spell automatically fails.

MINOR PHANTOM OBJECT

School illusion (figment) [mind-affecting]; **Level** sorcerer/wizard 4
Casting Time 1 minute
Components V, S
Range 0 ft.
Effect phantasmal, unattended, nonmagical object of nonliving plant matter, up to 1 cu. ft./level
Duration 10 minutes/level (D)
Save Will negates; **Spell Resistance** yes

This spell functions as the *minor creation spell*, except the object created is a semi-real phantasm. Any creature that interacts with the object may make a Will save, with success causing the object to cease to exist. A gnome casting this spell may make a Spellcraft check in place of any Craft check required to make a complex item.

RECHARGE INNATE MAGIC

School transmutation; **Level** alchemist 1, bard 1, cleric 1, druid 1, inquisitor 1, magus 1, sorcerer/wizard 1, witch 1
Casting Time 1 standard action
Components V, S
Range personal
Target you
Duration instantaneous

You channel magic energy into your own aura, recharging your innate magic abilities. You regain one use of all 0-level and 1st-level spell-like abilities you can use as a result of a racial trait.

HALF-ELVES

Elves have long drawn the covetous gazes of other races. Their generous lifespans, magical affinity, and inherent grace each contribute to the admiration or bitter envy of their neighbors. Of all their traits, however, none so entrance their human associates as their beauty. Since the two races first came into contact with each other, humans have held up elves as models of physical perfection, seeing in these fair folk idealized versions of themselves. For their part, many elves find humans attractive despite their comparatively barbaric ways, and are drawn to the passion and impetuosity with which members of the younger race play out their brief lives.

Sometimes this mutual infatuation leads to romantic relationships. Though usually short-lived, even by human standards, such trysts may lead to the birth of half-elves, a race descended from two cultures yet inheritor of neither. Half-elves can breed with one another, but even these "pureblood" half-elves tend to be viewed as bastards by humans and elves alike. Caught between destiny and derision, half-elves often view themselves as the middle children of the world.

Physical Description: Half-elves stand taller than humans but shorter than elves. They inherit the lean build and comely features of their elven lineage, but their skin color is normally dictated by their human side. While half-elves retain the pointed ears of elves, theirs are more rounded and less pronounced. Their eyes tend to be humanlike in shape, but feature an exotic range of colors from amber or violet to emerald green and deep blue. This pattern changes for half-elves of drow descent, however. Such elves are almost unfailingly marked with the white or silver hair of the drow parent, and more often than not have dusky gray skin that takes on a purplish or bluish tinge in the right light, while their eye color usually favors that of the human parent.

Society: Their lack of a unified homeland and culture forces half-elves to remain versatile, able to conform to nearly any environment. While often considered attractive to both races for the same reasons as their parents, half-elves rarely fit in with either humans or elves, as both races see too much evidence of the other in them. This lack of acceptance weighs heavily on many

HALF-ELF RACIAL TRAITS

+2 to One Ability Score: Half-elf characters gain a +2 bonus to one ability score of their choice at creation to represent their varied nature.

Medium: Half-elves are Medium creatures and have no bonuses or penalties due to their size.

Normal Speed: Half-elves have a base speed of 30 feet.

Low-Light Vision: Half-elves can see twice as far as humans in conditions of dim light.

Adaptability: Half-elves receive Skill Focus as a bonus feat at 1st level.

Elf Blood: Half-elves count as both elves and humans for any effect related to race.

Elven Immunities: Half-elves are immune to magic sleep effects and gain a +2 racial saving throw bonus against enchantment spells and effects.

Keen Senses: Half-elves receive a +2 racial bonus on Perception checks.

Multitalented: Half-elves choose two favored classes at first level and gain +1 hit point or +1 skill point whenever they take a level in either one of those classes.

Languages: Half-elves begin play speaking Common and Elven. Half-elves with high Intelligence scores can choose any languages they want (except secret languages, such as Druidic).

half-elves, yet others are bolstered by their unique status, seeing in their lack of a formalized culture the ultimate freedom. As a result, half-elves are incredibly adaptable, capable of adjusting their mind-sets and talents to whatever societies they find themselves in.

Even half-elves welcomed by one side of their heritage often find themselves caught between cultures, as they are encouraged, cajoled, or even forced into taking on diplomatic responsibilities between human and elven kind. Many half-elves rise to the occasion of such service, seeing it as a chance to prove their worth to both races. Others, however, come to resent the pressures and presumptions foisted upon them by both races and turn any opportunity to broker power, make peace, or advance trade between humans and elves into an exercise in personal profit.

Relations: Half-elves understand loneliness, and know that character is often less a product of race than of life experience. As such, they are often open to friendships and alliances with other races, and less likely than most to rely on first impressions when forming opinions of new acquaintances.

While many races join together to produce mixed offspring of notable power, such as half-orcs, half-dragons, and half-fiends, half-elves seem to have a unique position in the eyes of their progenitors and the rest of the world. Those humans who admire elvenkind see half-elves as a living link or bridge between the two races. But this attitude often foists unfair expectations and elevated standards upon half-elves, and quickly turns to derision when they do not live up to the grand destinies that others set for them. Additionally, those half-elves raised by or in the company of elves often have the human half of their parentage dubbed a mere obstacle, something to be overcome with proper immersion and schooling in the elven ways, and even the most well-meaning elven mentors often push their half-elven charges to reject a full half of themselves in order to "better" themselves. The exception is those few half-elves born of humans and drow. Not unlike most half-orcs, such unions are commonly born out of violence and savagery that leaves the child unwanted by its mother if not killed outright. Moreover, as the physical features of half-drow clearly mark their parentage, crafting a reputation founded on deeds and character instead of heritage is more challenging for them. Even the most empathetic of other half-elves balk at the sight of a half-drow.

Among other races, half-elves form unique and often unexpected bonds. Dwarves, despite their traditional mistrust of elves, see a half-elf's human parentage as something hopeful, and treat them as half-humans rather than half-elves. Additionally, while dwarves are long-lived, the lifespan of the stout folk is closer to a half-elf's own than that of either of her parents. As a result, half-elves

and dwarves often form lasting bonds, be they ones of friendship, business, or even competitive rivalry.

Gnomes and halflings often see half-elves as a curiosity. Those half-elves who have seen themselves pushed to the edges of society, truly without a home, typically find gnomes and halflings frivolous and worthy of disdain, but secretly envy their seemingly carefree ways. Clever and enterprising gnomes and halflings sometimes partner with a half-elf for adventures or even business ventures, using the half-elf's participation to lend their own endeavors an air of legitimacy that they cannot acquire on their own.

Perhaps the most peculiar and dichotomous relations exist between half-elves and half-orcs. Those half-orcs and half-elves who were raised among their non-human kin normally see one another as hated and ancient foes. However, half-elves who have been marginalized by society feel a deep, almost instant kinship with half-orcs, knowing their burdens are often that much harder because of their appearance and somewhat brutish nature. Not all half-orcs are inclined or able to understand such empathy, but those who do often find themselves with a dedicated diplomat, liaison, and apologist. For their own part, half-orcs usually return the favor by acting as bodyguards or intimidators, and take on other roles uniquely suited to their brawny forms.

Alignment and Religion: Half-elves' isolation strongly influences their characters and philosophies. Cruelty does not come naturally to them, nor does blending in or bending to societal convention—as a result, most half-elves are chaotic good. Half-elves' lack of a unified culture makes them less likely to turn to religion, but those who do generally follow the common faiths of their homeland. Others come to religion and worship later in their lives, especially if they have been made to feel part of a community through faith or the work of clerical figures.

Some half-elves feel the pull of the divine but live beyond the formal religious instruction of society. Such individuals often worship ideas and concepts like freedom, harmony, or balance, or the primal forces of the world. Still others gravitate toward long-forgotten gods, finding comfort and kinship in the idea that even deities can be overlooked.

Adventurers: Half-elves tend to be itinerants, wandering the lands in search of a place they might finally call home. The desire to prove themselves to the community and establish a personal identity—or even a legacy—drives many half-elf adventurers to lives of bravery. Some half-elves claim that despite their longevity, they perceive the passage of time more like humans than elves, and are driven to amass wealth, power, or fame early on in life so they may spend the rest of their years enjoying it.

Males Names: Calathes, Encinal, Iradli, Kyras, Narciso, Quinray, Seltyiel, Zirul.

Female Names: Cathran, Elsbeth, Iandoli, Kieyanna, Lialda, Maddela, Reda, Tamarie.

ALTERNATE RACIAL RULES

Due to their mixed heritage, half-elves exhibit great flexibility in their abilities.

Alternate Racial Traits

The following racial traits may be selected instead of existing half-elf racial traits. Consult your GM before selecting any of these new options.

Ancestral Arms: Some half-elves receive training in an unusual weapon. Half-elves with this racial trait receive Exotic Weapon Proficiency or Martial Weapon Proficiency with one weapon as a bonus feat at 1st level. This racial trait replaces the adaptability racial trait.

Arcane Training: Half-elves occasionally seek tutoring to help them master the magic in their blood. Half-elves with this racial trait have only one favored class, and it must be an arcane spellcasting class. They can use spell trigger and spell completion items for their favored class as if one level higher (or as a 1st-level character if they have no levels in that class). This racial trait replaces the multitalented racial trait.

Drow-Blooded: Some half-elves born of drow parents exhibit more drow traits than others—particularly many of the physical features of the drow—and have darkvision 60 feet and light blindness (*Bestiary* 301). This racial trait replaces the low-light vision racial trait.

Drow Magic: A few half-elves with drow ancestry exhibit the innate magic of that race. Half-elves with this trait have drow blood somewhere in their background, and can cast *dancing lights*, *darkness*, and *faerie fire* each once per day, using the half-elf's character level as the caster level for these spell-like abilities. This racial trait replaces the adaptability and multitalented racial traits.

Dual Minded: The mixed ancestry of some half-elves makes them resistant to mental attacks. Half-elves with this racial trait gain a +2 bonus on all Will saving throws. This racial trait replaces the adaptability racial trait.

Integrated: Many half-elves are skilled in the art of ingratiating themselves into a community as if they were natives. Half-elves with this racial trait gain a +1 bonus on Bluff, Disguise, and Knowledge (local) checks. This racial trait replaces the adaptability racial trait.

Sociable: Half-elves are skilled at charming others and recovering from faux pas. If half-elves with this racial trait attempt to change a creature's attitude with a Diplomacy check and fail by 5 or more, they can try to influence the creature a second time even if 24 hours have not passed. This racial trait replaces the adaptability racial trait.

Wary: Many half-elves have spent their long lives moving from place to place, often driven out by the hostility of others. Such experiences have made them wary of others' motivations. Half-elves with this trait gain a +1 racial bonus on Sense Motive and Bluff checks. This racial trait replaces the keen senses racial trait.

Water Child: Some half-elves are born of elves adapted to life on or near the water. These half-elves gain a +4 racial bonus on Swim checks, can always take 10 while swimming, and may choose Aquan as a bonus language. This racial trait replaces the adaptability and multitalented racial traits.

Racial Subtypes

You can combine various alternate racial traits to create half-elven subraces or variant races, such as the following.

Drow-Descended: These half-elves clearly bear the features of their dark elf parents, branding them immediately as a potential threat in the eyes of others no matter what their intent or character. These half-elves have the drow-blooded and drow magic alternate racial traits.

Elf-Raised: These half-elves represent those embraced by their elven relatives, and raised with all of the traditional cultural training and education typical of most full-blooded elves. These half-elves have the ancestral arms and arcane training alternate racial traits.

Human-Raised: These half-elves were born and raised into accepting human communities, often raised by generations of a single family, or through the charity of churches and temples. These half-elves have the integrated and wary racial traits.

Favored Class Options

The following favored options are available to all half-elves who have the listed favored class, and unless otherwise stated, the bonus applies each time you select the class reward.

Alchemist: Add +1 foot to the range increment of the alchemist's thrown splash weapons (including the alchemist's bombs). This option has no effect unless the alchemist has selected it 5 times (or another increment of 5); a range increment of 24 feet is effectively the same as a range increment of 20 feet, for example.

Barbarian: Add +1/4 to the bonus on Reflex saves and dodge bonus to AC against attacks made by traps granted by trap sense.

Bard: Add +1 to the bard's total number of bardic performance rounds per day.

Cavalier: Add +1 foot to the cavalier's mount's base speed. This option has no effect unless the cavalier has selected it 5 times (or another increment of 5); a speed of 54 feet is effectively a speed of 50 feet, for example. If the cavalier ever replaces his mount, the new companion gains this base speed bonus.

Cleric: Add +1/3 to the amount of damage dealt or damage healed when the cleric uses channel energy.

Druid: Select one cleric domain power at 1st level that is normally usable a number of times per day equal to 3 + the druid's Wisdom modifier. The druid adds +1/2 to the number of uses per day of that domain power. For druids whose nature bond gives them an animal companion, add +1 skill rank to the animal companion. If the druid ever replaces her animal companion, the new companion gains these bonus skill ranks.

Fighter: Add +1 to the fighter's CMD when resisting a disarm or overrun combat maneuver.

Gunslinger: Add +1/4 to the number of grit points in the gunslinger's grit pool.

Inquisitor: Add +1/4 to the number of times per day the inquisitor can change her most recent teamwork feat.

Magus: Add +1/4 to the magus's arcane pool.

Monk: Add +1/2 on Escape Artist checks and on Acrobatics checks to cross narrow surfaces.

Oracle: Add one spell known from the oracle spell list. This spell must be at least one level below the highest spell level the oracle can cast.

Paladin: Add +1 foot to the size of all the paladin's aura class features. This option has no effect unless the paladin has selected it 5 times (or another increment of 5); an aura of 14 feet is effectively the same as a 10-foot aura, for example.

Ranger: Add +1 skill rank to the ranger's animal companion. If the ranger ever replaces his companion, the new companion gains these bonus skill ranks.

Rogue: Add a +1/2 bonus on Bluff checks to feint and Diplomacy checks to gather information.

Sorcerer: Select one bloodline power at 1st level that is normally usable a number of times per day equal to 3 + the sorcerer's Charisma modifier. The sorcerer adds +1/2 to the number of uses per day of that bloodline power.

Summoner: Add +1/4 to the eidolon's evolution pool.

Witch: Add one spell from the witch spell list to the witch's familiar. This spell must be at least one level below the highest spell level she can cast. If the witch ever replaces her familiar, the new familiar knows these bonus spells.

Wizard: When casting wizard enchantment spells, add +1/3 to the effective caster level of the spell, but only to determine the spell's duration.

RACIAL ARCHETYPES

The following racial archetypes are available to half-elves.

Bonded Witch (Witch)

While all witches commune with the unknown, the blend of human ingenuity and adept learning mixed with elven blood gives some half-elves a unique conduit to channel the powers of the arcane. Bonded witches forsake familiars as vessels of power in favor of a specific object that grants them powers above and beyond those of their patron alone, as they tap into the powerful magic of the item itself. A bonded witch has the following class features.

Bonded Item (Sp): At 1st level, a bonded witch gains a bonded item instead of a familiar. This bonded item is similar to a wizard's arcane bond bonded item (*Core Rulebook* 78), and follows all the rules of such an item with the following exceptions.

A bonded witch's bonded item serves as a vessel for her spells and a conduit for communication with her patron. A bonded witch must commune with her bonded item each day to prepare her spells. The bonded item stores all of the spells that the bonded witch knows, and the bonded witch cannot prepare spells that are not stored within it. A bonded witch starts with the same number of spells and gains new spells the same way as a witch, and can even add spells by learning them from scrolls in the same way (*Advanced Player's Guide* 68), but a bonded witch cannot learn spells from another bonded item.

Since a bonded witch does not have a spellbook, starting at 2nd level, a bonded witch's bonded item can be used once per day to cast a spell dependent on the type of bonded object chosen by the bonded witch. The spell is treated like any other spell cast by the bonded witch, including its casting time, duration, and other effects dependent of the bonded witch's level. This spell cannot be further modified by metamagic feats or any other ability. As the bonded witch gains levels, the bonded item gains new spells that the bonded witch can cast in this way. She can cast any one of these spells once per day using her bonded object, but gains greater flexibility in what spells she can cast, and gains more powerful spells as she gains new levels. The bonded item spells associated with each item type are as follows.

Amulet: 2nd—*stonefist* (*Advanced Player's Guide* 247); 4th—*bear's endurance*; 6th—*burst of speed* (*Ultimate Combat* 225); 8th—*mnemonic enhancer*; 10th—*stoneskin*; 12th—*monstrous physique IV* (*Ultimate Magic* 229); 14th—*firebrand* (*Advanced Player's Guide* 222); 16th—*iron body*; 18th—*overwhelming presence* (*Ultimate Magic* 230).

Ring: 2nd—*shield*; 4th—*ablative barrier* (*Ultimate Combat* 221); 6th—*protection from energy*; 8th—*nondetection*; 10th—*life bubble* (*Advanced Player's Guide* 230); 12th—*resinous skin* (*Ultimate Combat* 242); 14th—*antimagic field*; 16th—*deflection* (*Advanced Player's Guide* 215); 18th—*spell immunity*.

Staff: 2nd—*shillelagh*; 4th—*warp wood*; 6th—*plant growth*; 8th—*arboreal hammer* (*Ultimate Magic* 206); 10th—*passwall*; 12th—*move earth*; 14th—*change staff*; 16th—*control plants*; 18th—*wooden phalanx* (*Ultimate Magic* 249).

Wand: 2nd—*magic missile*; 4th—*knock*; 6th—*fireball*; 8th—*restoration*; 10th—maximized *scorching ray*; 12th—*bull's strength* (mass); 14th—*greater restoration*; 16th—empowered and maximized *fireball*; 18th—empowered and maximized *fire shield*.

Weapon: 2nd—*warding weapon* (*Ultimate Combat* 248); 4th—*versatile weapon* (*Advanced Player's Guide* 254);

NEW ALCHEMIST DISCOVERY

The following discovery is favored by bramble brewers.

Defoliant Bomb*: These poisonous bombs clear away foliage, dealing extra damage to plant creatures.

When the alchemist creates a bomb, he can choose to have it deal extra damage against plant creatures but less damage against other creatures. Against creatures with the plant type, a defoliant bomb deals 1d8 points of damage, plus 1d8 points of damage for every odd-numbered level the alchemist possesses, instead of 1d6. Against all other creatures, the defoliant bomb only deals 1d4 points of damage, plus 1d4 points of damage for every odd-numbered level, instead of 1d6. This is a poison effect. A defoliant bomb kills all normal vegetation in the target's square and its splash area; any plant-based difficult terrain in the affected area becomes normal terrain.

6th—*greater magic weapon*; 8th—*telekinetic charge* (*Ultimate Combat* 247); 10th—*energy siege shot* (*Ultimate Combat* 228); 12th—*blade barrier*; 14th—*arcane cannon* (*Ultimate Combat* 223); 16th—*earthquake*; 18th—*ride the lightning* (*Ultimate Magic* 235).

This ability replaces the witch's familiar class feature.

Bramble Brewer (Alchemist)

Some half-elven alchemists merge human curiosity with their elven link to nature. Such alchemists can manipulate the forces of alchemy to create bombs that reshape terrain and defoliate swaths of vegetation or to create mutagens that bestow the resilience of oak or the tenacity of bamboo. A bramble brewer has the following class features.

Briar Bombs (Su): At 2nd level, a bramble brewer gains the tanglefoot bomb discovery (*Ultimate Magic* 17), but the entanglement's duration persists for a number of rounds equal to the bramble brewer's Intelligence modifier (minimum 1 round). Additionally, when a bramble brewer throws a tanglefoot bomb, it transforms all squares in its splash radius into difficult terrain that persists for as long as the bomb's entangling effect. Although these bombs deal no damage, for every 1d6 points of damage the bramble brewer's regular bombs deal, the briar bomb's splash radius increases by 5 feet. This ability replaces the 2nd-level discovery class feature.

Dendrite Mutagen (Su): At 1st level, a bramble brewer's mutagen still contains transformative power, but grants a treelike sturdiness rather than the feral power of standard mutagens. When imbibed, dendrite mutagen grants a +4 natural armor bonus, a +2 alchemical bonus to one physical ability score, and a −2 penalty to the corresponding mental ability score (as per the normal mutagen class feature; *Advanced Player's Guide* 28). In addition, the alchemist gains fast healing 1 as long as he is in an area of bright light (such as sunlight or inside the area of a *daylight* spell). This otherwise works like the standard mutagen class feature and replaces that ability.

A bramble brewer who selects the greater mutagen discovery can create a dendrite mutagen that still grants a +4 natural armor bonus, and also grants a +4 alchemical bonus to one physical ability score and a +2 bonus to a second physical ability score. The bramble brewer takes a −2 penalty to both associated mental ability scores as long as the mutagen persists, but his fast healing increases to 3 as long as he is in an area of bright light. This otherwise works like the greater mutagen discovery and replaces that ability.

A bramble brewer who selects the grand mutagen discovery can brew a dendrite mutagen that now grants a +6 natural armor bonus, a +6 alchemical bonus to one physical ability score, a +4 alchemical bonus to a second physical ability score, and a +2 alchemical bonus to a third physical ability score. The bramble brewer takes a −2 penalty to his Intelligence, Wisdom, and Charisma scores as long as the mutagen persists. The bramble brewer's fast healing increases to 5 as long as he is within an area of bright light. This otherwise works like the grand mutagen discovery and replaces that ability.

Grand Discovery (Su): At 20th level, a bramble brewer who selects the true mutagen grand discovery can create a dendrite mutagen that grants a +8 natural armor bonus and a +6 alchemical bonus to Strength, Dexterity, and Constitution. The bramble brewer takes a −2 penalty to his Intelligence, Wisdom, and Charisma scores as long as the mutagen persists. The bramble brewer's gains fast healing 10, but instead of only gaining fast healing in bright light, this fast healing persists in areas of bright or normal light. A bramble brewer must possess the grand mutagen discovery before selecting this discovery.

Discoveries: The following discoveries complement the bramble brewer archetype: precise bombs (*Advanced Player's Guide*); defoliant bomb (*Advanced Race Guide*); lingering spirit, strafe bomb, sunlight bomb (*Ultimate Magic*).

Wild Caller (Summoner)

Often a half-elf's ties to nature and elven heritage are so strong that they can dramatically affect the nature of his summonings. The wild caller calls eidolons that take more natural and savage forms and summons from nature rather than the Great Beyond. A wild caller has the following class features.

Spells: A wild caller does not have access to *summon monster* spells. Instead, he swaps out those spells on his spell list with *summon nature's ally* spells of the same level. This ability alters the normal spell list of the summoner.

Eidolon: The eidolon of a wild caller tends to take more natural and more savage forms than other summoners' eidolons. A wild caller gains 1/4 his class level as bonus evolution points in his eidolon's evolution pool, but his eidolon cannot take the following evolutions:

Advanced Player's Guide—1-point evolutions: magic attacks, skilled (while the eidolon can select this evolution, it can only do so with the following skills: Acrobatics, Climb, Escape Artist, Fly, Intimidate, Perception, Survival, and Swim); *2-point evolutions*: energy attacks, immunity, weapon training; *3-point evolutions*: damage reduction, frightful presence; *4-point evolutions*: breath weapon, spell resistance.

Ultimate Magic—1-point evolutions: basic magic, unnatural aura; *2-point evolutions*: channel resistance, head, minor magic, undead appearance; *3-point evolutions*: major magic; *4-point evolutions*: dimension door, incorporeal form, lifesense, no breath, ultimate magic.

This ability alters the normal summoner's eidolon class feature, but is otherwise identical to that class feature.

Summon Nature's Ally I (Sp): Starting at 1st level, a wild caller can cast *summon nature's ally* a number of times per day equal to 3 + his Charisma modifier. At 3rd level and every 2 levels thereafter, the power of this ability increases by one spell level, allowing him to summon more powerful creatures (to a maximum of *summon nature's ally IX* at 17th level). Furthermore, at 19th level, the wild caller cannot use *gate* as a spell-like ability, but can use either *summon elder worm* or *summon froghemoth* (*Ultimate Magic* 240) instead. This ability otherwise functions like the standard summoner's *summon monster I* ability and replaces that ability.

Wild Shadow (Ranger)

The isolation that some half-elves feel leads them to live a life of isolation amid the wild places of the world. Such rangers stalk the wild like shadows, creating close bonds with the wild itself instead of seeking the solace and aid of companions. While ill at ease within cities and other urban areas, they are adept at using the terrain to tactical advantage; they dart through brambles and rough terrain with uncommon grace and use the land itself to lock down enemies. A wild shadow has the following class features.

Wild at Heart (Ex): At 1st level, a wild shadow adds only 1/2 his class level when making wild empathy checks while in urban areas, and adds only 1/4 his class level to follow or identify tracks in such areas. In non-urban settings, he is considered two levels higher when determining the bonuses for such checks. This ability alters the track and wild empathy class features.

Favored Terrain (Ex): At 3rd level, when a wild shadow chooses a favored terrain, he cannot choose urban as the terrain type. Furthermore, at 8th level and every five levels thereafter, when he chooses a new favorite terrain type, he cannot choose the urban terrain type. This ability alters the favored terrain class feature.

Woodland Stride (Ex): This ability functions as the 7th-level ranger class feature of the same name, but the wild shadow gains it at 4th level instead. This ability replaces the hunter's bond class feature.

Unfettered Step (Ex): At 7th level, a wild shadow's woodland stride class feature functions in any difficult terrain within any of his favored terrains, even in areas that are enchanted or magically manipulated to impede

motion. This ability replaces the ranger's woodland stride class feature gained at 7th level.

Harrying Attack (Ex): At 11th level, a wild shadow can use his knowledge of terrain to make shrewd attacks in combat. Such attacks can make foes fumble or cause them to become entangled within areas of the wild shadow's favored terrain. As a standard action, the wild shadow denotes one target within line of sight and within one of his favored terrains as his harried prey. Once the foe is so designated, every time the wild shadow hits this harried prey with a melee or ranged weapon attack (either manufactured or natural), that creature is entangled for 1 round. A wild shadow can have no more than one harried prey at a time and that creature must correspond to one of his favored enemy types. He can dismiss this effect at any time as a free action, be he cannot select a new harried prey for 24 hours. If the wild shadow sees proof that his harried prey is dead, he can select a new harried prey after waiting 1 hour. This ability replaces the quarry class feature.

Wild Stalker (Ex): At 14th level, a wild shadow learns to better use natural surroundings to obscure his position in combat. Whenever a wild shadow is within one of his favored terrains and a feature of that terrain grants him cover, the bonuses to AC and Reflex saves for that cover improve by 1. Additionally, while he is within one of his favored terrains, if he gains concealment or total concealment, the miss chance of either type of concealment improves by 10%. Furthermore, at 16th level and 19th level, the bonuses granted by cover increase by 1 and the miss chance increases by another 10% (maximum +3 and +30% respectively at 20th level). This ability replaces the camouflage class feature.

Master of Terrain (Ex): At 19th level, a wild shadow can use his harrying attack against creatures other than his favored enemy or he can spend a standard action to designate up to two of his favored enemies as his harried prey instead. This ability replaces the improved quarry class feature.

NEW RACIAL RULES

The following options are available to half-elves. At the GM's discretion, other appropriate races may make use of some of these.

Half-Elven Equipment

Half-elves have access to the following equipment.

Golden Maple Leaves: These potent additives can only be culled from a rare maple tree known to grow exclusively in urban areas. These small, elaborately twisting trees are extremely slow to grow and mature—the leaves reach maturity only once every 3 years—and they are almost always grown and cultivated by half-elves. Additionally,

half-elves are keenly aware of the effort put into the leaves' growth and normally only sell the products of their labors to others of their kind. When the golden maple's delicate, five-pointed leaves finally take on their namesake's color, they can be cut, dried, and then ground into a fine powder, a process that requires a DC 15 Knowledge (nature) or Profession (herbalist) check. When used in conjunction with the Craft (alchemy) skill to create special substances and items like alchemical grease or tanglefoot bags, golden maple leaves reduce the Craft DC by 5 and add +1 to the DC of any save required by the alchemical item. A single dose of golden maple leaf powder is sufficient to augment the crafting of three alchemical items.

Star Charts: Many half-elves live in large cities or communities where they find it difficult to commune with nature. While some go on long sojourns to the wilderness, others spend their evenings on high, lonely rooftops, gazing at the stars. These lonely souls use star charts to track the movement of the stars and other celestial bodies. Anyone referencing one of these charts on a clear night can attempt a DC 20 Knowledge (geography) check to determine her approximate location and the month. In addition, these charts grant a +2 circumstance bonus on Survival checks made to avoid getting lost at night with a clear sky.

Half-Elven Equipment

Item	Cost	Weight
Golden maple leaves	50 gp	1/2 lb.
Star charts	200 gp	1/2 lb.

Half-Elven Feats

Half-elves have access to the following feats.

Discerning Eye

You are not easily fooled by illusions and forgeries.

Prerequisites: Elf or half-elf, keen senses racial trait.

Benefit: You receive a +2 racial bonus on saving throws against illusion spells and effects and a +2 bonus on Linguistic checks to detect forgeries. You can use the Linguistic skill to detect forgeries untrained.

Elven Spirit

Although you are of mixed heritage, you are closer to your elven relatives and the magic in their blood flows freely in your veins.

Prerequisite: Half-elf.

Benefit: You possess the elven magic racial trait of the elves, granting you a +2 racial bonus on caster level checks made to overcome spell resistance. In addition, you receive a +2 racial bonus on Spellcraft checks made to identify the properties of magic items. Alternatively, you can instead gain any one racial trait that elves can exchange for the elven magic racial trait.

Special: You can only take this feat at 1st level. If you take this feat, you cannot take the Human Spirit feat.

Exile's Path

A lifetime spent shunned by others and eschewing your heritage makes you resistant to efforts to pry inside of your mind.

Prerequisite: Half-elf.

Benefit: Once per day, when you fail a Will save against an enchantment spell or effect, you may reroll that saving throw, but must take the reroll result even if it's worse.

Half-Drow Paragon

Your drow blood is particularly strong.

Prerequisites: Drow-blooded and drow magic racial traits, half-elf.

Benefit: You count as a drow for any effects that relate to race. Furthermore, the spell-like abilities granted to you by your drow magic racial trait count as drow spell-like abilities for the purposes of any feat prerequisites.

Human Spirit

Your blood burns with the passion and unyielding quest for self-improvement displayed so prominently by your human relatives.

Prerequisite: Half-elf.

Benefit: You receive 1 bonus skill rank. Whenever you gain another Hit Die, you gain an additional skill rank. You cannot gain more than four skill ranks in this way.

Special: You can only take this feat at 1st level. If you take this feat, you cannot take the Elven Spirit feat.

Multitalented Mastery

You are adept at numerous disciplines.

Prerequisites: Character level 5th, half-elf, multitalented racial trait.

Benefit: All of your classes are considered favored classes. You gain either +1 hit point or +1 skill point whenever you take a level in any class. Apply these bonuses retroactively for all class levels that have not yet gained one of these bonuses.

Normal: Half-elves with the multitalented racial trait have two favored classes.

Neither Elf nor Human

You have removed yourself from your heritage so thoroughly that even magic does not recognize you.

Prerequisites: Exile's Path, Seen and Unseen, character level 11th, half-elf.

Benefit: You are not considered elven or human for the purpose of harmful spells or effects based on your type, like a *bane* weapon or a ranger's favored enemy class feature.

Seen and Unseen

Your anonymity makes you difficult to find through magical or mundane means, and you have learned how to combat both of your progenitor races.

Prerequisites: Exile's Path, character level 5th, half-elf.

Benefit: You gain a +2 bonus on all saving throws against scrying or divination effects. Additionally, you gain a +2 bonus on all Stealth checks, and elves, half-elves, and humans take a −4 penalty on all efforts to track you through the Survival skill.

Shared Manipulation

You can subtly bolster allies' ability to misdirect and infuriate their enemies.

Prerequisites: Cha 13, half-elf.

Benefit: As a move action, you can grant all friendly creatures within 30 feet who can see or hear you a +2 bonus on Bluff or Intimidate checks (choose which skill to affect each time you use this ability) for a number of rounds equal to your Charisma modifier (minimum 1 round).

Half-Elven Magic Items

Half-elves have access to the following magic items.

ANCESTRAL CLASP

Aura faint transmutation; **CL** 5th
Slot none; **Price** 10,000 gp; **Weight** 1/2 lb.

DESCRIPTION

Favored by half-elves seeking to distill their heritage into a combat edge, an ancestral clasp resembles a metal tube, open on both sides and covered in delicate elven calligraphy. Whenever a half-elf fits an ancestral clasp to the pommel, grip, or haft of a longbow, longsword, rapier, or shortbow, the character is treated as though she were proficient with that weapon. In addition, when an ancestral clasp is fitted to any weapon with the word "elven" in the title, the character treats the weapon as if it were a martial weapon, mirroring the Weapon Familiarity elven racial trait. A half-elf who already is proficient with one of the above weapons adorned with an ancestral clasp receives a +1 insight bonus on attack rolls with that weapon. Although this ability stems from the item's magic, the affected weapon is treated as nonmagical for the purpose of overcoming damage reduction. Affixing and removing an *ancestral clasp* is a standard action.

CONSTRUCTION

Requirements Craft Wondrous Item, *paragon surge*, creator must be a half-elf; **Cost** 5,000 gp

BROOCH OF BLENDING

Aura faint transmutation; **CL** 3rd
Slot neck; **Price** 2,000 gp; **Weight** —

DESCRIPTION

Occasionally, half-elves find it socially advantageous to blend in fully with either elves or humans. As a standard action, the wearer

of this brooch can transform his features to appear either entirely elven or entirely human. The magic of this brooch actually changes the wearer's features physically, granting him a +20 circumstance bonus on Disguise checks to appear as a member of the selected race. The transformation does not otherwise alter the wearer's features, and those who know him recognize him without a Perception check. This change remains until the brooch is used again or removed. This change does not radiate magic and cannot be seen with *detect magic*, although *true seeing* does reveal the alteration. This item only functions for half-elves, but there are versions that exist for half-orcs as well.

CONSTRUCTION

Requirements Craft Wondrous Item, *alter self*, creator must be a half-elf; **Cost** 1,000 gp

CLOAK OF THE DIPLOMAT

Aura moderate enchantment; **CL** 7th
Slot shoulders; **Price** 20,000 gp; **Weight** 1 lb.

DESCRIPTION

Half-elves are often called upon to mediate disputes when elves and humans come into conflict. This is due in part to their blood, but also to their natural skills as facilitators and diplomats. The *cloak of the diplomat* greatly aids them in this task. The cloak grants a +5 competence bonus on Diplomacy and Sense Motive checks. In addition, once per day, before making a Diplomacy or Sense Motive check, the wearer can decide to call upon the powers of the cloak to roll twice and take the better result. Finally, the wearer of this cloak can adjust a creature's attitude up to three steps when using Diplomacy, instead of the normal limit of two steps. However, the cloak's power does have one drawback. Should the wearer ever fail a Diplomacy check to adjust a creature's attitude by 5 or more, the creature's attitude is reduced by two steps instead of one.

CONSTRUCTION

Requirements Craft Wondrous Item, *charm person*, creator must have 5 ranks in Diplomacy and Sense Motive; **Cost** 10,000 gp

PURIFYING PEARL

Aura moderate conjuration and transmutation; **CL** 10th
Slot none; **Price** 19,000 gp; **Weight** —

DESCRIPTION

A favored tool of diplomats and those tasked with protecting the lives of regents and other important people, this small luminescent white pearl purifies putridity and poison in two ways. First, up to 10 cubic feet of food or drink that it touches per day is affected as if a *purify food and drink* spell had been cast upon the food or drink. Second, once per day, if placed in the mouth of a creature (as a standard action that provokes attacks of opportunity), the pearl acts as a *neutralize poison* spell cast on that creature (caster level 10th).

CONSTRUCTION

Requirements Craft Wondrous Item, *neutralize poison, purify food and water*; **Cost** 8,000 gp

RING OF THE SOPHISTICATE

Aura moderate transmutation and divination; **CL** 8th
Slot ring; **Price** 11,000 gp; **Weight** —

DESCRIPTION

A favorite ring of urban half-elves, humans, and halflings, this small and plain silver band is set with a single radiant-cut sapphire and decorated with a mazelike pattern engraved into the ring's metal. Often worn on the little finger, the ring grants its wearer a +4 competence bonus on Sense Motive and Knowledge (local) checks. Also, once per day on command, the wearer can use the ring to cast either *locate creature* or *locate object* (the wearer's choice). Furthermore, on command and at will, the wearer can instantly know the direction from her to the nearest tavern, pub, or similar watering hole as long as that establishment is in a settlement whose population is equivalent to that of a village or greater (*GameMastery Guide* 203) and which is within 20 miles of the wearer.

CONSTRUCTION

Requirements Forge Ring, *know direction, locate creature, locate object,* creator must have at least 4 ranks in both Sense Motive and Knowledge (local); **Cost** 5,500 gp

Half-Elven Spells

Half-elves have access to the following spells.

FORGETFUL SLUMBER

School enchantment (compulsion) [mind-affecting]; **Level** bard 4, sorcerer/wizard 4, witch 4
Casting Time 1 round
Components V, S, M (a few drops of river water)
Range close (25 ft. + 5 ft./2 levels)
Target one living creature **Duration** 1 minute/level
Saving Throw Will negates; **Spell Resistance** yes
This spell acts as the *deeper slumber* spell, but only affects one creature of 10 Hit Dice or fewer. In addition, a creature affected by this spell awakens with no knowledge of the events that led to the spell's casting. The target loses all memory from the 5 minutes prior to falling asleep. No effect short of a *miracle* or *wish* can restore memories lost by this spell.

PARAGON SURGE

School transmutation (polymorph); **Level** alchemist 3, cleric 3, magus 4, paladin 4, sorcerer/wizard 3, witch 3
Casting Time 1 standard action
Components V, S
Range personal (half-elf only)
Duration 1 minute/level
You surge with ancestral power, temporarily embodying all the strengths of both elvenkind and humankind

simultaneously, and transforming into a paragon of both races, something greater than elf or human alone. Unlike with most polymorph effects, your basic form does not change, so you keep all extraordinary and supernatural abilities of your half-elven form as well as all of your gear.

For the duration of the spell, you receive a +2 enhancement bonus to Dexterity and Intelligence and are treated as if you possessed any one feat for which you meet the prerequisites, chosen when you cast this spell.

RESILIENT RESERVOIR

School transmutation; **Level** magus 3, paladin 3, sorcerer/ wizard 4, witch 4
Casting Time 1 standard action
Components V, S
Range personal
Area special, see text
Duration 1 round/ level
Saving Throw none (see below); **Spell Resistance** yes

This spell creates a magical well of retribution that a caster can unleash with blinding speed.

Upon casting this spell, damage from melee attacks and touch spells gets transferred into a special pool that you then redirect before the spell's duration expires.

Each time you are struck by a melee attack or touch spell that deals hit point damage, 1 point of damage is negated and transferred into the reservoir created by this spell. The total number of points in the reservoir cannot exceed your caster level (to a maximum of 20 points at 20th level). As an immediate action, anytime before the spell's duration expires, you can release some or all of the energy of the reservoir, granting yourself an insight bonus on one skill check, attack roll, damage roll, or combat maneuver check, but you must do so before the roll is made. This bonus is equal to the number of points in the reservoir. For every five caster levels, you may call upon the reservoir one additional time (maximum of four times at 15th level).

If you are reduced to negative hit points while you are under the effect of this spell, the spell automatically release the remaining magic of the reservoir in a concussive blast of force. All creatures within a 15-foot radius take 1d6 points of force damage per 2 points remaining in the reserve (maximum of 10d6). A successful Reflex save halves this damage, and spell resistance applies to this effect.

URBAN GRACE

School transmutation; **Level** alchemist 1, bard 1, ranger 1, sorcerer/wizard 1, witch 1
Casting Time 1 standard action
Components V, S
Range personal
Duration 1 minute/level

You become one with the city around you, allowing you to move more easily through its crowds and buildings. For the duration of this spell, your base land speed increases by 10 feet. In addition, it does not cost you 2 squares of movement to enter a square with crowds, though the crowd still provides cover to you. This ability does not allow you to enter the space of enemy creatures without making the appropriate Acrobatics check. In addition, you receive a +4 circumstance bonus on Acrobatics checks made to move across uneven urban surfaces, such as roofs and broken pavement, and on Climb checks made to scale walls and other artificial surfaces. Whenever you make an Acrobatics check to make a long jump between two buildings or artificial structures, you are always treated as if you had a running start, regardless of the actual distance traveled.

HALF-ORCS

As seen by civilized races, half-orcs are monstrosities, the result of perversion and violence—whether or not this is actually true. Half-orcs are rarely the result of loving unions, and as such are usually forced to grow up hard and fast, constantly fighting for protection or to make names for themselves. Half-orcs as a whole resent this treatment, and rather than play the part of the victim, they tend to lash out, unknowingly confirming the biases of those around them. A few feared, distrusted, and spat-upon half-orcs manage to surprise their detractors with great deeds and unexpected wisdom—though sometimes it's easier just to crack a few skulls. Some half-orcs spend their entire lives proving to full-blooded orcs that they are just as fierce. Others opt for trying to blend into human society, constantly demonstrating that they aren't monsters. Their need to always prove themselves worthy encourages half-orcs to strive for power and greatness within the society around them.

Physical Description: Half-orcs average around 6 feet tall, with powerful builds and greenish or grayish skin. Their canine teeth often grow long enough to protrude from their mouths, and these "tusks," combined with heavy brows and slightly pointed ears, give them their notoriously bestial appearance. While half-orcs may be impressive, few ever describe them as beautiful. Despite these obvious orc traits, half-orcs are as varied as their human parents.

Society: Unlike half-elves, where at least part of society's discrimination is born out of jealousy or attraction, half-orcs get the worst of both worlds: physically weaker than their orc kin, they also tend to be feared or attacked outright by humans who don't bother making the distinction between full orcs and halfbloods. Even on the best of terms, half-orcs in civilized societies are not exactly accepted, and tend to be valued only for their physical abilities. On the other hand, orc leaders have been known to deliberately spawn half-orcs, as the halfbreeds make up for their lack of physical strength with increased cunning and aggression, making them natural leaders and strategic advisors.

Within orc tribes, half-orcs find themselves constantly striving to prove their worth in battle and with feats of strength. Half-orcs raised within orc tribes are more likely to file their tusks and cover themselves in tribal tattoos. Tribal leaders quietly recognize that half-orcs are often more clever than their orc cousins and often apprentice them to the tribe's shaman, where their cunning might eventually

HALF-ORC RACIAL TRAITS

+2 to One Ability Score: Half-orc characters gain a +2 bonus to one ability score of their choice at creation to represent their varied nature.

Medium: Half-orcs are Medium creatures and have no bonuses or penalties due to their size.

Normal Speed: Half-orcs have a base speed of 30 feet.

Darkvision: Half-orcs can see in the dark up to 60 feet.

Intimidating: Half-orcs receive a +2 racial bonus on Intimidate checks due to their fearsome nature.

Orc Blood: Half-orcs count as both humans and orcs for any effect related to race.

Orc Ferocity: Once per day, when a half-orc is brought below 0 hit points but not killed, he can fight on for 1 more round as if disabled. At the end of his next turn, unless brought to above 0 hit points, he immediately falls unconscious and begins dying.

Weapon Familiarity: Half-orcs are proficient with greataxes and falchions and treat any weapon with the word "orc" in its name as a martial weapon.

Languages: Half-orcs begin play speaking Common and Orc. Half-orcs with high Intelligence scores can choose from the following: Abyssal, Draconic, Giant, Gnoll, and Goblin.

strengthen the tribe. Apprenticeship to a shaman is a brutal and often short-lived distinction, however, and those half-orcs who survive it either become influential in the tribe or are eventually driven to leave.

Half-orcs have a much more mixed experience in human society, where many cultures view them as little more than monsters. They often are unable even to get normal work, and are pressed into service in the military or sold into slavery. In these cultures, half-orcs often lead furtive lives, hiding their nature whenever possible. The dark underworld of society is often the most welcoming place, and many half-orcs wind up serving as enforcers for thieves guilds or other types of organized crime.

Less commonly, human cities may allow half-orcs a more normal existence, even enabling them to develop small communities of their own. These communities are usually centered around the arena districts, the military, or mercenary organizations where their brute strength is valued and their appearance is more likely to be overlooked. Even surrounded by their own kind, half-orc life isn't easy. Bullying and physical confrontation comes easy to a people who have been raised with few other examples of behavior. It is, however, one of the best places for young half-orcs to grow up without prejudice, and these small enclaves are one of the few places where half-orc marriages and children are truly accepted and sometimes cherished.

Even more rarely, certain human cultures come to embrace half-orcs for their strength. There are stories of places where people see half-orc children as a blessing and seek out half-orc or orc lovers. In these cultures, half-orcs lead lives not much different from full-blooded humans.

Relations: Elves and dwarves tend to be the least accepting of half-orcs, seeing in them too great a resemblance to their racial enemies, and other races aren't much more understanding.

A lifetime of persecution leaves the average half-orc wary and quick to anger, yet people who break through his savage exterior might find a well-hidden core of empathy. Human societies with few orc problems tend to be the most accommodating, and half-orcs dwelling there can often find work as mercenaries and enforcers. Even in places where there is a general tolerance for half-orcs, however, many humans mistreat them when they can get away with it.

Half-orcs are envious of the measure of acceptance half-elves have within human and elven society and resent their physical beauty, which contrasts starkly to the half-orcs' brutish appearance. While half-orcs avoid antagonizing their half-breed cousins directly, they won't hesitate to undermine them if the opportunity presents itself.

Of all the other races, half-orcs are most sympathetic with halflings, who often have an equally rough lot in life. Half-orcs respect the halfling's ability to blend in and disappear and admire their perpetually cheerful outlook on life in spite of hardships. Halflings fail to appreciate this fact because they usually are too busy avoiding the large, intimidating half-orcs.

Alignment and Religion: Forced to live either among brutish orcs or as lonely outcasts in civilized lands, most half-orcs are bitter, violent, and reclusive. Evil comes easily to them, but they are not evil by nature—rather, most half-orcs are chaotic neutral, having been taught by long experience that there's no point doing anything but that which directly benefits themselves. Half-orcs worship the human or orc gods venerated in the area where they were raised. Those who live alongside humans most often worship human gods of war, freedom, or destruction. Half-orcs raised in orc tribes find themselves most drawn to the gods of blood, fire, and iron—depending more on what god the tribe worships rather than the half-orcs' personal preference. Many half-orcs are contrary about religion, either ignoring it entirely, or getting deeply involved in it and trying to find meaning in a life filled with hate and misunderstanding; even a half-orc divine spellcaster may wrestle with doubt and anger about religion and faith.

Adventurers: Staunchly independent, many half-orcs take to lives of adventure out of necessity, seeking to escape their painful pasts or improve their lot through force of arms. Others, more optimistic or desperate for acceptance, take up the mantle of crusaders in order to prove their worth to the world.

Half-orcs raised in orc societies often take up the brutish ways of those around them, becoming fighters, barbarians, or rangers. Half-orcs who survive their shaman training may eventually succeed their masters as tribal shamans, or flee the tribe and practice their magic as outcasts or explorers.

Half-orcs are just as likely to have children that possess an innate talent for sorcery as any other race, with the abyssal, destined, and elemental fire bloodlines being the most common types of sorcerers. Half-orcs are fascinated by alchemy, and its destructive capabilities make its usefulness obvious in any orc tribe. Half-orc alchemists treat themselves as living experiments, even to the point of trying to separate their orc and human halves through alchemy. Other alchemists use their powers to enhance their physical abilities and thus increase their status within orc communities.

In human societies, half-orcs have a few more options. Many find it easy to take advantage of the brute strength and work as mercenaries or caravan guards. Crime is another easy route for half-orcs, as there are plenty of criminals looking for a strong arm. Half-orc clerics in human communities are fairly rare; the more religious half-orcs more often turn to (or get pushed to) the martial aspects of religious service

and become paladins or inquisitors. Half-orcs usually lack the patience and money required to become a wizard.

Males names: Ausk, Davor, Hakak, Kizziar, Makoa, Nesteruk, Tsadok.

Female names: Canan, Drogheda, Goruza, Mazon, Shirish, Tevaga, Zeljka.

ALTERNATE RACIAL RULES

Half-orcs are as varied as humans and orcs in terms of culture and environment. The following rules represent some of those varied aspects and can be taken by any half-orc character. At the GM's discretion, a half-orc may also select from the alternate racial rules for orcs.

Alternate Racial Traits

The following racial traits may be selected instead of existing half-orc racial traits. Consult your GM before selecting any of these new options. A half-orc also has the option of selecting the squalid alternate racial trait (see page 139) in place of his orc ferocity racial trait.

Acute Darkvision: Some half-orcs have exceptionally sharp darkvision, gaining darkvision 90 feet. This racial trait replaces orc ferocity.

Beastmaster: Some half-orcs have a spiritual kinship with fantastical beasts, capturing them for sport or living and hunting with them. A half-orc with this trait treats whips and nets as martial weapons and gains a +2 racial bonus on Handle Animal checks. This racial trait replaces orc ferocity.

Bestial: The orc blood of some half-orcs manifests in the form of particularly prominent orc features, exacerbating their bestial appearances but improving their already keen senses. They gain a +2 racial bonus on Perception checks. This racial trait replaces orc ferocity.

Caveweight: Some half-orcs live far below the surface, seeking freedom in winding cave complexes. Half-orcs with this racial trait gain a +1 racial bonus on Knowledge (dungeoneering) and Survival checks made underground. This racial trait replaces the intimidating trait.

Chain Fighter: Some half-orcs have escaped from slavery and reforged the chains of their imprisonment into deadly weapons. Half-orcs with this racial trait are proficient with flails and heavy flails, and treat dire flails and spiked chains as martial weapons. This racial trait replaces weapon familiarity.

City-Raised: Half-orcs with this trait know little of their orc ancestry and were raised among humans and other half-orcs in a large city. City-raised half-orcs are proficient with whips and longswords, and receive a +2 racial bonus on Knowledge (local) checks. This racial trait replaces weapon familiarity.

Forest Walker: More at home in the forests and jungles of the world, these half-orcs are well adapted to their surroundings. Half-orcs with this trait have low-light vision and gain a +2 racial bonus on Climb checks. This racial trait replaces darkvision.

Gatecrasher: Many half-orcs revel in acts of wanton destruction. Half-orcs with this racial trait gain a +2 racial bonus on Strength checks to break objects and on sunder combat maneuver checks. This racial trait replaces orc ferocity.

Rock Climber: Half-orcs from mountainous regions are excellent climbers, and sometimes ambush prey by leaping down from above. Half-orcs with this racial trait gain a +1 racial bonus on Acrobatics and Climb checks. This racial trait replaces the intimidating trait.

Sacred Tattoo: Many half-orcs decorate themselves with tattoos, piercings, and ritual scarification, which they consider sacred markings. Half-orcs with this racial trait gain a +1 luck bonus on all saving throws. This racial trait replaces orc ferocity.

Scavenger: Some half-orcs eke out a leaving picking over the garbage heaps of society, and must learn to separate rare finds from the inevitable dross. Half-orcs with this racial trait receive a +2 racial bonus on Appraise checks and on Perception checks to find hidden objects (including traps and secret doors), determine whether food is spoiled, or identify a potion by taste. This racial trait replaces the intimidating trait.

Shaman's Apprentice: Only the most stalwart survive the years of harsh treatment that an apprenticeship to an orc shaman entails. Half-orcs with this trait gain Endurance as a bonus feat. This racial trait replaces the intimidating trait.

Skilled: Second- and third-generation half-orcs often favor their human heritage more than their orc heritage. Half-orcs with this trait gain 1 additional skill rank per level. This racial trait replaces darkvision.

Toothy: Some half-orcs' tusks are large and sharp, granting a bite attack. This is a primary natural attack that deals 1d4 points of piercing damage. This racial trait replaces orc ferocity.

Racial Subtypes

You can combine various alternate racial traits to create half-orc subraces or variant races, such as the following.

Arena-Bred: Many half-orcs are born and raised to fight in the arena, and in many cases have two half-orc parents or even a half-orc and a human parent. These arena-bred half-orcs lose the brutal physical appearance of their orc ancestors and look more human. They have the city-raised and skilled alternate racial traits.

Deep Kin: Some half-orcs are descended from clans that remained in the eternal darkness below the surface. Half-orcs from these clans tend to be smaller and more at home underground than those descended from surface-dwelling orcs. These half-orcs have the acute darkvision and cavewight alternate racial traits.

Feral: Half-orc children who are abandoned as infants or small children rarely survive in the wild, but a few manage to scrape out a meager existence as "wild children," tough enough to live but completely uncivilized. Feral half-orcs have the forest walker and toothy alternate racial traits.

Mountain Clan: Half-orcs from the more mountainous regions tend to be more agile and alert to the echoing sounds of their homeland. Mountain clan half-orcs have the bestial and rock climber racial traits.

Mystic: Orc shamans are brutal teachers who sometimes kill or maim their most promising students in order to eliminate what could be a potential rival. Half-orcs who survive years of abuse by an orc shaman master are deeply scarred and altered by the experience. Shaman trainees learn early that cunning and luck are often the only things that offer a chance of survival. They have the shaman's apprentice and tribal tattoo alternate racial traits.

Favored Class Options

The following options are available to all half-orcs who have the listed favored class, and unless otherwise stated, the bonus applies each time you select the class reward.

Alchemist: Add +1/2 to the alchemist's bomb damage.

Barbarian: Add +1 to the barbarian's total number of rage rounds per day.

Bard: Add +1 to the bard's total number of bardic performance rounds per day.

Cavalier: Add +1 hit point to the cavalier's mount companion. If the cavalier ever replaces his mount, the new mount gains these bonus hit points.

Cleric: Select one domain power granted at 1st level that is normally usable a number of times per day equal to 3 + the cleric's Wisdom modifier. The cleric adds +1/2 to the number of uses per day of that domain power.

Druid: Add +1/3 to the druid's natural armor bonus when using wild shape.

Fighter: Add a +2 bonus on rolls to stabilize when dying.

Gunslinger: Add a +1/3 bonus on attack rolls when using the pistol whip deed.

Inquisitor: Add a +1/2 bonus on Intimidate checks and Knowledge checks to identify creatures.

Magus: Add +1/2 point of fire damage to spells that deal fire damage cast by the magus.

Monk: Add +1 to the monk's CMD when resisting a grapple and +1/2 to the number of stunning attacks he can attempt per day.

Oracle: Add one spell known from the oracle spell list. This spell must be at least one level below the highest spell level the oracle can cast.

Paladin: Add +1/3 on critical hit confirmation rolls made while using smite evil (maximum bonus of +5). This bonus does not stack with Critical Focus.

Ranger: Add +1 hit point to the ranger's animal companion. If the ranger ever replaces his animal companion, the new animal companion gains these bonus hit points.

Rogue: Add +1/3 on critical hit confirmation rolls made while using sneak attack (maximum bonus of +5). This bonus does not stack with Critical Focus.

Sorcerer: Add +1/2 point of fire damage to spells that deal fire damage cast by the sorcerer.

Summoner: Add +1 hit point to the summoner's eidolon.

Witch: Add +1 skill rank to the witch's familiar. If the half-orc ever replaces her familiar, the new familiar gains these bonus skill ranks.

Wizard: Add a +1 bonus on concentration checks made due to taking damage while casting wizard spells.

RACIAL ARCHETYPES

The following racial archetypes are available to half-orcs.

Blood God Disciple (Summoner)

A half-orc summoner who devotes himself to one of the bloody orc gods may believe his eidolon is an avatar of that god rather than a mere supernatural creature. A blood god disciple generally fights by the avatar's side and offers it blood sacrifices in exchange for martial prowess. A blood god disciple has the following class features.

Blood Feast (Su): At 1st level, a blood god disciple can feed a recently fallen foe to his eidolon, allowing the outsider to channel some of its power into the summoner. The eidolon must spend a standard action to eat some of the opponent, which must be a living, corporeal creature killed or knocked unconscious by the eidolon or summoner in the past minute. This eating deals damage to the target as if the eidolon had attacked it with one natural attack (typically a bite). The fallen creature must have at least half as many Hit Dice as the summoner. Once the feeding is complete, the summoner may manifest one 1-point evolution. This lasts for 1 minute. The evolution's effects use the summoner's Hit Dice and ability scores rather than the eidolon's. The blood god disciple can use this ability a number of times per day equal to 3 + his Charisma modifier. He may only apply one use of this ability at a time (using it a second time replaces any evolution manifested with this ability), and can only manifest evolutions his eidolon has.

At 5th level, when the blood god disciple uses blood feast, he may manifest one 2-point evolution instead of a 1-point evolution. At 9th level, he may manifest up to two evolutions worth a total of 3 evolution points or fewer. At 13th level, he may manifest up to two evolutions

worth a total of 4 evolution points or fewer. At 17th level, he may manifest up to three evolutions worth a total of 5 evolution points or fewer.

This ability replaces the *summon monster I, III, V, VII,* and *IX* spell-like abilities.

Bloody Gift (Su): At 3rd level, when a blood god disciple uses blood feast to manifest an evolution, he may touch one ally and grant it that evolution as well. Each affected ally counts as one use per day of the blood feast ability. At 7th, 11th, 15th, and 19th level, the blood god disciple can affect an additional creature with this ability (each one counting as a use per day of blood feast). If the blood god disciple can manifest multiple evolutions per use of blood feast, his selected allies manifest these multiple evolutions as well. This ability replaces the *summon monster II* spell-like ability.

Avatar Gambit (Ex): At 7th level, when a blood god disciple dismisses his eidolon, he rages like a barbarian for a number of rounds equal to half his summoner

level (he may end this rage early just like a barbarian, but if he does so, any remaining rounds of rage from this ability are lost). This replaces the *summon monster IV* spell-like ability.

Rage Power (Ex): At 11th level and 15th level, a blood god disciple selects a barbarian rage power, which he may use when raging (whether from the avatar gambit ability or actual barbarian rage). This replaces the *summon monster VI* and *VIII* spell-like abilities.

Hateful Rager (Barbarian)

From a young age, many half-orcs are treated cruelly, bullied, ridiculed, and made outcasts. While some hide their shame, others foster a deep, burning hatred that they channel into a raw fury and unleash against their enemies. These half-orcs are called hateful ragers. A hateful rager has the following class features.

Reduced Rage (Ex): At 2nd level and every level thereafter, a hateful rager only gains 1 additional round of rage per day instead of the normal 2 additional rounds of rage per day.

Favored Enemy (Ex): At 2nd level, a hateful rager selects a favored enemy. This ability works identically to the ranger ability of the same name. At 8th, 14th, and 20th

level, the hateful rager selects another favored enemy and increases her bonus against one favored enemy type, as described in the ranger class.

While raging, the hateful rager makes every effort to fight a favored enemy rather than other opponents. If aware of the presence of a favored enemy, the hateful rager must make a DC 20 Will save each round to attack another creature; failure means the barbarian must attack the favored enemy or move closer to that enemy. She may freely attack creatures preventing her from reaching that favored enemy (regardless of whether they are actively trying to prevent her attacks or merely in the way). She can avoid harmful obstacles normally in her attempts to reach the target and is not forced to take the shortest route.

This ability replaces the barbarian's rage power gained at 2nd level. At 8th, 14th, and 20th levels, in place of a rage power she gains another favored enemy and increases her bonus against one favored enemy type.

Feed the Rage (Ex): At 5th level, a hateful rager gains 1 additional round of rage for each favored enemy she knocks unconscious or kills in combat. These current rounds of rage can only be used to add to the duration of her rage, and disappear when the rage ends. This ability replaces improved uncanny dodge.

Amplified by Hate (Ex): At 9th level, a hateful rager adds half her favored enemy bonus to the DC of any rage power she uses against a favored enemy. This ability replaces trap sense +3.

Rage Powers: The following rage powers complement the hateful rager archetype: intimidating glare, roused anger, terrifying howl (*Core Rulebook*); come and get me, inspire ferocity, overbearing advance, reckless abandon (*Advanced Player's Guide*).

Redeemer (Paladin)

As most half-orcs are outcasts, a half-orc paladin recognizes that often those who are monstrous are not necessarily evil and that sometimes even those who are evil became that way because of circumstances and misfortune. Some half-orc paladins take up these misunderstood creatures as their cause, standing up for the monstrous creatures and, when possible, leading them to the light. These paladins are called redeemers. A redeemer has the following class features.

Merciful Smite (Su): At 1st level, when a redeemer chooses to smite a creature, she can have all of her attacks against the target deal nonlethal damage. She does not take the normal –4 attack roll penalty for using a lethal weapon to deal nonlethal damage. She cannot use this ability to deal nonlethal damage to outsiders with the evil subtype, evil-aligned dragons, or undead creatures (these creatures take lethal damage from her smite). This

otherwise works like and replaces the standard paladin's smite evil.

Monstrous Rapport (Ex): At 1st level, redeemers gain a +2 bonus on Diplomacy checks to influence creatures who are commonly considered monstrous. This includes but is not limited to "monstrous" races such as goblins and orcs, monstrous humanoids, and other intelligent non-humanoid monsters. This ability replaces detect evil.

Pact of Peace (Sp): At 8th level, a redeemer can force a defeated creature to accept a binding pact of peace as a condition of its surrender, as if using *lesser geas*. Her caster level for this ability is equal to her paladin level. Rather than assigning a mission or task, the redeemer gives the creature a simple set of prohibitions to protect others. Example geas include "Leave this city and do not return" or "Do not attack caravans." The prohibition must be against an area no larger than 300 square miles or one specific group of people (such as a tribe or citizens of a particular city). This ability lasts 1 month per paladin level. This replaces aura of resolve.

Aura of Mercy (Su): At 11th level, a redeemer can expend two uses of her merciful smite ability to grant the merciful smite ability to all allies within 10 feet, using her bonuses. Allies must use this merciful smite ability by the start of the paladin's next turn and the bonuses last for 1 minute. Using this ability is a free action. Evil creatures gain no benefit from this ability. This replaces aura of justice.

Associates: A redeemer may ally with an evil creature as long as she feels the creature is capable of redemption. A redeemer may accept henchmen, followers, or cohorts who are not lawful good provided they demonstrate they are willing to follow her and seek betterment under her tutelage.

Skulking Slayer (Rogue)

Pushed into a life of crime by the society around them, half-orcs gravitate toward criminal activities that suit them best. Half-orc rogues leave subtle tactics and finesse to halflings and elves, and rely on brute strength and thuggery when they go about making mischief. Skulking slayers have turned the use of raw strength and surprise into an art form. A skulking slayer has the following class features.

Weapon and Armor Proficiency: The skulking slayer gains proficiency with greatclubs and whips, but loses proficiency with rapiers and hand crossbows.

Class Skills: The skulking slayer does not gain Disable Device, Linguistics, and Sleight of Hand as class skills.

Skill Ranks per Level: 6 + Int modifier.

Pass for Human (Ex): At 1st level, when trying to conceal her half-orc heritage, a skulking slayer gains a bonus on Disguise checks equal to half her level. When using disguise to appear as a specific individual,

skulking stalkers ignore the normal –2 penalty to appear as another race.

Underhanded Maneuvers (Ex): At 1st level, when she could normally make a sneak attack, a slayer may instead make a dirty trick or steal combat maneuver with a bonus on her roll. This bonus is equal to her number of sneak attack dice for a dirty trick combat maneuver, or 1-1/2 × her number of sneak attack dice for a steal combat maneuver. This ability replaces trapfinding.

Bonus Feats: At 2nd level, a skulking slayer can select the Surprise Follow-Through feat (see below) in place of a rogue talent. At 10th level, she can select the Improved Surprise Follow-Through feat in place of an advanced rogue talent.

Bold Strike (Ex): At 3rd level, when a skulking slayer charges and makes a sneak attack with a two-handed weapon, she rolls d8s instead of d6s for her sneak attack damage. This ability replaces trap sense +1 and +4.

Shifty (Ex): At 6th level, a skulking slayer gains a bonus on Bluff checks to feint equal to half her level. This ability replaces trap sense +2.

Unexpected Charge (Ex): At 9th level, a skulking slayer can make a Bluff check to feint as a swift action before a charge. This ability replaces trap sense +3.

Rogue Talents: The following rogue talents complement the skulking slayer archetype: combat trick, surprise attack (*Core Rulebook*); combat swipe, powerful sneak (*Advanced Player's Guide*); terrain mastery (*Ultimate Combat*).

Advanced Talents: The following advanced rogue talents complement the skulking slayer archetype: crippling strike (*Core Rulebook*); deadly sneak (*Advanced Player's Guide*); unwitting ally (*Ultimate Combat*).

NEW RACIAL RULES

The following options are available to half-orcs. At the GM's discretion, other appropriate races may also make use of some of these.

Half-Orc Equipment

Half-orcs have access to the following equipment.

Black Fester: This black paste is often applied on orc weapons before going on raids to stymie an enemy's healing magic. Like a poison, black fester stays on a weapon until the first time it strikes an opponent. It remains in the target's body for 1 hour. A creature exposed to black fester resists magical healing; a creature trying to magically heal the target must make a DC 10 caster level check to restore any hit points to the target.

Half-Orc Disguise Kit: This specifically designed kit was put together by half-orcs to help them appear more human. It includes skin cream to disguise green-gray skin color and other items designed to conceal or draw attention away from typical half-orc physical characteristics. Using this kit on a half-orc grants a +3 bonus on Disguise checks to appear human. Used on an orc, it only grants a +1 bonus on these checks.

Half-Orc Equipment

Item	Cost	Weight	Craft DC
Black fester (vial)	30 gp	—	25
Half-orc disguise kit	75 gp	1 lb.	—

Half-Orc Feats

Half-orcs and orcs have access to the following feats.

Beast Rider

You gain the service of a monstrous companion or mount.

Prerequisites: Animal companion or mount class feature, character level 7th, half-orc or orc.

Benefit: Select one of the following creature types: elephant, pteranodon, rhinoceros, stegosaurus, or triceratops. Add this creature type to your list of possible animal companions or mounts. When summoning a creature of the selected type to serve as a mount or companion, treat your effective druid level as if it were two levels higher (to a maximum of your character level). If the creature is large enough for you to ride, it gains the combat training general purpose (see Handle Animal) at no cost.

Blood Vengeance

Seeing an ally fall in combat fills you with a raging and murderous fury.

Prerequisites: Half-orc or orc, nonlawful.

Benefit: Whenever one of your allies is reduced to negative hit points or killed, you may enter a state similar to but less powerful than a barbarian's rage as a free action on your next turn. If you have the rage class feature and are already raging, your morale bonuses to Strength and Constitution increase by +2 for the duration of your rage. If you do not have the rage class feature, or you have no more rage rounds left, this weaker rage gives you all the benefits and penalties of a barbarian's rage, except your morale bonus to Strength and Constitution is only +2. In either case, this state lasts for 4 rounds.

As with a barbarian's rage, when this weaker rage ends, you are fatigued; if another ally falls before this duration ends, the weaker rage lasts for an additional 4 rounds. This feat does not allow you to enter a rage if you are fatigued. You may only use this feat if the fallen ally had at least as many Hit Dice as you (excluding conjured or summoned allies).

Destroyer's Blessing (Combat)

Breaking things adds to your power.

Prerequisites: Half-orc or orc, rage class feature.

Benefit: When you are raging and you succeed at a sunder combat maneuver, you regain 1 round of rage. If the sunder attempt causes the object to gain the broken condition, you heal 1 hit point. You can only gain these benefits once per round.

Ferocious Resolve

Your orc heritage allows you to fight on.

Prerequisites: Con 13, half-orc, orc ferocity racial trait.

Benefit: You gain the ferocity universal monster ability, allowing you to continue fighting at negative hit points. When using this ability, you gain a +2 bonus on Intimidate checks.

Normal: A half-orc with the orc ferocity racial trait can fight for 1 more round after he is brought below 0 hit points.

Ferocious Summons

Your summoned creatures gain your ferocity.

Prerequisites: Augment Summoning, Spell Focus (conjuration), half-orc or orc.

Benefit: Creatures you summon gain the ferocity universal monster ability.

Ferocious Tenacity (Combat)

You spit in the face of death.

Prerequisites: Ferocity racial trait, half-orc or orc, rage class feature.

Benefit: Once per day when raging, if you are hit by an attack that would deal enough hit points of damage to kill you (negative hit points equal to your Constitution score), as an immediate action you may expend 1 or more rounds of rage to negate some of this damage and keep yourself alive. Each round of rage you spend reduces the attack's damage by 1 point, but cannot reduce the damage taken below 1 hit point.

For example, if you are raging, have a raging Constitution score of 18, are currently at 2 hit points, and take 20 hit points of damage from a hit (which is enough to bring you to –18 hit points, thereby killing you), you may spend 1 round of rage to reduce the damage by 1 hit point (leaving you perilously close to death at –17 hit points); if you spend 17 rounds of rage, you reduce the damage to 1 (the minimum), leaving you with 1 hit point.

Note: If this damage still makes you fall unconscious, your rage ends just like it normally would, lowering your Constitution to its normal value and reducing your hit point total as normal. Therefore, it is possible to use this feat to prevent yourself from instantly dying, yet you still die because your negative hit points exceed your normal Constitution score—take your normal Constitution into account when deciding how many rounds of rage to spend with this feat.

Gore Fiend

Horrible wounds, whether on yourself or your enemies, make your blood sing.

Prerequisites: Half-orc or orc, rage class feature.

Benefit: When you are raging and you confirm a critical hit with a melee weapon or a critical hit is confirmed on you (whether by a melee weapon, spell, or ranged weapon), you regain 1 round of rage (up to your maximum for the day). You can only gain this benefit once per round.

Horde Charge (Teamwork)

When you charge with an ally, you are more deadly.

Prerequisites: Base attack bonus +1, half-orc or orc.

Benefit: When charging during the same round as an ally with this feat, you gain a +2 bonus on attack and damage rolls in addition to the normal bonus for charging. If you can make multiple attacks on a charge, this bonus only applies to the first attack.

Improved Surprise Follow-Through (Combat)

You follow up an attack with a surprising series of sweeping blows.

Prerequisites: Str 13, Cleave, Great Cleave, Power Attack, Surprise Follow Through, base attack bonus +8.

Benefit: When using Great Cleave, each opponent you attack on your turn (other than the first) is denied his Dexterity bonus against you.

Resilient Brute

You absorb punishment others find deadly.

Prerequisite: Half-orc or orc.

Benefit: Once per day, when a creature confirms a critical hit against you, you may treat half the damage as nonlethal damage. You cannot use this ability if you are immune to nonlethal damage. When your base attack bonus reaches +10, you may use this ability an additional time per day.

Surprise Follow-Through (Combat)

When striking one opponent, you catch its ally off guard.

Prerequisites: Str 13, Cleave, Power Attack, base attack bonus +1.

Benefit: When using Cleave or Great Cleave, the second foe you attack on your turn is denied its Dexterity bonus against you.

Sympathetic Rage (Combat)

Seeing an ally rage fills you with your own fury.

Prerequisites: Half-orc or orc, nonlawful.

Benefit: Whenever you are adjacent to an ally who is raging, you may choose to enter a similar but less powerful rage as a free action on your turn. This weaker rage gives you all the benefits and penalties of a barbarian's rage,

except your morale bonus to Strength and Constitution is only +2. There is no limit to how long you can rage, as long as you remain adjacent to a raging ally (for example, you could take a 5-foot step away from one raging ally toward another raging ally and maintain your rage). As with a barbarian's rage, when this weaker rage ends, you are fatigued. You cannot use this feat if you are fatigued.

Tenacious Survivor

Your spirit lingers long after any other's would have passed on.

Prerequisites: Con 13, Diehard, Endurance, half-orc or orc.

Benefit: When you are killed by hit point damage, your soul lingers in your body for a number of rounds equal to your Constitution bonus. You are still dead, but a creature can make a DC 10 Heal check as a standard action to realize that you can still be saved. You can be healed by magic as if you were alive. If you are healed enough hit points that you would no longer be dead, you are alive again, but you gain one permanent negative level.

Thrill of the Kill

Killing fuels your rage.

Prerequisites: Half-orc or orc, rage class feature.

Benefit: When you are raging and your attack reduces an enemy to negative hit points or kills it, you regain 1 round of rage. You may only use this feat if the fallen enemy had at least as many Hit Dice as you. You can only gain this benefit once per round.

Half-Orc Magic Items

Half-orcs have access to the following magic items.

CLOAK OF HUMAN GUISE

Aura faint illusion; **CL** 1st
Slot shoulders; **Price** 900 gp; **Weight** 1 lb.

DESCRIPTION

This plain cloak only has any effect when worn by a member of a half-human race such as a half-orc or half-elf. It alters the wearer's appearance similarly to a *hat of disguise*, but only to the extent that it conceals or alters the wearer's non-human physical traits so the creature appears fully human. Any feature that is plausibly human remains. For example, a half-orc wearing the cloak loses his green or gray skin color and pointed ears, has no visible tusks, and is otherwise completely able to pass as a human version of his normal self. Likewise, a half-elf wearing the cloak has round ears, humanlike eyes, and no other traits indicating elf ancestry. The wearer has no control over the specific guise, and those familiar with his normal appearance can recognize him in his human guise.

CONSTRUCTION

Requirements Craft Wondrous Item, disguise self; **Cost** 450 gp

RING OF FEROCIOUS ACTION

Aura faint transmutation; **CL** 5th
Slot ring; **Price** 3,000 gp; **Weight** 1 lb.

DESCRIPTION

This ring allows its wearer to persevere through physical or mental trauma that hampers his actions. The ring has 5 charges, renewed each day. At the start of his turn, if the wearer is staggered, as a free action he may spend a charge to activate the ring and ignore the staggered condition until his next turn.

CONSTRUCTION

Requirements Forge Ring, *haste*, *stabilize*; **Cost** 1,500 gp

SWIFT OBSIDIAN GREATAXE

Aura moderate transmutation; **CL** 10th
Slot none; **Price** 11,320 gp; **Weight** 12 lbs.

DESCRIPTION

The blade of this *+1 keen greataxe* is carved from jet-black obsidian. When the wielder charges an enemy, he receives a +10 foot enhancement bonus to his speed that round. Once per day, he can command the axe to grant all allies within 30 feet a +10 foot enhancement bonus to base speed for 1 round.

CONSTRUCTION

Requirements Craft Magic Arms and Armor, *expeditious retreat*, *keen edge*; **Cost** 5,820 gp

Half-Orc Spells

Half-orcs have access to the following spells.

BATTLE TRANCE

School enchantment (compulsion) [emotion, mind-affecting];
Level alchemist 3, antipaladin 3, cleric 4, inquisitor 3, ranger 3, witch 4
Casting Time 1 standard action
Components V, S
Range personal
Target you
Duration 1 minute/level
Save Will negates; **Spell Resistance** yes

You are transformed into a single-minded force of destruction. You gain the ferocity monster special ability, a number of temporary hit points equal to 1d6 + your caster level (maximum +10), and a +4 morale bonus on saving throws against mind-affecting effects. You cannot use the withdraw action or willingly move away from a creature that has attacked you.

When you use this spell, you immediately take 4 points of Intelligence damage. You must make a DC 20 concentration check to cast spells, and all other concentration checks to cast spells have a −5 penalty.

GHOST WOLF

School conjuration (creation); **Level** sorcerer/wizard 4, summoner 2

Casting Time 10 minutes
Components V, S, F (dire wolf tooth)
Range 0 ft.
Target one quasi-real wolflike creature
Duration 1 hour/level (D) or 1 round/level; see text
Saving Throw none (see description); **Spell Resistance** no

This spell conjures a Large, quasi-real, wolflike creature made of roiling black smoke. It functions as *phantom steed*, except as noted above. In addition, the creature radiates an aura of fear. Any creature with fewer than 6 Hit Dice within 30 feet (except the ghost wolf's rider) must make a Will save or become shaken for 1d4 rounds (this is a mind-affecting fear effect). A creature that makes its Will save is unaffected by the steed's fear aura for 24 hours.

The ghost wolf may also be used in combat. Once per round, the rider may direct the ghost wolf to attack in battle as a free action (bite +10, 1d8+6 points of damage); unlike an animal mount, this does not require a Ride check or any training. Once the ghost wolf attacks, it lasts for only 1 round per level thereafter.

HALF-BLOOD EXTRACTION

School transmutation (polymorph); **Level** alchemist 5, cleric 5, druid 5, sorcerer/wizard 5, witch 5
Casting Time 1 hour
Components V, S, M/DF (oils and poisons worth 3,000 gp)
Range touch
Target willing half-orc touched
Duration instantaneous
Saving Throw none; **Spell Resistance** no

You transform the target half-orc into a full-blooded orc. The target loses all of its half-orc racial traits and gains the orc racial traits.

LINEBREAKER

School transmutation; **Level** alchemist 1, antipaladin 1, inquisitor 1, magus 1, paladin 1, ranger 1
Casting Time 1 standard action
Components V, S
Range personal
Target you
Duration 1 minute/level

You gain a +20 foot bonus to your base speed when charging and a +2 bonus on combat maneuver checks made to bull rush or overrun.

SAVAGE MAW

School transmutation; **Level** antipaladin 1, cleric 2, druid 2, inquisitor 2, magus 2, ranger 1
Casting Time 1 standard action
Components V, S
Range personal

Target you
Duration 1 minute/level (D), special (see below)

Your teeth extend and sharpen, transforming your mouth into a maw of razor-sharp fangs. You gain a bite attack that deals 1d4 points of damage plus your Strength modifier. If you confirm a critical hit with this attack, it also deals 1 point of bleed damage. If you already have a bite attack, your bite deals 2 points of bleed damage on a critical hit. You are considered proficient with this attack. If used as part of a full-attack action, the bite is considered a secondary attack, is made at your full base attack bonus −5, and adds half your Strength modifier to its damage.

You can end this spell before its normal duration by making a bestial roar as a swift action. When you do, you can make an Intimidate check to demoralize all foes within a 30-foot radius that can hear the roar.

HALFLINGS

Optimistic and cheerful by nature, blessed with uncanny luck, and driven by a powerful wanderlust, halflings make up for their short stature with an abundance of bravado and curiosity. At once excitable and easy-going, halflings like to keep an even temper and a steady eye on opportunity, and are not as prone to violent or emotional outbursts as some of the more volatile races. Even in the jaws of catastrophe, halflings almost never lose their sense of humor. Their ability to find humor in the absurd, no matter how dire the situation, often allows halflings to distance themselves ever so slightly from the dangers that surround them. This sense of detachment can also help shield them from terrors that might immobilize their allies.

Halflings are inveterate opportunists. They firmly believe they can turn any situation to their advantage, and sometimes gleefully leap into trouble without any solid plan to extricate themselves if things go awry. Often unable to physically defend themselves from the rigors of the world, they know when to bend with the wind and when to hide away. Yet halflings' curiosity often overwhelms their good sense, leading to poor decisions and narrow escapes. While harsh experience sometimes teaches halflings a measure of caution, it rarely makes them completely lose faith in their luck or stop believing that the universe, in some strange way, exists for their entertainment and would never really allow them to come to harm.

Though their curiosity drives them to seek out new places and experiences, halflings possess a strong sense of hearth and home, often spending above their means to enhance the comforts of domestic life. Without a doubt, halflings enjoy luxury and comfort, but they have equally strong reasons to make their homes a showcase. Halflings consider this urge to devote time, money, and energy toward improving their dwellings a sign of both respect for strangers and affection for their loved ones. Whether for their own blood kin, cherished friends, or honored guests, halflings make their homes beautiful in order to express their feelings toward those they welcome inside. Even traveling halflings typically decorate their wagons or carry a few cherished keepsakes to adorn their campsites.

Physical Description: Halflings rise to a humble height of 3 feet. They prefer to walk barefoot, leading the bottoms of their feet to become roughly calloused. Tufts of thick, curly hair warm the tops of their broad, tanned feet.

HALFLING RACIAL TRAITS

+2 Dexterity, +2 Charisma, –2 Strength: Halflings are nimble and strong-willed, but their small stature makes them weaker than other races.

Small: Halflings are Small creatures and gain a +1 size bonus to their AC, a +1 size bonus on attack rolls, a –1 penalty to their CMB and CMD, and a +4 size bonus on Stealth checks.

Slow Speed: Halflings have a base speed of 20 feet.

Fearless: Halflings receive a +2 racial bonus on all saving throws against fear. This bonus stacks with the bonus granted by halfling luck.

Halfling Luck: Halflings receive a +1 racial bonus on all saving throws.

Keen Senses: Halflings receive a +2 racial bonus on Perception checks.

Sure-Footed: Halflings receive a +2 racial bonus on Acrobatics and Climb checks.

Weapon Familiarity: Halflings are proficient with slings and treat any weapon with the word "halfling" in its name as a martial weapon.

Languages: Halflings begin play speaking Common and Halfling. Halflings with high Intelligence scores can choose from the following: Dwarven, Elven, Gnome, and Goblin.

Their skin tends toward a rich cinnamon color and their hair toward light shades of brown. A halfling's ears are pointed, but proportionately not much larger than those of a human.

Halflings prefer simple and modest clothing. Though willing and able to dress up if the situation demands it, their racial urge to remain quietly in the background makes them rather conservative dressers in most situations. Halfling entertainers, on the other hand, make their livings by drawing attention, and tend to go overboard with gaudy and flashy costumes.

Society: Rather than place their faith in empires or great causes, many halflings prefer to focus on the simpler and humbler virtues of their families and local communities. Halflings claim no cultural homeland and control no settlements larger than rural assemblies of free towns. Most often, they dwell at the knees of their human cousins in human cities, eking out livings as they can from the scraps of larger societies. Many halflings lead perfectly fulfilling lives in the shadow of their larger neighbors, while some prefer more nomadic lives, traveling the world and experiencing all it has to offer.

Halflings rely on customs and traditions to maintain their own culture. They have an extensive oral history filled with important stories about folk heroes who exemplify particular halfling virtues, but otherwise see little purpose in studying history in and of itself. Given a choice between a pointless truth and a useful fable, halflings almost always opt for the fable. This tendency helps to explain at least something of the famous halfling adaptability. Halflings look to the future and find it very easy to cast off the weight of ancient grudges or obligations that drag down so many other races.

Relations: A typical halfling prides himself on his ability to go unnoticed by other races—a trait that allows many halflings to excel at thievery and trickery. Most halflings know full well the stereotypical view other races take of them as a result, and go out of their way to be forthcoming and friendly to the bigger races when they're not trying to go unnoticed. They get along fairly well with gnomes, although most halflings regard these eccentric creatures with a hefty dose of caution. Halflings respect elves and dwarves, but these races often live in remote regions far from the comforts of civilization that halflings enjoy, thus limiting opportunities for interaction. By and large, only half-orcs are shunned by halflings, for their great size and violent natures are a bit too intimidating for most halflings to cope with.

Halflings coexist well with humans as a general rule, but since some of the more aggressive human societies value halflings as slaves, they try not to grow too complacent. Halflings strongly value their freedom, especially the ability to travel in search of new experiences and the autonomy this requires. However, practical and flexible as always, enslaved halflings seldom fight back directly against their masters. When possible, they wait for the perfect opportunity and then simply slip away. Sometimes, if enslaved for long enough, halflings even come to adopt their owners as their new families. Though they still dream of escape and liberty, these halflings also make the best of their lives.

Alignment and Religion: Halflings are loyal to their friends and families, but since they dwell in a world dominated by races twice as large as themselves, they have come to grips with the fact that sometimes they need to scrape and scrounge for survival. Most halflings are neutral as a result. Though they usually make a show of respecting the laws and endorsing the prejudices of their communities, halflings place an even greater emphasis on the innate common sense of the individual. When a halfling disagrees with society at large, he will do what he thinks is best.

Always practical, halflings frequently worship the deity most favored by their larger and more powerful neighbors. They also usually cover their bets, however, by giving Desna her due. The goddess of both luck and travel seems a natural fit for most halflings and offering her a quick prayer every now and then is only common sense.

Adventurers: Their inherent luck coupled with their insatiable wanderlust makes halflings ideal candidates for lives of adventure. Though perfectly willing to pocket any valuables they come across, halflings often care more for the new experiences adventuring brings them than for any material reward. Halflings tend to view money as a means of making their lives easier and more comfortable, not as an end in and of itself.

Other such vagabonds often put up with this curious race in hopes that some of their mystical luck will rub off. Halflings see nothing wrong with encouraging this belief, not just in their traveling companions, but also in the larger world. Many try to use their reputation for luck to haggle for reduced fare when traveling by ship or caravan, or even for an overnight stay at an inn. They meet with mixed success, but there are just enough stories circulating about the good fortune that befalls people traveling with halflings to give even the most skeptical pause. Of course, some suspect that halflings deliberately spread these reports for just that reason.

Male Names: Antal, Boram, Hyrgan, Jamir, Lem, Miro, Sumak, Tribin, Uldar, Vraxim.

Female Names: Anafa, Bellis, Etune, Filiu, Irlana, Marra, Pressi, Rilka, Sistra, Wyssal, Yamyra.

ALTERNATE RACIAL RULES

Halflings are naturally blessed with good luck and adaptability to their surroundings. The following rules correspond with these attributes and may be used with any halfling character.

Alternate Racial Traits

The following racial traits may be selected instead of existing halfling racial traits. Consult your GM before selecting any of these new options.

Adaptable Luck: Some halflings have greater control over their innate luck. This ability gives them more options for how they can apply their good fortune from day to day, but also narrows its scope. Three times per day, a halfling can gain a +2 luck bonus on an ability check, attack roll, saving throw, or skill check. If halflings choose to use the ability before they make the roll or check, they gain the full +2 bonus; if they choose to do so afterward, they only gain a +1 bonus. Using adaptive luck in this way is not an action. This racial trait replaces halfling luck.

Craven: While most halflings are fearless, some are skittish, making them particularly alert. Halflings with this racial trait gain a +1 bonus on initiative checks and a +1 bonus on attack rolls when flanking. They take a –2 penalty on saves against fear effects and gain no benefit from morale bonuses on such saves. When affected by a fear effect, their base speed increases by 10 feet and they gain a +1 dodge bonus to Armor Class. This racial trait replaces fearless and halfling luck.

Fleet of Foot: Some halflings are quicker than their kin but less cautious. Halflings with this racial trait move at normal speed and have a base speed of 30 feet. This racial trait replaces slow speed and sure-footed.

Ingratiating: Halflings often survive at the whims of larger, more aggressive races. Because of this, they go out of their way to make themselves more useful, or at least entertaining, to larger folk. Halflings with this racial trait gain a +2 bonus on skill checks for a single Perform skill of their choice, and Perform is always a class skill for them. They also gain a +2 bonus on Craft and Profession checks. This racial trait replaces keen senses and sure-footed.

Low Blow: Some halflings train extensively in the art of attacking larger creatures. Halflings with this racial trait gain a +1 bonus on critical confirmation rolls against opponents larger than themselves. This racial trait replaces keen senses.

Outrider: Some halflings specialize in mounted combat. Halflings with this racial trait gain a +2 bonus on Handle Animal and Ride checks. This racial trait replaces sure-footed.

Polyglot: Some halflings, especially those who spend a lot of time traveling, develop a talent for learning new languages. These halflings gain a +2 racial bonus on Linguistics checks, and it is always a class skill for them. Halflings with this racial trait also begin play with the ability to speak Common, Halfling, and any one other language of their choice (except for secret languages, such as Druidic) in addition to bonus languages due to high Intelligence. They still gain the normal list of halfling bonus languages. This racial trait replaces keen senses and alters the halfling language racial trait.

Practicality: Halflings value hard work and common sense. Halflings with this racial trait gain a +2 bonus on any one Craft or Profession skill, as well as on Sense Motive checks and saves against illusions. This racial trait replaces fearless and sure-footed.

Shiftless: Halflings have a reputation for larceny and guile—and sometimes it's well deserved. Halflings with this racial trait gain a +2 racial bonus on Bluff and Sleight of Hand checks, and Sleight of Hand is always a class skill for them. This racial trait replaces sure-footed.

Swift as Shadows: Halflings possess incredible stealth even while moving through obstructed areas. Halflings with this racial trait reduce the penalty for using Stealth while moving by 5, and reduce the Stealth check penalty for sniping by 10. This racial trait replaces sure-footed.

Underfoot: Halflings must train hard to effectively fight bigger opponents. Halflings with this racial trait gain a +1 dodge bonus to AC against foes larger than themselves and a +1 bonus on Reflex saving throws to avoid trample attacks. This racial trait replaces halfling luck.

Wanderlust: Halflings love travel and maps. Halflings with this racial trait receive a +2 bonus on Knowledge (geography) and Survival checks. When casting spells or using abilities that provide or enhance movement, halflings treat their caster level as +1 higher than normal. This racial trait replaces fearless and halfling luck.

Warslinger: Halflings are experts at the use of the sling. Halflings with this racial trait can reload a sling as a free action. Reloading a sling still requires two hands and provokes attacks of opportunity. This racial trait replaces sure-footed.

Racial Subtypes

You can combine various alternate racial traits to create halfling subraces or variant races, such as the following.

Avenging: Unlike most halflings, members of this subtype actively look for trouble in their quest to avenge slights and wrongdoings. Whether resisting a local bully, monster, or troops of an oppressive ruler, halfling warriors of this secret subculture don masks and strike back on behalf of their community. These halflings have the low blow, underfoot, and warslinger alternate racial traits.

Nomadic: These halflings were born on the road and most follow it until the end of their days. They travel fast and light and never miss a chance for either profit or adventure. These halflings have the fleet-footed, polyglot, and wanderlust alternate racial traits.

Slave Born: These halflings come from lineages that have spent countless generations as property. Though usually free themselves, the weight of slavery still bears down on their souls, making them eager to please and prone to sudden fits of fear. These halflings have the craven and ingratiating alternate racial traits.

Favored Class Options

The following favored options are available to all halflings who have the listed favored class, and unless otherwise stated, the bonus applies each time you select the class reward.

Alchemist: Add one extract formula from the alchemist's list to the alchemist's formula book. This formula must be at least one level below the highest formula level the alchemist can create.

Barbarian: Add a +1/2 bonus to trap sense or +1/3 to the bonus from the surprise accuracy rage power.

Bard: Add +1/2 on Bluff checks to pass secret messages, +1/2 on Diplomacy checks to gather information, and +1/2 on Disguise checks to appear as an elven, half-elven, or human child.

Cavalier: Add +1/2 to the cavalier's effective class level for the purposes of determining the damage he deals when making an attack of opportunity against a challenged foe.

Cleric: Select one domain power granted at 1st level that is normally usable a number of times per day equal to 3 + the cleric's Wisdom modifier. The cleric adds +1/2 to the number of uses per day of that domain power.

Druid: Add a +1/4 luck bonus on the saving throws of the druid's animal companion.

Fighter: Add +1 to the fighter's CMD when resisting a trip or grapple attempt.

Gunslinger: Add +1/4 to the dodge bonus to AC granted by the nimble class feature (maximum +2) or +1/4 to the AC bonus gained when using the gunslinger's dodge deed.

Inquisitor: Add +1/4 to the number of times per day that an inquisitor can change her most recent teamwork feat.

Magus: The magus gains 1/6 of a new magus arcana.

Monk: Add +1 to the monk's CMD when resisting a grapple and +1/2 to the number of stunning attacks he can attempt per day.

Oracle: Add +1/2 to the oracle's level for the purpose of determining the effects of the oracle's curse ability.

Paladin: Add +1/2 hit point to the paladin's lay on hands ability (whether using it to heal or harm).

Ranger: Add a +1/4 dodge bonus to Armor Class against the ranger's favored enemies.

Rogue: Choose a weapon from the following list: sling, dagger, or any weapon with "halfling" in its name. Add a +1/2 bonus on critical hit confirmation rolls with that weapon (maximum bonus +4). This bonus does not stack with Critical Focus.

Sorcerer: Select one bloodline power at 1st level that is normally usable a number of times per day equal to 3 + the sorcerer's Charisma modifier. The sorcerer adds +1/2 to the number of uses per day of that bloodline power.

Summoner: Add +1 skill rank to the summoner's eidolon.

Witch: Add +1/4 to the witch's caster level when determining the effects of the spells granted to her by her patron.

Wizard: Add +1/2 to the wizard's effective class level for the purposes of determining his familiar's natural armor adjustment, Intelligence, and special abilities.

RACIAL ARCHETYPES & ORDERS

The following racial order and racial archetypes are available to halflings.

Community Guardian (Oracle)

The community guardian is chosen to protect and succor the weak and innocent within her community. Her calling also allows her to draw upon and focus the collective will in order to achieve those goals. A community guardian has the following class features.

Alignment: Any good.

Recommended Mysteries: ancestor (*Ultimate Magic* 53), life, lore, nature.

Class Skills: A community guardian adds Knowledge (local), Linguistics, Perception, and Survival to her list of class skills. These replace the additional class skills from her mystery.

Bonus Spells: *bless water* (2nd), *consecrate* (4th), *remove disease* (6th), *hallow* (10th), *heroes' feast* (12th). These bonus spells replace the oracle's mystery bonus spells from these levels.

Revelations: A community guardian must take the following revelations at the listed levels.

Spirit of Community (Ex): As a move action, you call upon the spirits of community. For the next round, you grant every ally within 30 feet a +1 competence bonus on a single skill check (of the ally's choice) that it makes before the end of this revelation's duration. Furthermore, allies within 30 feet can, as a free action, choose to forgo this bonus, and instead grant a single ally a +1 increase to its competence bonus granted by this ability (maximum +5). You can use this ability a number of times per day equal to 3 + your Charisma modifier. You must take this revelation at 1st level.

Renewing Radiance (Su): Once per day you can produce a burst of swirling white light that provides a measure of protection and renewal to allies within 30 feet for 1 round. On their turn, the allies can choose either to gain a +1 sacred bonus to AC for 1 round or to heal a number of hit points equal to 1d6 + your Charisma bonus (their choice). If an ally is dying, it is stabilized instead. At 7th level, the bonus to AC increases to +2, and the healing increases to 2d6 + your Charisma bonus hit points, and at 14th level the bonus to AC increases to +3, and the healing increases to 3d6 + your Charisma bonus hit points. You must take this revelation at 3rd level.

Filcher (Rogue)

A filcher steals valuables without their owners even realizing it. Whether cutting purses in the midst of combat or replacing prized items with fakes under the noses of their owners, the filcher is the master of the quick and quiet steal. A filcher has the following class features.

Quicker than the Eye (Ex): At 2nd level, a filcher develops an amazingly swift and delicate touch. When she uses Sleight of Hand, creatures take a penalty on their Perception checks to notice the attempt equal to half the filcher's class level. The filcher also subtracts her class level from the normal –20 penalty when attempting to make a Sleight of Hand check as a move action instead of as a standard action. Lastly, the filcher can withdraw

an object hidden on her person, including a weapon, as a move action instead of the usual standard action. This ability replaces evasion.

Rummage (Ex): At 3rd level, a filcher learns how to assess the value of items at the quickest glance. She can even make startlingly accurate guesses about particular items merely by observing the bulges they make in pouches, backpacks, or similar containers. She gains a +1 bonus on Appraise checks and an additional +1 bonus every three levels thereafter.

As a swift action, a filcher can make an Appraise check in order to determine the relative value of each object carried by her target (DC = 10 + 1 for every object the filcher is trying to ascertain the relative value of). Though she never learns the actual prices of items when using rummage, she does gain enough information to list these items in order, from the most valuable to the least valuable. She can, by taking a –20 penalty on the check, add to this assessment any items carried by her target that she cannot see. This ability replaces trap sense +1, +2, +3, +4, +5, and +6.

Filch (Ex): At 4th level, a filcher learns how pluck items off her opponents even in combat. She gains Improved Steal (*Advanced Player's Guide* 163) as a bonus feat and can use her Sleight of Hand bonus instead of her CMB when performing a steal combat maneuver (*Advanced Player's Guide* 322). If the filcher gains bonuses on combat maneuver checks from any feats, spells, magic items, or similar effects, they are added to the Sleight of Hand bonus when using the steal maneuver. This ability replaces uncanny dodge.

Superior Filching (Ex): At 8th level, a filcher becomes a master at separating owners from their property. She gains Greater Steal as a bonus feat, and opponents do not gain a +5 bonus to their CMD when she tries to remove items fastened to them. This ability replaces improved uncanny dodge.

Rogue Talents: The following rogue talents complement the filcher archetype: fast stealth, slow reactions (*Core Rulebook*); fast fingers, fast getaway (*Advanced Player's Guide*); black market connections, deft palm (*Ultimate Combat*).

Advanced Talents: The following advanced rogue talents complement the filcher archetype: skill mastery (*Core Rulebook*); fast tumble (*Advanced Player's Guide*); weapon snatcher (*Ultimate Combat*).

Order of the Paw (Cavalier)

Only dog- or wolf-riding halflings are eligible to join this order of cavaliers. When they do, they pledge to defend halflings, halfling settlements, and other innocent folks by patrolling the wilderness and seeking out possible threats to both individuals and whole communities. These cavaliers hunt down potential danger with a ruthless efficiency and determination that non-halflings find surprising and even somewhat alarming.

Edicts: The cavalier must strive to protect his community from rampaging monsters and fearsome conquers alike. His first priority is to aid halfling communities, but he also is sworn to protect those who cannot protect themselves from such threats in the wild. He must never take any action that would put a halfling community or an innocent creature in jeopardy. An order of the paw cavalier must take either a wolf or a dog as his mount.

Challenge: Whenever an order of the paw cavalier issues a challenge, his mount gains a +1 dodge bonus to AC as long it is threatening the target of the cavalier's challenge and the cavalier is riding the mount. This bonus increases by +1 for every four levels the cavalier possesses.

Skills: An order of the paw cavalier adds Knowledge (nature) and Survival to his list of class skills. He can make Knowledge (nature) checks untrained. Also, an order of the paw cavalier is adept at following tracks while mounted, using his mount's speed rather than his own to determine the penalty for tracking while moving, whether he is mounted or not.

Order Abilities: A cavalier belonging to the order of the paw gains the following abilities as he increases in level.

Danger Ward (Ex): At 2nd level, the cavalier can ready his allies for impending danger. As a standard action, he can ready all allies within 30 feet of the danger ahead, granting a bonus on a single type of saving throw (Fortitude, Reflex or Will) that he chooses when he grants this boon. At any point in the next minute, when these allies fail a saving throw of that type, they can choose to reroll the saving throw with a +4 competence bonus as an immediate action, but must take the results of the reroll even if it is worse. He can use this ability up to three times per day, once for each type of saving throw.

Canine Ferocity (Ex): At 8th level, when the cavalier uses his wolf or dog mount to perform a bull rush or overrun maneuver, the mount is considered to be one size category larger for the purposes of determining the size of creature it is maneuvering against and the mount's CMB. He also receives a bonus feat, chosen from the following list: Mounted Combat, Ride-By Attack, Skill Focus (Ride), Spirited Charge, Trample, or Unseat. He must qualify for the feat selected.

Giant Slayer (Ex): At 15th level, when the cavalier hits the target of his challenge with a melee attack, and that target is at least two size categories larger than the cavalier, he gains a bonus on damage rolls equal to 1/2 his cavalier level. This damage is multiplied on a critical hit.

Underfoot Adept (Monk)

An underfoot adept turns his diminutive stature and unorthodox footwork into a powerful weapon. Effortlessly moving across the battlefield, he ducks under the legs of larger creatures and then topples them with surprising attacks. An underfoot adept has the following class features.

Underfoot Grace (Ex): At 1st level, an underfoot adept uses his size and grace to avoid the attacks of those he passes. When using the Acrobatics skill to avoid attacks of opportunity by moving through a threatened area or an enemy's space, he only takes a −5 penalty when doing so at full speed, instead of the normal −10 penalty. This ability replaces the bonus feat gained at 1st level.

Underfoot Trip (Ex): At 1st level, an underfoot adept learns a number of maneuvers and grabs that can cause even the largest opponents to stumble and fall. He gains Improved Trip as a bonus feat, even if he does not meet the requirements. At 4th level, and every four levels thereafter, he acts as if he is one size larger for the purposes of determining the maximum size of creatures he can trip and when determining his CMB and CMD for purposes of a trip combat maneuver. This ability replaces stunning fist.

Improved Underfoot Grace (Ex): At 5th level, an underfoot adept's ability to avoid attacks of opportunity against those he passes improves. When using the Acrobatics skill to avoid attacks of opportunity, while moving through a threatened area or through an enemy's space, he takes no penalty when doing so at full speed. This ability replaces high jump.

NEW RACIAL RULES

The following options are available to halflings. At the GM's discretion, other appropriate races may also make use of some of these.

Halfling Equipment

Halflings have access to the following equipment.

Alchemical Preserves: Each small tin of this specially treated jam contains just enough of the gooey stuff to provide a halfling with a single serving of revitalizing nourishment. While any creature can eat these preserves as a standard action, it only affects halflings in a beneficial way. Halflings who eat the preserves recover from fatigue. Non-halflings who eat alchemical preserves become sickened for 1 round.

Billow Cape: This silk cape is constructed of many carefully arranged overlapping layers that are loosely stitched together. When exposed to a sudden influx of air, like that caused by falling, the cloak unfolds like a crude parachute. When falling, a creature wearing a billow cape is treated as if he had deliberately jumped from the height (*Core Rulebook* 443). When worn in areas of strong wind or greater (*Core Rulebook* 439), a billow cape hampers movement. In such wind conditions, the wearer treats all terrain as difficult terrain and takes a −4 penalty on

Fly checks. Because of the strange and somewhat fragile construction of this cape, only Small or smaller billow capes function properly. Larger billow capes take all the penalties resulting from high winds, but grant none of the benefits when the wearer falls.

Halfling Jugglesticks: This group of four brightly colored sticks is adorned with colorful streamers that can be juggled and manipulated to create displays and patterns. Halflings use them to even greater effect, gaining a +2 circumstance bonus on Perform (comedy) checks.

Roar Cord: This thin length of rope has many oddly shaped bits of hollow metal fixed along its length. As a standard action, a creature can swing a roar cord over its head to generate a variety of eerie noises. For the next round, any creature within 60 feet of the roar cord takes a –2 penalty on Perception checks that rely on sound and a –1 penalty on saving throws against fear effects. The roar cord can be used as a bardic instrument (string instrument) that grants the bard a +2 bonus on Perform checks when using the countersong bardic performance.

Halfling Equipment

Item	Cost	Weight	Craft DC
Alchemical preserves	50 gp	—	20
Billow cape	100 gp	4 lbs.	—
Halfling jugglesticks	25 gp	1 lb.	—
Roar cord	15 gp	1 lb.	—

Halfling Feats

Halflings have access to the following feats.

Adaptive Fortune

Your luck takes on almost legendary proportions.

Prerequisites: Fortunate One, adaptable luck racial trait, character level 10th, halfling.

Benefit: Increase the number of times per day you can use the adaptable luck racial trait by 1. Furthermore, when you use adaptable luck, increase the luck bonus for each type of use by 2.

Blundering Defense (Combat)

Your feverish and sometimes comical defensive techniques offer enough distraction to aid allies.

Prerequisites: Cautious Fighter, halfling.

Benefit: Whenever you fight defensively or use the total defense action, allies gain a luck bonus to AC and CMD equal to 1/2 the dodge bonus you gain from the action you are taking. Allies only gain this bonus while they are adjacent to you.

Cautious Fighter (Combat)

You care more about survival than victory.

Prerequisite: Halfling.

Benefit: When fighting defensively or using total defense, your dodge bonus to AC increases by 2.

Courageous Resolve

Even when others run, you tend to stand your ground.

Prerequisites: Craven racial trait or fearless racial trait, halfling.

Benefit: If you have the fearless racial trait, your racial bonus on saving throws against fear effects increases to +4. If you have the craven racial trait, you still take the –2 penalty on fear saves, but you can gain the benefit of morale bonuses on saving throws against fear effects.

Desperate Swing (Combat)

You land your most telling blows in desperate situations.

Prerequisites: Cautious Fighter, base attack bonus +1, halfling.

Benefit: Once per day, you can make a single melee attack while taking the total defense action. You take a –4 penalty on attack rolls when making this attack. You also gain a +4 bonus on critical confirmation rolls made while fighting defensively or making an attack of opportunity using this feat.

Fortunate One

You have an even greater knack than most halflings for adaptable luck.

Prerequisites: Adaptable luck racial trait, halfling.

Benefit: The number of times per day you can use the adaptable luck racial trait increases by 1.

Improved Low Blow (Combat)

You are adept at hitting larger opponents where it hurts.

Prerequisites: Base attack bonus +4, halfling, low-blow racial trait.

Benefit: Your bonus to confirm critical hits against opponents larger than yourself improves to +2. Furthermore, once per day, after you fail to hit with a critical hit confirmation roll, you can reroll the confirmation roll, but must take the new result even if it is worse.

Lucky Healer

Your luck allows you to draw from magical healing far more efficiently than most.

Prerequisites: Adaptive luck racial trait, halfling.

Benefit: Spend a use of your adaptive luck racial trait to reroll the damage healed from a single magical healing effect (such as a spell with "cure" in the title or channel energy). You regain a number of hit points equal to the new roll or the original roll, whichever is greater. Other creatures healed by the effect do not gain this benefit.

Lucky Strike (Combat)
Your luck increases the potency of your weapon attacks.

Prerequisites: Base attack bonus +5, adaptive luck racial trait, halfling.

Benefit: Spend a use of your adaptive luck racial trait to reroll the damage from a single weapon attack. You deal damage equal to the new damage roll, or the original roll, whichever is greater.

Risky Striker (Combat)
You can make yourself a little more vulnerable to larger creatures in order to land a devastating blow.

Prerequisites: Base attack bonus +1, halfling.

Benefit: You can choose to take a –1 penalty to AC to gain a +2 bonus on melee damage rolls against creatures two or more size categories larger than you. When your base attack bonus reaches +4 and every four levels thereafter, the damage increases by 2. The bonus damage is multiplied in the case of a critical hit. You can only choose to use this feat when you declare that you are making an attack action or a full-attack action with a melee weapon. The effects last until your next turn.

Sure and Fleet
You are both fast and careful.

Prerequisites: Fleet of foot racial trait, halfling.

Benefit: You gain a +2 racial bonus on Acrobatics and Climb checks.

Surprise Strike (Combat)
You actually seem to do more damage when frantically trying to avoid your enemies.

Prerequisites: Cautious Fighter, Desperate Swing, base attack bonus +6, halfling.

Benefit: Once per day, when fighting defensively or making an attack of opportunity while taking the total defense action with the Desperate Swing feat, you take no penalty on the attack roll.

Uncanny Defense (Combat)
Your instinct for self-preservation gives you many advantages.

Prerequisites: Cautious Fighter, base attack bonus +3, halfling.

Benefit: While fighting defensively or taking the total defense action, you gain a bonus on your Reflex saving throws and to your CMD equal to 1/2 of the dodge bonus to AC you gained from taking that action.

Halfling Magic Items
Halflings have access to the following magic items.

BOOK OF MARVELOUS RECIPES
Aura moderate conjuration; **CL** 11th
Slot none; **Price** 28,800; **Weight** 3 lbs.

DESCRIPTION

The pages of this thick and travel-worn leather book visibly rewrite themselves as a reader flips through them, creating a number of delicious recipes that seem to anticipate the current craving or culinary desires of the reader. The recipes can aid the reader in creating such dishes, allowing him to use the Profession (cook) skill untrained, or granting a +4 competence bonus on such checks if the reader is trained in that skill.

Furthermore, once per day, this book can be used to enhance a meal the reader is cooking. When used in this way, it grants the meal being cooked the effects of a *heroes' feast* spell (caster level 11th).

CONSTRUCTION

Requirements Craft Wondrous Item, *heroes' feast*, the creator must have at least 4 ranks in Profession (cook); **Cost** 14,400 gp

ESCAPE DUST
Aura faint conjuration; **CL** 3rd
Slot none; **Price** 300 gp; **Weight** —

DESCRIPTION

When a handful of this coarse, crystalline powder is thrown at a single creature, it circles around that creature and disrupts its ability to attack and see. Using this dust requires a ranged touch attack by its user (with a range increment of 5 feet), but doing so does not provoke attacks of opportunity. On a hit, the target is dazzled and cannot make attacks of opportunity or immediate actions for 1 round.

CONSTRUCTION

Requirements Craft Wondrous Item, *glitterdust*; **Cost** 150 gp

QUICKFINGERS GLOVES
Aura faint transmutation; **CL** 5th
Slot hands; **Price** 2,500 gp; **Weight** —

DESCRIPTION

These dark-colored, skin-tight gloves are typically made of either supple calfskin or silk. A wearer of these gloves with at least 1 rank in Sleight of Hand can perform such a check as a move action by taking a –10 penalty on the check rather than the normal –20. Both gloves must be worn for the magic to be effective.

CONSTRUCTION

Requirements Craft Wondrous Item, *cat's grace*, *haste*; **Cost** 1,250 gp

SOLIDSMOKE PIPEWEED
Aura moderate conjuration; **CL** 7th
Slot none; **Price** 1,000 gp; **Weight** —

DESCRIPTION

When smoked in any pipe, this pinch of magical tobacco produces a languid, milky-white smoke that the smoker can transform into useful objects. A halfling who puffs on the

pipe as a full-round action can shape the smoke into an object weighing no more than 5 pounds and having a maximum volume of 1 cubic foot. The halfling can, on following rounds, spend additional full-round actions to increase the object's weight by 2 additional pounds and its volume by another cubic foot. The halfling must succeed at an appropriate Craft check to make a complex item. If the halfling stops puffing on her pipe for any reason before she finishes creating the object, the figure in the smoke collapses and her pipe is extinguished. Objects created by *solidsmoke pipeweed* last for 24 hours before fading away into vapor. Objects created by the pipeweed have the same hardness, hit points, and other qualities as manufactured objects of their type, but look smoky and indistinct. Each pinch of *solidsmoke pipeweed* is sufficient for 3 full rounds of smoking. A single larger item must be created with a single pinch of *solidsmoke pipeweed*, so any item created with this pipeweed can't be larger than 9 pounds and 3 cubic feet.

A halfling cannot create an object designed to exactly duplicate or replace another specific object. For instance, while she could create a smoky lock with its own key, she could not puff smoke into an existing keyhole and then create a key that would open that particular lock.

This smoke is caustic and chokes non-halflings. It grants non-halflings no benefits, and each time they spend a standard action to smoke the pipeweed, they are sickened for 1 round.

CONSTRUCTION
Requirements Craft Wondrous Item, *minor creation*, creator must be a halfling; **Cost** 500 gp

SYMBOL OF LUCK
Aura faint evocation; **CL** 3rd
Slot none; **Price** 6,000 gp; **Weight** 1 lb.
DESCRIPTION
This translucent sphere of iron-hard glass changes shape to match its bearer's holy symbol within an hour of coming into her possession. After that transformation is complete, when this symbol is used by a halfling with the luck or adaptable luck racial trait to channel energy in order to heal, it also grants those healed a +1 luck bonus on saving throws for a number of rounds equal to the number of dice healed by the channel energy.
CONSTRUCTION
Requirements Craft Wondrous Item, *divine favor*, the creator must be a halfling; **Cost** 3,000 gp

Halfling Spells
Halflings have access to the following spells.

BLESSING OF LUCK AND RESOLVE
School enchantment (compulsion) [mind-affecting]; **Level** cleric 2, inquisitor 2, paladin 2

Casting Time 1 standard action
Components V, S
Range touch
Target one living creature touched
Duration 1 minute/level (D), special see below
A favored blessing of halfling clerics, this spell grants its target a +2 morale bonus on saving throws against fear effects. If the target has the fearless racial trait, it is immune to fear instead. If the target fails a saving throw against fear, it can end the spell as an immediate action to reroll the save with a +4 morale bonus, and must take the new result, even if it is worse.

BLESSING OF LUCK AND RESOLVE, MASS
School enchantment (compulsion) [mind-affecting]; **Level** cleric 6, inquisitor 6, paladin 4
Range close (25 ft. + 5 ft./2 levels)
Targets one creature/level, no two of which can be more than 30 ft. apart
This spell functions like *blessing of luck and resolve*, except that it affects multiple creatures.

ESCAPING WARD
School abjuration; **Level** bard 2, inquisitor 2, magus 2, ranger 2, sorcerer/wizard 2
Casting Time 1 standard action
Components V, S
Range personal
Target you
Duration 1 round/level
This ward grants you extra maneuverability when you avoid attacks against larger foes. While affected by this spell, when you are attacked and missed by a creature that is at least one size category larger than you, you can, as an immediate action, move up to 5 feet away from the attacking creature. You can increase this movement by 5 feet for every 5 caster levels. This movement does not provoke attacks of opportunity.

FEARSOME DUPLICATE
School illusion (figment); **Level** bard 3, inquisitor 3, sorcerer/wizard 3, witch 3
Casting Time 1 standard action
Components V, S
Range medium (100 ft. + 10 ft./level)
Effect monstrously distorted duplicate of you
Duration 1 minute/level (D)
Saving Throw Will disbelief (if interacted with); **Spell Resistance** yes
You create a larger and far more menacing version of yourself that you can send forth, manipulate like a puppet, and use to interact with others. You can make the duplicate up to two size categories larger than you are and determine

a theme as to how it alters your original appearance. However, this duplicate always retains some vestiges of your actual appearance. Creatures who already know you gain a +2 bonus on saving throws made to disbelieve this spell. Your duplicate has no actual substance, and you cannot use it to alter its surroundings or to attack or otherwise harm creatures it encounters. You can use the duplicate to speak, and interact verbally with creatures using the Bluff, Diplomacy, and Intimidate skills, and you gain a +2 competence bonus on Intimidate checks when using that skill through the duplicate.

You can see, hear, taste, and smell your duplicate's surroundings as if you are actually present using your Perception skill. While you also remain aware of your own immediate surroundings when controlling your duplicate, controlling it does take a toll on your senses. You take a –4 penalty on Perception checks while you control your duplicate.

The duplicate moves under your mental command, and while you need not act out its movements, you must take a standard action to control your duplicate for 1 round (concentrating on the spell) or it winks out of existence. You can maintain control of your duplicate even if you have no line of sight or line of effect to it.

The duplicate immediately winks out of existence if it is hit by an attack or in the area of a damaging effect, or if it moves beyond the maximum range of the spell.

VILLAGE VEIL

School illusion (figment) [mind-affecting]; **Level** bard 5, cleric 5, sorcerer/wizard 5, witch 5
Casting Time 1 standard action
Components V, S
Range long (400 ft. + 40 ft./level)
Area one 10-ft. cube per level
Duration 1 day/level
Saving Throw Will disbelief; **Spell Resistance** yes

You throw an illusion over an area to make creatures that view or interact with it believe it has suffered some great catastrophe or calamity that renders it utterly worthless for their needs. You must set a few general guidelines when casting the spell as to the nature of this disaster (fire, tornado, bandit raid, plague, etc.), after which the illusion fills in the remaining details to make it seem realistic. When casting the spell, you can grant creatures with particular, clearly identifiable physical traits (race, gender, age category, etc.) immunity to this spell. This allows all such eligible creatures to perceive the true nature of the affected area instead of its illusory appearance. Creatures without this immunity that fail their saving throws always perceive the affected area as having absolutely nothing of interest or worth to them. Unless they have reason for suspicion, they always move on without closely investigating the area. Creatures with sufficient reasons for suspicion who do choose to investigate the area gain another saving throw, this one with a +2 bonus, as they enter the village and directly interact with the illusion.

You can expand the area of this spell by casting it multiple times. Each time you do, you must effectively "attach" the spell to the existing area by using the same disaster and granting the same sorts of creatures immunity to its effects. If you fail to do this, the entire illusion, no matter how large, disappears.

HUMANS

Humans possess exceptional drive and a great capacity to endure and expand, and as such are currently the dominant race in the world. Their empires and nations are vast, sprawling things, and the citizens of these societies carve names for themselves with the strength of their sword arms and the power of their spells. Humanity is best characterized by its tumultuousness and diversity, and human cultures run the gamut from savage but honorable tribes to decadent, devil-worshiping noble families in the most cosmopolitan cities. Humans' curiosity and ambition often triumph over their predilection for a sedentary lifestyle, and many leave their homes to explore the innumerable forgotten corners of the world or lead mighty armies to conquer their neighbors, simply because they can.

Human society is a strange amalgam of nostalgia and futurism, being enamored of past glories and wistfully remembered "golden ages," yet at the same time quick to discard tradition and history and strike off into new ventures. Relics of the past are kept as prized antiques and museum pieces, as humans love to collect things—not only inanimate relics but also living creatures—to display for their amusement or to serve by their side. Other races suggest this behavior is due to a deep-rooted urge to dominate and assert power in the human psyche, an urge to take, till, or tame the wild things and places of the world. Those with a more charitable view believe humans are simply collectors of experiences, and the things they take and keep, whether living, dead, or never alive, are just tokens to remind themselves of the places they have gone, the things they have seen, and the deeds they have accomplished. Their present and future value is just a bonus; their real value is as an ongoing reminder of the inevitable progress of humanity.

Humans in many places are fascinated by older races and cultures, though at times they grow frustrated or even contemptuous of ancient and (to their mind) outmoded traditions. Their attitudes toward other races are thus a curious mix of exoticism and even fetishism, though usually with a very superficial level of understanding and appreciation of those cultures, alongside a deeply rooted arrogance that means most humans have a hard time regarding themselves as anything other than the default standard of society. Human scholars engaged in the study of other races—who might be assumed to be the most cosmopolitan and well versed in their nature and culture—have often proved no better than the less-learned members of their race when it comes to genuine closing of the social distance. Humans are gregarious, often friendly, and willing to mix and interact with others, but their sheer obliviousness to their offhanded marginalization of others is what so chagrins other races when dealing with them.

HUMAN RACIAL TRAITS

+2 to One Ability Score: Human characters gain a +2 racial bonus to one ability score of their choice at creation to represent their varied nature.

Medium: Humans are Medium creatures and receive no bonuses or penalties due to their size.

Normal Speed: Humans have a base speed of 30 feet.

Bonus Feat: Humans select one extra feat at 1st level.

Skilled: Humans gain an additional skill rank at first level and one additional rank whenever they gain a level.

Languages: Humans begin play speaking Common. Humans with high Intelligence scores can choose any languages they want (except secret languages, such as Druidic).

Of course, well-meaning, blundering ignorance and numerical superiority are not the only things that make other races suspicious of humans. Entirely too many examples can be found throughout history wherein human xenophobia and intolerance has led to social isolationism, civil oppression, bloody purges, inquisitions, mob violence, and open war. Humans are not the only race to hate what is different among them, but they seem to have a susceptibility to fear-mongering and suspicion, whether about race, language, religion, class, gender, or another difference. More moderate human citizens often sit idly by while their more extreme compatriots dominate the political and cultural conversation, yet there are also many who stand in opposition to extremists and embody a spirit of unity across the bounds of difference, transcending barriers and forming alliances and relationships both large and small across every color, creed, country, or species.

Physical Description: The physical characteristics of humans are as varied as the world's climes. From the dark-skinned tribesmen of the southern continents to the pale and barbaric raiders of the northern lands, humans possess a wide variety of skin colors, body types, and facial features. Generally speaking, humans' skin color assumes a darker hue the closer to the equator they live. At the same time, bone structure, hair color and texture, eye color, and a host of facial and bodily phenotypic characteristics vary immensely from one locale to another. Cheekbones may be high or broad, noses aquiline or flat, and lips full or thin; eyes range wildly in hue, some deep set in their sockets, and others with full epicanthic folds. Appearance is hardly random, of course, and familial, tribal, or national commonalities often allow the knowledgeable to identify a human's place of origin on sight, or at least to hazard a good guess. Humans' origins are also indicated through their traditional styles of bodily decoration, not only in the clothing or jewelry worn, but also in elaborate hairstyles, piercing, tattooing, and even scarification.

Society: Human society comprises a multitude of governments, attitudes, and lifestyles. Though the oldest human cultures trace their histories thousands of years into the past, when compared to the societies of other races like elves and dwarves, human society seems to be in a state of constant flux as empires fragment and new kingdoms subsume the old. In general, humans are known for their flexibility, ingenuity, and ambition. Other races sometimes envy humans their seemingly limitless adaptability, not so much biologically speaking but in their willingness to step beyond the known and press on to whatever might await them. While many or even most humans as individuals are content to stay within their comfortable routine, there is a dauntless spirit of discovery endemic to humans as a species that drives them in striving toward possibilities beyond every horizon.

Relations: Humans are fecund, and their drive and numbers often spur them into contact with other races during bouts of territorial expansion and colonization. In many cases, this tendency leads to violence and war, yet humans are also swift to forgive and forge alliances with races who do not try to match or exceed them in violence. Proud, sometimes to the point of arrogance, humans might look upon dwarves as miserly drunkards, elves as flighty fops, halflings as craven thieves, gnomes as twisted maniacs, and half-elves and half-orcs as embarrassments—but the race's diversity among its own members also makes many humans quite adept at accepting others for what they are. Humans may become so absorbed in their own affairs that they remain ignorant of the language and culture of others, and some take this ignorance to a hateful extreme of intolerance, oppression, and rarely even extermination of others they perceive as dangerous, strange, or "impure." Thankfully, while such incidents and movements may taint all of humanity in the eyes of some, they are more often the exception than the rule.

Alignment and Religion: Humanity is perhaps the most diverse of all the common races, with a capacity for both great evil and boundless good. Some humans assemble into vast barbaric hordes, while others build sprawling cities that cover miles. Taken as a whole, most humans are neutral, yet they generally tend to congregate in nations and civilizations with specific alignments. Humans also have the widest range of gods and religions, lacking other races' ties to tradition and eager to turn to anyone offering them glory or protection.

Adventurers: Ambition alone drives countless humans, and for many, adventuring serves as a means to an end, whether it be wealth, acclaim, social status, or arcane knowledge. A few pursue adventuring careers simply for the thrill of danger. Humans hail from myriad regions and backgrounds, and as such can fill any role within an adventuring party.

Names: Unlike other races, which generally cleave to specific traditions and shared histories, humanity's diversity has resulted in a nearly infinite set of names. The humans of a northern barbarian tribe have much different names than those hailing from a subtropical nation of sailors and traders. Even humans who speak the same language may have names that are as varied as their beliefs and appearances, depending on their origins.

ALTERNATE RACIAL RULES

Humans are as adaptable as they are varied. The following rules reflect this flexibility and can exhibit themselves in any human character.

Alternate Racial Traits

The following racial traits may be selected instead of existing human racial traits. Consult your GM before selecting any of these new options.

Adoptive Parentage: Humans are sometimes orphaned and adopted by other races. Choose one humanoid race without the human subtype. You start play with that race's languages and gain that race's weapon familiarity racial trait (if any). If the race does not have weapon familiarity, you gain either Skill Focus or Weapon Focus as a bonus feat that is appropriate for that race instead. This racial trait replaces the bonus feat trait.

Dual Talent: Some humans are uniquely skilled at maximizing their natural gifts. These humans pick two ability scores and gain a +2 racial bonus in each of those scores. This racial trait replaces the +2 bonus to any one ability score, the bonus feat, and the skilled traits.

Eye for Talent: Humans have great intuition for hidden potential. They gain a +2 racial bonus on Sense Motive checks. In addition, when they acquire an animal companion, bonded mount, cohort, or familiar, that creature gains a +2 bonus to one ability score of the character's choice. This racial trait replaces the bonus feat trait.

Focused Study: All humans are skillful, but some, rather than being generalists, tend to specialize in a handful of skills. At 1st, 8th, and 16th level, such humans gain Skill Focus in a skill of their choice as a bonus feat. This racial trait replaces the bonus feat trait.

Heart of the Fields: Humans born in rural areas are used to hard labor. They gain a racial bonus equal to half their character level to any one Craft or Profession skill, and once per day they may ignore an effect that would cause them to become fatigued or exhausted. This racial trait replaces skilled.

Heart of the Mountains: Humans born in the mountains are skilled at negotiating heights and precipices. They gain a +2 racial bonus on Climb checks and Acrobatics checks to move on narrow surfaces and uneven ground. Furthermore, they are considered acclimated to the effects of high altitude (*Core Rulebook* 430). This racial trait replaces skilled.

Heart of the Sea: Humans born near the sea are always drawn to it. They gain a +2 racial bonus on Profession (sailor) and Swim checks, and these are always class skills for them. They can hold their breath twice as long as normal, and spellcasters gain a +4 racial bonus on concentration checks when attempting to cast spells underwater. This racial trait replaces skilled.

Heart of the Slums: Humans who eke out a life in a city's teeming slums must be quick and clever. They gain a +2 racial bonus on Sleight of Hand and Stealth checks, and a +4 racial bonus on Survival checks in urban and underground settings. In addition, they may roll twice when saving against disease, taking the better roll. This racial trait replaces skilled.

Heart of the Snows: Humans born in chilly climes treat cold climates as one category less severe. They gain a +2 racial bonus on Fortitude saving throws against the effects of cold climates, on any check or saving throw to avoid slipping and falling, and to CMD against trip combat maneuvers. This bonus applies on Acrobatics and Climb checks made in slippery conditions. This racial trait replaces skilled.

Heart of the Streets: Humans from bustling cities are skilled with crowds. They gain a +1 racial bonus on Reflex saves and a +1 dodge bonus to Armor Class when adjacent to at least two other allies. Crowds do not count as difficult terrain for them. This racial trait replaces skilled.

Heart of the Sun: Humans born in tropical climates treat hot climates as one category less severe. They also gain a +2 racial bonus on Fortitude saving throws against the effects of a hot climate, as well as against the poison and distraction ability of swarms and vermin. This racial trait replaces skilled.

Heart of the Wilderness: Humans raised in the wild learn the hard way that only the strong survive. They gain a racial bonus equal to half their character level on Survival checks. They also gain a +5 racial bonus on Constitution checks to stabilize when dying and add half their character level to their Constitution score when determining the negative hit point total necessary to kill them. This racial trait replaces skilled.

Heroic: Some humans are born heroes. In campaigns that use the optional hero point system (*Advanced Player's Guide* 322–325), each time these humans gain a level, they gain 2 hero points instead of 1. If they take the Blood of Heroes feat, they gain 3 hero points each level instead of 2. This racial trait replaces the bonus feat trait.

Mixed Heritage: Often human civilization is defined by more than one characteristic. A human with this trait may select a second "Heart of the" racial trait. This replaces the bonus feat racial trait.

Silver Tongued: Human are often adept at subtle manipulation and putting even sworn foes at ease. Humans with this trait gain a +2 bonus on Diplomacy and Bluff checks. In addition, when they use Diplomacy to shift a creature's attitude, they can shift up to three steps up rather than just two. This racial trait replaces skilled.

Racial Subtypes

You can combine various alternate racial traits to create human subraces or variant races, such as the following.

Cosmopolitan: Adept as city living, these humans can navigate crowds and fulfill the need for skilled labor in such settlements. Replace the skilled racial trait with heart of the streets and the bonus feat racial trait with focused study.

Country Folk: These humans are suited to life in the countryside. Replace the skilled racial trait with heart of the fields and the bonus feat racial trait with focused study.

Gutter Rat: Often second-class citizens living in sprawling ghettos and slums, these humans work hard to eke out an existence in a city. Replace the skilled racial trait with heart of the slums and the bonus feat racial trait with mixed heritage (heart of the streets).

Imperious Human: Hailing from either an empire, an emerging nation, or a controlling city-state, these humans are arrogant expansionists, absorbing others to their causes and culture. Replace the skilled racial trait with silver tongued and the bonus feat racial trait with eye for talent.

Trailblazer: Adaptive and inventive, these humans must have quick wits and a dose of heroic luck to survive in the lands they settle. Replace the skilled racial trait with heart of the wilderness and the bonus feat racial trait with heroic. At the GM's discretion, you can swap out the heart of the wilderness racial trait for either heart of the mountains, heart of the sea, heart of the snows, or heart of the sun, depending on the type of terrain these humans are settling.

Versatile Human: While they lack some of the training of other humans, the natural talents of versatile humans more than make up for this lack. Replace the +2 bonus to any ability score, the skilled racial trait, and the bonus feat racial trait with dual talent.

Favored Class Options

The following options are available to all humans who have the listed favored class, and unless otherwise stated, the bonus applies each time you select the class reward.

Alchemist: Add one extract formula from the alchemist formula list to the character's formula book. This formula must be at least one level below the highest formula level the alchemist can create.

Barbarian: Add a +1/2 bonus to trap sense or +1/3 to the bonus from the superstitious rage power.

Bard: Add one spell known from the bard spell list. This spell must be at least one level below the highest spell level the bard can cast.

Cavalier: Add +1/4 to the cavalier's banner bonus.

Cleric: Add a +1 bonus on caster level checks made to overcome the spell resistance of outsiders.

Druid: Add a +1/2 bonus on Diplomacy and Intimidate checks to change a creature's attitude.

Fighter: Add +1 to the fighter's CMD when resisting two combat maneuvers of the character's choice.

Gunslinger: Add +1/4 point to the gunslinger's grit points.

Inquisitor: Add one spell known from the inquisitor spell list. This spell must be at least one level below the highest spell level the inquisitor can cast.

Magus: Add +1/4 point to the magus' arcane pool.

Monk: Add +1/4 point to the monk's *ki* pool.

Oracle: Add one spell known from the oracle spell list. This spell must be at least one level below the highest spell level the oracle can cast.

Paladin: Add +1 to the paladin's energy resistance to one kind of energy (maximum +10).

Ranger: Add +1 hit point or +1 skill rank to the ranger's animal companion. If the ranger ever replaces his companion, the new companion gains these bonus hit points or skill ranks.

Rogue: The rogue gains +1/6 of a new rogue talent.

Sorcerer: Add one spell known from the sorcerer spell list. This spell must be at least one level below the highest spell level the sorcerer can cast.

Summoner: Add +1 hit point or +1 skill rank to the summoner's eidolon.

Witch: Add one spell from the witch spell list to the witch's familiar. This spell must be at least one level below the highest spell level she can cast. If the witch ever replaces her familiar, the new familiar knows these bonus spells.

Wizard: Add one spell from the wizard spell list to the wizard's spellbook. This spell must be at least one level below the highest spell level the wizard can cast.

RACIAL ARCHETYPES & BLOODLINES

The following racial bloodline and racial archetypes are available to humans.

Buccaneer (Gunslinger)

Freebooters who cling to the convoluted codes that rule independent ships, the buccaneer is a gunslinger of the high seas. Their exploits are fueled by the thrill of danger and often by the temporary courage provided by grog. A buccaneer has the following class features.

Deeds: A buccaneer swaps four of the normal gunslinger deeds for the following deeds.

Seadog's Gait (Ex): At 1st level, the buccaneer gains Sea Legs (*Ultimate Combat* 117) as a bonus feat. If she spends 1 grit point, she can ignore difficult terrain until the end of her turn. This replaces the quick clear deed.

Pirate's Jargon (Ex): At 3rd level, the buccaneer's baffling palaver of nautical jargon and piratical cant provides a +2 bonus on Bluff and Intimidate checks. Furthermore, she can spend a swift action and 1 grit point to cause a single living creature within 30 feet to make a Will saving throw (DC = 10 + 1/2 her buccaneer level + her Charisma modifier) or become confused for 1 round. This is a mind-affecting language-dependent effect. This replaces the pistol whip deed.

Rope Swing (Ex): At 7th level, as long as the buccaneer has at least 1 grit point, she gains a bonus on Acrobatics and Climb checks equal to her gunslinger level when climbing or swinging on a rope. If she spends 1 grit point, her move

while climbing or swinging on a rope does not provoke attacks of opportunity. This replaces the dead shot deed.

Captain's Curse (Sp): At 11th level, a buccaneer can spend 2 grit points to use *old salt's curse* as a spell-like ability. At 15th level, she may use *black mark* instead. The caster level for these spell-like abilities is equal to the buccaneer's class level, and the save DC is equal to 10 + her buccaneer level + her Charisma modifier. This replaces the lightning reload deed.

Grit (Ex): Like the sea itself, a buccaneer is a force of nature. Instead of using her Wisdom modifier to determine the number of grit points she gains at the start of each day, she uses her Charisma modifier. This ability works in all other ways like the gunslinger's grit class feature.

Liquid Courage (Ex): At 2nd level, a buccaneer gains the ability to fortify her grit with strong drink. The act of drinking is a standard action that provokes attacks of opportunity, and each drink provides 1 grog point. Grog points can be used in place of grit points to fuel deeds or grit feats (including those requiring a minimum of 1 grit point to use). The buccaneer can gain a maximum number of grog points each day equal to her Constitution modifier (minimum 1), and they last for 1 hour or until used, whichever comes first. She gains a morale bonus on saves against fear and a dodge bonus to AC against attacks of opportunity equal to her current grog point total. This ability replaces the nimble ability.

Bonus Feat: In addition to combat and grit feats, a buccaneer can select from the following feats as her bonus feats: Expert Driver (water vehicles only; *Ultimate Combat* 100), Master Siege Engineer (*Ultimate Combat* 109), Siege Engineer (*Ultimate Combat* 118), Siege Gunner (*Ultimate Combat* 118), Skilled Driver (water vehicles only; *Ultimate Combat* 119).

Exotic Pet (Ex): At 5th level, a buccaneer gains a familiar as a wizard of half the buccaneer's class level (though the exotic pet never gains the ability to deliver touch spells or share spells). This pet is typically a monkey or parrot (use the stats for a raven familiar). Such animals are useful scouts, even in the thick of combat. As long as the pet is within 30 feet of the buccaneer, the buccaneer also gains the benefit of evasion. This ability replaces gun training 1.

Sword and Pistol: At 9th level, a buccaneer gains Sword and Pistol (*Ultimate Combat* 117) as a bonus feat even if she does not meet the prerequisites. This ability replaces gun training 2.

Gun Training (Ex): A buccaneer gains this ability only at 13th level with a single type of firearm.

Raider's Riposte (Ex): At 17th level, whenever an enemy misses a buccaneer with an attack of opportunity, it provokes an attack of opportunity from the buccaneer. This ability replaces gun training 4.

Feral Child (Druid)

Some youths, abandoned in the wilderness and then raised by animals, are so connected with their adoptive home and family that they become feral. Suspicious of civilized society, these foundlings often choose allegiance to the wild over their human forebears. A feral child has the following class features.

Weapon and Armor Proficiency: A feral child loses proficiency with the scimitar, scythe, and sickle and with shields.

Class Skills: A feral child adds Acrobatics to her list of class skills and removes Fly and Profession from her list of class skills.

Illiteracy: At 1st level, a feral child is unable to read and write, though she may learn by taking 1 rank of Linguistics. She does not gain Druidic as a free language and cannot select Sylvan as a bonus language.

Improved Unarmed Strike: At 1st level, a feral child gains Improved Unarmed Strike as a bonus feat.

Beast Family (Ex): At 1st level, a feral child may choose one specific type of animal as the type that raised her. She gains a +2 circumstance bonus on Handle Animal and wild empathy checks with animals of that type, and she can communicate with them as if using a continual *speak with animals* spell-like ability, but this ability is nonmagical.

Nature Bond (Ex): At 1st level, a feral child must select an animal companion as her nature bond.

Favored Terrain (Ex): At 3rd level, a feral child gains the favored terrain ability as a ranger of her class level. A feral child may not choose urban as a favored terrain. This ability replaces trackless step and a thousand faces.

Native Cunning (Ex): At 3rd level, a feral child gains trap sense as a barbarian of equal level, and in her favored terrain, she immediately receives a Perception check to notice traps within 10 feet, as the trap spotter rogue talent. In addition, at 3rd level and every three levels thereafter, she may choose one combat maneuver, and gains a bonus equal to her trap sense bonus to her CMD against that maneuver. This ability replaces wild shape.

Native Fortitude (Ex): At 4th level, a feral child gains a +1 bonus on saving throws against disease, exhaustion, fatigue, fear, and poison. When she is in her favored terrain, she instead applies her favored terrain bonus on such saving throws. She also recovers from ability damage, exhaustion, and fatigue at twice the normal rate. This ability replaces resist nature's lure.

Native Call (Su): At 9th level, when in her favored terrain, for any *summon nature's ally* spells a feral child uses to summon animals that are native to that terrain, she treats the duration of the spell as if she were 2 levels higher.

At 17th level, when the feral child uses *summon nature's ally* spells to summon such animals, those animals gain a +2 bonus to both their Strength and Constitution ability scores. This stacks with the effects of the Augmented Summoning feat.

This ability replaces venom immunity and timeless body.

Imperious Bloodline (Sorcerer)

A scion of forgotten kings, with a lineage rich with the dust of ancient empires spanning every golden age of humanity's history, an imperious embodies the apex of human potential, as well as human temerity and uninhibited hubris.

Class Skill: Perform (oratory).

Bonus Spells: *moment of greatness* (3rd; *Ultimate Combat* 237), *eagle's splendor* (5th), *heroism* (7th), *threefold aspect* (9th;

Advanced Player's Guide 249), *greater command* (11th), *pure strain* (13th), *greater age resistance* (15th; *Ultimate Magic* 205), *prediction of failure* (17th; *Ultimate Magic* 232), *overwhelming presence* (19th; *Ultimate Magic* 230).

Bonus Feats: Diehard, Endurance, Heroic Defiance (*Advanced Player's Guide* 162), Heroic Recovery (*Advanced Player's Guide* 162), Improved Initiative, Lingering Spell (*Advanced Player's Guide* 164), Magical Aptitude, Persuasive.

Bloodline Arcana: Whenever you cast a harmful spell, you gain a bonus equal to the spell's level on Intimidate checks made against any creature adversely effected by that spell until the end of your next turn. Adversely effected typically means damage, but it can also mean debilitating effects or conditions.

Bloodline Powers: You draw upon ancestors both legendary and forgotten.

Student of Humanity (Ex): At 1st level, you gain Diplomacy, Knowledge (history), Knowledge (local), Knowledge (nobility), and Linguistics as class skills. In addition, when using these skills to learn, study, or gather information about humans, you add an insight bonus equal to your Charisma bonus on such checks.

Heroic Echo (Su): At 3rd level, when you receive a morale bonus from any spell, spell-like ability, or magic item, including those you cast on yourself, that bonus increases by +1. At 9th level, this ability also applies to competence bonuses. If you receive a morale effect (or a competence effect at 9th level) that affects an area or multiple targets, as an immediate action you can share your increased bonus with all other recipients. This increase to other participants lasts a number of rounds equal to your Charisma bonus. You can use this ability once per day, plus one time per three levels after 3rd.

Take Your Best Shot (Su): At 9th level, if you are targeted by a harmful spell, spell-like ability, or supernatural ability and suffer no harm from it, whether because of a successful saving throw, spell resistance, the attack missing, or some other protection, as an immediate action you can make an Intimidate check to demoralize the creature that produced the effect, but only if the creature that used the harmful effect is within 30 feet and can clearly see and hear you.

At 13th level, you can use this ability after succeeding at a saving throw to reduce the effects of an attack (if no save is allowed, you cannot use this ability).

Heroic Legends (Su): At 15th level, you may inspire greatness or inspire heroics as a bard of your sorcerer level by sacrificing a spell slot as a swift or move action. The effect lasts a number of rounds equal to the sacrificed spell's level; this duration is doubled for human recipients.

Immortal Legend (Ex): At 20th level, you cease aging; no longer need to eat, drink, or sleep; and gain immunity to death effects and energy drain.

Wanderer (Monk)

Some monks wander the world in humility to learn and to share wisdom and philosophy from their teachers with those they meet, often aiding those who are in need. A wanderer has the following class features.

Class Skills: The wanderer adds Diplomacy, Knowledge (geography), Knowledge (local), Linguistics, and Survival to his list of class skills.

Far Traveler (Ex): At 1st level, the wanderer gains either one additional language known or proficiency in one exotic or martial weapon. At 4th level and every four levels thereafter, the wanderer may gain an additional language known or may retrain her weapon proficiency from this ability to a different exotic or martial weapon. This ability replaces the bonus feat gained at 1st level.

Long Walk (Ex): At 3rd level, the wanderer gains Endurance as a bonus feat, and the feat bonus doubles when he makes Constitution checks because of a forced march. In addition, a wanderer gains a +2 bonus on saving throws against spells and effects that cause exhaustion and fatigue. This ability replaces still mind.

Light Step (Su): At 5th level, a wanderer leaves no trail and cannot be tracked, though he can leave a trail if desired. By spending 1 point from his ki pool, he can use *ant haul* (*Advanced Player's Guide* 202), *feather step* (*Advanced Player's Guide* 221), *longstrider*, *pass without trace*, or *tireless pursuit* (*Advanced Player's Guide* 249) as a spell-like ability (with a caster level equal to his monk level). This ability replaces slow fall.

Inscrutable (Su): At 5th level, the wanderer gains a supernatural air of mystery. The DC to gain information or insight into the wanderer with Diplomacy, Knowledge skills, or Sense Motive increases by 5. In addition, by spending 1 point from his ki pool, the wanderer gains *nondetection* for 24 hours with a caster level equal to his monk level. This ability replaces high jump.

Wanderer's Wisdom (Ex): At 7th level, the wanderer can dispense excellent advice in the form of philosophical proverbs and parables. As a swift action, the wanderer can inspire courage or inspire competence as a bard of his monk level by spending 2 points from his ki pool. This affects one creature within 30 feet and lasts a number of rounds equal to the wanderer's Wisdom modifier (minimum 1 round). This ability is language-dependent. This ability replaces wholeness of body.

Disappear Unnoticed (Ex): At 12th level, the wanderer may use Stealth to hide even while being directly observed or when no cover or concealment is available, as long as he is adjacent to at least one creature of his size or larger, by spending 1 point from his ki pool. This effect lasts until the beginning of the wanderer's next turn and may be continued in consecutive rounds by spending 1 ki point each round. This ability replaces abundant step.

Free Step (Su): At 13th level, the wanderer gains continuous *freedom of movement* as a continuous spell-like ability. This ability replaces diamond soul.

NEW RACIAL RULES

The following options are available to humans. At the GM's discretion, other appropriate races may also make use of some of these.

Human Equipment

Humans have access to the following equipment.

Training Harness: This specialized gear must be tailored to a specific type of animal, using Table 6–8 on page 153 of the *Core Rulebook*. A training harness provides a +2 bonus on Handle Animal checks made with an animal wearing it.

Whip, Training: This short lash has a reach of only 10 feet, but is otherwise identical to a normal whip (*Core Rulebook* 149). The wielder gains a +2 circumstance bonus on Handle Animal checks to push a trained animal and on Intimidate checks made to demoralize any animal as long as the animal is within the whip's reach. When using the whip to demoralize a trained animal, the wielder may choose to fascinate the animal rather than causing it to become shaken for the same duration as the shaken condition, but the fascinate effect ends if line of sight between the wielder and the animal is broken.

Human Equipment

Item	Cost	Weight
Training harness	10 gp	10 lbs.
Whip, training	5 gp	2 lbs.

Human Feats

Humans have access to the following feats.

Bestow Luck

You are extremely lucky and sometimes your allies are as well.

Prerequisites: Defiant Luck, Inexplicable Luck, human.

Benefit: You gain an extra use per day of your Defiant Luck ability. You can also use your Inexplicable Luck ability to grant an ally that can see and hear its benefit as an immediate action.

Critical Versatility (Combat)

An open mind and combat training grant versatility to your critical hits.

Prerequisites: Fighter level 11th, human.

Benefit: Once per day, you can spend 1 hour practicing maneuvers to gain one single critical feat that you meet the prerequisites for. You gain the benefits of the chosen critical feat until you choose to practice a different critical feat.

Dauntless Destiny

Your ability to avert disaster is impressive.

Prerequisites: Cha 13, Fearless Curiosity, Intimidate 10 ranks, human.

Benefit: You gain a +1 bonus on saving throws against effects with the emotion descriptor; this bonus stacks with those granted by Fearless Curiosity and Intimidating Confidence. In addition, once per day you may reroll a natural 1 on a saving throw or an attack roll. If your reroll results in a successful saving throw or attack roll, as a free action you can make an Intimidate check to demoralize the target of your attack or the creature that forced you to make a saving throw, as long as the creature is within 30 feet and can see and hear you. This effect does not apply on saving throws against traps or other objects. This does not stack with other effects that allow you to reroll a saving throw or an attack roll. You may only make one reroll.

Defiant Luck

You can sometimes defiantly shrug off spells and attacks that would kill a lesser creature.

Prerequisite: Human.

Benefit: Once per day, after you roll a natural 1 on a saving throw or a critical hit is confirmed against you, you can either reroll that saving throw, or force the creature that confirmed the critical hit against you to reroll the critical confirmation roll. This does not stack with other effects that allow you to reroll a saving throw or an attack roll. You may only make one reroll.

Special: If you are using the optional hero point system (*Advanced Player's Guide* 322–324), you can also spend 1 hero point when a critical hit is confirmed against you to have the opponent reroll the critical hit confirmation roll.

Fast Learner

You progress gain extra versatility.

Prerequisites: Int 13, human.

Benefit: When you gain a level in a favored class, you gain both +1 hit point and +1 skill rank instead of choosing either one or the other benefit or you can choose an alternate class reward.

Fearless Curiosity

Your desire to see and experience the world overrides healthy caution.

Prerequisites: Cha 13, human.

Benefit: You gain a +1 bonus on saving throws against effects with the emotion descriptor. In addition, for any round in which you begin your turn affected by a fear effect, you gain a new save at the beginning of your turn to reduce the severity of the fear effect, from panicked to frightened, frightened to shaken, and shaken to unaffected.

Heroic Will

Your indomitable will breaks free from mental shackles.

Prerequisites: Iron Will, base Will save +4, human.

Benefit: Once per day as a standard action, you may attempt a new saving throw against a harmful condition requiring a Will save that is affecting you. If you are dominated, controlled, or cannot take an action because of the effect against which you are trying to make a new saving throw, you can make this saving throw at the start of the turn as no action, but on a success, your turn ends. You cannot use this feat to remove instantaneous effects, effects that do not require a Will save, or effects that do not allow a saving throw.

Huntmaster

You are an expert trainer of horses, hounds, falcons, or hunting cats.

Prerequisites: Handle Animal 1 rank; either the animal companion, divine bond (mount), or mount class feature; human.

Benefit: If you have the animal companion class feature, pick one of the following types of animal companions that this feat affects: bird, dog, small cat, or horse. If you have the divine bond (mount) or mount class feature, this feat always affects horses.

You gain a +2 bonus on Handle Animal and Knowledge (nature) checks with creatures of that type of animal. Furthermore, you are treated as one level higher when determining the abilities of your animal companion or mount, as long as it is of the chosen type.

Improved Improvisation

You are masterful in your improvisation.

Prerequisites: Int 13, Fast Learner, Improvisation, human.

Benefit: Your nonproficiency penalty with weapons, armor, and shields is halved. In addition, the bonus on all skill checks for skills you have no ranks in increases to +4 instead of +2.

Improvisation

You can figure out how to do almost anything.

Prerequisites: Int 13, Fast Learner, human.

Benefit: You gain a +2 bonus on all skill checks for skills you have no ranks in. Furthermore, you can use all trained skills untrained.

Inexplicable Luck

Others are often dumfounded by your luck.

Prerequisites: Defiant Luck, human.

Benefit: Once per day, as a free action before a roll is made, you gain a +8 bonus on any single d20 roll. You can also use this ability after the roll is made, but if you do, this bonus is reduced to +4.

Intimidating Confidence

You have boundless faith in your success.

Prerequisites: Cha 13, Fearless Curiosity, Intimidate 5 ranks, human.

Benefit: You gain a +1 bonus on saving throws against effects with the emotion descriptor; this bonus stacks with the bonus granted by Fearless Curiosity. When you confirm a critical hit, as a free action you can make an Intimidate check to demoralize one creature you threaten. If you have the Dazzling Display feat, you can make Intimidate checks to demoralize all creatures you threaten instead. You gain a +2 bonus on this check if your weapon has a ×3 critical modifier, or +4 if it has a ×4 critical modifier.

Martial Mastery (Combat)

You broaden your study of weapons to encompass multiple similar weapons.

Prerequisites: Martial Versatility, fighter level 16th, human.

Benefit: Each combat feat you have that applies to a specific weapon (e.g., Weapon Focus) can be used with all weapons in the same weapon group (*Ultimate Combat* 45).

Martial Versatility (Combat)

You further broaden your study of weapons to encompass multiple similar weapons.

Prerequisites: Fighter level 4th, human.

Benefit: Choose one combat feat you know that applies to a specific weapon (e.g., Weapon Focus). You can use that feat with any weapon within the same weapon group.

Special: You may take this feat more than once. Each time it applies to a different feat.

Surge of Success

Your success drives your further actions.

Prerequisite: Human.

Benefit: When you confirm a critical hit or roll a natural 20 on a saving throw, you gain a +2 circumstance bonus on a single attack roll, saving throw, skill check, or ability check of your choice before the end of your next turn. You must choose to use this bonus before you make the attack roll, saving throw, skill check, or ability check.

Human Magic Items

Humans have access to the following magic items.

BELT OF FORAGING

Aura faint divination; **CL** 3rd

Slot belt; **Price** 6,000 gp; **Weight** 1 lb.

DESCRIPTION

This belt allows its wearer to easily forage while in the wilderness. As long as the wearer of this belt has at least 1 rank in Survival, he need not make a check to get along in the wild;

he always succeeds at that Survival check as long as he moves at half his overland speed. He can still choose to make that check to provide food and water for one other creature for every 2 points by which his result exceeds DC 10. Furthermore, he can instead make a DC 20 Survival check to get along in the wild while moving at full speed instead of half speed. While doing so, he can provide food and water for one other creature for every 2 points by which his check result exceeds 20.

CONSTRUCTION

Requirements Craft Wondrous Item, *detect animals and plants*, creator must have at least 1 rank in Survival; **Cost** 3,000 gp

CROWN OF CONQUEST

Aura moderate enchantment; **CL** 7th

Slot head; **Price** 24,600 gp; **Weight** 3 lbs.

DESCRIPTION

This crown of steel and gold projects an aura of menacing power. The wearer gains a +4 competence bonus on Intimidate checks, and whenever he confirms a critical hit, the crown creates a *prayer* effect centered on the crown's wearer (caster level 5th).

If the wearer of the crown has the Leadership feat, he gains a +1 bonus to his Leadership score and any follower or cohort of the wearer gains a +1 bonus on attack rolls and saving throws against fear effects while within line of sight of the wearer.

CONSTRUCTION

Requirements Craft Wondrous Item, *bless*, *eagle's splendor*, *prayer*; **Cost** 12,300 gp

CROWN OF SWORDS

Aura faint evocation; **CL** 3rd

Slot head; **Price** 6,000 gp; **Weight** 3 lbs.

DESCRIPTION

This radiant crown of steel is bedecked with miniature mithral swords. A *crown of swords* can be used up to 10 times per day. When struck in combat, the wearer may spend one use as an immediate action to create a longsword-shaped *spiritual weapon* that then attacks her attacker. On the wearer's next turn, she may spend one additional use each round to continue attacking that target with the *spiritual weapon*; the *spiritual weapon* cannot be redirected and disappears if the target is killed or moves out of range. Multiple *spiritual weapons* may be created (even attacking the same target) if the wearer is attacked in subsequent rounds.

CONSTRUCTION

Requirements Craft Wondrous Item, *spiritual weapon*; **Cost** 3,000 gp

ROD OF STEADFAST RESOLVE

Aura moderate abjuration; **CL** 9th

Slot none; **Price** 38,305 gp; **Weight** 5 lbs.

DESCRIPTION

This rod functions as a +2 *light mace*. It takes the form of a light mace with a head in the shape of a clenched fist. While a creature wields this rod, it grants all its allies within a 20-foot-radius burst a +2 morale bonus on saving throws against fear and emotion effects, or a +4 morale bonus on such saves if the ally has the human subtype.

Also, once per day as an immediate action, the wielder can activate the rod to allow himself or a single ally within the rod's aura to reroll a failed saving throw against a spell or effect with the fear or emotion descriptor. The affected creature must take the result of the reroll, even if it is worse.

CONSTRUCTION

Requirements Craft Rod, *bless*, *calm emotion*, the creator must have the human subtype; **Cost** 19,305 gp

Human Spells

Humans have access to the following spells.

BESTOW INSIGHT

School enchantment (compulsion); **Level** bard 2, cleric 3, inquisitor 2, sorcerer/wizard 2, witch 2
Casting Time 1 standard action
Component V, S
Range touch
Target one creature touched
Duration 1 minute/level

When casting this spell, choose a single skill that you have at least one rank in. The target gains a +2 insight bonus on skill checks with this skill and is considered trained in that skill. The insight bonus increases by 1 for every four levels of the caster (maximum +6). Furthermore, once before the spell's duration, the target can choose to roll two checks and take the greater result. Doing so ends the spell's other effects.

BLACK MARK

School necromancy [curse, fear]; **Level** druid 7, witch 7
Casting Time 1 standard action
Components V, S, M (a flask of seawater)
Range touch
Target one creature
Duration permanent
Saving Throw Will negates; **Spell Resistance** yes

You mark the target with a black marking on its skin; the mark's exact appearance determined by you, but can be no larger than your hand. The *black mark* functions as a *mark of justice*, and when the mark is activated, the target becomes shaken anytime it is on or in the water more than a 5 feet from shore. In addition, as long as the *black mark* is active, the target is affected as if subject to *nature's exile* (*Advanced Player's Guide* 233), but all creatures with the aquatic or water subtype or with a swim speed are made

hostile, even those not of the animal type, though non-aquatic animals are not.

OLD SALT'S CURSE

School necromancy [curse]; **Level** druid 5, witch 5
Casting Time 1 standard action
Components V, S, M (a flask of seawater)
Range touch
Target one creature
Duration permanent
Saving Throw Will negates; **Spell Resistance** yes

You inflict a curse of the roiling sea upon the target, making it permanently sickened. Anytime the target is on or in the water more than a mile from shore, it also becomes staggered with seasickness. This curse cannot be dispelled, though *remove curse* or *break enchantment* can negate it.

2 FEATURED RACES

own!" Seoni yelled. In her hand, a marble-sized ball of flame sprang into being, roaring to consume her whole fist as she lifted it high and—

A rough arm shoved her back. "Are you insane?" Alahazra asked. "Do you really think fire's going to hurt an ifrit?"

Before them, the flaming warrior grinned, priceless scrolls turning to ash as they brushed against her glowing legs. She raised her sword.

"She's just an overgrown campfire," Alahazra said. She leveled her staff, its head crackling with lightning. "And what puts out fires better than a thunderstorm?"

FEATURED RACES

While the seven core races are the primary focus of the Pathfinder Roleplaying Game, they're not the only ones suitable to be played as characters. Other, even stranger races help populate the world, and—with the GM's permission—also work well as player character races, creating fun and exciting new roleplaying opportunities. This chapter details the most common of such races. From the nimble catfolk to the fiery ifrits and scavenging, birdlike tengus, these races have just as much motivation to be adventurers as do elves, gnomes, and humans. And while they may not be as common in the major population hubs of the Pathfinder campaign setting, each of the races detailed in this chapter presents its own unique background and abilities.

While many of these races are considered civilized, some are typically viewed as monsters, and may prove interesting challenges for roleplaying and character interaction. When playing drow, kobolds, orcs, or other such races, it is often best for party dynamics to take on the roles of characters who rebel against the norms of their races and societies—creatures who do not agree with their often brutal cultures, and instead wish to carve out a better existence for themselves among other races. When playing these races, even more so than for many other races, it is important to work with your GM to determine character motivations and backgrounds that work in the campaign.

This chapter provides details on the following races.

Aasimars: Creatures blessed with a celestial bloodline, aasimars seem human except for some exotic quality that betrays their otherworldly origin. While aasimars are nearly always beautiful, something simultaneously a part of and apart from humanity, not all of them are good, though very few are evil.

Catfolk: A race of graceful explorers, catfolk are both clannish and curious by nature. They tend to get along with races that treat them well and respect their boundaries. They love exploration, both physical and intellectual, and tend to be natural adventurers.

Dhampirs: The accursed spawn of vampires, dhampirs are living creatures tainted with the curse of undeath, which causes them to take damage from positive energy and gain healing from negative energy. While many members of this race embrace their dark sides, others are powerfully driven to rebel against their taint and hunt down and destroy vampires and their ilk.

Drow: Dark reflections of surface elves, drow are shadowy hunters who strive to snuff out the world's light. Drow are powerful magical creatures who typically serve demons, and only their chaotic nature stops them from becoming an even greater menace. A select few forsake their race's depraved and nihilistic society to walk a heroic path.

Fetchlings: Long ago, fetchlings were humans exiled to the Shadow Plane, but that plane's persistent umbra has transformed them into a race apart. These creatures have developed an ability to meld into the shadows and have a natural affinity for shadow magic. Fetchlings—who call themselves *kayal*—often serve as emissaries between the inhabitants of the Shadow Plane and the Material Plane.

Goblins: Crazy pyromaniacs with a tendency to commit unspeakable violence, goblins are the smallest of the goblinoid races. While they are a fun-loving race, their humor is often cruel and hurtful. Adventuring goblins constantly wrestle with their darkly mischievous side in order to get along with others. Few are truly successful.

Hobgoblins: These creatures are the most disciplined and militaristic of the goblinoid races. Tall, tough as nails, and strongly built, hobgoblins would be a boon to any adventuring group, were it not for the fact that they tend to be cruel and malicious, and often keep slaves.

Ifrits: Ifrits are a race descended from mortals and the strange inhabitants of the Plane of Fire. Their physical traits and personalities often betray their fiery origins, and they tend to be restless, independent, and imperious. Frequently driven from cities for their ability to manipulate flame, ifrits make powerful fire sorcerers and warriors who can wield flame like no other race.

Kobolds: Considering themselves the scions of dragons, kobolds have diminutive statures but massive egos. A select few can take on more draconic traits than their kin, and many are powerful sorcerers, canny alchemists, and cunning rogues.

Orcs: Savage, brutish, and hard to kill, orcs are often the scourge of far-flung wildernesses and cavern deeps. Many orcs become fearsome barbarians, as they are muscular and prone to bloody rages. Those few who can control their bloodlust make excellent adventurers.

Oreads: Creatures of human ancestry mixed with the blood of creatures from the Plane of Earth, oreads are as strong and solid as stone. Often stubborn and steadfast, their unyielding nature makes it hard for them to get along with most races other than dwarves. Oreads make excellent warriors and sorcerers who can manipulate the raw power of stone and earth.

Ratfolk: These small, ratlike humanoids are clannish and nomadic masters of trade. Often tinkers and traders, they are more concerned with accumulating interesting trinkets than amassing wealth. Ratfolk often adventure to find new and interesting curiosities rather than coin.

Sylphs: Ethereal folk of elemental air, sylphs are the result of human blood mixed with that of airy elemental folk. Like ifrits, oreads, and undines, they can become powerful elemental sorcerers with command over their particular elemental dominion. They tend to be beautiful and lithe, and have a knack for eavesdropping.

Tengus: These crowlike humanoid scavengers excel in mimicry and swordplay. Flocking into densely populated cities, tengus occasionally join adventuring groups out of curiosity or necessity. Their impulsive nature and strange habits can often be unnerving to those who are not used to them.

Tieflings: Diverse and often despised by humanoid society, tieflings are mortals stained with the blood of fiends. Other races rarely trust them, and this lack of empathy usually causes tieflings to embrace the evil, depravity, and rage that seethe within their corrupt blood. A select few see the struggle to smother such dark desires as motivation for grand heroism.

Undines: Like their cousins, the ifrits, oreads, and sylphs, undines are humans touched by planar elements. They are the scions of elemental water, equally graceful both on land and in water. Undines are adaptable and resistant to cold, and have an affinity for water magic.

GENERAL DESCRIPTION

Each race's entry begins with a general description of the race followed by specific entries for the race's physical description, society, relations with other races, alignment and religion, and common motivations for adventuring members of the race.

RACIAL TRAITS

Each race's entry features a sidebar listing the race's standard racial traits. This information includes the race's type, size, vision, and base speed, as well as a number of other traits common to most members of the race. With your GM's permission, you will also have the option to exchange these standard racial traits for a number of alternate racial traits, the rules for which are provided in the section below.

ALTERNATE RACIAL TRAITS

Members of each race can swap standard racial traits for the alternative racial traits listed in this section. Each alternate racial trait lists which standard trait it replaces. The full rules for swapping traits can be found in Chapter 1: Core Races.

FAVORED CLASS OPTIONS

Each race can take the listed favored class options instead of the normal favored class rewards (either +1 hp or +1 skill rank). The full rules for favored class options can be found in Chapter 1: Core Races.

RACIAL ARCHETYPES

This section presents two archetypes for each of the expanded races, with the exception of the kobold entry, where both an archetype and a sorcerer bloodline are

presented. Typically, only members of the section's race can take the listed archetype or bloodline, though such options rarely interact with the racial traits or alternate racial traits of that race. An archetype usually features a thematic link to the race, granting it class features that complement the abilities and the background of the race. Because adventurers are often societal outliers, sometimes these archetypes feature a theme that is the exception to the norm for racial tendencies. The class for each archetype or bloodline is listed in parentheses.

Aasimars: Purifier (oracle), tranquil guardian (paladin)

Catfolk: Cat burglar (rogue), nimble guardian (monk)

Dhampirs: Cruoromancer (wizard), kinslayer (inquisitor)

Drow: Cavern sniper (fighter), demonic apostle (cleric)

Fetchlings: Dusk stalker (ranger), shadow caller (summoner)

Goblins: Feral gnasher (barbarian), fire bomber (alchemist)

Hobgoblins: Fell rider (cavalier), ironskin monk (monk)

Ifrits: Immolator (inquisitor), wishcrafter (sorcerer)

Kobolds: Bushwhacker (gunslinger), kobold sorcerer (sorcerer bloodline)

Orcs: Dirty fighter (fighter), scarred witch doctor (witch)

Oreads: Shaitan binder (summoner), student of stone (monk)

Ratfolk: Gulch gunner (gunslinger), plague bringer (alchemist)

Sylphs: Sky druid (druid), wind listener (wizard)

Tengus: Shigenjo (oracle), swordmaster (rogue)

Tieflings: Fiend flayer (magus), fiendish vessel (cleric)

Undines: Undine adept (druid), watersinger (bard)

NEW RACIAL RULES

The final section of each race's entry provides new rules options for the race beyond archetypes, detailed in the following four categories.

Equipment: The equipment section for each race provides new rules for standard and alchemical equipment available to the race.

Feats: This section provides a host of new racial feats for members of this race. All of these feats have a race listed in their prerequisites, so members of other races cannot take them.

Magic Items: Magic items provided in this section are often created and used exclusively by members of the race. Some have effects that interact with racial traits, but others have broader uses, and can be used by members of other races.

Spells: The spells in this section are common to spellcasting members of this race. Sometimes they only target members of the race, but often they are just the race's well-guarded secrets; members of other races can learn to cast them with the GM's permission.

Aasimars

Aasimars are humans with a significant amount of celestial or other good outsider blood in their ancestry. While not always benevolent, aasimars are more inclined toward acts of kindness rather than evil, and they gravitate toward faiths or organizations associated with celestials. Aasimar heritage can lie dormant for generations, only to appear suddenly in the child of two apparently human parents. Most societies interpret aasimar births as good omens, though it must be acknowledged that some aasimars take advantage of the reputation of their kind, brutally subverting the expectations of others with acts of terrifying cruelty or abject venality. "It's always the one you least suspect" is the axiom these evil aasimars live by, and they often lead double lives as upstanding citizens or false heroes, keeping their corruption well hidden. Thankfully, these few are the exception and not the rule.

Physical Description: Aasimars look mostly human except for some minor physical trait that reveals their unusual heritage. Typical aasimar features include hair that shines like metal, jewel-toned eyes, lustrous skin color, or even glowing, golden halos.

Society: Aasimars cannot truly be said to have an independent society of their own. As an offshoot of humanity, they adopt the societal norms around them, though most find themselves drawn to those elements of society that work for the redress of injustice and the assuagement of suffering. This sometimes puts them on the wrong side of the law in more tyrannical societies, but aasimars can be careful and cunning when necessary, able to put on a dissembling guise to divert the attention of oppressors elsewhere. While corrupt aasimars may be loners or may establish secret societies to conceal their involvement in crime, righteous aasimars are often found congregating in numbers as part of good-aligned organizations, especially (though not always) churches and religious orders.

Relations: Aasimars are most common and most comfortable in human communities. This is especially true of those whose lineage is more distant and who bear only faint marks of their heavenly ancestry. It is unclear why the touch of the celestial is felt so much more strongly in humanity than other races, though it may be that humanity's inherent adaptability and affinity for change is responsible for the evolution of aasimars as a distinct race. Perhaps the endemic racial traits of other races are too deeply bred, too strongly present, and too resistant to change. Whatever dalliances other races may have had with the denizens of the upper planes, the progeny of such couplings are vanishingly rare and have never bred true.

However, even if they generally tend toward human societies, aasimars can become comfortable in virtually any environment. They have an easy social grace and are disarmingly personable. They get on well with half-elves, who share a similar not-quite-human marginal status, though their relations are often less cordial with half-orcs, who have no patience for aasimars' overly pretty words and faces. Elven courtiers sometimes dismiss aasimars as unsophisticated, and criticize them for relying on natural charm to overcome faux pas. Perhaps of all the known races, gnomes find aasimars most fascinating, and have an intense appreciation for their varied appearances as well as the mystique surrounding their celestial heritage.

Alignment and Religion: Aasimars are most often of good alignment, though this isn't necessarily universal, and aasimars that have turned their back on righteousness may fall into an unfathomable abyss of depravity. For the most part, however, aasimars favor deities of honor, valor, protection, healing, and refuge, or simple and prosaic faiths of home, community, and family. Some also follow the paths of art, music, and lore, finding truth and wisdom in beauty and learning.

Adventurers: Aasimars frequently become adventurers, as they often do not quite feel at home in human society and feel the pull of some greater destiny. Clerics, oracles, and paladins are most plentiful in their ranks, though bards, sorcerers, and summoners are not uncommon among those with a fondness for arcane magic. Aasimar barbarians are rare, but when born into such tribes they often rise to leadership and encourage their clans to embrace celestial totems.

Male Names: Aritian, Beltin, Cernan, Cronwier, Eran, Ilamin, Maudril, Okrin, Parant, Tural, Wyran, Zaigan.

Female Names: Arken, Arsinoe, Davina, Drinma, Imesah, Masozi, Nijena, Niramour, Ondrea, Rhialla, Valtyra.

ALTERNATE RACIAL TRAITS

The following racial traits may be selected instead of existing aasimar racial traits. Consult your GM before selecting any of these new options.

Celestial Crusader: Some aasimars follow their destiny to war against the powers of ultimate evil. These individuals gain a +1 insight bonus on attack rolls and to AC against evil outsiders and a +2 racial bonus on Knowledge (planes) and Spellcraft checks to identify evil outsiders or items or effects created by evil outsiders; they may use these skills untrained for this purpose. This racial trait replaces celestial resistance and skilled.

Deathless Spirit: Particularly strong-willed aasimars possess celestial spirits capable of resisting the powers of death. They gain resistance 5 against negative energy damage. They do not lose hit points when they gain a negative level, and they gain a +2 racial bonus on saving throws against death effects, energy drain, negative energy, and spells or spell-like abilities of the necromancy school. This racial trait replaces celestial resistance.

Exalted Resistance: An aasimar with this racial trait gains spell resistance equal to 5 + her level against spells and spell-like abilities with the evil descriptor, as well as any spells and spell-like abilities cast by evil outsiders. This racial trait replaces celestial resistance.

Halo: Some aasimars possess the ability to manifest halos. An aasimar with this racial trait can create *light* centered on her head at will as a spell-like ability. When using her halo, she gains a +2 circumstance bonus on Intimidate checks against evil creatures and on saving throws against becoming blinded or dazzled. This racial trait replaces the darkvision racial trait.

Heavenborn: Born in the celestial realms, aasimars with this racial trait gain a +2 bonus on Knowledge (planes) checks and they cast spells with the good or light descriptor at +1 caster level. This racial trait replaces the skilled and spell-like ability racial traits.

Immortal Spark: Aasimars with this racial trait defy the powers of death. They gain a +2 bonus on Knowledge (history) checks and saving throws against death effects and can use *lesser age resistance* (*Pathfinder RPG Ultimate Magic* 205) once per day as a spell-like ability. This racial trait replaces the skilled and spell-like ability racial traits.

Incorruptible: Occasionally, aasimars arise with the ability to further ward away evil. Aasimars with this racial trait can cast *corruption resistance* (*Pathfinder RPG Advanced Player's Guide* 212) against evil once per day as a spell-like ability. If an aasimar uses this ability on herself, the duration increases to 1 hour per level. This racial trait replaces the spell-like ability racial trait.

Scion of Humanity: Some aasimars' heavenly ancestry is extremely distant. An aasimar with this racial trait counts as an outsider (native) and a humanoid (human) for any effect related to race, including feat prerequisites and spells that affect humanoids. She can pass for human without using the Disguise skill. This

racial trait replaces the Celestial language and alters the native subtype.

Truespeaker: There are some aasimars whose language transcends all boundaries. They gain a +2 bonus on Linguistics and Sense Motive checks, and they learn two languages each time they gain a rank in Linguistics. This racial trait replaces skilled.

FAVORED CLASS OPTIONS

The following options are available to all aasimars who have the listed favored class, and unless otherwise stated, the bonus applies each time you select the favored class reward.

Bard: Choose one bardic performance; treat the bard as +1/2 level higher when determining the effects of that performance.

Cavalier: Add +1/4 to the cavalier's bonus on damage against targets of his challenge.

Cleric: Add +1/2 to damage when using positive energy against undead or using Alignment Channel to damage evil outsiders.

Inquisitor: Add +1/2 on Intimidate, Knowledge, and Sense Motive checks made against outsiders.

Oracle: Add +1/2 to the oracle's level for the purpose of determining the effects of one revelation.

Paladin: Add +1/6 to the morale bonus on saving throws provided by the paladin's auras.

Sorcerer: Add +1/4 to the sorcerer's caster level when casting spells with the good descriptor.

AASIMAR RACIAL TRAITS

+2 Wisdom, +2 Charisma: Aasimars are insightful, confident, and personable.

Native Outsider: Aasimars are outsiders with the native subtype.

Medium: Aasimars are Medium creatures and have no bonuses or penalties due to their size.

Normal Speed: Aasimars have a base speed of 30 feet.

Darkvision: Aasimars can see in the dark up to 60 feet.

Skilled: Aasimars have a +2 racial bonus on Diplomacy and Perception checks.

Spell-Like Ability: Aasimars can use *daylight* once per day as a spell-like ability (caster level equal to the aasimar's class level).

Celestial Resistance: Aasimars have acid resistance 5, cold resistance 5, and electricity resistance 5.

Languages: Aasimars begin play speaking Common and Celestial. Aasimars with high Intelligence scores can choose from the following languages: Draconic, Dwarven, Elven, Gnome, Halfling, and Sylvan.

Summoner: Add DR 1/evil to the summoner's eidolon. Each additional time the summoner selects this benefit, the DR/evil increases by +1/2 (maximum DR 10/evil).

RACIAL ARCHETYPES

The following racial archetypes are available to aasimars.

Purifier (Oracle)

The purifier seeks out signs of possession or mind control that manifest from unwilling (and often unwitting) servants for fiendish corruptors and their mortal minions. A purifier seeks liberation of mind, body, and spirit from the bondage of sin and the taint of the unholy. A purifier gains the following class features.

Recommended Mysteries: ancestor, battle, heavens, lore.

Bonus Spells: *veil of heaven* (2nd), *confess* (*Advanced Player's Guide* 212; 4th), *cast out* (*Advanced Player's Guide* 210; 6th), *denounce* (*Advanced Player's Guide* 215; 8th), *dispel evil* (10th), *banishment* (12th), *holy word* (14th), *mind blank* (16th), *freedom* (18th).

Diminished Spellcasting: A purifier can use one fewer spell per day of each level and does not automatically learn cure or inflict spells. Her number of oracle spells known is unchanged.

Revelations: A purifier must take the following revelations at the listed levels.

See Sin (Sp): At 3rd level, a purifier gains a bonus equal to 1/2 her oracle level on Sense Motive checks to sense enchantments, which she can make as a full-round action. She also gains a bonus equal to 1/2 her oracle level on Spellcraft checks to identify enchantment school spells and spells with the curse or emotion descriptor (see page 251 of *Ultimate Magic* for spells in the *Pathfinder RPG Core Rulebook* and *Advanced Player's Guide* that have the curse or emotion descriptor).

Celestial Armor (Su): At 7th level, a purifier's armor takes on a golden or silvery sheen and becomes light as a feather. Her armor weighs half as much as long as she wears it, and she also gains armor training as a fighter 4 levels lower than her oracle level. At 11th level, a purifier gains heavy armor proficiency.

Sin Eater (Su): At 11th level, a purifier can consume a curse, enchantment, or emotion effect by touch as a full-round action. She can do this a number of times per day equal to her Charisma modifier, and must make a Charisma check with a bonus equal to her oracle level against a DC of 11 + the caster level of the effect (or the Hit Dice of the creator for a supernatural effect). If the check succeeds, the effect is negated; however, the purifier is sickened for 1d4 rounds.

If the target is possessed (such as by a *magic jar* effect or a ghost's malevolence ability), the possessor is forced out on a successful check. Whether the check succeeds or fails, the possessor is sickened for 2d4 rounds.

Sacred Scourge (Su): At 5th level, a purifier may channel holy power to harm evil outsiders as a cleric of her level using the Alignment Channel feat. She may use this ability a number of times per day equal to 1 + her Charisma modifier.

Holy Terror (Su): At 9th level, a purifier may use her sacred scourge to panic evil outsiders as if using the Turn Undead feat against undead.

Celestial Master (Su): At 13th level, a purifier may use her sacred scourge to compel good outsiders to serve her, as if using the Command Undead feat against undead.

Tranquil Guardian (Paladin)

A tranquil guardian is a missionary of peace and tranquility, a soothing voice of succor in a violent and dangerous world. A tranquil guardian gains the following class features.

Touch of Serenity (Su): At 1st level, a tranquil guardian gains Touch of Serenity (*Advanced Player's Guide* 172) as a bonus feat, even if she does not meet the prerequisites. At 6th level, and every six levels thereafter, the duration of a tranquil guardian's Touch of Serenity increases by 1 round. Each round on its turn, the target may attempt a new Will save to end the effect. The duration does not stack; only the longest remaining duration applies. This ability replaces smite evil.

Serene Strike (Su): At 3rd level, when a tranquil guardian confirms a critical hit, she may convert all damage from her attack to nonlethal damage, and when she does, she can activate Touch of Serenity through her weapon or unarmed strike. Using serene strike is a free action. This ability replaces aura of courage.

Divine Bond (Su): A tranquil guardian who chooses a weapon as her divine bond may only increase her weapon's enhancement bonus or add the following properties to her weapon: *conductive* (*Advanced Player's Guide* 286), *defending*, *disruptive*, *grayflame* (*Advanced Player's Guide* 288), or *merciful*.

Aura of Calm (Su): At 8th level, a tranquil guardian is immune to all spells and spell-like abilities with the emotion descriptor, as well as all fear effects. Each ally within 10 feet of her gains a +4 morale bonus on saving throws against these effects.

This ability functions only while the tranquil guardian is conscious, not if she is unconscious or dead. This ability replaces aura of resolve.

Waves of Peace (Su): At 11th level, a tranquil guardian may expend 2 uses of her Touch of Serenity to affect each opponent within 5 feet of her with that effect. She does not need to touch the creature for the effect to take hold. This ability replaces aura of justice.

Apostle of Peace (Su): At 20th level, a tranquil guardian's DR increases to 10/evil, and whenever she channels positive energy or uses lay on hands to heal, she heals the maximum possible amount. In addition, any creature struck by her Touch of Serenity, even if it saves, must make an additional Will save (DC 10 + 1/2 her tranquil guardian level + her Charisma modifier) the next time it tries to attack. If it fails this save, the attack (including spells or special abilities) automatically fails. This ability replaces holy champion.

NEW RACIAL RULES

The following options are available to aasimars. At the GM's discretion, other appropriate races may make use of some of these new rules.

Aasimar Equipment

Aasimars have access to the following equipment.

Ambrosia: Upon consumption, this heavenly elixir, brewed from holy water and blessed herbs, grants a +2 sacred bonus on saving throws against negative energy, energy drain, and death effects for 1 hour, including saves to remove negative levels. Ambrosia affects undead and evil outsiders as holy water.

Anointing Oil: This sacred oil, infused with aromatic spices and distilled holy water, may be applied to a creature while casting a harmless divine spell with a range of touch, increasing the casting time to a full-round action but also increasing the caster's effective caster level by +1 for that spell.

Celestial Censer: This blessed thurible holds up to 10 pieces of incense, and burns at a rate of 1 stick per hour. If a smokestick is added to the incense in the censer while it burns, creatures with the evil subtype are dazzled for as long as they remain within the area of the resulting smoke.

Celestial Lamp: This polished lantern contains a *continual flame* and sheds light as a common lamp. If its font of consecrated crystal and metalwork is filled with holy water, the lamp's light is sanctified for 24 hours, adding a +1 bonus to the save DC of channeled positive energy or energy channeled to harm evil outsiders within a 30-foot radius.

Incense: This aromatic resin, imbued with fragrant oils, is often formed into sticks, cones, or balls and burned in ceremonies or during meditation. A piece of incense burns for 1 hour.

Aasimar Equipment

Item	Cost	Weight	Craft DC
Ambrosia (vial)	100 gp	1 lb.	25
Anointing oil	25 gp	1 lb.	20
Celestial censer	50 gp	3 lbs.	—
Celestial lamp	300 gp	2 lbs.	25
Incense (10 sticks)	10 gp	1 lb.	—

Aasimar Feats

Aasimars have access to the following feats.

Angel Wings

Feathered wings sprout from your back.

Prerequisites: Angelic Blood, aasimar, character level 10th.

Benefit: You gain a pair of gleaming feathered wings that grant a fly speed of 30 feet (average maneuverability) if wearing light armor or unencumbered, or 20 feet (poor maneuverability) with a medium or heavy load or medium or heavy armor. Fly is a class skill for you.

Angelic Blood

Your blood is infused with holy power.

Prerequisites: Con 13, aasimar.

Benefit: You gain a +2 bonus on saving throws against effects with the evil descriptor and on Constitution checks to stabilize when you are reduced to negative hit points (but not dead). Furthermore, each time you take bleed or blood drain damage, each undead creature or creature with the evil subtype that is currently adjacent to you also takes 1 point of damage.

Angelic Flesh

Your skin shines like burnished metal.

Prerequisites: Angelic Blood, aasimar.

Benefit: You take a –2 penalty on Disguise and Stealth checks but gain one of the following benefits, depending on the metallic affinity of your flesh (choose one).

Brazen: You gain fire resistance 5 and a +2 bonus on saves against fire effects.

Golden: You gain a +2 bonus on saves against blindness, dazzling, patterns, and effects with the light descriptor. When you cast spells or use spell-like abilities that are from the illusion (pattern) subschool or have the light descriptor, you do so at +1 caster level.

Silver: You gain a +2 bonus on saves against paralysis, petrification, and poison, and your unarmed strikes or natural weapons count as silver for the purpose of overcoming damage reduction.

Steel: You gain a +1 natural armor bonus to AC, and your unarmed strikes or natural weapons count as cold iron for the purpose of overcoming damage reduction.

Celestial Servant

Rather than being a normal animal or beast, your companion or familiar hails from the heavenly realms.

Prerequisites: Aasimar, animal companion, familiar, or mount class feature.

Benefit: Your animal companion, familiar, or mount gains the celestial template and becomes a magical beast, though you may still treat it as an animal when using Handle Animal, wild empathy, or any other spells or class abilities that specifically affect animals.

Channel Force

Your channel is bolstered by your faith, allowing you to move and damage your foes.

Prerequisites: Aasimar, channel energy 2d6.

Benefit: When you channel energy to deal damage, you may choose to affect only a single target within 30 feet. In addition to dealing damage, if that single target fails its saving throw, you may pull or push (*Pathfinder RPG Bestiary* 303) the target up to 5 feet for every 2d6 points of channel energy damage you are capable of dealing.

Greater Channel Force

Your eruptions of divine power move your enemies.

Prerequisites: Channel Force, Improved Channel Force, aasimar, channel energy 6d6.

Benefit: When using Improved Channel Force, you can affect all creatures in a 30-foot-radius burst.

Heavenly Radiance

Your heavenly light can be used in a variety of ways.

Prerequisites: Aasimar, *daylight* spell-like ability, sufficiently high level (see below).

Benefit: You gain one additional use per day of *daylight*. Choose one spell from the table below; by expending a use of *daylight*, you may use this spell as a spell-like ability. To select a spell, you must meet the minimum character level for its listing in the table. The save DC for this spell is Charisma-based.

Spell-Like Ability	Minimum Character Level
Flare burst (*Advanced Player's Guide* 223)	1st
Wake of light (*Advanced Player's Guide* 254)	3rd
Searing light	5th
Wandering star motes (*Advanced Player's Guide* 255)	7th
Sunbeam (one beam only)	9th

Special: You may take this feat multiple times. Each time you select it, you gain an additional use of *daylight* and may select another spell from the table.

Improved Channel Force

You move your enemies within a beam of righteous energy.

Prerequisites: Channel Force, aasimar, channel energy 4d6.

Benefit: When using Channel Force, you can affect all creatures in a 60-foot line or a 30-foot cone-shaped burst. You must choose to either push or pull all creatures within the affected area that fail their saves.

Metallic Wings

Your wing feathers are made of gleaming metal.

Prerequisites: Angelic Blood, Angelic Flesh, Angel Wings, aasimar, character level 11th.

Benefit: You gain two wing attacks. These are secondary natural attacks that deal 1d4 points of slashing damage (or 1d3 if you are Small).

Aasimar Magic Items

Aasimars favor the following magic items.

CELESTIAL SHIELD

Aura moderate evocation [good]; **CL** 7th
Slot shield; **Price** 13,170 gp; **Weight** 7 lbs.

DESCRIPTION

This bright silver or gold +2 *blinding heavy steel shield* is impossibly light and handy despite its size. It has no armor check penalty or arcane spell failure chance, and it allows the wielder to use *feather fall* on himself once per day. A creature wearing *celestial armor* while wielding a *celestial shield* may command the armor to provide *overland flight* rather than *fly* once per day.

CONSTRUCTION

Requirements Craft Magic Arms and Armor, *feather fall*, *overland flight*; **Cost** 6,670 gp

ELYSIAN SHIELD

Aura strong conjuration; **CL** 13th
Slot shield; **Price** 52,620 gp; **Weight** 45 lbs.

DESCRIPTION

This +2 *ghost touch tower shield* is engraved with funerary runes depicting the peaceful rest of the contented dead. The wielder of an *elysian shield* is immune to the create spawn ability of undead, and once per day as an immediate action can negate a single energy drain, ability drain, or ability damage attack by an undead creature. In addition, once per day as a standard action, the wielder can release a wave of positive energy that panics undead, as the Turn Undead feat (DC 20 Will negates).

CONSTRUCTION

Requirements Craft Magic Arms and Armor, Turn Undead, *death ward*, *etherealness*; **Cost** 26,390 gp

HALO OF MENACE

Aura moderate enchantment; **CL** 9th
Slot head; **Price** 84,000 gp; **Weight** 1 lb.

DESCRIPTION

When placed over the head, this halo of shimmering polished steel floats above it, though it still takes up the head slot. The halo constantly radiates a 20-foot-radius aura from its wearer. Any hostile creature within the aura must succeed at a DC 20 Will save or take a –2 penalties on attack rolls, saving throws, and AC for the next 24 hours or until it hits the wearer with an attack or damages it with a spell, spell-like ability, or supernatural ability. Chaotic creatures take a –2 penalty on this saving throw. A creature that has resisted or broken the effect of the halo of menace cannot be affected by the same wearer's aura for 24 hours. The aura is a mind-affecting effect.

CONSTRUCTION

Requirements Craft Wondrous Item, *order's wrath*, creator must be an aasimar or an archon; **Cost** 42,000 gp

Aasimar Spells

Aasimars have access to the following spells.

SACRED SPACE

School evocation [good]; **Level** cleric 2, paladin 2

Casting Time 1 standard action
Components V, S, M (a vial of ambrosia)
Range close (25 ft. + 5 ft./2 levels)
Area 20-ft.-radius emanation
Duration 2 hours/level
Saving Throw none; **Spell Resistance** no

This spell sanctifies an area with heavenly power. The DC to resist spells or spell-like abilities with the good descriptor or channeled energy that damages evil outsiders (as when using Alignment Channel) increases by +2. In addition, evil outsiders take a –1 penalty on attack rolls, damage rolls, and saving throws, and they cannot be called or summoned into a *sacred space*. If the *sacred space* contains an altar, shrine, or other permanent fixture dedicated to your deity, pantheon, or good-aligned higher power, the modifiers given above are doubled. You cannot cast *sacred space* in an area with a permanent fixture dedicated to a deity other than yours.

TRUESPEAK

School divination; **Level** bard 4, cleric 6, sorcerer/wizard 5, witch 5
Casting Time 1 standard action
Components V
Range personal
Target you
Duration 1 minute/level

You can communicate with any creature that is not mindless. As long as you can be heard, your speech is understandable to all creatures, each of which hears you as though you were conversing in its language or other natural mode of communication, and you hear their responses as though in your own native language. You may ask questions and receive answers, though this spell does not make creatures more friendly or cooperative than normal, and non-sentient creatures may give limited responses. While using *truespeak*, your language-dependent effects can affect any creature that is not mindless.

VEIL OF HEAVEN

School abjuration [good]; **Level** paladin 1
Casting Time 1 standard action
Components V, S, DF
Range personal or 5 ft.; see text
Target you or all creatures within 5 ft.; see text
Duration 10 minutes/level (D)
Saving Throw Will half; **Spell Resistance** none

You surround yourself with a veil of positive energy, making it harder for evil outsiders to harm you. For the duration of this spell, you gain a +2 sacred bonus to AC and on saves. Both of these bonuses apply only against attacks or effects created by outsiders with the evil subtype. You can dismiss this spell as a swift action to deal 1d8 points of damage + 1 point per paladin level to all such outsiders within 5 feet. A Will save halves this damage.

CATFOLK

Catfolk are a race of natural explorers who rarely tire of trailblazing, but such trailblazing is not limited merely to the search for new horizons in distant lands. Many catfolk see personal growth and development as equally valid avenues of exploration. While most catfolk are nimble, capable, and often active creatures, there is also a strong tendency among some catfolk to engage in quiet contemplation and study. Such individuals are interested in finding new solutions to age-old problems and questioning even the most steadfast philosophical certainties of the day. They are curious by nature, and catfolk culture never discourages inquisitiveness, but rather fosters and encourages it. Many are seen as quirky extroverts by members of other races, but within catfolk tribes there is no shame attached to minor peculiarities, eccentricities, or foolhardiness. All but the most inwardly focused catfolk enjoy being the center of attention, but not at the expense of their tribe, whether it's the one the catfolk are born into or the tribe they choose through the bonds of friendship with other creatures. Catfolk tend to be both generous and loyal to their family and friends.

Physical Description: In general, catfolk are lithe and slender, standing midway between dwarves and humans in stature. While clearly humanoid, they possess many feline features, including a coat of soft fine fur, slit pupils, and a sleek, slender tail. Their ears are pointed, but unlike those of elves, are more rounded and catlike. They manipulate objects as easily as any other humanoid, but their fingers terminate in small, sharp, retractable claws. These claws are typically not powerful enough to be used as weapons, but some members of the species—either by quirk of birth or from years of honing—can use them with deadly effect. Feline whiskers are not uncommon, but not universal, and hair and eye color vary greatly.

Society: While self-expression is an important aspect of catfolk culture, it is mitigated by a strong sense of community and group effort. In the wild, catfolk are a hunter-gatherer tribal people. The pursuit of personal power never comes before the health and wellbeing of the tribe. More than one race has underestimated this seemingly gentle people only to discover much too late that their cohesion also provides them great strength.

Catfolk prefer to be led by their most competent members, usually a council of sub-chieftains chosen by their peers, either though consensus or election. The sub-chiefs then choose a chieftain to lead in times of danger and to mediate disputes among the sub-chiefs. The chieftain is the most capable member of the tribe, and is often magically talented. Catfolk who settle in more urban and civilized areas still cling to a similar tribal structure, but often see friends outside the tribe, even those from other races, as part of their extended tribe. Within adventuring groups, catfolk who do not consider themselves the obvious choice as chieftain often defer to the person who most resembles their cultural ideal of a chieftain.

Relations: Adaptable and curious, catfolk get along with almost any race that extends reciprocal goodwill. They acclimate easily to halflings, humans, and especially elves. Catfolk and elves share a passionate nature, as well as a love of music, dance, and storytelling; elven communities often gently mentor catfolk tribes, though such elves are careful not to act in a patronizing manner toward their feline friends. Gnomes make natural companions for catfolk, as catfolk enjoy gnomes' strange and obsessive qualities. Catfolk are tolerant of kobolds as long as the reptilian beings respect the catfolk's boundaries. The feral nature of orcs stirs as much puzzlement as it does revulsion among catfolk, as they don't understand orcs' savagery and propensity for self-destruction. Half-orcs, on the other hand, intrigue catfolk, especially those half-orcs who strive to excel beyond the deleterious and hateful nature of their savage kin. Catfolk often view goblins and ratfolk as vermin, as they disdain the swarming and pernicious tendencies of those races.

Alignment and Religion: With community and unselfish cooperation at the center of their culture, as well as a good-natured curiosity and willingness to adapt to the customs of many other races, most catfolk tend toward good alignments. The clear majority of catfolk are also chaotic, as wisdom is not their strongest virtue; nevertheless, there are exceptions with cause. The gods Desna, Cayden Cailean, and Shelyn all speak to the souls of catfolk, and many tribes depict the latter two as catfolk themselves. The quest for self-improvement has led many an individual to explore different philosophies, including the worship of Irori.

Adventurers: Natural born trackers, the hunter-gatherer aspect of their tribes pushes many catfolk toward occupations as rangers and druids by default, but such roles don't always speak to their love of performance art, be it song, dance, or storytelling. Catfolk legends also speak of a rich tradition of great sorcerer heroes. Those catfolk who internalize their wanderlust often become wizards and monks, with many of those monks taking the path of the nimble guardian. While catfolk cavaliers and inquisitors are rare (steadfast dedication to a cause is often alien to the catfolk mindset) individuals who choose these paths are never looked down upon. Catfolk understand that exploration and self-knowledge can lead down many roads, and are accepting of nearly all professions and ways of life.

Male Names: Carruth, Drewan, Ferus, Gerran, Nyktan, Rouqar, Zithembe.

Female Names: Alyara, Duline, Hoya, Jilyana, Milah, Miniri, Siphelele, Tiyeri.

ALTERNATE RACIAL TRAITS

The following racial traits may be selected instead of typical catfolk racial traits. Consult your GM before selecting any of these new options.

Cat's Claws: Some catfolk have stronger and more developed claws than other members of their race, and can use them to make attacks. Catfolk with this racial trait have a pair of claws they can use as natural weapons. These claws are primary attacks that deal 1d4 points of damage. This racial trait replaces natural hunter.

Clever Cat: Catfolk's generally friendly disposition doesn't preclude craftiness. Some of them see social obstacles as games to be played and won. These catfolk receive a +2 racial bonus on Bluff, Diplomacy, and Sense Motive checks. This racial trait replaces natural hunter.

Climber: Catfolk hunters excel at hunting prey from trees and other high vantage points. Catfolk with this racial trait possess a climb speed of 20 feet (along with the +8 racial bonus on Climb checks a climb speed affords). This racial trait replaces sprinter.

Curiosity: Catfolk are naturally inquisitive about the world around them, though some are more curious than others. Such catfolk gain a +4 bonus on Diplomacy checks to gather information, and Knowledge (history) and Knowledge (local) are always class skills for them. If they choose a class that has either of these Knowledge skills as class skills, they gain a +2 racial bonus on those skills instead. This racial trait replaces natural hunter.

Nimble Faller: Some catfolk have an amazing sense of balance and keen knowledge of their own center of gravity. Catfolk with this trait land on their feet even when they take lethal damage from a fall. Furthermore, catfolk with this trait gain a +1 bonus to their CMD against trip maneuvers. This racial trait replaces sprinter.

Scent: Some catfolk favor a keen sense of smell over sensitive sight. Catfolk with this racial trait gain the

CATFOLK RACIAL TRAITS

+2 Dexterity, +2 Charisma, –2 Wisdom: Catfolk are sociable and agile, but often lack common sense.

Catfolk: Catfolk are humanoids with the catfolk subtype.

Medium: Catfolk are Medium creatures and have no bonuses or penalties due to their size.

Normal Speed: Catfolk have a base speed of 30 feet.

Low-Light Vision: In dim light, catfolk can see twice as far as humans.

Cat's Luck (Ex): Once per day when a catfolk makes a Reflex saving throw, he can roll the saving throw twice and take the better result. He must decide to use this ability before the saving throw is attempted.

Natural Hunter: Catfolk receive a +2 racial bonus on Perception, Stealth, and Survival checks.

Sprinter: Catfolk gain a 10-foot racial bonus to their speed when using the charge, run, or withdraw actions.

Languages: Catfolk begin play speaking Common and Catfolk. Catfolk with high Intelligence scores can choose from the following languages: Elven, Gnoll, Gnome, Goblin, Halfling, Orc, and Sylvan.

CATFOLK ROGUE TALENTS

The following rogue talents can only be taken by catfolk.

Deadly Scratch (Ex): A catfolk rogue with this talent can apply poison to her claws without accidentally poisoning herself. A catfolk rogue must have the cat's claws racial trait and the poison use class feature before taking this talent.

Disarming Luck (Ex): Once per day, when a catfolk rogue attempts to disable a device and fails by 5 or more, she can reroll the check as a free action. She must take the result of the reroll, even if it's worse than the original roll.

Graceful Faller (Ex): A catfolk rogue with this talent lands on her feet even when she takes lethal damage from a fall. If the catfolk rogue also has the nimble faller racial trait, she takes damage from any fall as if it were 20 feet shorter than it actually is.

Nimble Climber (Ex): A catfolk rogue with this talent gains a +4 bonus on Climb checks. If she has the climber racial trait, she can take 10 on her Climb checks even when in immediate danger or distracted.

Single-Minded Appraiser (Ex): A catfolk rogue with this talent is skilled at determining the value of sparkly things. She can always take 10 when appraising gems and jewelry.

Vicious Claws (Ex): A catfolk with this talent uses d8s to roll sneak attack damage instead of d6s, but only when she uses her claws to make the sneak attack. A catfolk rogue must have the cat's claws racial trait before taking this talent.

scent ability. This racial trait replaces the low-light vision racial trait.

FAVORED CLASS OPTIONS

The following options are available to all catfolk who have the listed favored class, and unless otherwise stated, the bonus applies each time you select the favored class reward.

Bard: Add +1/2 to the bard's bardic knowledge bonus.

Cavalier: Add +1/4 to the cavalier's banner bonus.

Druid: Add +1 hit points to the druid's animal companion. If the druid ever replaces her animal companion, the new animal companion gains these bonus hit points.

Oracle: Add one spell known from the oracle spell list. This spell must be at least one level below the highest spell level the oracle can cast.

Ranger: Choose a weapon from the following list: claws, kukri, longbow, longsword, short spear, or shortbow. Add +1/2 on critical hit confirmation rolls made while using that weapon (maximum bonus of +4). This bonus does not stack with Critical Focus.

Rogue: Add a +1/2 bonus on Bluff checks to feint and Sleight of Hands checks to pickpocket.

Sorcerer: Select one bloodline power at 1st level that is normally usable a number of times equal to 3 + the sorcerer's Charisma modifier. The sorcerer adds + 1/2 to the number of uses per day of that bloodline power.

RACIAL ARCHETYPES

The following racial archetypes are available to catfolk.

Cat Burglar (Rogue)

Gifted with finesse and stealth, catfolk make excellent burglars. Cat burglars are masters of breaking and entering, using their feline grace to make it seem as though no crime was ever committed in the first place. Few locks can withstand skilled cat burglars, and such nimble rogues are capable of bypassing traps without activating them and enabling associates to do the same. A cat burglar has the following class features.

Phantom Presence (Ex): At 4th level, a cat burglar masters stealthy movement and leaves no trace of her passing in dungeons and cities. While in dungeon and urban environments, she leaves no trail and cannot be tracked, though she can choose to leave behind a trail if she so desires. Furthermore, she can always choose to take 10 when making a Stealth check. This ability replaces uncanny dodge.

Trap Saboteur (Su): At 8th level, a cat burglar becomes a master of avoiding and manipulating traps and locks. She can attempt to open a lock as a standard action and takes 1/2 the normal amount of time to disable traps (minimum 1 round). When she has bypassed a trap without disarming it, she can also choose to suppress its trigger for up to 1 minute. If she does, she can also choose to end this suppression prematurely as a free action. This ability replaces uncanny dodge.

Rogue Talents: The following rogue talents complement the cat burglar archetype: fast stealth, quick disable (*Core Rulebook*); convincing fakes, dodge trap (*Advanced Race Guide*); fast picks (*Advanced Player's Guide*); terrain mastery (*Ultimate Combat*).

Advanced Talents: The following advanced rogue talents complement the cat burglar archetype: another day, fast tumble (*Advanced Player's Guide*); hide in plain sight (*Ultimate Combat*).

Nimble Guardian (Monk)

Some catfolk monks dedicate their graceful prowess to the defense of others, especially those dedicated to a similar ethos or who prove themselves as stalwart allies of the monk's cause. A nimble guardian has the following class features.

Defensive Aid (Ex): At 2nd level, a number of times per day equal to his Wisdom bonus, a nimble guardian can interpose herself between one adjacent ally and an attack or damage dealt in an area of effect. If an adjacent ally is the target of the attack or is required to make a Reflex saving throw against a damaging effect, as an immediate action the nimble guardian can grant that ally a +4 circumstance bonus to AC or on the saving throw against the effect. The nimble guardian must use this ability before the attack roll or saving throw is made. The nimble guardian can only use this ability if he is wearing light or no armor. This ability replaces evasion.

Nimble Reflexes (Ex): At 3rd level, a nimble guardian gains a +2 bonus on all Reflex saving throws. This ability replaces still mind.

Defensive Mastery (Ex): At 5th level, a nimble guardian gains 3 additional uses of her defensive aid ability per day. Furthermore, if an ally that gained the benefit of a use of defensive aid succeeds her Reflex saving throw, and the effect still deals damage on a successful saving throw, the nimble guardian can spend 1 *ki* point to negate that damage. Doing so is not an action. This ability replaces purity of body.

Guardian Feline (Su): At 7th level, a nimble guardian can transform himself into a feline creature by spending 2 *ki* points. The effect lasts for 1 hour or until the nimble guardian changes back. Changing form (to animal or back) is a standard action and does not provoke an attack of opportunity. The chosen form must be some form of feline (cheetah, lion, etc.). This ability is otherwise identical to *beast shape II*. At 9th level, this ability functions as *beast shape III*. This ability replaces wholeness of body.

Evasion (Ex): At 9th level, a nimble guardian gains evasion. This ability replaces improved evasion.

NEW RACIAL RULES

The following options are available to catfolk. At the GM's discretion, other appropriate races may make use of some of these new rules.

Catfolk Equipment

Catfolk have access to the following equipment.

Claw Blades: These subtle blades can only be used by catfolk with the cat's claws racial trait. Bought in a set of five, they fit over the wearer's claws on one hand. The blades grant the wearer a +1 enhancement bonus on claw attack rolls with that hand and change the weapon type from a natural weapon to a light slashing weapon. Catfolk with the cat's claws racial trait are proficient with this weapon. The claw blades can be enhanced like a masterwork weapon for the normal costs. The listed cost of the item is for one set of five claws for one hand.

Softpaw Boots: These soft and subtle boots are constructed of silk and specially cured leather. They are specially designed for catfolk feet. They work with the feline structure of the race's feet to soften footfalls and to reduce the imprints of their tracks. While wearing softpaw boots, a catfolk gains a +1 circumstance bonus on Stealth checks. Furthermore, the DC to notice or follow the tracks of a catfolk wearing softpaw boots increases by +2.

Trailscent Kit: This small box of specially prepared catfolk pheromones and alchemical reagents can be used to leave a small group of subtle but long-lasting scents that only catfolk can smell and decipher. Given a minute, a catfolk can create a scent mixture and apply it to a solid object, such as a tree, a wall, or even a smaller item such as a weapon or potion vial. When the catfolk does this, it leaves one of the following scent impressions: danger, food, shelter, or possession. The possession impression is always keyed to the specific catfolk using the kit, and signifies that she owns the territory or item. Other races can attempt to use this kit to create the danger, food, or shelter impression, but doing so requires a successful DC 20 Craft (alchemy) check. A catfolk can detect a particular scent applied with a trailscent kit from 30 feet away. If the scent is upwind, the range at which a catfolk can detect the scent increases to 60 feet; if it is downwind, the range drops to 15 feet. A catfolk with the scent racial quality doubles those distances. A scent impression lasts for 1 year or until it is washed away. Each kit has 10 uses.

Catfolk Equipment

Item	Cost	Weight	Craft DC
Claw blades	305 gp	2 lb.	—
Softpaw boots	25 gp	1 lb.	—
Trailscent kit	10 gp	5 lb.	25

Catfolk Feats

Catfolk have access to the following feats.

Black Cat

Bad luck befalls those who dare to cross you.

Prerequisite: Catfolk.

Benefit: Once per day as an immediate action, when you are hit by a melee attack, you can force the opponent who made the attack to reroll it with a −4 penalty. The opponent must take the result of the second attack roll. This is a supernatural ability.

Special: If you take this feat and don't already have all black fur, your fur turns completely black when you takes this feat.

Catfolk Exemplar

Your feline traits are more defined and prominent than those of other members of your race.

Prerequisite: Catfolk.

Benefit: You can take the Aspect of the Beast feat (*Advanced Player's Guide* 151) even if you do not meet the normal prerequisites. Furthermore, your catlike nature manifests in one of the following ways. You choose the manifestation when you take this feat, and cannot change it later.

Enhanced Senses (Ex): If you have low-light vision, you gain the scent catfolk racial trait. If you have the scent racial trait, you gain low-light vision.

Fast Sprinter (Ex): You gain a 10-foot racial bonus to your speed when using the charge, run, or withdraw actions. If you have the sprinter racial trait, your racial bonus to speed when using the charge, run, or withdraw action increases to a 20-foot bonus.

Sharp Claws (Ex): If you do not have the cat's claws racial trait or the claws of the beast manifestation from the Aspect of the Beast feat (*Advanced Player's Guide* 151), you gain the cat's claws racial trait. If you have either the cat's claws racial trait or the claws of the beast manifestation, your claw damage increases to 1d6.

Special: You can take this feat multiple times. Its effects do not stack. Each time you select it, you must choose a different manifestation.

Claw Pounce (Combat)

You can charge and make an attack with your paws.

Prerequisites: Str 13, Dex 15, Nimble Striker, base attack bonus +10, catfolk, cat's claws racial trait or Aspect of the Beast (claws of the beast manifestation).

Benefit: When you make a charge, you can make a full attack with your claws.

Normal: Charging is a special full-round action that limits you to a single attack.

Feline Grace

Your innate grace allows you to get out of the stickiest situations.

Prerequisites: Dexterity 13, catfolk.

Benefit: You gain a +2 bonus to your CMD against bull rush, grapple, overrun, repositioning, and trip combat maneuvers.

Nimble Striker (Combat)

You were born to charge your enemies and nobody does it better.

Prerequisites: Dex 13, base attack bonus +1, catfolk, sprinter racial trait.

Benefit: You do not take a –2 penalty to AC when you use the Cleave feat, Lunge feat, or when you charge.

Catfolk Magic Items

The following magic items are often created and used by catfolk.

CAT'S EYE CROWN

Aura moderate divination; **CL** 10th

Slot head (and none; see below); **Price** 18,000 gp; **Weight** 1 lb.

DESCRIPTION

This slender silver crown is decorated with a single cat's eye gemstone as a centerpiece. When the gem is attached to the crown, its wearer gains darkvision 60 feet, or increases her darkvision by 60 feet if she already possesses that sense. The gemstone is detachable, and can be rolled into rooms, dropped into holes, thrown through windows, or planted on a creature. Once per day, on command, the crown's wearer gains the benefit of the *clairaudience/clairvoyance* spell, but uses the cat's eye gemstone as that spell's sensor and gains darkvision when viewing through that sensor. If the stone is held or carried by a creature, even within a sack or some other container, the creature wearing the crown uses the senses of the creature carrying the gemstone as the sensor instead, whether or not the creature carrying the gemstone is aware of the stone's true purpose or even its existence. Destroying the gem (hardness 8, hp 5) severs the link, but a new cat's eye gemstone worth at least 100 gp can be fashioned and attuned to the crown. The attunement process takes 24 hours.

CONSTRUCTION

Requirements Craft Wondrous Item, *clairaudience/clairvoyance*, *darkvision*, creator must be catfolk; **Cost** 9,000 gp

DAREDEVIL SOFTPAWS

Aura faint enchantment; **CL** 3rd

Slot feet; **Price** 1,400 gp; **Weight** 1 lb.

DESCRIPTION

This pair of magical softpaw boots (see above) allows the catfolk wearing them to gain extra maneuverability while moving through hazardous areas. As a free action, the wearer can click her heels together to grant herself a +5 competence bonus on Acrobatics checks made to move through threatened squares or to move through an enemy's space without provoking attacks of opportunity for up to 10 rounds per day. The rounds need not be consecutive. Furthermore, anytime the wearer of the boots successfully moves though the space of an enemy without provoking an attack of opportunity, she gains a +2 bonus on attack rolls against that enemy until the end of her turn.

CONSTRUCTION

Requirements Craft Wondrous Item, *cat's grace*; **Cost** 700 gp

RENDING CLAW BLADE

Aura moderate transmutation; **CL** 11th

Slot none; **Price** 10,305 gp; **Weight** 1 lb.

DESCRIPTION

This set of *+1 keen claw blades* is most effective when the wearer has multiple claw attacks per round. When making a full attack with claws, if the wielder hits the same target with this weapon and a different claw attack or set of claw blades, he deals an extra 1d4 damage plus 1-1/2 times his Strength bonus. The wearer can deal this extra damage no more than once per round. This counts as a rend attack and does not stack with other abilities that grant rend attacks.

CONSTRUCTION

Requirements Craft Magic Arms and Armor, *bull's strength*, *keen edge*; **Cost** 5,305 gp

Catfolk Spells

Catfolk have access to the following spells.

NINE LIVES

School abjuration; **Level** cleric 8, witch 8

Casting Time 1 standard action

Range touch

Target one creature touched

Duration 1 hour/level

Saving Throw Will negates (harmless); **Spell Resistance** yes (harmless)

Despite its name, this powerful ward does not grant the target multiple lives, but rather gives the target the ability to get out of trouble and relieves harmful effects and conditions. For the spell's duration, the target can use any of the following abilities as an immediate action, but only up to a total of nine times, at which point the spell ends.

Cat's Luck: The target can use this ability when it fails a saving throw. The target can reroll the failed saving throw, but must take the new result even if it is worse.

Fortitude: The target uses this ability when a critical hit or sneak attack is scored against it. The critical hit or sneak attack is negated and the damage is instead rolled normally.

Rejuvenate: The target uses this ability when it is reduced to 0 or fewer hit points. The target is instantly healed 3d6 points of damage. If enough hit points are regained to bring the target to positive hit points, it does not fall unconscious. If it is not enough to leave the target with positive hit points, the target automatically stabilizes. Both of these effects work even if the damage was originally enough to kill the target.

Shake Off: The target uses this ability when it is under the effects of any of the following conditions: blinded, confused, cowering, dazed, dazzled, entangled, exhausted, fatigued, frightened, nauseated, panicked, shaken, sickened, or staggered. Using this ability ends one of those conditions.

Shimmy Out: The target uses this ability when it is grappled or pinned. The target automatically escapes the grapple as if it had succeeded at an Escape Artist check to escape the grapple.

Stay Up: The target uses this ability when it is tripped or otherwise knocked prone. The target steadies itself and stays upright.

STEAL BREATH

School transmutation [air]; **Level** bard 2, druid 2, sorcerer/wizard 2, witch 2

Casting Time 1 standard action

Components V, S

Range close (25 ft. + 5 ft./2 levels)

Target one living creature

Duration 1 round (see text)

Saving Throw Fortitude negates; see text; **Spell Resistance** yes

You pull the breath from a creature's lungs, dealing damage and leaving it unable to speak, use breath weapons, or cast spells with verbal components. If the target fails its saving throw, it takes 2d6 points of damage, and it cannot speak, use breath weapons, or anything else requiring breathing, and a visible line of swirling air leaves the target's mouth and enters your mouth.

If, during the duration, the target moves out of range or line of effect to you, the spell immediately ends. This spell has no effect on creatures that do not need to breathe air.

DHAMPIRS

The half-living children of vampires birthed by human females, dhampirs are progenies of both horror and tragedy. The circumstances of a dhampir's conception are often called into question but scarcely understood, as few mortal mothers survive the childbirth. Those who do often abandon their monstrous children and refuse to speak of the matter. While some speculate that dhampirs result when mortal women couple with vampires, others claim that they form when a pregnant woman suffers a vampire bite. Some particularly zealous scholars even contest dhampirs' status as a unique race, instead viewing them as humans suffering from an unholy affliction. Indeed, this hypothesis is strengthened by dhampirs' seeming inability to reproduce, their offspring inevitably humans (usually sorcerers with the undead bloodline). Regardless, they live and die just like any other mortal creatures, despite possessing a supernatural longevity akin to that of elves.

Hardship and suffering fill a dhampir's formative years. Most grow up as orphans, and despite their exquisite features and innate charm, they face a lifetime of prejudice, mistrust, fear, and persecution. Humans who witness the seemingly sinister nature of a dhampir child's supernatural powers or sensitivity to daylight display an array of reactions ranging from awe to terror to outright hatred. Eventually, a dhampir must learn to cope with these difficulties in order to find his place in the world. While most dhampirs succumb to the innate evil of their undead heritage and devolve into the monstrous fiends depicted by society, a few reject their unholy conceptions, instead vowing to avenge their mothers by hunting the very creatures that sired them.

Dhampirs keep few, if any, close companions. Ultimately, the majority of evil dhampirs regard their allies as little more than tools or fodder. Those whom they deem useful are judged by their merits as individuals, not by their race. However, even with those they feel attached to, most dhampirs are sullen and reserved. Some fear the persecution heaped upon them may be transferred to their companions, whereas others worry their own bloodlust will one day overwhelm them and they'll inadvertently turn upon their friends. In any case, an alliance with a dhampir almost always leads to an ill-fated conclusion.

Physical Description: Tall and slender and with well-defined musculature, dhampirs look like statuesque humans of unearthly beauty. Their hair, eye, and skin colors resemble unnerving versions of their mothers'; many possess a ghastly pallor, particularly in the sunlight, while those with dark complexions often possess skin the color of a bruise.

While many dhampirs can pass as humans in ideal conditions, their features are inevitably more pronounced and they move with an unnaturally fluid grace. All dhampirs have elongated incisors. While not true fangs, these teeth are sharp enough to draw blood, and many suffer a reprehensible desire to indulge in sanguinary delights, despite the fact that the act provides most no physical benefit.

Society: Dhampirs have no culture of their own, nor do they have any known lands or even communities. Often born in secret and abandoned at orphanages or left to die on the outskirts of town, they tend to live solitary lives as exiles and outcasts. Individuals acquire the cultural beliefs and teachings of the regions in which they grew up, and adopt additional philosophies over the course of their complex lives. This ability to adapt to a verity of circumstances provides dhampirs with a social camouflage that hides them from both predators and prey.

In rare instances, dhampirs might gather to form small groups or cabals dedicated to resolving their joint issues. Even so, the philosophies of such groups reflect the interests of the individuals involved, not any common dhampir culture.

Relations: As dhampirs are scions of evil, few races view them favorably. They share an affinity for those half-breeds whose sinister ancestry also sets them apart from human society, particularly tieflings and half-orcs. Humans view them with a combination of fear and pity, though such feelings often devolve into hatred and violence. Other humanoid races, such as dwarves, elves, and halflings, simply shun them. Similarly, dhampirs bear a deep-seeded loathing for living creatures, their hatred planted by jealousy and fed by frustration.

Alignment and Religion: Most dhampirs succumb to the evil within their blood. They are unnatural creatures, and the foul influence of their undead heritage makes an evil outlook difficult to overcome. Those who struggle against their wicked natures rarely progress beyond a neutral outlook.

Dhampirs who become vampire hunters tend to worship Sarenrae or Pharasma, depending on their moral stance. Those who have spiraled into evil and embraced their undead heritage typically worship the demon lord Zura the Vampire Queen or Urgathoa, goddess of the undead.

Adventurers: The life of an adventurer comes naturally to most dhampirs, since constant persecution condemns many to spend their days wandering. Evil dhampirs keep moving to maintain their secrecy and evade lynch mobs, while those who follow the path of vengeance venture forth in search of their despised fathers. Regardless of their reasons, most dhampirs simply feel more at home on the road than in a settlement. Having little formal training, a great many of these journeyers become fighters and rogues.

Almost universally, those inclined toward magic pursue the field of necromancy, though dhampir alchemists have been known to obsess over transforming their own bodies. Those who feel the call of the hunt often become inquisitors.

Names: Lacking a culture and unified traditions, dhampirs share humans' predilection for a diversity of names, and most keep their human birth names. Many dhampirs take their mother's surname, while others take the surname of the towns or regions in which they were born, or use a surname derived from a significant event.

ALTERNATE RACIAL TRAITS

The following racial traits may be selected instead of existing dhampir racial traits. Consult your GM before selecting any of these new options.

Dayborn: A few fortunate dhampirs were born during the day under the blessings of priests, and their blood has weaker ties to their undead bloodline than others of their kind. Such dhampirs are unhindered by daylight and lose the light sensitivity racial trait. This racial trait replaces the spell-like ability racial trait.

Fangs: On occasion, a dhampir may inherit his father's lengthy canines. Whenever the dhampir makes a grapple combat maneuver check to damage an opponent, he can choose to bite his opponent, dealing 1d3 points of damage as if using a natural bite attack. As a standard action, the dhampir can bite a creature that is bound, helpless, paralyzed, or similarly unable to defend itself. This racial trait replaces the spell-like ability racial trait.

Vampiric Empathy: Though dhampirs often relate poorly to humanoids, some share an affinity with baser creatures. These dhampirs gain the ability to communicate with bats, rats, and wolves as if under the effects of a *speak with animals* spell (caster level equal to 1/2 the dhampir's Hit Dice). In addition, they gain a +2 racial bonus on Diplomacy checks when dealing with these animals. Whenever these dhampirs initiate an exchange, animals begin with a starting attitude of indifferent. This is a supernatural ability. This racial trait replaces manipulative.

DHAMPIR RACIAL TRAITS

+2 Dexterity, +2 Charisma, −2 Constitution: Dhampirs are fast and seductive, but their racial bond to the undead impedes their mortal vigor.

Dhampir: Dhampirs are humanoids with the dhampir subtype.

Medium: Dhampirs are Medium creatures and have no bonuses or penalties due to their size.

Normal Speed: Dhampirs have a base speed of 30 feet.

Senses: Low-light vision and darkvision 60 feet.

Manipulative: +2 racial bonus on Bluff and Perception.

Undead Resistance: Dhampirs gain a +2 racial bonus on saving throws against disease and mind-affecting effects.

Light Sensitivity: Dhampirs are dazzled in areas of bright sunlight or within the radius of a *daylight* spell.

Negative Energy Affinity: Though a living creature, a dhampir reacts to positive and negative energy as if it were undead—positive energy harms it, while negative energy heals it.

Spell-Like Ability: A dhampir can use *detect undead* three times per day as a spell-like ability. The caster level for this ability equals the dhampir's class level.

Resist Level Drain (Ex): A dhampir takes no penalties from energy drain effects, though he can still be killed if he accrues more negative levels then he has Hit Dice. After 24 hours, any negative levels a dhampir takes are removed without the need for an additional saving throw.

Languages: Dhampirs begin play speaking Common. Those with high Intelligence scores can choose any language it wants (except secret languages, such as Druidic).

FAVORED CLASS OPTIONS

The following options are available to all dhampirs who have the listed favored class, and unless otherwise stated, the bonus applies each time you select the favored class reward.

Alchemist: Add +10 minutes to the duration of the alchemist's mutagens.

Cleric: Add +1 to the caster level of any channeling feat used to affect undead.

Fighter: Add a +2 bonus on rolls to stabilize when dying.

Inquisitor: Add a +1/2 bonus on Intimidate checks to demoralize humanoids.

Rogue: Add a +1/2 bonus on Stealth checks and Perception checks made in dim light or darkness.

Sorcerer: Add +1/2 point of negative energy damage to spells that deal negative energy damage.

Wizard: Add +1/4 to the wizard's caster level when casting spells of the necromancy school.

RACIAL ARCHETYPES

The following racial archetypes are available to dhampirs.

Cruoromancer (Wizard)

To those who know how to manipulate it, the blood of a dhampir can be a powerful component to magic. A cruoromancer infuses his necromantic magic with the power of his unique mixture of living blood and undead ichor. As his power increases in this strange arcane art, a cruoromancer finds potent ways to infuse his unique blood with necromancy spells. A cruoromancer has the following class features.

Blood Infusion (Su): When a cruoromancer casts a spell of the necromancy school, he can opt to infuse that spell with his undead-tainted blood as a swift action. As he increases in level, the power and effects of such infusions become more potent. Each time a cruoromancer uses blood infusion, he drains a portion of his own blood either by cutting himself with a blade or by opening a scab from a previous wound. When he does this, he takes an amount of damage equal to 1d4 + the level of the spell being infused. A cruoromancer can only affect a spell with a single type of blood infusion. At 1st level, he can infuse his necromancy spells in either of the following ways.

Focused Infusion: When the cruoromancer uses this infusion, he adds +1 to the DC of the infused necromancy spell.

Sickening Infusion: When the cruoromancer uses this infusion, any creature damaged by the infused necromancy spell becomes sickened for 1 round.

This ability replaces arcane bond.

Blood Command (Su): At 5th level, a cruoromancer can control up to 5 Hit Dice worth of undead creatures per caster level instead of the normal 4 Hit Dice of undead when casting the *animate dead* spell. He also gains the following blood infusion ability.

Commanding Infusion: When using this infusion with *animate dead*, the cruoromancer can create a number of Hit Dice of undead equal to three times his caster level instead of twice his caster level.

This ability replaces the 5th-level wizard bonus feat.

Blood Desecration (Su): At 10th level, a cruoromancer gains the following blood infusion.

Desecrating Infusion: When the cruoromancer uses this infusion, he can choose to center a *desecrate* effect on himself or a single target of the spell modified by this infusion (he chooses upon casting). This effect is like the *desecrate* spell, but lasts for 1 minute per caster level of the cruoromancer, and does not interact with altars, shrines, or permanent fixtures that boost the *desecrate* effect. This ability replaces the 10th-level wizard bonus feat.

Blood Ability (Su): At 15th level, a cruoromancer can choose to scry through a single undead creature he created with a spell modified by a commanding infusion. The undead creature is treated as if imbued with an *arcane eye* spell (caster level equal to the cruoromancer's wizard level). This ability replaces the 15th-level wizard bonus feat.

Perfect Infusion (Su): At 20th level, a cruoromancer can use his blood infusions without taking damage. This ability replaces the 20th-level wizard bonus spell.

Kinslayer (Inquisitor)

Appalled and guilt-ridden by the horrific circumstances of her birth, a kinslayer dedicates herself to eradicating the very creatures whose blood flows within her veins. She spends her life hunting and slaying those vampiric monsters for whom humans have become prey. A kinslayer has the following class features.

Judgment (Su): At 1st level, a kinslayer gains the following judgment.

Slayer's Brand (Su): When using this judgment, the kinslayer gains the ability to brand undead creatures with positive energy. To do so, she must make a successful melee touch attack against the undead creature. This attack deals an amount of positive energy damage equal to 1d6 + the kinslayer's Charisma score, and burns her personal symbol into the undead creature's flesh, bone, or even its incorporeal form. From that point onward, the kinslayer can sense the existence of the branded creature as if it were the target of a *locate creature* spell (caster level equal to 1/2 the kinslayer's inquisitor level). A slayer's brand lasts until the undead creature is destroyed or until the kinslayer uses this ability on another creature. This ability replaces the destruction judgment.

Greater Brand (Su): A 1st level, a kinslayer learns to modify her slayer's brand judgment as she gains levels. Whenever she gains the ability to learn a teamwork feat, she can instead opt to learn one of the following modifications to her slayer's brand judgment.

Branding Ray: The slayer's brand judgment can be used as a ranged touch attack with a range of 20 feet. A kinslayer can take this modification more than once. Whenever she does, she increases the range of her brand by 20 feet.

Debilitating Brand: A creature currently affected by the slayer's brand judgment takes a –2 penalty on attack rolls against the kinslayer who placed the brand.

Devastating Brand: When the kinslayer attacks a creature that she has branded with her slayer's brand, she threatens a critical hit on a roll of 19–20. If the kinslayer is good, she also gains a +2 sacred bonus on all rolls to confirm critical hits on a branded creature.

Dual Brand: The kinslayer can have up to two creatures branded at a time.

Holy Brand: The kinslayer can use her brand on creatures with the evil subtype as well as undead.

Searing Brand: The kinslayer's slayer's brand deals an additional 1d6 points of damage for every five inquisitor levels she has. If the creature hit with the slayer's brand is particularly vulnerable to bright light, the damage dice of her slayer's brand increases to d8s. A kinslayer must be at least 6th level to take this modification.

Silver Brand: The kinslayer can use her brand on lycanthropes and creatures with vulnerability to silver as well as undead.

Each time the kinslayer opts to take a greater brand, it replaces her ability to gain a teamwork feat at that level.

Undead Sense (Sp): At 2nd level, a kinslayer gains the ability to use *detect undead* as a spell-like ability (caster level equal to the kinslayer's inquisitor level) at will. If she detects the presence of undead, she can use her monster lore ability to attempt to determine the type of undead detected as well as to reveal any strengths or weaknesses the undead might have. If any of the detected undead are vampires, she gains a bonus on the check equal to her inquisitor level to immediately identify them as such.

This ability replaces *detect alignment.*

NEW RACIAL RULES

The following options are available to dhampirs. At the GM's discretion, other appropriate races may make use of some of these new rules.

Dhampir Equipment

The following equipment is used or made by dhampirs.

Heartstake Bolts: Specially crafted from solid darkwood, heartstake bolts are specifically designed to slay vampires. A heartstake bolt can be fired from any crossbow, but it imposes a –2 penalty on the attack roll and halves the range increment of the weapon. A vampire struck with a heartstake bolt takes the normal damage but must also succeed at a DC 20 Fortitude saving throw or fall to the ground helpless for 1 round. While the vampire

is helpless in this manner, a creature can attempt to use the heartstake bolt to finish off the vampire by driving it through the vampire's heart as a full-round action. Once the debilitating effect of the heartstake bolt has ended, the vampire can pull out the bolt as a move action. A vampire slain with a heartstake bolt is subject to the rules and limitations of slaying a vampire with a wooden stake as described under vampire weaknesses (*Bestiary* 270).

A heartstake bolt deals normal damage for the crossbow of its type.

Neck Guard: Made from hardened leather reinforced with a band of metal, this collar protects the wearer against vampire bites when worn around the throat. It provides a +1 armor bonus to AC against vampire bites or similar attacks that specifically target the wearer's throat. Unlike most armor bonuses, the neck guard's +1 bonus stacks with the armor bonus of light or medium armor, but it provides no additional bonus when worn with heavy armor.

Vampire Slayer's Kit: This small, latched wooden case contains numerous tools and devices used in hunting and slaying vampires. It contains 10 cloves of garlic, four masterwork wooden stakes, a hammer, a silvered mirror, 4 vials of holy water, 1 application of *silversheen*, and a masterwork holy symbol. It also contains numerous regents and powders used for treating wounds and making wards, salves, and other concoctions. In addition to its general usefulness, when displayed, a vampire slayer's kit grants its owner a +2 bonus on all Charisma-based skill checks made to investigate or seek out vampires.

Dhampir Equipment

Item	Cost	Weight
Heartstake bolts (5)	100 gp	3 lbs.
Neck guard	10 gp	1/4 lb.
Vampire slayer's kit	500 gp	8 lbs.

Dhampir Feats

Dhampirs have access to the following feats.

Blood Drinker

Consuming blood reinvigorates you.

Prerequisite: Dhampir.

Benefit: Choose one humanoid subtype, such as "goblinoid" (this subtype cannot be "dhampir"). You have acquired a taste for the blood of creatures with this subtype. Whenever you drink fresh blood from such a creature, you gain 5 temporary hit points and a +1 bonus on checks and saves based on Constitution. The effects last 1 hour. If you feed multiple times, you continue to gain hit points to a maximum of 5 temporary hit points for every three Hit Dice you have, but the +1 bonus on Constitution-based skill checks and saving throws does not stack.

Normally, you can only drink blood from an opponent who is helpless, grappled, paralyzed, pinned, unconscious, or similarly disabled. If you have a bite attack, you can drink blood automatically as part of your bite attack; otherwise, you must first cut your target by dealing 1 hit point of damage with a slashing or piercing weapon (though you may feed upon a creature with severe wounds or a bleed effect without cutting it first). Once you cut the target, you can drink from its wound as a standard action. Drinking blood deals 2 points of Constitution damage to the creature you feed upon.

The blood must come from a living creature of the specified humanoid subtype. It cannot come from a dead or summoned creature. Feeding on unwilling intelligent creatures is an evil act.

Blood Feaster

Consuming blood gives you superhuman strength.

Prerequisites: Blood Drinker, base attack bonus +6, dhampir.

Benefit: If you use your Blood Drinker feat to drain 4 or more points of Constitution from a living creature, you gain a +2 bonus on damage rolls and a +1 bonus on Strength-based skill checks. This bonus lasts for a number of rounds equal to 1/2 your Hit Dice.

Blood Salvage

You do not need to drink blood from a living creature to gain healing benefits.

Prerequisites: Blood Drinker, dhampir.

Benefit: You can use your Blood Drinker feat on a dead creature of the appropriate humanoid subtype. The creature must have died less than 6 hours beforehand.

Normal: You only benefit from the Blood Drinker feat if you consume fresh blood from a living creature.

Diverse Palate

Your taste for blood is broader than that of other dhampirs.

Prerequisites: Blood Drinker, dhampir.

Benefit: Choose a humanoid subtype or the monstrous humanoid type. You may use your Blood Drinker feat on creatures of this subtype or type.

Special: You can take this feat multiple times. Each time you select it, choose a new humanoid subtype or the monstrous humanoid.

Natural Charmer

You possess some of the dominating powers of your vampire progenitor.

Prerequisites: Cha 17, dhampir.

Benefit: You can take 20 on any Charisma-based skills to charm, convince, persuade, or seduce humanoids whose attitude is at least friendly to you. Taking 20 still requires 20 times the normal time to perform the skill.

Normal: You cannot take 20 on any check where you incur penalties for failure.

Dhampir Magic Items

Dhampirs have access to the following magic items.

AMULET OF CHANNELED LIFE
Aura moderate transmutation; **CL** 10th
Slot neck; **Price** 12,000 gp; **Weight** 1/2 lb.
DESCRIPTION
This amulet consists of a pale translucent gem in a dull gray metal setting etched with ancient runes. When worn by an individual with the negative energy affinity racial trait, it alters the effects of positive energy on his body. When targeted by positive energy that heals living creatures, the wearer instead

gains half the hit points the positive energy heals as temporary hit points. These temporary hit points go away after 10 minutes. This effect does not stack with *life channel* (see below) or other effects that convert healing positive energy to temporary hit points.

This item does not actually transpose positive energy into negative energy, it just affects the way the wearer's body reacts to positive energy. Only a living creature can benefit from this amulet; it provides no benefit to undead.

CONSTRUCTION

Requirements Craft Wondrous Item, *life channel*; **Cost** 6,000 gp

LENSES OF DARKNESS

Aura faint transmutation; **CL** 3rd

Slot eyes; **Price** 12,000 gp; **Weight** —

DESCRIPTION

Crafted from a dark-colored crystalline material and infused with magical darkness, these lenses fit over the wearer's eyes. When worn by a creature with light sensitivity or light blindness, these lenses protect the wearer against the effect of sunlight, the *daylight* spell, or similar light effects. Both lenses must be worn for the magic to be effective.

CONSTRUCTION

Requirements Craft Wondrous Item, *darkness*; **Cost** 6,000 gp

SYMBOL OF UNHOLY COMMAND

Aura faint necromancy; **CL** 3rd

Slot none; **Price** 8,000 gp; **Weight** 1 lb.

DESCRIPTION

This unholy symbol is carved entirely from human bone. When the wielder uses this unholy symbol as a focus for the Command Undead feat, he gains a +1 profane bonus to the DC of that feat.

Good creatures of 5 Hit Dice or less that attempt to touch the symbol must make a DC 15 Will save or be shaken for 1 round. Deliberate use of a *symbol of unholy command* is an evil act.

CONSTRUCTION

Requirements Craft Wondrous Item, Command Undead or *command undead*; **Cost** 4,000 gp

Dhampir Spells

Dhampirs have access to the following spells.

BLINDING RAY

School evocation [good, light]; **Level** cleric 2, inquisitor 3, paladin 2

Casting Time 1 standard action

Components V, S, DF

Range close (25 ft. + 5 ft./2 levels)

Effect one or more rays of light

Duration instantaneous (see text)

Saving Throw Fortitude negates; **Spell Resistance** yes

You blast your enemies with blinding rays of sunlight. You may fire one ray, plus one additional ray for every four levels beyond 3rd (to a maximum of three rays at 11th level). Each ray requires a ranged touch attack to hit. If a ray hits, it explodes into powerful motes of light, and the target must save or be blinded for 1 round. If the target has light blindness, light sensitivity, or is otherwise vulnerable to bright light, it instead must save or be blinded for 1d4 rounds and take 1d4 points of damage per two caster levels (maximum 5d4). Any creature blinded by a ray sheds light as a sunrod for the duration of its blindness. The rays may be fired at the same or different targets, but all rays must be aimed at targets within 30 feet of each other and fired simultaneously.

LIFE CHANNEL

School transmutation; **Level** cleric 2

Casting Time 1 standard action

Component V, S

Range touch

Target one touched creature with negative energy affinity

Duration 1 minute/level

Saving Throw Fortitude negates (harmless); **Spell Resistance** yes (harmless)

When cast on a creature with negative energy affinity, the target is able to convert channeled positive energy into temporary hit points. When subject to an effect that heals hit points only to living creatures (such as *cure light wounds* or channel positive energy), the target gains a number of temporary hit points equal to half the number of hit points that the positive energy would normally heal. These temporary hit points go away at the end of this spell's duration.

SPAWN WARD

School necromancy; **Level** cleric 5, inquisitor 5

Casting Time 1 standard action

Components V, S

Range touch

Target creature touched

Duration 10 minutes/level

Save Fortitude negates (harmless); **Spell Resistance** yes (harmless)

The target becomes resistant to the effects of energy drain and blood drain attacks made by undead creatures, and cannot be made into undead spawn if killed while the spell is in effect.

If the attacking undead's Hit Dice is less than or equal to your caster level, the blood drain or energy drain has no effect. If the attacking undead's Hit Dice are greater than your caster level, the undead must make a Fortitude save (against the DC of the spell) with each attack for those special abilities to have any effect. The spell only prevents the Constitution damage from blood drain and negative levels from energy drain, but not any other effects of these attacks.

DROW

Cruel and cunning, drow are a dark reflection of the elven race. Also called dark elves, they dwell deep underground in elaborate cities shaped from the rock of cyclopean caverns. Drow seldom make themselves known to surface folk, preferring to remain legends while advancing their sinister agendas through proxies and agents. Drow have no love for anyone but themselves, and are adept at manipulating other creatures. While they are not born evil, malignancy is deep-rooted in their culture and society, and nonconformists rarely survive for long. Some stories tell that given the right circumstances, a particularly hateful elf might turn into a drow, though such a transformation would require a truly heinous individual.

Physical Description: Drow are similar in stature to humans, but share the slender build and features of elves, including the distinctive long, pointed ears. Their eyes lack pupils and are usually solid white or red. Drow skin ranges from coal black to a dusky purple. Their hair is typically white or silver, though some variation is not unknown.

Society: Drow society is traditionally class-oriented and matriarchal. Male drow usually fulfill martial roles, defending the species from external threats, while female drow assume positions of leadership and authority. Reinforcing these gender roles, one in 20 drow are born with exceptional abilities and thus considered to be nobility, and the majority of these special drow are female. Noble houses define drow politics, with each house governed by a noble matriarch and composed of lesser families, business enterprises, and military companies. Each house is also associated with a demon lord patron. Drow are strongly driven by individual self-interest and advancement, which shapes their culture with seething intrigue and politics, as common drow jockey for favor of the nobility, and the nobility rise in power through a combination of assassination, seduction, and treachery.

Relations: Drow have a strong sense of racial superiority and divide non-drow into two groups: slaves, and those that are not yet slaves. In practice, however, races that may share similar inclinations (such as hobgoblins and orcs) and those who serve willingly may be treated as servitor races and granted a measure of trust and modest rank in drow society. Others, such as dwarves, gnomes, and halflings, are deemed fit only for the lash. Manipulative drow delight in exploiting the weak character of humans. While they claim no kinship with fetchlings, the drow harbor a curiosity toward the shadow race, as both are adaptations of races exposed to extreme and dangerous conditions. Finally, the drow's hatred of elves sets these beings apart from all other races, and the dark elves desire nothing more than to ruin everything about their surface cousins.

Alignment and Religion: Drow place a premium on power and survival, and are unapologetic about any vile choices they might make to ensure their survival. After all, they do not just survive adversity—they conquer it. They have no use for compassion, and are unforgiving of their enemies, both ancient and contemporary. Drow retain the elven traits of strong emotion and passion, but channel it through negative outlets, such as hatred, vengeance, lust for power, and raw carnal sensation. Consequently, most drow are chaotic evil. Demon lords are their chosen patrons, sharing their inclination toward power and destruction, and they also favor the goddess Lamashtu.

Adventurers: Conquerors and slavers, drow are driven to expand their territory, and many seek to settle ancient grudges upon elven and dwarven nations in ruinous and dreary sites of contested power on the surface. Male drow favor martial or stealth classes that put them close to their enemies and their homes, as either soldiers or spies. Female drow typically assume classes that lend themselves to leadership, such as bards and especially clerics. Both genders have an innate talent for the arcane arts, and may be wizards or summoners. Drow make natural antipaladins, but males are often discouraged from this path, as the feminine nobility feel discomforted by the idea of strong-willed males with autonomous instincts and a direct relationship with a demon lord.

Male Names: Arcavato, Drovic, Firyin, Kaelmourn, Mirrendier, Pharnox, Syrendross, Zov.

Female Names: Belmarniss, Cylellinth, Ilvaria, Johysis, Loscivia, Tyvorhan, Ulumbralya, Volundeil.

ALTERNATE RACIAL TRAITS

The following racial traits may be selected instead of existing drow racial traits. Consult your GM before selecting any of these new options.

Ambitious Schemer: Seduction and treachery are tools for advancement in drow society, even for the martially inclined. Drow with this racial trait may choose either Bluff or Diplomacy as a class skill, and gain a +2 bonus on such skill checks. This racial trait replaces keen sight.

Ancestral Grudge: The enmity between the drow and elves and dwarves is long-standing and deeply entrenched. Drow with this racial trait gain a +1 bonus on attack rolls against humanoids with the dwarf or elf subtypes (with the exception of drow) because of their special training against these reviled foes. This racial trait replaces poison use.

Blasphemous Covenant: Since their twisted beginnings, the drow have consorted with demons. Some drow have strong ties with these creatures and may call upon ancient and obscene associations to sway demonic cooperation. Drow with this racial trait gain a +2 bonus on Diplomacy checks made against unbound creatures with the demon subtype. Furthermore, demons conjured with any *summon* spell gain +2 hit points per Hit Die. Lastly, the cost of bribes or offerings for any *planar ally* spell cast by these drow to summon a demon is reduced by 20%. This racial trait replaces keen senses and poison use.

Darklands Stalker: The lands outside of drow cities, from rough-hewn tunnels to rocky caverns, are treacherous to navigate. Drow with this racial trait may move through difficult terrain without penalty while underground. In addition, drow with a Dexterity of 13 or higher gain Nimble Moves as a bonus feat. This racial trait replaces the spell-like abilities racial trait.

Seducer: Certain drow possess an innate understanding of the darkest desires that lurk in every heart. Drow with this racial trait add +1 to the saving throw DCs for spells and spell-like abilities of the enchantment school. In addition, drow with a Wisdom score of 15 or higher may use *charm person* once per day as a spell-like ability (caster level equal to the drow's character level). This racial trait replaces drow immunities.

Surface Infiltrator: Some drow dwell close to the surface lands, either because they serve drow causes or they were exiled. Drow with this racial trait gain low-light vision, allowing them to see twice as far as humans in conditions of dim light. This racial trait replaces the darkvision and light blindness racial traits.

FAVORED CLASS OPTIONS

The following options are available to all drow who have the listed favored class, and unless otherwise stated, the bonus applies each time you select the favored class reward.

Alchemist: Add +10 minutes to the duration of the alchemist's mutagens.

Antipaladin: The antipaladin adds +1/4 to the number of cruelties he can inflict.

Cleric: Select one domain power granted at 1st level that is normally usable a number of times per day equal to 3 + the cleric's Wisdom modifier. The cleric adds +1/2 to the number of uses per day of that domain power.

DROW RACIAL TRAITS

+2 Dexterity, +2 Charisma, –2 Constitution: Drow are nimble and manipulative.

Elf: Drow are humanoids with the elf subtype.

Medium: Drow are Medium creatures and receive no bonuses or penalties due to their size.

Normal Speed: Drow have a base speed of 30 feet.

Darkvision: Drow can see in the dark up to 120 feet.

Drow Immunities: Drow are immune to magic sleep effects and gain a +2 racial bonus on saving throws against enchantment spells and effects.

Keen Senses: Drow gain a +2 racial bonus on Perception checks.

Poison Use: Drow are skilled in the use of poison and never risk accidentally poisoning themselves.

Spell Resistance: Drow possess spell resistance equal to 6 plus their class levels.

Spell-Like Abilities: A drow can cast *dancing lights*, *darkness*, and *faerie fire*, once each per day, using her total character level as her caster level.

Light Blindness: Abrupt exposure to bright light blinds drow for 1 round; on subsequent rounds, they are dazzled as long as they remain in the affected area.

Weapon Familiarity: Drow are proficient with the hand crossbow, rapier, and short sword.

Languages: Drow begin play speaking Elven and Undercommon. Drow with high Intelligence scores can choose from the following languages: Abyssal, Aklo, Aquan, Common, Draconic, Drow Sign Language, Gnome, or Goblin.

Fighter: Choose the disarm or reposition combat maneuver. Add +1/3 to the fighter's CMB when attempting this maneuver (maximum bonus of +4).

Rogue: Add a +1/2 bonus on Bluff checks to feint and pass secret messages.

Sorcerer: Add one spell known from the sorcerer spell list. This spell must have the curse, evil, or pain descriptor, and be at least one level below the highest spell level the sorcerer can cast.

Wizard: Select one arcane school power at 1st level that is normally usable a number of times per day equal to 3 + the wizard's Intelligence modifier. The wizard adds +1/2 to the number of uses per day of that arcane school power.

RACIAL ARCHETYPES

The following racial archetypes are available to drow.

Cavern Sniper (Fighter)

Perfectly at home in the darkness, the cavern sniper capitalizes on stealth and ranged attacks imbued with his spell-like abilities to harass his opponents. The cavern sniper focuses on surprise, his innate magical abilities, and poison to take down unwary foes. The cavern sniper has the following class features.

Class Skills: The cavern sniper adds Stealth to his list of class skills and removes Intimidate from his list of class skills.

Imbued Shot (Su): At 1st level, the cavern sniper gains the ability to imbue his arrows or bolts with the effect of one of his drow *faerie fire*, *darkness*, or *deeper darkness* spell-like abilities (provided he has access to the ability) as a swift action. When such an arrow or bolt is fired, the spell's area is centered where the arrow or bolt lands. If the target of the attack has a space larger than 5 feet, the cavern sniper can choose which square of the creature's space is the center of the spell-like ability's effect, as long as that square is within line of sight of the cavern sniper. The cavern sniper can instead choose to target a single square within line of sight with an imbued arrow or bolt, and uses that square as the center of the spell-like ability's area of effect on a hit (AC 5). The arrow must be fired during the round it was imbued, or the spell-like ability is wasted. If the arrow or bolt misses, the use of the spell-like ability is wasted. This ability replaces the 1st-level fighter bonus feat.

Silent Shooter (Ex): At 2nd level, a cavern sniper gains a +2 bonus on Stealth checks made when loading a bow or crossbow, poisoning ammunition, and making sniping attempts. This bonus increases by +2 for every four levels beyond 2nd. This ability replaces bravery.

Quick and Deadly (Ex): At 4th level, the cavern sniper can move at full speed while using Stealth at no penalty and can

apply poison to a single arrow or crossbow bolt as a swift action. This ability replaces the 4th-level fighter bonus feat.

Sniper Training (Ex): At 5th level, the cavern sniper chooses the bow or crossbow weapon group and gains a +2 bonus on attack rolls and damage rolls. This bonus increases by +1 for every four levels beyond 5th. This ability replaces weapon training 1, 3, and 4.

Greater Imbued Shot (Su): At 9th level, the cavern sniper gains two extra uses of both his *faerie fire* and *darkness* spell-like abilities, but can only use these extra uses to imbue arrows and bolts with the imbued shot class feature. This ability replaces weapon training 2.

Weapon Mastery (Ex): At 20th level, when the cavern sniper gains weapon mastery, he must choose a weapon in either the bow or crossbow weapon group.

Demonic Apostle (Cleric)

In order to survive, the drow threw in their lot with demon lords. Thus, demon worship is common among the drow, and so are ranks of demonic apostles, who gain magical insight from their dark lords and crush their chaotic masters' enemies by channeling demonic energy. A demonic apostle has the following class features.

Demonic Magic: A demonic apostle must choose to channel negative energy, and must select either the Chaos or Evil domain or the Demon subdomain (*Advanced Player's Guide* 89) as her sole domain.

Demonic Familiar: At 1st level, a demonic apostle gains a familiar as a wizard equal to her cleric level, or if she already has a familiar, her cleric levels stack to determine the familiar's abilities. At 3rd level, her familiar gains the fiendish template (*Bestiary* 294). At 7th level, the demonic apostle exchanges her familiar for a quasit without the need to take the Improved Familiar feat.

Demonic Channel (Su): At 1st level, a demonic apostle can channel demonic energy to damage creatures of lawful and good alignment, or, at higher levels, bolster the abilities of chaotic evil allies.

Channeling this energy causes a 30-foot-radius burst centered on the cleric. Creatures within the burst that are lawful or good take 1d6 points of damage, plus 1d6 points of damage for every two levels the cleric possesses beyond 1st (2d6 at 3rd, 3d6 at 5th, and so on). Creatures that take damage from the channeled demonic energy receive a Fortitude save to halve the damage. The DC of this save is equal to 10 + 1/2 the demonic apostle's level + the demonic apostle's Charisma modifier. Lawful good creatures take a –2 penalty on this saving throw. At 5th level, chaotic evil allies within the burst are affected as if targeted by a *rage* spell with a duration of 1 round. At 9th level, lawful or good enemies are also sickened for 1d6 rounds if they fail their saving throw against the demonic channel. Channeling demonic energy is a standard action that does not provoke attacks of opportunity. This ability replaces channel energy.

NEW RACIAL RULES

The following options are available to drow. At the GM's discretion, other appropriate races may make use of some of these new rules.

Drow Equipment

Drow have access to the following equipment.

Riding Bat: Considered to be the fastest nonmagical transport in the Darklands, dire bats (*Bestiary* 30) are domesticated in captivity to serve as riding animals. Stables that accommodate these massive creatures are only commonly found in drow cities built in larger underground caverns, owing to the greater space required for training and exercise, though some drow outriders fly them almost to the surface. These creatures require exotic saddles to ride.

Riding Gecko: Larger than even what is commonly referred to as a giant gecko, these mammoth lizards have been specifically bred to be used as mounts for the drow. Prized for their ability to run along cave ceilings and sheer walls, these creatures require exotic saddles to ride. Use the statistics for a giant gecko with the giant template (*Pathfinder RPG Bestiary 3* 186, 291).

Spider Sac: Despite their name, spider sacs have nothing to do with spiders but rather are alchemical devices with a unique delivery system. Used for climbing as well as combat, these grayish, gourdlike pouches are made of a specially grown fungus with a tough but rubbery exterior. The fungoid is carefully harvested, pierced at one end, hollowed out, and then injected with a strong alchemical adhesive that hardens to a fibrous material almost instantly when exposed to air. When squeezed, a spider sac's adhesive shoots out to a maximum range of 10 feet and sticks to whatever it strikes, whereupon the strand dries instantly into a durable fibrous rope. For the purposes of climbing, treat a spider sac as a grappling hook except that all surfaces are AC 5. A spider sac can also be used as a lasso (*Advanced Player's Guide* 178) except with AC 10, 4 hit points, and a DC 24 Strength check to burst. A spider sac is a single-use item.

Drow Equipment

Item	Cost	Weight	Craft DC
Spider sac	30 gp	1 lb.	20

Drow Mounts

Mount	Cost	Weight
Bat, dire, riding	300 gp	—
Bat, dire, riding (combat trained)	450 gp	—
Gecko, riding	300 gp	—
Gecko, riding (combat trained)	400 gp	—

Drow Feats

Drow have access to the following feats.

Drow Nobility

Your blood courses with power, granting you greater spell-like abilities.

Prerequisites: Able to use drow spell-like abilities, drow.

Benefit: You may use *detect magic* as a spell-like ability at will, and add *feather fall* and *levitate* to the spell-like abilities that you may use once each per day. Your caster level is equal to your character level.

Greater Drow Nobility

You have mastered the lesser spell-like abilities of the drow, demonstrating true nobility.

Prerequisites: Cha 13, Drow Nobility, Improved Drow Nobility, able to use drow spell-like abilities, drow.

Benefit: Your *detect magic* spell-like ability is now constant. You may use your *dancing lights*, *deeper darkness*, *faerie fire*, *feather fall*, and *levitate* spell-like abilities at will.

Improved Drow Nobility

Your magical heritage is more potent than that of your peers, as demonstrated by your superior spell-like abilities.

Prerequisites: Cha 13, Drow Nobility, able to use drow spell-like abilities, drow.

Benefit: You may use your *dancing lights*, *faerie fire*, *feather fall*, and *levitate* spell-like abilities twice per day. Your *darkness* spell-like ability instead becomes *deeper darkness*, which you may use twice per day.

Improved Umbral Scion

You are a master of drow noble magic.

Prerequisites: Cha 13, Wis 13, Drow Nobility, Greater Drow Nobility, Improved Drow Nobility, Umbral Scion, able to use drow spell-like abilities, drow.

Benefit: You may use *dispel magic*, *divine favor*, and *suggestion* once per day as spell-like abilities. Your caster level is equal to your character level.

Noble Spell Resistance

Your ascension is complete; you have the spell resistance approaching that of a demon.

Prerequisites: Cha 13, Wis 13, Greater Drow Nobility, character level 13th, drow.

Benefit: Your spell resistance is equal to 11 + your character level.

Special: You receive a +1 circumstance bonus on Diplomacy and Intimidate checks made against any drow.

Shadow Caster

Your command over shadow and darkness create longer-lasting spell effects.

Prerequisites: Caster level 1st, drow.

Benefit: When you cast spells of the shadow subschool or spells with the darkness descriptor, you are considered two levels higher when determining the duration of those spells.

Spider Step

You tread where only arachnids dare.

Prerequisites: Character level 3rd, drow.

Benefit: You can cast *spider climb* once per day as a spell-like ability, using your character level as the caster level. Furthermore, you gain a +4 bonus on saving throws against the web special attacks of spiders and the effects of *web* and other similar spells (such as the *web cloud* spell).

Spider Summoner

You gain the ability to summon powerful spiders.

Prerequisites: Ability to cast *summon monster* or *summon nature's ally* spells, drow.

Benefit: When casting either a *summon monster* spell or a *summon nature's ally* spell, your options increase. Depending on the level of the spell, you can summon the spiders listed below.

Summon Monster: 1st level—giant crab spider* (*Bestiary 3* 254); 4th level—giant black widow* (*Bestiary 2* 256); 5th level—ogre spider* (*Bestiary 3* 256); 7th level—giant tarantula* (*Bestiary 2* 256)

Summon Nature's Ally: 1st level—giant crab spider (*Bestiary 3* 254); 4th level—giant black widow (*Bestiary 2* 256); 5th level—ogre spider (*Bestiary 3* 256); 7th level—giant tarantula (*Bestiary 2* 256)

Creatures marked with an asterisk (*) are summoned with the celestial template if you are good, and the fiendish template if you are evil. If you are neutral, you may choose which template to apply to the creature.

Furthermore, when you summon spiders using *summon monster* or *summon nature's ally*, the DC of the summoned monster's poison and web effects increases by 2.

Umbral Scion

New spell-like abilities are unlocked for you as you rise to ascendency among the drow people.

Prerequisites: Cha 13, Wis 13, Drow Nobility, Greater Drow Nobility, Improved Drow Nobility, able to use drow spell-like abilities, drow.

Benefit: Select one of the following: *dispel magic, divine favor,* or *suggestion.* You may use this spell once per day as a spell-like ability. Your caster level is equal to your character level.

Drow Magic Items

Drow have access to the following magic items.

GLOOM BLADE

Aura strong evocation; **CL** 13th
Slot none; **Price** 8,810 gp; **Weight** 2 lbs.

DESCRIPTION

As black as coal, this short sword grows more potent the farther it is kept from light. It acts as a *+1 short sword* when in dim light. In darkness, it acts as *+2 short sword*. When surrounded by supernatural darkness, such as in an area of *deeper darkness*, it acts a *+2 short sword* and bestows the benefit of the Blind-Fight feat to its wielder. In daylight or bright illumination, the sword temporarily loses all its magical enhancement bonuses and acts as a masterwork weapon, though it resumes its magical functions once it is no longer in the bright light.

CONSTRUCTION

Requirements Craft Magic Arms and Armor, *deeper darkness*; **Cost** 4,560 gp

LIVING GARMENTS

Aura faint transmutation; **CL** 3rd
Slot body; **Price** 5,000 gp; **Weight** 2 lbs.

DESCRIPTION

These sheer and silky robes, many of which are made of spider silk, are of the finest quality. On command, a *living garment* can make a number of subtle adjustments to itself, including coloring, fit, and basic design, accommodating and accentuating whatever mood the wearer wishes to convey. It always remains clean, and automatically repairs damage to itself at a rate of 1 hit point per round (hardness 0, 4 hit points). It also grants the wearer a +5 competence bonus on Diplomacy checks.

CONSTRUCTION

Requirements Craft Wondrous Item, *eagle's splendor, mending, prestidigitation*, creator must be a drow; **Cost** 2,500 gp

ROD OF SHADOWS

Aura moderate abjuration; **CL** 8th
Slot none; **Price** 64,305 gp; **Weight** 5 lbs.

DESCRIPTION

This ebon rod is so dark it seems to absorb the light around it. The rod functions as a *+2 light mace*, and allows its wielder to see in darkness as if it had the see in darkness ability (*Bestiary 2* 301). Three times per day, the wielder can use it to create a *deeper darkness* effect (caster level 8th). To use this ability, the rod's wielder must touch the object affected, which is a standard action that provokes attacks of opportunity.

CONSTRUCTION

Requirements Craft Rod, *deeper darkness, true seeing*; **Cost** 32,305 gp

Drow Spells

Drow have access to the following spells.

ANCESTRAL REGRESSION

School transmutation (polymorph); **Level** alchemist 2, antipaladin 3, cleric 2, sorcerer/wizard 3, witch 2
Casting Time 1 standard action
Components V, S
Range touch
Target willing drow touched
Duration 24 hours (D)
Saving Throw Will negates (harmless); **Spell Resistance** yes (harmless)

The target drow transforms into a surface elf. The drow loses her darkvision and light-blindness racial traits and gains the low-light vision racial trait in their place. The alignment and personality of the drow are not affected by the transformation, but the spell conceals her alignment as an *undetectable alignment* spell. The spell grants the target a +10 bonus on Disguise checks to pass as an elf, though she appears to be an elven analog of herself and can be recognized as such by other drow who know her.

WEB BOLT

School conjuration (creation); **Level** magus 1, sorcerer/wizard 1, witch 1
Casting Time 1 standard action
Components V, S
Range close (25 ft. + 5 ft./2 levels)
Effect fist-sized blob of webbing
Duration 1 min./level
Saving Throw Reflex negates; see text; **Spell Resistance** no

You launch a ball of webbing at a target, which must make a save or be affected as if by a *web* spell occupying only the creature's space. If the creature saves or breaks free of the webbing, the remaining webs dissolve and the square is not considered difficult terrain. The spell has no effect if the target is not on or adjacent to a solid surface that can support the webbing.

WEB CLOUD

School conjuration (creation); **Level** sorcerer/wizard 4, witch 4
Casting Time 1 standard action
Component V, S
Range medium (100 ft. + 10 ft./level)
Effect cloud spreads in 20-ft. radius, 20 ft. high
Duration 1 minute/level
Saving Throw Reflex partial; see text; **Spell Resistance** no

You create a cloud of flame-resistant strands of adhesive webbing that billows and flows much like a *cloudkill* spell. The cloud moves away from you at a rate of 10 feet per round, rolling along the surface of the ground.

Figure out the cloud's new spread each round based on its new point of origin, which is 10 feet farther away from the point of origin where the caster cast the spell. Creatures trapped in the webbing remain trapped even after the cloud passes, but the area the cloud leaves behind does not count as difficult terrain.

Because the webbing is heavier than air, it sinks to the lowest level of the land, even pouring down den or sinkhole openings. The cloud of webbing cannot penetrate liquids, nor can it be cast underwater.

The cloud otherwise acts like a *web* spell. A creature in the cloud at the start of its turn must save against the cloud or be affected. The webbing of this spell is flammable (see the *web* spell), but has fire resistance 5.

FETCHLINGS

Descended from humans trapped on the Shadow Plane, fetchlings are creatures of darkness and light intertwined. Generations of contact with that strange plane and its denizens have made fetchlings a race apart from humanity. While fetchlings acknowledge their origins, they exhibit little physical or cultural resemblance to their ancestors on the Material Plane, and are often insulted when compared to humans. Some members of the race also take offense at the name fetchling, as it was given to them by humans who saw them as little more than fetchers of rare materials from the Shadow Plane. Most fetchlings instead prefer to be called *kayal*, a word borrowed from Aklo that roughly translates to "shadow people" or "dusk dwellers."

Infused with the essence of the Shadow Plane and possessing human blood commingled with that of the Shadow Plane's natives, fetchlings have developed traits and abilities that complement their native plane's bleak and colorless terrain. Though most fetchlings treat the Shadow Plane as home, they often trade and deal with creatures of the Material Plane. Some fetchlings go so far as to create enclaves on the Material Plane in order to establish alliances and trade routes in areas where the boundary between the two planes is less distinct. These fetchlings often serve as merchants, middlemen, and guides for races on both sides of the planar boundary.

Physical Description: Superficially, fetchlings resemble unnaturally lithe—bordering on fragile—humans. Their adopted home has drained their skin and hair of bright colors. Their complexion ranges from stark white to deep black, and includes all the various shades of gray between those two extremes. Their eyes are pupilless and pronounced, and they typically glow a luminescent shade of yellow or greenish yellow, though rare individuals possess blue-green eyes. While their hair tends to be stark white or pale gray, many fetchlings dye their hair black. Some members of higher station or those who dwell on the Material Plane dye their hair with more striking colors, often favoring deep shades of violet, blue, and crimson.

Society: Fetchling are adaptable creatures, and as such display no singular preference for moral philosophy or the rule of law. Most mimic the cultural norms and governmental structures of those they live near or the creatures they serve. While fetchlings are arguably the most populous race on the Shadow Plane, they rarely rule over their own kind; most serve as vassals or subjects to the great umbral dragons of their homeland, or the bizarre nihiloi who dwell in the deeper darkness. Above all, fetchlings are survivors. Their tenacity, versatility, and devious pragmatism have helped them survive the harsh environs of the Shadow Plane and plots of the powerful

creatures dwelling within it. On the Material Plane, especially if unable to return to their home plane at will, fetchlings tend to cluster in small, insular communities of their own kind, mimicking the cultural norms and political structures of those they trade with.

Relations: Because of their shared ancestry, fetchlings interact most easily with humans, though they also find kinship with gnomes and other races that were cut off from their home planes or are not native to the Material Plane. Their pragmatism and adaptable nature put them at odds with warlike or destructive races, and when they do have to deal with orcs, goblinoids, or other savage cultures, fetchlings will often play the part of the fawning sycophant, a tactic learned from serving umbral dragons and one they see as key to their race's survival. Strangely, their relationship with dwarves and elves are rather strained. Dwarves find fetchlings duplicitous and creepy, while the tension with elves is so subtle and inexplicable that both races find it difficult to explain.

Alignment and Religion: Fetchlings—especially those living outside the Shadow Plane—worship a wide variety of gods. On the Shadow Plane, fetchlings primarily worship Desna and Zon-Kuthon, though while the former is venerated, the latter is more placated than worshiped. A smaller number of evil fetchlings worship demon lords of darkness and lust.

Adventurers: The Shadow Plane's ever-present hazards pose great danger to fetchling adventurers, but also great opportunity. Because of their servile status on their home plane, however, most fetchlings prefer to adventure on the Material Plane, which often offers more freedom and trading opportunities between the two planes. Fetchlings make excellent ninjas, oracles, rangers, rogues, and summoners.

Male Names: Arim, Drosil, Jegan, Somar, Yetar, Zoka.
Female Names: Acera, Amelisce, Inva, Renza, Zaitherin.

ALTERNATE RACIAL TRAITS

The following racial traits may be selected instead of existing fetchling racial traits. Consult your GM before selecting any of these new options.

Emissary: Rare fetchlings excel in the role of emissary between the Shadow Plane and the Material Plane. Once per day, such a fetchling can roll twice when making a Bluff or Diplomacy check and take the better roll. This racial trait replaces shadow blending.

Gloom Shimmer: Some fetchlings can manipulate shadowy energy in order to displace their location instead of transporting between shadows. Upon reaching 9th level, instead of gaining *shadow walk* as a spell-like ability, these fetchlings gain *displacement* as a spell-like ability usable twice per day. For this ability, a fetchling's caster level is equal to his total Hit Dice. This racial trait modifies the spell-like ability racial trait.

Shadow Magic: Fetchlings who spend their time studying the subtle magic of their adopted plane gain arcane insights on the use of shadow spells. These fetchlings gain a +1 racial bonus to the DC of any illusion (shadow) spells they cast. This racial trait replaces the skilled racial trait.

Subtle Manipulator: Rather than taking on the forms of others, some fetchling are adept at destroying the memories of other creatures. Instead of gaining *disguise self* as a spell-like ability, such fetchlings can use *memory lapse* (*Advanced Player's Guide* 232) once per day as a spell-like ability. For this ability, a fetchling's caster level is equal to his total Hit Dice. This racial trait modifies the spell-like ability racial trait.

World Walker: Fetchlings who have spent most of their lives on the Material Plane can become more acclimated to their new environments. Instead of gaining a +2 racial bonus on Knowledge (planes) checks, these fetchlings gain a +1 racial bonus on Knowledge (nature) and Knowledge (local) checks. This racial trait modifies the skilled racial trait.

FAVORED CLASS OPTIONS

The following options are available to all fetchlings who have the listed favored class, and unless otherwise stated, the bonus applies each time you select the favored class reward.

Oracle: Treat the oracle's level as +1/3 higher for the purposes of determining which of its racial spell-like abilities it can use.

Ranger: Add a +1/2 bonus on Perception and Survival checks made on the Plane of Shadow.

Rogue: Add a +1/2 bonus on Stealth and Sleight of Hand checks made while in dim light or darkness.

Sorcerer: Add +1/2 to either cold or electricity resistance (maximum resistance 10 for either type).

Summoner: The summoner's eidolon gains resistance 1 against either cold or electricity. Each time the summoner selects this reward, he increases his eidolon's resistance to one of those energy types by 1 (maximum 10 for any one energy type).

Wizard: Add one spell from the wizard spell list to wizard's spellbook. The spell must be at or below the highest level he can cast and be of the illusion (shadow) subschool or have the darkness descriptor.

FETCHLING RACIAL TRAITS

+2 Dexterity, +2 Charisma, –2 Wisdom: Fetchlings are quick and forceful, but often strange and easily distracted by errant thoughts.

Native Outsider: Fetchlings are outsiders with the native subtype.

Medium: Fetchlings are Medium creatures and receive no bonuses or penalties due to their size.

Normal Speed: Fetchlings have a base speed of 30 feet.

Darkvision: Fetchlings can see in the dark up to 60 feet.

Low-Light Vision: Fetchlings can see twice as far as humans in conditions of dim light.

Skilled: Fetchlings have a +2 racial bonus on Knowledge (planes) and Stealth checks.

Shadow Blending (Su): Attacks against a fetchling in dim light have a 50% miss chance instead of the normal 20% miss chance. This ability does not grant total concealment; it just increases the miss chance.

Shadowy Resistance: Fetchlings have cold resistance 5 and electricity resistance 5.

Spell-Like Abilities (Sp): A fetchling can use *disguise self* once per day as a spell-like ability. He can assume the form of any humanoid creature using this spell-like ability. When a fetchling reaches 9th level in any combination of classes, he gains *shadow walk* (self only) as a spell-like ability usable once per day, and at 13th level, he gains *plane shift* (self only, to the Shadow Plane or the Material Plane only) usable once per day. A fetchling's caster level is equal to his total Hit Dice.

Languages: Fetchlings begin play speaking Common. Fetchlings with a high Intelligence scores can choose from the following: Aklo, Aquan, Auran, Draconic, D'ziriak (understanding only, cannot speak), Ignan, Terran, and any regional human tongue.

Shadow Creature (CR +1)

Creatures with the shadow creature template dwell on the Shadow Plane, only rarely venturing onto other, brighter planes, and can be summoned by shadow callers. A shadow creature's CR increases by +1. A shadow creature's quick and rebuild rules are the same.

Rebuild Rules: Senses gains darkvision and low-light vision 60 ft.; **Defensive Abilities** gains energy resistance and DR as noted on the table below; **SR** gains SR equal to new CR + 5; **Special Abilities** *Shadow Blend (Su)* In any condition of illumination other than bright light, a shadow creature blends into the shadows, giving it concealment (20% miss chance). A shadow creature can suspend or resume this ability as a free action.

Shadow Creature Defenses

Hit Dice	Resist Cold and Electricity	DR
1–4	5	—
5–10	10	5/magic
11+	15	10/magic

RACIAL ARCHETYPES

The following racial archetypes are available to fetchlings.

Dusk Stalker (Ranger)

Hunters and guides through the Shadow Plane, dusk stalkers are rangers that thrive in shadow. Adept at hunting in dusk, darkness, and twilight, these rangers excel at manipulating shadows.

Class Skills: The dusk stalker adds Knowledge (planes) to his list of class skills and removes Knowledge (nature) from his list of class skills.

Shadow Guide: When a dusk stalker gains the favored terrain ability, that ability is modified in the following ways. At 3rd level, a dusk stalker picks his primary terrain normally, but only gains a +1 bonus on those checks while on a plane other than the Shadow Plane, and gains a +3 bonus on those checks while on the Shadow Plane. Each time he chooses to add a bonus in a favored terrain, he gains a +1 bonus on those checks while on a plane other than the Shadow Plane, and gains a +3 bonus on those checks while on the Shadow Plane. This ability modifies favored terrain.

Shadow Bond (Su): At 4th level, a dusk stalker creates a mystical bond with shadows. The shadows around a dusk stalker weave and swirl, confusing his enemies. When a dusk stalker is fighting in dim light or darkness (magical or otherwise), he gains a +4 insight bonus on Acrobatics checks made to move through an enemy's threatened area or through its space. Furthermore, a number of times per day equal to his Wisdom modifier, the dusk stalker can manipulate shadows

in a 5-foot square within 30 feet. That square must be in an area of dim light or darkness (magical or otherwise). Enemies with an Intelligence score within or adjacent to that 5-foot square take a –2 penalty to AC and on Reflex saving throws. The harassing shadows last for 1 round. This is a mind-affecting fear effect. This ability replaces hunter's bond.

Dark Sight (Su): At 12th level, a dusk stalker gains the see in darkness ability (*Bestiary 2* 301). This ability replaces camouflage.

Shadow Caller (Summoner)

While most summoners can call any manner of creature from across the planes to serve them in combat, supplementing the skills of their eidolon with a diverse range of creatures, others eschew this broad utility and instead concentrate upon calling forth entities from the Shadow Plane. A shadow caller has the following class features.

Class Skills: The shadow caller adds Stealth to his list of class skills and removes Use Magic Device from his list of class skills.

Shadow Summoning (Sp): When a shadow caller uses his *summon monster* ability or casts the *summon monster* spell, he typically summons creatures from the Shadow Plane or creatures closely associated with shadow. When a creature on the *summon monster* spell list indicates that it is summoned with either the celestial or the fiendish template based on the alignment of the caster, the creature summoned by the shadow caller has the shadow creature template instead (see sidebar). Furthermore, the *summon monster* lists are modified in the following ways (these changes also apply to using a higher-level summon spell to summon multiple creatures from a lower-level list).

Summon Monster I: No changes.

Summon Monster II: A shadow caller cannot summon Small elementals or lemures, but instead can summon zoogs (*Bestiary 3* 288).

Summon Monster III: A shadow caller cannot summon dretches or lantern archons, but can summon augur kytons (*Bestiary 3* 171).

Summon Monster IV: A shadow caller cannot summon Medium elementals, hell hounds, hound archons, or mephits, but can summon allips (*Bestiary 3* 12), gloomwings (*Bestiary 2* 133), and shadows (*Bestiary* 245).

Summon Monster V: A shadow caller cannot summon babau, bearded devils, bralani azatas, Large elementals, salamanders, or xills, but can summon shadow mastiffs (*Bestiary 3* 241) and shae (*Bestiary 3* 242).

Summon Monster VI: A shadow caller cannot summon Huge elementals, erinyes, lillend azatas, or succubi, but can summon cloakers (*Bestiary* 47).

Summon Monster VII: A shadow caller cannot summon bebiliths, bone devils, greater elementals, or vrocks, but can summon greater shadows (*Bestiary* 245).

Summon Monster VIII: A shadow caller can only summon derghodaemons (*Bestiary 3* 66) and young umbral dragons (*Bestiary 2* 102).

Summon Monster IX: A shadow caller can only summon interlocutor kytons (*Bestiary 3* 174) and nightwings (*Bestiary 3* 203).

This ability otherwise functions as and replaces the summoner's normal *summon monster* spell-like abilities.

Shadow Eidolon: A shadow caller's eidolon is at once a thing of shadow called from the deep of the Shadow Plane and his own shadow; the two are inseparable. When his eidolon manifests, his shadow lengthens and finally detaches from him as a creature unto itself. For as long as the shadow caller's eidolon is manifested, he and the eidolon do not have distinct shadows, regardless of the presence or absence of light. This lack of a shadow replaces the magical symbol that identifies the summoner and his eidolon.

This ability alters the summoner's eidolon ability.

New Evolutions

The following evolutions are available to all summoners.

2-Point Evolutions

Shadow Blend (Su): In any condition of illumination other than bright light, the eidolon disappears into the shadows, giving it concealment (20% miss chance). If it has the shadow form evolution, it instead gains total concealment (50% miss chance). The eidolon can suspend or resume this ability as a free action.

Shadow Form (Su): The eidolon's body becomes shadowy and more indistinct. This shadow form grants the eidolon constant concealment (20% miss chance), and its melee attacks affect incorporeal creatures as if it had the *ghost touch* weapon property. The eidolon's melee attacks deal only half damage to corporeal creatures.

NEW RACIAL RULES

The following options are available to fetchlings. At the GM's discretion, other appropriate races may make use of some of these new rules.

Fetchling Equipment

The following alchemical items either boost the strange physiology of fetchlings or augment their abilities to manipulate shadow and darkness.

Darklight Lantern: This lantern does not burn oil, but instead burns shadowcloy (see below). When shadowcloy is used as its fuel, this lantern creates a strange, hazy darkness that decreases the light level for 30 feet around it by one step (*Core Rulebook* 172). Unlike when shadowcloy is thrown at a single target, this haze does not decrease natural darkness to supernatural darkness. One flask of shadowcloy fuels a darklight lantern for 1 minute.

Gloom Sight Goggles: These nonmagical goggles are set with a piece of alchemically treated, black, obsidianlike stone found in the mountainous regions of the Shadow Plane. Gloom sight goggles interact with the unique eyes of fetchlings in such a way that when the goggles are worn over both eyes, they expand the range of a fetchling's darkvision to 90 feet, but the fetchling also gains the light sensitivity weakness (*Bestiary* 301). Other races cannot see through the lenses of these goggles, and they have no affect on fetchlings whose eyes have been modified by the Gloom Sight feat. Though they are alchemical rather than magical in nature, these goggles take up the magic item eye slot.

Shadowcloy: This thin black liquid is stored in airtight flasks because it evaporates quickly when exposed to air. Its cloying vapors cling to a target, obscuring vision for a short period of time. You can throw a shadowcloy flask as a splash weapon with a range increment of 10 feet. A direct hit means the target treats the ambient light as one category darker than normal (*Core Rulebook* 172), with a creature already in natural darkness treating it as supernatural darkness. This effect lasts for 1 round. A thrown shadowcloy flask has no effect on adjacent creatures or if it misses.

Fetchling Equipment

Item	Cost	Weight	Craft DC
Darklight lantern	20 gp	3 lbs.	—
Gloom sight goggles	200 gp	—	25
Shadowcloy flask	25 gp	1 lb.	20

Fetchling Feats

Fetchlings have access to the following feats.

Dark Sight

With further modification, your eyes can pierce the gloom of even magical darkness.

Prerequisites: Gloom Sight, fetchling.

Benefit: You gain the ability to see up to 15 feet clearly in magical darkness, such as that created by the *deeper darkness* spell.

Gloom Sight

With a combination of strange shadow magic and chirurgery, your eyes are permanently modified to see farther in darkness.

Prerequisite: Fetchling.

Benefit: You gain darkvision 90 ft., but gain the light sensitivity weakness (*Bestiary* 301).

Gloom Strike (Combat)

Few creatures are as accustomed to fighting in the shadows as you.

Prerequisites: Blind-Fight, fetchling.

Benefit: When you are within an area of dim light or darkness, you gain a +1 bonus on attack rolls against enemies that are also within dim light or darkness.

Improved Dark Sight

With further modification, your eyes see clearly in not only normal darkness, but in magical darkness as well.

Prerequisites: Dark Sight, Gloom Sight, fetchling.

Benefit: You gain the see in darkness ability (*Bestiary 2* 301) and lose the light sensitivity weakness, but gain the light blindness weakness (*Bestiary* 301).

Shadow Ghost

You can move between the Shadow Plane and the Material Plane more often.

Prerequisites: Fetchling, *shadow walk* spell-like ability.

Benefit: You gain the ability to use *shadow walk* an additional time each day.

Special: You may select this feat multiple times. Its effects stack.

Shadow Walker

You can pierce the veil between the Shadow Plane and the Material Plane more often, and to greater effect.

Prerequisites: Fetchling, *shadow walk* spell-like ability.

Benefit: You can expend one use of your shadow walk spell-like ability to use *dimension door* as a spell-like ability. Your start and end locations for this ability must be in dim light or darkness.

Fetchling Magic Items

Fetchlings have access to the following magic items.

AMULET OF HIDDEN LIGHT

Aura faint illusion; **CL** 3rd
Slot neck; **Price** 9,000 gp; **Weight** —

DESCRIPTION

This large amulet crafted of rough-cut glass can, on command, shed light as a sunrod. Unlike a normal light source, creatures outside this area cannot see the amulet's light.

CONSTRUCTION

Requirements Craft Wondrous Item, *light*, *invisibility*; **Cost** 4,500 gp

LAMBENT WINDOW

Aura moderate divination; **CL** 7th
Slot none; **Price** 20,000 gp; **Weight** 2 lbs.

DESCRIPTION

This small pane of glass in a frame made of black metal looks like a small hand mirror at first glance, but when a creature spends at least 1 minute staring into its reflection, the image shifts and changes, showing the landscape of another plane. If the *lambent window* is activated on the Material Plane, it shows the corresponding location on the Shadow Plane, along with any creatures at that location. Likewise, when used on the Shadow Plane, it shows the corresponding location on the Material Plane. This item only allows those staring into it to see the corresponding location on the other plane; they cannot hear through or gain other sensual information about the other side by way of the window. This effect can be used for up to 10 minutes per day. Those minutes need not be consecutive, and the 1 minute it takes to activate the *lambent window* does not count against this limit.

A person holding an active *lambent window* can use it as a special focus when casting *plane shift* or using *plane shift* as a spell-like ability to reach the specific location shown in the mirror, rather than 5–500 miles from the bearer's intended destination.

CONSTRUCTION

Requirements Craft Wondrous Item, *plane shift*, *scrying*; **Cost** 10,000 gp

LANTERN OF DANCING SHADOWS

Aura moderate transmutation; **CL** 6th
Slot none; **Price** 41,000 gp; **Weight** 2 lbs.

DESCRIPTION

This small lantern is made of thin, nearly transparent paper and black iron. The lantern burns for 6 hours on 1 pint of oil. The lantern's light causes the illumination level in a 30-foot radius to move one step toward dim light, from bright light to normal light, from normal light to dim light, or from darkness to dim light. The lantern has no effect in an area that is already in dim light. Nonmagical sources of light, such as torches and lanterns, do not increase the light level in the lantern's area. Magical light or darkness only change the light level in the lantern's area if they have a higher caster level than the lantern.

Once per day, the lit *lantern of dancing shadows* can be commanded to create quasi-real illusions from the shadows cast by its light, as the *shadow conjuration* spell. In addition, once per day, the lantern can be commanded to solidify shadows for a short period of time. These solidified shadows cause incorporeal creatures within the lantern's illumination radius (30 feet) to coalesce into semi-physical forms, as the *mass ghostbane dirge* spell (*Advanced Player's Guide* 225).

CONSTRUCTION

Requirements Craft Wondrous Item, *darkness*, *mass ghostbane dirge*, *shadow conjuration*; **Cost** 20,500 gp

Fetchling Spells

Fetchlings have access to the following spells.

GLOOMBLIND BOLTS

School conjuration (creation) [shadow]; **Level** magus 3, sorcerer/wizard 3, witch 3
Casting Time 1 standard action
Components V, S
Range medium (100 ft. + 10 ft./level)
Effect one or more bolts of energy
Duration instantaneous
Saving Throw Reflex negates; see text; **Spell Resistance** yes
You create one or more bolts of negative energy infused with shadow pulled from the Shadow Plane. You can fire one bolt,

plus one for every four levels beyond 5th (to a maximum of three bolts at 13th level) at the same or different targets, but all bolts must be aimed at targets within 30 feet of each other and require a ranged touch attack to hit. Each bolt deals 4d6 points of damage to a living creature or heals 4d6 points of damage to an undead creature. Furthermore, the bolt's energy spreads over the skin of creature, possibly blinding it for a short time. Any creature struck by a bolt must succeed at a Reflex saving throw or become blinded for 1 round.

SHADOWY HAVEN

School transmutation; **Level** sorcerer/wizard 4
Casting Time 1 standard action
Components V, S, M (a small black silk bag)
Range touch
Target one 5-foot square of floor touched
Duration 2 hours/level (D)
Saving Throw none; **Spell Resistance** no
This spell functions like *rope trick*, except the point of entry is through a 5-foot-square instead of a rope. The space holds as many as 10 creatures of any size.

When this spell is cast upon a 5-foot-square part of a wall, it creates an extradimensional space adjacent to the Plane of Shadow. Creatures in the extradimensional space are hidden beyond the reach of spells (including divinations) unless those spells work across planes. The space holds as many as 10 creatures (of any size). The entrance to the extradimensional space remains visible as an area that is darker than the ambient illumination.

Spells cannot be cast across the extradimensional interface, nor can area effects cross it. Those in the extradimensional space can see out of it as if a 5-foot-by-5-foot door or window were centered on the affected surface. The window is invisible (though it is within the shadowed entrance to the spell, which is visible), and even creatures that can see the window from the outside can't see through it. Anything inside the extradimensional space is ejected when the spell ends. Only one creature may enter or exit the extradimensional space at a time.

The entrance is only open when the area around it is in dim light. Any other level of light (brighter or darker) closes the entrance, trapping creatures inside the extradimensional space. If the entrance is closed when the spell expires, there is a 50% chance that creatures in it are ejected into the Shadow Plane instead of the location of the entrance. If this occurs, the creatures appear on the Shadow Plane 1d10 miles in a random direction from their corresponding location on the Material Plane. The spell has no effect if cast on a plane that is not adjacent to the Shadow Plane.

Because the extradimensional space is adjacent to the Shadow Plane, any *shadow walk* spell or similar effect that allows travel to the Shadow Plane is more accurate, reducing the distance creatures arrive off-target by half.

GOBLINS

Goblins are a race of childlike creatures with a destructive and voracious nature that makes them almost universally despised. Weak and cowardly, goblins are frequently manipulated or enslaved by stronger creatures that need destructive, disposable foot soldiers. Those goblins that rely on their own wits to survive live on the fringes of society and feed on refuse and the weaker members of more civilized races. Most other races view them as virulent parasites that have proved impossible to exterminate.

Goblins can eat nearly anything, but prefer a diet of meat and consider the flesh of humans and gnomes a rare and difficult-to-obtain delicacy. While they fear the bigger races, goblins' short memories and bottomless appetites mean they frequently go to war or execute raids against other races to sate their pernicious urges and fill their vast larders.

Physical Description: Goblins are short, ugly humanoids that stand just over 3 feet tall. Their scrawny bodies are topped with oversized and usually hairless heads with massive ears and beady red or occasionally yellow eyes. Goblins' skin tone varies based on the surrounding environment; common skin tones include green, gray, and blue, though black and even pale white goblins have been sighted. Their voracious appetites are served well by their huge mouths filled with jagged teeth.

Society: Violent but fecund, goblins exist in primitive tribal structures with constant shifts in power. Rarely able to sustain their own needs through farming or hunting and gathering, goblin tribes live where food is abundant or near places that they can steal it from. Since they are incapable of building significant fortifications and have been driven out of most easily accessible locations, goblins tend to live in unpleasant and remote locations, and their poor building and planning skills ensure that they dwell primarily in crude caves, ramshackle villages, and abandoned structures. Few goblins are good with tools or skilled at farming, and the rare items of any value that they possess are usually cast-off implements from humans or other civilized cultures.

Goblins' appetites and poor planning lead to small tribes dominated by the strongest warriors. Even the hardiest goblin leaders quickly find out that their survival depends on conducting frequent raids to secure sources of food and kill off the more aggressive youth of the tribe. Both goblin men and women are ugly and vicious, and both sexes are just as likely to rise to positions of power in a tribe.

Goblin babies are almost completely self-sufficient not long after birth, and such infants are treated almost like pets. Many tribes raise their children communally in cages or pens where adults can largely ignore them.

Mortality is high among young goblins, and when the adults fail to feed them or food runs low, youths learn at an early age that cannibalism is sometimes the best means of survival in a goblin tribe.

Relations: Goblins tend to view other beings as sources of food, which makes for poor relations with most civilized races. Goblins often survive on the fringes of human civilization, preying on weak or lost travelers and occasionally raiding small settlements to fuel their voracious appetites. They have a special animosity toward gnomes, and celebrate the capturing or killing of such victims with a feast. Of the most common races, half-orcs are the most tolerant of goblins, sharing a similar ancestry and experiencing the same hatred within many societies. Goblins are mostly unaware of half-orcs' sympathy, however, and avoid them because they are larger, meaner, and less flavorful than other humanoids.

Alignment and Religion: Goblins are greedy, capricious, and destructive by nature, and thus most are neutral or chaotic evil. When they bother to worship, goblins follow the goddess Lamashtu and to a lesser extent the four barghest hero-gods, Hadregash, Venkelvore, Zarongel, and Zogmugot.

Adventurers: Goblin adventurers are usually curious and inclined to explore the world, though they are often killed off by their own foolish misdeeds or hunted down for their random acts of destruction. Their pernicious nature makes interacting with civilized races almost impossible, so goblins tend to adventure on the fringes of civilization or in the wilds. Adventurous individuals who survive long enough often ride goblin dogs or other exotic mounts, and focus on archery to avoid close confrontation with larger enemies. Goblin spellcasters prefer fire magic and bombs over almost all other methods of spreading mayhem.

Male Names: Boorgub, Gogmurch, Rotfoot, Zobmaggle.
Female Names: Geedra, Goomluga, Hoglob, Luckums.

ALTERNATE RACIAL TRAITS

The following racial traits may be selected instead of existing goblin racial traits. Consult your GM before selecting any of these new options.

Cave Crawler: Some goblins are born and raised in caves and rarely see the light of day. Goblins with this trait gain a climb speed of 10 feet and the +8 racial bonus on Climb checks associated with having a climb speed. Goblins with this racial trait have a base speed of 20 feet and lose the fast movement racial trait.

City Scavenger: Goblins who live within the boundaries of human cities survive by scavenging for refuse and hunting stray animals. Goblins with this trait gain a +2 racial bonus on Perception and Survival checks, and can use Survival to forage for food while in a city. This racial trait replaces skilled.

Eat Anything: Raised with little or no proper food, many goblins have learned to survive by eating whatever they happen across and can digest nearly anything without getting sick. Goblins with this trait gain a +4 on Survival checks to forage for food and a +4 racial bonus on saves versus effects that cause the nauseated or sickened conditions. This racial trait replaces skilled.

Hard Head, Big Teeth: Goblins are known for their balloonlike heads and enormous maws, but some have even more exaggeratedly large heads filled with razor-sharp teeth. Goblins with this trait gain a bite attack as a primary natural attack that deals 1d4 points of damage. This racial trait replaces skilled.

Over-Sized Ears: While goblins' ears are never dainty, these goblins have freakishly large ears capable of picking up even the smallest sounds. Goblins with this racial trait gain a +4 bonus on Perception checks. This racial trait replaces skilled.

Tree Runner: In trackless rain forests and marshes, it can be difficult to find dry ground to build on. Goblin tribes living in such areas have learned to live in the treetops. These goblins gain a +4 racial bonus on Acrobatics and Climb checks. This racial trait replaces skilled.

Weapon Familiarity: Goblins' traditional weapons are the dogslicer and the horsechopper, weapons designed specifically to bring down their most hated foes. Goblins with this trait are proficient with the dogslicer and the horsechopper, and treat any weapon with the word "goblin" in it as martial weapons. This racial trait replaces skilled.

FAVORED CLASS OPTIONS

The following options are available to any goblins that have the listed favored class, and unless otherwise stated, the bonus applies each time you select the favored class reward.

Alchemist: The alchemist gains fire resistance 1. Each time this reward is selected, increase fire resistance by +1. This fire resistance does not stack with fire resistance gained from other sources.

Barbarian: Add +1/2 on critical hit confirmation rolls for attacks made with unarmed strikes or natural weapons (maximum bonus of +4). This bonus does not stack with Critical Focus.

Bard: Add +1 to the bard's total number of bardic performance rounds per day.

Cavalier: Add +1 hit points to the cavalier's mount companion. If the cavalier ever replaces his mount, the new mount gains these bonus hit points.

Druid: Add +1 hit points to the druid's animal companion. If the druid ever replaces her animal companion, the new animal companion gains these bonus hit points.

Gunslinger: Add +1/3 on critical hit confirmation rolls made with firearms (maximum bonus of +5). This bonus does not stack with Critical Focus.

Oracle: Add +1 on concentration checks made when casting spells with the fire descriptor.

Ranger: Gain a +1/2 bonus on damage dealt to dogs (and doglike creatures) and horses (and horselike creatures).

Rogue: Add a +1 bonus on the rogue's sneak attack damage rolls during the surprise round or before the target has acted in combat.

GOBLIN RACIAL TRAITS

+4 Dexterity, −2 Strength, −2 Charisma: Goblins are fast, but weak and unpleasant to be around.

Goblinoid: Goblins are humanoids with the goblinoid subtype.

Small: Goblins are Small creatures and gain a +1 size bonus to their AC, a +1 size bonus on attack rolls, a −1 penalty to their CMB and CMD, and a +4 size bonus on Stealth checks.

Fast: Goblins are fast for their size, and have a base speed of 30 feet.

Darkvision: Goblins can see in the dark up to 60 feet.

Skilled: +4 racial bonus on Ride and Stealth checks.

Languages: Goblins begin play speaking Goblin. Goblins with high Intelligence scores can choose from the following: Common, Draconic, Dwarven, Gnoll, Gnome, Halfling, and Orc.

Goblin Discoveries

The following discoveries are available to goblin alchemists.

Fire Brand (Su): An alchemist with this discovery can expend one daily bomb use to apply the bomb reagents to his weapon as a swift action. A weapon treated this way deals fire damage as if it had the *flaming* weapon special ability. At 10th level, the weapon is treated as if it had the *flaming burst* weapon special ability. The bomb reagents continue burning for 1 minute or until extinguished by dousing the weapon in water. An alchemist can use this ability with natural weapons, but he takes 1d6 points of fire damage per round for each natural weapon treated.

Rag Doll Mutagen (Su): When the alchemist imbibes a mutagen, his body and bones become rubbery and easy to contort. The alchemist gains a bonus equal to his class level on Escape Artist checks, can squeeze through places as if he were one size category smaller, and can make a Reflex save (DC equal to 15 + 1 for every 10 feet fallen) to take half damage from falling. At 10th level, all falling damage is considered nonlethal damage, and the alchemist can squeeze through places as if he were two size categories smaller than his size while under the effects of this mutagen.

Rocket Bomb (Su): Alchemists with this discovery can prepare special rockets to deliver their bombs. Rocket bombs travel farther and explode bigger than normal bombs, but cannot target individual creatures. Rocket bombs explode in a 20-foot radius, and all creatures in that area take the alchemist's normal splash damage. The range increment on a rocket bomb is 50 feet. Rocket bombs cannot be used with the precise bomb or fast bomb discoveries. An alchemist must be at least 6th level before selecting this discovery.

Scrap Bomb (Su): When the alchemist creates a bomb, he can choose to have it explode into shards of shrapnel that deal piercing damage. A creature that takes a direct hit from a scrap bomb takes 1 point of bleed damage per die of bomb damage unless it succeeds at a Reflex save.

Sorcerer: Add +1 spell known from the sorcerer spell list. This spell must be at least one level below the highest spell level the sorcerer can cast, and must have the fire descriptor.

Summoner: Add +1/4 evolution point to the eidolon's evolution pool. These bonus evolution points must be spent on evolutions that deal fire damage or protect the eidolon from fire (for example, resistance, energy attacks, immunity, breath weapon, and so on).

Witch: Add +1 spell from the witch spell list to the witch's familiar. This spell must be at least one level below the highest spell level she can cast. If the witch ever replaces her familiar, the new familiar knows these bonus spells.

Racial Archetypes

The following racial archetypes are available to goblins.

Feral Gnasher (Barbarian)

Feral gnashers grow up in the wild, either raised by animals or scraping by on their own, and soon learn to fend for themselves. These barbarians often utilize pieced-together armor and fight with their sharp teeth and whatever improvised weapons are within reach. A feral gnasher has the following class features.

Weapon and Armor Proficiency: A feral gnasher loses all martial weapon proficiencies except for greatclub and loses proficiency with medium armor.

Savage Bite (Ex): At 1st level, a feral gnasher gains a savage bite attack. This is a primary natural attack that deals 1d4 points of damage. If the goblin already has the hard head, big teeth racial trait, the damage increases to 1d6. At 10th level, the damage from a feral gnasher's bite increases to 1d6 (or 1d8 if the goblin has the hard head, big teeth racial trait) and deals ×3 damage on a critical hit. This ability replaces fast movement.

Impromptu Armament (Ex): At 2nd level, a feral gnasher gains Throw Anything as a bonus feat and can pick up an unattended object that can be wielded in one hand as a free action. Additionally, the feral gnasher can take Catch Off-Guard in place of a rage power. This replaces the rage power gained at second level.

Lockjaw (Ex): At 3rd level, a feral gnasher gains the grab ability with her bite attack. A feral gnasher can use this ability on a creature up to one size category larger than she is. This replaces trap sense +1.

Improvised Weapon Mastery (Ex): At 5th level, a feral gnasher gains Improvised Weapon Mastery as a bonus feat. This replaces improved uncanny dodge.

Improved Lockjaw (Ex): At 6th level, as long as a feral gnasher is controlling the grapple with her lockjaw attack, she does not gain the grappled condition, but is unable to move or use her mouth for anything other than grappling. This ability replaces trap sense +2.

Greater Lockjaw (Ex): At 9th level and again at 15th level, the size of a creature a feral gnasher is able to use her lockjaw's grab ability on increases by one size increment. This ability replaces trap sense +3 and trap sense +5.

Wicked Improvisation (Ex): At 12th level, a feral gnasher becomes more capable with improvised weapons and natural attacks. The feral gnasher gains a +1 competence bonus on damage rolls when using natural attacks or improvised weapons while raging. At 14th level and every two levels thereafter, the damage bonus increases by +1. This increase is not precision damage and is thus multiplied on a critical hit. This ability replaces trap sense +4.

Rage Powers: The following rage powers complement the feral gnasher archetype: increased damage reduction, scent, superstition (*Core Rulebook*); beast totem, beast totem (greater), beast totem (lesser) (*Advanced Player's Guide*); eater of magic, ghost rager (*Ultimate Combat*).

Fire Bomber (Alchemist)

Fire bombers are exceptionally good at using bombs to burn creatures and blow things up, but are not quite as good at creating other types of bombs or extracts. A fire bomber has the following class features.

Weapon and Armor Proficiency: A fire bomber treats torches as a simple weapon.

Fire Bombardier (Su or Ex): At 1st level, when a fire bomber throws a bomb that deals fire damage, all creatures in the splash radius take an additional point of damage per die of fire damage dealt. Fire bombers only add their Intelligence bonus to damage from bombs or alchemical substances that deal fire damage. This otherwise works like the alchemist's bomb and throw anything abilities. This ability alters bomb and throw anything.

Bonus Feats: A fire bomber can select the Burn! Burn! Burn!, Fire Tamer, or Flame Heart feat in place of a discovery.

Fiery Cocktail (Su): At 4th level, whenever a fire bomber uses a discovery that deals damage other than fire damage, he can split the damage dice evenly between the bomb's primary damage type and 1d6 points of fire damage; when there is an odd number of damage dice, the odd die of damage comes from the primary damage type. For example, an 8th-level fire bomber could throw a concussive bomb that deals 2d6 points of fire damage and 3d4 points of sonic damage. Additional effects from the bomb still apply, but the save DC for admixture bombs is reduced by 2. This replaces the alchemist's 4th-level discovery.

Fire Body (Ex): At 8th level, a fire bomber adds *elemental body I* to his extract list as a 3rd-level extract. *Elemental body* extracts prepared using fire body are limited to fire elementals only. This ability replaces poison resistance +6.

Improved Fire Body (Ex): At 10th level, fire bombers add *elemental body II* to their spell list as a 4th-level extract. *Elemental body* extracts prepared using improved fire body are limited to fire elementals only. This ability replaces poison immunity.

Greater Fire Body (Ex): At 14th level, fire bombers add *elemental body IV* to their spell list as a 5th-level extract. *Elemental body* extracts prepared using greater fire body are limited to fire elementals only. This ability replaces persistent mutagen.

Discoveries: The following discoveries complement the fire bomber archetype: fire brand, rocket bomb (see sidebar); explosive bombs, fast bombs, inferno bomb, precise bombs (*Advanced Player's Guide*); breath weapon bomb, explosive missile, immolation bomb (*Ultimate Combat*); bottled ooze, confusion bomb, strafe bomb (*Ultimate Magic*).

NEW RACIAL RULES

The following options are available to goblins. At the GM's discretion, other appropriate races may make use of some of these new rules.

Goblin Equipment

The following items are just some of the pieces of equipment used by goblins.

Bomb Launcher: These odd looking, egg-shaped contraptions have cleverly placed fins that improve bombs' accuracy. Goblin alchemists use these special containers to make their bombs more accurate when thrown long distances. Using a bomb launcher when throwing a bomb increases the bomb's range increment to 30 feet (or increases the range increment of a bomb with the rocket bomb discovery to 70 feet). Bomb launchers are destroyed when used.

Dogslicer: This short, curved sword is a favorite weapon of goblins, who show unusual cunning by drilling numerous holes in the blade to reduce the weapon's weight. Masterwork versions of a dogslicer lose the fragile special weapon ability.

TABLE 2-1: GOBLIN WEAPONS

Martial Weapons	Cost	Dmg (S)	Dmg (M)	Critical	Range	Weight	Type	Special
Light Melee Weapons								
Dogslicer	8 gp	1d4	1d6	19–20/×2	—	1 lb.	S	fragile*
Two-Handed Melee Weapons								
Horsechopper	10 gp	1d8	1d10	×3	—	12 lbs.	P or S	reach, trip

* **Fragile Weapons:** A fragile weapon gains the broken condition if the wielder rolls a natural 1 on an attack roll with the weapon. If a fragile weapon is already broken, rolling a natural 1 destroys it instead.

Horsechopper: Crafted by goblins to give themselves an advantage against horses, this weapon is essentially a halberd with an enlarged hook opposite the blade.

Mellowroot: Sneaky goblin chieftains give this orange paste to the tribe's warriors before proposing a particularly bold raid. Consuming mellowroot causes a euphoric feeling that makes you feel invulnerable. For 1 hour after consuming mellowroot, you gain a +5 alchemical bonus versus fear effects. However, while under the effects of mellowroot, you must make a DC 15 Will saving throw when you try to leave the threatened area of an opponent. If you fail the saving throw, you cannot leave the threatened area with that action but do not lose the action.

Stillgut: Drinking a vial of this bland, bluish liquid grants you a +5 alchemical bonus on Fortitude saves to avoid nausea or sickness for 1 hour. If you are already nauseated, you can drink stillgut as a move action. Drinking it in this fashion grants you a second saving throw (without the +5 bonus). Goblins often use stillgut so they can choke down meat or other foods in advanced stages of rot or decay.

Goblin Equipment

Items	Cost	Weight	Craft DC
Bomb launcher	10 gp	1/2 lb.	25
Mellowroot (vial)	25 gp	—	20
Stillgut (vial)	50 gp	—	25

Goblin Feats

Goblins have access to the following feats.

Burn! Burn! Burn!

You take the goblin love of arson and fire play to a whole new level.

Prerequisites: Disable Device 1 rank, goblin.

Benefit: You deal an extra 1d4 points of fire damage when you attack with fire from an alchemical or nonmagical source (such as with alchemical fire or torches) and gain a +4 competence bonus on Reflex saving throws made to avoid catching on fire or to put yourself out when on fire. Additional damage caused by this feat does not apply to magical attacks (such as an alchemist's bomb) or to splash damage.

Fire Hand (Combat)

Born with a torch in your hand, you have a gift with anything that burns.

Prerequisite: Goblin.

Benefit: You can wield a torch as a weapon without taking the nonproficient penalty and gain a +1 bonus on attack rolls with melee weapons that deal fire damage.

Fire Tamer

You know your way around even magical fire.

Prerequisite: Goblin.

Benefit: You gain a +2 bonus on saves against spells with the fire descriptor. Additionally, your scars mark you as a talented fire tamer, granting you a +2 circumstance bonus on Diplomacy and Intimidate checks when dealing with other goblins.

Flame Heart

You have mastered fire magic and alchemy.

Prerequisites: Fire Tamer, character level 5th, goblin.

Benefit: You gain fire resistance 5. When casting spells with the fire descriptor or throwing alchemist bombs that deal fire damage, treat your caster level or alchemist level as if you were 1 level higher.

Goblin Gunslinger (Combat)

You have learned how to fire the big guns.

Prerequisite: Goblin.

Benefit: You can wield Medium firearms without taking the penalty for an inappropriately sized weapon.

Normal: You take a –2 penalty when using an inappropriately sized weapon.

Tangle Feet (Combat)

Creatures who cross your path find themselves tripping over their own feet.

Prerequisites: Dodge, Mobility, Underfoot (Advanced Player's Guide 173), goblin, Small size or smaller.

Benefit: When you successfully make an Acrobatics check to avoid provoking an attack of opportunity from a larger opponent when you move through its threatened area or its space, you can make that opponent lose its balance until the end of its next turn as a free action. While that creature's balance is lost, if it attempts to move, it must make a successful DC 15 Acrobatics check or fall prone, wasting the move action. You can only affect one creature with this effect each round.

Goblin Magic Items

Goblins have access to the following magic item.

CLOAK OF FANGS

Aura moderate transmutation; **CL** 9th
Slot shoulders; **Price** 2,800 gp; **Weight** 1 lb.
DESCRIPTION
This rough-looking cloak covered in coarse animal hair is greatly prized by goblins. Wearing the cloak grants a +1 resistance bonus on saving throws. Furthermore, the wearer can force its teeth to grow rapidly up to five times per day as a swift action. The oversized teeth last for 1 round, during which time the wearer can make a bite attack. Treat this attack as a primary natural attack that deals 1d4 points of damage (or 1d6 if the wearer is Medium). If the wearer already has a bite attack, the damage of that bite attack increases by one step (see page 302 of the *Bestiary*).
CONSTRUCTION
Requirements Craft Wondrous Item, *alter self*, *resistance*; **Cost** 1,250 gp

Goblin Spells

Goblins have access to the following spells.

FIRE TRAIL

School transmutation [fire]; **Level** alchemist 3, magus 3, sorcerer/wizard 3
Casting Time 1 standard action
Components V, S
Range personal
Effect trail of flame that follows the caster's movements; see text
Duration 1 round/level
Saving Throw none; **Spell Resistance** yes
When you cast this spell, flammable liquid oozes from your pores, dripping onto the ground and spontaneously combusting. The flame does not harm you. During this spell's duration, each time you leave your space, you create a trail of fire that burns within the spaces you move through for 1 round before it burns out. You can leave up to 60 feet of flame trail each round, assuming you are Small or Medium. If you are larger than Medium, the maximum trail length is reduced based on your size. If you are Large, you can leave a trail up to 30 feet long (and 10 feet wide), and if you are Huge, you can leave a trail up to 15 feet long (and 15 feet wide); even larger casters can only leave a trail up to 10

feet long (and as wide as your space) each round. You choose where to leave a flame trail.

Creatures that start their turn adjacent to the flame trail take 1d6 points of fire damage. Creatures that start their turn within the flame trail or that enter an area of flame take a number of points of fire damage equal to 1d6 + 1 per caster level (maximum +10). If a creature moves into an area of the flame trail multiple times in a round, it takes this damage each time it enters the area of the flame trail. Flammable objects in or adjacent to the fire trail catch fire.

MUDBALL

School conjuration [earth]; **Level** druid 1, magus 1, sorcerer/ wizard 1, witch 1
Casting Time 1 standard action
Components V, S
Range close (25 ft. + 5 ft./2 levels)
Effect single fist-sized blob of sticky mud
Duration instantaneous
Saving Throw Reflex negates; see text; **Spell Resistance** no
When you cast this spell, you conjure a single ball of sticky mud and launch it at an enemy's face as a ranged touch attack. If the mudball hits, the target is blinded. Each round at the beginning of its turn, a creature blinded by this spell can attempt a Reflex saving throw to shake off the mud, ending the effect. The mudball can also be wiped off by the creature affected by it or by a creature adjacent to the creature affected by it as a standard action.

VOMIT TWIN

School conjuration (creation, teleportation); **Level** alchemist 3, magus 3, sorcerer/wizard 4, summoner 3
Casting Time 1 standard action
Components V, S
Range personal
Effect creates one ooze duplicate of the caster
Duration 1 round/level
Upon casting this spell, you vomit forth a disgusting ooze copy of yourself into a single adjacent square. As long as the twin exists, whenever you take a move action to move, the twin can move as well, although it does not need to follow you and cannot take any other actions. On subsequent rounds, at the start of your turn, you can instantaneously exchange places with your twin, as if using *teleport*. This is not an action and does not provoke an attack of opportunity.

The twin has a speed of 30 feet and provokes attacks of opportunity from movement as normal. It has an AC equal to 10 + 1/2 your caster level and a number of hit points equal to your caster level. If the twin is reduced to 0 hit points, it is destroyed, although you can create a new one on your turn as a standard action as long as the duration persists. You cannot have more than one vomit twin at a time.

HOBGOBLINS

Fierce and militaristic, hobgoblins survive by conquest. The raw materials to fuel their war machines come from raids, their armaments and buildings from the toil of slaves worked to death. Naturally ambitious and envious, hobgoblins seek to better themselves at the expense of others of their kind, yet in battle they put aside petty differences and fight with discipline rivaling that of the finest soldiers. Hobgoblins have little love or trust for one another, and even less for outsiders. Life for these brutes consists of duty to those of higher station, domination of those below, and the rare opportunities to seize personal glory and elevate their status.

Physical Description: Burly and muscled, hobgoblins stand a few inches shorter than the average human, and their long arms, thick torsos, and relatively short legs give them an almost apelike stature. Hobgoblins' skin is a sickly gray-green that darkens to mossy green after long exposure to the sun. Their eyes burn fiery orange or red, and their broad faces and sharply pointed ears give their features a somewhat feline cast. Hobgoblins lack facial hair, and even hobgoblin women are bald. Except for their size, hobgoblins bear a strong physical resemblance to their goblin cousins.

Society: Hobgoblins live in militaristic tyrannies, each community under the absolute rule of a hobgoblin general. Every hobgoblin in a settlement receives military training, with those who excel serving in the army and the rest left to serve more menial roles. Those deemed unfit for military service have little social status, barely rating above favored slaves. Despite this, hobgoblin society is egalitarian after a fashion. Gender and birth offer no barrier to advancement, which is determined almost solely by each individual's personal merit. Hobgoblins eschew strong attachments, even to their young. Matings are matters of convenience, and are almost always limited to hobgoblins of equal rank. Any resulting baby is taken from its mother and forcibly weaned after 3 weeks of age. Young mature quickly—most take no more than 6 months to learn to talk and care for themselves. Hobgoblins' childhoods last a scant 14 years, a mirthless span filled with brutal training in the art of war.

Relations: Hobgoblins view other races as nothing more than tools—implements to be enslaved, cowed, and put to work. Without slaves, hobgoblin society would collapse, so reliant is it on stolen labor. An injured, sickly, or defiant slave is like a broken tool, useless waste to be tossed out with the day's garbage. Not surprisingly, hobgoblin communities count no other races as their friends, and few as allies. Elves and dwarves earn special enmity, and are devilishly hard to break into proper slavery as both races hold blood feuds against goblinkind. Halflings

and half-orcs make especially prized slaves—the former for their agile skills and the ease of breaking them to the collar, and the latter for their talent at thriving under the harshest of conditions. Hobgoblins have little love for the rest of goblinkind, though they typically treat goblinoid slaves better than they do other races.

Alignment and Religion: Hobgoblin life is nothing if not ordered and hierarchical, and hobgoblins lean strongly toward the lawful alignments. While not innately evil, the callous and brutal training that fills the too-short childhood of hobgoblins leaves most embittered and full of hate. Hobgoblins of good alignment number the fewest, and almost exclusively consist of individuals raised in other cultures. More numerous but still rare are hobgoblins of chaotic bent, most often exiles cast out by the despots of their homelands. Religion, like most non-militaristic pursuits, matters little to the majority of hobgoblins. Most pay lip-service to one or more gods and occasionally make offerings to curry favor or turn aside ill fortune. Those hobgoblins who feel a stronger religious calling venerate fearsome, tyrannical gods and devils.

Adventurers: Hobgoblin adventurers tend to be iconoclasts, loners who chafe under the strict hierarchy of military life. Others have fled or been exiled in disgrace for showing weakness or cowardice. Some harbor dreams of one day returning to the hobgoblin flock flush with wealth and tales of great deeds. A few serve farsighted hobgoblin generals, who send the most promising youths out into the world that they might someday return as mighty heroes for the hobgoblin cause. Hobgoblins lean toward martial classes, particularly cavaliers, fighters, monks, and rogues. The arcane arts are distrusted in hobgoblin society and consequently their practitioners are rare, save for alchemists, who gain grudging praise and admiration for their pyrotechnic talents.

Male Names: Arak, Bekri, Doruk, Fethi, Grung, Hagla, Haluk, Kurat, Malgrim, Mevlut, Oktar, Saltuk, Turgut.

Female Names: Afet, Ceyda, Ela, Esma, Huri, Kurmu, Maral, Masal, Melda, Nisa, Nural, Sekla, Sena, Tansu, Vesile.

ALTERNATE RACIAL TRAITS

The following racial traits may be selected instead of existing hobgoblin racial traits. Consult your GM before selecting any of these new options.

Bandy-Legged: Bandy-legged hobgoblins have an even more exaggerated stature than other hobgoblins, with bowed legs and massive shoulders. Hobgoblins with this racial trait gain a +2 racial bonus on Climb and Ride checks, and a +2 racial bonus to their CMD against bull rush or trip attempts while on solid ground. The base speed of bandy-legged hobgoblins is reduced to 20 feet.

Battle-Hardened: Incessant drills make defense second nature to some hobgoblins. Hobgoblins with this racial trait gain a +1 bonus to CMD. This racial trait replaces sneaky.

Engineer: Hobgoblin engineers tinker endlessly with fire, explosives, and the engines of war. Hobgoblins with this racial trait gain a +2 racial bonus on Craft (alchemy) and Knowledge (engineering) checks. This racial trait replaces sneaky.

Fearsome: Some hobgoblins scorn caution and subtlety for swagger and bluster. Hobgoblins with this racial trait gain a +4 racial bonus on Intimidate checks. This racial trait replaces sneaky.

Magehunter: Hobgoblins hate and fear arcane casters. A magehunter gains a +2 racial bonus on Spellcraft checks made to identify a spell being cast and a +1 racial bonus on attack rolls against arcane spellcasters. He only gains this bonus against creatures that use spells, and not against those that only use spell-like abilities. This racial trait replaces sneaky.

Pit Boss: Slave blood fuels the hobgoblin war machine. Pit bosses extract the last breath of labor from their charges with a liberal touch of the lash. Hobgoblins with this racial trait gain proficiency with whips and a +1 racial bonus on combat maneuver checks made to disarm or trip with a whip. This racial trait replaces sneaky.

Scarred: A hobgoblin can scar himself with both blade and fire to toughen his hide into a mass of horny scars. Hobgoblins with this racial trait gain a +1 natural armor bonus to Armor Class. However, the repeated exposure to fire permanently damages their eyes. This racial trait replaces the darkvision racial trait.

Slave Hunter: Hobgoblin slavers excel at tracking down runaway slaves and surviving in filthy conditions. Hobgoblins with this racial trait gain a +2 racial bonus on Survival checks and a +2 racial bonus on Fortitude saves against disease. This racial trait replaces sneaky.

Unfit: Hobgoblins who failed to secure a position in the military hold the lowest status in hobgoblin society, and quickly learn the value of currying favor with their betters. Hobgoblins with this racial trait gain proficiency in a single martial weapon and +1 racial bonus on Bluff and Diplomacy checks. This racial trait replaces sneaky.

FAVORED CLASS OPTIONS

The following options are available to all hobgoblins who have the listed favored class, and unless otherwise stated, the bonus applies each time you select the favored class reward.

Alchemist: Add +1/2 to the number of bombs per day the alchemist can create.

Cavalier: Add a +1/2 bonus on Intimidate checks and Ride checks.

Cleric: Add +1/2 to negative energy spell damage, including inflict spells.

Fighter: Add a +1/2 circumstance bonus on critical hit confirmation rolls with a weapon of the fighter's choice (maximum bonus +4). This bonus does not stack with Critical Focus.

Gunslinger: Add +1/4 to the gunslinger's grit points.

Inquisitor: Add a +1 bonus on concentration checks made to cast inquisitor spells.

Monk: Add a +1/4 bonus on combat maneuver checks made to grapple or trip.

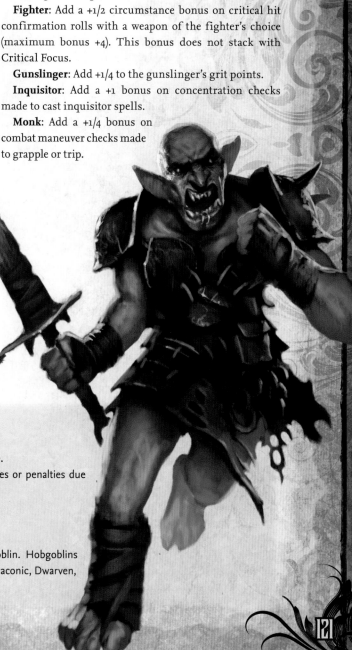

HOBGOBLIN RACIAL TRAITS

+2 Dexterity, +2 Constitution: Hobgoblins are fast and hardy.

Goblinoid: Hobgoblins are humanoids with the goblinoid subtype.

Medium: Hobgoblins are Medium creatures and have no bonuses or penalties due to their size.

Normal Speed: Hobgoblins have a base speed of 30 feet.

Darkvision: Hobgoblins can see in the dark up to 60 feet.

Sneaky: Hobgoblins receive a +4 racial bonus on Stealth checks.

Languages: Hobgoblins begin play speaking Common and Goblin. Hobgoblins with high Intelligence scores can choose from the following: Draconic, Dwarven, Infernal, Giant, and Orc.

Ranger: Add +1/4 to a single existing favored enemy bonus (maximum bonus +1 per favored enemy).

Rogue: Reduce the penalty for not being proficient with one weapon by 1. When the nonproficiency penalty for a weapon becomes 0 because of this ability, the rogue is treated as having the appropriate Martial or Exotic Weapon Proficiency feat for that weapon.

RACIAL ARCHETYPES

The following racial archetypes are available to hobgoblins.

Fell Rider (Cavalier)

The fell rider rides a bestial steed, a mount mastered by him alone. He tramples his enemies down, leaving twisted bodies in his wake, and fear rides with him.

Brute Steed (Ex): A fell rider's mount is unusually large and fierce. It gains a +2 bonus to Strength, but takes a –2 penalty to Dexterity. This otherwise works like the cavalier's mount ability and alters that ability.

Rampage (Ex): At 3rd level, a fell rider gains Trample as a bonus feat. The fell rider receives a +2 bonus on overrun attempts made while mounted. In addition, his mount gains a +2 bonus on damage rolls when making hoof attacks or using the trample monster ability, even when not overrunning. This ability replaces cavalier's charge.

Dread Rider (Ex): At 4th level, a fell rider gains a bonus equal to 1/2 his level on Intimidate checks made while mounted. Once per round as a free action, he can make an Intimidate check to demoralize a foe he has trampled or charged while mounted. This ability replaces expert trainer.

Fell Presence (Ex): At 5th level, a fell rider inspires dread while mounted. As long as the fell rider is mounted, all enemies within 60 feet receive a –2 penalty on savings throws against fear. At 10th level and every 5 levels thereafter, this penalty increases by –1. This ability replaces banner.

Deadly Rampage (Ex): At 11th level, a mounted fell rider no longer provokes attacks of opportunity when he attempts to overrun a creature. He can make a single melee attack against the creature as a free action if the overrun attempt succeeds. This ability replaces mighty charge.

Terror (Ex): At 14th level, a fell rider can rear up his mount as a standard action, spreading terror among his enemies.

Enemies within 60 feet who can see the fell rider must succeed at a Will save (DC 10 + 1/2 the fell rider's level + the fell rider's Charisma modifier) or be shaken for 1 round per level the fell rider possesses. Creatures with half or fewer Hit Dice than the fell rider become frightened instead. An opponent that succeeds at the saving throw is immune to that fell rider's terror ability for 24 hours. This ability is a mind-affecting fear effect, and replaces greater banner.

Unstoppable Rampage (Ex): At 20th level, a mounted fell rider can overrun up to four creatures as part of a single overrun combat maneuver. Each attempt made against a creature after the first receives a cumulative –5 penalty (for example, the fourth overrun attempt would be at a –15 penalty). If any overrun attempt fails, the fell rider cannot make further overrun attempts that round. Attacks made by the fell rider or his mount as part of the overrun, such as those provided by the Trample feat or the deadly rampage ability, receive a +4 bonus to hit, and any critical threats from these attacks automatically confirm. This ability replaces supreme charge.

Ironskin Monk (Monk)

Through discipline and training, an ironskin monk hardens his body to withstand punishing blows. Though slow on his feet, his calloused hands and feet can shatter stone and stagger foes.

Iron Skin (Ex): At 1st level, an ironskin monk gains a +1 bonus to his natural armor. This bonus stacks with any existing natural armor the ironskin monk already has. At 4th level, and every 4 levels thereafter, this bonus increases by +1. This ability replaces the monk's AC bonus ability and the ability to add his Wisdom bonus to his AC.

Bonus Feat: At 1st level, an ironskin monk adds Power Attack to his list of bonus feats. At 6th level, he adds Improved Sunder to the list. At 10th level, he adds Greater Sunder to the list. These bonus feat choices replace Dodge, Mobility, and Spring Attack on his bonus feat list.

Resilience (Ex): At 2nd level, an ironskin monk can shake off the physical effects of certain attacks. If he makes a Fortitude saving throw against an attack that has a reduced effect on a successful save, he instead avoids the effect entirely. This ability can be used only if the monk is wearing light armor or no armor. A helpless monk does not gain the benefits of resilience. This ability replaces evasion.

Ki Pool (Su): At 4th level, an ironskin monk can spend 1 point from his *ki* pool to gain a damage bonus equal to 1/2 his level against objects and constructs for 1 round. This replaces the ability to increase speed with *ki*.

Staggering Blow (Ex): At 5th level, an ironskin monk attacking with an unarmed strike can spend 1 point from his *ki* pool as a free action after a successful critical hit to stagger the creature struck for 1 round (Fort DC 10 + 1/2 the ironskin monk's level + the ironskin monk's Wisdom modifier negates). This ability replaces high jump.

Tough as Nails (Ex): At 6th level, an ironskin monk gains DR 1/—. Subtract 1 point from the damage the ironskin monk takes each time he is dealt damage from a weapon or a natural attack. This damage reduction increases by 1 point at 9th level and every 3 levels thereafter. Damage reduction can reduce damage to 0 but not below 0. This ability replaces fast movement and slow fall.

Evasion (Ex): At 9th level, an ironskin monk gains evasion. This ability replaces improved evasion.

Surefooted (Ex): At 17th level, an ironskin monk's speed is not reduced by difficult terrain. This ability replaces tongue of the sun and moon.

Unbreakable (Ex): At 20th level, an ironskin monk sets aside many of the frailties of mortal flesh. He becomes immune to death effects and stunning. He is not subject to ability damage or ability drain, and has a 75% chance of ignoring the extra damage dealt by critical hits and sneak attacks. This ability replaces perfect self.

NEW RACIAL RULES

The following options are available to hobgoblins. At the GM's discretion, other appropriate races may make use of some of these new rules.

Hobgoblin Equipment

Hobgoblins have access to the following equipment.

Brewed Reek: Animal musk, spoiled meat, pungent plants, and any other foul-smelling substances on hand go into a batch of brewed reek. When boiled, this mixture becomes a thick alchemical slime that adheres to anything it touches. You can hurl brewed reek as a splash weapon with a range increment of 10 feet. A creature struck with a direct hit must succeed at a DC 15 Fortitude save or be sickened for 2d6 rounds. If the target fails its save, it must make a second Fortitude save or be nauseated for 1 round. Creatures in the splash area must make a Fortitude save or be sickened for 1 round. A creature that drinks brewed reek does not get a saving throw and is sickened for 2d6 rounds and nauseated for 1 round.

Fetters: Fetters are manacles fitted around the ankles rather than the wrists, and use the same rules (*Core Rulebook* 156) for breaking, escape, and cost relative to size. A creature in fetters is entangled and can only move at half speed. In addition, a fettered creature must succeed at a DC 15 Acrobatics check to move more than its (reduced) speed in a round. If it fails the check by 5 or more, the creature falls prone.

Hobgoblin War Draught: This drink is a foul-smelling alchemical blend of raw alcohol, mashed grubs, and medicinal mushrooms. A hobgoblin under the effects of hobgoblin war draught ignores all penalties resulting from the fatigued and shaken conditions for 10 minutes, after which he must succeed at a DC 15 Fortitude save or be sickened for 1 hour. Anyone lacking the goblinoid subtype who drinks hobgoblin war draught must immediately make a DC 15 Fortitude save or be sickened for 1 hour; success means the drinker ignores all penalties resulting from the fatigued and shaken conditions for 1 minute, after which he is sickened for 10 minutes. Hobgoblin war draught has no effect on creatures that are immune to poison.

Manacle Barbs: Barbs added to these manacles wound a captive who does more than move slowly and with care. A creature secured in barbed manacles takes 1 point of piercing damage if it takes more than a single move action during a round. Rough movement of any kind, such as being struck in combat or falling prone, likewise causes 1 point of damage. Attempting to break out of barbed manacles with a Strength check deals 1d4 points of piercing damage to the captive regardless of the success of the attempt.

Fetters can also be fitted with barbs, but the wearer can avoid damage by not taking actions that involve moving its legs. Hobgoblins often use such fetters to secure artisans to their worktables. Securing a captive with multiple sets of manacles and/or fetters doesn't cause additional damage.

Unstable Accelerant: A volatile mix of incendiary reagents, unstable accelerant can be thrown just like alchemist's fire. In the hands of an alchemist, a flask of unstable accelerant can be used as part of creating a bomb, increasing its fire damage by +1d6 points. It has no effect on bombs that do not deal fire damage. If the bomb lasts for more than an instant, the extra damage only applies to the first round's damage.

Hobgoblin Equipment

Item	Cost	Weight	Craft DC
Brewed reek	40 gp	1 lb.	DC 25
Fetters	15 gp	2 lbs.	—
Fetters, masterwork	50 gp	2 lbs.	—
Hobgoblin war draught	10 gp	1 lb.	DC 20*
Manacle barbs	+15 gp	1 lb.	—
Unstable accelerant	50 gp	1/2 lb.	DC 25

* Craft DC 15 for hobgoblins

Hobgoblin Feats

Hobgoblins have access to the following feats.

Deafening Explosion

Your bombs explode with deafening force.

Prerequisites: Bomb class feature, hobgoblin.

Benefit: You may reduce your bomb damage by one die to give it the ability to deafen the creature struck by it. The bomb must deal fire, force, or sonic damage. If a creature takes a direct hit from your bomb, it must make a saving throw against the bomb's DC or be deafened for 1 minute. This deafening is in addition to any other effects the bomb would normally have.

Demoralizing Lash (Combat)

You cow your enemies with the lash of a whip.

Prerequisites: Base attack bonus +1, Intimidate 1 rank, hobgoblin.

Benefit: To use this feat, you must use a whip (or another weapon in the flails fighter weapon group) to attack a foe demoralized by an Intimidate check. If the attack hits, you extend the duration the creature is shaken by 1 round. This feat has no effect on creatures whose shaken conditions are from sources other than Intimidate checks.

Focusing Blow (Teamwork)

You and your allies work together to shake off mental effects.

Prerequisites: Hobgoblin Discipline, hobgoblin.

Benefit: An ally who also has this feat can deal damage to you in order to break an ongoing mind-affecting effect that allows a saving throw. The ally must cause at least 5 points of damage to you with an attack, spell, or other ability. You then reroll your saving throw, with a +1 bonus for every 5 additional points of damage the attack caused. If your save is successful, the mind-affecting effect ends. Only damage actually dealt counts for purposes of this feat; nonlethal damage and damage reduced or eliminated by damage reduction, resistances, and so on does not qualify.

Hobgoblin Discipline

The presence of other hobgoblins bolsters your resolve.

Prerequisites: Base attack bonus +1, hobgoblin.

Benefit: While you are within 30 feet of at least two other hobgoblins, you gain a +1 morale bonus on saving throws.

Taskmaster (Combat)

You intimidate weaker allies into reckless ferocity.

Prerequisites: Demoralizing Lash, Intimidate 5 ranks, hobgoblin.

Benefit: As a standard action, you spur an ally, who must have fewer Hit Dice than yourself, to reckless effort. For 1 minute, the ally gains a +1 morale bonus on attack rolls, weapon damage rolls, and Will saves against mind-affecting effects. However, the ally also takes a –2 penalty to AC and on skill checks. To affect an unwilling ally, you must succeed at an Intimidate check with the same DC used to demoralize your ally.

Special: If you have 10 or more ranks in Intimidate, the morale bonus increases to +2.

Terrorizing Display (Combat)

Your battle prowess frightens friend and foe alike.

Prerequisites: Dazzling Display, Demoralizing Lash, Taskmaster, Weapon Focus, Intimidate 10 ranks, hobgoblin, proficiency with selected weapon.

Benefits: When you use Dazzling Display, in addition to its normal effects, you can use it to spur allies within 30 feet as if you had used the Taskmaster feat. Use the same Intimidate check to determine the effects of Dazzling Display and this feat.

Hobgoblin Magic Items

Hobgoblins have access to the following weapon special abilities and magic items.

Cruel (weapon special ability): A *cruel* weapon feeds on fear and suffering. When the wielder strikes a creature that is frightened, shaken, or panicked with a *cruel* weapon, that creature becomes sickened for 1 round. When the wielder uses the weapon to knock unconscious or kill a creature, he gains 5 temporary hit points that last for 10 minutes.

Faint necromancy; CL 5th; Craft Magic Arms and Armor, *cause fear, death knell*; Price +1 bonus.

Deadly (weapon special ability): This special ability can only be placed on weapons that normally deal nonlethal damage, such as whips and saps. All damage a *deadly* weapon deals is lethal damage. A whip (or similar weapon that cannot damage creatures with armor or natural armor bonuses) with this special ability deals damage even to creatures with armor or natural armor. On command, the weapon suppresses this ability until told to resume it.

Faint necromancy; CL 5th; Craft Magic Arms and Armor, *inflict light wounds*; Price +1 bonus.

HOBGOBLIN BATTLE STANDARD

Aura moderate enchantment; **CL** 10th

Slot none; **Price** 50,000 gp (despair), 60,000 gp (ferocity), 45,000 gp (iron resolve); **Weight** 3 lbs.

DESCRIPTION

A battle standard is a cloth flag or standard, typically 2 feet wide and 4 feet long, meant to be carried and displayed on a lance, polearm, frame, or staff. It has no effect when not mounted properly or when lying on the ground. *Hobgoblin battle standards* normally depict the device or insignia of a tribe or nation, and different types of standards grant different effects.

A battle standard may be carried (on foot or mounted) or planted. In the latter case, the standard does not need a bearer, but if it is toppled or touched by an enemy, it loses its effectiveness until reclaimed and replanted by allies of its owner.

Despair: Enemies of the bearer of a *hobgoblin battle standard of despair* are sickened while within 60 feet of the banner. Any enemy that sustains a critical hit while sickened because of the standard must succeed at a Will saving throw (DC 15) or become dazed for 1 round.

Ferocity: Allies of the bearer of a *hobgoblin battle standard of ferocity* gain a +2 morale bonus on attack rolls, weapon damage rolls, and saving throws against mind-affecting effects as long as they are within 60 feet of the banner.

Iron Resolve: Allies of the bearer of a *hobgoblin battle standard of iron resolve* gain 10 temporary hit points and the benefits of the Diehard feat for as long as they are within 30 feet of the banner. The temporary hit points can only be gained once per day per creature.

CONSTRUCTION

Requirements Craft Wondrous Item, *crushing despair* (despair), *rage* (ferocity), *aid* and *bear's endurance* (iron resolve); **Cost** 25,000 gp (despair), 30,000 gp (ferocity), 22,500 gp (iron resolve)

HORSESHOES OF CRUSHING BLOWS

Aura faint evocation; **CL** 5th
Slot feet; **Price** 4,000 gp (+1), 16,000 gp (+2), 36,000 gp (+3), 64,000 gp (+4), 100,000 gp (+5); **Weight** 4 lbs. (for four)

DESCRIPTION

Horseshoes of crushing blows grant an enhancement bonus on attack and damage rolls made with hoof attacks; this bonus varies based on the item's price. Alternatively, as described for the *amulet of mighty fists*, they can grant melee weapon special abilities so long as they can be applied to unarmed attacks. *Horseshoes of crushing blows* cannot have a modified bonus (enhancement bonus plus special ability bonus equivalents) higher than +5. *Horseshoes of crushing blows* are crafted as sets of four, with each shoe in the set bearing the same enhancements. All four shoes must be worn by the same animal to be effective.

Horseshoes of crushing blows may be crafted out of special materials, gaining the usual benefits. For purposes of pricing, they count as a single one-handed weapon weighing 4 pounds (for example, *adamantine horseshoes of crushing blows* would cost an additional 3,000 gp). The materials needed to make *cold iron horseshoes of crushing blows* add no extra costs in and of themselves, but enhancing *cold iron horseshoes of crushing blows* increases the price by the usual 2,000 gp.

CONSTRUCTION

Requirements Craft Magic Arms and Armor, Craft Wondrous Item, creator's caster level must be at least three times the amulet's bonus, plus any requirements of the melee weapon special abilities; **Cost** 2,000 gp (+1), 8,000 gp (+2), 18,000 gp (+3), 32,000 gp (+4), 50,000 gp (+5)

SHACKLES OF DURANCE VILE

Aura moderate enchantment; **CL** 9th
Slot wrists; **Price** 16,200 gp; **Weight** 2 lbs.

DESCRIPTION

These masterwork iron manacles sap the will of their wearer. When attached to a humanoid creature as their command word is spoken, they affect their prisoner with a *dominate person* spell, except that if the prisoner fails its saving throw, the effect lasts for as long as the shackles are attached. Removing or destroying the shackles immediately breaks the enchantment. The shackles can be so used once per day. *Shackles of durance vile* can only be activated against a helpless, restrained, or willing creature; if attached to a creature still able to resist they function only as manacles, albeit superior ones. *Shackles of durance vile* have hardness 15, 20 hit points, and a superior lock. They have a break DC of 30 and an Escape Artist DC of 35.

CONSTRUCTION

Requirements Craft Wondrous Item, *dominate person*; **Cost** 8,200 gp

WOUND PASTE

Aura faint conjuration; **CL** 1st
Slot none; **Price** 50 gp; **Weight** 1/2 lb.

DESCRIPTION

Prized by slavers as an affordable way to stop a captive from bleeding to death, a dose of *wound paste* acts as a *stabilize* spell when slathered on a dying creature. Applying *wound paste* is a standard action that provokes an attack of opportunity. A pot of *wound paste* contains 5 doses.

CONSTRUCTION

Requirements Craft Wondrous Item, *stabilize*; **Cost** 25 gp

Hobgoblin Spells

Hobgoblins have access to the following spell.

AGONIZING REBUKE

School illusion (phantasm) [emotion, mind-affecting]; **Level** antipaladin 2, cleric 3, inquisitor 3, witch 3
Casting Time 1 standard action
Component V, S
Range close (25 ft. + 5 ft./2 level)
Target one living creature
Duration 1 round/level
Saving Throw Will negates; **Spell Resistance** yes.

With a word and a gesture, you instill such apprehension about attacking you in your target that doing so causes it mental distress and pain. Each time the target makes an attack against you, targets you with a harmful spell, or otherwise takes and action that would harm you, it takes 2d6 points of nonlethal damage.

IFRITS

Humans whose ancestry includes beings of elemental fire such as efreet, ifrits are a passionate and fickle race. No ifrit is satisfied with a sedentary life; like a wildfire, ifrits must keep moving or burn away into nothingness. Ifrits not only adore flames, but personify multiple aspects of them as well, embodying both fire's dynamic, ever-changing energy and its destructive, pitiless nature.

Physical Description: Ifrits vary in appearance as widely as their elemental ancestors do. Most have pointy ears, red or mottled horns on the brow, and hair that flickers and waves as if it were aflame. Some possess skin the color of polished brass or have charcoal-hued scales covering their arms and legs. Ifrits favor revealing and ostentatious clothing in bright oranges and reds, preferably paired with gaudy jewelry.

Society: Ifrits are most often born into human communities, and rarely form societies of their own. Those who grow up in a city are almost always imprisoned or driven off before they reach adulthood; most are simply too hot-headed and independent to fit into civilized society, and their predilection toward pyromania doesn't endear them to the local authorities. Those born into nomadic or tribal societies fare much better, since ifrits' instinctive urge to explore and conquer their surroundings can easily earn them a place among their tribe's leadership.

Relations: Even the best-natured ifrits tend to view other individuals as tools to use as they see fit, and as such they get along best with races they can charm or browbeat into submission. Half-elves and gnomes often find themselves caught up in an ifrit's schemes, while halflings, half-orcs, and dwarves usually bridle at ifrits' controlling nature. Strangely, ifrits sometimes form incredibly close bonds with elves, whose calm, aloof nature seems to counterbalance an ifrit's impulsiveness. Most ifrits refuse to associate with sylphs, but are otherwise on peaceable terms with the other elemental-touched races.

Alignment and Religion: Ifrits are a dichotomous people—on one hand, fiercely independent, and on the other, imperious and demanding. They are often accused of being morally impoverished, but their troublemaking behavior is rarely motivated by true malice. Ifrits are usually lawful neutral or chaotic neutral, with a few falling into true neutrality. Most ifrits lack the mindset to follow a god's teachings, and resent the strictures placed on them by organized faith. When ifrits do take to worship (usually venerating a fire-related deity), they prove to be zealous and devoted followers.

Adventurers: Ifrits adventure for the sheer thrill of it and for the chance to test their skill against worthy foes, but most of all they adventure in search of power. Once ifrits dedicate themselves to a task, they pursue it unflinchingly, never stopping to consider the dangers ahead of them. When this brashness finally catches up with them, ifrits often rely on sorcery or bardic magic to combat their resulting troubles.

Male Names: Aja, Denat, Efit, Elum, Jalij, Maqej, Urah.
Female Names: Alayi, Etwa, Maqan, Qari, Sami, Zetaya.

ALTERNATE RACIAL TRAITS

The following racial traits may be selected instead of existing ifrit racial traits. Consult your GM before selecting any of these new options.

Desert Mirage: Ifrits thrive in the deserts of the world, where their keen instincts and resistance to heat give them a huge edge over their competitors. Those with this trait gain a +2 racial bonus on Stealth checks in desert environments and on saves to resist starvation and thirst. This racial trait replaces fire affinity.

Efreeti Magic: Some ifrits inherit an efreeti ancestor's ability to magically change a creature's size. They can cast either *enlarge person* or *reduce person* (the ifrit chooses when using this ability) once per day as a spell-like ability (caster level equals the ifrit's level). The ifrit can use this ability to affect other ifrits as though they were humanoid creatures. This racial trait replaces the spell-like ability racial trait.

Fire in the Blood: Ifrits with this racial trait mimic the healing abilities of the mephits, gaining fast healing 2 for 1 round anytime they take fire damage (whether or not this fire damage gets through their fire resistance). The ifrits can heal up to 2 hit points per level per day with this ability, after which it ceases to function. This racial trait replaces fire affinity.

Fire Insight: Ifrit spellcasters sometimes find that their elemental heritage makes creatures of fire more willing to serve them. *Summon monster* and *summon nature's ally* spells that the ifrit casts last 2 rounds longer than normal when used to summon creatures with the fire subtype. This racial trait replaces fire affinity.

Fire-Starter: Ifrits with this racial trait derive sadistic satisfaction from watching others burn. Anytime the ifrit causes a creature to catch fire, he gains a +1 morale bonus on the next single attack roll, saving throw, skill check, or ability check that he makes in the next round. The ifrit only gains this bonus the first time he causes a particular creature to catch fire; subsequent times the creature catches fire provide no bonus. This racial trait replaces fire affinity.

Forge-Hardened: Not all ifrits are descended from efreet—some instead descend from azers or even salamanders. Such ifrits gain a +2 racial bonus on Craft (armor and weapons) checks and saves to resist fatigue and exhaustion. This racial trait replaces the spell-like ability racial trait.

Hypnotic: Ifrits with this racial trait evoke the entrancing nature of flame, adding +1 to the DC for all saving throws against spells or effects they cast that inflict the fascinated condition. Once per day, when a creature rolls a saving throw against such an effect from the ifrit, the ifrit can spend an immediate action to force that creature to reroll the saving throw and use the second result, even if it is worse. The ifrit must announce he is using this ability before the results of the first roll are revealed. This racial trait replaces fire affinity.

Wildfire Heart: Ifrits with this trait are as swift and dangerous as a blazing wildfire. They gain a +4 racial bonus on initiative checks. This racial trait replaces energy resistance.

FAVORED CLASS OPTIONS

The following options are available to all ifrits who have the listed favored class, and unless otherwise stated, the bonus applies each time you select the class reward.

Alchemist: Add +1/2 to the alchemist's bomb damage.

Bard: Add +1/6 to the number of people the bard can affect with the fascinate bardic performance.

Cleric: Add a +1/2 bonus on Knowledge (planes) checks relating to the Plane of Fire and creatures with the fire subtype.

Gunslinger: Add +1/2 to the bonus on initiative checks the gunslinger makes while using her gunslinger initiative deed.

Inquisitor: Add a +1/2 bonus on Intimidate checks made against creatures with the fire subtype and a +1/2 bonus on Knowledge (planes) checks relating to the Plane of Fire.

Oracle: Add +1/2 to the oracle's level for the purpose of determining the effects of one revelation.

Rogue: Add a +1/2 bonus on Acrobatics checks to jump and a +1/2 bonus on Intimidate checks to demoralize enemies.

Sorcerer: Choose a bloodline power from the elemental (fire) bloodline or the efreeti bloodline (*Ultimate Magic* 67) that the sorcerer can use. The sorcerer treats her class level as though it were +1/2 higher (to a maximum of +4) when determining the effects of that power.

IFRIT RACIAL TRAITS

+2 Dexterity, +2 Charisma, –2 Wisdom: Ifrits are passionate and quick, but impetuous and destructive.

Native Outsider: Ifrits are outsiders with the native subtype.

Medium: Ifrits are Medium creatures and receive no bonuses or penalties due to their size.

Normal Speed: Ifrits have a base speed of 30 feet.

Darkvision: Ifrits can see in the dark up to 60 feet.

Spell-Like Ability: *Burning hands* 1/day (caster level equals the ifrit's level).

Energy Resistance: Ifrits have fire resistance 5.

Fire Affinity: Ifrit sorcerers with the elemental (fire) bloodline treat their Charisma score as 2 points higher for all sorcerer spells and class abilities. Ifrit spellcasters with the Fire domain use their domain powers and spells at +1 caster level.

Languages: Ifrits begin play speaking Common and Ignan. Ifrits with high Intelligence scores can choose from the following: Aquan, Auran, Dwarven, Elven, Gnome, Halfling, and Terran.

RACIAL ARCHETYPES

The following racial archetypes are available to ifrits.

Immolator (Inquisitor)

The immolator puts her pyromaniacal urges to work in the service of a deity. She brings burning retribution down upon the enemies of her faith, consigning their souls to the sacrificial flames. An immolator has the following class features.

Servant of the Flame: An immolator must worship a deity whose portfolio includes the Fire domain. An immolator who selects the Fire domain (or one of its associated subdomains, if available) uses her domain powers at +1 caster level (this stacks with the ifrit's fire affinity racial trait).

Judgment (Su): An immolator gains the following judgment instead of the smiting judgment.

Immolation: The immolator channels purifying flame to consume her enemies. When dealing fire damage to an opponent, she treats the target's fire resistance as 5 lower than normal (minimum 0). At 6th level, she treats the target's resistance as 10 lower than normal, 15 lower than normal at 11th level, and 20 lower than normal at 16th level.

Burnt Offering (Su): At 5th level, as a swift action, an immolator can imbue one of her weapons with the *flaming* weapon special ability. Any creature slain by this weapon burns with magical flame; its body turns to ash, though its equipment is not harmed. This special ability only functions while the immolator wields the weapon. This ability lasts for a number of rounds per day equal to the immolator's level. These rounds do not need to be consecutive. At 12th level, this ability gives the immolator's weapon the *flaming burst* weapon special ability. This ability replaces bane and greater bane.

Judgment by Fire (Su): At 20th level, an immolator can call fiery judgment down upon a foe during combat. Whenever an immolator uses her judgment ability, she can invoke a judgment by fire on a foe as a swift action. Once declared, the immolator can make a single melee (or ranged attack, if the foe is within 30 feet) against the target. If the attack hits, the attack deals fire damage instead of weapon damage, and the target must make a successful Fortitude save or die (creatures immune to fire do not have to save). The DC of this save is equal to 10 + 1/2 the immolator's level + the immolator's Wisdom modifier. Regardless of whether the save is successful, the target creature is immune to the immolator's judgment by fire ability for 24 hours. Creatures killed in this manner explode in a burst of fire, dealing 10d6 points of fire damage to every creature within 5 feet (Reflex save for half damage, DC 10 + 1/2 the immolator's level + the immolator's Wisdom modifier). Once this ability has been used, it cannot be used again for 1d4 rounds. This ability modifies and functions as true judgment.

Wishcrafter (Sorcerer)

Wishcrafters are born with a talent for manipulating reality inherited from their efreeti ancestors. However, like the genies they are descended from, wishcrafters can only draw upon this power to fulfill the desires of others. A wishcrafter has the following class features.

Wishbound Arcana (Su): At 1st level, the wishcrafter can use the wishes of non-genie creatures other than herself in place of the normal verbal components of her spells. A creature can make a wish as a free action at any time, even during the wishcrafter's turn. The wishcrafter must be able to hear and understand a wish in order to use it as a spell component. A spell that doesn't normally have a verbal component gains one when cast using this ability. A wish doesn't need to mention the name of a specific spell, but must describe an outcome that can be accomplished by casting a spell the wishcrafter knows (for example, wishing to be bigger could supply the verbal component for *enlarge person*). A wishcrafter gains a +1 bonus to her caster level when using a creature's wish as a verbal component in this manner, but cannot include herself as a target of such spells. She can be affected by such a spell if it affects an area rather than a target or targets. A wishcrafter is under no compulsion to grant a creature's wish. Once the wishcrafter grants a creature's wish using this ability, she cannot use this ability to grant that creature any further wishes for 24 hours. This ability replaces bloodline arcana.

Expanded Wishcraft: At 3rd level and every 2 levels thereafter, the wishcrafter grows more adept at altering reality to fit the whims of others. She may add an additional spell selected from the sorcerer/wizard spell list to her list of spells known. This spell must be one level lower than the highest-level spell she can cast. A wishcrafter can only use these spells in conjunction with her wishbound arcana ability. For example, if she used this ability to learn *cat's grace*, she can only cast it when another creature wishes for it, and can't cast it on herself because it is a targeted spell. She cannot use these spells to craft or recharge magic items. These bonus spells replace the bloodline spells gained by the sorcerer's bloodline.

Heart's Desire (Su): At 7th level, as a swift action, a wishcrafter can force a single creature within 30 feet to confess its deepest desire. The target receives a Will save to negate this effect (DC 10 + 1/2 the wishcrafter's level + the wishcrafter's Charisma modifier). On a failed save, the creature must immediately wish aloud in a clear voice for something it truly desires, allowing the wishcrafter to activate her wishbound arcana ability if she knows a spell that can fulfill that wish. This is a mind-affecting effect. Regardless of whether the save is successful, a creature cannot be the target of the same wishcrafter's heart's desire ability again for 24 hours. The wishcrafter can use this ability a number of times per day equal to her Charisma bonus. This ability replaces the bloodline bonus feat gained at 7th level.

Twisted Wish (Su): At 13th level, a wishcrafter becomes adept at corrupting wishes to negatively affect the creature that wished them. When a wishcrafter affects a creature with a spell using its wish as a spell component, she may twist the wish, applying a −4 penalty to the creature's saving throws against the spell. The effects of wishes twisted this way are difficult to remove; the DC of caster level checks to dispel them increases by 5. This ability replaces the bloodline bonus feat gained at 13th level.

Perfect Wishcraft (Su): At 19th level, the wishcrafter perfects her ability to manipulate reality. Once per day, she may cast any spell on the sorcerer/wizard spell list as if it were on her list of spells known. Using this ability otherwise has all of the benefits and limitations of the wishbound arcana ability. This ability replaces the bloodline bonus feat gained at 19th level.

NEW RACIAL RULES

The following options are available to ifrits. At the GM's discretion, other appropriate races may make use of some of these new rules.

Ifrit Equipment

Ifrits have access to the following equipment.

Fire Ink: This rich yellow ink reacts with a creature's body heat to create a flickering, flamelike glow. It takes 10 minutes to apply fire ink, and 1 dose covers an approximately hand-sized area. Once applied, the ink glows as a candle for 24 hours. Four or more doses applied to the same part of the body glow as a torch for 24 hours. The alchemical reaction of the ink to the target's skin and body heat is painful and irritating, giving the target the sickened condition while the glow lasts. A DC 15 Heal check can temporarily soothe these sensations, negating the sickened condition for 1 hour. Creatures immune or resistant to fire are immune to this sickening effect. Ifrits are especially known for their fondness for fire ink, and ifrit fire-dancers often decorate their skin with flaming designs before performing. A concentrated version of the ink costs 10 times as much and can be used to make permanently glowing tattoos.

Ifrit's Blood: Ifrit alchemists claim to make this thick red oil from their own blood—hence the morbid name—but this claim is almost certainly false. Ifrit's blood ignites upon contact with air, but burns slowly and is unsuitable for use as a splash weapon. A creature can apply a flask of ifrit's blood to a weapon as a standard action, wreathing the weapon in vibrant red flames for 1 minute. The oil deals 1 point of fire damage on each successful attack with the weapon and deals 1 point of fire damage to the weapon itself, bypassing the weapon's hardness if any part of it is made of wood. If the oil is applied to a creature's natural weapons or unarmed strikes, the creature takes 1 point of fire damage each round (though its fire immunity or resistance still applies).

Ifrit Equipment

Item	Cost	Weight	Craft DC
Fire ink	1 gp	—	15
Ifrit's blood	50 gp	1 lb.	20

Ifrit Feats

Ifrits have access to the following feats.

Blazing Aura (Combat)

An inferno rages inside you, causing your body to radiate intense heat.

Prerequisites: Inner Flame, Scorching Weapons, character level 13th, ifrit.

Benefit: When you use Scorching Weapons, on your turn as a free action, you may create an aura of heat that lasts for 1 round. This aura deals 1d6 points of fire damage to any creature that begins its turn adjacent to you.

Blistering Feint (Combat)

Your foes flinch from the heat of your weapon, giving you an opportunity to slip past their defenses.

Prerequisites: Combat Expertise, Improved Feint, ifrit.

Benefit: You gain a +2 bonus on feint checks made while wielding a weapon that deals fire damage. Anytime you successfully feint a creature while using such a weapon, you may deal its fire damage to the enemy.

Elemental Jaunt

The spirits of your ancestral home call to you, beckoning you to return.

Prerequisites: Character level 15th, ifrit, oread, sylph, or undine.

Benefit: Once per day, you can cast *plane shift* as a spell-like ability with a caster level equal to your level to transport yourself and willing targets to an elemental plane that is appropriate to your race (ifrits to the Plane of Fire, oreads to the Plane of Earth, sylphs to the Plane of Air, and undines to the Plane of Water). While on that plane, you (but not anyone transported with you) are treated as though under the effect of the spell *planar adaptation* (*Advanced Player's Guide* 236).

Firesight

Fire no longer blinds you, and smoke conceals nothing from your gaze.

Prerequisite: Ifrit.

Benefit: You can see through fire and smoke without penalty, ignoring any cover or concealment bonuses from fire and smoke. This does not allow you to see anything you could not otherwise see (for example, invisible creatures are still invisible). You are immune to the dazzled condition.

Inner Flame (Combat)

Your body generates so much heat that your mere touch scorches your enemies.

Prerequisites: Scorching Weapons, character level 7th, ifrit.

Benefit: Your bonus on saves against fire attacks and spells with the fire descriptor or light descriptor increases to +4. When you use Scorching Weapons, the affected weapons deal an additional 1d6 points of fire damage instead of 1, and when you are grappling, you deal this damage to your grappling opponent on your turn.

Scorching Weapons (Combat)

Elemental fire stirs within your body, boiling your blood and rendering you resistant to flame.

Prerequisite: Ifrit.

Benefit: You gain a +2 bonus on saving throws against fire attacks and spells with the fire descriptor or light descriptor. As a swift action, you can make up to two held manufactured metallic weapons become red-hot for 1 round, dealing 1 additional point of fire damage with a successful hit. This does not stack with other effects that add fire damage to weapons, such as the *flaming* weapon special ability.

Ifrit Magic Items

Ifrits have access to the following weapon special ability and magic item.

Igniting (weapon special ability): An *igniting* weapon functions as a *flaming* weapon that also causes foes to catch fire (*Core Rulebook* 444) upon striking a successful critical hit. The target does not get a saving throw to avoid catching fire, but can make a save each round on its turn to put out the fire. The *flaming* ability must be active for the weapon to set enemies on fire.

Strong evocation; CL 12th; Craft Magic Arms and Armor, *flame blade*, *flame strike*, or *fireball*; Price +2 bonus.

CLOAK OF FIERY VANISHING

Aura faint abjuration and illusion; **CL** 5th
Slot shoulders; **Price** 2,600 gp; **Weight** 1 lb.

DESCRIPTION

This thick leather cloak is charred and blackened around the edges and smells faintly of soot. Once per day, when subject to an effect that deals fire damage, the wearer can spend an immediate action while obscured by the flames to become invisible, leaving behind an illusory pile of ashes and bones, as if he had been slain by the fire effect. The invisibility and the illusory remains last for 5 rounds or until the wearer attacks any creature. Creatures that study or interact with the ashes can make a DC 11 Will save to disbelieve the illusion, though this does not end the invisibility effect.

CONSTRUCTION

Requirements Craft Wondrous Item, *invisibility*, *silent image*;
   Cost 1,300 gp

Ifrit Spells

Ifrits have access to the following spells.

CHAINS OF FIRE

School evocation [fire]; **Level** magus 6, sorcerer/wizard 6
Components V, S, F (a drop of oil and a small piece of flint)
Range medium (100 ft. + 10 ft./level)
This spell functions like *chain lightning*, except as noted above, and the spell deals fire damage instead of electricity damage.

DEATH CANDLE

School necromancy [death, evil, fire]; **Level** antipaladin 1, cleric 2, inquisitor 2, witch 2
Casting Time 1 round
Components V, S
Duration instantaneous/1 round per HD of subject; see text
Saving Throw Fortitude negates; **Spell Resistance** yes
This spell functions like *death knell*, except instead of using the slain target's life energy to enhance yourself, you use it to summon a Small fire elemental resembling a burning, howling version of the slain creature. The elemental acts immediately on your turn and otherwise behaves as if you had summoned it with *summon monster II*. The elemental remains for a number of rounds equal to the Hit Dice of the slain creature.

FIRESTREAM

School evocation [fire]; **Level** magus 3, sorcerer/wizard 3
Casting Time 1 standard action
Components V, S
Range 20 ft.
Area 20-ft. line
Duration concentration, up to 1 round/level; see text
Saving Throw Reflex half; **Spell Resistance** yes
A rushing stream of fire sprays from your outstretched hand, dealing 2d6 points of fire damage to every creature in the area. Each round you continue to concentrate on the spell, you can select a new area for it to affect.

Firestream sets fire to combustibles and damages objects in the area. It can melt metals with low melting points, such as lead, gold, copper, silver, and bronze. If the damage caused to an interposing barrier shatters or breaks through it, the firestream may continue beyond the barrier if the area permits; otherwise it stops at the barrier just as any other spell effect does.

FURY OF THE SUN

School transmutation [curse, fire]; **Level** druid 2, witch 2
Casting Time 1 standard action
Components V, S
Range close (25 ft. + 5 ft./2 levels)
Targets one creature
Duration 10 minutes/level
Saving Throw Fortitude negates; **Spell Resistance** yes
You curse the target to suffer unbearable heat. On a failed saving throw, the target is immediately subjected to severe

heat (*Core Rulebook* 444), takes 1d4 points of nonlethal damage, and is suffering from heatstroke (fatigued). The target must save every 10 minutes as normal for severe heat (starting at DC 15 rather than the DC of this spell). Because this heat is internal, the target cannot avoid it using the normal methods for escaping heat dangers such as Survival checks or finding shade.

HEALING WARMTH

School abjuration; **Level** alchemist 4, cleric 4, druid 4, inquisitor 4
Casting Time 1 standard action
Components V, S
Range personal
Target you
Duration 1 minute/level
This spell grants you temporary immunity to fire damage as *protection from energy*. As a standard action, you may sacrifice 12 points of remaining energy absorption from the spell to heal a touched creature of 1d8 points of damage. Healing a creature provokes an attack of opportunity. When the spell has absorbed 12 points of fire damage per caster level (to a maximum of 120 points at 10th level), it is discharged.

SCORCHING ASH FORM

School transmutation [fire]; **Level** alchemist 4, sorcerer/wizard 4 **Components** S, M (a bit of gauze and a handful of ashes) **Duration** 1 minute/level
Saving Throw none; **Spell Resistance** no
This spell functions like *gaseous form*, except the target becomes a visible swirl of hot ash and smoke instead of harmless translucent gas. The target gains the fire subtype. Any creature that begins its turn sharing a space with the target takes 2d6 points of fire damage and must make a Fortitude save (DC 15, + 1 per previous check) or suffer the effects of smoke inhalation (*Core Rulebook* 444).

TOUCH OF COMBUSTION

School evocation [fire]; **Level** druid 1, inquisitor 1, magus 1, sorcerer/wizard 1, witch 1
Casting Time 1 standard action
Components V, S
Range touch
Target creature or object touched
Duration instantaneous
Saving Throw Reflex negates; see text; **Spell Resistance** yes
Your successful melee touch attack causes the target to ignite in a violent burst of flame, dealing 1d6 points of fire damage. If it fails its saving throw, the target also catches on fire (*Core Rulebook* 444). If the target catches fire, on the first round thereafter, creatures adjacent to it (including you) must each succeed at a Reflex save or take 1d4 points of fire damage.

Kobolds

Kobolds are weak, craven, and seethe with a festering resentment for the rest of the world, especially members of races that seem stronger, smarter, or superior to them in any way. They proudly claim kinship to dragons, but beneath all the bluster, the comparison to their glorious cousins leaves kobolds with a profound sense of inadequacy. Though they are hardworking, clever, and blessed with a natural talent for mechanical devices and mining, they spend their days nursing grudges and hatreds instead of celebrating their own gifts. Kobold tactics specialize in traps and ambushes, but kobolds enjoy anything that allows them to harm others without putting themselves at risk. Often, they seek to capture rather than to kill, taking out their frustrations on the helpless victims they drag back to their claustrophobic lairs.

Physical Description: Kobolds are small, bipedal reptilian humanoids. Most stand around 3 feet tall and weigh about 35 pounds. They have powerful jaws for creatures of their size and noticeable claws on their hands and feet. Often kobolds' faces are curiously devoid of expression, as they favor showing their emotions by simply swishing their tails. Kobolds' thick hides vary in color, and most have scales that match the hue of one of the varieties of chromatic dragons, with red scales being predominant. A few kobolds, however, have more exotic colors such as orange or yellow, which in some tribes raises or lowers an individual's status in the eyes of his fellows.

Society: Kobolds thrive in cramped quarters far from the light of the sun. Most live in vast warrens deep beneath the earth, but a few instead prefer to make their homes beneath tangles of overgrown trees and brush. Saving their malice for other races, most kobolds get along well with their own kind. While squabbles and feuds do occur, the elders who rule kobold communities tend to settle such conflicts swiftly. Kobolds delight in taking slaves, relishing the chance to torment and humiliate them. They are also cowardly and practical, and often end up bowing to more powerful beings. If these creatures are of another humanoid race, kobolds often scheme to free themselves from subjugation as soon as possible. If the overlord is a powerful draconic or monstrous creature, however, kobolds see no shame in submission, and often shower adoration on their new leader. This is especially true if the kobolds serve a true dragon, who they tend to worship outright.

Relations: Kobolds often seethe with hatred and jealousy, but their innate caution ensures that they only act on these impulses when they have the upper hand. If unable to safely indulge their urge to physically harm and degrade members of other races, they resort to careful insults and "practical jokes" instead.

They consider both dwarves and elves to be deadly rivals. Kobolds fear the brute power of half-orcs and resent humans for the dominant status that race enjoys. They believe half-elves blend the best qualities of both parent races, which strikes kobolds as fundamentally unfair. Kobolds believe halflings, small in stature, make wonderful slaves and targets for kobold rage and practical jokes. When the gnomes first arrived in the mortal realm, kobolds saw them as perfect victims. This sparked waves of retaliation and reprisal that have echoed on down through the centuries and earned the kobolds' permanent enmity.

Alignment and Religion: Kobolds readily knuckle under to superior force but rarely stop scheming to gain an edge over their oppressors. Most kobolds are lawful evil, though some, more concerned with procedure than their own personal advantage, become lawful neutral instead. Kobolds often pray to Asmodeus or Lamashtu in hopes of bringing ruin to their foes or power to themselves. A few others instead venerate Calistria, hoping for her blessing when making traps or striking back at the world they believe has so wronged them. In addition to these deities, kobolds, supremely opportunistic, also sometimes worship nearby monsters as a way of placating them or earning their favor.

Adventurers: Kobolds rarely leave their cozy warrens by their own choice. Most of those who set out on adventures are the last of their tribe, and such individuals often settle down again as soon as they find another kobold community willing to take them in. Kobolds who cannot rein in, or at least conceal, their spiteful and malicious natures have great difficulty surviving in the larger world.

Male Names: Draahzin, Eadoo, Ipmeerk, Jamada, Kib, Makroo, Olp, Yraalik, Zornesk.

Female Names: Adriaak, Harkail, Neeral, Ozula, Poro, Saassraa, Tarka.

ALTERNATE RACIAL TRAITS

The following racial traits may be selected instead of existing kobold racial traits. Consult your GM before selecting any of these new options.

Beast Bond: Some kobolds have a talent for training animals and beasts to help them both on and off the battlefield. Kobolds with this racial trait gain a +2 racial bonus on Handle Animal and Ride checks. Handle Animal and Ride are always class skills for them. This racial trait replaces crafty.

Dragon-Scaled: Some kobolds are hatched with scales of such vivid color that their connection to a particular sort of chromatic dragon seems undeniable. Whether this coloration is just a quirk of a stray egg or a trait shared by all the members of a tribe, these kobolds gain a resistance that makes them especially suited to work alongside dragons matching the color of the kobold's scales. Black-scaled and green-scaled kobolds with this racial trait gain acid resistance 5. Blue-scaled kobolds with this racial trait gain electricity resistance 5. Red-scaled kobolds with this racial trait gain fire resistance 5. White-scaled kobolds with this racial trait gain cold resistance 5. This racial trait replaces the armor racial trait.

Gliding Wings: Some kobolds are born with wings that, while too weak for actual flying, do allow them to fall at a very slow and safe pace. A kobold with wings can use them to glide. It can make a DC 15 Fly check to fall safely from any height without taking falling damage, as if using *feather fall*. When falling safely, it may make an additional DC 15 Fly check to glide, moving 5 feet laterally for every 20 feet it falls. This racial trait replaces crafty.

Jester: Some kobolds swallow their pride and survive by groveling, placating, and amusing the powerful. Kobolds with this racial trait gain a +2 racial bonus on Diplomacy and Perform checks. Diplomacy and Perform are always class skills for them. This racial trait replaces crafty.

FAVORED CLASS OPTIONS

The following options are available to all kobolds who have the listed favored class, and unless otherwise stated, the bonus applies each time you select the favored class reward.

Alchemist: Add +1/2 to the number of bombs per day the alchemist can create.

Bard: Treat the bard's level as +1/2 level higher for the purpose of determining the effect of the fascinate bardic performance.

Cavalier: Add 5 feet (up to 15 feet maximum) to the cavalier's mount's speed when it uses the charge or withdraw action.

Cleric: Add +1 to channel energy damage dealt to creatures denied their Dexterity bonus to AC (whether or not the creature has a Dexterity bonus to AC).

Druid: Add +1/2 to the druid's wild empathy bonus.

Fighter: Add +1/2 to damage rolls the fighter makes with weapon attacks against an opponent he is flanking or an opponent that is denied its Dexterity bonus to AC.

Gunslinger: Add +1/4 to the dodge bonus to AC granted by the nimble class feature (maximum +4).

Magus: Add a +1/2 bonus on concentration checks made to cast defensively.

Monk: Add +1/3 to the monk's AC bonus class ability.

Oracle: Add +1/4 to the armor or natural armor bonus granted by oracle spells she casts on herself.

Ranger: Add +1/4 to the number of opponents the ranger may select when using hunter's bond to grant a bonus to allies. All selected creatures must be of the same type.

Rogue: Add +1/2 to the rogue's trap sense bonus to AC.

Sorcerer: Choose acid, cold, electricity, or fire damage. Add +1/2 point of the chosen energy damage to spells that deal the chosen energy damage cast by the sorcerer.

KOBOLD RACIAL TRAITS

+2 Dexterity, –4 Strength, –2 Constitution: Kobolds are fast but weak.

Reptilian: Kobolds are humanoids with the reptilian subtype.

Small: Kobolds are Small creatures and gain a +1 size bonus to their AC, a +1 size bonus on attack rolls, a –1 penalty on their combat maneuver checks and to Combat Maneuver Defense, and a +4 size bonus on Stealth checks.

Normal Speed: Kobolds have a base speed of 30 feet.

Darkvision: Kobolds can see in the dark up to 60 feet.

Armor: Kobolds have a +1 natural armor bonus.

Crafty: Kobolds gain a +2 racial bonus on Craft (trapmaking), Perception, and Profession (miner) checks. Craft (traps) and Stealth are always class skills for a kobold.

Weakness: Light sensitivity.

Languages: Kobolds begin play speaking only Draconic. Kobolds with high Intelligence scores can choose from the following: Common, Dwarven, Gnome, and Undercommon.

Summoner: Add +1/4 to the summoner's shield ally bonus (maximum +2).

Witch: Add +5 feet to the distance at which her familiar grants the Alertness feat (maximum +20 feet).

RACIAL ARCHETYPES & BLOODLINES

The following racial archetype and racial bloodline are available to kobolds.

Bushwhacker (Gunslinger)

The bushwhacker specializes in the art of the ambush. For her, gunplay works best when it comes from a concealed position and is directed against a target that falls with the very first volley and is dead before the smoke clears. A bushwhacker has the following class features.

Trembling Grit (Ex): At 1st level, at the start of each day, a bushwhacker gains grit points equal to her Wisdom modifier – 1 (minimum of 1). In addition to all the ways any gunslinger can regain grit, a bushwhacker who reduces a helpless or unaware opponent to 0 hit points or fewer also regains 1 grit point. This expands the way in which the bushwhacker gains grit points, so a bushwhacker who gains grit points in this way only gains 1 grit point for reducing a helpless or unaware opponent, not 2 grit points. This otherwise works like the gunslinger's grit ability and alters that ability.

Craven Deeds (Ex): A bushwhacker replaces some of her deeds with the following deeds. This ability otherwise works like the gunslinger's deed ability and alters that ability.

Shifty Shot (Ex): At 3rd level, a bushwhacker with at least 1 grit point deals 1d6 points of extra damage when using her firearm to attack opponents denied their Dexterity bonus to AC (whether the target actually has a Dexterity bonus or not). Except for the requirement that she must use a firearm and must have at least 1 grit point to use it, this deed otherwise works identically to a rogue's sneak attack class feature (including the requirement that she must be within 30 feet of her target to deal this extra damage), and stacks with the sneak shot ability (see below) and sneak attack. This deed replaces the utility shot deed.

Long Range Shifty Shot (Ex): At 7th level, a bushwhacker can double the range at which she deals extra damage from a sneak attack or shifty shot (from 30 feet to 60 feet) with a firearm by spending 1 grit point. When she spends this grit point, she must still have at least 1 grit point left to deal extra damage from shifty shot if she is using this deed. This deed replaces the targeting deed.

Sneak Shot (Ex): At 4th level and every four levels thereafter, a bushwhacker deals 1d6 points of extra damage when using a firearm to attack opponents who are unable to properly defend themselves. Unlike with the shifty shot ability, she deals this extra damage regardless

of whether or not she has any grit points when making the attack. Except for the requirement that she makes a firearm attack, this works identically to a rogue's sneak attack class feature. This extra damage stacks with sneak attack and the damage from shifty shot. This ability replaces the bonus feats the gunslinger gains at 4th, 8th, 12th, 16th, and 20th level.

Kobold Sorcerer Bloodline

While many kobold sorcerers tout their purely draconic bloodline, over generations of eldritch training, some such spellcasters have created a bloodline that, while tinged with some draconic magic, is the embodiment of the race's virtue distilled into arcane form. Many practitioners of this bloodline go on to lead powerful kobold tribes.

Class Skill: Disable Device.

Bonus Spells: *alarm* (3rd), *create pit* (5th), *explosive runes* (7th), *dragon's breath* (9th), *transmute rock to mud* (11th), *guards and wards* (13th), *delayed blast fireball* (15th), *form of the dragon III* (17th), *imprisonment* (19th).

Bonus Feats: Alertness, Combat Casting, Defensive Combat Training, Dodge, Improved Initiative, Lightning Reflexes, Silent Spell.

Bloodline Arcana: Whenever you cast a spell against a creature that is denied its Dexterity bonus to AC, increase that spell's DC by +2.

Bloodline Powers: Like all kobolds, you have a natural talent for ambushing, creating traps, and mining. As your power increases, you discover ever more useful ways to blend your magic with these instinctive talents.

Trap Rune (Sp): At 1st level, as a standard action, you can sketch a single, nearly invisible magical rune on any 5-foot-square solid surface. When you create a rune, pick one of the following energy types: acid, cold, electricity, or fire. While the rune is active, the next creature other than you who steps on or touches the rune's area causes the rune to explode. The rune's explosion deals a number of points of energy damage equal to 1d8 + 1 per sorcerer level you possess to anything in its square. A Reflex saving throw halves the damage (DC 10 + 1/2 your sorcerer level + your Charisma modifier). The rune is considered a magical trap for the purpose of perceiving it or disabling it. The DC for both Perception and Disable Device checks is the same as the Reflex saving throw to halve the damage. You can use this ability a number of times per day equal to 3 + your Charisma modifier. Each rune lasts for 24 hours or until discharged.

Trap Sense (Ex): At 3rd level, you develop a sixth sense that helps you avoid traps. You gain a +2 bonus on Perception checks made to notice traps. You also gain a +1 bonus on Reflex saves to avoid traps and a +1 dodge bonus to AC against attacks made by traps. These bonuses increase

TABLE 2-2: KOBOLD TAIL ATTACHMENTS

Weapon	Cost	Dmg (S)	Dmg (M)	Crit	Range	Weight	Type	Special
Light Melee Weapons								
Long lash	15 gp	1d4	1d6	×2	—	1 lb.	S	reach
Pounder	1 gp	1d6	1d8	×2	—	4 lbs.	B	—
Razored	3 gp	1d6	1d8	19–20/×2	—	2 lbs.	S	—
Spiked	3 gp	1d6	1d8	×3	—	2 lbs.	P	—
Sweeper	7 gp	1d4	1d6	×2	—	3 lbs.	B	trip

by +1 at 7th level and for every four sorcerer levels you gain thereafter (to a maximum of +5 at 19th level). This bonus stacks with that provided by a rogue's trap sense and similar abilities.

Arcane Ambush (Su): At 9th level, as a swift action, you can expend a spell slot in order to grant you and your allies a bonus on attack and damage rolls. This bonus lasts 1 round, is equal to the level of the spell expended, and only applies to opponents your allies are flanking or opponents denied their Dexterity bonus against your allies. You grant this bonus to yourself plus up to one ally for every four sorcerer levels you possess (to a maximum of five allies at 20th level). The allies must be within 30 feet of you and you must have line of effect to each affected ally.

Earth Glide (Su): At 15th level, you gain the earth glide universal monster ability (*Bestiary 2* 296) with a speed equal to your base speed. This does not give you the ability to breathe while passing through earth, so you must hold your breath or use some alternate method to breathe while using this ability.

Nimble Walker (Su): At 20th level, you gain a +5 racial bonus on Reflex saving throws and on Acrobatics checks made to move through a creature's threatened area or through its space. You also gain the ability to breathe while passing through earth using your earth glide ability.

NEW RACIAL RULES

The following options are available to kobolds. At the GM's discretion, other appropriate races may make use of some of these new rules.

Kobold Equipment

Kobolds have access to the following equipment.

Alchemical Coal: A kobold who chews and swallows this alchemically treated piece of coal (a full-round action) can make one breath weapon attack during the next minute. If the kobold fails to make a breath attack before this minute expires, it is sickened for 1 hour. Other humanoid creatures that eat alchemical coal are sickened for 1 hour (though certain other creatures may be able to use them, at the GM's discretion). Creatures that are immune to poison are immune to the sickened effect. The type of breath weapon depends on the type of alchemical coal that is chewed by the kobold.

Blinding Cinders: This jagged bit of dusty red coal allows a kobold to breathe a 30-foot line of coarse cinders. The breath weapon deals 1d6 points of fire damage and blinds creatures in the area for 1 round. A creature that succeeds at a DC 15 Reflex saving throw takes half damage and is not blinded.

Choking Smoke: This crumbling chunk of chalky white coal allows a kobold to breathe a 15-foot cone of foul vapor that deals 1d6 points of acid damage and sickens a creature for 1d4 rounds. A creature that succeeds at a DC 15 Reflex saving throw takes half damage and is not sickened.

Cave Whistle: Fashioned from the spongy stem of a rare mushroom, this whistle produces a sound that only kobolds and dragons can hear. Kobolds often create complicated codes made up of notes that they use to coordinate ambushes and raids.

Kobold Tail Attachments: A kobold with the Tail Terror feat (see below) can slip this device over the tip of his tail to augment his natural attack. Each tail attachment provides just enough weight, balance, and striking power to increase the damage of his tail slap. It takes a full-round action to slip on a kobold tail attachment, and the kobold gains a +4 bonus against disarm attempts made to remove his tail attachment.

While a kobold is wearing a kobold tail attachment, the attack deals the tail attachment damage, and some attachments gain a special feature. Tail attachments are light weapons and can be improved by feats that can improve weapon attacks (such as Weapon Focus and Weapon Specialization). All kobold tail attachments make up a kobold tail attachment weapon group that can be improved by the fighter's weapon training class ability. Tail attachments can be constructed of special material and made into masterwork or magic items. There are five types of common tail attachments.

Long Lash: This slender cord has tiny bits of glass and stone embedded in its length.

Pounder: This squat ball is made from some sort of dull metal.

Razored: This metal wedge has a prickly edge on one of its sides.

Spiked: This narrow spike tapers to a sharp point.

Sweeper: When properly used, this sharply curved piece of metal can knock opponents off their feet. Unlike most trip weapons, you cannot drop it if you are tripped during your own trip attempt.

Kobold Equipment

Item	Cost	Weight	Craft DC
Alchemical coal (blinding cinders)	100 gp	—	25
Alchemical coal (choking smoke)	50 gp	—	20
Cave whistle	20 gp	—	—

Kobold Feats

Kobolds have access to the following feats.

Draconic Aspect

You possess some of the qualities of your dragon ancestors.

Prerequisite: Kobold.

Benefit: Your scales take on the color and some of the resistances of one of the chromatic dragons. Choose one

of the following chromatic dragon types: black (acid), blue (electricity), green (acid), red (fire), or white (cold). Your scales take on the color of that dragon, and you gain resistance 5 to the dragon color's corresponding energy type.

Special: If you have the dragon-scaled racial trait, your scale color does not change and you gain a +1 natural armor bonus instead.

Draconic Breath

You possess draconic defenses and a draconic breath weapon.

Prerequisites: Draconic Aspect, kobold.

Benefit: You gain a +2 bonus against sleep and paralysis effects. You gain a breath weapon that is determined by your scale coloration by either the Draconic Aspect feat or the dragon-scaled racial trait. Using a breath weapon is a standard action that does not provoke attacks of opportunity. You can use your breath weapon once per day. Creatures within the area of your breath weapon who succeed at a Reflex saving throw (DC 10 + your character level + your Constitution modifier) take only half damage.

Black (Su): You breathe a 30-foot line of acid that deals 2d6 points of acid damage.

Blue (Su): You breathe a 30-foot line of electricity that deals 2d6 points of electricity damage.

Green (Su): You breathe a 15-foot cone of acid that deals 2d6 points of acid damage.

Red (Su): You breathe a 15-foot cone of fire that deals 2d6 points of fire damage.

White (Su): You breathe a 15-foot cone of cold that deals 2d6 points of cold damage.

Special: Kobold sorcerers with either the Draconic or Kobold bloodline can use their Charisma modifier instead of their Constitution to determine the number of times per day they can use this breath weapon and the DC of this breath weapon.

Draconic Glide

You possess draconic defenses and wings that allow you to glide.

Prerequisites: Draconic Aspect, kobold.

Benefit: You gain a +2 bonus against sleep and paralysis effects. You grow a pair of wings that you can use to fall and glide at a safe pace. You can make a DC 15 Fly check to fall safely from any height without taking falling damage, as if using *feather fall*. When falling safely, you may make an additional DC 15 Fly check to glide, moving 5 feet laterally for every 20 feet you fall.

Special: If you have the gliding wings racial trait, instead of the above abilities, your base speed increases to 30 feet.

Draconic Paragon

You can shrug off sleep and paralysis effects as well as any dragon, and your draconic aspects improve.

Prerequisites: Draconic Aspect, either Draconic Breath or Draconic Glide, character level 10th, kobold.

Benefit: You gain an additional +2 bonus against sleep and paralysis effects. You can use your breath weapon twice per day and your breath weapon damage increases to 4d6 points of energy damage. Your wings from the Draconic Glide feat grow stronger, granting you a fly speed of 20 feet (average maneuverability).

Kobold Ambusher (Combat)

You are adept at moving fast and staying hidden.

Prerequisites: Stealth 4 ranks, kobold.

Benefit: You take no penalty on Stealth checks when you move up to your full speed. You can use the run or charge action and remain hidden, taking a –10 penalty on the check to do so.

Normal: When moving greater than half speed up to your full speed, you take a –5 penalty on Stealth checks. When you are able to run or charge while using Stealth, you take a –20 penalty on the Stealth check.

Kobold Sniper (Combat)

You snipe quickly, making it harder for others to find the location of your attack.

Prerequisites: Stealth 1 rank, kobold.

Benefit: When you are sniping, you only take a –10 penalty on your Stealth checks to stay hidden.

Normal: You take a –20 penalty on your Stealth check to maintain your obscured location while sniping.

Tail Terror (Combat)

You have strengthened your tail enough to make slap attacks with it.

Prerequisites: Base attack bonus +1, kobold.

Benefit: You can make a tail slap attack with your tail. This is a secondary natural attack that deals 1d4 points of bludgeoning damage. Furthermore, you can augment your tail slap attack with a kobold tail attachment. For the purpose of weapon feats, you are considered proficient with all kobold tail attachments.

Kobold Magic Items

Kobolds have access to the following magic items.

RUBBLE GLOVES

Aura faint transmutation; **CL** 5th
Slot hands; **Price** 8,000 gp; **Weight** 1 lb.

DESCRIPTION

These gloves are made of a fine metal mesh. If a creature wearing rubble gloves touches a 5-foot square of stone or earth floor, rubble roils to the surface, making the square difficult terrain. Using the gloves is a standard action that does not provoke attacks of opportunity. The wearer can use the gloves to create up to 20 squares of difficult terrain per day.

CONSTRUCTION

Requirements Craft Wondrous Item, *expeditious excavation*; **Cost** 4,000 gp

TRAPMAKER'S SACK

Aura moderate transmutation; **CL** 9th
Slot none; **Price** 20,000 gp; **Weight** 2 lbs.

DESCRIPTION

This heavy leather bag bulges only slightly but upon closer inspection appears to be chocked full of knives, gears, picks, shovels, and arrows. Once per day as a full-round action, the bearer can command the sack to create any mechanical trap of CR 4 or less (*Core Rulebook* 420–422), which appears at a designated spot within 50 feet. The bearer must make a Craft (traps) check with a DC equal to the normal DC for creating the trap (*Core Rulebook* 424). If successful, the trap instantly merges with the chosen area, exactly as if someone had actually built the trap in that spot. If the check fails, no trap appears. The sack can alter earth, stone, and wood to accommodate the trap without altering nearby terrain (including doors, pits, and so on).

CONSTRUCTION

Requirements Craft Wondrous Item, *fabricate*, creator must have 5 ranks in Craft (traps); **Cost** 10,000 gp

Kobold Spells

Kobolds have access to the following spell.

IMPROVE TRAP

School transmutation; **Level** antipaladin 2, druid 3, inquisitor 3, ranger 2, sorcerer/wizard 3, witch 3
Casting Time 1 minute
Components V, S
Range close (25 ft. + 5 ft./2 levels)
Target one trap
Duration instantaneous
Saving Throw Will negates (object); **Spell Resistance** yes (object)

When this spell is cast upon a trap, it improves one specific element of the trap chosen at the time of casting. The caster can improve the trap in any of the following ways (each one raises the trap's CR by +1).

- Increase DC of the Perception check required to locate the trap by +5.
- Increase DC of the Disable Device check required to disarm trap by +5.
- Increase the trap's attack bonus or saving throw by +2.

To cast this on a trap, you must know that the trap exists and its precise location. A trap can only have one improvement from this spell at a time. A second casting changes the improvement on the trap, but does not add another improvement.

ORCS

Orcs are aggressive, callous, and domineering. Bullies by nature, they respect strength and power as the highest virtues. On an almost instinctive level, orcs believe they are entitled to anything they want unless someone stronger can stop them from seizing it. They rarely exert themselves off the battlefield except when forced to do so; this attitude stems not just from laziness but also from an ingrained belief that work should trickle down through the pecking order until it falls upon the shoulders of the weak. They take slaves from other races, orc men brutalize orc women, and both abuse children and elders, on the grounds that anyone too feeble to fight back deserves little more than a life of suffering. Surrounded at all times by bitter enemies, orcs cultivate an attitude of indifference to pain, vicious tempers, and a fierce willingness to commit unspeakable acts of vengeance against anyone who dares to defy them.

Physical Description: Powerfully built, orcs typically stand just a few inches taller than most humans but have much greater muscle mass, their broad shoulders and thick, brawny hips often giving them a slightly lurching gait. They typically have dull green skin, coarse dark hair, beady red eyes, and protruding, tusklike teeth. Orcs consider scars a mark of distinction and frequently use them as a form of body art.

Society: Orcs usually live amid squalor and constant mayhem, and intimidation and brutal violence are the glue that holds orc culture together. They settle disputes by making increasingly grisly threats until, when a rival fails to back down, the conflict escalates into actual bloodshed. Orcs who win these ferocious brawls not only feel free to take whatever they want from the loser, but also frequently indulge in humiliating physical violation, casual mutilation, and even outright murder. Orcs rarely spend much time improving their homes or belongings since doing so merely encourages a stronger orc to seize them. In fact, whenever possible, they prefer to occupy buildings and communities originally built by other races.

Relations: Orcs admire strength above all things. Even members of enemy races can sometimes win an orc's grudging respect, or at least tolerance, if they break his nose enough times.

Orcs regard dwarves and elves with an odd mix of fierce hatred, sullen resentment, and a trace of wariness. They respect power, and, on some level, understand that these two races have kept them at bay for countless ages. Though they never miss a chance to torment a dwarf or elf who falls into their clutches, they tend to proceed cautiously unless certain of victory. Orcs dismiss halflings and gnomes as weaklings barely worth the trouble of enslaving. They often regard half-elves, who appear less threatening than full-blooded elves but have many elven features, as particularly appealing targets. Orcs view humans as race of sheep with a few wolves living in their midst. They freely kill or oppress humans too weak to fend them off but always keep one eye on the nearest exit in case they run into a formidable human.

Orcs look upon half-orcs with a strange mixture of contempt, envy, and pride. Though weaker than typical orcs, these half-breeds are also usually smarter, more cunning, and better leaders. Tribes led, or at least advised, by half-orcs are often more successful than those led by pure-blooded orcs. On a more fundamental level, orcs believe each half-orc also represents an orc exerting dominance over a weaker race.

Alignment and Religion: Orcs have few redeeming qualities. Most are violent, cruel, and selfish. Concepts such as honor or loyalty usually strike them as odd character flaws that tend to afflict members of the weaker races. Orcs are typically not just evil, but chaotic to boot, though those with greater self-control may gravitate toward lawful evil. Orcs pray to gods of fire, war, and blood, often creating tribal "pantheons" by combining these aspects into uniquely orc concepts.

Adventurers: Orcs usually leave their tribes only after losing out in a power struggle. Facing humiliation, slavery, or even death at the hands of their own kind, they opt instead to live and work with members of other races. Orcs who fail to rein in their tempers and the instinctive drive to dominate rarely last long once they strike out on their own. Though orcs who do manage to get by in other societies often enjoy the luxuries and comforts these societies can deliver, they still tend to dream of returning home, seizing power, and taking revenge.

Male Names: Arkus, Carrug, Felzak, Murdut, Prabur.

Female Names: Durra, Grillgiss, Ilyat, Krugga, Leffit, Olbin, Trisgrak.

ALTERNATE RACIAL TRAITS

The following racial traits may be selected instead of existing orc racial traits. Consult your GM before selecting any of these new options.

Dayrunner: Orcs refuse to yield to any foe, including the sun. Some spend hour upon hour glaring at the sun until their ruined eyes acclimatize to bright light. Orcs with this racial trait take a –2 penalty on all ranged attack rolls. This racial trait replaces light sensitivity.

Feral: Orcs have the ability to fend for themselves long before they master the rudiments of their language and culture. Having needed to hunt bugs and tiny animals for food to survive while still infants, feral orcs fight all the harder to survive when at the brink of death.

Orcs with this racial trait gain Survival as a class skill and gain a +1 racial bonus on melee weapon attack and damage rolls when at negative hit points. This racial trait replaces the orc's weapon familiarity and automatic languages. Feral orcs without additional languages due to high Intelligence scores or ranks in Linguistics can only communicate with grunts and gestures.

Smeller: Orcs with this racial trait gain a limited scent ability with half the normal range (*Bestiary* 304). This racial trait replaces ferocity and weapon familiarity.

Squalid: Some orcs exist in surroundings so filthy and pestilent that even other orcs would have difficulty living in them. Orcs with this racial trait gain a +2 racial bonus on saving throws made to resist nausea, the sickened condition, and disease. This racial trait replaces ferocity.

FAVORED CLASS OPTIONS

The following options are available to all orcs who have the listed favored class, and unless otherwise stated, the bonus applies each time you select the favored class reward.

Alchemist: Add +10 minutes to the duration of the alchemist's mutagens.

Barbarian: Add +1 to the barbarian's total number of rage rounds per day.

Cavalier: Add +1 to the cavalier's CMB when making bull rush or overrun combat maneuvers against a challenged target.

Druid: Add +1/2 to the damage dealt by the druid's animal companion's natural attacks.

Fighter: Add +2 to the fighter's Constitution score for the purpose of determining when he dies from negative hit points.

Ranger: Add +1 hit point to the ranger's animal companion. If the ranger ever replaces his animal companion, the new animal companion gains these bonus hit points.

Witch: Add one spell from the witch spell list to the witch's familiar. This spell must be at least one level below the highest spell level she can cast. If the witch ever replaces her familiar, the new familiar knows these bonus spells.

ORC RACIAL TRAITS

+4 Strength, –2 Intelligence, –2 Wisdom, –2 Charisma: Orcs are brutal and savage.

Orc: Orcs are humanoids with the orc subtype.

Medium: Orcs are Medium creatures and have no bonuses or penalties due to their size.

Normal Speed: Orcs have a base speed of 30 feet.

Darkvision: Orcs can see in the dark up to 60 feet.

Light Sensitivity: Orcs are dazzled in areas of bright sunlight or within the radius of a *daylight* spell.

Ferocity: Orcs can remain conscious and continue fighting even if their hit point totals fall below 0. Orcs are still staggered at 0 hit points or lower and lose 1 hit point each round as normal.

Weapon Familiarity: Orcs are always proficient with greataxes and falchions, and treat any weapon with the word "orc" in its name as a martial weapon.

Languages: Orcs begin play speaking Common and Orc. Orcs with high Intelligence scores can chose from the following: Dwarven, Giant, Gnoll, Goblin, Undercommon.

RACIAL ARCHETYPES

The following racial archetypes are available to orcs.

Dirty Fighter (Fighter)

The dirty fighter laughs at concepts like honor and fair play. He cares only for victory, no matter how he achieves it, and spends as much time mastering sneaky combat maneuvers as he does drilling with weapons or learning how to wear armor. A dirty fighter has the following class features.

Sidestep (Ex): At 2nd level, a dirty fighter learns how to evade his enemies when they react to his combat maneuvers. He gains a +1 dodge bonus to his AC against attacks of opportunity provoked by him while attempting a combat maneuver. This bonus increases by +1 for every four levels beyond 2nd level. This ability replaces bravery.

Maneuver Training (Ex): At 5th level, a dirty fighter becomes a master of dirty tricks. He gains a +2 bonus on dirty trick combat maneuver checks (*Advanced Player's Guide* 320) and +2 to his CMD when he is the target of a dirty trick combat maneuver. This ability replaces weapon training 1.

Speedy Tricks (Ex): At 9th level, a dirty fighter has perfected how to quickly perform dirty tricks. He can make a dirty trick combat maneuver as an attack instead of a standard action. This ability replaces weapon training 2.

Double Tricks (Ex): At 13th level, when a dirty fighter performs a combat maneuver, he may apply two different conditions to his target instead of one. Each penalty condition requires a separate action to remove. At 17th level, he may apply three different conditions. This ability replaces weapon training 3 and 4.

Scarred Witch Doctor (Witch)

The scarred witch doctor draws power from her ability to endure pain and suffering. She mutilates her own flesh, inflicting horrific scars, in order to attract the attention of her patron. Rather than call forth a familiar, she creates a repulsive fetish mask that she uses as a repository for her power. A scarred witch doctor has the following class features.

Constitution Dependent: A scarred witch doctor uses Constitution instead of Intelligence when determining the highest level of spells she can cast, her spell save DCs, number of spells known at 1st level, and any effects of her hexes normally determined by her Intelligence.

Hex Scar: Whenever a scarred witch doctor learns a hex, she must carve or brand a symbol in her flesh to represent this hex. She can disguise these scars with mundane or magical means, but they cannot be permanently removed.

Fetish Mask (Su): At 1st level, a scarred witch doctor forms a bond with a wooden mask. As she gains power, her connection to this mask causes it to grow ever more hideous and grotesque as it absorbs the weight of the self-induced pain that underlies her magic. Her spells derive from the insights her patron grants her while she's enduring the cuts, burns, and other sorts of mutilations she inflicts upon herself. Her fetish mask acts in all ways like a witch's familiar for the purpose of preparing and gaining spells. Rather than communing with a familiar to prepare spells each day, a scarred witch doctor hangs her mask on a wall, tree branch, or something similar and contemplates the agony it represents.

When wearing her fetish mask, a scarred witch doctor gains a +2 circumstance bonus on Heal and Intimidate checks and gains a +2 bonus on saving throws against effects that specifically cause pain or have the pain descriptor. If the mask is destroyed, the witch doctor can create another fetish mask (which almost immediately adopts the shocking appearance of the original) for the same price and time it takes a witch to replace a dead familiar.

At 5th level, the scarred witch doctor gains the ability to add magical abilities to her mask as if she had the Craft Wondrous Item feat.

This ability otherwise functions like and replaces the standard witch familiar.

Scarshield (Su): At 1st level, a scarred witch doctor learns how to harden her mutilated skin, gaining an enhancement bonus to her natural armor bonus equal to 1/2 her class level (minimum +1). She can use this ability for a number of minutes per day equal to her class level. These minutes do not need to be consecutive but she must spend them in 1-minute increments. This ability replaces the witch's 1st-level hex.

Hexes: The following hexes complement the scarred witch doctor archetype: evil eye, misfortune (*Advanced Player's Guide*); scar, unnerve beasts (*Ultimate Magic*).

Major Hexes: The following major hexes complement the scarred witch doctor archetype: agony, nightmare (*Advanced Player's Guide*); cook people, infected wounds (*Ultimate Magic*).

Grand Hexes: The following grand hexes complement the scarred witch doctor archetype: death curse, natural disaster (*Advanced Player's Guide*); dire prophecy (*Ultimate Magic*).

NEW RACIAL RULES

The following options are available to orcs. At the GM's discretion, other appropriate races may make use of some of these new rules.

Orc Equipment

Orcs have access to the following equipment.

Battle Mask: Made from wood, bone, or similar materials, this mask covers its wearer's actual appearance and identity by depicting a hateful, leering face instead. Because of a battle mask's excellent craftsmanship and exquisite details, the wearer gains a +1 bonus on Intimidate checks made to demoralize an opponent.

Tribal Standard: Mounted on a sturdy 15-foot pole, this flag inspires all orcs belonging to the tribe it represents. As long as they are within 60 feet and can see the standard, they gain a +1 morale bonus on saving throws against fear effects. The standard must be carried in one hand by a member of the tribe to have any effect (it provides no bonus if hung on a wall, draped over a throne, and so on). If the standard is brought low (such as by its bearer dropping it in the mud), defiled, destroyed, or captured, the tribe's members take a –1 penalty on attack rolls and saving throws versus fear effects for the next hour. If the orcs reclaim a captured standard, the penalties end and the bonus is restored.

War Spirit Pouch: This tiny bundle of sacred herbs and bones supposedly attracts the attention of helpful battle-spirits. By crushing the pouch as a standard action, an orc (or a creature from a suitably warlike culture) gains 1d4+1 temporary hit points. These temporary hit points go away after 10 minutes. A creature can only benefit from 1 spirit pouch at a time. Once used, the spirit pouch is destroyed.

Orc Equipment

Item	Cost	Weight	Craft DC
Battle mask	50 gp	2 lbs.	—
Tribal standard	50 gp	20 lbs.	—
War spirit pouch	50 gp	—	20

Orc Feats

Orcs have access to the following feats.

Born Alone

You are so tough and vicious that you killed and ate the rest of your litter while still in the womb.

Prerequisite: Orc.

Benefit: Whenever you kill or knock unconscious an opponent with a melee attack, you gain temporary hit points equal to your Constitution bonus (minimum 1) until your next turn. These temporary hit points do not stack. You do not gain this bonus if the opponent is helpless or has less than half your Hit Dice.

Bullying Blow (Combat)

With a simple hit, you more easily intimidate an opponent.

Prerequisites: Intimidate 1 rank, orc.

Benefit: As a standard action, you may make a melee attack with a –2 penalty on the attack roll. If the attack damages your opponent, you may make an Intimidate check to demoralize that opponent as a free action.

Normal: Intimidating an opponent is a standard action.

Ferocious Action

You ferocity is quick but shorter lived.

Prerequisites: Ferocity racial trait, orc.

Benefit: When you fall to 0 hit points or fewer, you lose 2 hit points each round, but you are not staggered. If you are in a rage (such as that caused by the barbarian rage class feature), you instead only lose 1 hit point per round.

Foment the Blood

You can unleash a wave of energy that drives orcs into a frenzy.

Prerequisites: Channel energy class feature, orc.

Benefit: When you channel energy, instead of creating its normal effect, you can give orcs a bonus on weapon damage and critical hit confirmation rolls until your next turn. This bonus is equal to the number of dice your channeled energy normally heals or harms. Your channel has its normal effect on other creatures in the area.

Grudge Fighter (Combat)

You feel great anger at anyone who dares to attack you, and this fury makes your own attacks that much stronger.

Prerequisite: Orc.

Benefit: You gain a +1 morale bonus on attack and damage rolls made against any creature that attacked you in the current combat.

Orc Weapon Expertise (Combat)

You can do more with the weapons orcs favor the most.

Prerequisites: Base attack bonus +1, orc.

Benefit: When you take this feat, choose one of the benefits below. Whenever you wield a weapon that has "orc" in its name, you gain the benefit you chose so long as you are actually proficient with that weapon.

Bully: Gain a +1 bonus on damage rolls against creatures at least one size smaller than you.

Defender: Gain a +1 shield bonus to your AC (or +2 if wielding a two-handed weapon).

Disrupter: Add +3 to opponents' concentration checks to cast a spell within your threatened area. This only applies if you are aware of the enemy's location and are capable of taking an attack of opportunity. If you have already used all of your available attacks of opportunity for the round, this increase does not apply.

Killer: Gain a +2 competence bonus on attack rolls made to confirm critical hits.

Thug: Deal +1 point of nonlethal damage with the weapon.

Trickster: Gain a +2 bonus on a single type of combat maneuver check that you can perform with that weapon.

This feat has no effect if you are not proficient with the weapon you're using.

Special: You can gain this feat multiple times. Each time you take this feat, you must choose a different benefit. You may only apply one of these benefits per round (chosen as a free action at the start of your turn).

Resolute Rager

Fear passes quickly while you are raging.

Prerequisites: Orc, rage class feature.

Benefit: While raging, when under the effect of a fear effect that allows a saving throw, you can make a new saving throw against that fear effect at the start of each of your turns before acting. If you make the new save, the fear effect ends.

Reverse-Feint (Combat)

You can goad an opponent into attacking you in order to make your counter attack all the more powerful.

Prerequisites: Toughness, base attack bonus +1, orc.

Benefit: As a move action, you can leave a gap in your defenses for one adjacent opponent to use. If the opponent attacks you on its next turn, it gains a +4 bonus on its attack roll. Whether or not the opponent successfully hits, you may attack it as an immediate action with a single melee attack, gaining a +2 bonus on your attack roll.

Trap Wrecker

You can smash traps instead of disarming them.

Prerequisites: Power Attack, Disable Device 1 rank, orc.

Benefit: You can attempt to disarm a trap by striking it with a melee weapon instead of making a Disable Device check. As a full-round action, make a melee attack against an Armor Class equal to the trap's Disable Device DC. If you miss, the trap activates. If you hit, roll damage. If this damage is at least half the trap's Disable Device DC, you disable the trap. If this damage is less than half the trap's Disable Device DC, the trap activates. You can only attempt this on nonmagical traps. You must be able to reach some part of the trap with your attack in order to use this feat. At the GM's discretion, some traps may not be susceptible to this feat.

Orc Magic Items

Orcs have access to the following weapon special ability and magic item.

Fury-Born (weapon special ability): A *fury-born* weapon draws power from the anger and frustration the wielder feels when battling foes that refuse to die. Each time the wielder damages an opponent with the weapon, its enhancement bonus increases by +1 when making attacks against that opponent (maximum total enhancement bonus of +5). This extra enhancement bonus goes away if the opponent dies, the wielder uses the weapon to attack a different creature, or 1 hour passes. Only melee weapons can have the *fury-born* ability.

Faint enchantment; CL 7th; Craft Magic Arms and Armor, *rage*; Price +2 bonus.

BONEBREAKER GAUNTLETS

Aura faint necromancy; **CL** 5th

Slot hands; **Price** 6,000 gp; **Weight** 2 lbs.

DESCRIPTION

These thick brass and leather gauntlets allow the wearer to tear through bone and muscle like paper. Once per day, as part of a melee attack, the wearer can activate the gauntlets to inflict a horrific injury on an opponent. If the attack hits, the target must make a DC 14 Will save. If the save fails, the gauntlets reduce the target's Strength, Dexterity, or Constitution (wearer's choice) by –6. This penalty cannot reduce the target's ability score below 1. The injury heals over time, reducing the penalty by 1 for each day that passes since the time of the injury, and is immediately removed by *heal*, *regenerate*, *restoration*, or any magic that can break a curse.

CONSTRUCTION

Requirements Craft Wondrous Item, *bestow curse*; **Cost** 3,000 gp

Orc Spells

Orcs have access to the following spells.

BLOOD BLAZE

School transmutation [fire]; **Level** alchemist 2, antipaladin 1, cleric 2, magus 2, sorcerer/wizard 2, witch 2
Casting Time 1 standard action
Components V, S
Range touch
Target creature touched
Duration 1 round/level (D)
Saving Throw Fortitude negates (harmless); **Spell Resistance** yes (harmless)

The target gains a 5-foot-radius aura that causes the blood of creatures in that area to ignite upon contact with air. Any creature (including the spell's target) within the aura that takes at least 5 points of piercing, slashing, or bleed damage from a single attack automatically creates a spray of burning blood. The spray strikes a creature in a randomly determined square adjacent to the injured creature. The spray deals 1d6 points of fire damage to any creature in that square, and 1 point of splash damage to all creatures within 5 feet of the spray's target, including the target of this spell. A creature can only create one spray of burning blood per round. Creatures that do not have blood (including oozes and most constructs and undead) do not create blood sprays when attacked.

BLOOD SCENT

School transmutation; **Level** alchemist 3, antipaladin 2, cleric 3, druid 3, inquisitor 3, ranger 2, sorcerer/wizard 3, witch 3
Casting Time 1 standard action
Components V, S
Range medium (100 ft. + 10 ft./level)
Targets one creature/2 levels, no two of which can be more than 30 ft. apart
Duration 1 minute/level (D)
Saving Throw Will negates (harmless); **Spell Resistance** yes (harmless)

You greatly magnify the target's ability to smell the presence of blood. The target is considered to have the scent universal monster ability, but only for purposes of detecting and pinpointing injured creatures (below full hit points). Creatures below half their full hit points or suffering bleed damage are considered strong scents for this ability.

Orcs and any creature under the effects of rage gain a +2 morale bonus on attack and damage rolls against creatures they can smell with this spell, or a +4 morale bonus if the target's blood counts as a strong scent.

ENEMY'S HEART

School necromancy [death, evil]; **Level** adept 2, antipaladin 2, cleric 2, witch 2
Casting Time 1 full-round action, special see below

Components V, S, M (target creature's heart)
Range touch
Target living creature touched
Duration concentration/1 minute per HD of the subject; see text
Saving Throw none; **Spell Resistance** yes

You cut out an enemy's heart and consume it, absorbing that enemy's power as your own. As part of casting this spell, you perform a coup de grace with a slashing weapon on a helpless, living adjacent target. If the target dies, you eat its heart to gain the spell's benefits. If the target survives, the spell is not wasted and you can try again as long as you continue concentrating on the spell. When you consume the heart, you gain the benefits of a *death knell* spell, except you gain 1d8 temporary hit points +1 per Hit Die of the target, and the bonus to Strength is a profane bonus.

SENTRY SKULL

School necromancy [evil]; **Level** antipaladin 1, cleric 2, sorcerer/wizard 2, witch 2
Casting Time 1 hour
Components V, S, M (an onyx gem worth at least 10 gp)
Range touch
Target severed head touched
Duration permanent (D); see text
Saving Throw none; **Spell Resistance** no

You restore the senses to the severed head of a humanoid or monstrous humanoid killed within the past 24 hours, creating a grisly sentinel. The head must be affixed to a pole, spear, tree branch, or other stable object, and the spell ends if the head or its object is moved. The head has darkvision 60 feet and low-light vision, can swivel in place to look in any direction, and has a +5 bonus on Perception checks.

If you are within 30 feet of the head, as a standard action you can shift your senses to it, seeing and hearing from its location and gaining the benefit of its darkvision and low-light vision, and you may use its Perception skill instead of your own. While your senses are in the severed head, your body is blind and deaf until you spend a free action to shift your senses back to your own body.

When you create the head, you can imprint it with a single triggering condition, similar to *magic mouth*. Once this triggering condition is set, it can never be changed. If you are within 30 feet of the head, you immediately know if it is triggered (if you have multiple active *sentry skulls*, you also know which one was triggered). This wakens you from normal sleep but does not otherwise disturb your concentration. For example, you could have a *sentry skull* alert you if any humanoid comes into view, if a particular rival approaches, if your guard animal is killed, and so on, as long as it occurs where the severed head can see it.

This spell does not give the head any ability to speak, think, or take any kind of action other than to turn itself, though it is a suitable target for other spells such as *magic mouth*.

OREADS

Oreads are humans whose ancestry includes the touch of an elemental being of earth somewhere along the line, often that of a shaitan genie. Stoic and contemplative, oreads are a race not easily moved, yet almost unstoppable when spurred to action. They remain a mystery to most of the world thanks to their reclusive nature, but those who seek them out in their secluded mountain hideaways find oreads to be quiet, dependable, and protective of their friends.

Physical Description: Oreads are strong and solidly built, with skin and hair colored stony shades of black, brown, gray, or white. While all oreads appear vaguely earthy, a few bear more pronounced signs of their elemental heritage—skin that shines like polished onyx, rocky outcroppings protruding from their flesh, glowing gemstones for eyes, or hair like crystalline spikes. They often dress in earthy tones, wearing practical clothing well suited to vigorous physical activity and preferring fresh flowers, simple gemstones, and other natural accents to complex manufactured jewelry.

Society: As a minor offshoot of the human race, oreads have no real established society of their own. Instead, most oreads grow up in human communities learning the customs of their parents. Adult oreads have a well-deserved reputation among other races for being hermits and loners. Few take well to the bustle of city life, preferring instead to spend their days in quiet contemplation atop some remote mountain peak or deep below the earth in a secluded cavern. Oreads with a greater tolerance for life among humans often join the city watch, or find some other way to serve their community in a position of responsibility.

Relations: Oreads feel comfortable in the company of dwarves, with whom they have much in common. They find gnomes too strange and many halflings far too brash, and so avoid these races in general. Oreads gladly associate with half-orcs and half-elves, feeling a sense of kinship with the other part-human races despite inevitable personality conflicts. Among the elemental-touched races, oreads have few friends but no true enemies.

Alignment and Religion: Oreads are, perhaps above all else, set in their ways, and any disruption of their routine is met with quiet disapproval. Oreads are fiercely protective of their friends, but don't seem particularly concerned with the well-being of those outside their small circle of acquaintances. As such, most oreads are lawful neutral. Religious life comes easily to the earth-touched. They appreciate the quiet, contemplative life of the monastic order, and most dedicate themselves to the worship of earth- or nature-related deities.

Adventurers: Oreads are initially hesitant adventurers. They dislike leaving their homes and don't handle the shock of new experiences well. Usually it takes some outside force to rouse oreads into action, often by threatening their homes, lives, or friends. Once the initial threat is dealt with, however, oreads often find they've grown accustomed to the adventuring life, and continue to pursue it through the rest of their days. Oreads make good monks and fighters thanks to their prodigious strength and self-discipline.

Male Names: Andanan, Jeydavu, Mentys, Oret, Sithundan, Urtar.

Female Names: Besthana, Echane, Ghatiyara, Irice, Nysene, Pashe.

ALTERNATE RACIAL TRAITS

The following racial traits may be selected instead of existing oread racial traits. Consult your GM before selecting any of these new options.

Crystalline Form: Oreads with this trait gain a +2 racial bonus to AC against rays thanks to their reflective crystalline skin. In addition, once per day, they can deflect a single ray attack targeted at them as if they were using the Deflect Arrows feat. This racial trait replaces earth affinity.

Earth Insight: Oread spellcasters sometimes find that their elemental heritage makes creatures of earth more willing to serve them. *Summon monster* and *summon nature's ally* spells that such oreads cast last 2 rounds longer than normal when used to summon creatures with the earth subtype. This racial trait replaces earth affinity.

Ferrous Growth: Oreads with this racial trait learn how to mimic the magic of their shaitan ancestors. Once per day, such an oread can cause a touched piece of nonmagical iron or steel to grow into an object up to 10 pounds in weight, such as a sword, crowbar, or light steel shield. This object remains in this form for 10 minutes or until broken or destroyed, at which point it shrinks back to its original size and shape. This racial trait replaces the spell-like ability racial trait.

Fertile Soil: Oread sorcerers with the verdant bloodline treat their Charisma score as 2 points higher for all sorcerer spells and class abilities. Oread clerics with the Plant domain use their domain powers and spells at +1 caster level. This racial trait replaces earth affinity.

Granite Skin: Rocky growths cover the skin of oreads with this racial trait. They gain a +1 racial bonus to natural armor. This racial trait replaces energy resistance.

Mountain-Born: Oreads are drawn to mountains and other high places, and after many generations they've grown well suited to their environment. Oreads with this racial trait gain a +2 racial bonus on Acrobatics checks

made to cross narrow ledges and on saves against altitude fatigue and sickness. This racial trait replaces the spell-like ability racial trait.

Stone in the Blood: Oreads with this racial trait mimic the healing abilities of the mephits, gaining fast healing 2 for 1 round anytime they are subject to acid damage (the acid damage does not need to overcome the oread's resistances or immunities to activate this ability). The oread can heal up to 2 hit points per level per day with this ability, after which it ceases to function. This racial trait replaces earth affinity.

Treacherous Earth: Once per day, an oread with this racial trait can will the earth to rumble and shift, transforming a 10-foot-radius patch of earth, unworked stone, or sand into an area of difficult terrain, centered on an area the oread touches. This lasts for a number of minutes equal to the oread's level, after which the ground returns to normal. This racial trait replaces the spell-like ability racial trait.

FAVORED CLASS OPTIONS

The following options are available to all oreads who have the listed favored class, and unless otherwise stated, the bonus applies each time you select the class reward.

Bard: Add +5 feet to the range of one of the bard's bardic performances (max +30 feet to any one performance).

Cleric: Add a +1/2 bonus on Knowledge (planes) checks relating to the Plane of Earth and creatures with the earth subtype.

Druid: Add a +1/2 bonus on Knowledge (nature) checks relating to plants and burrowing animals.

Fighter: Add +1 to the fighter's CMD when resisting a bull rush or drag attempt.

Monk: Add +1/3 on critical hit confirmation rolls made with unarmed strikes (maximum bonus of +5). This bonus does not stack with Critical Focus.

Paladin: Add +1/4 to the bonus the paladin grants her allies with her aura of courage and aura of resolve special abilities.

Ranger: Add +1/4 to the natural armor bonus of the ranger's animal companion. If the ranger ever replaces his animal companion, the new animal companion gains this bonus.

Summoner: Add a +1/4 natural armor bonus to the AC of the summoner's eidolon.

RACIAL ARCHETYPES

The following racial archetypes are available to oreads.

OREAD RACIAL TRAITS

+2 Strength, +2 Wisdom, –2 Charisma: Oreads are strong, solid, stable, and stoic.

Native Outsider: Oreads are outsiders with the native subtype.

Medium: Oreads are Medium creatures and have no bonuses or penalties due to their size.

Slow Speed: Oreads have a base speed of 20 feet.

Darkvision: Oreads can see in the dark up to 60 feet.

Spell-Like Ability: *Magic stone* 1/day (caster level equals the oread's total level).

Energy Resistance: Oreads have acid resistance 5.

Earth Affinity: Oread sorcerers with the elemental (earth) bloodline treat their Charisma score as 2 points higher for all sorcerer spells and class abilities. Oread clerics with the Earth domain use their domain powers and spells at +1 caster level.

Languages: Oreads begin play speaking Common and Terran. Oreads with high Intelligence scores can choose from the following: Aquan, Auran, Dwarven, Elven, Gnome, Halfling, Ignan, and Undercommon.

Shaitan Binder (Summoner)

Shaitan binders call upon a reflection of their genie ancestors to serve as their eidolons. A shaitan binder has the following class features.

Base Form: At 1st level, if a shaitan binder's eidolon has the biped base form, it gains a +2 bonus to one ability score. The shaitan binder must make this choice at 1st level. If at any time the shaitan binder's eidolon has another base form, it loses this bonus until it returns to biped form. A shaitan binder's eidolon does not gain the share spells ability.

Shaitan Magic (Su): At 4th level, a shaitan binder's eidolon gains the basic magic evolution (*Ultimate Magic*) as a free evolution. At 6th level, it gains the minor magic evolution (*Ultimate Magic*).

At 8th level, it gains the major magic evolution (*Ultimate Magic*) as a free evolution, and adds the following to the list of available spells for that evolution: *glitterdust* and *soften earth and stone*.

At 12th level, it gains the ultimate magic evolution (*Ultimate Magic*) as a free evolution, and adds the following to the list of available spells for that evolution: *meld into stone* and *stone shape*.

Although the shaitan binder gains the standard versions of these evolutions for free, he must pay the normal cost to upgrade them to the improved versions. This ability replaces shield ally and greater shield ally.

Earth Glide (Su): At 10th level, if a shaitan binder's eidolon has the burrow evolution, it gains the earth glide universal monster ability and can use this ability to travel at its full base speed. This ability replaces aspect.

Stone Curse (Su): At 18th level, a shaitan binder may select stone curse as a 4-point evolution. This allows the eidolon to trap creatures in stone like the shaitan stone curse ability (*Bestiary* 143). The DC to resist or break free of the stone curse is 10 + 1/2 the eidolon's Hit Dice + the eidolon's Strength score. This ability replaces greater aspect.

Noble Eidolon (Sp): At 20th level, a shaitan binder's eidolon gains the ability to grant its summoner's wishes. Once per day, the eidolon can cast *limited wish* as a spell-like ability. The eidolon's caster level is equal to its level. The wish must be spoken aloud by the shaitan binder, beginning with the words "I wish," and cannot duplicate a wish the eidolon has granted within the past 24 hours. If the eidolon uses this ability to duplicate a spell with a costly material component, the shaitan binder must provide that component. This ability replaces twin eidolon.

Student of Stone (Monk)

By following the path of the stone, students of stone give up much of monks' mobility in favor of sheer resilience. A student of stone has the following class features.

Hard as Stone (Ex): At 2nd level, whenever an opponent rolls to confirm a critical hit against a student of stone, treat the student of stone's AC as +4 higher than normal. This ability replaces evasion.

Strength of Stone (Ex): At 3rd level, a student of stone learns to draw strength from the earth. So long as both he and his opponent are touching the ground, the student of stone gains a +1 bonus on attack rolls, damage rolls, bull rush and trip combat maneuver rolls, and to his CMD when resisting a bull rush or trip attempt. This ability replaces fast movement.

Bonus Feat: At 6th level, a student of stone adds Elemental Fist (*Advanced Player's Guide*) to his list of available bonus feats. If the student of stone selects Elemental Fist as a bonus feat, he may only deal acid damage when using the feat. At 10th level, the student of stone adds Shaitan Style (*Ultimate Combat*) to his list of bonus feats, at 14th level, he adds Shaitan Skin (*Ultimate Combat*), and at 18th level, he adds Shaitan Earthblast (*Ultimate Combat*). This otherwise functions as and alters the bonus feat ability.

Bones of Stone (Su): At 7th level, as a swift action, a student of stone can spend 1 *ki* point to gain DR 2/magic until the beginning of his next turn. At 10th level, he can spend 1 *ki* point to gain DR 2/chaotic until his next turn. At 15th level, he can spend 1 *ki* point to gain DR 5/chaotic until his next turn. This ability replaces high jump.

Body of Stone (Ex): At 9th level, a student of stone gains the benefits of the *light fortification* armor property (*Core Rulebook* 463). This ability replaces improved evasion.

Soul of Stone (Su): At 12th level, as a swift action, a student of stone can spend 1 *ki* point to gain tremorsense 15 feet until his next turn. At 16th level, the range of this tremorsense increases to 30 feet. This ability replaces abundant step.

Stone Self: At 20th level, a student of stone becomes an earth outsider. He gains the earth subtype, as well as DR 5/chaotic, burrow speed 20 feet, and tremorsense 20 feet.

NEW RACIAL RULES

The following options are available to oreads. At the GM's discretion, other appropriate races may make use of some of these new rules.

Oread Equipment

Oreads have access to the following equipment.

Camouflage Lichen: Though oreads with obviously stony features are rare, almost all oreads have an essentially earthen quality to their skin that makes it perfect for cultivating plant life. Where other races would be appalled at the thought of plants taking root in their flesh, oreads see it as a natural and healthy extension of their elemental nature. For this reason, oread herbalists developed several strains of moss and lichen specifically adapted to grow on their bodies. Camouflage lichen is the most common variety of these oread plants. It takes 1 minute to apply a paste of camouflage lichen spores to the skin, and an additional 24 hours for the fungus to sprout. After this time, the oread is covered in a thin green layer of living plant matter, granting her a +4 bonus on Stealth checks made in green forest and jungle environments. Red-orange and white varieties exist, providing bonuses in appropriately colored environments (red-orange among autumn leaves or in red deserts, white in snow, and so on). Camouflage lichen has a short lifespan; it withers and dies 3 days after being applied, crumbling away into harmless powder. This item only works on oreads and other creatures with rocklike bodies.

Fleshgem: An oread adventurer discovered these small green gemstones when, after suffering a wound from falling on some jagged stones while exploring a cavern, she noticed pieces of beautiful green crystal growing from her skin. Oread jewelers found that these crystals, dubbed fleshgems, seemed to feed on the elemental energy that permeates an oread's flesh, growing from tiny chips of stone into large, elaborate gemstones. Essentially harmless, implanting fleshgems became a unique racial method of body alteration among oreads, equivalent to tattoos and piercings among other humanoids. Decorative fleshgems cost 1 gp and are merely ornamental. Fleshgem spikes, on the other hand, grow into elaborate crystalline shards that function as armor spikes, but the oread wearing them cannot wear armor over the spikes and even normal clothing requires special holes or seams to allow the spikes to stick out. Implanting a set of fleshgem spikes takes 10 minutes, and the resulting shard takes about a week to grow to full size. Removing a fleshgem takes 1 minute; the person removing the gem must make a successful DC 15 Heal check to avoid dealing 1d4 points of damage to the oread. The fleshgem spikes can be sundered or destroyed as if the growths were a worn object (hardness 1, 5 hp), but unless the embedded root of the fleshgem is removed, the shards grow back 1 week later.

Stonechipper Salve: This gritty, gray ointment weakens rocky materials. When applied to an object made of stone, it reduces the object's hardness by 3 for 10 minutes. As a standard action, a creature can apply the paste to affect one 5-foot-square or a Medium or smaller creature. The paste only affects hardness, not damage reduction or similar defenses.

Oread Equipment

Item	Cost	Weight	Craft DC
Camouflage lichen	100 gp	—	—
Fleshgem (decorative)	1 gp	—	—
Fleshgem (spikes)	50 gp	5 lbs.	—
Stonechipper salve	150 gp	1 lb.	20

Oread Feats

Oreads have access to the Elemental Jaunt feat (see page 129) and the following feats.

Dwarf Blooded
You have dwarven blood coursing through your veins.
Prerequisite: Oread.
Benefit: Your dwarven heritage manifests in two ways. First, your speed is never modified by armor or encumbrance, as the dwarf slow and steady racial trait. Second, you gain the stonecunning dwarf racial trait.

Echoes of Stone
Your senses are keener among the rocks and stones.
Prerequisite: Oread.
Benefit: You gain a +4 racial bonus on Perception checks underground, and on Survival checks to avoid becoming lost in caverns and rocky areas.

Murmurs of Earth
The earth opens up her secrets to your perceptions.
Prerequisites: Echoes of Stone, character level 9th, oread.
Benefit: You gain a limited form of tremorsense. As a move action, you become aware of all creatures within 15 feet that are in contact with the ground at that moment.

Oread Burrower
The ground parts for you at the slightest touch, allowing you to dig with great speed.
Prerequisites: Stony Step, character level 9th, oread.
Benefit: You gain a burrow speed equal to 1/2 your base speed. You can burrow through sand, dirt, clay, gravel, or similar materials, but not solid stone. You do not leave a hole behind, nor is your passage marked on the surface.

Oread Earth Glider
The earth welcomes you, showing you the secret paths through sand and soil.
Prerequisites: Oread Burrower, Stony Step, character level 13th, oread.
Benefit: You gain the earth glide universal monster ability and can use it to travel at your full base speed through sand, dirt, clay, gravel, or similar materials. If protected against fire damage, you can even burrow through lava. You can burrow through solid stone at 1/2 your base speed.

Stony Step
The earth recognizes its kinship with you and does not impede your movement.
Prerequisite: Oread.
Benefit: Whenever you move, you may move through 5 feet of earth- or stone-based difficult terrain (rubble, stone stairs, and so on) each round as if it were normal terrain.

The effects of this feat stack with similar feats such as Acrobatic Steps and Nimble Moves. This feat allows you to take a 5-foot step into this kind of difficult terrain.

Oread Magic Items

Oreads have access to the following shield special abilities.

Guarding (shield special ability): A *guarding* shield allows the wearer to transfer some or all of the shield's enhancement bonus to an adjacent creature's AC (this bonus stacks with all others). As a free action at the start of her turn before using any of the shield's other abilities, the wearer may choose an adjacent target and how much of the shield's enhancement bonus to allocate at the

start of her turn. The target's AC bonus lasts until the wearer's next turn or until the wearer and the target are ever more than 5 feet apart, at which point the target's bonus ends and the shield's enhancement bonus works normally for the wearer. This ability only affects a shield's enhancement bonus to Armor Class, not its enhancement bonus on attack rolls (if any) or any other shield abilities.

Moderate abjuration; CL 8th; Craft Magic Arms and Armor, *shield other*; Price +1 bonus.

Guarding, Greater (shield special ability): As the *guarding* property, except as a free action, the wearer selects any number of adjacent allies to receive the shield's bonus. All selected allies receive the same bonus. If a shielded target is ever more than 5 feet from the wearer, the effect ends for that target but not for any other targets.

Strong abjuration; CL 12th; Craft Magic Arms and Armor, *shield other*; Price +2 bonus.

BELT OF STONESKIN

Aura moderate abjuration; **CL** 10th
Slot belt; **Price** 60,000 gp; **Weight** 10 lbs.

DESCRIPTION

This belt is made of specially treated stone plates held together by thick iron chain. Every 24 hours, the belt's wearer gains DR 10/adamantine until the belt absorbs 100 points of damage, at which point the belt becomes useless for the remainder of the 24-hour period. When first worn, or after each time this belt is taken off, it must worn for 24 consecutive hours in order for its magic to take effect again.

CONSTRUCTION

Requirements Craft Wondrous Item, *stoneskin*, creator must be an oread or a creature with the earth subtype; **Cost** 30,000 gp

EARTHBIND ROD

Aura moderate transmutation; **CL** 6th
Slot none; **Price** 26,500 gp; **Weight** 5 lbs.

DESCRIPTION

This rod looks like nothing more than a large, strange sliver of rough granite. This rod's magic interacts with stone or earth to both steady its wielder and anchor creatures the rod touches. An *earthbind rod* functions like a +1 *light mace*, and it grants its wielder a +4 circumstance bonus to its CMD against bull rush, grapple, overrun, reposition, and trip combat maneuvers, but only if the wielder is an oread, has the earth subtype, or is standing on earth or stone. Three times per day, when the wielder hits a creature with this rod, as long as the target of this attack is standing on stone or earth, the wielder can attempt to entangle that creature (Fortitude DC 18 negates) for 1d4 rounds.

CONSTRUCTION

Requirements Craft Rod, *stone shape*; **Cost** 13,250 gp

MASK OF STONY DEMEANOR

Aura moderate transmutation; **CL** 6th
Slot head; **Price** 500 gp; **Weight** 4 lbs.

DESCRIPTION

When worn, this mask transforms the wearer's face into a stone statue and its voice into an emotionless monotone. Though it allows the wearer to speak, its facial expressions and voice betray little emotion, granting a +10 competence bonus on Bluff checks made to lie and a +5 competence bonus on Bluff checks made to feint, but also imposes a −5 penalty on Bluff checks made to pass a hidden message.

CONSTRUCTION

Requirements Craft Wondrous Item, *innocence* (*Advanced Player's Guide*), *stone shape*; **Cost** 250 gp

Oread Spells

Oreads have access to the following spells.

BINDING EARTH

School transmutation [earth]; **Level** druid 2, witch 2
Casting Time 1 standard action
Components V, S, DF
Range close (25 ft. + 5 ft./2 levels)
Target one creature or unattended object (see text)
Duration 1 round/level
Saving Throw Fortitude negates; **Spell Resistance** yes

If the target of this spell fails its Fortitude save, areas of earth and stone floor act as a snapping quagmire that pulls the target down and damages it if it attempts to move through such terrain.

If the target is a creature, it treats all areas of earth and stone it moves through as difficult terrain. Furthermore, for each 5 feet a creature moves through such areas, it takes 1d6 points of damage. Creatures with a burrow speed or the earth glide ability are unaffected by *binding earth*.

If cast on an unattended object resting on an area of stone or earth, the stone or earth warps and wraps around it, pulling it firmly to the ground. A DC 15 Strength check is required to pull the object free from snapping earth or stone.

BINDING EARTH, MASS

School transmutation [earth]; **Level** druid 6, witch 6
Target one creature or object/level, no two of which can be more than 30 ft. apart

This spell functions as *binding earth*, except as noted above.

MIGHTY FIST OF THE EARTH

School conjuration (creation) [earth]; **Level** cleric 1, druid 1
Casting Time 1 standard action
Components V, S, DF
Range close (25 ft. + 5 ft./2 levels)
Target one creature
Duration instantaneous

Saving Throw none; **Spell Resistance** yes

You create a fist-sized rock that flies toward one enemy. Make an unarmed strike attack roll against the target as if it were in your threatened area. If the attack is successful, the rock deals bludgeoning damage to the target as if you had hit the target with your unarmed strike. If you have a *ki* pool, as long as you have at least 1 point in your *ki* pool, the rock counts as a *ki* strike.

At 4th level, a qinggong monk (*Ultimate Magic* 51) may select this spell as a *ki* power costing 1 *ki* point to activate (if the monk has 0 *ki* points after activating this *ki* power, the rock does not count as a *ki* strike).

RAGING RUBBLE

School transmutation [earth]; **Level** bard 3, cleric 3, druid 3, sorcerer/wizard 3, witch 3
Casting Time 1 round
Components V, S, DF
Range close (25 ft. + 5 ft./2 levels)
Effect one swarm of stones
Duration concentration + 2 rounds
Saving Throw none; **Spell Resistance** yes

You animate an area of rubble, gravel, or other small stones, creating a dangerous, rolling area of debris. The animated rubble has a space of 10 feet and acts like a swarm, damaging (1d6 hit points) and distracting (DC 12) anything within it. As a move action, you can direct the rubble to move up to 10 feet. If the rubble is attacked, treat it as a Medium animated object with the young creature simple template and the swarm subtype.

STONE SHIELD

School conjuration (creation) [earth]; **Level** cleric 1, druid 1, magus 2, sorcerer/wizard 1, summoner 1
Casting Time 1 immediate action
Components V, S, DF
Range 0 ft.
Effect stone wall whose area is one 5-ft. square
Duration 1 round
Saving Throw none; **Spell Resistance** no

A 1-inch-thick slab of stone springs up from the ground, interposing itself between you and an opponent of your choice. The *stone shield* provides you with cover from that enemy (*Core Rulebook* 195) until the beginning of your next turn, granting you a +4 bonus to Armor Class and a +2 bonus on Reflex saving throws. If the opponent's attack misses you by 4 or less, the attack strikes the shield instead. The *stone shield* has hardness 8 and 15 hit points. If the shield is destroyed, the spell ends and the shield crumbles away into nothingness. Spells and effects that damage an area deal damage to the shield.

You cannot use this spell if you are not adjacent to a large area of earth or stone such as the ground or a wall. A qinggong monk (*Ultimate Magic*) may select this spell as a *ki* power at 4th level.

RATFOLK

Ratfolk are small, rodentlike humanoids; originally native to subterranean areas in dry deserts and plains, they are now more often found in nomadic trading caravans. Much like the pack rats they resemble, ratfolk are tinkerers and hoarders by nature, and as a whole are masters of commerce, especially when it comes to acquiring and repairing mechanical or magical devices. Though some are shrewd merchants who carefully navigate the shifting alliances of black markets and bazaars, many ratfolk love their stockpiles of interesting items far more than money, and would rather trade for more such prizes to add to their hoards over mere coins. It's common to see a successful crew of ratfolk traders rolling out of town with an even larger bundle than they entered with, the whole mess piled precariously high on a cart drawn by giant rats.

Physical Description: Typical ratfolk are average 4 feet tall and weigh 80 pounds. They often wear robes to stay cool in the desert or conceal their forms in cities, as they know other humanoids find their rodent features distasteful. Ratfolk have a strong attraction to shiny jewelry, especially copper, bronze, and gold, and many decorate their ears and tails with small rings made of such metals. They are known to train giant rats (dire rats with the giant creature simple template), which they often use as pack animals and mounts.

Society: Ratfolk are extremely communal, and live in large warrens with plenty of hidden crannies in which to stash their hoards or flee in times of danger, gravitating toward subterranean tunnels or tightly packed tenements in city slums. They feel an intense bond with their large families and kin networks, as well as with ordinary rodents of all sorts, living in chaotic harmony and fighting fiercely to defend each other when threatened. They are quick to use their stockpiles of gear in combat, but prefer to work out differences and settle disputes with mutually beneficial trades.

When a specific ratfolk warren grows overcrowded and the surrounding environment won't support a larger community, young ratfolk instinctively seek out new places in which to dwell. If a large enough group of ratfolk immigrants all settle down in a new, fertile area, they may create a new warren, often with strong political ties to their original homeland. Otherwise, individual ratfolk are inclined to simply leave home and take up residence elsewhere, or wander on caravan trips that last most of the year, reducing the pressure of overcrowding at home.

Relations: Ratfolk tend to get along quite well with humans, and often develop ratfolk societies dwelling in the sewers, alleys, and shadows of human cities. Ratfolk find dwarves too hidebound and territorial, and often mistake even mild criticisms from dwarves as personal attacks. Ratfolk have no particular feelings about gnomes and halflings, although in areas where those races and ratfolk must compete for resources, clan warfare can become dogma for generations. Ratfolk enjoy the company of elves and half-elves, often seeing them as the calmest and most sane of the civilized humanoid races. Ratfolk are particularly fond of elven music and art, and many ratfolk warrens are decorated with elven art pieces acquired through generations of friendly trade.

Alignment and Religion: Ratfolk individuals are driven by a desire to acquire interesting items and a compulsion to tinker with complex objects. The strong ties of ratfolk communities give them an appreciation for the benefits of an orderly society, even if they are willing to bend those rules when excited about accomplishing their individual goals. Most ratfolk are neutral, and those who take to religion tend to worship deities that represent commerce and family, including Abadar and Erastil.

Adventurers: Ratfolk are often driven by a desire to seek out new opportunities for trade, both for themselves and for their warrens. Ratfolk adventurers may seek potential markets for their clan's goods, keep an eye out for sources of new commodities, or just wander about in hopes of unearthing enough treasure to fund less dangerous business ventures. Ratfolk battles are often decided by cunning traps, ambushes, or sabotage of enemy positions, and accordingly young ratfolk heroes often take up classes such as alchemist, gunslinger, and rogue.

Male Names: Agiz, Brihz, Djir, Ninnec, Rerdahl, Rikkan, Skivven, Tamoq.

Female Names: Bessel, Fhar, Jix, Kitch, Kubi, Nehm, Rissi, Thikka.

ALTERNATE RACIAL TRAITS

The following racial traits may be selected instead of existing ratfolk racial traits. Consult your GM before selecting any of these new options.

Cornered Fury: Ratfolk can fight viciously when cut off from friends and allies. Whenever a ratfolk with this racial trait is reduced to half or fewer of his hit points, and has no conscious ally within 30 feet, he gains a +2 racial bonus on melee attack rolls and to Armor Class. This racial trait replaces swarming.

Scent: Some ratfolk have much more strongly developed senses of smell, instead of keen eyes and ears. These ratfolk have the scent ability, but take a –2 penalty on all Perception checks based primarily on sight or hearing. This racial trait replaces tinker.

Skulk: Some ratfolk can blend easily into their environments, and move with surprising grace. Ratfolk gain a +2 racial bonus on Stealth checks, and take only a

–5 penalty on Stealth checks made to hide from creatures they have distracted with a Bluff check (rather than the normal –10 penalty). This racial trait replaces tinker.

Unnatural: Some ratfolk unnerve normal animals, and train to defend themselves against the inevitable attacks from such creatures. These ratfolk take a –4 penalty on all Charisma-based skill checks to affect creatures of the animal type, and receive a +2 dodge bonus to AC against animals. An animal's starting attitude toward ratfolk is one step worse than normal. This racial trait replaces rodent empathy.

FAVORED CLASS OPTIONS

The following options are available to all ratfolk who have the listed favored class, and unless otherwise stated, the bonus applies each time you select the class reward.

Alchemist: The alchemist gains +1/6 of a new discovery.

Barbarian: When raging, add +1/4 to the barbarian's swarming trait's flanking bonus on attack rolls.

Druid: Add a +1 bonus on wild empathy checks made to influence animals and magical beasts that live underground.

Fighter: Add +1 to the fighter's CMD when resisting a bull rush or grapple attempt.

Gunslinger: Add a +1/2 bonus on initiative checks when the gunslinger has at least 1 grit point.

Monk: Add +1 feet to the speed the monk can move while making a Stealth check without taking a penalty. This has no effect unless the monk has selected this reward five times (or another increment of five). This does not allow the monk to use Stealth while running or charging.

Ranger: Add +1 to an animal companion's CMD when adjacent to the ranger. If the ranger ever replaces his animal companion, the new animal companion gains this bonus.

Rogue: Add a +1/2 bonus on Escape Artist checks.

Summoner: Add a +1 bonus on saving throws against poison made by the summoner's eidolon.

Witch: Add +5 feet to the range of one hex with a range other than "touch."

RACIAL ARCHETYPES

The following racial archetypes are available to ratfolk.

RATFOLK RACIAL TRAITS

+2 Dexterity, +2 Intelligence, –2 Strength: Ratfolk are agile and clever, yet physically weak.

Ratfolk: Ratfolk are humanoids with the ratfolk subtype.

Small: Ratfolk are Small and gain a +1 size bonus to their AC, a +1 size bonus on attack rolls, a –1 penalty on combat maneuver checks and to their CMD, and a +4 size bonus on Stealth checks.

Slow Speed: Ratfolk have a base speed of 20 feet.

Darkvision: Ratfolk can see in the dark up to 60 feet.

Rodent Empathy: Ratfolk gain a +4 racial bonus on Handle Animal checks made to influence rodents.

Swarming: Ratfolk are used to living and fighting communally, and are adept at swarming foes for their own gain and their foes' detriment. Up to two ratfolk can share the same square at the same time. If two ratfolk in the same square attack the same foe, they are considered to be flanking that foe as if they were in two opposite squares.

Tinker: Ratfolk gain a +2 racial bonus on Craft (alchemy), Perception, and Use Magic Device checks.

Languages: Ratfolk begin play speaking Common. Ratfolk with high Intelligence scores can choose from the following: Aklo, Draconic, Dwarven, Gnoll, Gnome, Goblin, Halfling, Orc, and Undercommon.

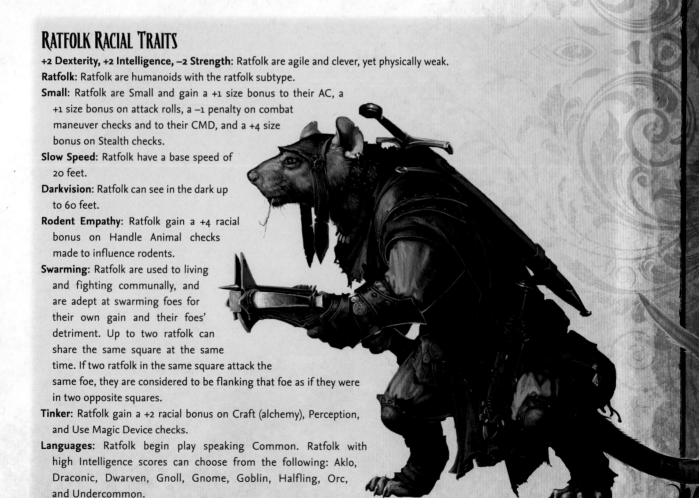

Gulch Gunner (Gunslinger)

Ratfolk warfare often occurs in cramped, claustrophobic spaces such as the ratfolk's own underground warrens and heavily trapped gulch fortresses, or the subterranean tunnels of goblins and similar foes. Since these battlegrounds often have tight corners and few areas with long lines of sight, those ratfolk who seek to master the use of firearms almost inevitably become experts in close-quarters combat. These gulch gunners often specialize in proficiency with a single pistol (easily handled in tight spaces) and wander from warren to warren selling their tunnel-shooting skills to the highest bidder. A gulch gunner has the following class features.

Class Skills: A gulch gunner adds Disable Device, Escape Artist, and Knowledge (dungeoneering) to her list of class skills and removes Knowledge (local), Ride, and Swim from her list of class skills.

Grit (Ex): At 1st level, a gulch gunner gains grit as a standard gunslinger. However, the close-combat focus

of the gulch gunner results in a slightly different set of circumstances for regaining grit.

Daring Adjacent Shot: The first time each round the gulch gunner makes a ranged firearm attack against an adjacent foe and provokes an attack of opportunity, she regains 1 grit point. Making an adjacent firearm attack against a helpless or unaware creature or on a creature that has fewer Hit Dice than half the gulch gunner's character level does not restore grit, nor do ranged attacks using some ability that prevents the gulch gunner from provoking an attack of opportunity. This ability replaces the ability to regain grit from a critical hit with a firearm.

Deeds: A gulch gunner has some unique deeds, which replace some of the standard gunslinger deeds as listed in each entry. These deeds follow all the general rules and restrictions of gunslinger deeds.

Flash and Shock (Ex): At 1st level, the gulch gunner can take advantage of the flash and sound of a firearm to throw off an attacker's aim at close range. When she makes an attack against a foe within her firearm's first range increment, she may spend 1 grit point to gain a +4 circumstance bonus to AC against that opponent until the beginning of her next turn. She can only perform this deed while wearing medium, light, or no armor, and while carrying no more than a light load. This deed replaces the deadeye deed.

Powder Burns (Ex): At 3rd level, the gulch gunner learns to maximize the damage dealt by a firearm at extremely close range. When the gulch gunner successfully hits an adjacent foe with a ranged firearm attack, she may spend 1 grit point to deal an additional 1d6 points of fire damage from the muzzle flash of her weapon. The target must also make a Reflex save (DC 10 + 1/2 the gulch gunner's level + the gulch gunner's Wisdom modifier) or catch on fire. This deed replaces the pistol whip deed.

Staggering Shot (Ex): At 15th level, when the gulch gunner hits an adjacent target with a ranged firearm attack, the target must also make a Fortitude save (DC 10 + 1/2 the gulch gunner's level + the gulch gunner's Wisdom modifier) or be staggered for 1d4 rounds. This deed replaces the menacing shot deed.

Belly Shot (Ex): At 9th level, a gulch gunner can press

her firearm directly against a vulnerable location of an adjacent target, dealing additional damage. When the gulch gunner successfully hits an adjacent target with a ranged firearm attack, she deals +1d6 points of damage. This damage increases to +2d6 at 13th level and to +3d6 at 17th level. Creatures immune to precision damage, critical hits, or sneak attacks do not take this additional damage. This ability replaces the gun training ability gained at 9th, 13th, and 17th level.

Plague Bringer (Alchemist)

The plague bringer sees disease as the ultimate weapon, and has worked tirelessly to master new diseases and disease-delivery systems. A plague bringer feels no more remorse at unleashing his armaments on his enemies than an archer does when firing an arrow in the heat of battle. Disease is a tool, and the plague bringer is its master. A plague bringer has the following class features.

Plague Vial (Su): At 1st level, a plague bringer can create a plague vial, an alchemically grown and concentrated disease sample. It takes 1 hour to prepare a plague vial, and once prepared, the vial remains potent until used. A plague bringer can only maintain 1 plague vial at a time—if he prepares a second vial, any existing plague vial becomes inert. A plague vial that is not in a plague bringer's possession becomes inert until a plague bringer picks it up again.

It's a standard action to drink a plague vial. Upon being imbibed, the plague vial infects the plague bringer's blood, sweat, tears, and other bodily fluids for 10 minutes per class level. Any creature that harms him with melee attacks (except with reach weapons) must make a Fortitude save (DC 10 + 1/2 the plague bringer's level + the plague bringer's Intelligence modifier) or become sickened for 1 round per plague bringer level. The plague bringer is immune to the effect of his own plague vial, but not that of another's plague vial. The effects of multiple plague vials do not stack.

As a standard action, the plague bringer can infect a weapon with this sickness (typically by licking it or wiping his blood or pus on it). The disease on the weapon works like a poisoned weapon, except the source is a disease instead of a poison (so a dwarf's resistance to poison does not apply).

Anyone other than a plague bringer (including another alchemist) who drinks a plague vial must make a saving throw against the vial's DC or become nauseated for 1 hour. Unless he learns how to brew a mutagen by taking the mutagen discovery (see *Ultimate Magic*), he can never benefit from a mutagen and reacts to it as if he were a non-alchemist. At any particular time, a plague bringer can only be under the effect of either a plague vial or a

RATFOLK DISCOVERIES

The following new discoveries can be taken by any alchemist who meets the prerequisites, but are more common among ratfolk.

Greater Plague Bomb: The effects of the smoke created by an alchemist's bomb duplicates the effects of *greater contagion* (see *Ultimate Magic*) instead of *fog cloud*, filling an area equal to twice the bomb's splash radius for 1 round per level. An alchemist must be at least 16th level and must possess the plague bomb (see *Ultimate Magic*) and smoke bomb discoveries before selecting this discovery.

Lingering Plague: Any creature that must make a save against a disease caused by the alchemist's extract or other class ability must make a second save 1 round later to avoid doubling the duration of the disease effect. If the disease doesn't have a duration, this discovery reduces its onset time and frequencies by half. An alchemist must be at least 8th level before selecting this discovery.

mutagen (not both); drinking another immediately ends the effects of any ongoing plague vial or mutagen.

All limitations to mutagens apply to plague vials as if they were the same substance. The infuse mutagen discovery and persistent mutagen class ability apply to plague vials. The sticky poison discovery applies to a weapon infected with a plague vial. The plague vial is a disease effect. This ability replaces mutagen.

Disease Resistance (Ex): At 2nd level, a plague bringer gains a +2 bonus on all saving throws against disease. This bonus increases to +4 at 5th level, and to +6 at 8th level. At 10th level, a plague bringer becomes completely immune to disease (including magical diseases). This ability replaces all increments of poison resistance and poison immunity.

Discoveries: The following discoveries complement the plague bringer archetype: explosive bomb, precise bombs, smoke bomb (*Advanced Player's Guide*); breath weapon bomb, fast bomb, nauseating bomb (*Ultimate Combat*); plague bomb (*Ultimate Magic*).

NEW RACIAL RULES

The following options are available to ratfolk. At the GM's discretion, other appropriate races may make use of some of these new rules.

Ratfolk Equipment

Ratfolk have access to the following equipment.

Blight Tonic: Blight tonic increases the potency of a creature's disease attack transmitted by physical contact, such as a dire rat's filth fever. The next time a creature

must save against the drinker's disease save DC, the DC for the initial infection increases by +2. The tonic lasts for 10 minutes or until the next time a creature must save against the drinker's disease DC, whichever comes first.

Pox Burster: A pox burster is an alchemically preserved animal bladder or gourd that has been filled with toxic, rotting materials. You can throw a pox burster as a splash weapon. Treat this attack as a ranged touch attack with a range increment of 10 feet. A direct hit forces a target to immediately make a DC 13 Fortitude save or contract filth fever. Every space adjacent to the target square of the pox burster is covered in disease-causing filth. For the next minute, any creature that is injured while in one of these spaces must also make a DC 9 Fortitude save or contract filth fever.

Stink Ink: Stink ink is a special, pungent, musk-based ink that allows its user to encode information with smell rather than visually. Stink ink dries clear but its sharp, extremely localized smell can be picked out by those with sensitive enough noses to make it possible to read by sense of smell. Only creatures with the keen senses trait or scent ability can read stink ink without aid of some form of magic. Reading or writing something with stink ink takes twice as long as going through the same amount of information written in normal ink.

Stink Ink, Arcane: Most common among ratfolk alchemists, arcane stink ink is used to inscribe formulae or spells into formula books and spellbooks. Like normal stink ink, the arcane version can only be read by creatures with the scent ability (although *read magic* works normally on spells and arcane formulae inscribed with stink ink). Using arcane stink ink to inscribe a spell or formula into a book costs +10% of the normal amount (*Core Rulebook* 219).

Tailblade: A tailblade is a small, sharp knife designed to be strapped to the tip of a wielder's tail. It takes a full-round action to strap on or remove a tailblade. The wearer can loosely attach the tailblade (without strapping it securely in place) as a move action, but using a loosely attached tailblade gives the wielder a –4 penalty on all attack rolls made with the weapon, and other creatures get a +4 bonus on disarm combat maneuver checks to disarm the tailblade. A ratfolk wielding a tailblade can make a tail attack, adding its Strength modifier to the tailblade's damage. Ratfolk are considered proficient with such attacks and can apply feats or effects appropriate to natural attacks to tail attacks made with a tailblade. If used as part of a full attack action, attacks with a tailblade are considered secondary attacks.

Ratfolk Equipment

Item	Cost	Weight	Craft DC
Blight tonic	150 gp	1 lb.	20
Pox burster	50 gp	1 lb.	20
Stink ink	5 gp	1 lb.	15
Stink ink, arcane	special	1 lb.	—

Ratfolk Feats

Ratfolk have access to the following feats.

Burrowing Teeth

You have teeth and claws that suit you well to digging.

Prerequisites: Sharpclaw, Tunnel Rat, ratfolk.

Benefit: You gain a burrow speed equal to 1/2 your base speed. You can burrow through sand, dirt, clay, gravel, or similar materials, but not solid stone. You do not leave a hole behind, nor is your passage marked on the surface.

Sharpclaw (Combat)

Your nails are large and strong.

Prerequisite: Ratfolk.

Benefit: You gain two claw attacks. These are primary natural attacks that deal 1d4 points of damage.

Tunnel Rat

You are a master of fighting in confined spaces.

Prerequisites: Ratfolk, swarming racial trait.

Benefit: You count as one size smaller than normal for the purpose of squeezing.

Ratfolk Magic Items

Ratfolk have access to the following magic items.

CAP OF HUMAN GUISE

Aura faint illusion; **CL** 3rd
Slot head; **Price** 800 gp; **Weight** —

DESCRIPTION

This threadbare hat allows its wearer to alter her appearance as with a *disguise self* spell, except she can only appear as a plainly dressed Small human child, adult halfling, or adult gnome, such as a peasant, blacksmith, or shopkeeper. The wearer can slightly alter the cap's appearance as part of the disguise, but otherwise must match the overall unremarkable look of the illusory form.

CONSTRUCTION

Requirements Craft Wondrous Item, *disguise self*; **Cost** 400 gp

TABLE 2-3: RATFOLK WEAPONS

Martial Weapons	Cost	Dmg (S)	Dmg (M)	Critical	Range	Weight	Type	Special
Light Melee Weapons								
Tailblade	11 gp	1d2	1d3	20/×2	—	1/2 lb.	S	—

CLOAK OF THE SCUTTLING RAT

Aura faint transmutation; **CL** 5th
Slot shoulders; **Price** 6,000 gp; **Weight** 1 lb.

DESCRIPTION

This unassuming cloak initially appears to be made of plain leather. When the wearer speaks the command word, however, the *cloak of the scuttling rat* wraps itself around the individual, transforming her into a dire rat as if using *beast shape I*. The wearer can remain in dire rat form for up to 5 minutes per day. This duration need not be consecutive, but it must be used in 1-minute increments.

CONSTRUCTION

Requirements Craft Wondrous Item, *beast shape I*; **Cost** 3,000 gp

PIPES OF THE WARREN GUARDIAN

Aura faint conjuration; **CL** 5th
Slot none; **Price** 6,000 gp; **Weight** —

DESCRIPTION

These finely crafted yellow-ivory pipes are bound in bronze and decorated with bits of amber. If the possessor learns the proper tune, once per day he can use these pipes to summon 1d4+1 dire rats as if using *summon monster III*. The summoned dire rats also have the swarming racial trait, and count as ratfolk for the purposes of the ratfolk's swarming racial trait.

CONSTRUCTION

Requirements Craft Wondrous Item, *summon monster III*; **Cost** 3,000 gp

RING OF RAT FANGS

Aura faint transmutation; **CL** 3rd
Slot ring; **Price** 5,000 gp; **Weight** —

DESCRIPTION

This bone ring is the shape of an elongated rat biting its own tail. The wearer gains a bite attack as a primary natural attack. This attack deals 1d4 points of piercing damage for a Medium wearer or 1d3 points of damage for a Small wearer. After about a week of wearing the ring, the wearer's appearance becomes more ratlike, though she still looks like a member of her original race (for example, a human might gain prominent teeth).

CONSTRUCTION

Requirements Forge Ring, *magic fang*, *polymorph*; **Cost** 2,500 gp

RING OF SWARMING STABS

Aura faint transmutation; **CL** 5th
Slot ring; **Price** 6,000 gp; **Weight** —

DESCRIPTION

This ring is crafted of hardened leather strips, into which bits of fur, feathers, bone, and ivory have been woven. Twice per day, when the wearer is flanking an opponent, he can as a swift action deal an additional 1d6 points of damage on a successful melee attack against that opponent. This is a sneak attack for any effects that reduce or negate such damage.

CONSTRUCTION

Requirements Forge Ring, *guidance*, creator must be able to sneak attack; **Cost** 3,000 gp

Ratfolk Spells

Ratfolk have access to the following spells.

ALCHEMICAL TINKERING

School transmutation; **Level** cleric 2, sorcerer/wizard 1, witch 1
Casting Time 1 standard action
Components V, S
Range touch
Target firearm or alchemical item touched
Duration 1 minute/level
Saving Throw Fortitude negates (object); **Spell Resistance** yes

You transform one alchemical item or firearm into another alchemical item or firearm of the same or lesser cost. Magic items are unaffected by this spell. At the end of the spell's duration, alchemical items used while transformed are destroyed and do not return to a usable state and firearms transformed revert back to their original type.

DELAY DISEASE

School conjuration (healing); **Level** alchemist 2, cleric 2, druid 2, inquisitor 2, paladin 2, ranger 2, witch 1
Casting Time 1 standard action
Components V, S, DF
Range touch
Target creature touched
Duration 1 day
Saving Throw Fortitude negates (harmless); **Spell Resistance** yes (harmless)

The target becomes temporarily immune to disease. Any disease to which it is exposed during the spell's duration does not affect the target until the spell's duration has expired. If the target is currently infected with a disease, you must make a caster level check against the disease's DC to suspend it for the duration of the spell; otherwise, that disease affects the target normally. *Delay disease* does not cure any damage a disease may have already done.

SICKENING STRIKES

School transmutation [disease]; **Level** alchemist 2, antipaladin 2, druid 2, magus 3, ranger 4, witch 2
Casting Time 1 standard action
Components V, S
Range personal
Target you
Duration 1 round/level
Saving Throw Fortitude negates; see text; **Spell Resistance** yes

You are imbued with disease, and any creature you strike with a melee attack must make a Fortitude save or be sickened for 1 minute. Creatures that are immune to disease are immune to this sickened effect.

SYLPHS

Born from the descendants of humans and beings of elemental air such as djinn, sylphs are a shy and reclusive race consumed by intense curiosity. Sylphs spend their lives blending into the crowd, remaining unnoticed as they spy and eavesdrop on the people around them. They call this hobby "listening to the wind," and for many sylphs it becomes an obsession. Sylphs rely on their capable, calculating intellects and on knowledge gleaned from eavesdropping to deliver them from danger.

Physical Description: Sylphs tend to be pale and thin to the point of appearing delicate, but their skinny bodies are often more resilient than they look. Many sylphs can easily pass for humans with some effort, though the complex blue markings that swirl across their skin reveal their elemental ancestry. Sylphs also bear more subtle signs of their heritage, such as a slight breeze following them wherever they go. These signs become more pronounced as a sylph experiences intense passion or anger, spontaneous gusts of wind tousling the sylph's hair or hot blusters knocking small items off of shelves.

Society: Sylphs are usually born to human parents, and so are raised according to human customs. Most sylphs dislike the attention they receive growing up in human society, so it's common for them to leave home soon after coming of age. They rarely abandon civilization altogether, however, preferring instead to find some new city or settlement where they can go unnoticed among (and spy upon) the masses. A sylph who happens upon another sylph unnoticed instantly becomes obsessed with her kin, spying on and learning as much about the other as she possibly can. Only after weighing all the pros and cons and formulating plans for every potential outcome will the sylph introduce herself to the other. Rarely, two sylphs will discover each other's presence in a community at the same time. What ensues thereafter is a sort of cat-and-mouse game, a convoluted dance in which each sylph spies on the other as both attempt to gain the upper hand. Sylphs who meet this way always become either inseparable friends or intractable enemies.

Relations: Sylphs enjoy prying into the affairs of most other races, but have little taste for actually associating with most of them. Sylphs can relate on some level with elves, who share their tendency toward aloofness, but often spoil any possible relationship by violating the elven sense of privacy. Dwarves distrust sylphs intensely, considering them flighty and unreliable. They form excellent partnerships with halflings, relying on the short folk's courage and people skills to cover their own shortcomings. Sylphs are amused by the annoyed reactions they provoke in ifrits, and find oreads too boring to give them much attention.

Alignment and Religion: Sylphs have little regard for laws and traditions, for such strictures often prohibit the very things sylphs love—subterfuge and secrecy. This doesn't mean sylphs are opposed to law, merely that they use the most expedient means available to accomplish their goals, legal or not. Most sylphs are thus neutrally aligned. Sylphs are naturally drawn to mystery cults, and to deities who focus on secrets, travel, or knowledge.

Adventurers: An inborn urge to get to the bottom of things drives many sylphs to the adventuring life. A sylph who runs across the trail of a mystery will never be satisfied until she has uncovered every thread of evidence, followed up on every lead, and found the very heart of the trouble. Such sylphs make plenty of enemies by poking around into other peoples' affairs, and usually turn to their roguish talents or wizardry to defend themselves.

Male Names: Akaash, Eydan, Hanuun, Siival, Vasaam.

Female Names: Inam, Keeya, Lissi, Nava, Radaya, Tena.

ALTERNATE RACIAL TRAITS

The following racial traits may be selected instead of existing sylph racial traits. Consult your GM before selecting any of these new options.

Air Insight: Sylph spellcasters sometimes find that their elemental heritage makes creatures of air more willing to serve them. *Summon monster* and *summon nature's ally* spells that the sylph casts last 2 rounds longer than normal when used to summon creatures with the air subtype. This racial trait replaces air affinity.

Breeze-Kissed: Breezes seem to follow most sylphs wherever they go, but some sylphs are better able to control these winds than others. A sylph with this racial trait surrounds herself with swirling winds, gaining a +2 racial bonus to AC against nonmagical ranged attacks. The sylph can calm or renew these winds as a swift action. Once per day, the sylph can channel this wind into a single gust, making a bull rush or trip combat maneuver attempt against one creature within 30 feet. Whether or not the attempt succeeds, the winds are exhausted and no longer provide a bonus to the sylph's AC for 24 hours. This is a supernatural ability. This racial trait replaces air affinity.

Like the Wind: A sylph with this racial trait gains a +5 foot bonus to her base speed. This racial trait replaces energy resistance.

Sky Speaker: Sylphs with this racial trait feel kinship toward the creatures of the air, and can use *speak with animals* once per day to speak to birds or other flying animals. Her caster level for these effects is equal to her level. This racial trait replaces the sylph's spell-like ability racial trait.

Storm in the Blood: A sylph with this racial trait gains fast healing 2 for 1 round anytime she takes electricity damage (whether or not this electricity damage gets through her electricity resistance). The sylph can heal up to 2 hit points per level per day with this ability, after which it ceases to function. This racial trait replaces air affinity.

Thunderous Resilience: Sylphs with this racial trait gain sonic resistance 5. This racial trait replaces energy resistance.

Weather Savvy: Some sylphs are so in tune with the air and sky that they can sense the slightest change in atmospheric conditions. Sylphs with this trait can spend a full-round action to predict the weather in an area for the next 24 hours. The sylph's prediction is always accurate, but cannot account for spells or supernatural effects that might alter the forecast. This racial trait replaces the sylph's spell-like ability racial trait.

Whispering Wind: Some sylphs are especially thin and wispy, as though they were made more of air than flesh. Sylphs with this racial trait gain a +4 racial bonus on Stealth checks. This racial trait replaces the sylph's spell-like ability racial trait.

FAVORED CLASS OPTIONS

The following options are available to all sylphs who have the listed favored class, and unless otherwise stated, the bonus applies each time you select the class reward.

Cleric: Add a +1/2 bonus on Knowledge (planes) checks relating to the Plane of Air and creatures with the air subtype.

Druid: Add a +1/2 bonus on Knowledge (nature) checks relating to weather and flying animals.

Inquisitor: Add a +1/2 bonus on Stealth checks while motionless and on opposed Perception checks.

Oracle: Add +1/2 to the oracle's level for the purpose of determining the effects of one revelation.

Rogue: Add a +1/2 bonus on Acrobatics checks to jump and a +1/2 bonus on Sense Motive checks.

Sorcerer: Choose a bloodline power from the djinni or elemental (air) bloodline that the sorcerer can use. The sorcerer treats her class level as though it were +1/2 higher (to a maximum of +4) when determining the effects of that power.

Witch: Add a +1/2 bonus on Stealth checks and Perception checks made by the witch's familiar. If the sylph ever replaces her familiar, the new familiar gains these bonus skill ranks.

Wizard: Select one arcane school power from the air or wood elemental schools that the wizard can currently use. The wizard treats her class level as though it were +1/2 higher (to a maximum of +4) when determining the effects of that power.

SYLPH RACIAL TRAITS

+2 Dexterity, +2 Intelligence, −2 Constitution: Sylphs are quick and insightful, but slight and delicate.

Native Outsider: Sylphs are outsiders with the native subtype.

Medium: Sylphs are Medium creatures and have no bonuses or penalties due to their size.

Normal Speed: Sylphs have a base speed of 30 feet.

Darkvision: Sylphs can see in the dark up to 60 feet.

Spell-Like Ability: *Feather fall* 1/day (caster level equals the sylph's total level).

Energy Resistance: Sylphs have electricity resistance 5.

Air Affinity: Sylph sorcerers with the elemental (air) bloodline treat their Charisma score as 2 points higher for all sorcerer spells and class abilities. Sylph spellcasters with the Air domain use their domain powers and spells at +1 caster level.

Languages: Sylphs begin play speaking Common and Auran. Sylphs with high Intelligence scores can choose from the following: Aquan, Dwarven, Elven, Gnome, Halfling, Ignan, and Terran.

RACIAL ARCHETYPES

The following racial archetypes are available to sylphs.

Sky Druid (Druid)

Some druids develop ties not to a particular landscape, but instead to the endless blue expanse of the skies. Such are the sky druids, who are more at home soaring through air than standing on the ground. A sky druid has the following class features.

Weapon and Armor Proficiency: A sky druid loses medium armor proficiency.

Nature Bond (Ex): At 1st level, a sky druid who chooses an animal companion must select one with a fly speed. If choosing a domain, the sky druid must choose from the Air, Animals, Liberation, and Weather domains, or subdomains appropriate to those domains.

Sky's Embrace (Su): At 2nd level, a sky druid no longer takes falling damage, as though she were constantly under the effect of *feather fall*. Additionally, she may take ranks in the Fly skill regardless of whether she has a natural fly speed, and may use her Fly skill in place of Acrobatics when making jump checks. This ability replaces woodland stride.

Resist Storm (Ex): At 4th level, a sky druid gains a +4 bonus on saving throws against spells with the air or electricity descriptors and against effects that control or modify the weather (such as *sleet storm*). This ability replaces resist nature's lure.

Skymaster (Su): At 5th level, a sky druid can use the *fly* spell (self only) for a number of minutes per day equal to her druid level. These minutes do not need to be consecutive. This ability replaces trackless step.

Wild Shape (Su): At 6th level, a sky druid gains the ability to use wild shape. When a sky druid takes the form of a creature with a fly speed, this ability functions at her class level + 1. For all other forms, her effective druid level for the ability is equal to her actual sky druid level. This ability otherwise functions as and replaces wild shape.

Soaring Form (Ex): At 9th level, a sky druid is no longer affected by altitude sickness or natural or magical wind. This ability replaces venom immunity.

Into the Wild Blue (Su): At 13th level, a sky druid gains a fly speed equal to twice her base land speed (good maneuverability). This ability replaces a thousand faces.

Wind Listener (Wizard)

The wind listener takes a sylph's natural curiosity to the extreme, enhancing his natural skill at subterfuge and eavesdropping with potent arcane magic. A wind listener has the following class features.

Class Skills: A wind listener adds Perception to his list of class skills.

Arcane School: A wind listener cannot select divination or illusion as a prohibited school.

Spontaneous Divination (Su): At 1st level, a wind listener can reshape stored spell energy into divination spells he did not prepare ahead of time. The wind listener can "lose" any prepared spell that is not a cantrip in order to cast a divination spell of the same spell level or lower. The new spell must be one the wind listener knows and is capable of casting. Spells cast with this ability increase their casting time to a full-round action (if the spell's normal casting time is longer than a full-round action, it remains unchanged). This ability replaces arcane bond.

Abjuration Sense (Ex): At 5th level, a wind listener develops a sixth sense for spotting spells designed to guard against his investigations. He gains a bonus on Perception checks equal to 1/2 his level to notice spells of the abjuration school and on Spellcraft checks to identify abjuration effects, spells, and magic items. This ability replaces the bonus feat gained at 5th level.

Wispy Form (Ex): At 10th level, the wind listener gains the ability to become airy and translucent as a standard action, gaining DR 10/magic and the effects of *improved invisibility* for a number of rounds per day equal to his level. These rounds need not be consecutive. Like the natural invisibility universal monster ability (*Bestiary 2* 299), this ability is not subject to *invisibility purge*. This ability replaces the bonus feat gained at 10th level.

Listening to the Wind (Sp): At 15th level, the wind listener can call upon spirits of the air to uncover lost lore about a legendary person, place, or thing. Invoking the spirits takes 10 minutes, during which time the wind listener must be free of distractions and able to concentrate. Once called, the spirits seek out information on the subject of the wind listener's inquiries. This functions as the spell *legend lore* (caster level equal to the wind listener's level), except that the wind listener is free to engage in other activities while spirits investigate on his behalf. The time required for the air spirits to return with this information is equal to what the casting time of the spell *legend lore* would have been if the wind listener had cast it. The wind listener can use this ability once per week, and only if he does not currently have air spirits searching for information. If the air spirits are currently searching for information, the wind listener can end their task early as a standard action, dismissing the magical effect and not returning any information. This ability replaces the bonus feat gained at 15th level.

NEW RACIAL RULES

The following equipment, feats, magic items, and spells are available to sylphs. At the GM's discretion, other appropriate races may make use of some of these new rules.

Sylph Equipment

Sylphs have access to the following equipment.

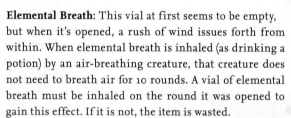

Elemental Breath: This vial at first seems to be empty, but when it's opened, a rush of wind issues forth from within. When elemental breath is inhaled (as drinking a potion) by an air-breathing creature, that creature does not need to breath air for 10 rounds. A vial of elemental breath must be inhaled on the round it was opened to gain this effect. If it is not, the item is wasted.

Wing Cloak: This strange piece of equipment only works for sylphs and similar creatures, whose light, airy bodies can be borne upon the winds. Looking like a fine silk traveler's cloak, a wing cloak is secretly reinforced with a series of wooden struts that, when locked into place, stretch the cloak's fabric into a rudimentary wing. Arranging the struts into a wing or reversing the change is a move action. When the cloak is shaped into a wing, the wearer can make a DC 15 Fly check to fall safely from any height without taking falling damage, as if using *feather fall*. When falling, the wearer may make an additional DC 15 Fly check to glide, moving 5 feet laterally for every 20 feet she falls. Readying and using a wing cloak requires two hands and provokes an attack of opportunity. A wing cloak has hardness 0 and 5 hit points. If the wing cloak is broken, the Fly DCs to use it increase by +10.

Sylph Equipment

Item	Cost	Weight	Craft DC
Elemental breath	80 gp	1/2 lb.	20
Wing cloak	1,200 gp	1 lb.	—

Sylph Feats

Sylphs have access to the Elemental Jaunt feat (see page 129) and the following feats.

Airy Step

The air responds to your innate elemental nature, protecting you from harm and cushioning your falls.

Prerequisite: Sylph.

Benefit: You gain a +2 bonus on saving throws against effects with the air or electricity descriptors and effects that deal electricity damage. You may ignore the first 30 feet of any fall when determining falling damage.

Cloud Gazer

Your insight into your elemental heritage gives you a clarity of sight few humans possess.

Prerequisite: Sylph.

Benefit: You can see through fog, mist, and clouds, without penalty, ignoring any cover or concealment bonuses from such effects. If the effect is created by magic, this feat instead triples the distance you can see without penalty.

Inner Breath

Your body is suffused with elemental air that provides for all your respiratory needs.

Prerequisites: Character level 11th, sylph.

Benefit: You no longer need to breathe. You are immune to effects that require breathing (such as inhaled poison). This does not give you immunity to cloud or gas attacks that do not require breathing, such as *cloudkill*.

Wings of Air

The winds lift you, carrying you where you want to go.

Prerequisites: Airy Step, character level 9th, sylph.

Benefit: Your bonus on saves against effects with the air or electricity descriptors and effects that deal electricity damage increases to +4. In addition, you gain a supernatural fly speed equal to your base speed (good maneuverability). You may only fly with this ability when wearing light armor or no armor.

Sylph Magic Items

Sylphs have access to the following armor special ability and magic item.

Cloudburst (armor special ability): This armor is usually decorated with engravings of storm clouds and lightning bolts. If an attack strikes the wearer and deals at least 10 points of electricity damage, the armor becomes visibly charged with electricity for 1 round. As a swift action on the wearer's next turn that does not provoke an attack of opportunity, she may use *shocking grasp* as a spell-like ability, dealing 1d6 points of electricity damage for every 10 points of damage dealt to the wearer since her last turn (maximum 5d6 for 50 or more points of electrical damage taken). Determine the effect of the *shocking grasp* based on how much damage the triggering electrical attack would have dealt the wearer before any applicable resistances or immunities.

Faint abjuration and evocation; CL 5th; Craft Magic Arms and Armor; *resist energy, shocking grasp*; Price +5,000 gp.

ELIXIR OF FORCEFUL EXHALATION

Aura faint evocation; **CL** 3rd

Slot none; **Price** 900 gp; **Weight** 1 lb.

DESCRIPTION

This fizzy, sky-blue liquid leaves its drinker feeling buoyant, yet bloated. The drinker gains a +4 competence bonus on Acrobatics checks made to make high or long jumps and on Swim checks for up to 1 hour after consuming the elixir. As a standard action, the drinker can exhale a 15-foot-long *gust of wind*. The drinker can exhale up to three gusts, after which the elixir's effect is discharged and the skill bonuses end. Unused gusts dissipate after 1 hour.

CONSTRUCTION

Requirements Craft Wondrous Item, *gust of wind*; **Cost** 450 gp

Sylph Spells

Sylphs have access to the following spells.

ABSORBING INHALATION

School transmutation [air]; **Level** alchemist 4, druid 4, sorcerer/wizard 4

Casting Time 1 standard action

Components V, S

Range close (25 ft. + 5 ft./2 levels)

Target one cloud-like effect, up to one 10-ft. cube/level

Duration 1 round/level; see text

Saving Throw see text; **Spell Resistance** no

You grant your lungs inhuman strength and capacity, allowing you to harmlessly and completely inhale one gas, fog, smoke, mist, or similar cloud-like effect. If the targeted cloud is a magical effect, you must succeed at a caster level check (DC 11 + the effect's caster level) to inhale it. Inhaling the cloud removes it from the area, leaving normal air in its place. If the cloud is too large for you to affect with a single casting of this spell, you may instead inhale a portion of the cloud, but you must inhale the portion of the cloud closest to you. This spell has no effect on gaseous creatures. It can only affect an instantaneous-duration cloud (such as a breath weapon) if you ready an action to cast the spell in response.

While inhaled, the cloud does not harm you. You may keep the cloud harmlessly contained within you for up to 1 round per level, but you must hold your breath to do so (even if you do not normally have to breathe). If the cloud has a duration, the time the cloud is contained within you counts toward that duration. As a standard action, you may release the stored cloud as a breath weapon, filling a 60-foot cone (or the cloud's original area, if smaller than a 60-foot cone). Any creature in the breath's area is subject to its normal effects, making saving throws and spell resistance checks as appropriate against the cloud's original DC. The exhaled cloud resumes its duration, if any. Exhaling the stored cloud ends this spell. If you do not exhale the cloud before this spell's duration expires, you suffer the cloud's effects and automatically fail any saving throw to resist it.

CLOUD SHAPE

School transmutation [air]; **Level** druid 4, ranger 4, sorcerer/wizard 4

Range personal

Target you

Duration 10 minutes/level (D)

This spell functions like *gaseous form*, except you assume the shape of a Colossal cloud with a space of 30 feet. You choose the general appearance of the cloud (white, stormy, fluffy, flat, and so on), after which your appearance cannot be changed. Even the closest inspection cannot reveal that the cloud in question is actually a magically concealed creature. To all normal tests you are, in fact, a cloud, although a *detect magic* spell reveals a moderate transmutation aura on the cloud. Your fly speed in cloud form is 30 feet.

GUSTING SPHERE

School evocation [air]; **Level** druid 2, magus 2, sorcerer/wizard 2

Casting Time 1 standard action

Components V, S

Range medium (100 ft. + 10 ft./level)

Effect 5-ft.-diameter sphere of air

Duration 1 round/level

Saving Throw Fortitude negates (object) or Reflex negates; see text; **Spell Resistance** yes

A swirling ball of wind rolls in whichever direction you point, hurling those it strikes with great force. The sphere is treated in all ways as an area of severe wind (*Core Rulebook* 439), applying a –4 penalty on ranged weapon attacks that pass through it. The sphere moves 30 feet per round. As part of this movement, it can ascend or jump up to 30 feet to strike a target. If it enters a space containing a Medium or smaller creature, it stops moving for that round and generates a sharp thrust of wind to bull rush the creature. The sphere's CMB for bull rush combat maneuvers uses your caster level in place of its base attack bonus, with a +2 bonus for its Strength score (14). Whether or not the bull rush is successful, the creature takes 1d6 points of nonlethal bludgeoning damage from the attack. If the bull rush fails, the creature is still subject to the severe winds from the sphere as long as they remain in the same square as it. A *gusting sphere* rolls over objects or barriers that are less than 4 feet tall.

The sphere moves as long as you actively direct it (a move action for you); otherwise, it merely stays at rest. A *gusting sphere* immediately dissipates if it exceeds the spell's range.

MIASMATIC FORM

School transmutation [air, poison]; **Level** alchemist 4, sorcerer/wizard 4
Components S, M (contact or inhaled poison worth 100 gp)
Duration 1 minute/level
Saving Throw none; see text; **Spell Resistance** no
This spell functions like *gaseous form*, except the target's vaporous body is dangerous to creatures that touch it. A creature can make a Fortitude save (DC 14 + your Intelligence modifier) on its turn to resist the vapors. When you cast this spell, you select one of the following options.

Stinking cloud: The target's body nauseates creatures that fail their saving throws, as *stinking cloud* (Fortitude negates, see text). This form of the spell does not require a material component.

Poisonous cloud: The target's body is deadly poison, dealing 1d2 points of Constitution damage to creatures that fail their saves (Fortitude halves). This form of the spell requires a material component.

PATH OF THE WINDS

School evocation [air]; **Level** druid 6, sorcerer/wizard 6
Casting Time 1 standard action
Components V, S,
Range 100 ft.
Effect 40-ft.-high downdraft of wind in a 100-foot line
Duration concentration + 1 round
Saving Throw Fortitude negates; **Spell Resistance** yes
With a sweeping gesture, you call forth mighty winds to clear a path ahead of you. The winds are the equivalent of a windstorm (*Core Rulebook* 439). During the first round of the spell, the winds sweep the designated area clear of anything

of Small or smaller size, blowing it outward to the sides of the spell's effect (50% chance of landing on either side). You may move within the effect without penalty, though all other creatures are subject to the wind's effects. On the second and all later rounds of the spell, the edges of the effect are treated as a wind wall. If the effect includes a body of water or other liquid, the winds create a channel up to 40 feet deep into the surface of the liquid. On your turn as a move action, you can move the effect of this spell, either rotating it at one of its ends up to 45 degrees, or moving it up to 50 feet in line with its current orientation (toward you or away from you).

WIND BLADES

School transmutation [air]; **Level** druid 5, magus 5, sorcerer/wizard 5, witch 5
Casting Time 1 standard action
Components V, S
Range touch
Target creature touched
Duration 1 round/level
Saving Throw Will negates; **Spell Resistance** yes
You harden the air around the target into jagged invisible blades that deal damage based on how fast the target moves. On its turn, the target takes 1d6 points of slashing damage if it moves at least 5 feet, plus 1d6 points of slashing damage for each additional 10 feet of movement. Movement that doesn't pass through air (such as burrowing, swimming, or teleportation) doesn't cause this damage.

In areas of strong wind (*Core Rulebook* 439), the target takes damage on its turn, even if it doesn't move. The wind deals 1d8 points of slashing damage for strong wind, plus 1d8 for every wind category above strong. This extra damage does not occur from instantaneous wind effects (such as *gust of wind*), only from wind effects that last at least 1 round.

WINDY ESCAPE

School transmutation [air]; **Level** bard 1, druid 1, magus 1, sorcerer/wizard 1
Casting Time 1 immediate action
Components V, S
Range personal
Target you
Duration instantaneous
You respond to an attack by briefly becoming vaporous and insubstantial, allowing the attack to pass harmlessly through you. You gain DR 10/magic against this attack and are immune to any poison, sneak attacks, or critical hit effect from that attack.

You cannot use *windy escape* against an attack of opportunity you provoked by casting a spell, using a spell-like ability, or using any other magical ability that provokes an attack of opportunity when used.

TENGUS

The crowlike tengus are known as a race of scavengers and irrepressible thieves. Covetous creatures predominantly motivated by greed, they are vain and easily won over with flattery. Deceptive, duplicitous, and cunning, tengus seek circumstances in which they can take advantage of the situation, often at the expense of others, including their own kind. They can be highly competitive, but impulsive and rash. Some claim their behavior is innate, while others believe their selfish mannerisms are cultural and developed as a learned adaptation that has enabled their people to endure through centuries of oppression.

Tengus are natural survivalists. For many, only theft and guile have afforded them the temporary luxuries other races take for granted. In the past, both humans and powerful races such as giants sought the bird-folk as slaves and servitors. Many tengus scavenged for survival, scraping for food in the shadows of cities or living as subsistence hunters and gatherers in the wild. Their descendants now struggle to find their place in contemporary society, often competing against negative stereotypes or driven to embrace them, and they rely on thievery and swordplay to get by in a harsh and unforgiving world.

Physical Description: Tengus are avian humanoids whose features strongly resemble crows. They have broad beaks and both their arms and their legs end in powerful talons. Though tengus are unable to fly, iridescent feathers cover their bodies—this plumage is usually black, though occasionally brown or blue-back. Their skin, talons, beaks, and eyes are similarly colored, and most non-tengus have great difficulty telling individuals apart. Tengus who wish to be more easily identified by other humanoids may bleach certain feathers or decorate their beaks with dyes, paint, or tiny glued ornaments. Though they are about the same height as humans, they have slight builds and tend to hunch over. A tengu's eyes sit slightly back and to the sides of his head, giving him binocular vision with a slightly more panoramic field of view than other humanoids. Like many avians, tengus have hollow bones and reproduce by laying eggs.

Society: Tengus live in close-knit communities in which they keep to themselves. In urban centers, they tend to group in communal slums, while those living in rural areas establish isolated settlements. Overall, they remain secretive about their culture, which is a combination of old traditions laced with newer bits of culture scavenged from the races common in the neighboring regions. Cultural scavenging also extends to language, and regional dialects of Tengu are peppered with terms and colloquialisms from other languages.

Unsurprisingly, tengus have a knack for language and pick up new ones quickly.

Most tengu communities tend to follow a tribal structure. Tribal rules remain loose and subjective, and tribe members settle any conflicts through public arbitration (and occasionally personal combat). While every tengu has a voice in her society, in most settlements, tengus still defer to their revered elders for wisdom and advice.

Relations: Few races easily tolerate tengus. Of the most common races, only humans allow them to settle within their cities with any regularity. When this occurs, tengus inevitably form their own ghettos and ramshackle communities, typically in the most wretched neighborhoods. Regardless of their tolerance, most humans maintain as little contact with tengus as possible. Tengus occasionally make friends with halflings and gnomes, but only when they share mutual interests. Conversely, most dwarves have no patience for tengus whatsoever. Other races tend to view tengus in a similar fashion to humans, though many actively discourage them from settling in their realms.

Alignment and Religion: Tengus tend to be neutral, though those who allow their impulsiveness to get the better of them lean toward chaotic neutral. Religious beliefs vary from tribe to tribe; some worship the traditional tengu gods (most of which are aspects of better-known deities), while others take to the worship of human gods or celestial spirits. Tengus can be fickle with regard to their patrons, quickly abandoning religious customs when they cease to provide any tangible benefit. Many embrace polytheism, picking and choosing to uphold the tenets of whatever deities best suit them at the time.

Adventurers: With little at home to leave behind, many tengus turn to a life of adventure seeking fame, fortune, and glory. A common tengu belief portrays a life on the road as a series of experiences and trials that form a path to enlightenment. Some take this to mean a path of spiritual empowerment; others view it as a way to perfect their arts or swordsmanship. Perhaps in spite of the prejudices upheld by outsiders, many tengu adventurers embrace their stereotypes. These individuals seek to succeed by epitomizing tengu racial qualities, and proudly flaunt their heritage. Despite their avian frailty, with their quick reflexes and quicker wits, tengus make excellent rogues and rangers, while those with a strong connection to the spirit world often become oracles. Those disciplined in the practice of martial arts take jobs as mercenaries and bodyguards in order to profit from their talents.

Male Names: Bukka, Chak-Chak, Chuko, Ebonfeather, Highroost, Kraugh, Pezzack, Taicho, Tchoyoitu, Xaikon.

Female Names: Aerieminder, Aikio, Cheetchu, Daba, Gildedhackle, Kankai, Mikacha, Ruk, Zhanyae.

ALTERNATE RACIAL TRAITS

The following racial traits may be selected instead of existing tengu racial traits. Consult your GM before selecting any of these new options.

Carrion Sense: Many tengus have a natural ability to sniff out carrion. While their sense of smell isn't as keen as that of other species, it is particularly attuned to the scent of injuries or death. Tengus with this racial trait have a limited scent ability, which only functions for corpses and badly wounded creatures (50% or fewer hit points). This racial trait replaces gifted linguist.

Claw Attack: Tengus with this racial trait have learned to use their claws as natural weapons. They gain two claw attacks as primary natural attacks that deal 1d3 points of damage, and are treated as having the Improved Unarmed Strike feat for the purpose of qualifying for other feats. This racial trait replaces swordtrained.

Exotic Weapon Training: Instead of swords, some tengus are trained in exotic weaponry. Such tengus choose a number of eastern weapons (*Ultimate Combat* 131) equal to 3 + their Intelligence bonus, and gain proficiency with these weapons. This racial trait replaces swordtrained.

Glide: Some tengus can use their feathered arms and legs to glide. Tengus with this racial trait can make a DC 15 Fly check to fall safely from any height without taking falling damage, as if using *feather fall*. When falling safely, a tengu may make an additional DC 15 Fly check to glide, moving 5 feet laterally for every 20 feet he falls. This racial trait replaces gifted linguist.

FAVORED CLASS OPTIONS

The following options are available to all tengus who have the listed favored class, and unless otherwise stated, the bonus applies each time you select the class reward.

Barbarian: Add +1/3 to the bonus from the superstitious rage power.

Fighter: Add +1 to the fighter's CMD when resisting a grapple or trip attempt.

Monk: Add +1/4 point to the monk's *ki* pool.

Oracle: Add +1/2 to the oracle's level for the purpose of determining the effects of the oracle's curse ability.

Rogue: Choose a weapon from those listed under the tengu's swordtrained ability. Add a +1/2 bonus on critical hit confirmation rolls with that weapon (maximum bonus +4). This bonus does not stack with Critical Focus.

Sorcerer: Select one bloodline power at 1st level that is normally usable a number of times per day equal to 3 + the sorcerer's Charisma modifier. The sorcerer adds +1/2 to the number of uses per day of that bloodline power.

TENGU RACIAL TRAITS

+2 Dexterity, +2 Wisdom, –2 Constitution: Tengus are fast and observant, but relatively fragile and delicate.

Tengu: Tengus are humanoids with the tengu subtype.

Medium: Tengus are Medium creatures and receive no bonuses or penalties due to their size.

Normal Speed: Tengus have a base speed of 30 feet.

Senses: Tengus have low-light vision.

Sneaky: Tengus gain a +2 racial bonus on Perception and Stealth checks.

Gifted Linguist: Tengus gain a +4 racial bonus on Linguistics checks, and learn 2 languages each time they gain a rank in Linguistics rather than 1 language.

Swordtrained: Tengus are trained from birth in swordplay, and as a result are automatically proficient with swordlike weapons (including bastard swords, daggers, elven curve blades, falchions, greatswords, kukris, longswords, punching daggers, rapiers, scimitars, short swords, and two-bladed swords).

Natural Weapon: A tengu has a bite attack that deals 1d3 points of damage.

Languages: Tengus begin play speaking Common and Tengu. Tengus with high Intelligence scores can choose any languages they want (except for secret languages, such as Druidic).

Witch: Add one spell from the witch spell list to the witch's familiar. This spell must be at least one level below the highest spell level she can cast. If the witch ever replaces her familiar, the new familiar knows these bonus spells.

RACIAL ARCHETYPES

The following racial archetypes are available to tengus.

Shigenjo (Oracle)

The shigenjo walks the path of enlightenment and transcendence by seeking oneness with the celestial spirits. In doing so, she unlocks the martial potential of her own spiritual power. A shigenjo has the following class features.

Class Skills: A shigenjo adds Knowledge (nature), Knowledge (religion), Knowledge (planes), and Survival to her list of class skills. These replace the additional class skills from her mystery.

Alignment: Any neutral.

Recommended Mysteries: ancestor, battle, fire, heavens, lore, metal, nature, stone, time, waves, wood.

Bonus Spells: *true strike* (2nd), *alter self* (4th), *divine power* (8th), *magic jar* (12th), *ki shout* (14th, *Ultimate Magic*), *moment of prescience* (16th). These bonus spells replace the shigenjo's mystery bonus spells at these levels.

Ki Pool (Su): At 7th level, a shigenjo gains a pool of *ki* points, supernatural energy she can use to accomplish amazing feats. The number of points in the shigenjo's *ki* pool is equal to 1/3 her oracle level + her Charisma modifier. The *ki* pool is replenished each morning after 8 hours of rest or meditation; these hours do not need to be consecutive. If the shigenjo possesses levels in another class that grants points to a *ki* pool, *ki* points gained from the shigenjo class stack with those gained from the other class to determine the total number of *ki* points in the combined pool, but only one ability score modifier is added to the total. The choice of which score to use is made when the second class ability is gained, and once made, the choice is permanent. The shigenjo can use *ki* points from this pool to power the abilities of every class she possesses that grants a *ki* pool.

As long as she has at least 1 point in her *ki* pool, a shigenjo can make a *ki* strike as a monk whose level is equal to her oracle level – 3. As a swift action, she may spend 1 point of *ki* to gain one of the following benefits.

Ki Magic: Add +1 to the DC of the next spell she casts on her turn.

Ki Curse: Treat her oracle level as 5 higher for the purpose of determining the effects of her curse for the next round.

Ki Insight: Gain a +4 insight bonus on Spellcraft checks for 1 round.

This ability replaces the shigenjo's 7th-level revelation.

Quivering Palm (Su): At 15th level, a shigenjo may learn quivering palm as the monk ability of the same name in place of a revelation. She treats her oracle level as her monk level for this ability, and the DC is based on her Charisma bonus instead of her Wisdom bonus.

Final Revelation: Upon reaching 20th level, you achieve true enlightenment and becomes one with the celestial spirits. You gain the ability to speak with any creature that uses a language. For a number of days equal to your Wisdom score, you can ignore the negative effects of extreme weather, starvation, thirst, and exhaustion. If you die, your powerful connection to the celestial realm allows you to be reborn 3 days later (as *reincarnate*). This replaces the final revelation of the shigenjo's mystery.

Swordmaster (Rogue)

A swordmaster meditates to strengthen her spiritual connection to her blade. She strives to perfect her skills by mastering six deadly trances. A swordmaster has the following class features.

Class Skills: The swordmaster adds Knowledge (nature) and Survival to her list of class skills and removes Disguise and Knowledge (dungeoneering) from her list of class skills.

Trance (Ex): At 3rd level, a swordmaster learns to focus her martial prowess using an intense meditative trance. Under the influence of a trance, the swordmaster can perform fantastic martial feats. Entering a trance is a full-round action that provokes attacks of opportunity. The swordmaster can maintain the trance for a number of rounds per day equal to 4 + her Wisdom modifier. At each level beyond 3rd, she can remain in the trance for 1 additional round. She can end her trance as a free action. Following a trance, the swordmaster is fatigued for a number of rounds equal to 2 × the number of rounds she spent in the trance. A swordmaster cannot enter a new trance while fatigued but can otherwise enter a trance multiple times during a single encounter or combat. If a swordmaster falls unconscious, her trance immediately ends.

At 3rd level, the swordmaster chooses one trance from the list below. She chooses another trance at 6th, 9th, 12th, 15th, and 18th level. She can only use one type of trance at a time.

Crane Trance (Ex): The swordmaster's blade rises and falls with the graceful sweeping arcs of the mountain crane. When in this trance, a swordmaster gains the benefits of the Crane Style feat (*Ultimate Combat* 93).

Dragon Trance (Ex): Like the dragon, the swordmaster has honed the steadiness of her mind and body. When in this trance, a swordmaster gains the benefits of the Dragon Style feat (*Ultimate Combat* 98).

Leopard Trance (Ex): Using the swiftness of the leopard, a swordmaster's evasive footwork confuses her opponents.

When in this trance, a swordmaster gains the benefits of the Mobility feat.

Monkey Trance (Ex): As the monkey springs, the swordmaster leaps from the reach of her enemies. While in this trance, a swordmaster can make an Acrobatics check opposed by an opponent's CMD. If she succeeds, she may move 5 feet as a swift action within the opponent's threatened area; this movement does not provoke attacks of opportunity and does not count as a 5-foot step.

Serpent Trance (Ex): Like the serpent, the swordmaster's quick movements allow her to catch her opponent unawares. While in this trance, a swordmaster receives a +4 bonus on Bluff checks made to feint during combat.

Tiger Trance (Ex): The swordmaster pounces upon her opponents, striking with the ferocity and brute force of a wild tiger. While in this trance, a swordmaster can make a combat maneuver check against an opponent within charge range. If she succeeds, she may charge that opponent and make a full attack against that opponent.

This ability replaces all increments of trap sense.

Rogue Talents: The following rogue talents complement the swordmaster archetype: combat trick, stand up, surprise attack, weapon training (*Core Rulebook*); befuddling strike, positioning strike (*Advanced Player's Guide*).

Advanced Talents: The following advanced rogue talents complement the swordmaster archetype: crippling strike, defensive roll (*Core Rulebook*); hunter's surprise, redirect attack (*Advanced Player's Guide*); confounding blade (*Ultimate Combat*).

NEW RACIAL RULES

The following options are available to tengus. At the GM's discretion, other appropriate races may make use of some of these new rules.

Tengu Equipment

Tengus have access to the following equipment.

Signal Kite Kit: Though wingless, tengus have long cast their thoughts toward the sky and flight. Built from paper glued to bamboo frames, their kites are painted with various colors and pictures. In addition to flying kites as a leisure activity, tengus also fly kites of various shades and patterns to send signal messages. Tengus have developed an extensive code of signals and can use their kites to display complex messages visible at great distances. A signal kite kit includes six small colored kites that can be hooked together in different patterns to facilitate complex messages. The kit also includes a spool and 300 feet of twine. Sending or interpreting a signal kite's message functions as described in the Bluff skill, but the sender and anyone trying to understand the message must also know Tengu.

Terror Kite: This small kite is usually painted with a fierce face and bright colors and is edged with serrated

wooden blades. Its twine is strengthened by soaking it in glue and sometimes with crushed glass to give it a slight cutting edge. The kite has hardness 5 and 3 hit points. Participants in a kite battle make alternating sunder combat maneuvers against each other's kites; each successful maneuver allows a competitor to roll 1d6 points of damage against the opponent's kite. When a kite reaches 0 hit points, it is broken or its string is cut, and its player loses the match. In some matches, points are awarded for touching the kite's top to the opponent's string, with the winner being the first to reach a set point total. Those interested in kite-fighting may select the terror kite as a weapon for the purpose of feats such as Weapon Focus and Weapon Specialization, and apply these bonuses on kite damage rolls and on their sunder combat maneuver attempts made while using terror kites.

Wing Oil: Tengus mix special salves to protect their feathers from the elements. This one-ounce vial of wing oil gives a feathered creature a +1 bonus on all saving throws to resist the effects of cold weather. Its effects last 24 hours.

Tengu Equipment

Item	Cost	Weight	Craft DC
Signal kite kit	5 gp	—	—
Terror kite	20 gp	—	—
Wing oil	1 gp	—	20

Tengu Feats

Tengu have access to the following feats.

Blood Beak (Combat)

Your bleed attack is bloody and dangerous.

Prerequisites: Base attack bonus +5, natural weapon racial trait, tengu.

Benefit: Increase the damage of your beak attack to 1d6. Furthermore, when you confirm a critical hit with your beak attack, you also deal 1 point of bleed damage.

Special: The bleed effect from this feat stacks with that of the Bleeding Critical feat and similar effects, adding 1 point to your bleed damage.

Carrion Feeder

Like many scavengers, you can stomach foods that would make weaker creatures ill.

Prerequisite: Tengu.

Benefit: You gain a +2 racial bonus on saving throws against diseases and ingested poisons (but not other poisons). You receive a +2 bonus on Survival skill checks to find food for yourself (and only yourself).

Long-Nose Form

You can shift into the form of a human with an unusually long nose.

Prerequisites: Character level 3rd, tengu.

Benefit: Once per day, you can assume the form of a human whose nose is the length of your beak. This spell-like ability functions as *alter self* with a caster level equal to your level. While in this form you gain the scent ability and a +2 bonus to your Strength score. Because your long nose in this form clearly indicates you are not fully human, you do not gain the normal bonus to Disguise checks for using a polymorph effect (however, you could possibly explain the nose as an unfortunate curse or deformity, or hide it with an item such as a plague doctor's mask).

Scavenger's Eye

Your gaze is naturally drawn to valuable glittering objects.

Prerequisite: Tengu.

Benefit: You gain a +2 bonus on Appraise checks. You may determine the most valuable item in a hoard as a standard action and gain an additional +2 bonus on the

Appraise check to do so. In addition, if you fail an Appraise check by 5 or more, you treat the check as if you had failed by less than 5.

Normal: Determining the most valuable object in a treasure hoard takes 1 full-round action.

Tengu Raven Form

You can shift into the form of a giant black raven.

Prerequisites: Tengu Wings, character level 7th, tengu.

Benefit: Once per day, you can take the form of a Large black bird resembling a raven, granting you a fly speed of 60 feet (good maneuverability), a +4 size bonus to your Strength, a –2 penalty to your Dexterity, and a +4 natural armor bonus. This spell-like ability otherwise functions as *beast shape II* with a caster level equal to your level.

Tengu Wings

You can grow wings that allow you to fly.

Prerequisites: Character level 5th, tengu.

Benefit: Once per day, you can sprout a pair of giant black crow's wings, granting you a fly speed of 30 feet (average maneuverability). This spell-like ability otherwise functions as *beast shape I* (though you do not gain any other benefits of that spell) with a caster level equal to your level.

Tengu Magic Items

Tengus have access to the following magic items.

BLACK FEATHER FAN

Aura faint evocation; **CL** 5th
Slot none; **Price** 10,000 gp; **Weight** 1 lb.

DESCRIPTION

This elaborate fan is made with a dozen black feathers set into a metal handle embossed with a stylized crest. The bearer can use it to create a *gust of wind*, *whispering wind*, or *wind wall*. The fan's effects can be used 3 times per day, in any combination.

CONSTRUCTION

Requirements Craft Wondrous Item, *gust of wind*, *whispering wind*, *wind wall*; **Cost** 5,000 gp

---

BLACK JADE RAVEN (FIGURINE OF WONDROUS POWER)

Aura moderate conjuration and transmutation; **CL** 11th
Slot none; **Price** 9,100 gp; **Weight** 1 lb.

DESCRIPTION

This fist-sized piece of black jade is exquisitely tooled into the shape of a raven with outstretched wings. Upon command, it transforms into a black raven (use the stats for an eagle) or a giant black raven (use the stats for a giant eagle). Both forms of the raven have Improved Steal (*Advanced Player's Guide*) as a bonus feat. The raven understands Common but cannot speak. It can answer questions related to its abilities or what it has seen by cawing once for "yes" and twice for "no."

The raven can maintain its non-figurine status for only 24 hours per week. This duration need not be continuous, but it must be used in 1-hour increments. After three transformations into its giant raven form (though not its smaller version), the statuette loses all magical properties.

CONSTRUCTION

Requirements Craft Wondrous Item, *animate objects*; **Cost** 4,550 gp

RED FEATHER FAN

Aura moderate evocation; **CL** 6th
Slot none; **Price** 5,000 gp; **Weight** 1 lb.

DESCRIPTION

This fan is made of copper fashioned into a dozen small feathers mounted on a ring-shaped bone handle. Once per day, the bearer can hold it and speak a command word to counterspell a darkness effect (as if using *daylight*) or counterspell a light effect (as if using *deeper darkness*). If activated in an area of overlapping light and darkness effects, the fan randomly counterspells one of them, leaving the other intact.

CONSTRUCTION

Requirements Craft Wondrous Item, *daylight*, *deeper darkness*; **Cost** 2,500 gp

TENGU DRINKING JUG

Aura faint transmutation; **CL** 3rd
Slot none; **Price** 1,000 gp; **Weight** 2 lbs.

DESCRIPTION

This looks like a one-gallon stoneware jug with white glaze, black birds painted around the middle, and a cork stopper tied about the neck with a hemp cord. Any liquid placed within the jug becomes safe to drink, as though affected by *purify food and drink* (though the jug only affects liquids). Three times per day, the bearer can command the jug to alter the temperature of its contents so that it ranges anywhere from ice cold to boiling hot. Once per day, the bearer can command water placed into the jug to transform into plum liquor, sake, or tea. A tengu jug holds up to 1 gallon of any liquid.

CONSTRUCTION

Requirements Craft Wondrous Item, *prestidigitation*, *purify food and drink*; **Cost** 500 gp

Tengu Spells

Tengus have access to the following spells.

COMMUNE WITH BIRDS

School divination; **Level** bard 2, druid 1, ranger 1, sorcerer/wizard 2, witch 2
Casting Time 1 standard action
Components V, S

Range personal
Target you
Duration 10 minutes; see text

You utter a question in the form of a low-pitched bird call that can be heard up to a mile away, and can understand the responses given by birds in the area. Over the next 10 minutes, the birds reply as if you had asked them the question using *speak with animals*, giving you a general consensus answer to the question based on their knowledge. For example, you could ask if there is drinkable water in the area, the location of predators or other creatures, directions to a mountaintop or other natural feature, and so on, and the local bird communities would answer to the best of their ability.

If there are no birds in range, the spell has no effect and you do not get a response. Any creature using *speak with animals* (or a similar ability) who hears this bird call can understand your question, though it may not be able to reply in a way you can hear.

THEFT WARD

School abjuration; **Level** cleric 1, inquisitor 1, sorcerer/wizard 1, witch 1
Casting Time 1 standard action
Components V, S
Range touch
Target one object
Duration 1 day

You ward a single object in your possession against theft. You gain a +10 bonus on Perception checks to notice someone trying to take the object from you.

WINTER FEATHERS

School abjuration; **Level** cleric 1, druid 1, inquisitor 1, ranger 1, sorcerer/wizard 1
Casting Time 1 standard action
Components V, S
Range touch
Target feathered creature touched
Duration 24 hours
Saving Throw Will negates (harmless); **Spell Resistance** yes (harmless)

The target's feathers thicken and fluff up to ward against winter's chill. The target suffers no harm from being in a cold environment, and can exist comfortably in conditions as low as −50 degrees Fahrenheit without having to make Fortitude saves. The creature's equipment is likewise protected. This spell doesn't provide any protection from cold damage, nor does it protect against other environmental hazards associated with cold weather (such as slipping on ice, blindness from snow, and so on).

When you cast this spell, you may have the target's feathers turn white for the duration, granting it a +4 circumstance bonus on Stealth checks to hide in ice and snow.

Tieflings

Simultaneously more and less than mortal, tieflings are the offspring of humans and fiends. With otherworldly blood and traits to match, tieflings are often shunned and despised out of reactionary fear. Most tieflings never know their fiendish sire, as the coupling that produced their curse occurred generations earlier. The taint is long-lasting and persistent, often manifesting at birth or sometimes later in life, as a powerful, though often unwanted, boon. Despite their fiendish appearance and netherworld origins, tieflings have a human's capacity of choosing their fate, and while many embrace their dark heritage and side with fiendish powers, others reject their darker predilections. Though the power of their blood calls nearly every tiefling to fury, destruction, and wrath, even the spawn of a succubus can become a saint and the grandchild of a pit fiend an unsuspecting hero.

Physical Description: No two tieflings look alike; the fiendish blood running through their veins manifests inconsistently, granting them an array of fiendish traits. One tiefling might appear as a human with small horns, a barbed tail, and oddly colored eyes, while another might manifest a mouth of fangs, tiny wings, and claws, and yet another might possess the perpetual smell of blood, foul incenses, and brimstone. Typically, these qualities hearken back in some way to the manner of fiend that spawned the tiefling's bloodline, but even then the admixture of human and fiendish blood is rarely ruled by sane, mortal laws, and the vast flexibility it produces in tieflings is a thing of wonder, running the gamut from oddly beautiful to utterly terrible.

Society: Tieflings on the Material Plane rarely create their own settlements and holdings. Instead, they live on the fringes of the land where they were born or choose to settle. Most societies view tieflings as aberrations or curses, but in cultures where there are frequent interactions with summoned fiends, and especially where the worship of demons, devils, or other evil outsiders is legal or obligatory, tieflings might be much more populous and accepted, even cherished as blessings of their fiendish overlords.

Tieflings seldom see another of their own kind, and thus they usually simply adopt the culture and mannerisms of their human parents. On other planes, tieflings form enclaves of their own kind. But often such enclaves are less than harmonious—the diversity of tiefling forms and philosophies is an inherent source of conflict between members of the race, and cliques and factions constantly form in an ever-shifting hierarchy where only the most opportunistic or devious gain advantage. Only those of common bloodlines or those who manage to divorce their worldview from the inherently selfish, devious, and evil nature of their birth manage to find true acceptance, camaraderie, and common ground among others of their kind.

Relations: Tieflings face a significant amount of prejudice from most other races, who view them as fiend-spawn, seeds of evil, monsters, and lingering curses placed upon the world. Far too often, civilized races shun or marginalize them, while more monstrous ones simply fear and reject them unless forced or cowed into acceptance. But half-elves, half-orcs, fetchlings and—most oddly—aasimars tend to view them as kindred spirits who are too often rejected or who don't fit into most societies by virtue of their birth. The widespread assumption that tieflings are innately evil—ill-founded though it may be—prevents many from easily fitting into most cultures on the Material Plane except in exceedingly cosmopolitan or planar-influenced nations.

Alignment and Religion: Despite their fiendish heritage and the insidious influence of prejudice, tieflings can be of any alignment. Many of them fall prey to the dark desires that haunt their psyches, and give in to the seduction of the whispering evil within, yet others steadfastly reject their origins and actively fight against evil lures and the negative assumptions they face from others by performing acts of good. Most, however, strive to simply find their own way in the world, though they tend to adopt a very amoral, neutral view when they do. Though many creatures just assume that tieflings worship devils and demons, their religious views are as varied as their physical forms. Individual tieflings worship all manner of deities, but they are just as likely to shun religion all together. Those who give in to the dark whispers that haunt the psyche of all tieflings serve all manner of powerful fiends.

Adventurers: Tieflings rarely integrate into the mortal societies they call home. Drawn to the adventuring life as a method of escape, they hope to make a better life for themselves, to prove their freedom from their blood's taint, or to punish a world that fears and rejects them. Tieflings make skilled rogues, powerful wizards and magi, and especially puissant sorcerers as their potent blood empowers them. Those who succumb to the evil within often become powerful clerics of fiendish powers.

Male Names: Baru, Dellisar, Maldrek, Molos, Sarvin, Shoremoth, Temerith, Voren, Zoren.

Female Names: Allizsah, Indranna, Kasidra, Kilarra, Mellisan, Mordren, Nisha.

ALTERNATE RACIAL TRAITS

The following racial traits may be selected instead of existing tiefling racial traits. Consult your GM before selecting any of these new options.

Beguiling Liar: Many tieflings find that the best way to get along in the world is to tell others what they want to hear. These tieflings' practice of telling habitual falsehoods grants them a +4 racial bonus on Bluff checks to convince an opponent that what they are saying is true when they tell a lie. This racial trait replaces skilled.

Fiendish Sprinter: Some tieflings have feet that are more bestial than human. Whether their feet resemble those of a clawed predator or are the cloven hooves common to many of their kind, tieflings with this trait gain a 10-foot racial bonus to their speed when using the charge, run, or withdraw actions. This racial trait replaces skilled.

Maw or Claw: Some tieflings take on the more bestial aspects of their fiendish ancestors. These tieflings exhibit either powerful, toothy maws or dangerous claws. The tiefling can choose a bite attack that deals 1d6 points of damage or two claws that each deal 1d4 points of damage. These attacks are primary natural attacks. This racial trait replaces the spell-like ability racial trait.

Prehensile Tail: Many tieflings have tails, but some have long, flexible tails that can be used to carry items. While they cannot wield weapons with their tails, they can use them to retrieve small, stowed objects carried on their persons as a swift action. This racial trait replaces fiendish sorcery.

Scaled Skin: The skin of these tieflings provides some energy resistance, but is also as hard as armor. Choose one of the following energy types: cold, electricity, or fire. A tiefling with this trait gains resistance 5 in the chosen energy type and also gains a +1 natural armor bonus to AC. This racial trait replaces fiendish resistance.

Soul Seer: Rare tieflings have a peculiar sight that allows them to see the state of a creature's soul.

They can use *deathwatch* at will as spell-like ability. This racial trait replaces the spell-like ability and fiendish sorcery racial traits.

Vestigial Wings: Some tieflings possess a pair of undersized, withered, or stunted wings like a mockery of those of their fiendish forebearer. Sometimes these wings are leathery, like those of a bat. Other times they are covered with a scattering of black, red, or violet feathers. Rare manifestations can take even more bizarre forms. These wings do not provide the lift required for actual flight, but do have enough power to aid flight attained by some other method, and grant a +4 racial bonus on Fly skill checks. This racial trait replaces skilled.

FAVORED CLASS OPTIONS

The following options are available to all tieflings who have the listed favored class, and unless otherwise stated, the bonus applies each time you select the class reward.

TIEFLING RACIAL TRAITS

+2 Dexterity, +2 Intelligence, –2 Charisma: Tieflings are quick in body and mind, but are inherently strange and unnerving.
Native Outsider: Tieflings are outsiders with the native subtype.
Medium: Tieflings are Medium creatures and receive no bonuses or penalties due to their size.
Normal Speed: Tieflings have a base speed of 30 feet.
Darkvision: Tieflings see in the dark for up to 60 feet.
Skilled: Tieflings gain a +2 racial bonus on Bluff and Stealth checks.
Spell-Like Ability: Tieflings can use *darkness* once per day as a spell-like ability. The caster level for this ability equals the tiefling's class level.
Fiendish Resistance: Tieflings have cold resistance 5, electricity resistance 5, and fire resistance 5.
Fiendish Sorcery: Tiefling sorcerers with the Abyssal or Infernal bloodlines treat their Charisma score as 2 points higher for all sorcerer class abilities.
Languages: Tieflings begin play speaking Common and either Abyssal or Infernal. Tieflings with high intelligence scores can choose from the following: Abyssal, Draconic, Dwarven, Elven, Gnome, Goblin, Halfling, Infernal, and Orc.

Alchemist: Add +1/2 to the alchemist's bomb damage.

Cleric: Add a +1 bonus on caster level checks made to overcome the spell resistance of outsiders.

Druid: Add a +1 bonus on wild empathy checks made to improve the attitude of fiendish animals.

Inquisitor: Add a +1/2 bonus on Intimidate checks and Knowledge checks to identify creatures.

Magus: Add +1/4 point to the magus's arcane pool.

Paladin: Add +1 to the amount of damage the paladin heals with lay on hands, but only when the paladin uses that ability on herself.

Rogue: Add +1/2 to sneak attack damage dealt to creatures with the outsider type.

Sorcerer: Add +1/2 to the number of times per day a sorcerer can use the corrupting touch infernal bloodline power, or +1 to the total number of rounds per day the sorcerer can use the claws abyssal bloodline power. The sorcerer must possess the applicable power to select these bonuses.

Summoner: Add +1 hit point or +1 skill rank to the summoner's eidolon.

Witch: The witch's familiar gains resistance 1 against cold, electricity, or fire. Each time the witch selects this reward, increase the familiar's resistance to one of these energy types by 1 (maximum 5 for any one type). If the witch ever replaces her familiar, the new familiar has these resistances.

Wizard: Select one arcane school power at 1st level that is normally usable a number of times per day equal to 3 + the wizard's Intelligence modifier. The wizard adds +1/2 to the number of uses per day of that arcane school power.

RACIAL ARCHETYPES

The following racial archetypes are available to tieflings.

Fiend Flayer (Magus)

Some tiefling magi can tap the dark energy of their fiendish blood to enhance their arcane and combat talents. By physically carving away their tainted flesh, they can use its dark energies to enhance their powers, call forth weapons from thin air, and bypass enemies' strongest defenses. A fiend flayer has the following class features.

Infernal Mortification (Su): At 1st level, a fiend flayer can sacrifice some of his own infernal blood to add to his arcane pool. Sacrificing blood in this way is a standard action. For every 2 points of Constitution damage the fiend flayer takes in this way, his arcane pool increases by 1 point. Any arcane pool points gained in this way and not spent disappear the next time the magus prepares his spells. Unlike normal ability score damage, this damage cannot be healed by way of *lesser restoration*. Only time can heal the Constitution damage taken by way of infernal mortification. This ability cannot be used if the fiend flayer's Constitution damage is equal to or greater than 1/2 his Constitution score.

Magus Arcana: A fiend flayer gains access to the following magus arcana. He cannot select any arcana more than once.

Fiendblade (Su): As a swift action, as long as the fiend flayer used infernal mortification that day to increase his arcane pool, he can conjure forth a weapon using this arcana. Doing so costs 2 points from his arcane pool. The weapon can take the form of any single one-handed melee weapon the fiend flayer is proficient with. This weapon starts as a weapon with a +1 enhancement bonus, but for every four levels beyond 3rd the fiend flayer possesses, the weapon gains another +1 enhancement bonus, to a maximum of +5 at 19th level. This summoned weapon lasts for 1 minute.

At 5th level, these bonuses can be used to add any of the following weapon properties to the fiendblade: *anarchic, axiomatic, dancing, flaming, burst, frost, icy burst, keen, shock, shocking burst, speed,* or *unholy.*

These bonuses and properties are decided when the arcane pool points are spent and cannot be changed until the next time the fiend flayer uses this arcana. Another creature cannot wield the fiendblade; if it leaves the hand of the fiend flayer, it dissipates in a wisp of red smoke that smells of burning blood.

A fiend flayer can only have one fiendblade in existence at a time. If he uses this ability again, the first fiendblade disappears.

Bypassing Strike (Su): The fiend flayer can expend 1 point from his arcane pool as a swift action to allow one melee or spellstrike attack he makes before the end of his turn to ignore an evil outsider target's damage reduction.

Fiendish Vessel (Cleric)

Many clerics pray to or make evil bargains with fiendish powers, devoting body and soul to the insane plans and wicked aims of their despicable patrons. But these mortal clerics are often just shallow beings searching for quick power or the caress of true and final oblivion—few truly grasp the full scope of the entities they worship. Fiendish vessels, through their fiendish heritage, share an innate connection with their patron, and that connection grants them understanding and power. A fiendish vessel has the following class features.

Alignment: Unlike normal clerics, a fiendish vessel's alignment must match her patron's.

Domains: A fiendish vessel must select the Daemon, Demon, or Devil subdomain (*Advanced Player's Guide* 88–90) as one of her domain choices, based on the fiendish patron she chooses to serve.

Channel Evil (Su): At 1st level, a fiendish vessel, rather than channeling positive or negative energy, instead channels the pure evil power of her fiendish patron. This ability is similar to channeling negative energy,

TABLE 2-4: FIENDISH PATRONS

Unlike most clerics, fiendish vessels must pick either the god Asmodeus or one of the following archdevils, demon lords, or Horsemen as their patron. The following describes some of the more common patrons. A more complete list of archdevils and demon lords can be found on pages 231 of the *Pathfinder Campaign Setting: Inner Sea World Guide*.

ARCHDEVILS

Archdevil	AL	Areas of Concern	Domains	Favored Weapon
Baalzebul	LE	Arrogance, flies, lies	Air, Death, Evil, Law	Spear
Belial	LE	Adultery, deception, desire	Charm, Destruction, Evil, Law	Ranseur
Dispater	LE	Cities, prisons, rulership	Evil, Law, Nobility, Trickery	Heavy mace
Mephistopheles	LE	Contracts, devils, secrets	Evil, Knowledge, Law, Rune	Trident

DEMON LORDS

Demon Lord	AL	Areas of Concern	Domains	Favored Weapon
Abraxas	CE	Forbidden lore, magic, snakes	Chaos, Evil, Knowledge, Magic	Whip
Baphomet	CE	Beasts, labyrinths, minotaurs	Animal, Chaos, Evil, Strength	Glaive
Dagon	CE	Deformity, the sea, sea monsters	Chaos, Destruction, Evil, Water	Trident
Shax	CE	Envy, lies, murder	Chaos, Destruction, Evil, Nobility	Dagger

THE FOUR HORSEMEN

Horseman	AL	Areas of Concern	Domains	Favored Weapon
Apollyon	NE	Pestilence	Air, Darkness, Destruction, Evil	Scythe
Charon	NE	Death	Death, Evil, Knowledge, Water	Quarterstaff
Szuriel	NE	War	Evil, Fire, Strength, War	Greatsword
Trelmarixian	NE	Famine	Earth, Evil, Madness, Weather	Spiked gauntlet

but instead of healing undead and dealing damage to living creatures, this blast of evil energy automatically heals evil creatures and debilitates good creatures within its burst.

Channeling this evil causes a burst that affects all creatures in a 30-foot radius centered on the fiendish vessel. In the case of evil creatures, the amount of damage healed is equal to 1d4 points of damage and increases by 1d4 at every two levels beyond 1st (to a maximum of 10d4 at 19th level). Good creatures in the burst receive a Will saving throw to negate this damage. Good creatures that fail their saving throws are sickened for 1d4 rounds. Good creatures with a number of Hit Dice less than or equal to the fiendish vessel's class level – 5 that fail their saving throws are nauseated for 1 round and then sickened for 1d4 rounds instead. The DC of this save is equal to 10 + 1/2 the fiendish vessel's level + the fiendish vessel's Charisma bonus. Neutral creatures are unaffected by this burst of evil energy.

A fiendish vessel may channel this energy a number of times per day equal to 3 + her Charisma modifier. Doing so is a standard action that does not provoke attacks of opportunity. A fiendish vessel can choose whether or not to include herself in this effect. A fiendish vessel must present her unholy symbol or use her familiar as the divine focus for this ability.

For the purposes of feats that affect channel energy, this ability counts as channeling negative energy. If the feat changes the way the fiendish vessel channels or deals damage with her channeling, use the amount of damage this ability heals evil creatures to determine the damage-dealing potential of the affected ability. For instance, if a 5th-level fiendish vessel takes the Channel Smite feat, her channeling deals an additional 3d4 points of damage to living creatures on a successful hit (though they may save to negate the damage).

This ability replaces channel energy.

Fiendish Familiar: At 3rd level, a fiendish vessel's patron rewards her with a fiendish servant. The fiendish vessel gains an imp, quasit, or cacodaemon familiar based on the patron she worships. If she worships Asmodeus or an archdevil, she gets an imp; if she worships a demon lord, she gets a quasit; and if she worships one of the Four Horsemen, she gains a cacodaemon. This ability is identical to the wizard's arcane bond with a familiar and the Improved Familiar feat, using the fiendish vessel's character level in place of the wizard level.

This tiny fiend acts like a perverse, manifest moral compass. Furthermore, this familiar can act as a living divine focus and unholy symbol for her spellcasting if the fiendish vessel so desires, which means that when she

uses her channel evil ability, its burst can be centered on the familiar instead, as long as that familiar is within 30 feet and line of sight. A fiendish vessel's familiar tends to be fawning and subservient to the fiendish vessel. Should her familiar die, the fiendish vessel's patron replaces the familiar with an identical one within 1 week, without the need for a special ritual. Furthermore, the fiendish familiar gains the following special abilities beyond the standard familiar special abilities.

Fiendish Augury (Sp): At 3rd level, the fiendish vessel can ask the familiar whether a particular course of action will bring good or bad results for her in the immediate future. This ability acts like the *augury* spell, with a caster level equal to the fiendish vessel's level, with the familiar acting as the mouthpiece for the spell. This ability can be used once per day.

Fiendish Divination (Sp): At 9th level, the fiendish vessel can use a more powerful form of divination to gain intelligence from her patron through her fiendish familiar. This ability acts like the *divination* spell, with a caster level equal to the fiendish vessel's level; the familiar acts as the mouthpiece for the spell. This ability can be used once per day.

Extra Divination (Sp): At 13th level, the fiendish vessel can gain intelligence from her patron more often each day. She can use fiendish divination up to 3 times per day.

Fiendish Summoning: When casting *summon monster* spells, a fiendish vessel is limited to summoning fiendish creatures and evil outsiders of the same alignment as her patron.

NEW RACIAL RULES

The following options are available to tieflings. At the GM's discretion, other appropriate races may make use of some of these new rules.

Tiefling Equipment

Tieflings have access to the following equipment.

Fiendgore Unguent: When this unguent—prepared with vile alchemical reagents and the gore of fiends—is applied to a wounded tiefling or evil outsider (not currently at maximum hit points), it momentarily transforms the essence of the target into something even more fearsome and demonic. While under the effects of a fiendgore unguent, a tiefling or an evil outsider gains a +2 circumstance bonus on Intimidate checks and a +1 circumstance bonus to the DC of all spells with the fear descriptor that they cast. Applying the unguent is a delicate process, requiring a full-round action, and can only be properly applied to a willing or helpless creature. If applied to a creature other than a tiefling or an evil outsider, it sickens the creature instead. The unguent's effects (either beneficial or harmful) last for 1 minute.

Tiefling Equipment

Item	Cost	Weight	Craft DC
Fiendgore unguent	75 gp	1 lb.	20

Tiefling Feats

Tieflings have access to the following feats.

Armor of the Pit

Your fiendish traits take the form of a protective scaly skin.

Prerequisite: Tiefling.

Benefit: You gain a +2 natural armor bonus.

Special: If you have the scaled skin racial trait, you instead gain resistance 5 to two of the following energy types that you don't have resistance to already: cold, electricity, and fire.

Expanded Fiendish Resistance

You gain extra fiendish resistances.

Prerequisite: Tiefling.

Benefit: Pick one of the following energy types that you do not already have resistance to: acid, cold, electricity, or fire. You gain resistance 5 to that energy type.

Special: You can take this feat multiple times. Each time you do, pick another energy type you do not have resistance to. You gain resistance 5 to that energy type.

Fiend Sight

Your eyes develop keener sight in dim light and darkness.

Prerequisites: Darkvision 60 ft., tiefling.

Benefit: You gain low-light vision and your darkvision improves to 120 ft.

Special: You can take this feat twice. When you take it a second time, you gain the see in darkness universal monster ability (*Bestiary* 2 301).

Grasping Tail

Your tail becomes more useful.

Prerequisite: Tiefling.

Benefit: You can use your tail to grab stowed items. While you cannot wield weapons with your tail, you can use it to retrieve small, stowed objects carried on your person as a swift action.

Special: If you have the prehensile tail racial trait, you can use your tail to grab unattended items within 5 feet as a swift action as well as to grab stowed objects carried on your person; you can hold such objects with your tail, though you cannot manipulate them with your tail (other than to put them in your hand).

Tiefling Magic Items

Tieflings have access to the following magic items.

DARKSIRE AMULET

Aura faint abjuration; **CL** 3rd

Slot neck; **Price** 9,000 gp; **Weight** 1 lb.

DESCRIPTION

This small iron locket contains some token—a scale, a shaving of a horn or claw, or lock of burning hair—from a fiend. When worn by a tiefling, if he has cold, electricity, or fire resistance, this amulet increases that resistance by 5. Furthermore, it provides a +4 insight bonus on Diplomacy skill checks made to influence evil outsiders.

CONSTRUCTION

Requirements Craft Wondrous Item, *resist energy*, creator must be a tiefling, half-fiend, or true fiend ; **Cost** 4,500 gp

HALO OF INNER CALM

Aura strong abjuration; **CL** 15th

Slot head; **Price** 16,000 gp; **Weight** 1 lb.

DESCRIPTION

This silvery ring looks like a halo. When worn by a tiefling it hovers just above his head, though it still uses the head magic item slot. It helps to calm the baser emotions and the dark whispers that plague tieflings, granting the wearer a +4 resistance bonus on saving throws against all spells with the emotion descriptor. When worn by a tiefling of a good alignment, it provides spell resistance 13 against spells with the evil descriptor and a +2 sacred bonus on saving throws.

CONSTRUCTION

Requirements Craft Wondrous Item, creator must be a tiefling of good alignment, *holy aura*; **Cost** 8,000 gp

Tiefling Spells

Tieflings have access to the following spells.

DAMNATION STRIDE

School conjuration (teleportation) [fire]; **Level** sorcerer/wizard 5, summoner 4, witch 5

Casting Time 1 standard action

Target self and creatures within a 10-foot-radius burst (see below)

Duration 1 minutes/level

Saving Throw Reflex half, see text; **Spell Resistance** no

This spell functions like *dimension door*, except you leave behind a burst of fire. Choose one corner of your starting square. A 10-foot-radius burst of flame explodes from that corner the moment you leave, dealing 4d6 points of fire damage (Reflex negates).

HELLMOUTH LASH

School transmutation [acid, electricity, or fire]; **Level** sorcerer/wizard 4, witch 4

Casting Time 1 standard action

Components V, S

Range personal

Target you

Duration 1 round/level (D)

Upon casting this spell, your tongue transforms into an energy whip weapon that can deal acid, electricity, or fire damage. You choose what type of energy damage the spell deals when you cast it. You attack with your tongue as if it were a whip, except you make touch attacks with it and it can harm creatures with armor or natural armor bonuses. You are considered proficient with this weapon. A successful touch attack with the tongue deals 1d8 points of energy damage per two caster levels (maximum of 5d8 points of damage at 10th level).

While the spell is in effect, you cannot speak, cast spells requiring verbal components, or activate items requiring command words.

The spell has the acid, electricity, or fire descriptor, depending on what type of energy damage you chose when you cast it.

UNDINES

Undines are humans who trace their ancestry to creatures from the Plane of Water. Even at first glance, one notices the potency of their ancestry, for an undine's very flesh mimics the color of lakes, seas, and oceans. Whether they have the blood of marids or water mephits as their kin, all undines define themselves through their ancestry. They perceive their individual differences as gifts and explore the supernatural aspects of their unique heritage to the fullest.

The undines are a proud race and show little outward fear. While good-natured and somewhat playful among their own kind, they behave with slightly more reserve and seriousness in the company of non-undines. They have excellent emotional control, and can edge their tempers from calm to raging and back again within but a few minutes. While some might dub their behavior erratic, undines are simply a bit more outwardly melodramatic than most races. Certainly, they are not moody and do not become angered, excited, or otherwise emotional without provocation. As close friends, some find them overly possessive, though they are also extremely protective of those they care about.

Undines tend to settle near water, usually in warmer climates. Though land-dwellers, they spend a fair amount of time in the water. For this reason, most dress sparsely, wearing only enough clothing to protect themselves from the elements, and few wear shoes. They avoid wearing jewelry around their necks and keep their hair slicked back and tied into tight knots. This prevents hair or other objects from becoming a distraction or hindrance while swimming. Similarly, undines pursuing martial classes choose weapons that they can wield efficiently on land as well as in water.

Physical Description: Undines display a wide variation of skin tones, ranging from pale turquoise to deep blue to sea green. An undine's straight, thick hair tends to be of a similar, yet slightly darker color than her skin. All have limpid blue eyes. Physically, undines most resemble humans, and their physiques show human diversity in regard to overall height and body type. Aside from their coloration, their most racially defining traits remain their fin-like ears and webbed hands and feet.

Society: Undines define themselves as a unique race and are capable of producing undine offspring. While they remain able to interbreed with humans, they tend to keep to themselves, and form small, reclusive communities near bodies of water, or in some cases, floating settlements. A typical undine community lives under the guidance of a small council comprising officials appointed by consensus. Council positions can be held indefinitely, though a community unhappy with the performance of a council member can call for her resignation.

Intermarriage in undine communities is common, with children raised communally. A fair amount of regional diversity exists in undine culture, as influenced by the specific ancestry of independent settlements. It should also be noted that not all undine in a single settlement claim the same ancestry, as undines may marry other undines from outside their own communities.

Relations: Undines hold no biases or prejudices toward any particular races. Their communities rely primarily on trade, giving them ample opportunity to interact with a diverse range of outsiders and foreigners. They have no qualms about establishing neighborhoods within the settlements of other races, provided adequate respect is given to both the undines and any nearby bodies of water. Still, in such instances, a given undine community does what it can to retain its autonomy.

Undines get along quite well with elves and gnomes. Often these races share protective duties over forested lakes and streams. Similarly, they interact favorably with good or neutral aquatic humanoids, sharing many common interests. They barter most freely with humans and dwarves for resources such as metal and cloth.

Alignment and Religion: Most undines are neutral. Their principle interests lie in the welfare of their people, and thus their moral concerns focus upon the community and upon themselves. This neutral view also allows them to interact with a broad scope of non-undine races with whom they trade. While not deeply religious, undines possess a strong spiritual connection to both their supernatural ancestors and to water itself. Those who pursue nonsecular paths almost always worship the gods of their ancestors or gods whose portfolios feature some aspect of water.

Adventurers: On occasion, an undine leaves her people to seek out a life of adventure. Like water itself, some undines simply feel compelled to move, and adventuring gives them an ample excuse for living on the road. Others adventure for less wholesome reasons, and exile is a common punishment for crimes within undine society. With few other options, most exiles turn to adventuring hoping to find a new place in the world. Undines' affinity toward water makes them particularly good druids, while undine sorcerers usually have aquatic bloodlines.

Male Names: Aven, Dharak, Ghiv, Jamash, Maakor, Ondir, Radid, Shiradahz.

Female Names: Afzara, Baarah, Calah, Iryani, Maarin, Nylgune, Pari, Radabeh, Urdahna.

ALTERNATE RACIAL TRAITS

The following racial traits might be selected instead of existing undine racial traits. Consult your GM before selecting any of these new options.

Acid Breath: Undines whose outsider heritage can be traced to a water mephit can wield acid as a weapon.

Such an undine has a breath weapon that is a 5-foot cone of acidic water usable once per day. The breath deals 1d8 points of acid damage per two character levels (maximum 5d8). A Reflex saving throw (DC 10 + 1/2 the undine's level + the undine's Constitution modifier) halves the damage. This racial trait replaces the spell-like ability racial trait.

Amphibious: Some undines are born with a permanent bond to water. Undines with this racial trait gain the aquatic subtype and amphibious special quality. This racial trait replaces the spell-like ability racial trait.

Deepsight: The eyes of some undines are especially adapted to the lightless depths of the oceans, but not to air-filled environments. An undine with this racial trait has darkvision 120 feet when underwater, but otherwise has no darkvision at all. This racial trait replaces darkvision.

Flesh Chameleon: Some undines can change their coloration to match human skin tones. As a standard action, an undine with this racial trait can change her natural blue hue to match any normal human skin tone, and can revert to normal as a free action. This grants a +4 racial bonus on Disguise checks to appear human. This racial trait replaces energy resistance.

Hydrated Vitality: An undine with this racial trait gains fast healing 2 for 1 round anytime she submerges completely within a body of natural salt water, fresh water, or brackish water. Stagnant, poisoned, or trapped water (such as an artificial pit or a *bag of holding*) does not activate this ability. The undine can heal up to 2 hit points per level per day with this ability, after which it ceases to function. This racial trait replaces water affinity.

Nereid Fascination: Some undines can trace their ancestry to nereids as well as to outsiders. Once per day as a standard action, such an undine can create a 20-foot-radius aura that causes humanoids within the aura's range to become fascinated with her for a number of rounds equal to 1/2 the undine's character level (minimum 1). Targets may resist with a Will save (DC 10 + 1/2 the undine's level + the undine's Charisma modifier). This is a supernatural ability. This racial trait replaces the spell-like ability racial trait.

Ooze Breath: Some undines' outsider heritage can be traced to ooze mephits. These undines have a breath weapon that is a 5-foot cone of slime usable once per day. The slime deals 1d4 points of acid damage per two character levels (maximum 5d4) and sickens creatures in the area for 3 rounds. A successful Reflex saving throw (DC 10 + 1/2 the undine's level + the undine's Constitution modifier) halves the damage and negates the sickened effect. This racial trait replaces the spell-like ability racial trait.

Terrain Chameleon: Some undines can change their coloration to blend in with underwater terrain, mixing browns, grays, and greens to resemble kelp or other natural water plants. As a standard action, an undine with this racial trait can change her coloration,

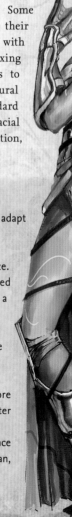

UNDINE RACIAL TRAITS

+2 Dexterity, +2 Wisdom, −2 Strength: Undines are both perceptive and agile, but tend to adapt rather than match force with force.

Native Outsider: Undines are outsiders with the native subtype.

Medium: Undines are Medium creatures and receive no bonuses or penalties due to their size.

Normal Speed: Undines have a base speed of 30 feet on land. They also have a swim speed of 30 feet, can move in water without making Swim checks, and always treat Swim as a class skill.

Darkvision: Undines can see in the dark up to 60 feet.

Spell-Like Ability: *Hydraulic push* (*Advanced Player's Guide*) 1/day (caster level equals the undine's level).

Energy Resistance: Undines have cold resistance 5.

Water Affinity: Undine sorcerers with the elemental (water) bloodline treat their Charisma score as 2 points higher for all sorcerer spells and class abilities. Undine clerics with the Water domain cast their Water domain powers and spells at +1 caster level.

Languages: Undines begin play speaking Common and Aquan. Undines with high Intelligence scores can choose from the following: Auran, Dwarven, Elven, Gnome, Halfling, Ignan, and Terran.

gaining a +4 bonus on Stealth checks in underwater environments. She can return to normal as a free action. This racial trait replaces energy resistance.

Water Sense: Undines with this racial trait can sense vibrations in water, granting them blindsense 30 feet against creatures in contact with the same body of water. This racial trait replaces energy resistance.

FAVORED CLASS OPTIONS

The following options are available to all undines who have the listed favored class, and unless otherwise stated, the bonus applies each time you select the class reward.

Bard: Add a +1 bonus on Perform checks to use the countersong bardic performance against creatures with the aquatic or water subtypes.

Cleric: Add a +1 bonus on caster level checks to overcome the spell resistance of creatures with the aquatic or water subtype.

Druid: Add a +1 bonus on wild empathy checks to influence animals and magical beasts with the aquatic subtype.

Monk: Add +1 to the monk's CMD when resisting a grapple and +1/3 to the number of stunning attacks he can attempt per day.

Sorcerer: Add a +1 bonus on caster level checks to cast spells underwater.

Summoner: If the summoner's eidolon has an aquatic base form (*Ultimate Magic* 74), add +5 feet to the range of the summoner's life link ability.

Wizard: Add one spell from the cleric, druid, or wizard spell list with the water descriptor to the wizard's spellbook. This spell must be at least one level below the highest spell level he can cast. This spell is treated as one level higher unless it also appears on the wizard spell list.

RACIAL ARCHETYPES

The following racial archetypes are available to undines.

Undine Adept (Druid)

An undine adept dedicates herself to preserving the knowledge of the first undines and ensuring her people's ancient connections to the natural world remain undisturbed. They serve as the keepers of the roots of the undine people and as their protectors. An undine adept has the following class features.

Domains: An undine adept who chooses a domain must choose the Community or Water domain, or any subdomain of those domains.

Amphibious (Su): At 2nd level, the undine adept gains the aquatic subtype and the amphibious universal monster ability, allowing her to breathe water or air. This ability replaces woodland stride.

Augment Summoning (Su): At 3rd level, any creature with the water subtype the undine adept summons with either *summon monster* or *summon nature's ally* gains the benefits of the Augment Summoning feat. This replaces trackless step.

Resist Water's Call (Su): At 4th level, an undine adept gains a +4 bonus on saving throws against the spell-like and supernatural abilities of outsiders with the aquatic or water subtype, fey with the aquatic or water subtype, and spells and effects with the water descriptor. This ability replaces resist nature's lure.

Wild Shape (Su): At 6th level, an undine adept gains the ability to use wild shape. When an undine takes the form of a creature with the aquatic or water subtype, this ability functions at her class level + 1. For all other forms, her effective druid level for the ability is equal to her actual undine adept level. This ability otherwise functions as and replaces wild shape.

Commune with Water Spirits: At 9th level, an undine adept adds *commune* to her druid spell list. She may use this spell whether she worships a deity or elemental forces. This ability replaces venom immunity.

Watersinger (Bard)

The watersinger's song reaches from the depths of his soul into the elemental waters from which life first sprang. His voice commands water, bending and shaping it to his desire.

Bardic Performance: A watersinger has some unique bardic performances, which replace some of the standard bardic performances as listed in each entry. These bardic performances follow all the general rules and restrictions of a bard's bardic performances.

Watersong (Su): At 1st level, a watersinger can use bardic performance to manipulate and control the shape of water within 30 feet. A successful Perform check allows the bard to animate and control a 5-foot-cube of water. The watersinger can command the water to take various forms, bend, rise, fall, or sustain a shape, and can make it support weight as if it were solid ice. For example, the watersinger could create a pillar of water (to provide cover), ladder, channel, bridge, stairs, slide, and so on. The manipulated water is as slippery as normal ice. This ability cannot create forms more fragile or complex than what could be carved in normal ice. While under the bard's control, the water has hardness 0 and 3 hit points per inch of thickness. At level 3, the manipulated water gains hardness 1, and this increases by +1 for every 3 bard levels beyond that. At 5th, 10th, 15th, and 20th level, the volume affected increases by an additional 5-foot cube (these cubes must be adjacent to each other). The manipulated water retains its shape for 1 round after the bard stops spending bardic performance rounds to maintain it. This ability replaces fascinate, suggestion, and mass suggestion.

Waterstrike (Su): At 3rd level, the watersinger can spend 1 round of bardic performance to command any water he is currently manipulating with his watersong performance to lash out and strike an opponent with a slam attack. The watersinger uses his base attack bonus and Charisma bonus to make this attack, and deals 1d6 points of bludgeoning damage plus his Charisma bonus. The attack can originate from any square of water the bard is manipulating, and the water can get a flanking bonus or help a combatant get one, but cannot make attacks of opportunity. The water can make multiple attacks per round if your base attack bonus allows you to do so. At 10th level, the water's slam damage increases to 1d8 points and the water gains a reach of 10 feet. At 15th level, the water's slam damage increases to 2d6 points. At 20th level, the water's slam damage increases to 2d8 points. This performance replaces inspire competence.

Lifewater (Su): At 5th level, the watersinger can spend 1 round of bardic performance as a standard action to manipulate the water, blood, and other fluids within a creature's body, causing the target to become sickened for 1d4 rounds. Alternatively, he may use this ability to attempt a reposition combat maneuver (*Advanced Player's Guide*), using his base attack bonus and his Charisma modifier as his CMB. This ability has a range of 30 feet, only works on creatures whose bodies contain fluid, and does not affect creatures that are immune to critical hits. This performance replaces the use of lore master gained at 5th level (though a watersinger still gains the use of lore master once per day at 11th level and twice per day at 17th).

Watersinger Spells: A watersinger adds certain water-themed spells to his spell list. He adds these abilities to his spell list as soon as his bard level allows him to cast spells of that spell level. 0—*create water*; 1st—*hydraulic push* (*Advanced Player's Guide*), *slipstream* (*Advanced Player's Guide*); 2nd—*aqueous orb* (*Advanced Player's Guide*), *hydraulic torrent* (*Advanced Player's Guide*), *water walk*; 3rd—*fluid form* (*Advanced Player's Guide*), *ride the waves* (*Ultimate Magic*); 4th—*control water*, *communal water walk* (*Ultimate Combat*); 5th—*vortex* (*Advanced Player's Guide*); 6th—*seamantle* (*Advanced Player's Guide*).

NEW RACIAL RULES

The following equipment, feats, magic items, and spells are available to undines. At the GM's discretion, other appropriate races may make use of some of these new rules.

Undine Equipment

Undines have access to the following equipment.

Chain Belts: While undines dress sparingly, they often wear 10-foot-long belts of fine linked chain about their waists. The belts contain hinged links to which the wearer can affix various objects such as tools, small weapons, and other valuables, including links of silver and platinum, or small hammered plates of gold set with gems. If worn properly, the belt can hold up to 30 pounds of small items. A swimming undine can unwrap the belt as swift action if she needs to remove it to decrease her weight load.

Potion Sponge: This egg-sized sponge is covered in a layer of waterproof edible wax, designed to absorb 1 dose of a potion. Chewing a potion sponge and swallowing its liquid contents is a full-round action. A creature of at least Large size can swallow the sponge in its entirely; other creatures must spit out the sponge once it's depleted (a free action). Unlike a potion that is drunk from a vial, a potion sponge can be used underwater. A potion can be poured from a vial into a sponge potion (or squeezed from a sponge into a vial) as a full-round action. The potion sponge is immune to attacks that specifically target crystal, glass, ceramic, or porcelain, such as *shatter*. It otherwise works like a potion vial.

Undine Weaponshaft: Undines incorporate a unique design when crafting shafted weapons such as quarterstaves, spears, and tridents. Instead of a solid shaft, the weapon is built around a pipe of wood or metal, with the butt end sealed and the front end left open. As a full-round action, an undine can make a single melee attack with the weapon and use her *hydraulic push* spell-like ability against the target of that melee attack. The weapon otherwise functions like a standard weapon of its type, and can be made of special materials (such as mithral or adamantine) and masterwork quality.

Undine Equipment

Item	Cost	Weight	Craft DC
Chain belt	15 gp	1/4 lb.	—
Potion sponge	2 gp	—	15
Undine weaponshaft	+300 gp	—	—

Undine Feats

Undines have access to the Elemental Jaunt feat (see page 129) and the following feats.

Aquatic Ancestry

You favor your outsider ancestry and are better adapted to life in the water.

Prerequisite: Undine.

Benefit: You gain the amphibious special quality. Your swim speed increases by +10 feet.

Hydraulic Maneuver

You can use your *hydraulic push* to disarm or trip.

Prerequisites: *Hydraulic push* spell-like ability, undine.

Benefit: You may use *hydraulic push* to attempt a bull rush, disarm, dirty trick (blind or dazzle, see *Advanced Player's Guide*), or trip combat maneuver. Each time you

use *hydraulic push*, you must decide which of the allowed combat maneuvers you want to perform. You may use this feat with your *hydraulic push* racial spell-like ability, your class-granted use of *hydraulic push*, or any *hydraulic push* spells you cast, but not with magic items or other external sources that use that spell.

Normal: *Hydraulic push* can only be used to make a bull rush combat maneuver.

Steam Caster

You imbue your fire spells with elemental water, transforming them into powerful gouts of steam.

Prerequisite: Undine.

Benefit: You may increase the casting time of a fire spell to a full-round action, infusing it with elemental power (spells with a casting time of 1 full-round action or longer do not have an increased casting time). The spell is treated as if it had the water descriptor. All fire effects of the altered spell instead manifest as superheated steam. The altered spell works normally underwater without requiring a caster level check. Unlike fire, the steam cannot ignite objects or set creatures on fire. As the spell still deals fire damage, fire resistance or immunity still applies to the spell's effects.

Triton Portal

You can channel your inner magic to summon allies.

Prerequisites: Character level 5th, *hydraulic push* spell-like ability, undine.

Benefit: Once per day, you may expend your racial *hydraulic push* ability to instead cast *summon nature's ally III* as a spell-like ability with a caster level equal to your character level. This use of the ability can only summon a Small water elemental or 1d3 dolphins. Using this ability is a full-round action.

Water Skinned

Your touch extinguishes small flames.

Prerequisite: Undine.

Benefit: As a standard action, you can extinguish a small nonmagical fire with a touch, affecting anything up to the size of a large campfire. This ability does not affect fires with a total area greater than 5 square feet. Touching the fire in this way does not harm you.

Undine Magic Items

Undines have access to the following magic item.

SHARK TOOTH AMULET

Aura faint abjuration; **CL** 5th
Slot neck; **Price** 9,000 gp; **Weight** —

DESCRIPTION

This amulet is crafted of a single massive petrified shark tooth suspended on kelp twine and grants its wearer combat

potency while underwater. While wearing this amulet, its wearer can use melee weapons normally, taking no penalty to attack and dealing full damage with such attacks. This amulet also allows the wearer to make thrown range weapon attacks underwater, though such attacks take a –2 penalty on attack rolls and their range increment is halved.

CONSTRUCTION

Requirements Craft Wondrous Item, *touch of the sea* (*Advanced Player's Guide*), the crafter must be an undine or have the water subtype; **Cost** 4,500 gp

SHAWL OF LIFE-KEEPING

Aura faint conjuration (healing); **CL** 3rd
Slot shoulders; **Price** 1,000 gp; **Weight** —

DESCRIPTION

This magical shawl is woven from silken, diaphanous material. Once per day, the wearer can speak a command word to transfer some of her life energy into the shawl (up to 10 hit points). If she is wearing the shawl and is reduced to –1 hit points or below, the shawl immediately heals her an amount equal to the number of hit points stored in the shawl. This healing cannot prevent the wearer from being killed. The life energy stored in the shawl lasts for 24 hours or until it heals the wearer, whichever comes first. If the shawl is destroyed, the stored life energy is lost.

While the shawl is storing a creature's life energy, it retains a connection to that creature. If another creature holds the shawl in hand, the creature whose life energy is stored in the shawl takes a –2 penalty on Fortitude and Reflex saving throws against all effects from the current bearer of the shawl.

CONSTRUCTION

Requirements Craft Wondrous Item, *cure light wounds*, *stabilize*; **Cost** 500 gp

SLIPPERS OF THE TRITON

Aura moderate abjuration; **CL** 7th
Slot feet; **Price** 56,000 gp; **Weight** 1 lb.

DESCRIPTION

Once they are slipped on, these web-toed slippers allow the wearer to breathe water and grant extra maneuverability while within such environments. If the wearer has no swim speed, it gains a 30 foot swim speed. If the wearer has a swim speed, it gains a +10 foot enhancement bonus to its swim speed.

CONSTRUCTION

Requirements Craft Wondrous Item, *ride the waves* (*Ultimate Magic*); **Cost** 28,000 gp

Undine Spells

Undines have access to the following spells.

MARID'S MASTERY

School transmutation [water]; **Level** cleric 1, druid 1, ranger 1, sorcerer/wizard 1, witch 1

Casting Time 1 standard action

Components V, S

Range touch

Target creature touched

Duration 1 minute/level

Saving Throw Will negates (harmless); **Spell Resistance** yes (harmless)

The target gains a +1 bonus on attack and damage rolls if it and its opponent are touching water. If the opponent or the target is touching the ground, the target takes a –4 penalty on attack and damage rolls.

NEREID'S GRACE

School enchantment (charm) [mind-affecting]; **Level** druid 1, witch 1

Casting Time 1 standard action

Components V, S

Range touch

Target you

Duration 1 round/level

You radiate the unearthly grace of a nereid. If you are not wearing armor (or your armor is not visible, such as when using *glamered* armor), you gain a deflection bonus to your Armor Class and CMD equal to your Charisma bonus.

NIXIE'S LURE

School enchantment (charm) [mind-affecting, sonic]; **Level** bard 4, druid 3, sorcerer/wizard 3, summoner 4, witch 3

Casting Time 1 standard action

Components V, S

Range 300 ft.

Target all creatures within a 300-ft.-radius burst centered on you

Duration concentration + 1 round/level (D)

Saving Throw Will negates; **Spell Resistance** yes

This spell creates an unearthly and infectious song that seductively summons all who hear it. *Nixie's lure* affects a maximum of 24 Hit Dice of creatures. Creatures in the area who fail their saves are lured by the song and move toward you using the most direct means available. If the path leads them into a dangerous area such as through fire or off a cliff, the creatures each receive a second saving throw to end the effect before moving into peril. Creatures lured by the spell's song can take no actions other than to defend themselves. A victim within 5 feet of you simply stands still and for the duration of the spell remains fascinated.

UNDINE'S CURSE

School necromancy [evil]; **Level** sorcerer/wizard 1, witch 1

Casting Time 1 standard action

Components V, S

Range close (25 ft. + 5 ft./2 levels)

Target one creature

Duration 1 hour/level

Saving Throw Will negates; **Spell Resistance** yes

The target loses its body's natural ability to breathe automatically. As long as it remains conscious and is able to take physical actions, it keeps breathing and is able to function normally. If it is ever unconscious (including sleeping) or unable to take physical actions, it stops breathing and begins to suffocate. Creatures that do not have to breathe are immune to this spell.

3 Uncommon Races

Bird men!" Harsk laughed and drew his dagger with his free hand. "So that's what the witch meant. Fair enough—I could use a drumstick or three."

Seelah shushed him and raised her sword, letting the feral creatures see the holy symbol embedded in its hilt. "Hail, neighbors," she called. "We mean you no harm."

Inside the ruins, more glowing eyes appeared. Black wings unfurled, hiding the moon. Somewhere in the night, a voice screeched a wordless hunting cry.

"I think you're going to want to revise that statement," Harsk said. "In three... two..."

UNCOMMON RACES

Some races are so uncommon that their very existence may be the subject of debate. Living on the fringes of the wilderness, in hidden grottos deep beneath the surface, under the ocean waves, or among the clouds of the night sky, few members of these races hear the call of adventure.

The 14 races presented in this chapter are all suitable to be played as PCs, but their rarity or isolation often sets them apart. While all are exotic, the reasons for their rarity are as diverse as their forms. The changeling, an offspring of a hag and a mortal lover, is an uncommon player race because of the improbability of such a foul union. Other races, like the kitsune, nagaji, samsarans, and wayangs, are often more common in certain far-flung lands but are rarely seen in most others. Still other races, like the gillmen, gripplis, merfolk, strix, and svirfneblin, typically distrust outsiders and keep to their own remote and insular communities.

While these races are rare, the same can be said of anyone willing to become an adventurer. Such an activity is not for those who crave a normal life, and these races also produce the rare spirit who strikes out into the wild places of the world in search of excitement and exploration. With your GM's permission, you can select any of the following uncommon races for your player character. Each racial section provides all the information you need to create a character along with a number of new options available to characters of that race. This chapter details the following uncommon races.

Changelings: The offspring of hags and their mortal lovers, changelings are abandoned and raised by foster parents. Always female, changelings all hear a spiritual call during puberty to find their true origins. Tall and slender, with dark hair and eyes mismatched in color, changelings are eerily attractive.

Duergar: Gray skinned, deep-dwelling dwarves who hate their lighter skinned cousins, duergar view life as constant toil ending only in death. Though these dwarves are typically evil, honor and keeping one's word means everything to them, and a rare few make loyal adventuring companions.

Gillmen: Survivors of a land-dwelling culture whose homeland was destroyed, gillmen were saved and transformed into an amphibious race by the aboleths. Though in many ways they appear nearly human, gillmen's bright purple eyes and gills set them apart from humanity. Reclusive and suspicious, gillmen know that one day the aboleths will call in the debt owed to them.

Gripplis: Furtive frogfolk with the ability to camouflage themselves among fens and swamps, gripplis typically keep to their wetland homes, only rarely interacting with the outside world. Their chief motivation for leaving their marshy environs is to trade in metal and gems.

Kitsune: These shapeshifting, foxlike folk share a love of mischief, art, and the finer things in life. They can appear as a single human as well as their true form, that of a foxlike humanoid. Kitsune are quick-witted, nimble, and gregarious, and because of this, a fair number of them become adventurers.

Merfolk: These creatures have the upper torso of a well-built and attractive humanoid and a lower half consisting of a finned tail. Though they are amphibious and extremely strong swimmers, their lower bodies make it difficult for them to move on land. Merfolk can be shy and reclusive. Typically keeping to themselves, they are distrustful of land-dwelling strangers.

Nagaji: It is believed that nagas created the nagaji as a race of servants and that the nagaji worship their creators as living gods. Due to their reptilian nature and strange mannerisms, these strange, scaly folk inspire fear and wonder in others not of their kind. They are resistant to both poison and mind-affecting magic.

Samsarans: Ghostly servants of karma, samsarans are creatures reincarnated hundreds if not thousands of times in the hope of reaching true enlightenment. Unlike humans and other races, these humanoids remember much of their past lives.

Strix: Hunted to dwindling numbers by humans, who see them as winged devils, strix are black-skinned masters of the nighttime sky. Their territorial conflicts have fueled their hatred for humans. This longstanding feud means that these nocturnal creatures often attack humans on sight.

Sulis: Also called suli-jann, these humanoids are the descendants of mortals and jann. These strong and charismatic individuals manifest mastery over elemental power in their adolescence, giving them the ability to manipulate earth, fire, ice, or electricity. This elemental power tends to be reflected in the suli's personality as well.

Svirfneblin: Gnomes who guard their hidden enclaves within dark tunnels and caverns deep under the earth, svirfneblin are as serious as their surface cousins are whimsical. They are resistant to the magic of the foul creatures that share their subterranean environs, and wield powerful protective magic. Svirfneblin are distrustful of outsiders and often hide at their approach.

Vanaras: These mischievous, monkeylike humanoids dwell in jungles and warm forests. Covered in soft fur and sporting prehensile tails and handlike feet, vanaras are strong climbers. These creatures are at home both on the ground and among the treetops.

Vishkanyas: Strangely beautiful on the outside and poisonous on the inside, vishkanyas see the world through slitted serpent eyes. Vishkanyas possess a serpent's grace and ability to writhe out of their enemies' grasp with ease. Vishkanyas have a reputation for being both seductive and manipulative. They can use their saliva or blood to poison their weapons.

Wayangs: The small wayangs are creatures of the Plane of Shadow. They are so attuned to shadow that it even shapes their philosophy, believing that upon death they merely merge back into darkness. The mysteries of their shadowy existence grant them the ability to gain healing from negative energy as well as positive energy.

GENERAL DESCRIPTION

Each race's entry begins with a brief and general description of the race followed by specific entries for the race's physical description, society, relations with other races, alignment and religion, and common motivation for adventuring members of the race. This description provides enough information to create a comprehensive background and personality for a character of this race.

RACIAL TRAITS

Each race's entry features a sidebar listing the race's standard racial traits. This information includes the race's type, size, vision, and base speed, as well as a number of other traits common to most members of the race. With your GM's permission, you will also have the option to exchange these standard racial traits for a number of alternate racial traits, the rules for which are provided in the section below.

ALTERNATE RACIAL TRAITS

Members of each race can swap standard racial traits for the alternate racial traits listed in this section. Each alternate racial trait lists which standard trait it replaces. The full rules for swapping traits can be found in Chapter 1: Core Races.

FAVORED CLASS OPTIONS

Each race can take the listed favored class options instead of the normal favored class rewards (either +1 hp or +1 skill rank). The full rules for favored class options can be found in Chapter 1: Core Races.

RACIAL ARCHETYPES

This section presents a single racial archetype for each of the uncommon races. Typically, only members of the section's race can take the listed archetype. An archetype usually features a thematic link to the race, granting it class features that complement the abilities and the background of the race. Because adventurers are often societal outliers, sometimes these archetypes feature a theme that is the exception to the norm for racial

tendencies. At the GM's discretion, a member of another race can take most of these archetypes either because they fit a character concept or because the character was raised or trained by a member of the race that can typically select the archetype. Such exceptions should be rare for the archetypes detailed in this chapter, however, since these races are not common in most campaigns. The following is a list of all the archetypes featured in this chapter, listed by race. The class for each archetype is listed in parentheses.

Changelings: Dreamweaver (witch)
Duergar: Gray disciple (monk)
Gillmen: Eldritch raider (rogue)
Gripplis: Bogborn alchemist (alchemist)
Kitsune: Kitsune trickster (rogue)
Merfolk: Wave warden (ranger)
Nagaji: Naga aspirant (druid)
Samsarans: Reincarnated oracle (oracle)
Strix: Airborne ambusher (fighter)
Sulis: Elemental knight (magus)
Svirfneblin: Deep bomber (alchemist)
Vanaras: Treetop monk (monk)
Vishkanyas: Deadly courtesan (rogue)
Wayangs: Shadow puppeteer (bard)

NEW RACIAL RULES

The final section of each race entry provides new rules options for the race other than archetypes in any of the following four categories. Not all the races in this chapter include entries for each of these sections.

Equipment: The equipment section for each race provides new rules for standard and alchemical equipment available to the race. Often such equipment is available on the open market and members of other races can purchase it, but many times, especially in the case of alchemical equipment, it has no effect, lesser effects, or even detrimental effects on members of other races.

Feats: This section provides a host of new racial feats for members of this race. These feats often play off a particular theme of the race and in many cases expand or empower racial traits of that race. All of these feats have the associated race in their prerequisites, so members of other races cannot take them.

Magic Items: Magic items provided in this section are often created and used exclusively by members of the race. Some have effects that interact with racial traits, but others have broader uses, and can be used by members of other races.

Spells: The spells in this section are common to spellcasting members of the race. Sometimes they only target members of the race, but often they are just the race's well-guarded secrets; members of other races can learn to cast them with GM permission.

Changelings

Changelings are the offspring of hags and their lovers taken through magic or madness. Dropped off on doorsteps of prospective foster parents, changelings are raised by strangers. Typically tall, slender, dark haired, and attractive, changelings otherwise resemble their fathers' race. They are always female, and their mismatched colored eyes and abnormally pale skin hint at their true heritage. At puberty, changelings receive "the call," a hypnotic spiritual voice that beckons them to travel and discover their true origins. Changelings who ignore this call choose their own destiny; those who heed it discover their "mother" and may come into great power by transforming into hags themselves.

ALTERNATE RACIAL TRAITS

The following racial traits may be selected instead of existing changeling racial traits. Consult your GM before selecting any of these new options.

Mist Child: When the changeling has concealment or total concealment, the miss chance of attacks against her increases by 5%. This racial trait replaces hulking changeling.

Object of Desire: The changeling adds +1 to her caster level when casting *charm person* and *charm monster*. This replaces green widow.

Ocean's Daughter: The changeling gains a +1 trait bonus on Swim checks. She automatically succeeds at Swim checks made to avoid nonlethal damage from swimming. This racial trait replaces sea lungs.

FAVORED CLASS OPTIONS

The following options are available to all changelings who have the listed favored class, and unless otherwise stated, the bonus applies each time you select the favored class reward.

Oracle: Add +1/2 to the oracle's level for the purpose of determining the effects of the oracle's curse ability.

Rogue: The rogue gains 1/6 of a new rogue talent.

Witch: Add one spell from the witch spell list to the witch's familiar. This spell must be at least one level below the highest spell level she can cast. If the witch ever replaces her familiar, the new familiar knows these bonus spells.

RACIAL ARCHETYPES

The following racial archetype is available to changelings.

CHANGELING RACIAL TRAITS

+2 Wisdom, +2 Charisma, –2 Constitution: Changelings are frail, but are clever and comely.

Medium: Changelings are Medium creatures and have no bonuses or penalties due to their size.

Humanoid: Changelings are humanoids with the changeling subtype.

Normal Speed: Changelings have a base speed of 30 feet.

Hag Racial Trait: The changeling inherits one of the following racial traits, depending on her mother's hag type:

Hulking Changeling (Annis Hag): The changeling gains a +1 racial bonus on melee damage.

Green Widow (Green Hag): The changeling gains a +2 racial bonus on Bluff checks against creatures that are sexually attracted to her.

Sea Lungs (Sea Hag): The changeling may hold her breath for a number of rounds equal to three times her Constitution before she risks drowning.

Claws: Changelings' fingernails are hard and sharp, granting them two claw attacks (1d4 points of damage each).

Natural Armor: Changelings have a +1 natural armor bonus.

Darkvision: Changelings can see in the dark up to 60 feet.

Languages: Changelings begin play speaking Common and the primary language of their host society. Changelings with high Intelligence scores can choose from the following: Aklo, Draconic, Dwarven, Elven, Giant, Gnoll, Goblin, and Orc.

Dreamweaver (Witch)

A changeling dreamweaver draws upon her hag heritage to ply the dream realms in order to touch mortal minds and souls, for good or ill. A dreamweaver witch has the following class features.

Class Skills: The dreamweaver adds Sense Motive to her list of class skills and removes Healing from her list of class skills.

Patron: A dreamweaver's patron is normally portents or stars (*Pathfinder RPG Ultimate Magic* 83).

Spells: A dreamweaver replaces some of her patron's spells with the following: 2nd—*sow thoughts* (see below), 4th—*dust of twilight* (*Pathfinder RPG Advanced Player's Guide*), 6th—*deep slumber*, 8th—*modify memory*, 10th—*dream*, 12th—*cloak of dreams* (*Advanced Player's Guide*), 14th—*ethereal jaunt*, 16th—*moment of prescience*, 18th—*astral projection*.

Dream Spinner (Su): At 2nd level, when a dreamweaver casts a mind-affecting spell on a target that is sleeping because of her slumber hex or a spell she cast, she adds +1 to the mind-affecting spell's DC. If the target succeeds at the saving throw against the spell, it does not wake up, nor does it have any recollection of having resisted a spell. If appropriate, the dreamweaver may incorporate elements of a mind-affecting spell (i.e., *sow thought*, *suggestion*, and so on) into the target's subconscious so it believes the spell's effects originated in its dreams (the details of how these elements fit into the dream is up to the GM). This ability replaces the witch's hex gained at 2nd level.

Dream Thief (Su): At 6th level, a dreamweaver can alter the sleeping mind of any creature that is sleeping because of her slumber hex or a spell she cast. She can reshape one of the target's memories as if using *modify memory*. Alternatively, she may insert herself into the dreaming memories of the target, prompting the target's mind to show her some specific information; the dreamer's subconscious may resist, or try to deceive her with out-of-context memories, similar to the way a corpse can resist when questioned with *speak with dead*. A Will save negates either effect (DC equal to that of the witch's hex). Whether or not the save is successful, a creature cannot be the target of this hex again for 1 day. This ability replaces the witch's hex gained at 6th level.

Dream Possession (Su): At 10th level, a dreamweaver can take control of any creature that is sleeping because of her slumber hex or a spell she cast. This effect functions as *magic jar*, using the witch's familiar acting as the soul receptacle. A Will save negates either effect (DC equal to that of the witch's hex). Whether or not the save is successful, a creature cannot be the target of this hex again for 1 day. This ability replaces the witch's hex gained at 10th level.

Hexes: The following hexes complement the dreamweaver archetype: charm, slumber (*Advanced Player's Guide*); beast of ill-omen (*Ultimate Magic*).

Major Hexes: The following major hexes complement the dreamweaver archetype: nightmare, vision (*Advanced Player's Guide*).

Grand Hexes: The following major hexes complement the dreamweaver archetype: eternal slumber (*Advanced Player's Guide*); dire prophecy (*Ultimate Magic*).

NEW RACIAL RULES

The following options are available to changelings. At the GM's discretion, other appropriate races may also make use of some of these.

Changeling Feats

Changelings have access to the following feat.

Mother's Gift

You inherit a special boon from your hag parent.

Prerequisite: Changeling.

Benefit: Your dark legacy manifests in one of the following ways. You choose the manifestation when you choose the feat, and once selected it cannot be changed.

Hag Claws (Ex): You gain a +1 bonus on attack and damage rolls with your claws.

Surprisingly Tough (Ex): Your natural armor bonus increases by +1.

Uncanny Resistance (Su): You gain spell resistance equal to 6 + your character level.

Special: You can gain this feat up to three times. Its effects do not stack. Each time you take the feat, you must select a different manifestation.

Changeling Spells

Changelings have access to the following new spell.

SOW THOUGHT

School enchantment (compulsion) [mind-affecting]; **Level** bard 1, sorcerer/wizard 1, witch 1

Casting Time 1 standard action

Components V, S

Range close (25 ft. + 5 ft./2 levels)

Target one creature

Duration permanent

Save Will negates; **Spell Resistance** yes

You plant an idea, concept, or suspicion in the mind of the subject. The target genuinely believes that the idea is his own, but is not required to act upon it. If the idea is contrary to the target's normal thoughts (such as making a paladin think, "I should murder my friends") the target may suspect mind-altering magic is at play. The idea must be fairly clear, enough so that it can be conveyed in one or two sentences. You do not need to share a common language for the spell to succeed, but without a common language you can only sow the most basic rudimentary ideas.

DUERGAR

Duergar dwell in subterranean caverns far from the touch of light. They detest all races living beneath the sun, but that hatred pales beside their loathing of their surface-dwarf cousins. Dwarves and duergar once were one race, but the dwarves left the deeps for their mountain strongholds. Duergar still consider themselves the only true dwarves, and the rightful heirs of all beneath the world's surface. In appearance, duergar resemble gray-skinned dwarves, bearded but bald, with cold, lightless eyes. They favor taking captives in battle over wanton slaughter, save for surface dwarves, who are slain without hesitation. Duergar view life as ceaseless toil ended only by death. Though few can be described as anything other than vile and cruel, duergar still value honor and rarely break their word.

ALTERNATE RACIAL TRAITS

The following racial traits may be selected instead of existing duergar racial traits. Consult your GM before selecting any of these new options.

Blood Enmity: Duergar have long warred against their dwarven cousins and the hated drow. Duergar with this racial trait receive a +1 racial bonus on attack rolls against humanoid creatures of the dwarf or elf subtypes. This racial trait replaces the *invisibility* spell-like ability.

Daysighted: The cruel light of the sun harms some duergar less than others. Such duergar lack the light sensitivity racial trait, but have darkvision of only 60 feet.

Deep Magic: Duergar spellcasters labor long to overcome the inborn spell resistance held by so many of their underground foes. Duergar with this racial trait receive a +2 racial bonus on caster level checks made to overcome spell resistance and a +2 racial bonus on dispel checks. This racial trait replaces the *enlarge person* and *invisibility* spell-like abilities.

Dwarf Traits: Duergar can select any dwarf racial trait that replaces stability. They can select dwarf racial traits that replace the hardy dwarf racial trait by giving up duergar immunities instead.

FAVORED CLASS OPTIONS

The following options are available to all duergar who have the listed favored class, and unless otherwise stated, the bonus applies each time you select the favored class reward.

Cleric: Add a +1/2 bonus on checks made to craft magic items.

Fighter: Add +1 to the fighter's CMD when resisting a bull rush or trip attempt.

Inquisitor: Add +1/6 to the number of times per day the inquisitor can use the judgment class feature.

DUERGAR RACIAL TRAITS

+2 Constitution, +2 Wisdom, –4 Charisma: Duergar are hearty and observant, but also belligerent.

Medium: Duergar are Medium creatures and have no bonuses or penalties due to their size.

Dwarf: Duergar are humanoids with the dwarf subtype.

Slow and Steady: Duergar have a base speed of 20 feet, but their speed is never modified by armor or encumbrance.

Superior Darkvision: Duergar can see in the dark up to 120 feet.

Duergar Immunities: Duergar are immune to paralysis, phantasms, and poison. They gain a +2 racial bonus on saves against spells and spell-like abilities.

Stability: Duergar receive a +4 racial bonus to their CMD against bull rush or trip attempts while on solid ground.

Spell-Like Abilities: A duergar can use *enlarge person* and *invisibility* once each per day, using its character level as its caster level and affecting itself only.

Light Sensitivity: Duergar are dazzled in areas of bright light.

Languages: Duergar begin play speaking Common, Dwarven, and Undercommon. Duergar with high Intelligence scores can choose from the following: Aklo, Draconic, Giant, Goblin, Orc, and Terran.

RACIAL ARCHETYPES

The following racial archetype is available to duergar.

Gray Disciple (Monk)

The gray disciple contemplates the inner voice of duergar magic and the silent eternity of stone, mastering these dual mysteries and combining them to deadly effect.

Fade from Sight (Sp): At 4th level, as a swift action, the gray disciple can become invisible (as the *invisibility* spell) for 1 round by spending 1 *ki* point. To use this ability, the gray disciple must already have *invisibility* as a spell-like ability. This ability replaces slow fall and still mind.

Gray Heart (Sp): At 6th level, as a swift action, the gray disciple can enlarge himself (as the *enlarge person* spell) for 1 minute by spending 1 *ki* point. To use this ability, the gray disciple must already have *enlarge person* available as a spell-like ability. This ability replaces high jump and the bonus feat gained at 6th level.

Born in Darkness (Sp): At 7th level, as a standard action, the gray disciple can radiate *darkness* (as the spell, except originating from the disciple's person) for 1 round per level by spending 1 *ki* point. This ability replaces wholeness of body.

Earth Glide (Su): At 12th level, as a swift action, the gray disciple can spend a *ki* point to walk through solid stone for 1 round. This functions as the earth glide universal monster ability. The gray disciple may continue earth gliding as long as he spends 1 *ki* point every round as a swift action. If he ceases earth gliding within a solid object, he is violently ejected and takes 5d6 points of damage. The gray disciple is not harmed by damage caused to material he is earth gliding through, but a *stone to flesh* spell cast upon it causes violent ejection as described above. This ability replaces abundant step.

Entomb (Su): At 15th level, a gray disciple can phase a foe into solid rock, killing it instantly. To use this ability, he expends 1 ki point as part of a bull rush or reposition combat maneuver against a creature adjacent to unworked earth or stone. If the attempt succeeds, the gray disciple pushes his foe inside the rock using his earth glide ability. If the creature succeeds at a Reflex save (DC 10 + 1/2 the gray disciple's monk level + the gray disciple's Wisdom modifier), it is ejected in the nearest open space and takes 5d6 points of damage. If it fails, it dies instantly as its body merges with the surrounding stone. Entomb is usable once per day, but a failed bull rush or reposition attempt does not count as a use of the ability. Entomb has no effect on creatures that can earth glide, are incorporeal, or

can otherwise can survive merging with a solid object. This ability replaces quivering palm.

Earthen Thrall (Sp): At 17th level, a gray disciple can attempt to control a creature with the earth subtype once per day. This ability is treated as *dominate monster* (DC 10 + 1/2 the gray disciple's monk level + the gray disciple's Wisdom modifier), but is only effective against creatures with the earth subtype, and the gray disciple can keep only a single creature enthralled. If he attempts to control a second creature with this ability, the first creature is automatically released from domination whether or not the second attempt succeeds. This ability replaces tongue of the sun and moon and empty body.

NEW RACIAL RULES

The following options are available to duergar. At the GM's discretion, other appropriate races may make use of these options.

Duergar Equipment

Duergar have access to the following equipment.

Spellscorch: Refined from rare underground crystals, this poison causes a burning headache that impedes spellcasting. If the target fails its Fortitude save, for the next minute the target must make a Concentration check with a DC equal to 10 + spell level to cast a spell, and all other concentration checks to cast spells take a –5 penalty.

Duergar Feats

Duergar have access to the following feats.

Giant Steps

When enlarged, your speed increases.

Prerequisites: Duergar, slow and steady racial trait.

Benefit: When your size increases to Large or larger, your base speed increases by 20 feet. This increase applies only if the effect that changed your size does not alter your speed.

Lingering Invisibility

You remain briefly translucent after losing *invisibility*.

Prerequisite: Duergar.

Benefit: When your *invisibility* ends, you gain concealment for 1 round per minute of duration the invisibility effect had remaining (minimum 1 round). This only occurs if the invisibility is from your racial spell-like ability or a spell you cast. Effects that negate invisibility negate this concealment.

TABLE 3-1: DUERGAR POISON

Name	Type	Fort DC	Onset	Frequency	Effect	Cure	Cost
Spellscorch	injury	14	—	1/rd. for 4 rds.	see text	1 save	200 gp

GILLMEN

Gillmen are the remnants of a race of surface-dwelling humanoids whose homeland was drowned in a great cataclysm at the hands of the aboleth. The aboleths rescued a few survivors, warping them into an amphibious race to serve as emissaries to the surface world. Modern gillmen remain reclusive and suspicious, scarred by both the loss of their ancient heritage and the sure knowledge that aboleths do nothing without expecting to profit from it. Physically gillmen have expressive brows, pale skin, dark hair, and bright purple eyes. Three slim gills mark each side of their necks, near the shoulder, but they are otherwise close enough in appearance to humans that they can pass as such (for a time) without fear of detection.

ALTERNATE RACIAL TRAITS

The following racial traits may be selected instead of existing gillman racial traits. Consult your GM before selecting any of these new options.

Riverfolk: Some gillmen groups live in colonies along vast riverways, and have adapted to living on land for much longer periods. Gillmen with this trait have a thin coating of natural oil that keeps their skin from cracking even without water. However, this natural oil also makes such gillmen particularly susceptible to flames, and they gain vulnerability to fire. This racial trait replaces water dependent.

Slimehunter: Gillmen with this trait are from lineages that have fought against aboleths since the aberrations rescued their human ancestors. They receive a +2 racial bonus on saving throws against aboleth spells, spell-like abilities, and supernatural abilities. This racial trait replaces enchantment resistance.

Throwback: Some gillmen are throwbacks to their land-dwelling human ancestors. Gillmen with this racial trait do not have the amphibious trait, have the human subtype instead of the aquatic subtype, have no swim speed or bonuses to the Swim skill, cannot breathe water, and do not have the water dependent racial trait.

FAVORED CLASS OPTIONS

The following options are available to all gillmen who have the listed favored class, and unless otherwise stated, the bonus applies each time you select the favored class reward.

Fighter: Add +1 to the fighter's CMD when resisting two combat maneuvers of the character's choice.

Rogue: The rogue gains 1/6 of a new rogue talent.

Sorcerer: Add one spell known from the sorcerer spell list. This spell must be at least one level below the highest spell level the sorcerer can cast.

Wizard: Add one spell from the wizard spell list to the wizard's spellbook. This spell must be at least one level below the highest spell level he can cast.

GILLMAN RACIAL TRAITS

+2 Constitution, +2 Charisma, –2 Wisdom: Gillmen are vigorous and beautiful, but their domination by the aboleths has made them weak-willed.

Medium: Gillmen are Medium creatures and have no bonuses or penalties due to their size.

Aquatic: Gillmen are humanoids with the aquatic subtype.

Normal Speed: Gillmen have a base speed of 30 feet on land. As aquatic creatures, they also have a swim speed of 30 feet, can move in water without making Swim checks, and always treat Swim as a class skill.

Amphibious: Gillmen have the aquatic subtype, but can breathe both water and air.

Enchantment Resistance: Gillmen gain a +2 racial saving throw bonus against non-aboleth enchantment spells and effects, but take a –2 penalty on such saving throws against aboleth sources.

Water Dependent: A gillman's body requires constant submersion in fresh or salt water. Gillmen who spend more than 1 day without fully submerging themselves in water risk internal organ failure, painful cracking of the skin, and death within 4d6 hours.

Languages: Gillmen begin play speaking Common and Aboleth. Gillmen with high Intelligence scores can choose from the following: Aklo, Aquan, Draconic, and Elven.

RACIAL ARCHETYPES

The following racial archetype is available to gillmen.

Eldritch Raider (Rogue)

An eldritch raider is a rogue who seeks to unravel the mysteries of the destruction of the gillmen's homeland. They explore old ruins that date back to the days of the old human empire and track down relics and lore from its glory days. An eldritch raider has the following class features.

Class Skills: An eldritch raider adds Knowledge (arcana), Knowledge (history), and Spellcraft to her list of class skills and removes Disguise, Perform, and Sleight of Hand from her list of class skills.

Skill Ranks per Level: 6 + Int modifier.

Detect Magic (Sp): At 2nd level, an eldritch raider gains the ability to use *detect magic* at will. The eldritch raider treats her rogue level as her caster level for this ability. This ability counts as the minor magic rogue talent for purposes of qualifying for other rogue talents. This ability replaces the rogue talent rogues gained at 2nd level.

Eldritch Intuition (Ex): At 3rd level, an eldritch raider gains an intuitive sense that allows her to more easily activate sorcerer and wizard spell completion and spell trigger items. She gains a +1 bonus on Use Magic Device checks for this purpose. This bonus increases to +2 at 6th level, +3 at 9th level, +4 at 12th level, +5 at 15th level, and +6 at 18th level. This ability replaces the trap sense class feature.

New Talents: An eldritch raider has access to the following new advanced talents when selecting rogue advanced talents.

Major Eldritch Magic (Sp): The eldritch raider gains the ability to cast a 3rd-level spell from the sorcerer/wizard spell list two times per day as a spell-like ability. The caster level for this ability is equal to her rogue level. The save DC for this spell is 13 + her Intelligence modifier. The eldritch raider must have an Intelligence of at least 13 to select this talent. The eldritch raider must have the major magic, minor eldritch magic, and minor magic rogue talents before choosing this talent.

Minor Eldritch Magic (Sp): The eldritch raider gains the ability to cast a 2nd-level spell from the sorcerer/wizard spell list two times per day as a spell-like ability. The caster level for this ability is equal to her rogue level. The save DC for this spell is 12 + her Intelligence modifier. The eldritch raider must have an Intelligence of at least 12 to select this talent. The eldritch raider must have the major magic and minor magic rogue talents before choosing this talent.

Rogue Talents: The following rogue talents complement the eldritch raider archetype: major magic, minor magic,

quick disable, trap spotter (*Core Rulebook*); fast picks (*Advanced Player's Guide*); black market connections, esoteric scholar, ninja trick (slow metabolism, wall climber) (*Ultimate Combat*).

Advanced Talents: The following advanced rogue talents complement the eldritch raider archetype: dispelling attack, improved evasion, slippery mind (*Core Rulebook*); major eldritch magic, minor eldritch magic (*Advanced Race Guide*); thoughtful reexamination (*Advanced Player's Guide*); familiar, hard to fool (*Ultimate Combat*).

NEW RACIAL RULES

The following options are available to gillmen. At the GM's discretion, other appropriate races may make use of these as well.

Gillman Equipment

Gillmen have access to the following equipment.

Sea-Knife: A sea-knife is a long-handled weapon with a short blade. It is designed to be strapped to the ankle or foot of the wielder, pointing downward and jutting out beyond the wearer's leg. Donning or removing a sea-knife is a full-round action. The wearer cannot use a leg with a sea-knife strapped to it for walking or running. A sea-knife can be used as a light melee weapon when the wielder is swimming, flying, or prone. This allows the wielder to use a two-handed weapon, or wield a weapon with one hand and carry a shield, and still make off-hand attacks with the sea-knife. Attacks made with a sea-knife take a –2 circumstance penalty on attack rolls in addition to all other attack penalties.

Gillman Spells

Gillmen have access to the following new spell.

ABOLETH'S LUNG

School transmutation; **Level** cleric 2, druid 2, sorcerer/wizard 2, witch 2

Casting Time 1 standard action

Components V, S, M/DF (piece of seaweed)

Range touch

Target living creatures touched

Duration 1 hour/level; see text

Saving Throw Will negates; **Spell Resistance** yes

The targets are able to breathe water, freely. However, they can no longer breathe air. Divide the duration evenly among all the creatures you touch. This spell has no effect on creatures that can already breathe water.

TABLE 3-2: GILLMAN WEAPON

Martial Weapons	Cost	Dmg (S)	Dmg (M)	Critical	Range	Weight	Type	Special
Sea-knife	8 gp	1d3	1d4	19–20/×2	—	1 lb.	S	—

GRIPPLIS

Gripplis stand just over 2 feet tall and have mottled green-and-brown skin. Most gripplis are primitive hunter gatherers, living on large insects and fish found near their treetop homes, and are unconcerned about events outside their swamps. The rare grippli who leaves the safety of the swamp tends to be a ranger or alchemist seeking to trade for metals and gems.

ALTERNATE RACIAL TRAITS

The following racial traits may be selected instead of existing grippli racial traits. Consult your GM before selecting any of these new options.

Glider: Gripplis' aerodynamic bodies and thick webbing between the toes enable a falling grippli to treat the distance fallen as half the actual distance. The grippli can steer himself while falling, moving horizontally up to a number of feet equal to half the vertical distance fallen. The grippli cannot use this trait if it is wearing heavy armor, is carrying a heavy load, or is unable to react to the fall (such as being helpless). This racial trait replaces swamp stride.

Jumper: Gripplis with this trait are always considered to have a running start when making Acrobatics checks to jump. This racial trait replaces camouflage.

Princely: The grippli gains proficiency with rapiers and a +2 racial bonus on Diplomacy and Intimidate checks. This racial trait replaces swamp stride and weapon familiarity.

Toxic Skin (Ex): Once per day as a swift action, a grippli can create a poison that can be applied to a weapon or delivered as a touch attack. Alternatively, the grippli can smear the poison on its own body as a standard action, affecting the first creature to hit it with an unarmed strike or natural weapon. The poison loses its potency after 1 hour. The grippli is immune to its own poison. This racial trait replaces swamp stride and camouflage.

Grippli Poison: Skin or weapon—contact or injury; *save* Fort DC 10 + 1/2 the grippli's Hit Dice plus its Constitution modifier; *frequency* 1/round for 6 rounds; *effect* 1d2 Dexterity damage; *cure* 1 save.

FAVORED CLASS OPTIONS

The following options are available to all gripplis who have the listed favored class, and unless otherwise stated, the bonus applies each time you select the favored class reward.

Alchemist: Add +1/4 to the number of toxic skin uses per day.

Druid: Add a +1/2 bonus on concentration checks. This bonus doubles in a forest or swamp terrain.

Gunslinger: Add a +1/4 bonus on attack rolls when making a utility shot or a dead shot.

Rogue: Add a +1/2 bonus on Perception checks while in a forest or swamp.

Ranger: Add a +1 racial bonus on Swim skill checks. When this bonus reaches +8, the ranger gains a swim speed of 15 feet (this does not grant the ranger another +8 racial bonus on Swim checks).

GRIPPLI RACIAL TRAITS

+2 Dexterity, +2 Wisdom, –2 Strength: Gripplis are nimble and alert, but spindly.

Small: Gripplis are Small creatures and gain a +1 size bonus to their AC, a +1 size bonus on attack rolls, a –1 penalty to their CMB and CMD, and a +4 size bonus on Stealth checks.

Grippli: Gripplis are humanoids with the grippli subtype.

Normal Speed: Gripplis have a base speed of 30 feet and a climb speed of 20 feet.

Darkvision: Gripplis can see in the dark up to 60 feet.

Camouflage: Gripplis receive a +4 racial bonus on Stealth checks in marshes and forested areas.

Swamp Stride (Ex): A grippli can move through difficult terrain at its normal speed while within a swamp. Magically altered terrain affects a grippli normally.

Weapon Familiarity: Gripplis are proficient with nets.

Languages: Gripplis begin play speaking Common and Grippli. Gripplis with high Intelligence scores can choose from the following: Boggard, Draconic, Elven, Gnome, Goblin, and Sylvan.

RACIAL ARCHETYPES

The following racial archetype is available to gripplis.

Bogborn Alchemist (Alchemist)

Some grippli alchemists are particularly attuned to the swamps and the dangerous creatures that inhabit them; these serve as their laboratories and research subjects, respectively. These bogborn alchemists have the following class features.

Class Skills: A bogborn alchemist adds Swim to his list of class skills.

Amphibious Mutagen (Ex): At 1st level, when a bogborn alchemist uses a mutagen, he may choose to have his mutagen form enhanced for aquatic movement. This gives him the amphibious special quality, his feet elongate, and the webbing between his fingers and toes expands, granting a swim speed of 15 feet. This replaces throw anything.

Discovery Options: A bogborn alchemist can select the toxic skin grippli racial trait in place of an alchemical discovery.

Discoveries: The following discoveries complement the bogborn alchemist archetype: chameleon (*Advanced Race Guide*); concentrate poison, sticky poison (*Advanced Player's Guide*); nauseating flesh, poison conversion (*Ultimate Combat*); bottled ooze, tanglefoot bomb, tentacle (*Ultimate Magic*).

NEW RACIAL RULES

The following options are available to gripplis. At the GM's discretion, other appropriate races may also make use of some of these.

Grippli Equipment

Gripplis have access to the following equipment.

Black Marsh Spider Venom: This potent spider venom causes victims to become disoriented and lose muscle control until eventually they collapse.

Grippli Feats

Gripplis have access to the following feat.

Agile Tongue

Your long pink tongue is capable of manipulating small items and even stealing objects.

Prerequisite: Grippli.

Benefit: You have a prehensile tongue with a range of 10 feet. You can pick up items weighing no more than 5 pounds, make Sleight of Hand checks, perform the steal or disarm combat maneuvers, or make melee touch attacks with your tongue.

GRIPPLI DISCOVERIES

The following new discoveries can be taken by any alchemist who meets the prerequisites, but are more common among gripplis.

Chameleon (Su): An alchemist with this discovery can shift the colors of his skin and equipment to blend in with the surrounding terrain. He gains a +4 enhancement bonus on Stealth checks. At 10th level, the bonus on Stealth checks increases to +8.

Deadly Excretions (Ex): When using his toxic skin ability, the alchemist can choose to excrete a Constitution poison instead of a Dexterity poison. This poison works the same as the normal grippli toxic skin poison except that a failed save deals 1 point of Constitution damage. The alchemist must be at least 8th level and must have the toxic skin racial trait before selecting this discovery.

Underwater Demolition (Ex): The alchemist gains the ability to throw bombs underwater (normally, thrown weapons cannot be used underwater), including throwing from the air into the water. If the bomb travels through water, the range increment is reduced to 5 feet.

Grippli Magic Items

Gripplis have access to the following magic item.

BUBBLE VAULT
Aura faint transmutation; **CL** 5th
Slot none; **Price** 1,500 gp; **Weight** —
DESCRIPTION
This tiny pearl swells to form a 1-foot-diameter soap-like bubble when placed in water. Up to 5 cubic feet of goods can be placed inside the *bubble vault*. On command, the bubble sinks to the bottom of the water, automatically burying itself 1 foot deep in the bottom ground if there is mud or other loose material present. If the command word is spoken three times within 30 feet of the bubble, it rises to the surface of the water, at which time it can be opened and the items within it retrieved. Once opened, the bubble reverts to its pearl form for 24 hours. The bubble is watertight but does not otherwise magically protect or preserve its contents. If forced open, it has hardness 1 and 5 hit points.
CONSTRUCTION
Requirements Craft Wondrous Item, *shrink item*, *unseen servant*; **Cost** 750 gp

TABLE 3-3: GRIPPLI POISON

Name	Type	Fort DC	Onset	Frequency	Effect	Cure	Cost
Black spider marsh poison	injury	14	—	1/rd. for 6 rds.	1d4 Dex and confused for 1 rd.	2 consecutive saves	800 gp

KITSUNE

Kitsune, or fox folk, are vulpine shapeshifters known for their love of both trickery and art. Kitsune possess two forms: that of an attractive human of slender build with salient eyes, and their true form of an anthropomorphic fox. Despite an irrepressible penchant for deception, kitsune prize loyalty and make true companions. They delight in the arts, particularly riddles and storytelling, and settle in ancestral clans, taking their wisdom from both the living and spirits.

Quick-witted and nimble, kitsune make excellent bards and rogues. It is not uncommon for one to pursue sorcery, while those few born with white fur and pale eyes usually become oracles.

ALTERNATE RACIAL TRAITS

The following racial traits may be selected instead of existing kitsune racial traits. Consult your GM before selecting any of these new options.

Fast Shifter (Su): You were born with an innate talent for switching between your natural forms. Using your racial change shape ability is a move action instead of a standard action. This racial trait replaces kitsune magic.

Gregarious (Ex): Even among your own kind, your gift for making friends stands out. Whenever you successfully use Diplomacy to win over an individual, that creature takes a –2 penalty to resist any of your Charisma-based skill checks for the next 24 hours. This racial trait replaces agile.

FAVORED CLASS OPTIONS

The following options are available to all kitsune who have the listed favored class, and unless otherwise stated, the bonus applies each time you select the favored class reward.

Bard: Add a +1/2 bonus on Bluff checks to lie and a +1/2 bonus on Diplomacy checks to gather information.

Druid: Add a +1/2 bonus on Diplomacy and Intimidate checks to change a creature's attitude.

Oracle: Reduce the penalty for not being proficient for one weapon by 1. When the nonproficiency penalty for a weapon becomes 0 because of this ability, the oracle is treated as having the appropriate Martial or Exotic Weapon Proficiency feat for that weapon.

Rogue: The rogue gains 1/6 of a new rogue talent.

Sorcerer: Add +1/4 to the DC of enchantment spells.

RACIAL ARCHETYPES

The following racial archetype is available to kitsune.

KITSUNE RACIAL TRAITS

+2 Dexterity, +2 Charisma, –2 Strength: Kitsune are agile and companionable, but tend to be physically weak.

Medium: Kitsune are Medium creatures and have no bonuses or penalties due to their size.

Kitsune: Kitsune are humanoids with the kitsune and shapechanger subtypes.

Normal Speed: Kitsune have a base speed of 30 feet.

Low-Light Vision (Ex): Kitsune can see twice as far as humans in conditions of dim light.

Change Shape (Su): A kitsune can assume the appearance of a specific single human form of the same sex. The kitsune always takes this specific form when she uses this ability. A kitsune in human form cannot use her bite attack, but gains a +10 racial bonus on Disguise checks made to appear human. Changing shape is a standard action. This ability otherwise functions as *alter self*, except that the kitsune does not adjust her ability scores.

Agile (Ex): Kitsune receive a +2 racial bonus on Acrobatics checks.

Kitsune Magic (Ex/Sp): Kitsune add +1 to the DC of any saving throws against enchantment spells that they cast. Kitsune with a Charisma score of 11 or higher gain the following spell-like ability: 3/day—*dancing lights*.

Natural Weapons (Ex): In her natural form, a kitsune has a bite attack that deals 1d4 points of damage.

Languages: Kitsune begin play speaking Common and Sylvan. Kitsune with high Intelligence scores can choose from the following: any human language, Aklo, Celestial, Elven, Gnome, and Tengu.

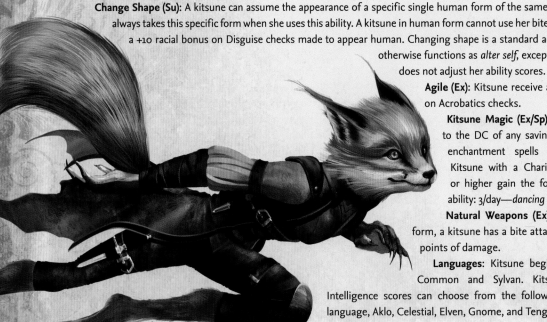

Kitsune Trickster (Rogue)

The kitsune trickster combines her sharpened wit with minor arcane powers of charm and persuasion. She uses her talents to spin convincing lies, riddles, and stories. A trickster has the following class features.

Kitsune's Guile (Ex): At 1st level, a trickster relies on her intellect as much as her personality. She adds her Intelligence modifier on Bluff, Diplomacy, Disguise, and Sense Motive checks. This ability replaces trapfinding.

Kitsune's Charm (Sp): At 3rd level, a kitsune trickster can use *charm person* once per day as a spell-like ability (caster level equal to her rogue level – 2). At 6th level, and every three levels thereafter, the kitsune trickster gains an additional daily use of this ability. This ability replaces trap sense.

Rogue Talents: The following rogue talents complement the kitsune trickster archetype: major magic, minor magic (*Core Rulebook*); false friend, obfuscate story, steal the story (see below); charmer, coax information, honeyed words (*Advanced Player's Guide*); convincing lie (*Ultimate Combat*).

Advanced Talents: The following advanced rogue talents complement the kitsune trickster archetype: skill mastery, slippery mind (*Core Rulebook*); master of disguise (*Advanced Player's Guide*); rumormonger (*Ultimate Combat*).

NEW RACIAL RULES

The following options are available to kitsune. At the GM's discretion, other appropriate races may also make use of some of these.

Kitsune Feats

Kitsune have access to the following feats. See page 5 of *Pathfinder Player Companion: Dragon Empires Primer* for the Fox Shape, Swift Kitsune Shapechanger, and Vulpine Pounce feats.

Magical Tail

You grow an extra tail that represents your growing magical powers.

Prerequisite: Kitsune.

Benefit: You gain a new spell-like ability, each usable twice per day, from the following list, in order: *disguise self, charm person, misdirection, invisibility, suggestion, displacement, confusion, dominate person*. For example, the first time you select this feat, you gain *disguise self* 2/day; the second time you select this feat, you gain *charm person* 2/day. Your caster level for these spells is equal to your Hit Dice. The DCs for these abilities are Charisma-based.

Special: You may select this feat up to eight times. Each time you take it, you gain an additional ability as described above.

Realistic Likeness

When you are in human form, you can take the shape of a specific individual.

ROGUE TALENTS

The following new rogue talents can be taken by any rogue who meets the prerequisites, but they are more common among kitsune.

False Friend (Ex): A rogue with this talent gains a +4 bonus when making Bluff checks to convince someone she has never met or who doesn't know her well that they are previously acquainted or know each other well.

Obfuscate Story (Ex): While another individual attempts to give an account of an event, the rogue makes an opposed Diplomacy check to deftly interject comments or statements over the course of the storytelling that cause the individual to muddle his ability to recall accurate or specific details. If the rogue succeeds, her target remains unaware that the rogue's interjections caused the confusion. However, if she fails, the target is allowed a Sense Motive check (DC equal to the rogue's failed Diplomacy check) to figure out that she made deliberate attempts to confuse the story.

Steal the Story (Ex): After muddling another's account using obfuscate story, the rogue may make another opposed Diplomacy check to alter the details further in order to discredit, insult, or humiliate the target. If the check succeeds, the target takes a penalty on Diplomacy and Intimidate checks against anyone who heard the altered story. This penalty is equal to the rogue's Intelligence, Wisdom, or Charisma bonus (whichever is highest), and lasts until the target is able to repair his reputation or discredit the rogue. The rogue must have the obfuscate story talent to select this talent.

Prerequisite: Kitsune.

Benefit: You can precisely mimic the physical features of any individual you have encountered. When you use your racial change shape ability, you can attempt to take the form of an individual, granting you a +10 circumstance bonus on Disguise checks made to fool others with your impersonation.

Kitsune Magic Items

Kitsune have access to the following magic item.

KITSUNE STAR GEM

Aura faint transmutation; **CL** 1st (1st), 3rd (2nd), or 5th (3rd)
Slot none; **Price** 750 gp (1st), 3,000 gp (2nd), 6,750 gp (3rd);
Weight —

DESCRIPTION

This magical jewel glows like *faerie fire*, shedding light as a candle. It acts as *pearl of power*, except it only allows a kitsune to recover a spent use of a spell-like ability of the appropriate spell level.

CONSTRUCTION

Requirements Craft Wondrous Item, creator must be a kitsune; **Cost** 365 gp (1st), 1,500 gp (2nd), or 3,375 gp (3rd)

MERFOLK

Merfolk have the upper torsos of well-built and attractive humans and lower halves consisting of the tail and fins of a great fish. Their hair and scales span a wide range of hues, with merfolk in a given region closely resembling each other. Merfolk can breathe air freely but move on dry land only with difficulty, and rarely spend long periods out of water. As a race, merfolk are insular and distrustful of strangers, but individuals, especially adventuring merfolk, break the mold and can be quite garrulous. Merfolk concern themselves more with nature and the arts than with morality and ethical debates, and have a strong inclination toward neutral alignments.

ALTERNATE RACIAL TRAITS

The following racial traits may be selected instead of existing merfolk racial traits. Consult your GM before selecting any of these new options.

Darkvision: Some merfolk favor the lightless depths over shallower waters. Merfolk with this racial trait gain darkvision with a range of 60 feet and light sensitivity. This racial trait replaces low-light vision.

Seasinger: The beautiful voices of the merfolk are legendary. A seasinger gains a +2 racial bonus on Perform (sing) checks and a +1 racial bonus to the save DC of language-dependent spells. This racial trait replaces low-light vision.

Strongtail: A few merfolk have broad, strong tails that are more suited for land travel than the typical merfolk tail. Merfolk with this racial trait have a land speed of 15 feet and a swim speed of 30 feet.

FAVORED CLASS OPTIONS

The following options are available to all merfolk who have the listed favored class, and unless otherwise stated, the bonus applies each time you select the favored class reward.

Druid: Add +1 hit point to the druid's animal companion. If the merfolk ever replaces her animal companion, the new animal companion gains these bonus hit points.

Ranger: Add +1 hit point to the ranger's animal companion. If the ranger ever replaces his animal companion, the new animal companion gains these bonus hit points.

Sorcerer: Add +1/2 to the sorcerer's caster level when determining the range of any spells with the water descriptor.

RACIAL ARCHETYPES

The following racial archetype is available to merfolk.

Wave Warden (Ranger)

The wave warden patrols beneath the sea, preserving the safety and secrets of merfolk communities. Though he fares best beneath the water, dry land is no haven to his quarry.

Deep Sentinel (Ex): A wave warden adds half his level (minimum +1) on Perception checks made to notice creatures underwater. This ability replaces track.

MERFOLK RACIAL TRAITS

+2 Dexterity, +2 Constitution, +2 Charisma: Merfolk are graceful, hale, and beautiful.

Medium: Merfolk are Medium creatures and have no bonuses or penalties due to their size.

Slow Speed: Merfolk have a base speed of 5 feet. They have a swim speed of 50 feet.

Aquatic: Merfolk are humanoids with the aquatic subtype.

Amphibious: Merfolk are amphibious, but prefer not to spend long periods out of the water.

Low-Light Vision: Merfolk have low-light vision.

Armor: Merfolk have a +2 natural armor bonus.

Legless: Merfolk have no legs, and cannot be tripped.

Languages: Merfolk begin play speaking Common and Aquan. Merfolk with high Intelligence scores can choose from the following: Aboleth, Aklo, Draconic, Elven, and Sylvan.

Aquatic Prowess Feat (Ex): At 2nd level and every four levels thereafter, a wave warden selects a bonus feat that improves his prowess in aquatic environments. He can choose these feats even if he does not meet the prerequisites. Initially, he may choose from the following feats: Dodge, Mobility, Net Adept (*Ultimate Combat*), Net and Trident (*Ultimate Combat*), Net Maneuvering (*Ultimate Combat*), Precise Shot, Rapid Reload, Sea Hunter, and Two-Weapon Fighting. At 6th level, he adds Improved Two-Weapon Fighting, Net Trickery (*Ultimate Combat*), and Spring Attack to the list. At 10th level, he adds Greater Two-Weapon Fighting and Improved Precise Shot to the list. This ability otherwise functions like and replaces the standard ranger's combat style bonus feats, including the limitations on armor worn.

Favored Terrain (Ex): At 3rd level, a wave warden gains water as a favored terrain. At 8th level and every five levels thereafter, his bonus in aquatic terrain increases by +2. He does not gain additional favored terrains. This otherwise functions like the standard ranger's favored terrain ability and replaces that ability.

Seaborn (Ex): At 7th level, a wave warden may move through any sort of aquatic growth (such as coral or seaweed) or across a wet surface at his normal speed and without taking damage or suffering any other impairment. Obstacles that are enchanted or magically manipulated to impede motion still affect him. This ability replaces woodland stride.

Watery Summons (Sp): At 8th level, a wave warden can summon allies once per day as a full-round action. This functions as *summon nature's ally III*, except it can only be used to summon creatures with the aquatic or water subtypes. At 11th level, this ability improves to *summon nature's ally IV*, with this progression continuing every three levels thereafter. The warden's caster level is equal to his ranger level. This ability replaces swift tracker.

NEW RACIAL RULES

The following options are available to merfolk. At the GM's discretion, other appropriate races may also make use of some of these.

Merfolk Equipment

Merfolk have access to the following equipment.

Underwater Crossbow: An underwater crossbow functions like its normal counterpart above water, and can be used underwater. When fired underwater, the crossbow has a range increment of 20 feet. Anyone proficient with a normal crossbow can use an underwater crossbow.

Merfolk Equipment

Ranged Weapons	Cost	Weight
Underwater crossbow, heavy	100 gp	8 lbs.
Underwater crossbow, light	70 gp	4 lbs.

Merfolk Feats

Merfolk have access to the following feat.

Sea Hunter (Combat)

Your blows knock swimming opponents off balance.

Prerequisites: Combat Expertise, merfolk.

Benefit: When you make a successful melee attack against a swimming target, as a free action you can attempt to knock the target off balance. Treat this as a trip combat maneuver. If you succeed, the target is considered off balance (see Table 13–7: Combat Adjustments Underwater on page 433 of the *Core Rulebook*) until it recovers its balance, usually by making a Swim check on its turn. This feat has no effect on creatures with a swim speed, those using magic such as *freedom of movement*, and creatures that can't be tripped.

Merfolk Magic Items

Merfolk have access to the following magic item.

SEAFOAM SHAWL

Aura faint transmutation; **CL** 5th
Slot shoulders; **Price** 6,000 gp; **Weight** 1 lb.

DESCRIPTION

This shawl of delicate lace grants the benefits of the *fins to feet* spell (see below) once per day.

CONSTRUCTION

Requirements Craft Wondrous Item, *fins to feet*; **Cost** 3,000 gp

Merfolk Spells

Merfolk have access to the following spell.

FINS TO FEET

School transmutation (polymorph); **Level** druid 3, sorcerer/wizard 3, witch 3
Casting Time 1 standard action
Components V, S
Range touch
Target willing creature touched
Duration 1 hour/level (D)
Save none; **Spell Resistance** yes

You transform the target's fins, flippers, or tail into legs and feet, allowing it to walk on land. The target loses its swim speed but gains a base speed appropriate for a humanoid of its size (speed 30 if a Medium or larger creature, speed 20 if Small). If the creature is immersed in water for 1 round, the transformation reverts, allowing it to swim normally. One round after leaving the water, the transformation occurs again, allowing it to walk.

This spell only works on merfolk, tritons, seals, fish, and other creatures whose bodies or limbs are used mainly for swimming and are not suitable for walking. It does not give the target the ability to breathe air.

NAGAJI

The nagaji are a race of ophidian humanoids with scaled skin that mimics the dramatic appearance of true nagas. Like serpents, they have forked tongues and lidless eyes, giving them an unblinking gaze that most other races find unnerving. Their physical forms are otherwise humanlike, raising wary speculation about their origins. It is widely believed that true nagas created them as a servitor race, through crossbreeding, magic, or both, and indeed nagaji revere nagas as living gods. Nagaji often inspire awe and fear among other humanoids, as much for their mysterious ancestry as for their talent for both swords and sorcery.

ALTERNATE RACIAL TRAITS

The following racial trait may be selected instead of an existing nagaji racial trait. Consult your GM before selecting this option.

Hypnotic Gaze (Sp): The nagaji's gaze is so intense it stops others in their tracks. Once per day, it can attempt to hypnotize a single target, as per the spell *hypnotism* (caster level equal to the nagaji's Hit Dice). The DC of this effect is equal to 11 + the nagaji's Charisma modifier. The effects of the hypnotic gaze only last a single round. This racial trait replaces serpent's sense.

FAVORED CLASS OPTIONS

The following options are available to all nagaji who have the listed favored class, and unless otherwise stated, the bonus applies each time you select the favored class reward.

Alchemist: Add +1 on Craft (alchemy) checks to craft poison and +1/3 on the DCs of poisons the alchemist creates.

Fighter: Add +1 to the fighter's CMD when resisting a grapple or trip attempt.

Monk: Add +1/4 point to the monk's *ki* pool.

Summoner: Add +1 hit point to the summoner's eidolon.

RACIAL ARCHETYPES

The following racial archetype is available to nagaji.

Naga Aspirant (Druid)

The naga aspirant follows the ancient beliefs and engages in the rituals of a druidic sect dedicated to the transcendence of her nagaji form through absolute devotion to nagas and naga gods. Through acting as a herald to the naga deities, the aspirant is rewarded with the ability to unlock her ultimate spirit form and become a true naga. A naga aspirant has the following class features.

Aspirant's Bond (Ex): A naga aspirant gains a spiritual connection to the serpentine deities worshiped by the nagas. At 1st level, and each time she gains a druid level, she may add one of the following spells to her druid spell list.

0—*acid splash, bleed, daze, mage hand, open/close, ray of frost*; 1st—*charm person, divine favor, expeditious retreat, mage armor, magic missile, ray of enfeeblement, shield, shield of faith, silent image, true strike*; 2nd—*acid arrow, detect thoughts, invisibility, mirror image, scorching ray, see invisibility*; 3rd—*dispel magic, displacement, fireball, lightning bolt, suggestion*; 4th—*divine power, greater invisibility*.

This ability replaces spontaneous casting.

NAGAJI RACIAL TRAITS

+2 Strength, +2 Charisma, –2 Intelligence: Nagaji are strong and have forceful personalities, but tend to ignore logic and mock scholastic pursuits.

Medium: Nagaji are Medium creatures and have no bonuses or penalties due to their size.

Reptilian: Nagaji are humanoids with the reptilian subtype.

Normal Speed: Nagaji have a base speed of 30 feet.

Low-Light Vision: Nagaji can see twice as far as humans in conditions of dim light.

Armored Scales: Nagaji have a +1 natural armor bonus from their scaly flesh.

Resistant (Ex): Nagaji receive a +2 racial saving throw bonus against mind-affecting effects and poison.

Serpent's Sense (Ex): Nagaji receive a +2 racial bonus on Handle Animal checks against reptiles, and a +2 racial bonus on Perception checks.

Languages: Nagaji begin play speaking Common and Draconic. Nagaji with high Intelligence scores can choose from the following: any human tongue, Abyssal, Aklo, Celestial, Draconic, Giant, Infernal, and Sylvan.

Aspirant's Enlightenment (Ex): At 4th level, a naga aspirant gains a +4 bonus on saving throws against the spell-like abilities, supernatural abilities, and poison of nagas. This ability replaces resist nature's lure.

Naga Shape (Su): At 6th level, the naga aspirant can use her wild shape ability (gained at 4th level, as normal) to assume the form of a true naga. This effect functions in a similar manner to a *shapechange* spell with the following exception. The druid's true naga form is unique, representing her personal evolution. When taking naga form, the nagaji's body transforms into that of a large serpent, though she keeps her own head. The naga aspirant loses her limbs and her size increases by one category, granting her a +4 size bonus to Strength and Constitution, a –2 penalty to Dexterity, and a +2 enhancement bonus to her natural armor bonus. She gains a +10 enhancement bonus to land speed and a bite attack that deals 1d6 points of damage. She can cast verbal spells in this form, but cannot cast spells with other components without metamagic or feats such as Natural Spell. This otherwise works like and replaces wild shape.

Augmented Form (Su): At 9th level and every four levels thereafter, a naga aspirant can choose one of the following abilities to enhance her naga form. Once chosen, this augmentation cannot be changed and always applies to her naga form. The caster level for these abilities is equal to her druid level, and unless otherwise stated, the DC is equal to 10 + 1/2 the druid's class level + the druid's Charisma bonus. This ability replaces venom immunity, a thousand faces, and timeless body.

Charming Gaze (Sp): The druid gains a gaze attack that affects creatures within 30 feet as a *charm person* spell.

Darkvision (Su): The druid gains darkvision with a range of 60 feet.

Detect Thoughts (Su): The druid can use *detect thoughts* at will.

Guarded Thoughts (Ex): The druid gains a +2 racial bonus on saves against charm effects and immunity to any form of mind reading (such as *detect thoughts*).

Poison Immunity (Ex): The druid gains immunity to all poisons. The druid's naga form must have at least one poison-based natural attack in order to select this ability.

Poisonous Sting (Ex): The druid's stinger becomes venomous. The naga form must have a tail stinger to take this ability. Sting—injury; save Fort DC 10 + 1/2 the druid's class level + the druid's Constitution modifier; *frequency* 1 round; *effect* sleep for 2d4 minutes; *cure* 1 save.

Spit Venom (Ex): The naga form can spit her venom up to 30 feet as a standard action. This is a ranged touch attack with no range increment. Any opponent hit by this attack must make a successful save (see above) to avoid the effect. The naga form must have a venomous bite to take this ability.

Sting (Ex): The naga form grows a stinger on the end of her tail, granting her a sting natural attack that deals 1d6 points of piercing damage.

Swim (Ex): The naga form gains a swim speed equal to her base speed.

Tough Scales (Ex): The druid's enhancement bonus to her natural armor increases by +2. The druid may select this ability more than once. Its effects stack.

Venomous Bite (Ex): The naga form's bite attack becomes poisonous. Bite—injury; save Fortitude DC 10 + 1/2 the druid's class level + the druid's Constitution modifier; *frequency* 1/round for 6 rounds; *effect* 1 Constitution damage, *cure* 1 save.

True Naga (Su): At 20th level, a naga aspirant metamorphoses into a unique naga. Her wild shape form becomes her natural form, though she can transform into her original nagaji shape at will. Her creature type permanently changes to aberration. This ability replaces wildshape (at will).

NEW RACIAL RULES

The following options are available to nagaji. At the GM's discretion, other appropriate races may also make use of some of these.

Nagaji Feats

Nagaji have access to the following feat.

Spit Venom (Combat)

You have mastered the nagaji warrior technique of spitting venom into your opponent's eyes.

Prerequisite: Nagaji.

Benefit: As a full-round action, you can spit poison up to 10 feet as a ranged touch attack. If you hit, the target must make a successful Fortitude save or be blinded for 1d6 rounds. The DC of this save is equal to 10 + 1/2 your total Hit Dice + your Constitution modifier. You can use this ability once per day plus one additional time per day for every three Hit Dice you have.

Nagaji Magic Items

Nagaji have access to the following magic item.

NAGAJI SCALE POLISH

Aura moderate evocation; **CL** 7th
Slot none; **Price** 1,400 gp; **Weight** 1/2 lb.

DESCRIPTION

This small clay urn contains a scintillating paste which works like *imbue with spell ability*, except the spell effect is not limited to cleric spells. Any caster may casts spells into the jar. The creature that applies the paste to its scales (a standard action) gains the ability to cast the imbued spells (assuming it has enough Hit Dice and the requisite ability scores). Only a reptilian creature (such as a dragon or a humanoid with the reptilian subtype) can use the polish to cast spells.

CONSTRUCTION

Requirements Craft Wondrous Item, *imbue with spell ability* or *mnemonic enhancer*; **Cost** 700 gp

SAMSARANS

Mysterious humanoids with pale blue flesh and transparent blood like the waters of a trickling brook, samsarans are ancient creatures even in their youth. A samsaran's life is not a linear progression from birth to death, but rather a circle of birth to death to rebirth. Whenever a samsaran dies, it reincarnates anew as a young samsaran to live a new life. Her past memories remain vague and indistinct—and each new incarnation is as different a creature and personality as a child is to a parent.

Samsarans appear similar to humans, with dark hair and solid white eyes with no pupils or irises. Skin tones are generally shades of light blue.

ALTERNATE RACIAL TRAITS

The following racial trait may be selected instead of existing samsaran racial traits. Consult your GM before selecting this new options.

Mystic Past Life (Su): You can add spells from another spellcasting class to the spell list of your current spellcasting class. You add a number of spells equal to 1 + your spellcasting class's key ability score bonus (Wisdom for clerics, and so on). The spells must be the same type (arcane or divine) as the spellcasting class you're adding them to. For example, you could add *divine power* to your druid class spell list, but not to your wizard class spell list because *divine power* is a divine spell. These spells do not have to be spells you can cast as a 1st-level character. The number of spells granted by this ability is set at 1st level. Changes to your ability score do not change the number of spells gained. This racial trait replaces shards of the past.

FAVORED CLASS OPTIONS

The following options are available to all samsarans who have the listed favored class, and unless otherwise stated, the bonus applies each time you select the favored class reward.

Monk: Add a +1/2 bonus on the monk's saving throws to resist death attacks.

Oracle: Add one spell known from the oracle spell list. This spell must be at least one level below the highest spell level the oracle can cast.

Rogue: The rogue gains 1/6 of a new rogue talent.

Wizard: Add one spell from the wizard spell list to the wizard's spellbook. This spell must be at least one level below the highest spell level the wizard can cast.

SAMSARAN RACIAL TRAITS

All samsarans are humanoids with the samsaran subtype. They have the following racial traits.

+2 Intelligence, +2 Wisdom, –2 Constitution: Samsarans are insightful and strong-minded, but their bodies tend to be frail.

Medium: Samsarans are Medium creatures and have no bonuses or penalties due to their size.

Normal Speed: Samsarans have a base speed of 30 feet.

Low-Light Vision (Ex): Samsarans can see twice as far as humans in conditions of dim light.

Lifebound (Ex): Samsarans gain a +2 racial bonus on all saving throws made to resist death effects, saving throws against negative energy effects, Fortitude saves made to remove negative levels, and Constitution checks made to stabilize if reduced to negative hit points.

Samsaran Magic (Sp): Samsarans with a Charisma score of 11 or higher gain the following spell-like abilities: 1/day—*comprehend languages*, *deathwatch*, and *stabilize*. The caster level for these effects is equal to the samsaran's level.

Shards of the Past (Ex): A samsaran's past lives grant her bonuses on two particular skills. A samsaran chooses two skills—she gains a +2 racial bonus on both of these skills, and they are treated as class skills regardless of what class she actually takes.

Languages: Samsarans begin play speaking Common and Samsaran. Samsarans with high Intelligence scores can choose from the following: any human language, Abyssal, Aquan, Auran, Celestial, Draconic, Giant, Ignan, Infernal, Nagaji, Tengu, and Terran.

RACIAL ARCHETYPES

The following racial archetype is available to samsarans.

Reincarnated Oracle (Oracle)

A reincarnated oracle draws her knowledge and power from the experiences of her previous lives. Her memories guide her through a spiritual ascension leading the way to her ultimate incarnation. A reincarnated oracle has the following class features.

Recommended Mysteries: ancestor, lore, time.

Oracle's Curse: A reincarnated oracle must choose the haunted or tongues curse at 1st level.

Bonus Spells: *see alignment* (*Ultimate Combat*, 2nd), *detect thoughts* (4th), *contact other plane* (10th), *moment of prescience* (16th), *overwhelming presence* (*Ultimate Magic*, 18th). These spells replace the oracle's mystery bonus spells at these levels.

Revelations: A reincarnated oracle must take the following revelations at one of the listed levels.

Location Memories (Su): As a swift action, you may search your past lives for memories of or insight about your current location. This grants you the scent ability, low-light vision, and a +2 insight bonus on Perception and Survival checks for 1 minute. You can use this ability a number of times per day equal to 3 + your Charisma modifier. You must take this revelation at 1st level or 3rd level.

Spirit Memories (Su): Once per day, you call upon the unfulfilled desires and goals of your past lives and project their frustration and despair through your eyes at a target. This is a gaze attack affecting one creature. The target must make a Will save (DC 10 + 1/2 your oracle level + your Charisma modifier) or be sickened and staggered for 1 round. This is a mind-affecting compulsion effect. You can use this ability a number of times per day equal to 3 + your Charisma modifier. You must take this revelation at 1st, 3rd, or 7th level.

NEW RACIAL RULES

The following options are available to samsarans. At the GM's discretion, other appropriate races may also make use of some of these.

Samsaran Equipment

Samsarans have access to the following equipment.

Samsaran Life Wheel: This handheld wooden spool spins freely within a boxlike housing. Inscribed upon the exterior of the spool are dozens of samsaran prayers along with names or symbols associated with a samsaran's past lives. Samsarans believe that spinning the wheel during meditation strengthens the spiritual connections between their former lives. If a samsaran meditates with her wheel for at least 10 minutes about a Knowledge (history) question relating to her own history or the histories of her past lives, she gains a +1 insight bonus on the check.

Samsaran Equipment

Item	Cost	Weight
Samsaran life wheel	25 gp	1/2 lb.

Samsaran Feats

Samsaran have access to the following feat.

Life's Blood

Your blood flows with eternal life, and its healing powers allow you use your blood to heal others.

Prerequisite: Samsaran.

Benefit: At will as a full-round action, you may perform a special bloodletting ritual through which you sacrifice some of your own vitality to heal another creature. When using this feat, you take 1d4 points of damage and apply your blood to the wounds of a living creature, healing it for a number of hit points equal to the amount of damage you took from the ritual. This is a supernatural ability. Only you can perform this bloodletting. A creature cannot be healed by this ability more than once per day.

Samsaran Magic Items

Samsarans have access to the following magic item.

INCENSE OF MANY FATES

Aura moderate divination; **CL** 11th

Slot none; **Price** 3,300 gp; **Weight** 1 lb.

DESCRIPTION

When used during meditation, this incense allows a samsaran's consciousness to pass through past or future lives to learn more about an important person, place, or thing. This functions like *legend lore*, but only works if the subject is at hand. The transcendental state lasts 1 hour, during which she can take no other actions. If she is disrupted during the meditation, the incense's effect is lost. Creatures other than samsarans can use this incense, but the connections to other lives are weaker and require a deeper meditation that takes 24 hours. Each block of incense lasts for 1 use.

CONSTRUCTION

Requirements Craft Wondrous Item, *legend lore*; **Cost** 1,650 gp

Samsaran Spells

Samsarans have access to the following spell.

KARMIC BLESSING

School divination [good]; **Level** cleric 1, witch 1

Casting Time 1 standard action

Components V, S

Range touch

Target creature touched

Duration 1 round/level

Save Will negates (harmless); **Spell Resistance** yes (harmless)

The target treats one skill of your choice as a class skill.

STRIX

Human neighbors tell horrific tales of slaughter woven with frightened suspicion when speaking of strix. Strix, however, tell a tale of encroachment and a struggle for land and resources. For ages, humans invaded strix lands fighting bloody battles against the fierce, black-skinned creatures they thought to be winged devils. Over time, strix have developed a hatred for humankind and now fiercely protect their dwindling numbers.

ALTERNATE RACIAL TRAITS

The following racial traits may be selected instead of existing strix racial traits. Consult your GM before selecting any of these new options.

Dayguard: Familiar with watching over its tribe during the day, the strix gains a +2 racial bonus on Perception checks and treats Perception as a class skill. This racial trait replaces nocturnal.

Frightening: The strix looks particularly menacing and use this to its advantage, gaining a +2 racial bonus on Intimidate checks. This racial trait replaces nocturnal.

Nimble: The strix receives a +1 racial bonus on Reflex saves. This replaces the suspicious racial trait.

Tough: The strix receives a +1 racial bonus on Fortitude saves. This racial trait replaces suspicious.

Wing-Clipped: The flight of wing-clipped strix is weaker than normal, whether from deformity or injury. Their fly speed is 20 feet (poor) instead of the normal fly speed, and they must make a DC 30 Fly check to fly upward. Ostracized by their tribes and forced to deal with other races, these strix compensate for their weakness by gaining a +2 racial bonus on Bluff, Climb, and Diplomacy checks.

FAVORED CLASS OPTIONS

The following options are available to all strix who have the listed favored class, and unless otherwise stated, the bonus applies each time you select the favored class reward.

Barbarian: Add +1 to the barbarian's total number of rage rounds per day.

Fighter: Add +1/4 to the attack roll bonus from the strix's hatred racial trait.

Monk: Add +1/4 point to the monk's *ki* pool.

Ranger: Add +1/2 round to the duration of the bonus granted to the companions of the ranger using his hunter's bond ability.

STRIX RACIAL TRAITS

+2 Dexterity, -2 Charisma: Strix are swift and elusive, but tend to be stubborn and swift to anger.

Strix: Strix are humanoids with the strix subtype.

Medium: Strix are Medium creatures and have no bonuses or penalties due to their size.

Normal Speed: Strix have a base speed of 30 feet on land. They also have a fly speed of 60 feet (average).

Low-Light Vision: Strix can see twice as far as humans in conditions of dim light.

Darkvision: Strix can see in the dark up to 60 feet.

Hatred: Strix receive a +1 racial bonus on attack rolls against humanoid creatures with the human subtype because of their special training against these hated foes.

Nocturnal: Strix gain a +2 racial bonus on Perception and Stealth checks in dim light or darkness.

Suspicious: Strix receive a +2 racial bonus on saving throws against illusion spells and effects.

Languages: Strix begin play speaking Strix. Those with high Intelligence scores can choose from the following: Auran, Common, Draconic, Giant, Gnome, Goblin, Infernal.

RACIAL ARCHETYPES

The following racial archetype is available to strix.

Airborne Ambusher (Fighter)

Driven by suspicion and hatred, strix doggedly guard their territories, making deadly use of their flight. Using swift strikes from above, strix plummet onto their foes with lethal force.

Weapon and Armor Proficiency: An airborne ambusher is not proficient with heavy armor or tower shields.

Class Skills: An airborne ambusher adds Fly to his list of class skills and removes Climb from his list of class skills.

Combat Flyer (Ex): At 2nd level, an airborne ambusher may use his fighter bonus feats to select Flyby Attack and Hover. This replaces bravery.

Aerobatics (Ex): At 5th level, an airborne ambusher may make a Fly check instead of an Acrobatics check to move through a threatened area or an enemy's space. This replaces weapon training 1.

Flying Dodger (Ex): At 9th level, when an airborne ambusher flies at least half its fly speed on its turn, it gains a +1 dodge bonus to AC for 1 round. This bonus increases to +2 at 11th level and +4 at 17th level. This ability replaces weapon training 2.

Plummeting Charge (Ex): At 13th level, if an airborne ambusher flies at least half its fly speed as part of a charge, it gains a +2 racial bonus on the attack roll (in addition to the normal charge bonus) and a +4 bonus on its critical confirmation roll. These bonuses improve to +4 and +6 at 17th level. This replaces weapon training 3 and 4.

NEW RACIAL RULES

The following options are available to strix. At the GM's discretion, other appropriate races may also make use of some of these.

Strix Equipment

Strix have access to the following equipment.

Snag Net: This short, wide net is covered in barbed loops and slipknots. It works like a typical net exotic weapon, except it has the trip weapon special feature. If you entangle an opponent and hold the trailing rope, on your turn in place of a melee attack you may make a trip combat maneuver check against that opponent; if you succeed, you may trip the opponent or deal 1 point of piercing damage to the opponent. The concentration DC to cast while entangled in a snag net is 17 + the spell's level. The Escape Artist DC to escape a snag net is 22.

Strix Feats

Strix have access to the following feat.

Stretched Wings

You strengthen your crippled wings.

Prerequisites: Str 13, Skill Focus (Fly), strix, wing-clipped racial trait.

Benefit: Your strix racial fly speed increases to 60 feet (average). You ignore the wing-clipped trait's Fly check requirement to fly upward.

Strix Magic Items

Strix have a fondness for magic items like this one.

STONEMIST CLOAK

Aura faint conjuration (creation) and illusion; **CL** 3rd
Slot shoulders; **Price** 3,500 gp; **Weight** 1 lb.

DESCRIPTION

In rocky or mountainous areas, when this stone-gray cloak is worn with the hood drawn up around the head, the wearer gains a +5 competence bonus on Stealth checks. Once per day, the wearer can create an area of fog equivalent to *obscuring mist*.

CONSTRUCTION

Requirements Craft Wondrous Item, *invisibility*, *obscuring mist*; **Cost** 1,750 gp

---

Strix Spells

Strix have access to the following spell.

STRONG WINGS

School transmutation; **Level** druid 1, ranger 1, sorcerer/wizard 1, witch 1
Casting Time 1 standard action
Components V, S
Range touch
Target creature touched
Duration 1 minute/level
Save Fortitude negates (harmless); **Spell Resistance** yes (harmless)

The target's wings grow more powerful, causing its fly speed to increase by +10 feet and its maneuverability to improve by one category (to a maximum of good). This increase counts as an enhancement bonus. This spell has no effect on wingless creatures or winged creatures that cannot fly.

TABLE 3-4: STRIX WEAPON

Exotic Weapons	Cost	Dmg (S)	Dmg (M)	Critical	Range	Weight	Type	Special
Two-Handed Melee Weapons								
Net, snag	30 gp	see text	see text	—	10 ft.	10 lbs.	P	Trip, see text

SULIS

Sulis, or suli-jann, are the descendents of mortals and jann. They manifest their otherworldly heritage in adolescence, or when awakened by an encounter with a genie. Strong and attractive, these dynamic individuals can call forth elemental energies to augment their prowess in combat. Neither genie nor quite human, sulis stand in two worlds and often feel as if they don't belong to either.

ALTERNATE RACIAL TRAITS

The following racial trait may be selected instead of existing suli racial traits. Consult your GM before selecting this new option.

Energy Strike (Su): A suli with this racial trait has a stronger connection to one energy type than to the other three used by sulis. Choose one energy type: acid, cold, electricity, or fire. The suli's elemental assault ability can only deal energy damage of this type. The suli has resistance 5 to this energy type and no racial resistance to the other three types. While her elemental assault is active, the suli gains an additional ability based on the chosen energy type.

Earthfoot (acid): Whenever the suli moves through difficult terrain related to earth and stone (rubble, mud, sand, and so on), she may move through 5 feet of that difficult terrain each round as if it were normal terrain. This allows the suli to take a 5-foot step into that difficult terrain. Other kinds of difficult terrain (ice, caltrops, foliage, and so on) affect the suli normally.

Firehand (fire): Instead of adding damage to a melee attack, the suli may hurl a piece of her arm-flames as if it were a thrown weapon. The suli makes a ranged touch attack; if the attack hits, the target takes 1d6 points of fire damage. The flames have a range increment of 10 feet.

Icewalk (cold): The suli can walk on water-based liquids as if using *water walk*, except instead of hovering above the surface, she creates a temporary layer of ice that supports her and immediately melts once she moves away from it. This ice is not slippery to the suli and does not affect her balance or speed, though other ice affects her normally. Other creatures cannot travel on this ice, but the suli may carry a creature while moving.

Shockshield (electricity): Once per round as an immediate action, the suli can shock a creature that touches or attacks her with a natural attack, unarmed strike, or metal melee weapon, dealing 1d6 points of electricity damage to the creature.

This racial trait otherwise works like and replaces elemental assault.

FAVORED CLASS OPTIONS

The following options are available to all sulis who have the listed favored class, and unless otherwise stated, the bonus applies each time you select the favored class reward.

SULI RACIAL TRAITS

+2 Strength, +2 Charisma, –2 Intelligence: Sulis are brawny and charming, but slow-witted.

Native Outsider: Sulis are outsiders with the native subtype.

Medium: Sulis are Medium creatures and have no bonuses or penalties due to their size.

Normal Speed: Sulis have a base speed of 30 feet.

Low-Light Vision: Sulis can see twice as far as humans in dim light.

Negotiator: Sulis are keen negotiators, and gain a +2 racial bonus on Diplomacy and Sense Motive checks.

Elemental Assault (Su): Once per day as a swift action, a suli can shroud her arms in acid, cold, electricity, or fire. This lasts for one round per level, and can be dismissed as a free action. Unarmed strikes with her arms or hands (or attacks with weapons held in those hands) deal +1d6 points of damage of the appropriate energy type.

Energy Resistance 5: Sulis have resistance to acid 5, cold 5, electricity 5, and fire 5.

Languages: Sulis begin play speaking Common and one elemental language (Aquan, Auran, Ignan, or Terran). Sulis with high Intelligence scores can choose from the following: Aquan, Auran, Draconic, Ignan, and Terran.

Magus: Add +1/4 point to the magus's arcane pool.

Monk: Add +1/2 point of damage to elemental assault.

Ranger: Add +1 to acid resistance, cold resistance, electricity resistance, or fire resistance.

RACIAL ARCHETYPES

The following racial archetype is available to sulis.

Elemental Knight (Magus)

Elemental knights are born with elemental energies surging through their blood and discover the secret of reconciling and focusing this primal power into the arcane. An elemental knight has the following class features.

Elemental Arcana (Su): At 3rd level, elemental knights may select the following magus arcana available only to them.

Assault Synergy (Su): As a swift action, the elemental knight can expend 1 round of duration from elemental assault to add +1d6 points of energy damage to an offensive spell he casts that round. The spell must have the acid, cold, electricity or fire descriptor. This extra energy damage matches the energy damage of the spell. At 10th level, he may expend 2 rounds instead of 1 to add +2d6 points of energy damage to the spell.

Energy Reflection (Su): This functions like the reflection magus arcana, except it only works on spells that deal acid, cold, electricity, or fire damage. As long as the elemental knight spends at least 1 point from her arcane pool to activate this arcana, he may expend rounds of elemental assault as if they were arcane pool points. For example, the knight could spend 1 arcane pool point and 3 rounds of elemental assault to reflect a spell of 4th-level or lower. The elemental knight must be at least 12th level before selecting this arcana.

Energy Resistance Boost (Su): As a swift action, the elemental knight can expend 1 point from his arcane pool or 1 round of elemental assault to increase all of his racial energy resistances by +5 for 1 round.

Elemental Matrix (Su): At 4th level, an elemental knight gains Incremental Elemental Assault (see below) as a bonus feat. In addition, at 4th level, as a swift action, an elemental knight may expend rounds of duration from her elemental assault ability. For every 4 rounds expended, he gains 1 arcane pool point. This ability replaces spell recall.

Magus Arcana: The following magus arcana complement the elemental knight archetype: empowered magic, pool strike, spell shield.

NEW RACIAL RULES

The following options are available to sulis. At the GM's discretion, other appropriate races may also make use of some of these.

Suli Equipment

Sulis have access to the following equipment.

Elemental Flux: This flask of alchemical powder reacts to the elemental power in suli blood. Adding at least 1 hit point worth of suli blood to it creates an alchemical splash weapon. The splash weapon works like a flask of acid, except the damage is a random energy type (acid, cold, electricity, or fire). A DC 10 Craft (alchemy) check identifies what energy type the activated flask has. The activated flux retains its power for 24 hours before becoming inert material. The Craft (alchemy) DC to create this is 20.

Suli Equipment

Item	Cost	Weight	Craft DC
Elemental flux (flask)	20 gp	1 lb.	20

Suli Feats

Sulis have access to the following feats.

Extra Elemental Assault

You have unlocked greater elemental power.

Prerequisite: Suli.

Benefit: Your elemental assault ability lasts an additional 2 rounds per day.

Special: You can take this feat multiple times. Its effects stack.

Incremental Elemental Assault

You may activate and quench your elemental assault ability multiple times per day.

Prerequisite: Suli.

Benefits: You may use your elemental assault ability in 1-round increments, up to a maximum number of rounds per day equal to your character level. These rounds do not have to be consecutive. Activating the ability is a swift action; ending it is a free action.

Normal: You can use elemental assault once per day. It lasts a number of rounds equal to your class level.

Suli Spells

Sulis have access to the following spell.

IMBUE WITH ELEMENTAL MIGHT

School evocation [see text]; **Level** cleric 2, magus 2, sorcerer/wizard 2

Components V, S

Duration 24 hours or until discharged (D)

Save Will negates (harmless); **Spell Resistance** yes (harmless)

This spell functions like *imbue with spell ability*, except you transfer the use of your elemental assault ability to the target. The target must have an Intelligence score of at least 5 to use the ability. The imbued elemental assault functions exactly like yours, except the ability's duration is based on the target's level or Hit Dice. Once you cast this spell, you cannot use your elemental assault ability until the duration of the spell is over.

SVIRFNEBLIN

In the dark below earth, svirfneblin protect their enclaves, keeping their small communities safe from the terrors of the lightless depths. Serious creatures with slate-gray skin, these gnomes vary greatly from their surface cousins by choosing to live in the shadowy depths and protect the world above from the foul creatures sharing their chambers, vaults, and tunnels.

ALTERNATE RACIAL TRAITS

The following racial traits may be selected instead of existing svirfneblin racial traits. Consult your GM before selecting any of these new options.

Healthy: Svirfneblin gain a +4 bonus on Fortitude saves against disease and poison, including magical diseases. This racial trait replaces fortunate.

Stoneseer: Svirfneblin add +1 to the caster level of any spells with the earth descriptor they cast. Svirfneblin also gain the following spell-like abilities: Constant—*nondetection*; 1/day—*magic stone, stone shape, stone tell*; caster level equals the svirfneblin's class levels. This racial trait replaces svirfneblin magic.

FAVORED CLASS OPTIONS

The following options are available to all svirfneblin who have the listed favored class, and unless otherwise stated, the bonus applies each time you select the favored class reward.

Alchemist: Add one extract formula from the alchemist's list to the alchemist's formula book. This formula must be at least one level below the highest formula level the alchemist can create.

Oracle: Add one spell known from the oracle spell list. This spell must be at least one level below the highest spell level the oracle can cast.

Ranger: Add DR 1/magic to the ranger's animal companion. Each additional time the ranger selects this benefit, the DR/magic increases +1/2 (maximum DR 10/magic). If the ranger ever replaces his animal companion, the new companion gains this DR.

SVIRFNEBLIN RACIAL TRAITS

–2 Strength, +2 Dexterity, +2 Wisdom, –4 Charisma: Svirfneblin are fast and observant but relatively weak and emotionally distant.

Gnome: Svirfneblin are humanoids with the gnome subtype.

Small: Svirfneblin are Small creatures and gain a +1 size bonus to their AC, a +1 size bonus on attack rolls, a –1 penalty to their CMB and CMD, and a +4 size bonus on Stealth checks.

Defensive Training: Svirfneblin gain a +2 dodge bonus to Armor Class.

Senses: Svirfneblin have darkvision 120 ft. and low-light vision.

Fortunate: Svirfneblin gain a +2 racial bonus on all saving throws.

Skilled: Svirfneblin gain a +2 racial bonus on Stealth checks; this improves to a +4 bonus underground. They gain a +2 racial bonus on Craft (alchemy) checks and Perception checks.

Hatred: Svirfneblin receive a +1 bonus on attack rolls against humanoid creatures of the reptilian and dwarven subtypes due to training against these hated foes.

Stonecunning: Svirfneblin gain stonecunning as dwarves (*Core Rulebook* 21).

Spell Resistance: Svirfneblin have SR equal to 11 + their class levels.

Svirfneblin Magic: Svirfneblin add +1 to the DC of any illusion spells they cast. Svirfneblin also gain the following spell-like abilities: Constant—*nondetection*; 1/day—*blindness/deafness, blur, disguise self*; caster level equals the svirfneblin's class levels.

Languages: Svirfneblin begin play speaking Gnome and Undercommon. Those with high Intelligence scores can choose from the following: Aklo, Common, Draconic, Dwarven, Elven, Giant, Goblin, Orc, and Terran.

RACIAL ARCHETYPES

The following racial archetype is available to svirfneblin.

Deep Bomber (Alchemist)

Consumed with keeping hidden from the horrors below the surface, svirfneblin use their racial proclivity for alchemy and their inherent talent for obfuscation to strike their enemies from the darkness and retreat unseen. A deep bomber has the following class features.

Silent Bomb: At 2nd level, when the deep bomber creates a bomb, he can choose to have it explode without making any noise, although those damaged by it may cry out. This ability replaces poison use.

Targeting Bomb*: At 3rd level, when the deep bomber creates a bomb, he can choose to have its detonation include a *faerie fire* effect that applies to all creatures within the splash radius (including the target, if any). This ability replaces swift alchemy (the deep bomber gains swift alchemy at 18th level and never gains instant alchemy).

Stonekin: At 6th level, the deep bomber automatically learns *tree shape* as a 2nd-level extract, except instead of a tree, he takes the form of a stalagmite that is the same size as his current size. At 7th level, he automatically learns *meld into stone* as a 3rd-level extract. This ability replaces swift poisoning.

Discoveries: The following discoveries complement the deep bomber archetype: delayed bomb, dispelling bomb, fast bombs, infusion, madness bomb, poison bomb.

NEW RACIAL RULES

The following options are available to svirfneblin. At the GM's discretion, other appropriate races may also make use of some of these.

Svirfneblin Equipment

Svirfneblin have access to the following equipment.

Jolting Dart: This alchemically grown crystal dart builds up an electrical charge when thrown. A creature struck by the dart takes normal piercing damage and 1d6 points of electricity damage. Anyone proficient in darts can use a jolting dart. Once thrown, the dart is destroyed.

Svirfneblin Feats

Svirfneblin have access to the following feat.

Stoic Pose

You can hold yourself as still as a statue, evading detection.

Prerequisite: Svirfneblin.

SVIRFNEBLIN DISCOVERIES

The following new discoveries can be taken by any alchemist who meets the prerequisites, but are more common among svirfneblin.

Darkness Bomb*: When the alchemist creates a bomb, he can choose to have it suppress light sources on the target. This extinguishes nonmagical light sources carried by the target and dispels magical light sources for 1 round/level as *deeper darkness*.

Glassfoot Bomb*: When the alchemist creates a bomb, he can choose to have it cover the ground in volatile jagged crystals in addition to its normal effects. These crystals act like caltrops, evaporating into a smelly but harmless gas in 2d6 rounds.

Benefit: By spending 5 rounds finding a suitable location, you can hold yourself so still that you appear to be a Small object such as a pile of rocks. This allows you to make a Stealth check without cover or concealment, as long as you do not move or take any other actions.

Svirfneblin Spells

Svirfneblin have access to the following spells.

EARTH GLIDE

School transmutation [earth]; **Level** alchemist 4, druid 4, sorcerer/wizard 4

Casting Time 1 standard action

Components V, S

Range touch

Target creature touched

Duration 1 round/level

Saving Throw Will negates (harmless); **Spell Resistance** yes (harmless)

The target can pass through stone, dirt, or almost any other sort of earth except metal as easily as a fish swims through water, traveling at a speed of 5 feet. If protected against fire damage, it can move through lava. This movement leaves behind no tunnel or hole, nor does it create any ripple or other sign of its presence. It requires as much concentration as walking, so the subject can attack or cast spells normally, but cannot charge or run. Casting *move earth* on an area containing the target flings the target back 30 feet, stunning it for 1 round (DC 15 Fortitude negates). This spell does not give the target the ability to breathe underground, so when passing through solid material, the creature must hold its breath.

TABLE 3-5: SVIRFNEBLIN WEAPON

Martial Weapons	Cost	Dmg (S)	Dmg (M)	Critical	Range	Weight	Type	Special
Ranged Weapons								
Jolting dart	100 gp	1d3	1d4	×2	20 ft.	1/2 lb.	P	See text

Vanaras

Vanaras are intelligent, monkeylike humanoids that live in deep, warm forests and lush jungles. A vanara's body is covered in a thin coat of soft fur, and individuals with chestnut, ivory, and even golden coats are common. Despite their fur, vanaras can grow lengthy hair on their head just as humans can, and both male and female vanaras take pains to wear elaborate hairstyles for important social functions. The hair on a vanara's head matches the color of its fur. All vanaras have long, prehensile tails and handlike feet capable of well-articulated movements. A vanara stands slightly shorter and weighs slightly less than a typical human.

ALTERNATE RACIAL TRAITS

The following racial traits may be selected instead of existing vanara racial traits. Consult your GM before selecting any of these new options.

Tree Stranger: Some vanaras have spent their lives among humans in centers of learning instead of traditional treetop homes. These vanaras treat all Knowledge skills as class skills, but lose their climb speed racial trait.

Whitecape: The rare whitecape vanara clans have more in common with savanna-dwelling baboons than the jungle-dwelling monkeys that most vanaras resemble. Their stooping build grants them a +4 racial bonus to CMD when resisting a bull rush or trip. These vanaras usually have a thick mane of hair on the head and shoulders (called a "cape") and shorter tails. This racial trait replaces prehensile tail.

FAVORED CLASS OPTIONS

The following options are available to all vanaras who have the listed favored class, and unless otherwise stated, the bonus applies each time you select the favored class reward.

Alchemist: Add +1/2 to the alchemist's bomb damage.

Druid: Add a +1/2 bonus on wild empathy checks and a +1/2 bonus on Handle Animal skill checks.

Fighter: Add +1 to the fighter's CMD when resisting a reposition or trip attempt.

Monk: Add a +1 bonus on Acrobatics checks made to jump.

Ranger: Add +1/4 dodge bonus to Armor Class against the ranger's favored enemies.

Rogue: The rogue gains 1/6 of a new rogue talent.

RACIAL ARCHETYPES

The following racial archetype is available to vanaras.

Treetop Monk (Monk)

While many vanaras follow traditional monastic training and traditions, others learn to blend exotic combat and the mysterious forces of *ki* with the natural world, allowing them to move through trees and overgrowth to deliver devastating attacks. A treetop monk has the following class features.

Branch Runner (Ex): At 3rd level, a treetop monk adds half the base speed bonus from his fast movement ability to his racial climb speed. This ability replaces still mind.

Vanara Racial Traits

+2 Dexterity, +2 Wisdom, –2 Charisma. Vanaras are agile and insightful, but are also rather mischievous.

Vanara: Vanaras are humanoids with the vanara subtype.

Medium: Vanaras are Medium creatures and have no bonuses or penalties due to their size.

Normal Speed: Vanaras have a base speed of 30 feet and a Climb speed of 30 feet.

Low-Light Vision: A vanara can see twice as far as a human in dim light.

Nimble: Vanaras have a +2 racial bonus on Acrobatics and Stealth checks.

Prehensile Tail: A vanara has a long, flexible tail that she can use to carry objects. She cannot wield weapons with her tail, but the tail allows her to retrieve a small, stowed object carried on her person as a swift action.

Languages: Vanaras begin play speaking Common and Vanaran. Vanaras with high Intelligence scores can choose from the following: Aklo, Celestial, Elven, Gnome, Goblin, and Sylvan.

Wood Affinity (Su): At 5th level, a treetop monk may expend 1 point from his *ki* pool as a free action to treat a wooden object as if it were not broken for 1 minute (this includes a weapon with a wooden haft such as an axe or spear). At 8th level, as a free action, a treetop monk can expend 1 point from his *ki* pool to use the Lunge feat with any wooden or wood-hafted melee weapon. This ability replaces purity of body.

Freedom of Movement (Su): At 12th level, a treetop may expend 1 point from his *ki* pool as a swift action to gain the effects of *freedom of movement* for 1 round. This ability replaces abundant step.

NEW RACIAL RULES

The following options are available to vanaras. At the GM's discretion, other appropriate races may also make use of some of these.

Vanara Equipment

Vanaras are known to use equipment crafted from the following material.

Whipwood: Vanara woodworkers craft this extremely flexible material in a time-consuming process. Whipwood is actually a composite of several bendable wooden fibers woven and fused together to form a flexible but sturdy unit. Only wooden weapons or weapons with wooden hafts (such as axes and spears) can be made out of whipwood. A creature wielding a whipwood weapon treats its CMD as +2 higher for the purpose of avoiding sunder attempts against that weapon. A whipwood weapon's hit points increase by +5. Whipwood loses its special qualities if under the effect of an *ironwood* spell.

Type of Whipwood Item	Cost Modifier
Wooden or wood-hafted weapon	+500 gp

Vanara Feats

Vanaras have access to the following feat.

Tree Hanger (Combat)

You can use your tail to defend against trip attacks and to hang from nearby protrusions.

Prerequisites: Acrobatics 1 rank, vanara.

Benefit: You gain a +2 bonus to your CMD against all trip attacks. If your square has a branch or other sturdy large object that you could hang from, as a swift action you may make a DC 15 Acrobatics check to jump upward and use your tail to hang from that object. While hanging, you can't be tripped, you ignore the effects of difficult terrain in your square, and you gain a +2 bonus to your CMD against bull rush, drag, and reposition attacks. If you leave that square (including if you are moved against your will), you lose your grip on the object and are no

longer hanging. While hanging, you cannot use your tail for anything else.

Vanara Magic Items

Vanaras have access to the following magic items.

MERIDIAN BELT

Aura moderate transmutation; **CL** 9th

Slot belt; **Price** 1,000 gp; **Weight** 1 lb.

DESCRIPTION

This narrow cloth belt has a silver buckle in the shape of four rings. The belt allows a creature to wear a magic ring on each foot in addition to the ring on each hand, though only two rings function at any given time. As a swift action, the wearer can change which of his rings are active (both hands, both feet, left hand and right foot, and so on). For example, a creature could wear a *ring of protection*, *ring of energy resistance*, *ring of swimming*, and *ring of counterspells*, switching between any two of them as a swift action each round as it desires.

The belt does not change the type of action required to activate a ring (for example, activating a *ring of invisibility* is still a standard action), but allows the wearer to easily switch between the constant powers of several worn rings. While the belt is worn, wearing a ring on a foot counts toward the attunement process of certain rings (such as a *ring of sustenance*) even if the belt isn't used to make that ring active during that attunement period.

CONSTRUCTION

Requirements Craft Wondrous Item, *polymorph*; **Cost** 500 gp

Vanara Spells

Vanaras have access to the following spell.

PREHENSILE PILFER

School transmutation; **Level** alchemist 3, bard 3, magus 3, sorcerer/wizard 3

Casting Time 1 standard action

Components V, S

Range touch

Target creature touched

Duration 1 round/level (D)

Saving Throw Fortitude negates (harmless); **Spell Resistance** yes (harmless)

The target's tail moves and acts more quickly, almost with a mind of its own. When making a full-attack action, the target may use its tail to make a dirty trick or steal combat maneuver as a swift action. For the purpose of this attack, the target's tail is a natural weapon with a reach of 5 feet. This spell has no effect on creatures lacking a prehensile tail. If the target already has an extra attack from *haste* or a similar effect, this spell only allows the tail to make dirty trick and steal combat maneuvers, but does not grant an extra attack.

VISHKANYAS

Vishkanyas are a race of exotic humanoids with poisonous blood. Possessed of an alien beauty, these graceful humanoids see the world through serpentine eyes of burnished gold. Their supple skin is covered with tiny scales, often of a light green, which are sometimes arrayed in patterns not unlike those of a serpent. They cannot be generalized as good or evil, but since they truly speak with forked tongues, they are content to accept the gold they're offered and leave questions of morality to others.

ALTERNATE RACIAL TRAITS

The following racial traits may be selected instead of existing vishkanya racial traits. Consult your GM before selecting any of these new options.

Sensual: You are trained in drawing attention to yourself. You gain a +2 bonus on any one Perform skill. This racial trait replaces keen senses.

Subtle Appearance: You have normal (humanlike) eyes, and your beauty is more conventional. You gain a +4 bonus on Disguise checks to look fully human. This racial trait replaces low-light vision.

FAVORED CLASS OPTIONS

The following options are available to all vishkanyas who have the listed favored class, and unless otherwise stated, the bonus applies each time you select the favored class reward.

Bard: Add +1 to the bard's total number of bardic performance rounds per day.

Rogue: Add +1 to the rogue's CMD when resisting a grapple or reposition attempt.

Sorcerer: Select one bloodline power at 1st level that is normally usable a number of times per day equal to 3 + the sorcerer's Charisma modifier. The sorcerer adds +1/2 to the number of uses per day of that bloodline power.

RACIAL ARCHETYPES

The following racial archetype is available to vishkanyas.

Deadly Courtesan (Rogue)

Skilled at manipulation and diversion, the deadly courtesan builds up those around her and periodically takes them down. She can be a spy, entertainer, assassin,

VISHKANYA RACIAL TRAITS

+2 Dexterity, +2 Charisma, −2 Wisdom: Vishkanyas are graceful and elegant, but they are often irrational.

Vishkanya: Vishkanyas are humanoids with the vishkanya subtype.

Medium: Vishkanyas are Medium creatures and have no bonuses or penalties due to their size.

Normal Speed: Vishkanyas have a base speed of 30 feet.

Low-Light Vision: Vishkanyas can see twice as far as humans in conditions of dim light.

Keen Senses: Vishkanyas receive a +2 racial bonus on Perception checks.

Limber: Vishkanyas receive a +2 racial bonus on Escape Artist and Stealth checks.

Poison Resistance: A vishkanya has a racial bonus on saving throws against poison equal to its Hit Dice.

Poison Use: Vishkanyas are skilled in the use of poison and never accidentally poison themselves when using or applying poison.

Toxic: A number of times per day equal to his Constitution modifier (minimum 1/day), a vishkanya can envenom a weapon that he wields with his toxic saliva or blood (using blood requires the vishkanya to be injured when he uses this ability). Applying venom in this way is a swift action.

Vishkanya Venom: Injury; *save* Fort DC 10 + 1/2 the vishkanya's Hit Dice + the vishkanya's Constitution modifier; *frequency* 1/round for 6 rounds; *effect* 1d2 Dex; *cure* 1 save.

Weapon Familiarity: Vishkanyas are always proficient with blowguns, kukri, and shuriken.

Languages: Vishkanyas begin play speaking Common and Vishkanya. Vishkanyas with high Intelligence scores can choose from the following: Aklo, Draconic, Elven, Goblin, Sylvan, and Undercommon.

bodyguard, or just an intimate to someone who needs it most. A deadly courtesan has the following class features.

Class Skills: At 1st level, a deadly courtesan adds Knowledge (history) and Knowledge (nobility) to her list of class skills and removes Knowledge (dungeoneering) from her list of class skills.

Bardic Performance (Su): At 2nd level, a deadly courtesan gains the bardic performance ability and the fascinate bardic performance. Her fascinate DC is 10 + 1/2 her rogue level + her Charisma modifier. She can use this bardic performance for a number of rounds per day equal to 1 + her Charisma modifier. At each level after 2nd, she can use bardic performance for 1 additional round per day. If the courtesan also has bard levels, she may use these rounds for either class's fascinate bardic performance, and her bard and rogue levels stack for determining her fascinate DC. This ability replaces the rogue trick gained at 2nd level.

Inspire Competence (Su): At 3rd level, a deadly courtesan can use her bardic performance to inspire competence. The bonus begins at +2 and increases by +1 for every six levels the courtesan has attained beyond 3rd (+3 at 9th and +4 at 15th). This ability replaces all levels of trap sense.

Performance Strike (Sp): At 8th level, as a swift action, a deadly courtesan may expend rounds of bardic performance to gain a morale bonus on one attack roll. The amount of the bonus is equal to the number of bardic performance rounds expended (maximum bonus equal to 1/2 her deadly courtesan level). This ability replaces improved uncanny dodge.

Rogue Talents: The following rogue talents complement the deadly courtesan archetype: finesse rogue, stand up (*Core Rulebook*); charmer, coax information, fast fingers, honeyed words (*Advanced Player's Guide*); convincing lie, deft palm (*Ultimate Combat*).

Advanced Talents: The following advanced rogue talents complement the deadly courtesan archetype: slippery mind (*Core Rulebook*); master of disguise (*Advanced Player's Guide*); rumormonger, unwitting ally (*Ultimate Combat*).

NEW RACIAL RULES

The following options are available to vishkanyas. At the GM's discretion, other appropriate races may also make use of some of these.

Vishkanya Equipment

Vishkanyas have access to the following equipment.

Poison Tattoo: This henna-like paste creates a dark brown tattoo on the hands or feet that fades over the next 2d6 days. The tattoo temporarily boosts the strength of a vishkanya's natural poison, increasing the DC of the next weapon envenomed with the vishkanya's blood or saliva by +2 (once used, the tattoo is merely decorative and does not affect the creature's poison). A typical tattoo consists of intricate whorls and spiritual symbols on the hands or feet.

Vishkanya Equipment

Item	Cost	Weight	Craft DC
Poison tattoo	50 gp	—	20

Vishkanya Feats

Vishkanyas have access to the following feat.

Sleep Venom

You can change the nature of your toxic spittle to put your enemies to sleep.

Prerequisite: Vishkanya.

Benefit: As a swift action, you may alter the effects of your venom so the target falls unconscious. This changes the initial and secondary effect of your venom to the following: *initial effect* staggered for 1d4 rounds; *secondary effect* unconsciousness for 1 minute. You must make the decision to alter your venom before you apply it to a weapon.

Normal: Vishkanya venom deals Dexterity damage.

Vishkanya Magic Items

Vishkanyas have access to the following magic item.

CORSET OF THE VISHKANYA

Aura faint transmutation; **CL** 3rd
Slot chest; **Price** 3,000 gp; **Weight** 1 lb.

DESCRIPTION

This black corset fits neatly beneath armor. As a free action, the wearer can compress herself to fit through tight spaces as though affected by a *squeeze* spell for up to 10 rounds per day. While using the corset's magic, she gains a +5 bonus on Escape Artist checks.

CONSTRUCTION

Requirements Craft Wondrous Item, *grease*, *squeeze* (see below); **Cost** 1,500 gp

Vishkanya Spells

Vishkanyas have access to the following spell.

SQUEEZE

School transmutation (polymorph); **Level** alchemist 2, sorcerer/wizard 2, witch 2

Casting Time 1 standard action
Components V, S
Range touch
Target creature touched
Duration 1 minute/level
Save Fortitude negates (harmless); **Spell Resistance** yes (harmless)

The target becomes flexible regardless of its actual size and mass. It can move through areas at least half its size with no penalty for squeezing. It can move through a space at least one-quarter its width using the penalties for squeezing through a space at least half its width.

WAYANGS

The wayangs are a race of small supernatural humanoids who trace their ancestry to the Plane of Shadows. They are extremely gaunt, with pixielike stature and skin the color of deep shadow. Deeply spiritual, they follow a philosophy known as "The Dissolution," which teaches that in passing they may again merge into the shadow. They readily express their beliefs through ritual scarification and skin bleaching, marking their bodies with raised white dots in ornate spirals and geometric patterns. Shy and elusive, they live in small, interdependent tribes. Wayangs rarely associate with outsiders.

ALTERNATE RACIAL TRAITS

The following racial trait may be selected instead of existing wayang racial traits. Consult your GM before selecting this new option.

Dissolution's Child: Once per day, you may change your appearance to look as if you were little more than a 4-foot-tall area of shadow. Your physical form still exists and you are not incorporeal—only your appearance changes. This works like *invisibility*, except it only lasts 1 round per level (maximum 5 rounds). This is a supernatural ability. This racial trait replaces shadow magic.

FAVORED CLASS OPTIONS

The following options are available to all wayangs who have the listed favored class, and unless otherwise stated, the bonus applies each time you select the favored class reward.

Bard: Add one spell known from the wizard's illusion school spell list. This spell must be at least one level below the highest spell level the bard can cast. The spell is treated as being one level higher, unless it is also on the bard spell list.

Oracle: Add one spell known from the wizard's illusion school spell list. This spell must be at least one level below the highest spell level the oracle can cast. That spell is treated as one level higher unless it is also on the oracle spell list.

Sorcerer: Add +1/2 point of damage to any illusion spells of the shadow subschool cast by the sorcerer.

Summoner: Add +1 skill rank to the summoner's eidolon.

RACIAL ARCHETYPES

The following racial archetype is available to wayangs.

Shadow Puppeteer (Bard)

A shadow puppeteer invokes amazing and terrifying shadow puppet shows, producing supernatural effects by

WAYANG RACIAL TRAITS

+2 Dexterity, +2 Intelligence, –2 Wisdom: Wayang are nimble and cagey, but their perception of the world is clouded by shadows.

Wayang: Wayangs are humanoids with the wayang subtype.

Small: Wayangs are Small creatures and gain a +1 size bonus to their AC, a +1 size bonus on attack rolls, a –1 penalty on their CMB and to CMD, and a +4 size bonus on Stealth checks.

Slow Speed: Wayangs have a base speed of 20 feet.

Darkvision: Wayangs can see in the dark up to 60 feet.

Light and Dark (Su): Once per day as an immediate action, a wayang can treat positive and negative energy effects as if she were an undead creature, taking damage from positive energy and healing damage from negative energy. This ability lasts for 1 minute once activated.

Lurker: Wayangs gain a +2 racial bonus on Perception and Stealth checks.

Shadow Magic: Wayangs add +1 to the DC of any saving throws against spells of the shadow subschool that they cast. Wayangs with a Charisma score of 11 or higher also gain the following spell-like abilities: 1/day—*ghost sound*, *pass without trace*, and *ventriloquism*. The caster level for these effects is equal to the wayang's level. The DC for these spells is equal to 10 + the spell's level + the wayang's Charisma modifier.

Shadow Resistance: Wayangs get a +2 racial bonus on saving throws against spells of the shadow subschool.

Languages: Wayangs begin play speaking Common and Wayang. Wayangs with high Intelligence scores can choose from the following: any human language, Abyssal, Aklo, Draconic, Goblin, Infernal, Nagaji, Samsaran, and Tengu.

creating and manipulating shadow. A shadow puppeteer has the following class feature.

Bardic Performance: A shadow puppeteer gains the following types of bardic performance. The character must be able to perform shadow puppetry in order to activate any of these abilities. Shadow puppetry uses Perform (act), and requires a light source. These abilities replace all levels of inspire courage and inspire competence.

Shadow Servant (Sp): At 1st level, the puppeteer can create a *shadow servant* to perform simple tasks. The shadow servant is identical to an *unseen servant* (caster level equal to the shadow puppeteer's bard level), except it appears as a formless shadow. Shadow servant relies on visual components.

Shadow Puppets (Sp): At 1st level, a shadow puppeteer can use bardic performance to create one quasi-real shadowy creature resembling a monster from the *summon monster I* list. These shadowy creatures otherwise work like *shadow conjuration*, and targets interacting with them get a Will saving throw (DC 10 + 1/2 your bard level + your Charisma bonus) to treat them as only 20% real. At 4th level and every three levels thereafter, this ability acts like the next higher version of *summon monster* (*summon monster II* at 4th level and so on).

NEW RACIAL RULES

The following options are available to wayangs. At the GM's discretion, other appropriate races may also make use of some of these.

Wayang Equipment

Wayangs have access to the following equipment.

Shadow Stencils: This set of 10 elaborate metal stencils are used in shadow puppetry to cast shadows of highly stylized figures and objects. If used to aid in the creation of any type of shadow spell or effect (including shadow puppet bardic performances), a wayang adds a +1 competence bonus to her saving throw DC. Using a shadow stencil requires one hand.

Wayang Equipment

Item	Cost	Weight
Shadow stencil set	30 gp	2 lbs.

Wayang Feats

Wayangs have access to the following feat.

Shadowy Dash

In dim light, you resemble little more than a shadow.

Prerequisite: Wayang.

Benefit: Whenever you are in an area of dim light or darkness, you can move at full speed using Stealth without taking the normal –5 penalty for doing so.

Normal: When moving at more than half your speed and up to your normal speed, you take a –5 penalty on Stealth checks.

Wayang Magic Items

Wayangs have access to the following magic item.

BAG OF SHADOW CLOUDS
Aura moderate illusion; **CL** 7th
Slot none; **Price** 30,240 gp; **Weight** 1 lb.

DESCRIPTION

Anyone peering into this bag of deep gray cloth sees nothing but empty blackness. Within the bag exists an extradimensional space linked to the Plane of Shadow. Three times per day, as a move action, the bearer can reach within the bag and pull out 1d4 semisolid shards of shadow. The bag's bearer can use each shard of shadow as a thrown weapon targeting a single 5-foot square. When it hits, it acts as a *darkness* spell, but only affecting one 5-foot square. As a move action, the bearer of the bag can move a shadow cloud up to 10 feet in any direction. Whether or not they are thrown, the shards of shadow and shadow clouds last 10 minutes before dissipating.

CONSTRUCTION

Requirements Craft Wondrous Item, *darkness*, *shadow conjuration*; **Cost** 15,120 gp

Wayang Spells

Wayangs have access to the following spells.

SHADOW ANCHOR
School illusion (shadow) [shadow]; **Level** bard 2, sorcerer/wizard 2, witch 2
Casting Time 1 standard action
Components S
Range touch
Target creature touched
Effect a shadowy shadow tether
Duration 1 round/level (D); see text
Save Will negates; **Spell Resistance** yes

The target's shadow becomes a flexible tether to its current square. The creature can move up to 5 feet from that square without penalty. Moving farther than 5 feet from the tether point requires the target to make a bull rush combat maneuver check against a CMB of 10 + 1/2 your caster level + your Intelligence modifier (if a witch or wizard) or Charisma modifier (if a bard or sorcerer). The target takes a –1 penalty for every 5 feet of distance between it and its tethered square. Failing this check means the target's move is wasted and it cannot move farther away. If it fails this check by 10 or more, it is pulled 5 feet toward the tether square and is knocked prone. If it beats the check by 10 or more, the spell ends. This spell does not work on creatures that do not cast shadows or reflections. If the target uses a teleportation effect or leaves the current plane, the spell ends.

4 Race Builder

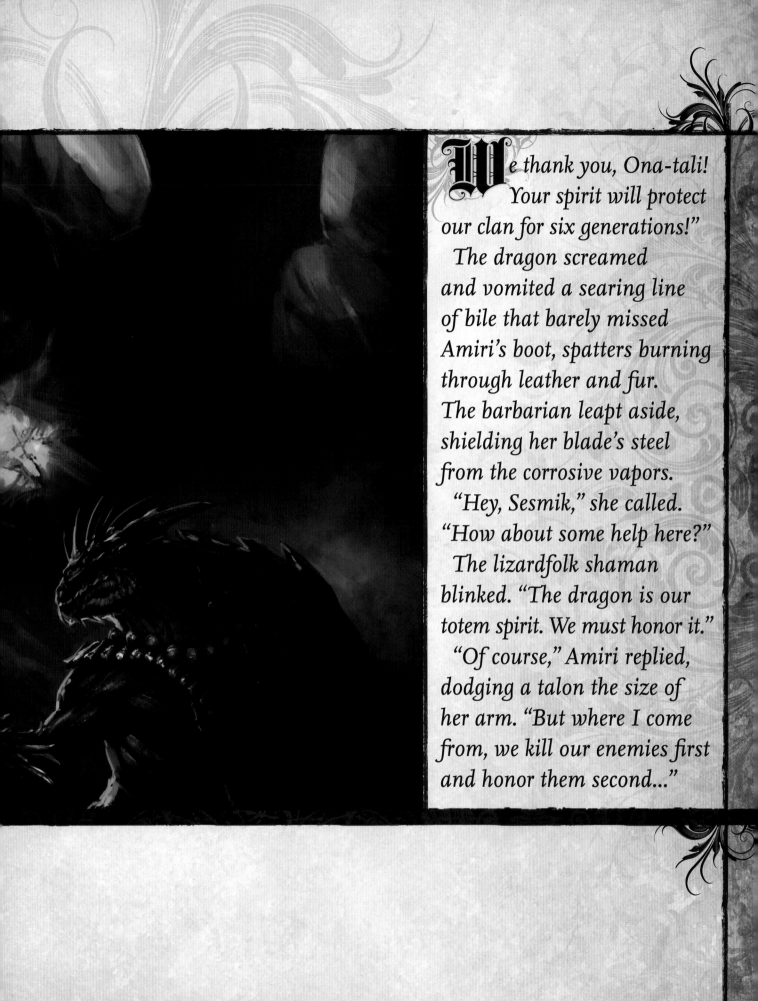

We thank you, Ona-tali! Your spirit will protect our clan for six generations!" The dragon screamed and vomited a searing line of bile that barely missed Amiri's boot, spatters burning through leather and fur. The barbarian leapt aside, shielding her blade's steel from the corrosive vapors.

"Hey, Sesmik," she called. "How about some help here?"

The lizardfolk shaman blinked. "The dragon is our totem spirit. We must honor it."

"Of course," Amiri replied, dodging a talon the size of her arm. "But where I come from, we kill our enemies first and honor them second..."

Race Builder

There comes a point in nearly every campaign when someone—either one of the players or the GM—wants to create a new race. Sometimes the GM needs a new race to fill a story or ecological niche in her campaign world. Such races may be as simple as elves who dwell in an arctic climate or as complex as clockwork giants from another plane of existence. Perhaps a player wants to play a monstrous race, or has been inspired by some piece of fiction or flight of creative fancy and wants to create a race for a new character concept not yet seen in Pathfinder. The following rules allow GMs, or even players with GM oversight, to create new races that are balanced and mesh with the core races.

In addition, these rules allow you to create powerful races meant to take on more challenging encounters than those typically faced by the core races. You can create new races, model a race after an existing monster, or even "power up" core races in order to play those races side-by-side with more powerful new races.

RACE EXAMPLES

This chapter features numerous examples of races designed with the race builder. Sidebars early in the chapter offer detailed examples of races found in the *Pathfinder RPG Bestiary*, *Bestiary 2*, and *Bestiary 3* that would normally have racial Hit Dice, skills, and other abilities. PC members of such races, however, calculate these benefits based solely on their class. Note that these races are only an approximation of their monstrous counterparts and may not match exactly. Later in the chapter, sidebars detail entirely new races created using the race builder rules. Lastly, the final section of the chapter breaks down the points and abilities of core races and many of the featured and uncommon races.

CREATING A NEW RACE

This race builder allows you to create a new race by buying racial qualities and racial traits with Race Points (RP). There are a number of differences between racial qualities and racial traits. The main difference is that racial qualities are mandatory (you must make a choice for each category of racial qualities provided in these rules), whereas racial traits are optional. There are six categories of racial qualities, including type, subtypes (if any), size, base speed, ability score modifiers, and languages. Racial traits present a number of interesting options for the race you are creating, from expanded modes of movement and bonuses on skill checks to even stranger powers, like a frightening croak attack or the ability to change shape. Racial traits are split up into a number of different categories, such as defense, offense, and magical traits.

Before you buy racial qualities and traits, you must determine the power level of your race. The GM decides this based on the needs of her campaign. The power level of the race determines the number of RP you get to build the race, as well as the maximum number of racial traits you can choose from each racial trait category and what kinds of traits you can take from those categories.

Sometimes racial qualities and traits cost 0 RP or a negative number of RP, which means they can be taken for free or gain back RP, respectively. In the case of racial qualities, choosing a 0-point option still counts toward your choice for that racial quality category, and in the case of racial traits, such choices still count toward the maximum number of traits per racial trait category.

There are three power levels: standard, advanced, and monstrous. Standard races can only take standard racial traits, while advanced races can take both standard and advanced racial traits, and monstrous races can take standard, advanced, and monstrous racial traits. Table 4–1 summarizes the number of RP you can spend as well as the maximum number of traits per racial trait category you can take based on your power level.

TABLE 4-1: RACIAL POINTS AND TRAIT MAXIMUMS BY POWER LEVEL

Power Level	RP Range	Traits per Category
Standard	1–10	3
Advanced	11–20	4
Monstrous	20+	5

Once you have determined the race's power level, follow each of the steps below to create your race.

STEP 1: CONCEPT

A race is more than just a group of individuals with similar qualities and traits. A race is a collection of people with a shared history and cultural identity. While the race builder presents many options for creating new races, and it may be tempting to treat each section as a buffet of options to help you ferret out the most optimal choices for your character, it is generally more beneficial for your campaign world to conceptualize your race first. Before choosing options, consider answering some questions about your race and its culture. Answering these questions can aid you in making reasonable choices about the qualities and traits of your race so that it can better fit in the game world—rather than just being a collection of seemingly random options. Such questions might include the following.

- Where does your race tend to live and why?
- What does your race look like? How does the members' appearance help them adapt to their typical environment?

- What is your race's history? Does it have a creation myth? Were there pivotal events in the race's history?
- What kinds of relationships does your race have with other races? Does it have allies? Competitors? Enemies? Hated foes?
- What classes does your race tend to favor?

If you are using these rules and you are not the GM, make sure you work closely with your GM to create a race that fills a definite niche and need in her campaign world.

STEP 2: RACIAL QUALITIES

The next step is to choose your race's qualities. You must select an option from each of the following quality categories. Qualities or aspects of qualities often serve as prerequisites for racial traits.

Type Quality

This is the race's creature type. A race's creature type is similar to the corresponding creature type found in the *Pathfinder RPG Bestiary*, with a few important differences. The first difference is that each race type assumes members of the race are roughly humanoid in shape and have two arms, two legs, a torso, and a head. This is important so that a race can take advantage of all the various magic item slots available to characters and can utilize the standard weapon and armor options. The second difference is that all of these race types are 0-Hit Dice creatures, which means that their Hit Dice, base attack bonus, saving throw progression, skill points, class skills, and weapon and armor proficiencies are based on the class levels each member of a race takes.

Like other racial qualities, each type has a point cost. The baseline creature type—humanoid—costs 0 RP, and offers the most flexibility when choosing other racial traits and racial abilities, while a more expensive type typically grants less flexibility. The cost of the race's type also determines which of these types you can choose from based on the power level of the race you are creating. You cannot pick a type with an RP cost equal to or higher than the maximum RP cost of the power level of the race you are building. This means you must build an advanced race if you want to make a race with the undead type, or a monstrous race if you are building a race with the construct type. If you want to make a construct- or undead-themed creature at lower power levels, see the Special Subtypes sidebar on page 218 for some lower-cost options.

Sometimes a race type may grant racial traits as features. For instance, the construct type grants members of that race darkvision 60 feet. If this is the case, the cost of that racial trait is already paid for when you buy the type quality, and this trait does not count toward the maximum when you buy racial traits from the corresponding racial trait category. For instance,

RACES WITHOUT CONSTITUTION

Generating ability scores for most of the races you create with these rules—even advanced and monstrous races—uses the standard methods found on page 15 of the *Pathfinder RPG Core Rulebook*. Races without Constitution scores are the exception, and require some slight changes to the ability score generation methods. The changes are as follows, corresponding to the five methods found in the *Core Rulebook*.

Standard: Roll 4d6, discarding the lowest result as normal, and sum the results, but only do this five times, and assign them as you see fit, skipping Constitution.

Classic: Roll 3d6 and sum the results five times, and assign them as you see fit, skipping Constitution.

Heroic: Roll 2d6 and add 6 to the sum of each. Do this five times and assign them as you see fit, skipping Constitution.

Dice Pool: Instead of a pool of 24d6, races without Constitution get a pool of 20d6 to assign to the ability scores, except for Constitution. These characters still must assign a minimum of 3d6 in each of the other ability scores. Increase the number for high-powered games.

Purchase: When using the purchase method for ability scores, assume members of races without Constitution have a Constitution score of 10 and buy the rest of the abilities normally using the points allocated for the campaign's power level.

when buying other vision traits for a construct race, the darkvision 60 feet feature that race already has does not count toward the limit of five traits from the senses racial trait category for the race. Traits granted by the race type still count for meeting any other trait prerequisites.

The humanoid type requires that you pick at least one subtype for your race, and the outsider (native) type allows you to make a decision about what other plane your race may have ties to. Keep track of your race's creature type, any subtypes it has, and any planes it has ties to. Sometimes a race's type, subtypes, or planar ties serve as prerequisites for some racial traits. For instance, you must have the ratfolk subtype to take the rodent empathy racial trait, and you must have ties to Abaddon, the Abyss, or Hell in order to take the fiendish sorcery racial trait.

Aberration (3 RP)

Aberrations have bizarre anatomies, strange abilities, alien mindsets, or any combination of the three. An aberration has the following features.

- Aberrations have the darkvision 60 feet racial trait.
- Aberrations breathe, eat, and sleep.

Special Subtypes

Two of the creature types—construct and undead—create interesting player options, but are too expensive if you are trying to create a race within the strictures of the standard power level. If you are making a standard race and still want it to be a construct or undead race, consider the two special subtypes detailed below, the half-construct and half-undead. Each of these includes much of the flavor of the types they are related to, but grants fewer abilities and immunities. These subtypes can be added to any of the race types except for construct and undead. When you apply these subtypes to the humanoid type, choose another subtype as the creature's other half. For example, you could make a creature that is humanoid (half-construct, human).

Half-Construct (7 RP)

A half-construct race is a group of creatures that are artificially enhanced or have parts replaced by constructed mechanisms, be they magical or mechanical. A half-construct race has the following features.

- Half-constructs gain a +2 racial bonus on saving throws against disease, mind-affecting effects, poison, and effects that cause either exhaustion or fatigue.
- Half-constructs cannot be raised or resurrected.
- Half-constructs do not breathe, eat, or sleep, unless they want to gain some beneficial effect from one of these activities. This means that a half-construct can drink potions to benefit from their effects and can sleep in order to regain spells, but neither of these activities is required for the construct to survive or stay in good health.

Half-Undead (5 RP)

Half-undead races are strange or unholy fusions of the living and the undead. Players interested in playing a half-undead race might also consider the dhampir (*Bestiary 2* 89), the progeny of a vampire and a human. A half-undead race has the following features.

- Half-undead have the darkvision 60 feet racial trait.
- Half-undead gain a +2 racial bonus on saving throws against disease and mind-affecting effects.
- Half-undead take no penalties from energy-draining effects, though they can still be killed if they accrue more negative levels than they have Hit Dice. After 24 hours, any negative levels they've gained are removed without any additional saving throws.
- Half-undead creatures are harmed by positive energy and healed by negative energy. A half-undead creature with the fast healing special quality still benefits from that quality.

Construct (20 RP)

A construct race is a group of animated objects or artificially created creatures. A construct race has the following features.

- Constructs have no Constitution score. Any DCs or other statistics that rely on a Constitution score treat a construct as having a score of 10 (no bonus or penalty).
- Constructs have the low-light vision racial trait.
- Constructs have the darkvision 60 feet racial trait.
- Constructs are immune to all mind-affecting effects (charms, compulsions, morale effects, patterns, and phantasms).
- Constructs cannot heal damage on their own, but can often be repaired via exposure to a certain kind of effect (depending on the construct's racial abilities) or through the use of the Craft Construct feat. Constructs can also be healed through spells such as *make whole*. A construct with the fast healing special quality still benefits from that quality.
- Constructs are not subject to ability damage, ability drain, fatigue, exhaustion, energy drain, or nonlethal damage.
- Constructs are immune to any effect that requires a Fortitude save (unless the effect also works on objects or is harmless).
- Constructs do not risk death due to massive damage, but they are immediately destroyed when reduced to 0 hit points or fewer.
- Constructs cannot be raised or resurrected.
- Constructs are hard to destroy, and gain bonus hit points based on their size, as shown on the following table.

Construct Size	Bonus Hit Points
Tiny	—
Small	10
Medium	20
Large	30

- Constructs do not breathe, eat, or sleep, unless they want to gain some beneficial effect from one of these activities. This means that a construct can drink potions to benefit from their effects and can sleep in order to regain spells, but neither of these activities is required to survive or stay in good health.

Dragon (10 RP)

A dragon is a reptilian creature with magical or unusual abilities. A dragon race has the following features.

- Dragons have the darkvision 60 feet racial trait.
- Dragons have the low-light vision racial trait.
- Dragons are immune to magical sleep effects and paralysis effects.
- Dragons breathe, eat, and sleep.

Fey (2 RP)

A fey is a creature with supernatural abilities and connections to nature or to some other force or place. A fey race has the following features.
- Fey have the low-light vision racial trait.
- Fey breathe, eat, and sleep.

Humanoid (0 RP)

Humanoid races have few or no supernatural or spell-like abilities, but most can speak and have well-developed societies. Humanoids are usually Small or Medium, unless they have the giant subtype, in which case they are Large. Every humanoid creature also has a subtype to match its race, such as human, giant, goblinoid, reptilian, or tengu. If you are making a new humanoid race, you should either find an existing subtype to match or make a new one by using the name of the race as the subtype. If you are making a half-breed race, it should have the racial type of both parent races. For example, a half-elf has both the human and the elf subtypes. Subtypes are often important to qualify for other racial abilities and feats. If a humanoid has a racial subtype, it is considered a member of that race in the case of race prerequisites. A humanoid race has the following features.
- Humanoids breathe, eat, and sleep.

Monstrous Humanoid (3 RP)

Monstrous humanoids are similar to humanoids, but have monstrous or animalistic features. They often have magical abilities as well. A monstrous humanoid race has the following features.
- Monstrous humanoids have the darkvision 60 feet racial trait.
- Monstrous humanoids breathe, eat, and sleep.

Outsider (native) (3 RP)

A native outsider is at least partially composed of the essence (but not necessarily the matter) of some plane other than the Material Plane. Some creatures start out as some other type and become outsiders when they attain a higher (or lower) state of spiritual existence. When making a native outsider race, it is sometimes important to pick a single Outer Plane that race is tied to. For example, tieflings are tied to Abaddon, the Abyss, or Hell. Such ties can be important for qualifying for other racial abilities, but it's not required that a native outsider be tied to another plane. A native outsider race has the followings features.
- Native outsiders have the darkvision 60 feet racial trait.
- Native outsiders breathe, eat, and sleep.

Plant (10 RP)

This type encompasses humanoid-shaped vegetable creatures. Note that regular plants, such as those found in ordinary gardens and fields, lack Wisdom and Charisma scores and are not creatures, but objects, even though they are alive. A plant race has the following features.
- Plants have the low-light vision racial trait.
- Plants are immune to all mind-affecting effects (charms, compulsions, morale effects, patterns, and phantasms).
- Plants are immune to paralysis, poison, polymorph, sleep effects, and stunning.
- Plants breathe and eat, but do not sleep, unless they want to gain some beneficial effect from this activity. This means that a plant creature can sleep in order to regain spells, but sleep is not required to survive or stay in good health.

Undead (16 RP)

Undead races are once-living creatures animated by spiritual or supernatural forces. An undead race has the following features.
- Undead have no Constitution score. Undead use their Charisma score in place of their Constitution score when calculating hit points, Fortitude saves, and any special ability that relies on Constitution (such as when calculating a breath weapon's DC).
- Undead have the darkvision 60 feet racial trait.
- Undead are immune to all mind-affecting effects (charms, compulsions, morale effects, patterns, and phantasms).
- Undead are immune to bleed damage, death effects, disease, paralysis, poison, sleep effects, and stunning.
- Undead are not subject to nonlethal damage, ability drain, or energy drain, and are immune to damage to physical ability scores (Constitution, Dexterity, and Strength), as well as to exhaustion and fatigue effects.
- Undead are harmed by positive energy and healed by negative energy. An undead creature with the fast healing special quality still benefits from that quality.
- Undead are immune to any effect that requires a Fortitude save (unless the effect also works on objects or is harmless).
- Undead do not risk death from massive damage, but are immediately destroyed when reduced to 0 hit points or fewer.
- Undead are not affected by *raise dead* and *reincarnate* spells or abilities. *Resurrection* and *true resurrection* can affect undead creatures. These spells turn undead creatures back into the living creatures they were before becoming undead.
- Undead do not breathe, eat, or sleep, unless they want to gain some beneficial effect from one of these activities. This means that an undead creature can drink potions to benefit from their effects and can sleep in order to regain spells, but neither of these activities is required to survive or stay in good health.

Size Quality

The next step is to pick a size quality for your race. Most races are Medium or Small, which have no prerequisites, but you can also elect to make your race either Large or Tiny with the following modifications at the listed point cost.

Large (7 RP): *Prerequisite*: Humanoids taking this quality must have the giant subtype; *Benefit*: Large creatures gain a +2 size bonus to Strength and a −2 size penalty to Dexterity. Large races take a −1 size penalty to their AC, a −1 size penalty on attack rolls, a +1 bonus on combat maneuver checks and to their CMD, and a −4 size penalty on Stealth checks. A Large creature takes up a space that is 10 feet by 10 feet and has a reach of 5 feet.

Medium (0 RP): Medium races have no bonuses or penalties due to their size. A Medium creature has a space of 5 feet by 5 feet and a reach of 5 feet.

Small (0 RP): Small races gain a +1 size bonus to their AC, a +1 size bonus on attack rolls, a −1 penalty on combat maneuver checks and to their CMD, and a +4 size bonus on Stealth checks. Small races have a space of 5 feet by 5 feet and a reach of 5 feet.

Tiny (4 RP): *Prerequisites*: Aberration, construct, dragon, fey, outsider (native), or plant type; *Benefit*: Tiny creatures gain a +2 size bonus to Dexterity and a −2 size penalty to Strength. Tiny races gain a +2 size bonus to their AC, a +2 size bonus on attack rolls, a −2 penalty on combat maneuver checks and to their CMD, and a +8 size bonus on Stealth checks. Tiny characters take up a space of 2-1/2 feet by 2-1/2 feet, so up to four of these characters can fit into a single square. Tiny races typically have a natural reach of 0 feet, meaning they can't reach into adjacent squares. They must enter an opponent's square to attack it in melee. This provokes an attack of opportunity from the opponent. Since they have no natural reach, they do not threaten the squares around them. Other creatures can move through those squares without provoking attacks of opportunity. Tiny creatures typically cannot flank an enemy.

Base Speed Quality

The next step is to pick the base speed quality for your race. Some racial traits can increase speed or grant other movement types, but these traits usually require the normal speed quality as a prerequisite. You have the following options.

Normal Speed (0 RP): The race has a base speed of 30 feet.

CENTAUR

Type	
Monstrous humanoid	2 RP
Size	
Large	7 RP
Base Speed	
Normal	0 RP
Ability Score Modifiers	
Flexible (+2 Str, +2 Wis)	2 RP
Languages	
Standard	0 RP
Racial Traits	
Ability Score Racial Traits	
Advanced Constitution (+2)	4 RP
Advanced Dexterity (+2)	4 RP
Advanced Strength (+2)	4 RP
Defense Racial Traits	
Natural armor	2 RP
Movement Racial Traits	
Fast (+10 feet)	1 RP
Senses Racial Traits	
Darkvision 60 ft.	— RP
Other Racial Traits	
Quadruped	2 RP
Total	**28 RP**

Slow Speed (–1 RP): The race has a base speed of 20 feet. If the race is Medium, its members' speed is never modified by armor or encumbrance.

Ability Score Modifier Quality

The next step is to determine the ability score modifier quality for your race. In many ways, choosing this quality is one of the most important choices when creating a new race, as it determines many of the native abilities of that race.

With the exception of the human heritage modifier quality, when you choose a race's ability score modifiers, you are choosing what ability scores are modified for every member of that race. Only the human heritage modifier quality allows individual members to decide which ability score is modified during character creation.

Most of the ability score modifier qualities divide ability scores into two broad categories that each represent three of the six abilities: physical (Strength, Dexterity, and Constitution) and mental (Intelligence, Wisdom, and Charisma).

With the exception of the human heritage modifier quality, bonuses granted to ability scores with one of these qualities count as racial bonuses for the purpose of qualifying for racial trait prerequisites.

Advanced (4 RP): *Prerequisites:* Advanced or monstrous power level; *Modifiers:* Pick either mental or physical ability scores. Members of this race gain a +2 bonus to all of those scores, a +4 bonus to one score of the other type, and a –2 penalty to one other ability score of the other type.

Flexible (2 RP): Members of this race gain a +2 bonus to any two ability scores.

Greater Paragon (2 RP): Members of this race gain a +4 bonus to one ability score, a –2 penalty to one physical ability score, and a –2 penalty to one mental ability score.

Greater Weakness (–3 RP): Pick either mental or physical ability scores. Members of this race take a –4 penalty to one of those ability scores, a –2 penalty to another of those ability scores, and a +2 bonus to the other ability score.

Human Heritage (0 RP): *Prerequisites:* Human subtype; *Modifiers:* Members of this race gain a +2 to any single ability score of your choice during character creation.

Mixed Weakness (–2 RP): Pick either mental or physical ability scores. Members of this race gain a +2 bonus to one ability score of that type and a –2 penalty to another ability score of that type. They also gain a +2 bonus to one ability score of the other type and a –4 penalty to another ability score of the other type.

Paragon (1 RP): Members of this race gain a +4 bonus to a single ability score, and a –2 penalty to either all physical or all mental ability scores. If the bonus is to a single physical ability score, the penalties apply to all mental ability scores, and vice versa.

Specialized (1 RP): Pick either mental or physical ability scores. Members of this race gain a +2 bonus to two ability scores of the chosen type, and a –2 penalty to one ability score of the other type.

Standard (0 RP): Members of this race gain a +2 bonus to one physical ability score, a +2 bonus to one mental ability score, and a –2 penalty to any other ability score.

Weakness (–1 RP): Members of this race gain a +2 bonus to one physical ability score, a +2 bonus to one mental ability score, and a –4 penalty to any other ability score.

CHALLENGING ADVANCED AND MONSTROUS RACES

Because they have powerful racial traits and abilities, advanced and monstrous races require greater challenges, especially at lower levels. The basic guideline for accomplishing this is to treat a group of characters with advanced and monstrous races as a level or more higher for a number of levels based on their total RP spent, using the following chart. Calculate the party's adjusted average party level, and use that number, rather than the actual APL, when creating encounters and adventures for the group. For groups with mixed power levels, average the RP and round the result to the nearest multiple of 10.

Avg RP	Average Party Level			
	1–5	6–10	11–15	16–20
20	+1 level	+0 level	+0 level	+0 level
30	+2 level	+1 level	+0 level	+0 level
40	+3 level	+2 level	+1 level	+0 level

Language Quality

The next step is to pick the race's language quality. This quality determines the starting languages and bonus languages for the race. There are three options. In cases where the language trait instructs you to choose a racial language, that language is either the race's racial language (if any; feel free to create a new language for the race if you wish), Draconic (if it is a humanoid with the reptilian subtype), or, if the race is of the outsider (native) type, one of the planar languages (Abyssal, Aquan, Auran, Celestial, Ignan, Infernal, or Terran) of the corresponding plane. (Creatures tied to Abaddon can take either Abyssal or Infernal as a racial language.) If your race is native to the Darklands, you can replace Common with Undercommon. See the Linguistics skill entry on pages 100–102 of the *Core Rulebook* for a list of languages.

Construct and undead races usually have the racial language of the race that created them.

Linguist (1 RP): Members of this race start with Common plus their racial language (if any). Furthermore, members of this race with high Intelligence scores can learn any languages they want (except Druidic and other secret languages).

Humanoid Subtypes as Prerequisites

There are a number of racial traits that require a certain humanoid subtype as a prerequisite. This is usually the case when a racial trait mentions a race in its name. As the GM, you can view these subtype prerequisites as suggestions and indicators as to what kinds of races or humanoid subtypes would usually take these traits. Feel free to change the name or racial subtype prerequisite of such a trait to better fit the race you are building.

Standard (0 RP): Members of this race start with Common plus their racial language (if any). Furthermore, choose up to seven languages (except for Druidic or other secret languages). Members of this race with high Intelligence scores can choose from any of these additional languages.

Xenophobic (0 RP): Members of this race start with their racial language only. Races without a racial language cannot take this array. Furthermore, choose up to four languages (except for Druidic or other secret languages), one of which must be Common (or Undercommon, if the race is native to the Darklands). Members of this race with high Intelligence scores can choose from any of these additional languages.

STEP 3: RACIAL TRAITS

Once you have chosen all your racial qualities, you may then choose your racial traits with your remaining RP.

Racial traits are divided into several categories: ability score, defense, feat and skill, magical, movement, offense, senses, weakness, and other racial traits. The number of racial traits you can buy from each category depends on the power level of the race you are creating—standard races can pick no more than three traits from each category, advanced races can pick no more than four traits from each category, and monstrous races can pick no more than five traits from each category. Furthermore, traits in each category are organized by type—standard, advanced, and monstrous. Standard races can only select traits from the standard section of each category, advanced races can select traits from the standard or advanced sections, and monstrous races can select from any section.

Unless stated otherwise, all racial traits are extraordinary abilities, and each racial trait can only be taken once.

The following format is used for all racial traits.

Name (RP Cost): Each racial trait begins with its name. The number of RP each trait costs is listed in parentheses directly after the name. For racial traits you can take more than once, this is the number of RP you pay each time you take the traits, unless stated otherwise in the Special line of the trait description.

Prerequisites: Some racial traits have prerequisites. Your race must meet any prerequisites listed in this entry before you can take the trait. Some traits require a specific type or subtype, while others require that you take other racial traits or qualities before you take it.

Benefit: This is the benefit the racial trait grants the members of the race you are creating.

Special: This includes additional facts about the racial trait.

Ability Score Racial Traits

The following racial traits add to the base ability score modifiers chosen in the ability score modifier quality.

Advanced Traits

Advanced Charisma (4 RP): *Prerequisites:* None; *Benefit:* Members of this race receive a +2 racial bonus to Charisma. *Special:* This bonus can be taken multiple times, but each additional time it is taken, its cost increases by 1 RP. Its effects stack.

Advanced Constitution (4 RP): *Prerequisites:* None; *Benefit:* Members of this race receive a +2 racial bonus to Constitution. *Special:* This bonus can be taken multiple times, but each additional time it is taken, its cost increases by 1 RP. Its effects stack.

Advanced Dexterity (4 RP): *Prerequisites:* None; *Benefit:* Members of this race receive a +2 racial bonus to Dexterity. *Special:* This bonus can be taken multiple times, but each additional time it is taken, its cost increases by 1 RP. Its effects stack.

Advanced Intelligence (4 RP): *Prerequisites:* None; *Benefit:* Members of this race receive a +2 racial bonus to Intelligence. *Special:* This bonus can be taken multiple times, but each additional time it is taken, its cost increases by 1 RP. Its effects stack.

Advanced Strength (4 RP): *Prerequisites:* None; *Benefit:* Members of this race receive a +2 racial bonus to Strength. *Special:* This bonus can be taken multiple times, but each additional time it is taken, its cost increases by 1 RP. Its effects stack.

Advanced Wisdom (4 RP): *Prerequisites:* None; *Benefit:* Members of this race receive a +2 racial bonus to Wisdom. *Special:* This bonus can be taken multiple times, but each additional time it is taken, its cost increases by 1 RP. Its effects stack.

Defense Racial Traits

The following racial traits augment the defenses of members of the race.

Standard Traits

Ancient Foe (3 RP): *Prerequisites:* None; *Benefit:* Choose one monster type or one subtype of the humanoid type. Members of this race gain a +2 dodge bonus to AC against monsters of that type and a +2 racial bonus on combat maneuver checks made to grapple creatures of that type.

Battle-Hardened (4 RP): *Prerequisites:* None; *Benefit:* Members of this race gain a +1 to CMD.

Bond to the Land (2 RP): *Prerequisites:* None; *Benefit:* Members of this race gain a +2 dodge bonus to AC when in a specific terrain type selected from the ranger's list of favored terrains. This choice is made at character creation, and cannot be changed.

Breeze-Kissed (4 RP): *Prerequisite:* Outsider (native) with ties to the Plane of Air or fey type; *Benefit:* Members of this race are surrounded by swirling winds, gaining a +2 racial bonus to AC against nonmagical ranged attacks. They can calm or renew these winds as a swift action. Once per day, a member of this race can channel this wind into a single gust, making a bull rush or trip combat maneuver attempt against one creature within 30 feet. Doing so exhausts the user's breeze-kissed ability for 24 hours. This is a supernatural ability.

Cat's Luck (1 RP): *Prerequisite:* The race has at least a +2 racial bonus to Dexterity; *Benefit:* Members of this race gain the following extraordinary ability: Once per day, when a member of this race makes a Reflex saving throw, it can roll the saving throw twice and take the better result. It must decide to use this ability before attempting the saving throw.

Celestial Resistance (3 RP): *Prerequisite:* Outsider (native) with ties to Elysium, Heaven, or Nirvana; *Benefit:* Members of this race gain acid resistance 5, cold resistance 5, and electricity resistance 5.

Cornered Fury (4 RP): *Prerequisites:* None; *Benefit:* Whenever a member of this race is reduced to half its hit points or fewer and has no conscious ally within 30 feet, it gains a +2 racial bonus on melee attack rolls and to Armor Class.

Crystalline Form (2 RP): *Prerequisite:* Outsider (native) with ties to the Plane of Earth, construct type, or half-construct subtype; *Benefit:* Members of this race have reflective, crystalline skin that grants them a +2 racial bonus to AC against rays. Once per day, they can deflect a single ray attack targeted at them as if they were using the Deflect Arrows feat.

Deathless Spirit (3 RP): *Prerequisites:* None; *Benefit:* Members of this race gain resistance 5 against negative energy damage. They do not lose hit points when they gain a negative level, and they gain a +2 racial bonus on saving throws against death effects, energy drain, negative energy, and spells or spell-like abilities of the necromancy school.

DRIDER

Type	
Aberration	3 RP
Size	
Large	7 RP
Base Speed	
Normal	0 RP
Ability Score Modifiers	
Flexible (+2 Con, +2 Wis)	2 RP
Languages	
Standard	0 RP
Racial Traits	
Ability Score Racial Traits	
Advanced Constitution (+2)	4 RP
Advanced Dexterity (+2)	4 RP
Advanced Strength (+2)	4 RP
Defense Racial Traits	
Greater spell resistance	3 RP
Natural armor	2 RP
Movement Racial Traits	
Climb	2 RP
Senses Racial Traits	
Darkvision 60 ft.	— RP
Other Racial Traits	
Quadruped (8 legs)	4 RP
Total	**35 RP**

Defensive Training, Greater (4 RP): *Prerequisites*: None; *Benefit*: Members of this race gain a +2 dodge bonus to Armor Class.

Defensive Training, Lesser (1 RP): *Prerequisites*: None; *Benefit*: Choose one subtype of humanoid. Members of this race gain a +4 dodge bonus to AC against humanoids of the chosen subtype.

Desert Runner (2 RP): *Prerequisites*: None; *Benefit*: Members of this race receive a +4 racial bonus on Constitution checks and Fortitude saves to avoid fatigue and exhaustion, as well as any other ill effects from running, forced marches, starvation, thirst, and hot or cold environments.

Dual-Minded (1 RP): *Prerequisite*: Humanoid with two subtypes or race with half-construct or half-undead subtype; *Benefit*: Members of this race gain a +2 bonus on all Will saving throws.

Duergar Immunities (4 RP): *Prerequisites*: Dwarf subtype, at least a +2 racial bonus to Constitution; *Benefit*: Members of this race are immune to paralysis, phantasms, and poison. They also gain a +2 racial bonus on saving throws against spells and spell-like abilities.

Elven Immunities (2 RP): *Prerequisite*: Elf subtype; *Benefit*: Members of this race are immune to magic sleep effects and gain a +2 racial bonus on saving throws made against enchantment spells and effects.

Energy Resistance (1 RP): *Prerequisite*: Outsider (native) with ties to an elemental plane; *Benefit*: Pick one of the following energy types that corresponds to the plane the race has ties to: acid (earth), cold (water), electricity (air), or fire (fire). Members of this race have resistance 5 to the corresponding energy type. *Special*: This trait can be taken more than once. Each time it is taken, select an additional energy type that corresponds to another elemental plane the race has ties to.

Eternal Hope (2 RP): *Prerequisites*: None; *Benefit*: Members of this race gain a +2 racial bonus on saving throws against fear and despair effects. Also, once per day, after a natural roll of 1 on a d20 roll, members of this race may reroll and use the second result.

GARGOYLE

Type	
Monstrous humanoid	3 RP
Size	
Medium	0 RP
Base Speed	
Normal speed	0 RP
Ability Score Modifiers	
Paragon (+4 Con, −2 Int, −2 Wis, −2 Cha)	1 RP
Languages	
Standard	0 RP
Racial Traits	
Ability Score Racial Traits	
Advanced Strength (+2)	4 RP
Defense Racial Traits	
Damage reduction (10/magic)	6 RP
Improved natural armor (+3)	6 RP
Natural armor	2 RP
Feat and Skill Racial Traits	
Skill bonus (+2 Stealth)	2 RP
Movement Racial Traits	
Flight (50 ft., average)	8 RP
Offense Racial Traits	
Bite	1 RP
Claws	2 RP
Natural attack (gore)	1 RP
Senses Racial Traits	
Darkvision 60 ft.	— RP
Total	**36 RP**

Exalted Resistance (3 RP): *Prerequisite*: Outsider (native) with ties to Elysium, Heaven, or Nirvana; *Benefit*: Members of this race gain spell resistance equal to 6 + their character level against spells and spell-like abilities with the evil descriptor, as well as any spells and spell-like abilities cast by evil outsiders.

Fearless (1 RP): *Prerequisites*: None; *Benefit*: Members of this race gain a +2 racial bonus on all saving throws against fear effects. *Special*: This bonus stacks with the bonus granted by the lucky (greater or lesser) racial trait.

Fiendish Resistance (3 RP): *Prerequisite*: Outsider (native) with ties to Abaddon, the Abyss, or Hell; *Benefit*: Members of this race gain cold resistance 5, electricity resistance 5, and fire resistance 5.

Fire in the Blood (3 RP): *Prerequisite*: Outsider (native) with ties to the Plane of Fire or dragon type; *Benefit*: Members of this race gain fast healing 2 for 1 round anytime they take fire damage (whether or not this fire damage overcomes their fire resistance, if any). Members of this race can heal up to 2 hit points per level per day with this ability, after which it ceases to function.

Halo (2 RP): *Prerequisite*: Outsider (native) with ties to Elysium, Heaven, or Nirvana; *Benefit*: Members of this race can create *light* centered on their head at will as a spell-like ability. When using the halo, a member of this race gains a +2 circumstance bonus on Intimidate checks against evil creatures and on saving throws against becoming blinded or dazzled.

Hardy (3 RP): *Prerequisite*: The race has at least a +2 racial bonus to Constitution; *Benefit*: Members of this race gain a +2 racial bonus on saving throws against poison, spells, and spell-like abilities.

Healthy (2 RP): *Prerequisite*: The race has at least a +2 racial bonus to Constitution; *Benefit*: Members of this race gain a +4 bonus on Fortitude saves against disease and poison, including magical diseases.

Hydrated Vitality (3 RP): *Prerequisite*: Outsider (native) with ties to the Plane of Water, fey type, or plant type; *Benefit*: Members of this race gain fast healing 2 for 1 round anytime they submerge completely within a body of natural salt water, fresh water, or brackish water. Stagnant, poisoned, or trapped water (such as water within an artificial pit or a *bag of holding*) does not activate this ability. Members of this race can heal up to 2 hit points per level per day with this ability, after which it ceases to function.

Illusion Resistance (1 RP): *Prerequisites*: None; *Benefit*: Members of this race gain a +2 racial bonus on saving throws against illusion spells or effects.

Lifebound (2 RP): *Prerequisite*: A Constitution score; *Benefit*: Members of this race gain a +2 racial bonus on all saving throws made to resist death effects, saving throws against negative energy effects, Fortitude saves made to remove negative levels, and Constitution checks made to stabilize if reduced to negative hit points.

Lucky, Lesser (2 RP): *Prerequisites*: None; *Benefit*: Members of this race gain a +1 racial bonus on all saving throws.

Mist Child (1 RP): *Prerequisites*: None; *Benefit*: Whenever a member of this race has concealment or total concealment, the miss chance of attacks against her increases by 5%.

Mountain-Born (1 RP): *Prerequisites*: None; *Benefit*: Members of this race gain a +2 racial bonus on Acrobatics checks made to cross narrow ledges and on saving throws against altitude fatigue and sickness.

Natural Armor (2 RP): *Prerequisites*: None; *Benefit*: Members of this race gain a +1 natural armor bonus to their Armor Class.

Plagueborn (1 RP): *Prerequisites*: None; *Benefit*: Members of this race gain a +2 racial bonus on saving throws against disease, ingested poisons, and becoming nauseated or sickened.

Poison Resistance (3 RP): *Prerequisites*: None; *Benefit*: Members of this race gain a racial bonus on saving throws against poison effects equal to their Hit Dice.

Resist Level Drain (1 RP): *Prerequisite*: Negative energy affinity racial trait; *Benefit*: Members of this race take no penalty from energy-draining effects, though a member of this race can still be killed if it accrues more negative levels than it has Hit Dice. After 24 hours, any negative levels a member of this race has accrued are removed without the need for any additional saving throws.

Resistant (2 RP): *Prerequisites*: None; *Benefit*: Members of this race gain a +2 racial bonus on saving throws against mind-affecting effects and poison.

Shadow Blending (1 RP): *Prerequisite*: Shadow resistance racial trait; *Benefit*: Attacks made against members of this race while they are within areas of dim light have a 50% miss chance instead of the normal 20% miss chance. This trait does not grant total concealment; it just increases the miss chance. This is a supernatural ability.

Shadow Resistance (2 RP): *Prerequisites*: None; *Benefit*: Members of this race gain cold resistance 5 and electricity resistance 5.

Spell Resistance, Greater (3 RP): *Prerequisites*: None; *Benefit*: Members of this race gain spell resistance equal to 11 + their character level.

Spell Resistance, Lesser (2 RP): *Prerequisites*: None; *Benefit*: Members of this race gain spell resistance equal to 6 + their character level.

Stability (1 RP): *Prerequisites*: None; *Benefit*: Members of this race receive a +4 racial bonus to their CMD when resisting bull rush or trip attempts while standing on the ground.

Stone in the Blood (3 RP): *Prerequisite*: Outsider (native) with ties to the Plane of Earth, construct type, dragon type, or half-construct subtype; *Benefit*: Members of this race gaining fast healing 2 for 1 round anytime they take

acid damage (whether or not this acid damage overcomes their acid resistance, if any). A member of this race can heal up to 2 hit points per level per day with this ability, after which it ceases to function.

Storm in the Blood (3 RP): *Prerequisite:* Outsider (native) with ties to the Plane of Air, dragon type, fey type, or plant type; *Benefit:* Members of this race gain fast healing 2 for 1 round anytime they take electricity damage (whether or not this electricity damage overcomes their electricity resistance, if any). A member of this race can heal up to 2 hit points per level per day with this ability, after which it ceases to function.

Stubborn (2 RP): *Prerequisites:* None; *Benefit:* Members of this race gain a +2 racial bonus on Will saving throws to resist spells and spell-like abilities of the enchantment (charm) and enchantment (compulsion) subschools. In addition, if a member of this race fails such a save, it receives another save 1 round later to prematurely end the effect (assuming the spell or spell-like ability has a duration greater than 1 round). This second save is made at the same DC as the first. If the member of the race has a similar ability from another source (such as a rogue's slippery mind class feature), it can only use one of these abilities per round, but can try the other on the second round if the first reroll ability fails.

Undead Resistance (1 RP): *Prerequisites:* None; *Benefit:* Members of this race gain a +2 racial bonus on saving throws against disease and mind-affecting effects.

Unnatural (2 RP): *Prerequisites:* None; *Benefit:* Members of this race unnerve normal animals, and train to defend themselves against the inevitable attacks from such creatures. Members of this race take a –4 penalty on all Charisma-based skill checks to affect creatures of the animal type, and receive a +4 dodge bonus to AC against animals. Animals' starting attitude toward members of this race is one step worse than normal.

Advanced Traits

Fey Damage Resistance (3 RP): *Prerequisite:* Fey type; *Benefit:* Members of this race gain DR 5/cold iron.

Improved Natural Armor (1 RP): *Prerequisite:* Natural armor racial trait; *Benefit:* Members of this race gain a +1 natural armor bonus. *Special:* This racial trait can be taken multiple times. Each additional time you take this trait, increase its cost by 1 RP. Its effects stack.

Improved Resistance (2 RP): *Prerequisite:* Resistance 5 to any energy type; *Benefit:* Members of this race increase their resistance to one energy type to 10. *Special:* This racial trait can be taken multiple times. Each additional time you take this trait, increase its cost by 1 RP, and increase one other resistance to 10.

Lucky, Greater (4 RP): *Prerequisites:* None; *Benefit:* Members of this race gain a +2 racial bonus on all saving throws.

Moon-Touched Damage Resistance (3 RP): *Prerequisites:* None; *Benefit:* Members of this race gain DR 5/silver.

Skeletal Damage Reduction (2 RP): *Prerequisite:* Undead type; *Benefit:* Members of this race gain DR 5/bludgeoning.

Monstrous Traits

Damage Reduction (4 RP; see special): *Prerequisites:* None; *Benefit:* Members of this race gain DR 5/magic. *Special:* This can be increased to DR 10/magic for an additional 2 RP. The type of DR can be changed to one of the alignments (chaos, evil, good, or law) if the race is of the outsider (native) type with ties to the appropriate plane (chaos for a race with ties to a lawful-aligned plane, evil for a race with ties to a good-aligned plane, etc.) for an additional 2 RP.

Elemental Immunity (4 RP): *Prerequisite:* Outsider (native) with ties to an elemental plane; *Benefit:* Pick one of the following energy types that corresponds to the plane the race has ties to: acid (earth), cold (water), electricity (air), or fire (fire). Members of this race are immune to the chosen energy type. *Special:* This trait can be taken more than once. Each additional time you take this trait, increase its cost by 1 RP. Each time it is taken, select another energy type that corresponds to another elemental plane the race has ties to. If a race has vulnerability to fire and immunity to cold, it gains the cold subtype. If a race has vulnerability to cold and immunity to fire, it gains the fire subtype.

Fast Healing (6 RP): *Prerequisites:* None; *Benefit:* Members of this race regain 1 hit point each round. Except for where noted here, fast healing is just like natural healing. Fast healing does not restore hit points lost from starvation, thirst, or suffocation, nor does it allow a creature to regrow lost body parts. Fast healing continues to function (even at negative hit points) until a member of this race dies, at which point the effects of fast healing immediately end. *Special:* This trait can be taken multiple times. Each time fast healing is taken, its cost increases by 1 RP.

Rock Catching (2 RP): *Prerequisite:* Large size quality; *Benefit:* Members of this race can catch Small, Medium, or Large rocks (or projectiles of similar shape). Once per round, a member of this race that would normally be hit by a rock can make a Reflex saving throw to catch it as a free action. The DC is 15 for a Small rock, 20 for a Medium rock, and 25 for a Large rock (if the projectile provides a magical bonus on attack rolls, the DC increases by that amount). The member of this race must be aware of the attack in order to make a rock catching attempt.

Feat and Skill Racial Traits

Feat and skill racial traits typically grant bonuses on particular skills or grant bonus feats.

Standard Traits

Beguiling Liar (2 RP): *Prerequisites:* None; *Benefit:* Members of this race gain a +4 racial bonus on Bluff checks to convince an opponent that what they are saying is true when they tell a lie.

Camouflage (1 RP): *Prerequisites:* None; *Benefit:* Choose a ranger favored terrain type. Members of this race gain a +4 racial bonus on Stealth checks while within that terrain type.

Cave Dweller (1 RP): *Prerequisites:* None; *Benefit:* Members of this race gain a +1 bonus on Knowledge (dungeoneering) and Survival checks made underground.

Craftsman (1 RP): *Prerequisites:* None; *Benefit:* Member of this race gain a +2 racial bonus on all Craft or Profession checks to create objects from metal or stone.

Curiosity (4 RP): *Prerequisites:* None; *Benefit:* Members of this race are naturally inquisitive about the world around them. They gain a +4 bonus on Diplomacy checks to gather information, and Knowledge (history) and Knowledge (local) become class skills for them. If they choose a class that has either of these Knowledge skills as class skills, they gain a +2 racial bonus on those skills instead.

Emissary (1 RP): *Prerequisites:* None; *Benefit:* Once per day, members of this race can roll twice when making a Bluff or Diplomacy check and take the better roll.

Flexible Bonus Feat (4 RP): *Prerequisites:* None; *Benefit:* Members of this race select one extra feat at 1st level.

Focused Study (4 RP): *Prerequisites:* None; *Benefit:* At 1st, 8th, and 16th level, members of this race gain Skill Focus in a skill of their choice as a bonus feat.

Gift of Tongues (2 RP): *Prerequisite:* Standard or linguist language quality; *Benefit:* Members of this race gain a +1 racial bonus on Bluff and Diplomacy checks, and they learn one additional language every time they put a rank in the Linguistics skill.

Gifted Linguist (2 RP): *Prerequisite:* Standard or linguist language quality; *Benefit:* Members of this race gain a +4 racial bonus on Linguistics checks, and they learn one additional language every time they put a rank in the Linguistics skill.

Greed (1 RP): *Prerequisites:* None; *Benefit:* Members of this race gain a +2 bonus on Appraise checks to determine the price of nonmagical goods that contain precious metals or gemstones.

Gregarious (1 RP): *Prerequisite:* The race has at least a +2 racial bonus to Charisma; *Benefit:* When members of this race successfully use Diplomacy to win over an individual, that creature takes a −2 penalty on attempts to resist any of the member's Charisma-based skills for the next 24 hours.

GNOLL

Type	
Humanoid (gnoll)	0 RP
Size	
Medium	0 RP
Base Speed	
Normal	0 RP
Ability Score Modifiers	
Flexible (+2 Str, +2 Con)	2 RP
Languages	
Xenophobic	0 RP
Racial Traits	
Defense Racial Traits	
Natural armor	2 RP
Senses Racial Traits	
Darkvision 60 ft.	2 RP
Total	**6 RP**

Integrated (1 RP): *Prerequisites:* None; *Benefit:* Members of this race gain a +1 bonus on Bluff, Disguise, and Knowledge (local) checks.

Master Tinker (2 RP): *Prerequisites:* None; *Benefit:* Members of this race gain a +1 bonus on Disable Device and Knowledge (engineering) checks. Members of this race are also treated as proficient with any weapon they have personally crafted.

Nimble Faller (2 RP): *Prerequisite:* The race has at least a +2 racial bonus to Dexterity; *Benefit:* Members of this race land on their feet even when they take lethal damage from a fall. Furthermore, they gain a +1 bonus to their CMD against trip attempts.

Scavenger (2 RP): *Prerequisites:* None; *Benefit:* Members of this race gain a +2 racial bonus on Appraise and Perception checks to find hidden objects (including traps and secret doors), determine whether food is spoiled, or identify a potion by taste.

Shards of the Past (4 RP): *Prerequisites:* None; *Benefit:* Members of this race have past lives that grant them two particular Knowledge skills. Each member of this race

picks two Knowledge skills. The member of this race gains a +2 racial bonus on both of these skills, and those skills are treated as class skills regardless of what class the member of this race actually takes.

Silent Hunter (2 RP): *Prerequisites:* None; *Benefit:* Members of this race reduce the penalty for using Stealth while moving by 5 and can make Stealth checks while running at a –20 penalty (this number includes the penalty reduction from this trait).

Silver Tongued (3 RP): *Prerequisites:* None; *Benefit:* Members of this race gain a +2 bonus on Diplomacy and Bluff checks. In addition, when they use Diplomacy to shift a creature's attitude, they can do so up to three steps up rather than just two.

Skill Bonus (2 RP): *Prerequisites:* None; *Benefits:* Pick a single skill. Members of this race gain a +2 racial bonus on skill checks made with this skill. Alternatively, pick two related skills—each member of this race gains a +1 racial bonus on these skills during character creation. *Special:* This trait can be taken up to three times. Each time it is taken, choose a different skill (+2 bonus) or two different skills (+1 bonus on one of character's choice).

Skill Training (1 RP): *Prerequisites:* None; *Benefit:* Pick up to two skills. These skills are always considered class skills for members of this race.

Skilled (4 RP): *Prerequisites:* None; *Benefit:* Members of this race gain an additional skill rank at 1st level and one additional skill rank whenever they gain a level.

LIZARDFOLK

Type	
Humanoid (reptilian)	0 RP
Size	
Medium	0 RP
Base Speed	
Normal	0 RP
Ability Score Modifiers	
Flexible (+2 Str, +2 Con)	2 RP
Languages	
Xenophobic	0 RP
Racial Traits	
Defense Racial Traits	
Natural armor	2 RP
Movement Racial Traits	
Swim	1 RP
Offense Racial Traits	
Bite	1 RP
Claws	2 RP
Total	**8 RP**

Sneaky (5 RP): *Prerequisites:* None; *Benefit:* Members of this race gain a +4 racial bonus on Stealth checks.

Sneaky Rider (6 RP): *Prerequisites:* None; *Benefit:* Members of this race gain a +4 racial bonus on Ride and Stealth checks.

Sociable (1 RP): *Prerequisites:* None; *Benefit:* When members of this race attempt to change a creature's attitude with a Diplomacy check and fail by 5 or more, they can try to influence the creature a second time even if 24 hours have not passed.

Stalker (1 RP): *Prerequisites:* None; *Benefit:* Perception and Stealth are always class skills for members of this race.

Static Bonus Feat (2 RP): *Prerequisites:* None; *Benefit:* Choose one feat with no prerequisites. All members of this race gain this feat as a bonus feat at 1st level.

Stonecunning (1 RP): *Prerequisites:* None; *Benefit:* Members of this race receive a +2 bonus on Perception checks to notice unusual stonework, such as traps and hidden doors located in stone walls or floors. They receive a check to notice such features whenever they pass within 10 feet of them, whether or not they are actively looking.

Underground Sneak (5 RP): *Prerequisite:* Race is native to the Darklands; *Benefit:* Members of this race gain a +2 racial bonus on Craft (alchemy), Perception, and Stealth checks. The bonus on Stealth checks increases to a +4 bonus while underground.

Urbanite (1 RP): *Prerequisites:* None; *Benefit:* Members of this race gain a +2 racial bonus on Diplomacy checks made to gather information and Sense Motive checks made to get a hunch about a social situation.

Water Child (4 RP): *Prerequisites:* None; *Benefit:* Members of this race gain a +4 racial bonus on Swim checks, can always take 10 while swimming, and may choose Aquan as a bonus language.

Advanced Traits

Nimble Attacks (2 RP): *Prerequisites:* None; *Benefit:* Members of this race receive Weapon Finesse as a bonus feat.

Quick Reactions (2 RP): *Prerequisites:* None; *Benefit:* Members of this race receive Improved Initiative as a bonus feat.

Magical Racial Traits

The following racial traits augment a race's ability to use magic or grant spell-like abilities.

Standard Traits

Arcane Focus (1 RP): *Prerequisites:* None; *Benefit:* Members of this race gain a +2 racial bonus on concentration checks made to cast arcane spells defensively.

Change Shape, Greater (6 RP): *Prerequisite:* Aberration, dragon, fey, humanoid, or monstrous humanoid type; *Benefit:* Members of this race gain the following supernatural ability: a member of this race can assume the appearance of a Small or Medium humanoid as the *alter self* spell, save that it does not adjust its ability scores.

Change Shape, Lesser (3 RP): *Prerequisite:* Aberration, dragon, fey, humanoid, or monstrous humanoid type; *Benefit:* Members of this race gain the following supernatural ability: A member of this race can assume the appearance of a single form of a single humanoid race of its size. The form is static and cannot be changed each time it takes this form. The creature gains a +10 racial bonus on Disguise checks made to appear as the member of the race whose appearance it assumes. Changing its shape is a standard action. This trait otherwise functions as *alter self,* save that the creature does not adjust its ability scores.

Deep Magic (3 RP): *Prerequisite:* Native of the Darklands; *Benefit:* Members of this race gain a +2 racial bonus on caster level checks made to overcome spell resistance and a +2 racial bonus on dispel checks.

Dissolution's Child (5 RP): *Prerequisite:* Outsider (native) with ties to the Shadow Plane, fey type, undead type, or half-undead subtype; *Benefit:* Members of this race gain the following supernatural ability: Once per day, a member of this race can change its appearance to look as if it were little more than a 4-foot-tall area of shadow. Its physical form still exists and it is not incorporeal—only its appearance changes. This racial trait works like *invisibility,* except the effect only lasts 1 round per level (maximum 5 rounds).

Dreamspeaker (2 RP): *Prerequisites:* None; *Benefit:* Members of this race gain a +1 bonus to the saving throw DCs of spells of the divination school and spells that produce sleep effects that they cast. In addition, members of this race with a Charisma score of 15 or higher may use *dream* once per day as a spell-like ability (caster level is equal to the user's character level).

Elemental Affinity (1 RP): *Prerequisite:* Outsider (native) with ties to an elemental plane; *Benefit:* If a member of the race is a sorcerer with the elemental bloodline corresponding to the elemental plane it has ties to (i.e., air, earth, fire, or water), it treats its Charisma score as 2 points higher for all sorcerer spells and class abilities. Furthermore, a member of this race able to cast domain spells that correspond to the elemental plane the race has ties to casts its domain powers and spells at +1 caster level. This trait does not give members of this race early access to level-based powers; it only affects powers that they could already use without this trait.

Elemental Summoner (2 RP): *Prerequisites:* None; *Benefit:* Choose one of the following elemental subtypes— air, earth, fire, or water. When summoning a creature with the chosen subtype with a *summon* spell, increase the duration of that spell by 2 rounds.

Elven Magic (3 RP): *Prerequisite:* Elf subtype; *Benefit:* Members of this race gain a +2 bonus on caster level checks made to overcome spell resistance. In addition, they also receive a +2 racial bonus on Spellcraft checks made to identify the properties of magic items.

Enclave Protector (2 RP): *Prerequisites:* None; *Benefit:* Members of this race add +1 to the caster level of any abjuration spells they cast. Members of this race also gain the following spell-like abilities: constant—*nondetection;* 1/day—*faerie fire, obscure object, sanctuary.* The caster level for these effects is equal to the user's character level.

Envoy (1 RP): *Prerequisites:* None; *Benefit:* Members of this race with an Intelligence score of 11 or higher gain the following spell-like abilities: 1/day—*comprehend languages, detect magic, detect poison, read magic.* The caster level for these effects is equal to the user's character level.

Fell Magic (3 RP): *Prerequisites:* None; *Benefit:* Members of this race gain +1 to the DC of any saving throws against necromancy spells that they cast. Members of this race with a Wisdom score of 11 or higher also gain the following spell-like abilities: 1/day—*bleed, chill touch, detect poison, touch of fatigue.* The caster level for these effects is equal to the user's character level. The DC for these spell-like abilities is equal to 10 + the spell's level + the user's Wisdom modifier.

Ferrous Growth (2 RP): *Prerequisite:* Outsider (native) with ties to the Plane of Earth; *Benefit:* Once per day, a member of this race can cause a touched piece of iron or steel to grow into an object weighing up to 10 pounds, such as a sword, crowbar, or light steel shield. This object remains in this form for 10 minutes or until broken or destroyed, at which point it shrinks back to its original size and shape.

Fertile Soil (2 RP): *Prerequisite:* Outsider (native) with ties to the Plane of Earth, fey type, or plant type; *Benefit:* Sorcerer members of this race with the verdant bloodline treat their Charisma score as 2 points higher for all sorcerer spells and class abilities. Clerics who are members of this race with the Plant domain use their domain powers and spells at +1 caster level. This trait does not give members of this race early access to level-based powers; it only affects powers that they could already use without this trait.

Fiendish Sorcery (1 RP): *Prerequisite:* Outsider (native) with ties to Abaddon, the Abyss, or Hell; *Benefit:* If a member of this race is a sorcerer with the Abyssal or Infernal bloodline, it treats its caster level as 1 higher when casting bonus spells and bloodline powers. This trait does not give members of this race early access to level-based powers; it only affects powers that they could already use without this trait.

Gnome Magic (2 RP): *Prerequisite:* Gnome subtype; *Benefit:* Members of this race gain a +1 bonus to the DC of any saving throws against illusion spells that they cast. Members of this race with a Charisma score of 11 or higher also gain the following spell-like abilities: 1/day—*dancing lights, ghost sounds, prestidigitation, speak with animals.* The caster level for these effects is equal to the user's level. The DC for the spell-like abilities is equal to 10 + the spell's level + the user's Charisma modifier.

Heavenborn (3 RP): *Prerequisite:* Outsider (native) with ties to Elysium, Heaven, or Nirvana; *Benefit:* Members of this race gain a +2 bonus on Knowledge (planes) checks, and they cast spells with the good or light descriptor at +1 caster level.

Hypnotic (2 RP): *Prerequisites:* None; *Benefit:* Members of this race add +1 to the DC for all saving throws against spells or effects they cast that inflict the fascinated condition. Once per day, when a creature rolls a saving throw against such an effect from a member of this race, the member of the race can force that creature to reroll the saving throw and use the second result, even if it is worse.

Hypnotic Gaze (3 RP): *Prerequisites:* None; *Benefit:* Members of this race gain the following supernatural ability: Once per day, a member of this race can attempt to hypnotize a single target as per the spell *hypnotism* (caster level equal to its character level). The effects of the hypnotic gaze last only 1 round.

Immortal Spark (7 RP): *Prerequisite:* Outsider (native) with ties to Elysium, Heaven, or Nirvana; *Benefit:* Members of this race gain a +2 bonus on Knowledge (history) checks and saving throws against death effects and can use *lesser age resistance* (*Pathfinder RPG Ultimate Magic* 205) once per day as a spell-like ability.

Lightbringer (2 RP): *Prerequisites:* None; *Benefit:* Members of this race are immune to light-based blindness and dazzle effects, and are treated as one level higher when determining the effects of any light-based spells or effects they cast (including spell-like and supernatural abilities). If a member of this race has an Intelligence of 10 or higher, it may use *light* at will as a spell-like ability.

Magical Linguist (2 RP): *Prerequisites:* None; *Benefit:* Members of this race gain a +1 bonus to the DC of spells they cast that have the language-dependent descriptor or that create glyphs, symbols, or other magical writings. They also gain a +2 racial bonus on saving throws against such spells. Members of this race with a Charisma score of 11 or higher also gain the following spell-like abilities: 1/day—*arcane mark, comprehend languages, message, read magic.* The caster level for these spell-like abilities is equal to the user's character level.

Nereid Fascination (3 RP): *Prerequisite:* Outsider (native) with ties to the Plane of Water or fey type; *Benefit:* Members of this race gain the following supernatural ability: Once per day, a member of this race can create a 20-foot-radius burst that causes humanoids within the aura's range to become fascinated with the user (as the bard's fascinate bardic performance). Affected humanoids may resist this effect by making a successful Will saving throw (DC 10 + 1/2 the user's character level + the user's Charisma modifier).

Object of Desire (1 RP): *Prerequisites:* None; *Benefit:* Members of this race add +1 to their caster level when casting *charm person* and *charm monster.*

Pyromaniac (3 RP): *Prerequisites:* None; *Benefit:* Members of this race are treated as +1 level higher when casting spells with the fire descriptor, using granted powers of the Fire domain, using bloodline powers of the fire elemental bloodline, using the revelations of the oracle's flame mystery, and determining the damage of alchemist bombs that deal fire damage. This trait does not give members of this race early access to level-based powers; it only affects powers that they could already use without this trait. If a member of this race has a Charisma score of 11 or higher, it also gains the following spell-like abilities: 1/day—*dancing lights, flare, prestidigitation, produce flame.* The caster level for these spell-like abilities is equal to the user's character level.

Samsaran Magic (2 RP): *Prerequisite:* Samsaran subtype; *Benefit:* Members of this race with a Charisma score of 11 or higher gain the following spell-like abilities: 1/day—*comprehend languages, deathwatch, stabilize.* The caster level for these effects is equal to the user's character level.

Seducer (2 RP): *Prerequisite:* The race has at least a +2 racial bonus to Charisma; *Benefit:* Members of this race add +1 to the saving throw DCs for their spells and spell-like abilities of the enchantment school. In addition, members of this race with a Wisdom score of 15 or higher may use *charm person* once per day as a spell-like ability (caster level is equal to the user's character level).

Shadow Caster (2 RP): *Prerequisites:* None; *Benefit:* Members of this race add +1 to the saving throw DCs for their spells and spell-like abilities of the illusion (shadow) subschool.

Shadow Magic (2 RP): *Prerequisites:* None; *Benefit:* Members of this race add +1 to the DC of any saving throws against spells of the shadow subschool that they cast. Members of this race with a Charisma score of 11 or higher also gain the following spell-like abilities: 1/day—*ghost sound, pass without trace, ventriloquism.* The caster level for these spell-like abilities is equal to the user's character level.

OGRE

Type	
Humanoid (giant)	0 RP
Size	
Large	7 RP
Base Speed	
Normal	0 RP
Ability Score Modifiers	
Paragon (+4 Str, –2 Int, –2 Cha, –2 Wis)	1 RP
Languages	
Xenophobic	0 RP
Racial Traits	
Ability Score Racial Traits	
Advanced Constitution (+2)	4 RP
Advanced Wisdom (+2)	4 RP
Defense Racial Traits	
Improved natural armor (+1)	1 RP
Natural armor	2 RP
Offense Racial Traits	
Reach	1 RP
Senses Racial Traits	
Darkvision 60 ft.	2 RP
Low-light vision	1 RP
Total	23 RP

Soul Seer (4 RP): *Prerequisite:* Outsider (native); *Benefit:* Members of this race gain the use of *deathwatch* as a constant spell-like ability.

Spell-Like Ability, Lesser (Variable, see Special): *Prerequisites:* None; *Benefit:* Choose a 2nd-level or lower spell that does not attack a creature or deal damage. Members of this race can use this spell as a spell-like ability once per day. The caster level of the spell is equal to the user's character level. *Special:* This trait costs as many RP as the level of the spell chosen (minimum 1 RP). This trait can be taken up to three times. Each time you take an additional spell, adjust the RP cost of this trait appropriately.

Stoneseer (2 RP): *Prerequisites:* None; *Benefit:* Members of this race add +1 to the caster level of any spells with the earth descriptor they cast. Members of this race also gain the following spell-like abilities: constant—*nondetection*; 1/day—*magic stone, stone shape, stone tell.* The caster level for these spell-like abilities is equal to the user's character level.

Stonesinger (1 RP): *Prerequisites:* None; *Benefit:* Members of this race are treated as 1 level higher when casting spells with the earth descriptor or using powers of the Earth domain, bloodline powers of the earth elemental bloodline, and revelations of the oracle's stone mystery. This trait does not give members of this race early access to level-based powers; it only affects powers they could already use without this trait.

Svirfneblin Magic (2 RP): *Prerequisite:* Gnome subtype; *Benefit:* Members of this race add +1 to the DC of any illusion spells they cast. They also gain the following spell-like abilities: constant—*nondetection*; 1/day—*blindness/deafness, blur, disguise self.* The DC for the spells is equal to 10 + the spell's level + the caster's Charisma modifier.

Treacherous Earth (2 RP): *Prerequisite:* Outsider (native) with ties to the Plane of Earth or fey type; *Benefit:* Members

GATHLAIN

These strange fey creatures have a symbiotic relationship with an ivy-like plant that serves as their wings. The relationship is so close, it is impossible to separate fey from plant. Gathlains are sometimes helpful, often mischievous, and native to deep primeval forests and jungles, but are also prone to wanderlust and adventuring.

Type	
Fey	2 RP
Size	
Small	0 RP
Base Speed	
Normal	0 RP
Ability Score Modifiers	
Standard (+2 Cha, -2 Con, +2 Dex)	0 RP
Languages	
Standard	0 RP
Racial Traits	
Defense Racial Traits	
Natural armor	2 RP
Magical Racial Traits	
Spell-like ability, lesser (*entangle, feather step* [*Advanced Player's Guide* 221])	2 RP
Movement Racial Traits	
Flight (40 ft. poor)	6 RP
Senses Racial Traits	
Low-light vision	— RP
Total	**12 RP**

of this race gain the following supernatural ability: Once per day, a member of this race can will the earth to rumble and shift, transforming a 10-foot-radius patch of earth, unworked stone, or sand into an area of difficult terrain centered on a square it can touch. This lasts for a number of minutes equal to the user's level, after which the ground returns to normal.

Weather Savvy (1 RP): *Prerequisite*: Outsider (native) with ties to the Plane of Air or fey type; *Benefit*: Members of this race are so in tune with the air and sky they can sense the slightest change in atmospheric conditions. They can spend a full-round action to predict the weather in an area for the next 24 hours. This prediction is always accurate, but cannot account for spells or supernatural effects that might alter the forecast.

Advanced Traits

Constant Spell-Like Divination (3 RP): *Prerequisites*: None; *Benefit*: Choose one of the following spells: *detect magic, detect poison, detect secret doors, detect undead*. Members of this race can use this spell as a constant spell-like ability. The caster level of the spell-like ability is equal to the user's character level.

Shadow Travel (5 RP): *Prerequisite*: Outsider (native) with ties to the Shadow Plane; *Benefit*: When a member of this race reaches 9th level in any combination of classes, she gains the ability to use *shadow walk* (self only) as a spell-like ability once per day, and at 13th level, she can use *plane shift* (self only to the Shadow Plane or the Material Plane only) as a spell-like ability once per day. The caster level of these spell-like abilities is equal to the user's character level.

Spell-Like Ability, Greater (Variable, see Special): *Prerequisites*: None; *Benefit*: Choose a 3rd-level or 4th-level spell that does not attack a creature or deal damage. Members of this race can use this spell as a spell-like ability once per day. The caster level of the spell is equal to the user's character level. *Special*: This trait costs as many RP as the level of the spell chosen. This trait can be taken up to three times. Each time you take an additional spell, adjust the RP cost of this trait appropriately.

Monstrous Traits

Spell-Like Ability, At-Will (Variable, see Special): *Prerequisites*: None; *Benefit*: Choose a 3rd-level or lower spell that does not attack a creature or deal damage. Members of this race can use this spell as an at-will spell-like ability. The caster level of the spell is equal to the user's character level. *Special*: This trait costs as many RP as twice the level of spell chosen (minimum 2). Up to five spells can be chosen when you take this trait. Each time you take an additional spell, adjust the RP cost of this trait appropriately.

Movement Racial Traits

The following racial traits augment a race's ability to move about the world.

Standard Traits

Climb (2 RP): *Prerequisites*: None; *Benefit*: Members of this race have a climb speed of 20 feet, and gain the +8 racial bonus on Climb checks that a climb speed normally grants.

Darklands Stalker (4 RP): *Prerequisite*: Native to the Darklands; *Benefit*: Members of this race can move unhindered through difficult terrain while underground. In addition, members of this race with a Dexterity score of 13 or higher gain Nimble Moves as a bonus feat.

Fleet-Footed (3 RP): *Prerequisite*: The race has at least a +2 racial bonus to Dexterity; *Benefit*: Members of this race receive Run as a bonus feat and a +2 racial bonus on initiative checks.

Gliding Wings (3 RP): *Prerequisites*: None; *Benefit*: Members of this race take no damage from falling (as if subject to a constant nonmagical *feather fall* spell). While in midair, members of this race can move up to 5 feet in any horizontal direction for every 1 foot they fall, at a speed of 60 feet per round. A member of a race with gliding wings cannot gain height with these wings alone; it merely coasts in other directions as it falls. If subjected to a strong wind or any other effect that causes a creature with gliding wings to rise, it can take advantage of the updraft to increase the distance it can glide.

Jumper (2 RP): *Prerequisite*: The race has at least a +2 racial bonus to Dexterity; *Benefit*: Members of this race are always considered to have a running start when making Acrobatics checks to jump.

Mountaineer (1 RP): *Prerequisites*: None; *Benefit*: Members of this race are immune to altitude sickness and do not lose their Dexterity bonus to AC when making Climb checks or Acrobatics checks to cross narrow or slippery surfaces.

Sprinter (1 RP): *Prerequisite*: Normal speed; *Benefit*: Members of this race gain a +10 foot racial bonus to their speed when using the charge, run, or withdraw actions.

Swift as Shadows (3 RP): *Prerequisite*: The race has at least a +2 racial bonus to Dexterity; *Benefit*: Members of this race reduce the penalty for using Stealth while moving at full speed by 5, and reduce the Stealth check penalty for sniping by 10.

Swim (2 RP): *Prerequisites*: None; *Benefit*: Members of this race have a swim speed of 30 feet and gain the +8 racial bonus on Swim checks that a swim speed normally grants.

Terrain Stride (1 RP): *Prerequisite*: Normal speed; *Benefit*: Choose a ranger favored terrain type. Members of this race can move through natural difficult terrain at their normal speed while within the chosen terrain. Magically altered terrain affects them normally.

Vestigial Wings (2 RP): *Prerequisites:* None; *Benefit:* Members of this race have wings that do not provide the lift required for actual flight, but do have enough power to aid flight attained by some other method, and grant a +4 racial bonus on Fly checks.

Advanced Traits

Burrow (3 RP): *Prerequisite:* Normal speed; *Benefit:* Members of this race gain a burrow speed of 20 feet. *Special:* This trait can be taken twice. The second time it is taken, the burrow speed increases to 30 feet.

Fast (1 RP): *Prerequisite:* Normal speed; *Benefit:* Members of this race gain a +10 foot bonus to their base speed. *Special:* This trait can be taken more than once, but each time it is, the cost increases by 1 RP. Its effects stack.

Flight (4 RP): *Prerequisites:* None; *Benefit:* Members of this race have a fly speed of 30 feet with clumsy maneuverability. *Special:* This trait can be taken more than once. For each additional 2 RP spent, the race's fly speed increases by +10 feet, and the maneuverability improves by one step.

Powerful Swimmer (1 RP): *Prerequisite:* Swim racial trait; *Benefit:* Members of this race receive a +10 foot bonus to their swim speed. *Special:* This trait can be taken twice. Its effects stack.

Monstrous Traits

Expert Climber (4 RP): *Prerequisite:* Climb racial trait; *Benefit:* Members of this race can cling to cave walls and even ceilings as long as the surface has hand- and footholds. In effect, members of this race are treated as being constantly under the effects of a nonmagical *spider climb* spell, save that members of this race cannot cling to smooth surfaces. This trait doubles the normal +8 racial bonus on Climb checks normally granted to creatures with a climb speed (to a total +16 bonus).

Offense Racial Traits

The following racial traits augment a race's fighting prowess.

Standard Traits

Bite (1 RP): *Prerequisites:* Small or larger size; *Benefit:* Members of this race gain a natural bite attack, dealing damage equivalent to that of a creature two size categories lower than normal for their size (*Bestiary* 302; 1d2 for Small races, 1d3 for Medium, etc.). The bite is a primary attack, or a secondary attack if the creature is wielding manufactured weapons. *Special:* This trait can be taken up to two times. The second time it is taken, the bite damage increases by one size category.

Breath Weapon (1 RP): *Prerequisites:* Aberration, construct, dragon, humanoid (reptilian), monstrous humanoid, or outsider (native) with ties to an elemental plane; *Benefit:* Choose one of the following energy types: acid, cold, electricity, or fire. If the creature is an outsider (native), it must have ties to an elemental plane, and it must pick an energy that corresponds to the plane it has ties to (acid [earth], cold [water], electricity [air], or fire [fire]). Then pick either a 15-foot cone or a 20-foot line. Once per day, as a standard action, members of this race can make a supernatural breath weapon attack that deals 1d6 points of the damage type chosen in the area chosen. All creatures within the affected area must make a Reflex saving throw to avoid taking damage. The save DC against this breath weapon is 10 + 1/2 the user's character level + the user's Constitution modifier. Those who succeed at the save take no damage from the attack. *Special:* You can take this trait more than once. Each time you do so, the cost of this trait increases by 1 RP. When do, you can augment the breath weapon in the following ways (augmentations marked with an asterisk [*] can be taken more than once).

Extra Breath*: The member of this race can use its breath weapon an additional time per day.

Increased Area: Increase the cone's size to 30 feet or the line to 50 feet.

Increased Damage*: Increase the damage by an additional d6.

Powerful Breath: The breath weapon deals half damage on a failed saving throw.

Celestial Crusader (7 RP): *Prerequisite:* Outsider (native) with ties to Elysium, Heaven, or Nirvana; *Benefit:* Members of this race gain a +1 insight bonus on attack rolls and to AC against evil outsiders and a +2 racial bonus to identify evil outsiders or items or effects evil outsiders create with Knowledge (planes) or Spellcraft; they may use these skills untrained for this purpose.

Elemental Assault (1 RP): *Prerequisite:* Dragon type or outsider (native) with ties to an elemental plane; *Benefit:* Pick one of the following energy types that corresponds to the plane the race has ties to: acid (earth), cold (water), electricity (air), or fire (fire). Members of this race gain the following supernatural ability: Once per day as a swift action, a member of this race can call on the elemental power lurking in its veins to shroud its arms in the energy type that corresponds to the elemental plane its race has ties to. Unarmed strikes with its elbows or hands (or attacks with weapons held in those hands) deal +1d6 points of damage of the appropriate energy type. This lasts for 1 round per character level. The creature may end the effects of its elemental assault early as a free action.

Ferocity (4 RP): *Prerequisites:* None; *Benefit:* Members of this race gain the following extraordinary ability: If the hit points of a member of this race fall below 0 but it is not yet dead, it can continue to fight. If it does, it is staggered, and loses 1 hit point each round. It still dies when its hit points reach a negative amount equal to its Constitution score.

Gatecrasher (2 RP): *Prerequisites:* None; *Benefit:* Members of this race gain a +2 racial bonus on Strength checks to break objects and a +2 racial bonus on combat maneuver checks to sunder.

Hatred (1 RP): *Prerequisites:* None; *Benefit:* Choose two subtypes of humanoids or outsiders or one creature type other than humanoid or outsider. Members of this race gain a +1 racial bonus on attack rolls against creatures of these subtypes or this type.

Kneecapper (1 RP): *Prerequisite:* Small; *Benefit:* Members of this race gain a +4 racial bonus on combat maneuver checks to trip an opponent.

Magehunter (4 RP): *Prerequisites:* None; *Benefit:* Members of this race gain a +2 racial bonus on Spellcraft checks made to identify a spell being cast and a +1 racial bonus on attack rolls against arcane spellcasters. Members of this race only gain this bonus against creatures that use spells, not against those that only use spell-like abilities.

Orc Ferocity (2 RP): *Prerequisite:* Orc subtype; *Benefit:* Once per day, when a member of this race is reduced to fewer than 0 hit points but is not killed, it can fight on for 1 more round as if disabled. At the end of its next turn, unless brought to above 0 hit points, it immediately falls unconscious and begins to die.

Poison Use (1 RP): *Prerequisites:* None; *Benefit:* Members of this race are skilled with poison and never risk accidentally poisoning themselves when applying it to weapons.

Relentless (1 RP): *Prerequisites:* None; *Benefit:* Members of this race gain a +2 bonus on combat maneuver checks made to bull rush or overrun an opponent. This bonus

KASATHA

Hunters and raiders of the wasteland, the clannish, four-armed kasatha guard their territories by way of lightning-fast raids and terrifying assaults. As young adults, some members of this race roam the world for a full year looking for adventure and treasure to bring back to their clans. A renegade few decide to forsake their clan and spend their life adventuring.

Type	
Humanoid (kasatha)	0 RP
Size	
Medium	0 RP
Base Speed	
Normal	0 RP
Ability Score Modifiers	
Flexible (+2 Dex, +2 Wis)	2 RP
Languages	
Standard	0 RP
Racial Abilities	
Defense Racial Traits	
Defensive training, greater	4 RP
Desert runner	2 RP
Feat and Skill Racial Traits	
Stalker	1 RP
Movement Racial Traits	
Jumper	2 RP
Terrain stride (desert)	1 RP
Other Racial Traits	
Multi-armed (4 arms)	8 RP
Total	**20 RP**

only applies while both the member of this race and its opponent are standing on the ground.

Sky Sentinel (3 RP): *Prerequisites:* None; *Benefit:* Members of this race gain a +1 racial bonus on attack rolls, a +2 dodge bonus to AC, and a +2 bonus on Perception checks against flying creatures. In addition, enemies on higher ground gain no attack roll bonus against members of this race.

Slapping Tail (3 RP): *Prerequisites:* None; *Benefit:* Members of this race have a tail they can use to make attacks of opportunity with a reach of 5 feet. The tail is a natural attack that deals 1d6 points of damage plus the user's Strength modifier if Small, 1d8 points of damage plus the user's Strength modifier if Medium, or 1d10 points of damage plus 1-1/2 times the user's Strength modifier if Large. *Special:* If a Large creature has the reach trait, its tail also gains reach.

Stench Aura (4 RP): *Prerequisite:* Monstrous humanoid type, reptilian subtype, or undead type; *Benefit:* Members of this race secrete a terrible scent as a 15-foot aura that nearly every other creature finds offensive. All living creatures (except those with the stench aura ability) within the aura must succeed at a Fortitude saving throw (DC 10 + 1/2 the user's character level + the user's Constitution modifier) or be sickened for 5 rounds. Creatures that succeed at the saving throw cannot be sickened by the same creature's stench aura for 24 hours. A *delay poison* or *neutralize poison* spell or similar effect removes the effect from the sickened creature. This is a poison effect. *Special:* This trait can be taken up to two times. The second time it is taken, the size of the aura increases to 30 feet, and the duration of the effect increases to 10 rounds.

Sticky Tongue (2 RP): *Prerequisite:* Medium or larger size; *Benefit:* Members of this race can make melee attacks with their long, sticky tongues. This is a secondary attack. A creature hit by this attack cannot move more than 10 feet away from the attacker and takes a –2 penalty to AC as long as the tongue is attached (this penalty does not stack if multiple tongues are attached). The tongue

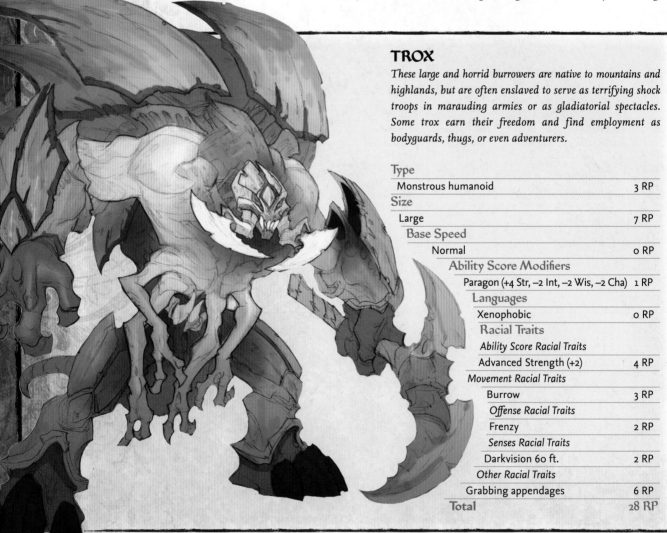

TROX

These large and horrid burrowers are native to mountains and highlands, but are often enslaved to serve as terrifying shock troops in marauding armies or as gladiatorial spectacles. Some trox earn their freedom and find employment as bodyguards, thugs, or even adventurers.

Type	
Monstrous humanoid	3 RP
Size	
Large	7 RP
Base Speed	
Normal	0 RP
Ability Score Modifiers	
Paragon (+4 Str, –2 Int, –2 Wis, –2 Cha)	1 RP
Languages	
Xenophobic	0 RP
Racial Traits	
Ability Score Racial Traits	
Advanced Strength (+2)	4 RP
Movement Racial Traits	
Burrow	3 RP
Offense Racial Traits	
Frenzy	2 RP
Senses Racial Traits	
Darkvision 60 ft.	2 RP
Other Racial Traits	
Grabbing appendages	6 RP
Total	28 RP

can be removed by the target or an adjacent ally by making an opposed Strength check against the attacking creature as a standard action or by dealing 2 points of damage to the tongue (AC 11, damage does not reduce the sticky-tongued creature's hit points). A member of this race cannot move more than 10 feet away from a creature stuck to its tongue, but it can release its tongue from the target as a free action. A member of this race can only have one creature attached to its tongue at a time. *Special*: This trait can be taken up to two times. The second time it is taken, members of this race gain the ability to pull a creature attached to their tongue 5 feet toward them as a swift action.

Swarming (1 or 2 RP): *Prerequisite*: Medium or smaller size; *Benefit*: Members of this race are used to living and fighting communally with other members of their race. Up to two members of this race can share the same square at the same time. If two members of this race that are occupying the same square attack the same foe, they are considered to be flanking that foe as if they were in two opposite squares. *Special*: If the race is Small or smaller, this trait costs 1 RP. If the race is Medium, it costs 2 RP.

Terrifying Croak (2 RP): *Prerequisites*: None; *Benefit*: Members of this race gain the following supernatural ability: Once per hour as a standard action, a member of this race can emit a thunderous croak. Any creature not of its subtype (if humanoid) or type (if another race type) must make a successful Will saving throw (DC 10 + 1/2 the user's character level + the user's Charisma modifier) or become shaken for 1d4 rounds. A target that successfully saves cannot be affected by the user's terrifying croak for 24 hours. Creatures that are already shaken become frightened for 1d4 rounds instead. This is a sonic, mind-affecting effect.

Toxic (1 RP): *Prerequisite*: Aberration, dragon, plant, or undead type, or grippli, half-undead, reptilian, or vishkanya subtype; *Benefit*: Members of this race gain the following extraordinary ability: A number of times per day equal to its Constitution modifier (minimum 1/day), a member of this race can envenom a weapon that it wields with its toxic saliva or blood (using blood requires the creature to be injured when it uses this ability). Applying venom in this way is a swift action. When you take this trait, choose one of the following venoms.

Life-Stealing Venom: Injury; *save* Fort DC 10 + 1/2 the user's Hit Dice + the user's Constitution modifier; *frequency* 1/round for 6 rounds; *effect* 1 Con; *cure* 1 save.

Paralytic Venom: Injury; *save* Fort DC 10 + the 1/2 user's Hit Dice + the user's Constitution modifier; *frequency* 1/round for 6 rounds; *effect* 1d2 Dex; *cure* 1 save.

Weakening Venom: Injury; *save* Fort DC 10 + 1/2 the user's Hit Dice + the user's Constitution modifier; *frequency* 1/round for 6 rounds; *effect* 1d2 Str; *cure* 1 save.

Weapon Familiarity (1 RP): *Prerequisites*: None; *Benefit*: Choose up to two weapons, or one weapon and a racial weapon group. When choosing a racial weapon group, you must choose a group that includes the same name as one of your subtypes. Members of this race are proficient with those weapons. For the purposes of weapon familiarity, all bows are considered one weapon. *Special*: This trait can be taken up to two times. The second time it is taken, the race becomes proficient with another two weapons or one weapon and a racial weapon group.

Wyrmscourged (3 RP): *Prerequisites*: None; *Benefit*: Members of this race gain a +1 bonus on attack rolls and a +2 dodge bonus to AC and on saving throws against the extraordinary, supernatural, and spell-like abilities of dragons. In addition, they gain a +2 racial bonus on Knowledge (arcana) checks to identify dragons and can make such checks untrained.

Advanced Traits

Claws (2 RP): *Prerequisites*: None; *Benefit*: Members of this race receive two claw attacks. These are primary natural attacks. The damage is based on the creature's size (*Bestiary* 302).

Frenzy (2 RP): *Prerequisites*: None; *Benefit*: Once per day, whenever a member of this race takes damage, it flies into a frenzy for 1 minute, gaining a +2 racial bonus to Constitution and Strength, but a −2 penalty to AC.

Frightful Gaze (6 RP): *Prerequisites*: None; *Benefit*: Members of this race gain the following supernatural ability: Creatures within 30 feet of a member of this race that meet its gaze must succeed at a Will saving throw (DC 10 + the 1/2 user's character level + the user's Charisma modifier) or stand paralyzed in fear for 1 round. This is a mind-affecting fear effect. A target that successfully saves cannot be affected by the user's frightful gaze for 24 hours.

Natural Attack (1 RP): *Prerequisites*: None; *Benefit*: Pick one of the following natural attacks: gore, hoof (if the race has hooves), slam, talons, or wings (if the race has flight). Members of this race receive one natural attack of the chosen type. Gore, slam, and talons are primary natural attacks, while hoof and wings are secondary natural attacks. The damage is based on the creature's size (*Bestiary* 302). *Special*: This trait can be taken multiple times. Each time, pick a different natural attack.

Reach (1 RP): *Prerequisite*: Large size; *Benefit*: Members of this race have a reach of 10 feet.

Swordtrained (4 RP): *Prerequisites*: None; *Benefit*: Members of this race are trained from birth in swordplay, and as a result are automatically proficient with swordlike weapons (including bastard swords, daggers, elven curve blades, falchions, greatswords, kukris, longswords, punching daggers, rapiers, scimitars, short swords, and two-bladed swords).

QUADRUPEDS AND MAGIC ITEM SLOTS

Creating a race with more than two legs adversely affects that race's ability to use standard feet slot magic items. The best way to deal with this is to create variant magic item versions of the various boots, shoes, and slippers that can be worn by this race. Allow members of these races to find *ankle bracelets of speed* or *horseshoes of spider climb* that act just like their traditional magic item counterparts, but fit the new race's form.

Tripping Tail (3 RP): *Prerequisite:* Slapping tail trait; *Benefit:* When a member of this race hits with its slapping tail, it can make a trip attack as a free action that does not provoke attacks of opportunity.

Monstrous Traits

Elemental Weapons (6 RP): *Prerequisite:* Outsider (native) with ties to an elemental plane; *Benefit:* Pick one of the following energy types that corresponds to the plane the race has ties to: acid (earth), cold (water), electricity (air), or fire (fire). Members of this race deal 1d6 points of energy damage of the selected type whenever they strike a foe with a natural attack, unarmed strike, or melee weapon.

Powerful Charge (2 RP): *Prerequisite:* Natural attack trait; *Benefit:* Select one of the race's natural attacks. Whenever a member of this race charges, it deals twice the number of damage dice with the selected natural attack plus 1-1/2 times its Strength bonus.

Rock Throwing (3 RP): *Prerequisite:* Large size; *Benefit:* Members of this race are accomplished rock throwers and gain a +1 racial bonus on attack rolls with thrown rocks. A member of this race can hurl rocks up to two categories smaller than its size. A "rock" is any large, bulky, and relatively regularly shaped object made of any material with a hardness of at least 5. A thrown rock has a range increment of 120 feet. The creature can hurl the rock up to five rage increments. Damage from a thrown rock is 2d6 plus 1-1/2 times the throwing creature's Strength bonus.

Senses Racial Traits

All races start with normal vision. The following traits augment their vision or otherwise enhance their senses.

Standard Traits

Carrion Sense (1 RP): *Prerequisites:* None; *Benefit:* Members of this race have a natural ability to sniff out carrion. This functions like the scent ability, but only for corpses and badly wounded creatures (creatures with 25% or fewer hit points).

Darkvision 60 Feet (2 RP): *Prerequisites:* None; *Benefit:* Members of this race can see in the dark up to 60 feet.

Darkvision 120 Feet (3 RP): *Prerequisites:* None; *Benefit:* Members of this race can see in the dark up to 120 feet.

Deepsight (2 RP): *Prerequisite:* Amphibious racial trait; *Benefit:* Members of this race are specially adapted to the lightless depths of the oceans, but not to air-filled environments. They can see in the dark up to 120 feet while underwater, but do not gain this benefit out of water.

Low-Light Vision (1 RP): *Prerequisites:* None; *Benefit:* Members of this race can see twice as far as a race with normal vision in conditions of dim light.

Minesight (2 RP): *Prerequisites:* None; *Benefit:* Members of this race have darkvision 90 feet; however, they are automatically dazzled in bright light and take a –2 penalty on saving throws against effects with the light descriptor.

Water Sense (1 RP): *Prerequisite:* Outsider (native) with ties to the Plane of Water or amphibious racial trait; *Benefit:* Members of this race can sense vibrations in water, granting them blindsense 30 feet against creatures that are touching the same body of water.

Advanced Traits

Scent (4 RP): *Prerequisites:* None; *Benefit:* Members of this race gain the scent ability (*Bestiary* 304).

See in Darkness (4 RP): *Prerequisites:* None; *Benefit:* Members of this race can see perfectly in darkness of any kind, including that created by spells such as *deeper darkness*.

Monstrous Traits

All-Around Vision (4 RP): *Prerequisites:* None; *Benefit:* Members of this race have some way of seeing all around them, granting them a +4 racial bonus on Perception checks and making them immune to flanking.

Blindsense 30 Feet (4 RP): *Prerequisites:* None; *Benefit:* Using nonvisual senses such as acute smell or hearing, members of this race notice things they cannot see. Members of this race usually do not need to make Perception checks to pinpoint the location of a creature within 30 feet, provided they have line of effect to that creature. A creature that members of this race cannot see still has total concealment against individuals with blindsense, and members of this race still have the normal miss chance when attacking creatures that have concealment. Visibility still affects the movement of members of this race. Members of this race are still denied their Dexterity bonus to AC against attacks from creatures they cannot see.

Weakness Racial Traits

The following racial traits apply weaknesses to members of the race. All weakness racial traits cost negative RP, which means they subtract from a race's total RP spent for the purposes of meeting the race's power level restrictions.

Standard Traits

Light Blindness (–2 RP): *Prerequisite:* Darkvision or see in darkness trait; *Weakness:* Abrupt exposure to bright light blinds members of this race for 1 round; on subsequent rounds, they are dazzled as long as they remain in the affected area.

Light Sensitivity (–1 RP): *Prerequisite:* Darkvision; *Weakness:* Members of this race are dazzled as long as they remain in an area of bright light.

Negative Energy Affinity (–1 RP): *Prerequisites:* None; *Weakness:* A member of this race is alive, but reacts to positive and negative energy as if it were undead—positive energy harms it, while negative energy heals it.

Resurrection Vulnerability (–1 RP): *Prerequisite:* Half-undead subtype or undead type; *Weakness:* A *raise dead* spell cast on a member of this race can destroy it (Will negates). Using the spell in this way does not require a material component.

Vulnerable to Sunlight (–2 RP): *Prerequisite:* Native to the Darklands or the Plane of Shadow; *Weakness:* Members of this race take 1 point of Constitution damage after every hour they are exposed to sunlight.

Advanced Traits

Elemental Vulnerability (–2 RP): *Prerequisite:* Outsider (native) with ties to an elemental plane; *Weakness:* Pick one of the following energy types: acid, cold, electricity, or fire. Members of this race have vulnerability to the chosen energy type. They cannot posses any racial trait that grants them resistance or immunity to this energy type. *Special:* This trait can be taken multiple times. Each time it is taken, choose a different energy type. If a race has vulnerability to fire and immunity to cold, it gains the cold subtype. If a race has vulnerability to cold and immunity to fire, it gains the fire subtype.

Sunlight Powerlessness (–2 RP): *Prerequisite:* Half-undead subtype or undead type; *Weakness:* Members of this race are powerless in natural sunlight (this does not include light created by effects such as a *daylight* spell). A member of this race caught in natural sunlight cannot attack and is staggered.

WYRWOOD

The original wyrwoods were created centuries ago to serve a wizard as spies and emotionless apprentices. The wizard's downfall came about when he granted them free will, which in addition to their cold, calculating intelligence heralded the birth of a strange new race. The wyrwoods murdered their former master and stole the secrets of their own creation, which they jealously guard and rigorously control.

Type	
Construct	20 RP
Size	
Small	0 RP
Base Speed	
Normal	0 RP
Ability Score Modifiers	
Standard (+2 Dex, +2 Int, –2 Cha)	0 RP
Languages	
Standard	0 RP
Racial Traits	
Senses Racial Traits	
Darkvision 60 ft.	— RP
Low-light vision	— RP
Total	**20 RP**

Other Racial Traits

This category covers various traits that other categories do not, which can augment your race in a number of different ways.

Standard Traits

Amphibious (2 RP): *Prerequisite*: Swim racial trait; *Benefit*: Members of this race are amphibious and can breathe both air and water.

Heroic (4 RP): *Prerequisites*: None; *Benefit*: In campaigns that use the optional hero point system (*Pathfinder RPG Advanced Player's Guide* 322), each time a member of this race gains a level, it gains 2 hero points instead of 1. If it takes the Blood of Heroes feat, it gains 3 hero points each level instead of 2.

Hold Breath (1 RP): *Prerequisites*: None; *Benefit*: Members of this race can hold their breath for a number of rounds equal to four times their Constitution score before risking drowning or suffocating.

Light and Dark (1 RP): *Prerequisites*: None; *Benefit*: Members of this race gain the following supernatural ability: Once per day as an immediate action, a member of this race can treat positive and negative energies as if it were an undead creature, taking damage from positive energy and healing damage from negative energy. This ability lasts for 1 minute once activated.

Multitalented (2 RP): *Prerequisites*: None; *Benefit*: Members of this race choose two favored classes at 1st level and gain +1 hit points or +1 skill rank whenever they take a level in either of those classes.

Prehensile Tail (2 RP): *Prerequisites*: None; *Benefit*: Members of this race have a long, flexible tail that can be used to carry objects. They cannot wield weapons with their tails, but they can retrieve small, stowed objects carried on their persons as a swift action.

Rodent Empathy (1 RP): *Prerequisite*: Ratfolk subtype; *Benefit*: Members of this race gain a +4 bonus on Handle Animal checks made to influence rodents.

WYVARAN

Thought to be a fusion of kobolds and wyverns, wyvarans are often found leading kobold tribes, serving wyverns, or even dwelling among true dragons. Like wyverns, they are territorial creatures, but also have an acute sense of honor. Depending on how they are treated, wyvarans can become powerful allies or deadly enemies.

Type	
Dragon	10 RP
Size	
Medium	0 RP
Base Speed	
Normal	0 RP
Ability Score Modifiers	
Standard (+2 Dex, –2 Int, +2 Wis)	0 RP
Languages	
Standard	0 RP
Racial Traits	
Movement Racial Traits	
Flight (30 ft., clumsy)	4 RP
Offense Racial Traits	
Slapping tail	3 RP
Senses Racial Traits	
Darkvision 60 ft.	— RP
Low-light vision	— RP
Total	17 RP

Treespeech (2 RP): *Prerequisite*: Plant type; *Benefit*: Members of this race have the ability to converse with plants as if subject to a continual *speak with plants* spell.

Advanced Traits

Grabbing Appendages (6 RP): *Prerequisites*: Any type except humanoid, Large size; *Benefit*: Members of this race have a small group of appendages that are useful for little more than to aid in grappling. Members of this race gain Improved Grapple as a bonus feat, and can maintain a grapple and still make attacks with their main appendages.

Monstrous Traits

Multi-Armed (4 RP): *Prerequisites*: None; *Benefit*: Members of this race possess three arms. A member of this race can wield multiple weapons, but only one hand is its primary hand, and all others are off hands. It can also use its hands for other purposes that require free hands. *Special*: This trait can be taken up to twice. When it is taken a second time, the race gains a fourth arm.

Quadruped (2 RP): *Prerequisites*: Any type except humanoid, Large size, normal speed; *Benefit*: Members of this race possess four legs and two arms, granting them a +4 racial bonus to CMD against trip attempts and a +10 foot bonus to their base speed. In addition, members of this race use weapons and armor as if they were Medium (instead of Large). *Special*: The number of legs can be increased by 2 for each additional 1 RP spent. Each such increase grants an additional +4 racial bonus to CMD against trip attempts, but no other bonus.

CORE RACE EXAMPLES

Presented in this section are the seven core races from the *Pathfinder RPG Core Rulebook*, built with the race builder rules.

Dwarves

Type
Humanoid (dwarf)	0 RP

Size
Medium	0 RP

Base Speed
Slow	−1 RP

Ability Score Modifiers
Standard (+2 Con, +2 Wis, −2 Cha)	0 RP

Languages
Standard	0 RP

Racial Traits
Defense Racial Traits	
Defensive training, lesser	1 RP
Hardy	3 RP
Stability	1 RP
Feat and Skill Racial Traits	
Greed	1 RP
Stonecunning	1 RP

Offense Racial Traits	
Hatred	1 RP
Weapon familiarity	2 RP
Senses Racial Traits	
Darkvision 60 ft.	2 RP
Total	**11 RP**

Elves

Type
Humanoid (elf)	0 RP

Size
Medium	0 RP

Base Speed
Normal	0 RP

Ability Score Modifiers
Standard (+2 Dex, −2 Con, +2 Int)	0 RP

Languages
Standard	0 RP

Racial Traits
Defense Racial Traits	
Elven immunities	2 RP
Feat and Skill Racial Traits	
Skill bonus (Perception)	2 RP
Magical Racial Traits	
Elven magic	3 RP
Offense Racial Traits	
Weapon familiarity	2 RP
Senses Racial Traits	
Low-light vision	1 RP
Total	**10 RP**

Gnomes

Type
Humanoid (gnome)	0 RP

Size
Small	0 RP

Base Speed
Slow	−1 RP

Ability Score Modifiers
Standard (−2 Str, +2 Con, +2 Cha)	0 RP

Languages
Standard	0 RP

Racial Traits
Defense Racial Traits	
Defensive training, lesser	1 RP
Illusion resistance	1 RP
Feat and Skill Racial Traits	
Skill bonus (Perception)	2 RP
Skill bonus (choose one Craft or Profession)	2 RP
Magical Racial Traits	
Gnome magic	2 RP
Offense Racial Traits	
Hatred	1 RP

Weapon familiarity	1 RP
Senses Racial Traits	
Low-light vision	1 RP
Total	10 RP

Half-Elves

Type	
Humanoid (elf, human)	0 RP
Size	
Medium	0 RP
Base Speed	
Normal	0 RP
Ability Score Modifiers	
Human heritage	0 RP
Languages	
Linguist	1 RP
Racial Traits	
Defense Racial Traits	
Elven immunities	2 RP

Feat and Skill Racial Traits	
Skill bonus (Perception)	2 RP
Static bonus feat (Skill Focus)	2 RP
Senses Racial Traits	
Low-light vision	1 RP
Other Racial Traits	
Multitalented	2 RP
Total	10 RP

Half-Orcs

Type	
Humanoid (human, orc)	0 RP
Size	
Medium	0 RP
Base Speed	
Normal	0 RP
Ability Score Modifiers	
Human heritage	0 RP
Languages	
Standard	0 RP
Racial Traits	
Offense Racial Traits	
Orc ferocity	2 RP
Weapon familiarity	2 RP
Feat and Skill Racial Traits	
Skill bonus (Intimidate)	2 RP
Senses Racial Traits	
Darkvision 60 ft.	2 RP
Total	8 RP

Halflings

Type	
Humanoid (halfling)	0 RP
Size	
Small	0 RP
Base Speed	
Slow	−1 RP
Ability Score Modifiers	
Standard (−2 Str, +2 Dex, +2 Cha)	0 RP
Languages	
Standard	0 RP
Racial Traits	
Defense Racial Traits	
Fearless	1 RP
Lucky, lesser	2 RP
Feat and Skill Racial Traits	
Skill bonus (Acrobatics)	2 RP
Skill bonus (Climb)	2 RP
Skill bonus (Perception)	2 RP
Offense Racial Traits	
Weapon familiarity	1 RP
Total	9 RP

240

Humans

Type	
Humanoid (human)	0 RP
Size	
Medium	0 RP
Base Speed	
Normal	0 RP
Ability Score Modifiers	
Human	0 RP
Languages	
Linguist	1 RP
Racial Traits	
Feat and Skill Racial Traits	
Flexible bonus feat	4 RP
Skilled	4 RP
Total	**9 RP**

EXPANDED RACE EXAMPLES

The following races are derived from some of the most "character-friendly" races of the monsters presented in the *Pathfinder RPG Bestiary*, *Bestiary 2*, and *Bestiary 3*.

Aasimars

Type	
Outsider (native)	3 RP
Size	
Medium	0 RP
Base Speed	
Normal	0 RP
Ability Score Modifiers	
Flexible (+2 Wis, +2 Cha)	2 RP
Languages	
Standard	0 RP
Racial Traits	
Defense Racial Traits	
Celestial resistance	3 RP
Feat and Skill Racial Traits	
Skill bonus (Diplomacy)	2 RP
Skill bonus (Perception)	2 RP
Magical Racial Traits	
Spell-like ability, greater	3 RP
Senses Racial Traits	
Darkvision 60 ft.	— RP
Total	**15 RP**

Catfolk

Type	
Humanoid (catfolk)	0 RP
Size	
Medium	0 RP
Base Speed	
Normal	0 RP

Ability Score Modifiers	
Standard (+2 Dex, −2 Wis, +2 Cha)	0 RP
Languages	
Standard	0 RP
Racial Traits	
Defense Racial Traits	
Cat's luck	1 RP
Feat and Skill Racial Traits	
Skill bonus (Perception)	2 RP
Skill bonus (Stealth)	2 RP
Skill bonus (Survival)	2 RP
Movement Racial Traits	
Sprinter	1 RP
Senses Racial Traits	
Low-light vision	1 RP
Total	**9 RP**

Dhampirs

Type	
Humanoid (dhampir)	0 RP
Size	
Medium	0 RP
Base Speed	
Normal	0 RP
Ability Score Modifiers	
Standard (+2 Dex, −2 Con, +2 Cha)	0 RP
Languages	
Linguist	1 RP
Racial Traits	
Defense Racial Traits	
Resist level drain	1 RP
Undead resistance	1 RP
Feat and Skill Racial Traits	
Skill bonus (Bluff)	2 RP
Skill bonus (Perception)	2 RP
Magical Racial Traits	
Spell-like ability, lesser	3 RP
Senses Racial Traits	
Darkvision 60 ft.	2 RP
Low-light vision	1 RP
Weakness Racial Traits	
Light sensitivity	−1 RP
Negative energy affinity	−1 RP
Total	**11 RP**

Drow

Type	
Humanoid (elf)	0 RP
Size	
Medium	0 RP
Base Speed	
Normal	0 RP

Ability Score Modifiers

Standard (+2 Dex, –2 Con, +2 Cha)	0 RP

Languages

Standard	0 RP

Racial Traits

Defense Racial Traits	
Elven immunities	2 RP
Spell resistance, lesser	2 RP
Feat and Skill Racial Traits	
Skill bonus (Perception)	2 RP
Magical Racial Traits	
Spell-like ability, lesser	4 RP
Offense Racial Traits	
Poison use	1 RP
Weapon familiarity	2 RP
Senses Racial Traits	
Darkvision 120 ft.	3 RP

Weakness Racial Traits

Light blindness	–2 RP
Total	**14 RP**

Drow Nobles

Type

Humanoid (elf)	0 RP

Size

Medium	0 RP

Base Speed

Normal	0 RP

Ability Score Modifiers

Advanced (+4 Dex, –2 Con, +2 Int, +2 Wis, +2 Cha)	4 RP

Languages

Standard	0 RP

Racial Traits

Defense Racial Traits	
Elven immunities	2 RP
Spell resistance, greater	3 RP
Feat and Skill Racial Traits	
Skill bonus (Perception)	2 RP
Magical Racial Traits	
Spell-like ability, lesser	1 RP
Spell-like ability, greater	6 RP
Spell-like ability, constant	3 RP
Spell-like ability, at will	16 RP
Offense Racial Traits	
Poison use	1 RP
Weapon familiarity	2 RP
Senses Racial Traits	
Darkvision 120 ft.	3 RP
Weakness Racial Traits	
Light blindness	–2 RP
Total	**41 RP**

Duergar

Type

Humanoid (dwarf)	0 RP

Size

Medium	0 RP

Base Speed

Slow	–1 RP

Ability Score Modifiers

Weakness (+2 Con, +2 Wis, –4 Cha)	–1 RP

Languages

Standard	0 RP

Racial Traits

Defense Racial Traits	
Duergar immunities	4 RP
Stability	1 RP
Magical Racial Traits	
Spell-like ability, lesser	3 RP
Senses Racial Traits	
Darkvision 120 ft.	3 RP

Weakness Racial Traits	
Light sensitivity	−1 RP
Total	**8 RP**

Fetchlings

Type	
Outsider (native)	3 RP
Size	
Medium	0 RP
Base Speed	
Normal	0 RP
Ability Score Modifiers	
Standard (+2 Dex, −2 Wis, +2 Cha)	0 RP
Languages	
Standard	0 RP
Racial Traits	
Defense Racial Traits	
Shadow blending	1 RP
Shadowy resistance	2 RP
Feat and Skill Racial Traits	
Skill bonus (Knowledge [planes])	2 RP
Skill bonus (Stealth)	2 RP
Magical Racial Traits	
Spell-like ability, lesser	1 RP
Shadow travel	5 RP
Senses Racial Traits	
Darkvision 60 ft.	— RP
Low-light vision	1 RP
Total	**17 RP**

Goblins

Type	
Humanoid (goblinoid)	0 RP
Size	
Small	0 RP
Base Speed	
Normal	0 RP
Ability Score Modifiers	
Greater paragon (−2 Str, +4 Dex, −2 Cha)	2 RP
Languages	
Standard	0 RP
Racial Traits	
Feat and Skill Racial Traits	
Sneaky rider	6 RP
Senses Racial Traits	
Darkvision 60 ft.	2 RP
Total	**10 RP**

Gripplis

Type	
Humanoid (grippli)	0 RP
Size	
Small	0 RP

Base Speed	
Normal	0 RP
Ability Score Modifiers	
Standard (−2 Str, +2 Dex, +2 Wis)	0 RP
Languages	
Standard	0 RP
Racial Traits	
Feat and Skill Racial Traits	
Camouflage	1 RP
Movement Racial Traits	
Climb	1 RP
Terrain stride (swamp)	1 RP
Offense Racial Traits	
Weapon familiarity	1 RP
Senses Racial Traits	
Darkvision 60 ft.	2 RP
Total	**6 RP**

Hobgoblins

Type	
Humanoid (goblinoid)	0 RP

Size	
Medium	0 RP
Base Speed	
Normal	0 RP
Ability Score Modifiers	
Flexible (+2 Dex, +2 Con)	2 RP
Languages	
Standard	0 RP
Racial Traits	
Feat and Skill Racial Traits	
Sneaky	5 RP
Senses Racial Traits	
Darkvision 60 ft.	2 RP
Total	**9 RP**

Ifrits

Type	
Outsider (native)	3 RP

Size	
Medium	0 RP
Base Speed	
Normal	0 RP
Ability Score Modifiers	
Standard (+2 Dex, −2 Wis, +2 Cha)	0 RP
Languages	
Standard	0 RP
Racial Traits	
Defense Racial Traits	
Energy resistance (fire)	1 RP
Magical Racial Traits	
Elemental affinity (fire)	1 RP
Spell-like ability, lesser	1 RP
Senses Racial Traits	
Darkvision 60 ft.	— RP
Total	**6 RP**

Kobolds

Type	
Humanoid (reptilian)	0 RP
Size	
Small	0 RP
Base Speed	
Normal	0 RP
Ability Score Modifiers	
Greater weakness (−4 Str, +2 Dex, −2 Con)	−3 RP
Languages	
Standard	0 RP
Racial Traits	
Defense Racial Traits	
Natural armor	2 RP
Feat and Skill Racial Traits	
Skill bonus (Craft [trapmaking])	2 RP
Skill bonus (Profession [miner])	2 RP
Skill training (Craft [trapmaking] and Profession [miner])	1 RP
Senses Racial Traits	
Darkvision 60 ft.	2 RP
Weakness Racial Traits	
Light sensitivity	−1 RP
Total	**5 RP**

Orcs

Type	
Humanoid (orc)	0 RP
Size	
Medium	0 RP
Base Speed	
Normal	0 RP
Ability Score Modifiers	
Paragon (+4 Str, −2 Int, −2 Wis, −2 Cha)	1 RP

Languages

Standard	0 RP

Racial Traits

Offense Racial Traits	
Ferocity	4 RP
Weapon familiarity	2 RP
Senses Racial Traits	
Darkvision 60 ft.	2 RP
Weakness Racial Traits	
Light sensitivity	−1 RP
Total	**8 RP**

Oreads

Type

Outsider (native)	3 RP

Size

Medium	0 RP

Base Speed

Slow	−1 RP

Ability Score Modifiers

Standard (+2 Str, +2 Wis, −2 Cha)	0 RP

Languages

Standard	1 RP

Racial Traits

Defense Racial Traits	
Energy resistance (acid)	1 RP
Magical Racial Traits	
Elemental affinity (earth)	1 RP
Spell-like ability, lesser	1 RP
Senses Racial Traits	
Darkvision 60 ft.	— RP
Total	**6 RP**

Ratfolk

Type

Humanoid (ratfolk)	0 RP

Size

Small	0 RP

Base Speed

Slow	−1 RP

Ability Score Modifiers

Standard (−2 Str, +2 Dex, +2 Int)	0 RP

Languages

Standard	0 RP

Racial Traits

Feat and Skill Racial Traits	
Skill bonus (Craft [alchemy])	2 RP
Skill bonus (Perception)	2 RP
Skill bonus (Use Magic Device)	2 RP
Offense Racial Traits	
Swarming	1 RP
Senses Racial Traits	
Darkvision 60 ft.	2 RP
Other Racial Traits	
Rodent empathy	1 RP
Total	**9 RP**

Sulis

Type

Outsider (native)	3 RP

Size

Medium	0 RP

Base Speed

Normal	0 RP

Ability Score Modifiers

Standard (+2 Str, −2 Int, +2 Cha)	0 RP

Languages

Standard	0 RP

Racial Traits

Defense Racial Traits	
Energy resistance (all)	4 RP
Feat and Skill Racial Trait	
Skill bonus (Diplomacy)	2 RP
Skill bonus (Sense Motive)	2 RP
Offense Racial Traits	
Elemental assault (all)	4 RP
Senses Racial Traits	
Darkvision 60 ft.	— RP
Low-light vision	1 RP
Total	**16 RP**

Svirfneblin

Type

Humanoid (gnome)	0 RP

Size

Small	0 RP

Base Speed

Slow	−1 RP

Ability Score Modifiers

Mixed weakness (−2 Str, +2 Dex, +2 Wis, −4 Cha)	−2 RP

Languages

Standard	0 RP

Racial Traits

Defense Racial Traits	
Defensive training, greater	3 RP
Lucky, greater	4 RP
Spell resistance, greater	3 RP
Feat and Skill Racial Traits	
Skill bonus (Craft [alchemy])	2 RP
Skill bonus (Perception)	2 RP
Stonecunning	1 RP
Underground sneak	5 RP
Magical Racial Traits	
Svirfneblin magic	2 RP
Offense Racial Traits	
Hatred	1 RP

Senses Racial Traits	
Darkvision 120 ft.	3 RP
Low-light vision	1 RP
Total	**24 RP**

Sylphs

Type Outsider (native)	3 RP
Size	
Medium	0 RP
Base Speed	
Normal	0 RP
Ability Score Modifiers	
Standard (+2 Dex, –2 Con, +2 Int)	0 RP
Languages	
Standard	0 RP
Racial Traits	
Defense Racial Traits	
Energy resistance (electricity)	1 RP

Magical Racial Traits	
Spell-like ability, lesser	1 RP
Elemental affinity (air)	1 RP
Senses Racial Traits	
Darkvision 60 ft.	— RP
Total	**6 RP**

Tengus

Type	
Humanoid (tengu)	0 RP
Size	
Medium	0 RP
Base Speed	
Normal	0 RP
Ability Score Modifiers	
Standard (+2 Dex, –2 Con, +2 Wis)	0 RP
Languages	
Linguist	1 RP
Racial Traits	
Feat and Skill Racial Traits	
Gifted linguist	2 RP
Skill bonus (Perception)	2 RP
Skill bonus (Stealth)	2 RP
Offense Racial Traits	
Natural weapon	1 RP
Swordtrained	4 RP
Senses Racial Traits	
Low-light vision	1 RP
Total	**13 RP**

Tieflings

Type	
Outsider (native)	3 RP
Size	
Medium	0 RP
Base Speed	
Normal	0 RP
Ability Score Modifiers	
Standard (+2 Dex, +2 Int, –2 Cha)	0 RP
Languages	
Standard	0 RP
Racial Traits	
Defense Racial Traits	
Fiendish resistance	3 RP
Feat and Skill Racial Traits	
Skill bonus (Bluff)	2 RP
Skill bonus (Stealth)	2 RP
Magical Racial Traits	
Fiendish sorcery	1 RP
Spell-like ability, lesser	2 RP
Senses Racial Traits	
Darkvision 60 ft.	— RP
Total	**13 RP**

Undines

Type
Outsider (native)	3 RP

Size
Medium	0 RP

Base Speed
Normal	0 RP

Ability Score Modifiers
Standard (−2 Str, +2 Dex, +2 Wis)	0 RP

Languages
Standard	0 RP

Racial Traits

Defense Racial Traits
Energy resistance (cold)	1 RP

Magical Racial Traits
Elemental affinity (water)	1 RP
Spell-like ability, lesser	1 RP

Movement Racial Traits
Swim	1 RP

Senses Racial Traits
Darkvision 60 ft.	— RP

Total	**7 RP**

Vanaras

Type
Humanoid (vanara)	0 RP

Size
Medium	0 RP

Base Speed
Normal	0 RP

Ability Score Modifiers
Standard (+2 Dex, +2 Wis, −2 Cha)	0 RP

Language
Standard	0 RP

Racial Traits

Feat and Skill Racial Traits
Skill bonus (Acrobatics)	2 RP
Skill bonus (Stealth)	2 RP

Movement Racial Traits
Climb	1 RP

Senses Racial Traits
Low-light vision	1 RP

Other Racial Traits
Prehensile tail	2 RP

Total	**8 RP**

Vishkanyas

Type
Humanoid (vishkanya)	0 RP

Size
Medium	0 RP

Base Speed
Normal	0 RP

Ability Score Modifiers
Standard (+2 Dex, −2 Wis, +2 Cha)	0 RP

Languages
Standard	0 RP

Racial Traits

Defense Racial Traits
Poison resistance	3 RP

Feat and Skill Racial Traits
Skill bonus (Escape Artist)	2 RP
Skill bonus (Perception)	2 RP
Skill bonus (Stealth)	2 RP

Offense Racial Traits
Toxic	1 RP
Weapon familiarity	2 RP

Senses Racial Traits
Low-light vision	1 RP

Total	**13 RP**

APPENDIX 1: AGE

You can choose or randomly generate your character's age. If you choose it, it must be at least the minimum age for the character's race and class (see the Random Starting Ages tables). Alternatively, roll the dice indicated for your class on the appropriate table and add the result to the minimum age of adulthood for your race to determine your character's age.

With age, a character's physical ability scores decrease and his mental ability scores increase (see the Aging Effects tables). The effects of each aging step are cumulative. However, none of a character's ability scores can be reduced below 1 in this way.

When a character reaches venerable age, secretly roll his maximum age (on the appropriate Aging Effects table) and record the result, which the player does not know. A character who reaches his maximum age dies of old age sometime during the following year.

TABLE 5-1: CORE RACE RANDOM STARTING AGES

Race	Adulthood	Intuitive[1]	Self-Taught[2]	Trained[3]
Dwarf	40 years	+3d6	+5d6	+7d6
Elf	110 years	+4d6	+6d6	+10d6
Gnome	40 years	+4d6	+6d6	+9d6
Half-elf	20 years	+1d6	+2d6	+3d6
Half-orc	14 years	+1d4	+1d6	+2d6
Halfling	20 years	+2d4	+3d6	+4d6
Human	15 years	+1d4	+1d6	+2d6

TABLE 5-2: FEATURED RACE RANDOM STARTING AGES

Race	Adulthood	Intuitive[1]	Self-Taught[2]	Trained[3]
Aasimar	60 years	+4d6	+6d6	+8d6
Catfolk	15 years	+1d4	+1d6	+2d6
Dhampir	110 years	+4d6	+6d6	+10d6
Drow	110 years	+4d6	+6d6	+10d6
Fetchling	20 years	+1d6	+2d6	+3d6
Goblin	12 years	+1d4	+1d6	+2d6
Hobgoblin	14 years	+1d4	+1d6	+2d6
Ifrit	60 years	+4d6	+6d6	+8d6
Kobold	12 years	+1d4	+1d6	+2d6
Orc	12 years	+1d4	+1d6	+2d6
Oread	60 years	+4d6	+6d6	+8d6
Ratfolk	12 years	+1d4	+1d6	+2d6
Sylph	60 years	+4d6	+6d6	+8d6
Tengu	15 years	+1d4	+1d6	+2d6
Tiefling	60 years	+4d6	+6d6	+8d6
Undine	60 years	+4d6	+6d6	+8d6

TABLE 5-3: UNCOMMON RACE RANDOM STARTING AGES

Race	Adulthood	Intuitive[1]	Self-Taught[2]	Trained[3]
Changeling	15 years	+1d4	+1d6	+2d6
Duergar	40 years	+3d6	+5d6	+7d6
Gillman	20 years	+1d6	+2d6	+3d6
Grippli	12 years	+1d4	+1d6	+2d6
Kitsune	15 years	+1d4	+1d6	+2d6
Merfolk	15 years	+1d4	+1d6	+2d6
Nagaji	20 years	+1d6	+2d6	+3d6
Samsaran	60 years	+4d6	+6d6	+8d6
Strix	12 years	+1d4	+1d6	+2d6
Suli	15 years	+1d4	+1d6	+2d6
Svirfneblin	40 years	+4d6	+6d6	+9d6
Vanara	14 years	+1d4	+1d6	+2d6
Vishkanya	15 years	+1d4	+1d6	+2d6
Wayang	40 years	+4d6	+5d6	+6d6

1 This category includes barbarians, oracles, rogues, and sorcerers.

2 This category includes bards, cavaliers, fighters, gunslingers, paladins, rangers, summoners, and witches.

3 This category includes alchemists, clerics, druids, inquisitors, magi, monks, and wizards.

TABLE 5-4: CORE RACE AGING EFFECTS

Race	Middle Age[1]	Old[2]	Venerable[3]	Maximum Age
Dwarf	125 years	188 years	250 years	250 + 2d% years
Elf	175 years	263 years	350 years	350 + 4d% years
Gnome	100 years	150 years	200 years	200 + 3d% years
Half-elf	62 years	93 years	125 years	125 + 3d20 years
Half-orc	30 years	45 years	60 years	60 + 2d10 years
Halfling	50 years	75 years	100 years	100 + 5d20 years
Human	35 years	53 years	70 years	70 + 2d20 years

TABLE 5-5: FEATURED RACE AGING EFFECTS

Race	Middle Age[1]	Old[2]	Venerable[3]	Maximum Age
Aasimar	150 years	200 years	250 years	250 + 6d% years
Catfolk	35 years	53 years	70 years	70 + 2d20 years
Dhampir	175 years	263 years	350 years	350 + 4d% years
Drow	175 years	263 years	350 years	350 + 4d% years
Fetchling	62 years	93 years	125 years	125 + 3d20 years
Gnome	100 years	150 years	200 years	200 + 3d% years
Goblin	20 years	30 years	40 years	40 + 1d20 years
Hobgoblin	30 years	45 years	60 years	60 + 2d10 years
Ifrit	150 years	200 years	250 years	250 + 6d% years
Kobold	20 years	30 years	40 years	40 + 1d20 years
Orc	20 years	30 years	40 years	40 + 1d20 years
Oread	150 years	200 years	250 years	250 + 6d% years
Ratfolk	20 years	30 years	40 years	40 + 1d20 years
Sylph	150 years	200 years	250 years	250 + 6d% years
Tengu	35 year	53 years	70 years	70 + 2d20 years
Tiefling	150 years	200 years	250 years	250 + 6d% years
Undine	150 years	200 years	250 years	250 + 6d% years

TABLE 5-6: UNCOMMON RACE AGING EFFECTS

Race	Middle Age[1]	Old[2]	Venerable[3]	Maximum Age
Changeling	35 years	53 years	70 years	70 + 2d20 years
Duergar	125 years	188 years	250 years	250 + 2d% years
Gillman	62 years	93 years	125 years	125 + 3d20 years
Grippli	20 years	30 years	40 years	40 + 1d20 years
Kitsune	32 year	50 years	65 years	65 + 3d12 years
Merfolk	35 years	53 years	70 years	70 + 2d20 years
Nagaji	60 years	90 years	120 years	120 + 3d20 years
Samsaran	150 years	200 years	250 years	250 + 6d% years
Strix	20 years	30 years	40 years	40 +1d20 years
Suli	35 years	53 years	70 years	70 + 2d20 years
Svirfneblin	100 years	150 years	200 years	200 + 3d% years
Vanara	30 years	45 years	60 years	60 + 2d10 years
Vishkanya	35 years	53 years	70 years	70 + 2d20 years
Wayang	100 years	150 years	200 years	200 + 1d% years

1 At middle age, −1 to Str, Dex, and Con and +1 to Int, Wis, and Cha.

2 At old age, −2 to Str, Dex, and Con and +1 to Int, Wis, and Cha.

3 At venerable age, −3 to Str, Dex, and Con and +1 to Int, Wis, and Cha.

APPENDIX 2: HEIGHT AND WEIGHT

To determine a character's height, roll the modifier dice indicated on the appropriate Random Height & Weight table and add the result, in inches, to the base height for your character's race and gender. To determine a character's weight, multiply the result of the modifier dice by the weight multiplier and add the result to the base weight for your character's race and gender.

Table 5-7: Core Race Random Height & Weight

Race	Base Height	Base Weight	Modifier	Weight Multiplier
Dwarf, male	3 ft. 9 in.	150 lbs.	2d4	x7 lbs.
Dwarf, female	3 ft. 7 in.	120 lbs.	2d4	x7 lbs.
Elf, male	5 ft. 4 in.	100 lbs.	2d8	x3 lbs.
Elf, female	5 ft. 4 in.	90 lbs.	2d6	x3 lbs.
Gnome, male	3 ft. 0 in.	35 lbs.	2d4	x1 lb.
Gnome, female	2 ft. 10 in.	30 lbs.	2d4	x1 lb.
Half-elf, male	5 ft. 2 in.	110 lbs.	2d8	x5 lbs.
Half-elf, female	5 ft. 0 in.	90 lbs.	2d8	x5 lbs.
Half-orc, male	4 ft. 10 in.	150 lbs.	2d12	x7 lbs.
Half-orc, female	4 ft. 5 in.	110 lbs.	2d12	x7 lbs.
Halfling, male	2 ft. 8 in.	30 lbs.	2d4	x1 lb.
Halfling, female	2 ft. 6 in.	25 lbs.	2d4	x1 lb.
Human, male	4 ft. 10 in.	120 lbs.	2d10	x5 lbs.
Human, female	4 ft. 5 in.	85 lbs.	2d10	x5 lbs.

Table 5-8: Featured Race Random Height & Weight

Race	Base Height	Base Weight	Modifier	Weight Multiplier
Aasimar, male	5 ft. 2 in.	110 lbs.	2d8	x5 lbs.
Aasimar, female	5 ft. 0 in.	90 lbs.	2d8	x5 lbs.
Catfolk, male	4 ft. 10 in.	120 lbs.	2d8	x5 lbs.
Catfolk, female	4 ft. 5 in.	85 lbs.	2d8	x5 lbs.
Dhampir, male	4 ft. 10 in.	120 lbs.	2d10	x5 lbs.
Dhampir, female	4 ft. 5 in.	85 lbs.	2d10	x5 lbs.
Drow, male	5 ft. 4 in.	90 lbs.	2d6	x3 lbs.
Drow, female	5 ft. 4 in.	100 lbs.	2d8	x3 lbs.
Fetchling, male	5 ft. 4 in.	90 lbs.	2d6	x3 lbs.
Fetchling, female	5 ft. 2 in.	80 lbs.	2d6	x3 lbs.
Goblin, male	2 ft. 8 in.	30 lbs.	2d4	x1 lb.

Race	Base Height	Base Weight	Modifier	Weight Multiplier
Goblin, female	2 ft. 6 in.	25 lbs.	2d4	x1 lb.
Hobgoblin, male	4 ft. 2 in.	165 lbs.	2d8	x5 lbs.
Hobgoblin, female	4 ft. 0 in.	145 lbs.	2d8	x5 lbs.
Ifrit, male	5 ft. 2 in.	110 lbs.	2d8	x5 lbs.
Ifrit, female	5 ft. 0 in.	90 lbs.	2d8	x5 lbs.
Kobold, male	2 ft. 6 in.	25 lbs.	2d4	x1 lb.
Kobold, female	2 ft. 4 in.	20 lbs.	2d4	x1 lb.
Orc, male	5 ft. 1 in.	160 lbs.	2d12	x7 lbs.
Orc, female	4 ft. 9 in.	120 lbs.	2d12	x7 lbs.
Oread, male	4 ft. 0 in.	150 lbs.	2d6	x7 lbs.
Oread, female	3 ft. 9 in.	120 lbs.	2d6	x7 lbs.
Ratfolk, male	3 ft. 7 in.	65 lbs.	2d4	x3 lbs.
Ratfolk, female	3 ft. 4 in.	50 lbs.	2d4	x3 lbs.
Sylph, male	5 ft. 2 in.	110 lbs.	2d8	x5 lbs.
Sylph, female	5 ft. 0 in.	90 lbs.	2d8	x5 lbs.
Tengu, male	4 ft. 0 in.	65 lbs.	2d6	x3 lbs.
Tengu, female	3 ft. 10 in.	55 lbs.	2d6	x3 lbs.
Tiefling, male	4 ft. 10 in.	120 lbs.	2d10	x5 lbs.
Tiefling, female	4 ft. 5 in.	85 lbs.	2d10	x5 lbs.
Undine, male	4 ft. 10 in.	120 lbs.	2d10	x5 lbs.
Undine, female	4 ft. 5 in.	85 lbs.	2d10	x5 lbs.

Table 5-9: Uncommon Race Random Height & Weight

Race	Base Height	Base Weight	Modifier	Weight Multiplier
Changeling, female	4 ft. 2 in.	85 lbs.	2d4	x5 lbs.
Duergar, male	3 ft. 9 in.	150 lbs.	2d4	x7 lbs.
Duergar, female	3 ft. 7 in.	120 lbs.	2d4	x7 lbs.
Gillman, male	4 ft. 10 in.	120 lbs.	2d10	x5 lbs.
Gillman, female	4 ft. 5 in.	85 lbs.	2d10	x5 lbs.
Grippli, male	1 ft. 7 in.	25 lbs.	2d4	x1 lb.
Grippli, female	1 ft. 5 in.	20 lbs.	2d4	x1 lb.
Kitsune, male	4 ft. 10 in.	100 lbs.	2d8	x5 lbs.
Kitsune, female	4 ft. 5 in.	85 lbs.	2d8	x5 lbs.
Merfolk, male	5 ft. 10 in.	145 lbs.	2d10	x5 lbs.
Merfolk, female	5 ft. 8 in.	135 lbs.	2d10	x5 lbs.
Nagaji, male	5 ft. 9 in.	180 lbs.	2d10	x7 lbs.
Nagaji, female	5 ft. 6 in.	160 lbs.	2d10	x7 lbs.
Samsaran, male	5 ft. 4 in.	110 lbs.	2d8	x5 lbs.
Samsaran, female	5 ft. 6 in.	110 lbs.	2d8	x5 lbs.
Strix, male	5 ft. 4 in.	125 lbs.	2d8	x5 lbs.
Strix, female	5 ft. 2 in.	115 lbs.	2d8	x5 lbs.
Suli, male	4 ft. 10 in.	120 lbs.	2d10	x5 lbs.
Suli, female	4 ft. 5 in.	85 lbs.	2d10	x5 lbs.
Svirfneblin, male	3 ft. 0 in.	35 lbs.	2d4	x1 lb.
Svirfneblin, female	2 ft. 10 in.	30 lbs.	2d4	x1 lb.
Vanara, male	4 ft. 8 in.	105 lbs.	2d8	x5 lbs.
Vanara, female	4 ft. 2 in.	90 lbs.	2d8	x5 lbs.
Vishkanya, male	5 ft. 3 in.	85 lbs.	2d8	x5 lbs.
Vishkanya, female	5 ft. 1 in.	75 lbs.	2d8	x5 lbs.
Wayang, male	3 ft. 0 in.	35 lbs.	2d4	x1 lb.
Wayang, female	2 ft. 10 in.	30 lbs.	2d4	x1 lb.

APPENDIX 3: SPELLS

Spells are organized by class and level. The page number the spell appears on is in parentheses following the spell.

Alchemist Spells

1st-Level Alchemist Spells: *blend* (29), *linebreaker* (59), *recharge innate magic* (39), *urban grace* (49)

2nd-Level Alchemist Spells: *ancestral regression* (107), *blood blaze* (143), *delay disease* (155), *minor dream* (39), *sickening strikes* (155), *squeeze* (209)

3rd-Level Alchemist Spells: *battle trance* (58), *blood scent* (143), *fire trail* (119), *paragon surge* (48), *prehensile pilfer* (207), *vomit twin* (119)

4th-Level Alchemist Spells: *absorbing inhalation* (160), *earth glide* (205), *healing warmth* (131), *miasmatic form* (161), *scorching ash form* (131)

5th-Level Alchemist Spells: *half-blood extraction* (59)

Antipaladin Spells

1st-Level Antipaladin Spells: *blood blaze* (143), *death candle* (131), *ironbeard* (19), *linebreaker* (59), *savage maw* (59), *sentry skull* (143)

2nd-Level Antipaladin Spells: *agonizing rebuke* (125), *blood scent* (143), *enemy's heart* (143), *improve trap* (137), *sickening strikes* (155)

3rd-Level Antipaladin Spells: *ancestral regression* (107), *battle trance* (58)

Bard Spells

1st-Level Bard Spells: *jitterbugs* (39), *recharge innate magic* (39), *sow thought* (185), *toilsome chant* (19), *urban grace* (49), *windy escape* (161)

2nd-Level Bard Spells: *bestow insight* (79), *commune with birds* (167), *escaping ward* (68), *shadow anchor* (211), *steal breath* (95)

3rd-Level Bard Spells: *death from below* (39), *fearsome duplicate* (68), *minor dream* (39), *prehensile pilfer* (207), *raging rubble* (149)

4th-Level Bard Spells: *forgetful slumber* (48), *nixie's lure* (179), *truespeak* (89)

5th-Level Bard Spells: *village veil* (69)

Cleric Spells

1st-Level Cleric Spells: *ironbeard* (19), *karmic blessing* (199), *marid's mastery* (178), *mighty fist of the earth* (148), *recharge innate magic* (39), *stone shield* (149), *theft ward* (167), *winter feathers* (167)

2nd-Level Cleric Spells: *aboleth's lung* (189), *alchemical tinkering* (155), *ancestral regression* (107), *blessing of luck and resolve* (68), *blinding ray* (101), *blood blaze* (143), *death candle* (131), *delay disease* (155), *enemy's heart* (143), *groundswell* (19), *imbue with elemental might* (203), *life channel* (101), *sacred space* (89), *savage maw* (59), *sentry skull* (143), *whispering lore* (29)

3rd-Level Cleric Spells: *agonizing rebuke* (125), *bestow insight* (79), *blood scent* (143), *paragon surge* (48), *raging rubble* (149)

4th-Level Cleric Spells: *battle trance* (58), *healing warmth* (131), *ward of the season* (29)

5th-Level Cleric Spells: *half-blood extraction* (59), *spawn ward* (101), *village veil* (69)

6th-Level Cleric Spells: *blessing of luck and resolve, mass* (68), *truespeak* (89)

8th-Level Cleric Spells: *nine lives* (95)

Druid Spells

1st-Level Druid Spells: *blend* (29), *commune with birds* (167), *marid's mastery* (178), *mighty fist of the earth* (149), *mudball* (119), *nereid's grace* (179), *recharge innate magic* (39), *stone shield* (149), *strong wings* (201), *touch of combustion* (131), *whispering lore* (29), *windy escape* (161), *winter feathers* (167)

2nd-Level Druid Spells: *aboleth's lung* (189), *binding earth* (149), *delay disease* (155), *fury of the sun* (131), *groundswell* (19), *gusting sphere* (160), *savage maw* (59), *sickening strikes* (155), *steal breath* (95)

3rd-Level Druid Spells: *blood scent* (143), *fins to feet* (195), *improve trap* (137), *nixie's lure* (179), *raging rubble* (149), *ward of the season* (29)

4th-Level Druid Spells: *absorbing inhalation* (160), *cloud shape* (160), *earth glide* (205), *healing warmth* (131)

5th-Level Druid Spells: *half-blood extraction* (59), *old salt's curse* (79), *wind blades* (161)

6th-Level Druid Spells: *binding earth, mass* (149), *path of the winds* (161)

7th-Level Druid Spells: *black mark* (79)

Inquisitor Spells

1st-Level Inquisitor Spells: *linebreaker* (59), *recharge innate magic* (39), *theft ward* (167), *touch of combustion* (131), *winter feathers* (167)

2nd-Level Inquisitor Spells: *bestow insight* (79), *blessing of luck and resolve* (68), *death candle* (131), *delay disease* (155), *escaping ward* (68), *savage maw* (59)

3rd-Level Inquisitor Spells: *agonizing rebuke* (125), *battle trance* (58), *blinding ray* (101), *blood scent* (143), *fearsome duplicate* (68), *improve trap* (137)

4th-Level Inquisitor Spells: *healing warmth* (131)

5th-Level Inquisitor Spells: *spawn ward* (101)

6th-Level Inquisitor Spells: *blessing of luck and resolve, mass* (68)

Magus Spells

1st-Level Magus Spells: *blend* (29), *ironbeard* (19), *linebreaker* (59), *mudball* (119), *recharge innate magic* (39), *touch of combustion* (131), *web bolt* (107), *windy escape* (161)

2nd-Level Magus Spells: *blood blaze* (143), *escaping ward* (68), *groundswell* (19), *gusting sphere* (160), *imbue with elemental might* (203), *savage maw* (59), *stone shield* (149)

3rd-Level Magus Spells: *fire trail* (119), *firestream* (131), *gloomblind bolts* (113), *prehensile pilfer* (207), *resilient reservoir* (49), *sickening strikes* (155), *vomit twin* (119)

4th-Level Magus Spells: *paragon surge* (48)

5th-Level Magus Spells: *wind blades* (161)

6th-Level Magus Spells: *chains of fire* (131)

Paladin Spells

1st-Level Paladin Spells: *ironbeard* (19), *linebreaker* (59), *veil of heaven* (89)

2nd-Level Paladin Spells: *blessing of luck and resolve* (68), *blinding ray* (101), *delay disease* (155), *sacred space* (89)

3rd-Level Paladin Spells: *resilient reservoir* (49)

4th-Level Paladin Spells: *blessing of luck and resolve, mass* (68), *paragon surge* (48)

Ranger Spells

1st-Level Ranger Spells: *blend* (29), *commune with birds* (167), *ironbeard* (19), *linebreaker* (59), *marid's mastery* (178), *savage maw* (59), *strong wings* (201), *urban grace* (49), *whispering lore* (29), *winter feathers* (167)

2nd-Level Ranger Spells: *blood scent* (143), *delay disease* (155), *escaping ward* (68), *groundswell* (19), *improve trap* (137)

3rd-Level Ranger Spells: *battle trance* (58), *ward of the season* (29)

4th-Level Ranger Spells: *cloud shape* (160), *sickening strikes* (155)

Sorcerer/Wizard Spells

1st-Level Sorcerer/Wizard Spells: *alchemical tinkering* (155), *blend* (29), *marid's mastery* (178), *mudball* (119), *recharge innate magic* (39), *sow thought* (185), *stone shield* (149), *strong wings* (201), *theft ward* (167), *touch of combustion* (131), *undine's curse* (179), *urban grace* (49), *web bolt* (107), *windy escape* (161), *winter feathers* (167)

2nd-Level Sorcerer/Wizard Spells: *aboleth's lung* (189), *bestow insight* (79), *blood blaze* (143), *commune with birds* (167), *death from below* (39), *escaping ward* (68), *gusting sphere* (160), *imbue with elemental might* (203), *jitterbugs* (39), *sentry skull* (143), *shadow anchor* (211), *squeeze* (209), *steal breath* (95)

3rd-Level Sorcerer/Wizard Spells: *ancestral regression* (107), *blood scent* (143), *fearsome duplicate* (68), *fins to feet* (195), *fire trail* (119), *firestream* (131), *gloomblind bolts* (113), *improve trap* (137), *minor dream* (39), *nixie's lure* (179), *paragon surge* (48), *prehensile pilfer* (207), *raging rubble* (149)

4th-Level Sorcerer/Wizard Spells: *absorbing inhalation* (160), *cloud shape* (160), *earth glide* (205), *forgetful slumber* (48), *ghost wolf* (58), *hellmouth lash* (173), *miasmatic form* (161), *minor phantom object* (39), *resilient reservoir* (49), *scorching ash form* (131), *shadowy haven* (113), *vomit twin* (119), *web cloud* (107)

5th-Level Sorcerer/Wizard Spells: *damnation stride* (173), *half-blood extraction* (59), *major phantom object* (39), *truespeak* (89), *village veil* (69), *wind blades* (161)

6th-Level Sorcerer/Wizard Spells: *chains of fire* (131), *path of the winds* (161)

Summoner Spells

1st-Level Summoner Spells: *stone shield* (149)

2nd-Level Summoner Spells: *ghost wolf* (58)

3rd-Level Summoner Spells: *vomit twin* (119)

4th-Level Summoner Spells: *damnation stride* (173), *nixie's lure* (179)

Witch Spells

1st-Level Witch Spells: *alchemical tinkering* (155), *blend* (29), *delay disease* (155), *karmic blessing* (199), *marid's mastery* (178), *mudball* (119), *nereid's grace* (179), *recharge innate magic* (39), *sow thought* (185), *strong wings* (201), *theft ward* (167), *touch of combustion* (131), *undine's curse* (179), *urban grace* (49), *web bolt* (107), *whispering lore* (29)

2nd-Level Witch Spells: *aboleth's lung* (189), *ancestral regression* (107), *bestow insight* (79), *binding earth* (149), *blood blaze* (143), *commune with birds* (167), *death candle* (131), *enemy's heart* (143), *fury of the sun* (131), *minor dream* (39), *sentry skull* (143), *shadow anchor* (211), *sickening strikes* (155), *squeeze* (209), *steal breath* (95)

3rd-Level Witch Spells: *agonizing rebuke* (125), *blood scent* (143), *fearsome duplicate* (68), *fins to feet* (195), *gloomblind bolts* (113), *improve trap* (137), *nixie's lure* (179), *paragon surge* (48), *raging rubble* (149), *ward of the season* (29)

4th-Level Witch Spells: *battle trance* (58), *forgetful slumber* (48), *hellmouth lash* (173), *resilient reservoir* (49), *web cloud* (107)

5th-Level Witch Spells: *damnation stride* (173), *half-blood extraction* (59), *old salt's curse* (79), *truespeak* (89), *village veil* (69), *wind blades* (161)

6th-Level Witch Spells: *binding earth, mass* (149)

7th-Level Witch Spells: *black mark* (79)

8th-Level Witch Spells: *nine lives* (95)

INDEX

Feat names are capitalized. Combat feats are followed by an asterisk. Magic items are presented in italics.

OPEN GAME LICENSE Version 1.0a